Teach Us To Number

Williams'
Exhaustive Concordance of
Bible Numbers

by

J.G. Williams
B.S., M.B.S., Ph.D.

Verity & Charity Publications
PO Box 422, Portage, WI

Teach Us
To Number

Williams'
Exhaustive Concordance of
Bible Numbers

ISBN 978-1503359178

Published and Distributed by

Verity & Charity Publications
PO Box 422
Portage, WI

www.veritycharity.com

TABLE OF CONTENTS

INTRODUCTION

> *"So teach us to number our days, so that we may apply our hearts unto wisdom."*
> *Psalm 90:12*

God created numbers. His magnificent creation as well as subsequent human history is brimming with things that can be counted, weighed, measured and quantified from every conceivable vantage point. Our Lord in his infinite wisdom saw fit to record many thousands of these measurements in his holy word. Each instance of the Lord recording how many, how long or how much provides yet another example of the Spirit breathed words of God by which we are to live – words that *"were written aforetime..for our learning, that we through patience and comfort of the scriptures might have hope."* (Rom. 15:4) This concordance is an exhaustive record of those numbers.

In the winter of 1995 this author was on furlough in a church in Montana. Around the dinner table, we began discussing the topic of Paul's fateful sea voyage in Acts chapter twenty-seven. A question arose that began the almost twenty year journey that led to the publication of this concordance. If every word and fact of Scripture is indeed inspired, why did the Holy Spirit record for us that there were exactly 276 people on board Paul's ship? The answer to this question I still do not know, but the immediate difficulty on that afternoon was ascertaining how many times the number 276 appears in Scripture. In Acts 27:37, the Holy Spirit did not record the number of souls on this ship as "276" or even as "two hundred and seventy-six," but instead as "two hundred threescore and sixteen." After some concordance work that afternoon, we were pretty sure there was only one reference to this number in the Bible, but because of variations *we could not be sure.*

Subsequently in my Bible reading, the realization that the same number could appear in many different forms began to take hold. For instance, consider the number 39. This number never appears in Scripture as "thirty nine," but it would take considerable effort to discover this. A written concordance would require a laborious effort of comparing all the instances of "thirty" and "nine" only to return a non-result. An electronic search of "thirty" and "nine" returns five hits. One of these raises a false flag in Ezra 2:42 that actually turns out to be 139 – the others are simply the two words occurring in the same verse. If we try the ordinal number "thirty ninth" we come up empty.

So is 39 absent from Scripture? No. There are in fact four occurrences. Three of these are the ordinal number 39th that appear in two different formats one would be unlikely to search for:

> 2Ki 15:13 – "nine and thirtieth"
> 2Ki 15:17 – "nine and thirtieth"
> 2Ch 16:12 – "thirty and ninth"

The last occurrence of 39 is found II Cor. 11:24 in reference to the whippings suffered by the apostle Paul when he received, *"forty stripes save one."* 40 – 1 = 39! Generally speaking, who among us would have had the patience to track down these variations and think of all the possible combinations? How could we even be sure after our study that we have in fact found **all** the occurrences of any given number that we are investigating? The purpose of this volume is to accomplish that task for you.

Teach Us To Number – Williams' Exhaustive Concordance of Bible Numbers is based on the premise of 1Cor 2:13 that the Holy Spirit teaches by comparing things that are similar. This concordance employs a user-friendly format designed to help you find all of the occurrences of the same number, fraction, mixed number or date. To do this it is arranged in three easy-to-use sections:

1) *The Concordance of Bible Numbers –* **Section One**

   ➢ All of the numbers of the Bible will be found here

> Begins with **Zero** and goes up to **Billions** and then on into **Infinity**
> Fractions less than one will be found between **Zero** & **One**
> Each number heading begins with the cardinal number (eg. 39) followed by the ordinal number (eg. 39th) and then any variations for that number that might exist
> The indefinite numbers (eg. few, many, one's, hundred's, etc.) will be found towards the end of this section after the definite numbers (eg. 1, 2, 1000, 603,500, etc.) have run out

2) ***The Directory of Dates*** – **Section Two**

> The first part of this section includes all of the generic dates that could happen in any given year – generally these will only have a month and day mentioned in Scripture
> The second part of this section includes all of the specific dates mentioned in the Bible that refer to someone's life or some event in history – generally these will include a year as well as a month and day

3) ***The Index of Numbered Items*** – **Section Three**

> This section is largely the opposite of the first – rather than beginning with the number, it begins with the item being counted
> Listed alphabetically from **Abomination** to **Yoke**

Specific hints and tips can be found in the introduction to each section.

The student should note that there are number of things that ***Teach Us To Number*** does not include and is not designed to do:

1)	This concordance is primarily designed to record the numbers that actually appear in Scripture – it does not count or add things up to arrive at results that are not specifically recorded or mentioned in the Bible. For instance the Bible records that David picked up **five** smooth stones when he went out to face Goliath – later in the chapter he chooses "a" stone out of the bag and kills the giant. In this volume you will find the reference to **five** in Section One and the same reference in Section Three under **Stones**. You will not find any reference to the ***four*** remaining stones as Scripture does not specifically mention them. Neither will you find a reference to the ***one*** stone that David used as Scripture does not specifically mention it as being "one."

2)	This concordance makes no reference to the numbers that compose verse references. The text of Scripture composes the inspired words of God, not the chapter and verse divisions. Although a message on the 1:1's or 3:16's of Scripture may be an interesting study, this volume only deals with the numbers given by the Spirit of God in the **text** of Scripture.

3)	This concordance does not profess to be a study in Bible numerology. Although it may provide the foundation for you to ascertain whether there is any significance to the number 7, 11 or 40 in Scripture, this volume does not delve into this topic beyond the odd general comment.

4)	This concordance does not provide statistics on total numbers of words. We suggest you consult other resources if you wish to know how many words are in the book of Ruth or how many times the word Jersualem appears in Scripture. Now if you wish to know how many times the number 17 or 330 appears in Scripture, you will find ***Teach Us To Number*** far easier in arriving at the correct answer than a standard concordance. You may look up these numbers in Section One and easily count them yourself.

The author's desire is that over time preachers and students of the word will come to see the use of this aid in sermon and lesson preparation as well their own personal study.   To God be the glory as he teaches us to number!

J.G. Williams

August 23, 2012
Blenheim, New Zealand

CONCORDANCE OF BIBLE NUMBERS
SECTION ONE

Introduction

Section One includes all of the actual numbers referred to in the text of Scripture as well as a host of terms that are used in the Bible to count things (eg. many, few, none, etc.).   Please note carefully the following tips that will assist you in finding the information for which you are searching:

> This section is numbered chronologically from **Zero** to **Infinity**.

> Fractions less than one are found in chronological order between **Zero** and **One**.

> A *cardinal number* tells how many (eg. 3, 99 or 700) while an *ordinal number* tells in what order (eg. 1st, 9th or 100th).   For each number the cardinal numbers are listed first and then the ordinal numbers.   Many of the numbers under eleven have other variations (eg. single, twice, tenfold, etc.) that will be listed alphabetically after the cardinal and/or ordinal number to which they refer.

> Each number will only be listed where it is a complete number in its own right:

>> *Example one – "fifty and three thousand and four hundred"* from Num. 1:43 will only be found under the heading of 53,400 – its component parts will **not** be found under 50, 3, 1000, 3000, 4, or 400. You will find that this particular trait is what makes *Teach Us To Number* such a valuable reference tool!
>> *Example two – "three tenth deals of fine flour"* from Lev. 14:10 is intended to convey the fraction three-tenths. As such, it will not be found under the cardinal number three or the ordinal number tenth – instead it will be found under the appropriate fraction 3/10.

> *Italics* indicate a number inferred, but not explicitly stated in instances that the author thought worthy of inclusion.   For example, *"I have bought five yoke of oxen"* from Luke 14:19 is included under the number **Ten** (as well as the number **Five**) even though the verse does not explicitly state that there are ten oxen.   Questionable or overlapping instances such as this one have often been included in the appropriate, multiple locations of this volume to assist the student in easily finding the information for which they are searching.   By the same token, the author's desire was to avoid extrapolating too many inferences from any given reference when it is obvious that this was not the Holy Spirit's intent.   For instance, *"reigned a full month in Samaria"* from 2Ki 15:13 strongly infers **thirty** (days) and was thus recorded; it could include **four** (weeks) and **1/12th** (year) as well, but as these numbers are not mentioned in 2Ki 15:13, they were deemed beyond the intent of the verse.

> All of the numbers in Scripture appear in Section One, but not necessarily in Section Three. Where a number is counting something (thus being used as an adjective or adverb), it will also be found under the appropriate heading in the *Index of Numbered Items.*   When a number is used as a prounoun and does not count something (eg. *"love* **one** *another"* or *"deprived of you* **both***"*) it will only be found here in Section One.

> Dates are found in Section Two.   The component parts of a date (eg. eleven months, ten days or 600th year) will be found in this Section One, but will usually be followed by the designation, *SEE DATES*.   Such references should not be confused with other occasions where months, days and years are being counted but are not part of a date persay (eg. Gen1:13 – *"the third day"*).

> In the listings that follow each number, each Bible reference is followed by 4-10 words from the verse as space would allow. Although often edited for brevity's sake, the author's intention was to include enough words to help the student quickly grasp the context of the number if possible. Any deviation from the actual words of the King James Bible was not intended and every effort has been made to faithfully quote from the verse being referenced.

0 – Zero

The word zero does not appear in the King James Bible. However, this section includes the following terms that convey the concept of zero:

a)	No	e)	Nought
b	None	f)	Naught
c)	No one (some usages)	g)	Not one
d)	Nothing		

No

"No" (1323x) is generally used in the sense of zero when found as an adjective clearly modifying a noun. "No" in this context will almost always answer the question "how many?" For the purposes of this section, the answer is of course zero. In the following list "no" has usually been excluded when used as an adverb (modifying an adjective or another adverb) or when used in the place of "not."

In some cases the counting effect of "no" is carried over to several nouns by the use of the conjunction "nor" – eg. *Whatsover hath no fins nor scales in the waters..."* (Lev 11:12)   Such instances have been recorded in the *Index of Numbered Items.*

Gen 8:9 – "the dove found no rest"
Gen 11:30 – "But Sarai..had no child"
Gen 13:8 – " Let there be no strife"
Gen 15:3 – "to me thou hast given no seed"
Gen 16:1 – "wife bare him no children"
Gen 26:29 – "That thou wilt do us no hurt"
Gen 30:1 – "she bare Jacob no children"
Gen 31:50 – "no man is with us"
Gen 37:22 – "lay no hand upon him"
Gen 37:24 – "pit..there was no water in it"
Gen 38:21 – "There was no harlot in this place"
Gen 38:22 – "there was no harlot in this place"
Gen 40:8 – "dream, and there is no interpreter"
Gen 41:44 – "shall no man lift up his hand"
Gen 45:1 – "there stood no man with him"
Gen 47:4 – "thy servants have no pasture"
Gen 47:13 – "there was no bread in all the land"
Exo 2:12 – "he saw that there was no man"
Exo 5:16 – "There is no straw given"
Exo 5:18 – "there shall no straw be given you"
Exo 8:22 – "no swarms of flies shall be there"
Exo 9:26 – "was there no hail"
Exo 12:16 – "no manner of work shall be done"
Exo 12:19 – "no leaven found in your houses"
Exo 12:43 – "shall no stranger eat thereof"
Exo 12:48 – "no uncircumcised person shall eat"
Exo 13:3 – "shall no leavened bread be eaten"
Exo 13:7 – "shall no leavened bread be seen"
Exo 14:11 – "no graves in Egypt"
Exo 15:22 – "and found no water"
Exo 16:18 – "he that gathered little had no lack"
Exo 16:19 – "Let no man leave of it"
Exo 16:29 – "let no man go out of his place"
Exo 17:1 – "there was no water for the people"
Exo 20:3 – "no other gods before me"
Exo 21:8 – "he shall have no power"
Exo 21:22 – "yet no mischief follow"

Exo 22:2 – "no blood be shed for him"
Exo 22:10 – "no man seeing it"
Exo 23:8 – "And thou shalt take no gift"
Exo 23:13 – "make no mention of..other gods"
Exo 23:32 – "make no covenant with them"
Exo 30:9 – "offer no strange incense"
Exo 30:12 – "that there be no plague"
Exo 33:4 – "no man did put on..ornaments"
Exo 33:20 – "shall no man see me, and live"
Exo 34:3 – "no man shall come up with thee"
Exo 34:14 – "thou shalt worship no other god"
Exo 34:17 – "shalt make thee no molten gods"
Exo 35:3 – "Ye shall kindle no fire"
Lev 2:11 – "No meat offering..shall be made"
Lev 2:11 – "ye shall burn no leaven"
Lev 5:11 – "he shall put no oil upon it"
Lev 6:30 – "no sin offering..shall be eaten"
Lev 7:23 – "Ye shall eat no manner of fat"
Lev 7:26 – "ye shall eat no manner of blood"
Lev 11:12 – "Whatsoever hath no fins nor scales"
Lev 12:4 – "she shall touch no hallowed thing"
Lev 13:21 – "there be no white hairs therein"
Lev 13:26 – "there be no white hair"
Lev 13:31 – "there is no black hair in it"
Lev 13:32 – "there be in it no yellow hair"
Lev 16:17 – "shall be no man in the tabernacle"
Lev 16:29 – "do no work at all"
Lev 17:12 – "No soul of you shall eat blood"
Lev 17:14 – "eat the blood of no manner of flesh"
Lev 19:15 – "do no unrighteousness in judgment"
Lev 19:35 – "do no unrighteousness in judgment"
Lev 20:14 – "there be no wickedness among you"
Lev 21:3 – "sister..which hath had no husband"
Lev 21:21 – "No man that hath a blemish"
Lev 22:10 – "no stranger eat of the holy thing"
Lev 22:13 – "priest's daughter..have no child"
Lev 22:21 – "shall be no blemish therein"

Lev 23:3 – "ye shall do no work therein"
Lev 23:7 –"do no servile work therein"
Lev 23:8 – "do no servile work therein"
Lev 23:21 – "do no servile work therein"
Lev 23:25 – "do no servile work therein"
Lev 23:28 – "do no work in that same day"
Lev 23:31 – "do no manner of work"
Lev 23:35 – "do no servile work therein"
Lev 23:36 – "do no servile work therein"
Lev 25:31 – "villages which have no wall"
Lev 25:36 – "Take thou no usury of him"
Lev 26:1 – "Ye shall make you no idols"
Lev 26:37 – "no power..before your enemies"
Lev 27:26 – "no man shall sanctify it"
Lev 27:28 – "no devoted thing.. shall be sold"
Num 1:53 – "that there be no wrath"
Num 3:4 – "they had no children"
Num 5:8 – "But if the man have no kinsman"
Num 5:13 – "there be no witness against her"
Num 5:15 – "he shall pour no oil upon it"
Num 5:19 – "If no man have lain with thee"
Num 6:3 – "shall drink no vinegar of wine"
Num 6:5 – "no razor come upon his head"
Num 6:6 – "he shall come at no dead body"
Num 8:19 – "that there be no plague"
Num 8:26 – "shall do no service..Levites"
Num 16:40 – "no stranger.. offer incense"
Num 18:5 – "that there be no wrath"
Num 18:20 – "Thou shalt have no inheritance"
Num 18:23 – "Levites..have no inheritance"
Num 18:24 – "Levites..have no inheritance"
Num 18:32 – "ye shall bear no sin"
Num 19:2 – "heifer..wherein is no blemish"
Num 19:15 – "vessel, which hath no covering"
Num 20:2 – "no water for the congregation"
Num 20:5 – "it is no place of seed, or of figs"
Num 21:5 – "for there is no bread"
Num 22:26 – "where was no way to turn"
Num 23:23 – "no enchantment against Jacob"
Num 26:33 – "Zelophehad..had no sons"
Num 26:62 – "there was no inheritance given"
Num 27:3 – "Our father..had no sons."
Num 27:4 – "our father..hath no son?"
Num 27:8 – "If a man die, and have no son"
Num 27:9 – "And if he have no daughter"
Num 27:10 – "if he have no brethren"
Num 27:11 – "if his father have no brethren"
Num 27:17 – "sheep which have no shepherd"
Num 28:18 – "do no manner of servile work"
Num 28:25 – "ye shall do no servile work"
Num 28:26 – "ye shall do no servile work"
Num 29:1 – "ye shall do no servile work"
Num 29:12 – "ye shall do no servile work"
Num 29:35 – "ye shall do no servile work"
Num 33:14 – "no water for the people"
Num 35:31 – "no satisfaction for..a murderer"
Num 35:32 – "take no satisfaction for him"
Deu 1:39 – "no knowledge between good..evil"
Deu 4:12 – "heard..voice..but saw no similitude"
Deu 4:15 – "ye saw no manner of similitude"
Deu 7:2 – "make no covenant with them"

Deu 7:16 – "thine eye shall have no pity"
Deu 7:24 – "no man..able to stand before thee"
Deu 8:15 – "where there was no water"
Deu 10:9 – "Levi hath no part nor inheritance"
Deu 11:17 – "shut up the heaven..no rain"
Deu 11:25 – "no man be able to stand before you"
Deu 12:12 – "no part nor inheritance with you"
Deu 14:27 – "Levite..hath no part nor inheritance"
Deu 14:29 – "Levite..hath no part nor inheritance"
Deu 15:4 – "there shall be no poor among you"
Deu 15:19 – "shalt do no work with the firstling"
Deu 16:3 – "Thou shalt eat no leavened bread"
Deu 16:4 – "no leavened bread seen with thee"
Deu 16:8 – "thou shalt do no work therein"
Deu 18:1 – "Levi..no part nor inheritance"
Deu 18:2 – "no inheritance among..brethren"
Deu 20:12 – "if it will make no peace with thee"
Deu 21:14 – "if thou have no delight in her"
Deu 22:26 – "in..damsel no sin worthy of death"
Deu 23:14 – "no unclean thing in thee"
Deu 23:17 – "no whore of the daughters of Israel"
Deu 23:22 – "it shall be no sin in thee"
Deu 24:1 – "she find no favour in his eyes"
Deu 24:6 – "No man shall take the..millstone"
Deu 25:5 – "If brethren..have no child"
Deu 28:26 – "no man shall fray them away"
Deu 28:29 – "no man shall save thee"
Deu 28:32 – "shall be no might in thine hand"
Deu 28:65 – "shalt thou find no ease"
Deu 32:12 – "was no strange god with him"
Deu 32:20 – "children in whom is no faith"
Deu 32:39 – "there is no god with me"
Deu 34:6 – "no man knoweth of his sepulcher"
Jos 8:20 – "they had no power to flee"
Jos 8:31 – "no man hath lift up any iron"
Jos 10:14 – "And there was no day like that"
Jos 11:20 – "that they might have no favour"
Jos 14:4 – "they gave no part unto the Levites"
Jos 17:3 – "But Zelophehad..had no sons"
Jos 18:7 – "the Levites have no part among you"
Jos 22:25 – "ye have no part in the LORD"
Jos 22:27 – "Ye have no part in the LORD"
Jos 23:9 – "no man hath been able to stand"
Jdg 2:2 – "And ye shall make no league"
Jdg 5:19 – "they took no gain of money"
Jdg 6:4 – "left no sustenance for Israel"
Jdg 11:39 – "and she knew no man"
Jdg 13:5 – "no razor shall come on his head"
Jdg 13:7 – "drink no wine nor strong drink"
Jdg 17:6 – "there was no king in Israel"
Jdg 18:1 – "there was no king in Israel"
Jdg 18:7 – "no magistrate in the land"
Jdg 18:10 – "there is no want of any thing"
Jdg 18:28 – "And there was no deliverer"
Jdg 19:1 – "there was no king in Israel"
Jdg 19:15 – "no man that took them"
Jdg 19:18 – "no man that receiveth me to house"
Jdg 19:19 – "there is no want of any thing"
Jdg 19:30 – "There was no such deed done"
Jdg 21:12 – "that had known no man"
Jdg 21:25 – "there was no king in Israel"

1Sa 1:2 – "Hannah had no children"
1Sa 1:11 – "no razor come upon his head"
1Sa 2:9 – "by strength shall no man prevail"
1Sa 2:24 – "it is no good report that I hear"
1Sa 3:1 – "there was no open vision"
1Sa 6:7 – "on which there hath come no yoke"
1Sa 10:27 – "brought him no presents"
1Sa 11:3 – "if there be no man to save us"
1Sa 13:19 – "Now there was no smith found"
1Sa 14:6 – "there is no restraint to the LORD"
1Sa 14:26 – "no man put his hand to his mouth"
1Sa 17:32 – "Let no man's heart fail"
1Sa 17:50 – " no sword in the hand of David"
1Sa 20:21 – "peace to thee, and no hurt"
1Sa 20:34 – "did eat no meat the second day"
1Sa 21:1 – "alone, and no man with thee?"
1Sa 21:2 – "Let no man know any thing"
1Sa 21:4 – "There is no common bread"
1Sa 21:6 – "no bread there but the showbread"
1Sa 21:9 – "sword..for there is no other save that"
1Sa 25:31 – "this shall be no grief unto thee"
1Sa 26:12 – "gat them away, and no man saw"
1Sa 28:10 – "there shall no punishment happen"
1Sa 28:20 – "there was no strength in him"
1Sa 29:3 – "I have found no fault in him"
1Sa 30:12 – "he had eaten no bread"
2Sa 1:21 – "let there be no dew, neither..rain"
2Sa 6:23 – "Therefore Michal..had no child"
2Sa 12:6 – "because he had no pity"
2Sa 13:12 – "no such thing ought to be done"
2Sa 13:16 – "There is no cause"
2Sa 14:25 – "there was no blemish in him"
2Sa 15:3 – "no man deputed of the king"
2Sa 15:26 – "I have no delight in thee"
2Sa 18:13 – "no matter hid from the king"
2Sa 18:18 – "I have no son to keep my name"
2Sa 18:20 – "thou shalt bear no tidings"
2Sa 18:22 – "thou hast no tidings ready?"
2Sa 20:1 – "We have no part in David"
2Sa 20:10 – "Amasa took no heed to the sword"
2Sa 21:4 – "have no silver nor gold of Saul"
1Ki 1:1 – "but he gat no heat"
1Ki 3:2 – "there was no house built"
1Ki 3:18 – "no stranger with us in the house"
1Ki 6:18 – "there was no stone seen"
1Ki 8:16 – "I chose no city out..of Israel"
1Ki 8:23 – "there is no God like thee"
1Ki 8:35 – "When..there is no rain"
1Ki 8:46 – "there is no man that sinneth not"
1Ki 9:22 – "did Solomon make no bondmen"
1Ki 10:12 – "there came no such almug trees"
1Ki 13:9 – "Eat no bread, nor drink water"
1Ki 13:17 – "Thou shalt eat no bread"
1Ki 13:22 – "Eat no bread, and drink no water"
1Ki 17:7 – " had been no rain in the land"
1Ki 17:17 – "there was no breath left in him"
1Ki 18:10 – "there is no nation or kingdom"
1Ki 18:23 – "lay it on wood..put no fire under"
1Ki 18:23 – "and put no fire under"
1Ki 18:25 – "but put no fire under"
1Ki 18:26 – "But there was no voice"

1Ki 21:4 – "And Ahab..would eat no bread"
1Ki 21:5 – "so sad, that thou eatest no bread?"
1Ki 22:17 – "These have no master"
1Ki 22:18 – "prophesy no good concerning me"
1Ki 22:47 – "There was then no king in Edom"
2Ki 1:16 – "because there is no God in Israel"
2Ki 1:17 – "because he had no son"
2Ki 3:9 – "there was no water for the host"
2Ki 4:14 – "Verily she hath no child"
2Ki 4:41 – "there was no harm in the pot"
2Ki 5:15 – "there is no God in all the earth"
2Ki 7:5 – "there was no man there"
2Ki 7:10 – "there was no man there"
2Ki 10:31 – "Jehu took no heed to walk"
2Ki 12:7 – "receive no more money"
2Ki 12:8 – "receive no more money"
2Ki 17:4 – "brought no present to the king"
2Ki 19:18 – "for they were no gods"
2Ki 22:7 – "there was no reckoning made"
2Ki 23:10 – "no man might make his son"
2Ki 23:18 – "let no man move his bones"
2Ki 23:25 – "like unto him was there no king"
2Ki 25:3 – "there was no bread for the people"
1Ch 2:34 – "Now Sheshan had no sons"
1Ch 12:17 – "there is no wrong in mine hands"
1Ch 16:21 – "suffered no man to do..wrong"
1Ch 16:22 – "do my prophets no harm"
1Ch 22:16 – "Of the gold..there is no number"
1Ch 23:22 – "Eleazar died, and had no sons"
1Ch 24:2 – "Nadab and Abihu..had no children"
1Ch 24:28 – "Eleazar, who had no sons"
2Ch 6:5 – "I chose no city..of Israel"
2Ch 6:14 – "there is no God like thee"
2Ch 6:26 – "heaven is shut up..there is no rain"
2Ch 6:36 – "there is no man which sinneth not"
2Ch 7:13 – "shut up heaven..there be no rain"
2Ch 8:9 – "did Solomon make no servants"
2Ch 9:4 – "there was no more spirit in her"
2Ch 14:6 – "he had no war in those years"
2Ch 14:11 – "them that have no power"
2Ch 15:5 – "there was no peace to him"
2Ch 15:19 – "And there was no more war"
2Ch 17:10 – "no war against Jehoshaphat"
2Ch 18:16 – "sheep that have no shepherd"
2Ch 19:7 – "there is no iniquity with the LORD"
2Ch 20:12 – "no might against this..company"
2Ch 21:19 – "people made no burning for him"
2Ch 22:9 – "Ahaziah..no power to keep..kingdom"
2Ch 32:15 – "no god..able to deliver his people"
2Ch 35:18 – "And there was no passover"
2Ch 36:16 – "wrath..arose..there was no remedy"
2Ch 36:17 – "no compassion upon..man..maiden"
Ezr 4:16 – "have no portion on this side the river"
Ezr 9:14 – "should be no remnant nor escaping"
Ezr 10:6 – "he did eat no bread, nor drink water"
Neh 2:14 – "there was no place for the beast"
Neh 2:17 – "that we be no more a reproach"
Neh 2:20 – "ye have no portion, nor right"
Neh 6:1 – "wall..there was no breach left therein"
Neh 6:8 – "no such things done as thou sayest"
Neh 13:19 "there should no burden be brought"

Neh 13:26 – "Solomon..was there no king like him"
Est 5:12 – "queen did let no man come in"
Est 8:8 – "the writing..may no man reverse"
Est 9:2 – "no man could withstand them"
Job 3:7 – "let no joyful voice come therein"
Job 4:18 – "he put no trust in his servants"
Job 5:19 – "there shall no evil touch thee"
Job 9:25 – "days..flee away, they see no good"
Job 10:18 – "Oh that..no eye had seen me!"
Job 11:3 – "shall no man make thee ashamed?"
Job 12:2 – "No doubt but ye are the people"
Job 12:14 – "there can be no opening"
Job 12:24 – "wilderness where there is no way"
Job 13:4 – "ye are all physicians of no value"
Job 15:3 – "speeches wherewith..can do no good"
Job 15:15 – "he putteth no trust in his saints"
Job 15:19 – "no stranger passed among them"
Job 15:28 – "houses which no man inhabiteth"
Job 16:18 – "let my cry have no place"
Job 18:17 – "he shall have no name in the street"
Job 19:7 – "but there is no judgment"
Job 19:16 – "and he gave me no answer"
Job 20:21 – "shall no man look for his goods"
Job 24:7 – "they have no covering in the cold"
Job 24:15 – "No eye shall see me"
Job 24:22 – "and no man is sure of life"
Job 26:2 – "the arm that hath no strength"
Job 26:3 – "him that hath no wisdom"
Job 26:6 – "destruction hath no covering"
Job 28:7 – "a path which no fowl knoweth"
Job 28:18 – "No mention shall be made"
Job 30:13 – "they have no helper"
Job 30:17 – "my sinews take no rest"
Job 32:3 – "three friends..had found no answer"
Job 32:5 – "no answer..of these three men"
Job 32:19 – "belly is as wine which hath no vent"
Job 34:22 – "There is no darkness"
Job 36:16 – "where there is no straitness"
Job 38:26 – "on the earth, where no man is"
Job 41:16 – "no air can come between them"
Job 42:2 – "no thought..withholden from thee"
Job 42:15 – "no women found so fair"
Psa 3:2 – "There is no help for him in God"
Psa 5:9 – "no faithfulness in their mouth"
Psa 6:5 – "in death there..no remembrance of thee"
Psa 14:1 – " The fool..said..There is no God"
Psa 14:4 – "workers of iniquity no knowledge"
Psa 19:3 – "There is no speech nor language"
Psa 23:4 – "I will fear no evil"
Psa 32:2 – "in whose spirit there is no guile"
Psa 32:9 – "horse..mule..have no understanding"
Psa 33:16 – "There is no king saved by..an host"
Psa 34:9 – "no want to them that fear him"
Psa 36:1 – "there is no fear of God before his eyes"
Psa 38:3 – "There is no soundness in my flesh"
Psa 38:7 – "there is no soundness in my flesh"
Psa 38:14 – "in whose mouth are no reproofs"
Psa 40:17 – "make no tarrying, O my God"
Psa 50:9 – "take no bullock out of thy house"
Psa 53:1 – "fool hath said..There is no God"
Psa 53:4 – "workers of iniquity no knowledge"

Psa 53:5 – "great fear, where no fear was"
Psa 55:19 – "Because they have no changes"
Psa 63:1 – "thirsty land, where no water is"
Psa 69:2 –"mire, where there is no standing"
Psa 70:5 – "O LORD, make no tarrying"
Psa 72:12 – "him that hath no helper"
Psa 73:4 – "no bands in their death"
Psa 78:64 – "widows made no lamentation"
Psa 81:9 – "no strange god be in thee"
Psa 84:11 – "no good thing will he withhold"
Psa 88:4 – "a man that hath no strength"
Psa 91:10 – "There shall no evil befall thee"
Psa 92:15 – "no unrighteousness in him"
Psa 101:3 – "no wicked thing before mine eyes"
Psa 102:27 – "thy years shall have no end"
Psa 105:14 – "suffered no man to do them wrong"
Psa 105:15 – "do my prophets no harm"
Psa 107:4 – "they found no city to dwell in"
Psa 107:40 – "wilderness, where there is no way"
Psa 119:3 – "They also do no iniquity"
Psa 142:4 –" no man that would know me"
Psa 143:2 – "shall no man living be justified"
Psa 144:14 – "that there be no complaining"
Psa 146:3 – "man, in whom there is no help"
Pro 1:24 – "and no man regarded"
Pro 3:30 – "if he have done thee no harm"
Pro 6:7 – "having no guide, overseer, or ruler"
Pro 8:24 – "When there were no depths"
Pro 8:24 – "when there were no fountains"
Pro 10:22 – "he addeth no sorrow with it"
Pro 11:14 – "Where no counsel is, the people fall"
Pro 12:21 – "shall no evil happen to the just"
Pro 12:28 – "pathway thereof there is no death"
Pro 14:4 – "Where no oxen are..crib is clean"
Pro 17:16 – "seeing he hath no heart to it"
Pro 17:20 – "a froward heart findeth no good"
Pro 17:21 – "the father of a fool hath no joy"
Pro 18:2 – "fool hath no delight in understanding"
Pro 21:10 – "findeth no favour in his eyes"
Pro 21:30 – "no wisdom..against the LORD"
Pro 21:30 – "no..understanding..against the LORD"
Pro 21:30 – "no..counsel..against the LORD"
Pro 22:24 – "no friendship with an angry man"
Pro 24:20 – "no reward to the evil man"
Pro 25:28 – "no rule over his own spirit"
Pro 26:20 – "no wood..the fire goeth out"
Pro 26:20 – "no talebearer, the strife ceaseth"
Pro 28:1 – "wicked flee when no man pursueth"
Pro 28:3 – "sweeping rain which leaveth no food"
Pro 28:17 – "let no man stay him"
Pro 28:24 – "It is no transgression"
Pro 29:9 – "rage or laugh, there is no rest"
Pro 29:18 – "no vision, the people perish"
Pro 30:20 – "I have done no wickedness"
Pro 30:27 – "The locusts have no king"
Pro 31:11 – "he shall have no need of spoil"
Ecc 1:9 – "no new thing under the sun"
Ecc 1:11 – "no remembrance of former things"
Ecc 2:11 – "was no profit under the sun"
Ecc 2:16 – "no remembrance of the wise"
Ecc 3:11 – "no man can find out the work"

Ecc 3:12 – "there is no good in them"
Ecc 3:19 – "a man hath no preeminence"
Ecc 4:1 – "and they had no comforter"
Ecc 4:1 – "but they had no comforter"
Ecc 4:8 – "no end of all his labour"
Ecc 4:16 – "There is no end of all the people"
Ecc 5:4 – "he hath no pleasure in fools"
Ecc 6:3 – "also that he have no burial"
Ecc 6:6 – "yet hath he seen no good"
Ecc 7:21 – "take no heed unto all words"
Ecc 8:5 – "shall feel no evil thing"
Ecc 8:8 – "no man..hath power over the spirit"
Ecc 8:15 – "no better thing under the sun"
Ecc 9:1 – "no man knoweth..love or hatred"
Ecc 9:8 – "let thy head lack no ointment"
Ecc 9:10 – "no work..in the grave"
Ecc 9:10 – "no..device..in the grave"
Ecc 9:10 – "no..knowledge..in the grave"
Ecc 9:10 – "no..wisdom, in the grave"
Ecc 9:15 – "no man remembered that..poor man"
Ecc 12:1 – "I have no pleasure in them"
Ecc 12:12 – "making many books there is no end"
Son 4:7 – "there is no spot in thee"
Son 5:6 – "but he gave me no answer"
Son 8:8 – "sister..she hath no breasts"
Isa 1:6 – "there is no soundness in it"
Isa 1:30 – "a garden that hath no water"
Isa 5:6 – "that they rain no rain upon it"
Isa 5:8 – "till there be no place"
Isa 5:13 – "because they have no knowledge"
Isa 8:20 – "because there is no light in them"
Isa 9:7 – "peace there shall be no end"
Isa 9:17 – "LORD shall have no joy"
Isa 9:19 – "no man shall spare his brother"
Isa 13:14 – "a sheep that no man taketh up"
Isa 13:18 – "they shall have no pity"
Isa 14:8 – "no feller is come up against us"
Isa 15:6 – "there is no green thing"
Isa 16:10 – "there shall be no singing"
Isa 23:1 – "so that there is no house"
Isa 23:10 – "there is no more strength"
Isa 23:12 – "shalt thou have no rest"
Isa 24:10 – "that no man may come in"
Isa 25:2 – "palace of strangers to be no city"
Isa 27:11 – "it is a people of no understanding"
Isa 28:8 – "so that there is no place clean"
Isa 29:16 – "He had no understanding?"
Isa 30:7 – "help in vain, and to no purpose"
Isa 33:8 – "he regardeth no man"
Isa 33:21 – "shall go no galley with oars"
Isa 35:9 – "No lion shall be there"
Isa 37:19 – "for they were no gods"
Isa 40:20 – "he hath no oblation"
Isa 40:28 – "no searching of his understanding"
Isa 40:29 – "them that have no might"
Isa 41:28 – "I beheld, and there was no man"
Isa 43:10 – "before me there was no God"
Isa 43:11 – "beside me there is no saviour"
Isa 43:12 – "there was no strange god among you"
Isa 43:24 – "bought me no sweet cane"
Isa 44:6 – "beside me there is no God"

Isa 44:8 – "yea, there is no God"
Isa 44:12 – "he drinketh no water, and is faint"
Isa 45:5 – "there is no God beside me"
Isa 45:9 – "He hath no hands?"
Isa 45:14 – "is none else, there is no God"
Isa 45:20 – "they have no knowledge"
Isa 45:21 – "there is no God else beside me"
Isa 47:1 – "there is no throne, O..Chaldeans"
Isa 47:6 – "thou didst shew them no mercy"
Isa 48:22 – "is no peace..unto the wicked"
Isa 50:2 – "when I came, was there no man?"
Isa 50:2 – "or have I no power to deliver?"
Isa 50:2 – "there is no water..dieth for thirst"
Isa 50:10 – "walketh in darkness..hath no light"
Isa 52:11 – "touch no unclean thing"
Isa 53:2 – "he hath no form nor comeliness"
Isa 53:2 – "no beauty that we..desire him"
Isa 53:9 – "he had done no violence"
Isa 54:17 – "No weapon..formed..shall prosper"
Isa 55:1 – "he that hath no money; come..buy"
Isa 57:1 – "no man layeth it to heart"
Isa 57:10 – "There is no hope"
Isa 57:21 – "is no peace..to the wicked"
Isa 58:3 – "thou takest no knowledge?"
Isa 59:8 – "no judgment in their goings"
Isa 59:10 – "we grope as if we had no eyes"
Isa 59:15 – "it displeased him..no judgment"
Isa 59:16 – "saw that there was no man"
Isa 59:16 – "there was no intercessor"
Isa 60:15 – "no man went through thee"
Isa 62:7 – "And give him no rest"
Jer 2:6 – "land that no man passed through"
Jer 2:11 – "gods, which are yet no gods?"
Jer 2:13 – "cisterns, that can hold no water"
Jer 2:25 – "There is no hope"
Jer 2:30 – "they received no correction"
Jer 3:3 – "hath been no latter rain"
Jer 4:22 – "to do good they have no knowledge"
Jer 4:23 – "heavens, and they had no light"
Jer 4:25 – "and, lo, there was no man"
Jer 5:7 – "sworn by them that are no gods"
Jer 6:10 – "they have no delight in it"
Jer 6:14 – "peace; when there is no peace"
Jer 6:23 – "cruel, and have no mercy"
Jer 7:32 – "bury..till there be no place"
Jer 8:6 – "no man repented..wickedness"
Jer 8:11 – "peace; when there is no peace"
Jer 8:13 – "shall be no grapes on the vine"
Jer 8:15 – "looked for peace, but no good"
Jer 8:22 – "Is there no balm in Gilead"
Jer 8:22 – "is there no physician there?"
Jer 10:14 – "there is no breath in them"
Jer 11:23 – "shall be no remnant of them"
Jer 12:11 – "no man layeth it to heart"
Jer 12:12 – "no flesh shall have peace"
Jer 14:3 – "came..and found no water"
Jer 14:4 – "there was no rain in the earth"
Jer 14:5 – "because there was no grass"
Jer 14:6 – "because there was no grass"
Jer 14:19 – "there is no healing for us?"
Jer 14:19 – "peace, and there is no good"

Jer 16:19 – "things wherein there is no profit"
Jer 16:20 – "gods..they are no gods?"
Jer 17:21 – "bear no burden.. sabbath day"
Jer 17:24 – " bring in no burden through..gates"
Jer 17:24 – "Sabbath..do no work therein"
Jer 18:12 – "There is no hope"
Jer 19:11 – "till there be no place to bury"
Jer 22:3 – "do no wrong, do no violence"
Jer 22:28 – "vessel wherein is no pleasure?"
Jer 22:30 – "no man of his seed shall prosper"
Jer 23:17 – "No evil shall come upon you"
Jer 25:6 – "I will do you no hurt"
Jer 25:35 – "shepherds..no way to flee"
Jer 30:13 – "thou hast no healing medicines"
Jer 30:17 – "Zion, whom no man seeketh after"
Jer 35:6 – "We will drink no wine"
Jer 35:6 – "Ye shall drink no wine"
Jer 35:8 – "to drink no wine all our days"
Jer 36:19 – "let no man know where ye be"
Jer 38:6 – "in..dungeon there was no water"
Jer 38:24 – "Let no man know of these words"
Jer 39:12 – "and do him no harm"
Jer 40:15 – "slay Ishmael..no man shall know"
Jer 41:4 – "slain Gedaliah, and no man knew it"
Jer 44:2 – "Jerusalem..no man dwelleth"
Jer 44:5 – "burn no incense unto..gods"
Jer 44:17 – "had we plenty..and saw no evil"
Jer 45:3 – "Woe is me..I find no rest"
Jer 48:8 – "no city shall escape"
Jer 48:33 – "shouting shall be no shouting"
Jer 48:38 – "vessel wherein is no pleasure"
Jer 49:1 – "Hath Israel no sons?"
Jer 49:18 – "Sodom..no man shall abide there"
Jer 49:33 – "Hazor..no man abide there"
Jer 49:36 – "there shall be no nation"
Jer 50:14 – "against Babylon..spare no arrows"
Jer 50:40 – "so shall no man abide there"
Jer 51:17 – "there is no breath in them"
Jer 51:43 – "land wherein no man dwelleth"
Jer 52:6 – "famine..there was no bread"
Lam 1:3 – "Judah..she findeth no rest"
Lam 1:6 – "like harts that find no pasture"
Lam 1:9 – "she had no comforter"
Lam 2:9 – "prophets..no vision from the LORD"
Lam 2:18 – "give thyself no rest"
Lam 4:4 – "bread, and no man breaketh it"
Lam 4:6 – "no hands stayed on her"
Lam 5:5 – "we labour, and have no rest"
Eze 13:10 – "Peace; and there was no peace"
Eze 13:16 – "and there is no peace"
Eze 14:15 – "no man may pass through"
Eze 15:5 – "it was meet for no work"
Eze 16:34 – "no reward is given unto thee"
Eze 16:41 – "shalt give no hire any more"
Eze 18:32 – "I have no pleasure in..death "
Eze 19:14 – "she hath no strong rod"
Eze 22:26 – "no difference..holy..profane"
Eze 24:6 – "let no lot fall upon it"
Eze 24:17 – "make no mourning for the dead"
Eze 28:3 – "no secret that they can hide"
Eze 28:9 – "thou shalt be a man, and no God"

Eze 29:11 – "No foot of man shall pass through"
Eze 29:18 – "yet had he no wages, nor his army"
Eze 33:11 – "no pleasure..death of the wicked"
Eze 34:5 – "because there is no shepherd"
Eze 34:8 – "because there was no shepherd"
Eze 36:29 – "and lay no famine upon you"
Eze 37:8 – "there was no breath in them"
Eze 39:10 – "take no wood out of the field"
Eze 44:2 – "gate..no man shall enter in by it"
Eze 44:9 – "No stranger..shall enter..sanctuary"
Eze 44:17 – "no wool shall come upon them"
Eze 44:25 – "shall come at no dead person"
Eze 44:28 – "give them no possession in Israel"
Dan 1:4 – "Children in whom was no blemish"
Dan 2:10 – "there is no king, lord, nor ruler"
Dan 2:35 – "that no place was found for them"
Dan 3:25 – "four men..they have no hurt"
Dan 3:27 – " the fire had no power"
Dan 3:29 – "no other God that can deliver"
Dan 4:9 – "Belteshazzar..no secret troubleth thee"
Dan 6:2 – "the king should have no damage"
Dan 6:15 – " no decree nor statute..be changed"
Dan 6:22 – "O king, have I done no hurt"
Dan 6:23 – "no manner of hurt was found"
Dan 8:4 – "no beasts might stand before him"
Dan 8:7 – "no power in the ram to stand"
Dan 10:3 – "I ate no pleasant bread"
Dan 10:8 – "remained no strength in me"
Dan 10:16 – "I have retained no strength"
Dan 10:17 – "remained no strength in me"
Hos 4:1 – "there is no truth..in the land"
Hos 4:1 – "there is no..mercy..in the land"
Hos 4:1 – "no..knowledge of God in the land"
Hos 4:4 – "Yet let no man strive"
Hos 4:6 – "thou shalt be no priest to me"
Hos 8:7 – "it hath no stalk"
Hos 8:7 – "the bud shall yield no meal"
Hos 8:8 – "a vessel wherein is no pleasure"
Hos 9:16 – "Ephraim..shall bear no fruit"
Hos 10:3 – "shall say, We have no king"
Hos 13:4 – "know no god but me"
Hos 13:4 – "for there is no saviour beside me"
Joe 1:18 – "herds of cattle..have no pasture"
Joe 3:17 – "shall no strangers pass through"
Amo 3:4 – "a lion..hath no prey?"
Amo 3:5 – "Can a bird fall..where no gin is"
Amo 5:20 – "day of the LORD..no brightness"
Amo 7:14 – "answered Amos..I was no prophet"
Mic 3:7 – "for there is no answer of God"
Mic 4:9 – "is there no king in thee?"
Mic 5:12 – "shalt have no more soothsayers"
Mic 7:1 – "there is no cluster to eat"
Nah 3:18 – "and no man gathereth them"
Nah 3:19 – "is no healing of thy bruise"
Hab 1:14 – "fishes..that have no ruler"
Hab 2:19 – "there is no breath at all"
Hab 3:17 – "the fields shall yield no meat"
Hab 3:17 – "shall be no herd in the stalls"
Zep 2:5 – "there shall be no inhabitant"
Zep 3:5 – "LORD..he will not do iniquity"
Zep 3:5 – "the unjust knoweth no shame"

Zep 3:6 – "so that there is no man"
Zec 1:21 – "no man did lift up his head"
Zec 7:14 – "no man passed through"
Zec 8:10 – "there was no hire for man"
Zec 8:17 – "love no false oath"
Zec 9:8 – "no oppressor shall pass through"
Zec 9:11 – "the pit wherein is no water"
Zec 10:2 – "there was no shepherd"
Zec 13:5 – "I am no prophet"
Zec 14:17 – "upon them shall be no rain"
Zec 14:18 – "family..that have no rain"
Mal 1:10 – "I have no pleasure in you"
Mat 6:1 – "no reward of your Father"
Mat 6:24 – "No man can serve two masters"
Mat 6:25 – "Take no thought for your life"
Mat 6:31 – "Therefore take no thought"
Mat 6:34 – "Take..no thought for the morrow"
Mat 8:4 – "See thou tell no man"
Mat 8:28 – "that no man might pass by"
Mat 9:16 – "No man putteth a piece of..cloth"
Mat 9:30 – "See that no man know it"
Mat 9:36 – "as sheep having no shepherd"
Mat 10:19 – "take no thought how..ye..speak"
Mat 11:27 – "no man knoweth the Son"
Mat 12:39 – "shall no sign be given to it"
Mat 13:5 – "had no deepness of earth"
Mat 13:6 – "had no root, they withered away"
Mat 16:4 – "no sign be given unto it"
Mat 16:7 – "we have taken no bread"
Mat 16:8 – "ye have brought no bread"
Mat 16:20 – "tell no man that he was..Christ"
Mat 17:8 – "saw no man, save Jesus only"
Mat 17:9 – "Tell the vision to no man"
Mat 19:18 – "Thou shalt do no murder"
Mat 20:7 – "Because no man hath hired us"
Mat 20:13 – "Friend, I do thee no wrong"
Mat 21:19 – "Let no fruit grow on thee"
Mat 22:23 – "say that there is no resurrection"
Mat 22:24 – "a man die, having no children"
Mat 22:25 – "seven brethren.. having no issue"
Mat 22:46 – "And no man was able to answer"
Mat 23:9 – "And call no man your father"
Mat 24:4 – "Take heed that no man deceive you"
Mat 24:22 – "there should no flesh be saved"
Mat 25:3 – "and took no oil with them"
Mat 25:42 – "ye gave me no meat"
Mat 25:42 – "ye gave me no drink"
Mat 26:55 – "and ye laid no hold on me"
Mar 2:17 – "have no need of the physician"
Mar 2:21 – "No man also seweth"
Mar 2:22 – "no man putteth new wine"
Mar 3:27 – "No man can enter into"
Mar 4:5 – "it had no depth of earth"
Mar 4:6 – "it had no root, it withered away"
Mar 4:7 – "choked it..yielded no fruit"
Mar 4:17 – "have no root in themselves"
Mar 4:40 – "how is it that ye have no faith?"
Mar 5:3 – "no man could bind him"
Mar 5:37 – "suffered no man to follow him"
Mar 5:43 – "that no man should know it"
Mar 6:5 – "could there do no mighty work"

Mar 6:8 – "no scrip, no bread, no money"
Mar 6:31 – "no leisure so much as to eat"
Mar 7:24 – "would have no man know it"
Mar 7:36 – "that they should tell no man"
Mar 8:12 – "There shall no sign be given"
Mar 8:16 – "because we have no bread"
Mar 8:17 – "because ye have no bread?"
Mar 8:30 – "they should tell no man of him"
Mar 9:3 – "as no fuller on earth can white"
Mar 9:8 – "they saw no man any more"
Mar 9:9 – "tell no man what..they had seen"
Mar 9:39 – "no man which shall do a miracle"
Mar 10:29 – "no man that hath left house"
Mar 11:14 – "No man eat fruit of thee"
Mar 12:14 – "carest for no man"
Mar 12:18 – "say there is no resurrection"
Mar 12:19 – "brother die..leave no children"
Mar 12:20 – "seven brethren.. dying left no seed"
Mar 12:22 – "seven had her, and left no seed"
Mar 12:34 – "no man after that durst ask"
Mar 13:11 – "take no thought beforehand"
Mar 13:20 – "no flesh should be saved"
Mar 13:32 – "day..hour knoweth no man"
Luk 1:7 – "And they had no child"
Luk 1:33 – "of his kingdom..shall be no end"
Luk 2:7 – "no room for them in the inn"
Luk 3:14 – "Do violence to no man"
Luk 4:24 – "No prophet is accepted"
Luk 5:14 – "charged him to tell no man"
Luk 5:36 – "No man putteth a piece"
Luk 5:37 – "And no man putteth new wine"
Luk 5:39 – "No man also having drunk old wine"
Luk 7:44 – " gavest me no water for my feet"
Luk 7:45 – "Thou gavest me no kiss"
Luk 8:13 – "these have no root"
Luk 8:14 – "bring no fruit to perfection"
Luk 8:16 – "No man..lighted a candle"
Luk 8:27 – "certain man..ware no clothes"
Luk 8:51 – "he suffered no man to go in"
Luk 8:56 – "should tell no man what was done"
Luk 9:21 – "to tell no man that thing"
Luk 9:36 – "told no man in those days"
Luk 9:62 – "No man..hand to the plough"
Luk 10:4 – "salute no man by the way"
Luk 10:22 – "no man knoweth who the Son is"
Luk 11:20 – "no doubt the kingdom of God"
Luk 11:29 – "shall no sign be given it"
Luk 11:33 – "No man..lighted a candle"
Luk 11:36 – "body..having no part dark"
Luk 12:11 – "no thought how..what..answer"
Luk 12:17 – "no room..to bestow my fruits"
Luk 12:22 – "Take no thought for your life"
Luk 12:33 – "where no thief approacheth"
Luk 15:7 – "persons, which need no repentance"
Luk 15:16 – "no man gave unto him"
Luk 16:13 – "No servant can serve two masters"
Luk 18:29 – "no man that hath left house"
Luk 20:31 – "left no children, and died"
Luk 22:36 – "he that hath no sword"
Luk 22:53 – "stretched forth no hands"
Luk 23:4 – "I find no fault in this man"

Luk 23:14 – "found no fault in this man"
Luk 23:22 – "I have found no cause of death"
Joh 1:18 – "No man hath seen God at any time"
Joh 1:47 – "an Israelite..in whom is no guile!"
Joh 2:3 – "They have no wine"
Joh 3:2 – "no man can do these miracles"
Joh 3:13 – "And no man hath ascended"
Joh 3:32 – "no man receiveth his testimony"
Joh 4:9 – "Jews have no dealings..Samaritans"
Joh 4:17 – "I have no husband"
Joh 4:17 – "I have no husband"
Joh 4:27 – "no man said, What seekest thou?"
Joh 4:38 – "whereon ye bestowed no labour"
Joh 4:44 – "a prophet hath no honour"
Joh 5:7 – "Sir, I have no man"
Joh 5:22 – "the Father judgeth no man"
Joh 6:44 – "No man can come to me"
Joh 6:53 – "ye have no life in you"
Joh 6:65 – "no man can come unto me"
Joh 7:4 – "no man..doeth any thing in secret"
Joh 7:13 – "no man spake openly of him"
Joh 7:18 – "no unrighteousness is in him"
Joh 7:27 – "no man knoweth whence he is"
Joh 7:30 – "no man laid hands on him"
Joh 7:44 – "but no man laid hands on him"
Joh 7:52 – "out of Galilee ariseth no prophet"
Joh 8:10 – "hath no man condemned thee?"
Joh 8:11 – "She said, No man, Lord."
Joh 8:15 – "I judge no man"
Joh 8:20 – "and no man laid hands on him"
Joh 8:37 – "my word hath no place in you"
Joh 8:44 – "because there is no truth in him"
Joh 9:4 – "the night cometh..no man can work"
Joh 9:41 – "ye should have no sin"
Joh 10:18 – "No man taketh it from me"
Joh 10:29 – "no man is able to pluck them out"
Joh 10:41 – "John did no miracle"
Joh 11:10 – "because there is no light in him"
Joh 13:8 – "thou hast no part with me"
Joh 13:28 – "no man at the table knew"
Joh 14:6 – "no man cometh unto the Father"
Joh 15:13 – "Greater love hath no man"
Joh 15:22 – "they have no cloke for their sin"
Joh 16:22 – "your joy no man taketh from you"
Joh 16:29 – "plainly, and speakest no proverb"
Joh 18:38 – "Pilate..I find in him no fault at all"
Joh 19:4 – "that I find no fault in him"
Joh 19:6 – "for I find no fault in him"
Joh 19:9 – "But Jesus gave him no answer."
Joh 19:11 – "no power at all against me"
Joh 19:15 – "We have no king but Caesar"
Act 1:20 – "and let no man dwell therein"
Act 4:17 – "speak..to no man in this name"
Act 5:13 – "durst no man join himself"
Act 5:23 – "we found no man within"
Act 7:11 – "our fathers found no sustenance"
Act 9:7 – "hearing a voice, but seeing no man"
Act 9:8 – "eyes..opened, he saw no man"
Act 10:34 – "God is no respecter of persons"
Act 12:18 – "no small stir among the soldiers"
Act 13:28 – "no cause of death in him"

Act 13:37 – "But he..saw no corruption"
Act 15:9 – "no difference between us and them"
Act 15:24 – "we gave no such commandment"
Act 15:28 – "lay upon you no greater burden"
Act 16:28 – "Do thyself no harm"
Act 18:10 – "no man shall set on thee..hurt thee"
Act 18:15 – "I will be no judge of such matters"
Act 19:23 – "arose no small stir about that way"
Act 19:24 – "no small gain unto the craftsmen"
Act 19:26 – "they be no gods..made with hands"
Act 19:40 – "no cause..may give an account"
Act 20:33 – "coveted no man's silver..gold"
Act 21:25 – "they observe no such thing"
Act 21:39 – "a citizen of no mean city"
Act 23:8 – "say that there is no resurrection"
Act 23:9 – "We find no evil in this man"
Act 23:22 – "see thou tell no man"
Act 25:10 – "to the Jews have I done no wrong"
Act 25:11 – "no man may deliver me unto them"
Act 25:26 – "I have no certain thing to write"
Act 27:22 – "no loss of any man's life"
Act 28:4 – "No doubt this man is a murderer"
Act 28:5 – "shook off the beast..felt no harm"
Act 28:6 – "saw no harm come to him"
Act 28:18 – "there was no cause of death in me"
Act 28:31 – "no man forbidding him"
Rom 2:11 – "no respect of persons with God"
Rom 3:18 – "no fear of God before their eyes"
Rom 3:20 – "no flesh be justified in his sight"
Rom 3:22 – "for there is no difference"
Rom 4:15 – "there is no transgression"
Rom 5:13 – "when there is no law"
Rom 7:3 – "so that she is no adulteress"
Rom 7:18 – "in me..dwelleth no good thing"
Rom 8:1 – "therefore now no condemnation"
Rom 10:12 – "no difference..Jew..Greek"
Rom 10:19 – "by them that are no people"
Rom 12:17 – "Recompense to no man evil"
Rom 13:1 – "there is no power but of God"
Rom 13:8 – "Owe no man any thing"
Rom 13:10 – "Love worketh no ill"
Rom 14:7 – "no man dieth to himself"
Rom 14:13 – "no man put a stumblingblock"
1Co 1:7 – "come behind in no gift"
1Co 1:10 – "there be no divisions among you"
1Co 1:29 – "That no flesh should glory"
1Co 2:11 – "things of God knoweth no man"
1Co 2:15 – "he himself is judged of no man"
1Co 3:11 – "other foundation can no man lay"
1Co 3:18 – "Let no man deceive himself."
1Co 3:21 – "let no man glory in men"
1Co 4:11 – "and have no certain dwellingplace"
1Co 7:25 – "no commandment of the Lord"
1Co 7:37 – "no necessity, but hath power"
1Co 8:13 – "I will eat no flesh while the world"
1Co 10:13 – "no temptation taken you"
1Co 10:24 – "Let no man seek his own"
1Co 10:25 – "eat, asking no question"
1Co 10:27 – "no question..conscience sake"
1Co 11:16 – "we have no such custom"
1Co 12:3 – "no man speaking by the Spirit"

1Co 12:3 – "no man can say that Jesus is the Lord"
1Co 12:21 – "I have no need of thee"
1Co 12:21 – "I have no need of you"
1Co 12:24 – "our comely parts have no need"
1Co 12:25 – "be no schism in the body"
1Co 13:5 – "thinketh no evil"
1Co 14:2 – "for no man understandeth him"
1Co 14:28 – "if there be no interpreter"
1Co 15:12 – "is no resurrection of the dead"
1Co 15:13 – "be no resurrection of the dead"
1Co 16:2 – "be no gatherings when I come"
1Co 16:11 – "Let no man therefore despise"
2Co 2:13 – "I had no rest in my spirit"
2Co 3:10 – "had no glory in this respect"
2Co 5:16 – "know we no man after the flesh"
2Co 5:21 – "who knew no sin"
2Co 6:3 – "Giving no offence in any thing"
2Co 7:2 – "we have wronged no man"
2Co 7:2 – "we have corrupted no man"
2Co 7:2 – "we have defrauded no man"
2Co 7:5 – "our flesh had no rest"
2Co 8:15 – "had gathered little had no lack"
2Co 8:20 – "no man should blame us"
2Co 11:9 – "I was chargeable to no man"
2Co 11:10 – "no man shall stop me"
2Co 11:15 – "Therefore it is no great thing"
2Co 11:16 – "Let no man think me a fool"
2Co 13:7 – "I pray to God that ye do no evil"
Gal 2:16 – "shall no flesh be justified"
Gal 3:11 – "no man is justified by the law"
Gal 3:15 – "no man disannulleth, or addeth"
Gal 5:4 – "Christ is become of no effect"
Gal 5:23 – "against such there is no law"
Gal 6:17 – "let no man trouble me"
Eph 2:12 – "having no hope, and without God"
Eph 4:29 – "Let no corrupt communication"
Eph 5:5 – "no whoremonger.. in the kingdom"
Eph 5:6 – "Let no man deceive you"
Eph 5:11 – "have no fellowship with..darkness"
Eph 5:29 – "no man ever yet hated his own flesh"
Php 2:7 – "made himself of no reputation"
Php 2:20 – "I have no man likeminded"
Php 3:3 – "have no confidence in the flesh"
Php 4:15 – "no church communicated"
Col 2:16 – "Let no man therefore judge you"
Col 2:18 – "Let no man beguile you"
Col 3:25 – "there is no respect of persons"
1Th 3:3 – "no man should be moved by these"
1Th 4:6 – "That no man go beyond..defraud"
1Th 4:13 – "as others which have no hope"
1Th 5:1 – "ye have no need that I write"
2Th 2:3 – "Let no man deceive you"
2Th 3:14 – "have no company with him"
1Ti 4:12 – "Let no man despise thy youth"
1Ti 5:22 – "Lay hands suddenly on no man"
1Ti 6:16 – "light which no man can approach"
1Ti 6:16 – "whom no man hath seen"
2Ti 2:4 – "No man that warreth entangleth"
2Ti 2:14 – "about words to no profit"
2Ti 4:16 – "At my first answer no man stood"

Tit 2:8 – "having no evil thing to say of you"
Tit 2:15 – "Let no man despise thee."
Tit 3:2 – "To speak evil of no man"
Heb 5:4 – "no man taketh this honour"
Heb 7:13 – "of which no man gave attendance"
Heb 8:7 – "no place have been sought"
Heb 9:17 – "it is of no strength at all"
Heb 9:22 – "shedding of blood is no remission"
Heb 10:6 – "thou hast had no pleasure"
Heb 10:38 – "soul shall have no pleasure"
Heb 12:11 – "no chastening..seemeth..joyous"
Heb 12:14 – "no man shall see the Lord"
Heb 12:17 – "found no place of repentance"
Heb 13:10 – "whereof they have no right to eat"
Heb 13:14 – "have we no continuing city"
Jas 1:13 – "Let no man say when..tempted"
Jas 1:17 – "with whom is no variableness"
Jas 2:13 – "that hath shewed no mercy"
Jas 3:8 – "the tongue can no man tame"
Jas 3:12 – "no fountain both yield salt..fresh"
1Pe 2:22 – "Who did no sin"
1Pe 3:10 – "his lips that they speak no guile"
2Pe 1:20 – "no prophecy of the scripture"
1Jn 1:5 – "in him is no darkness at all"
1Jn 1:8 – "say that we have no sin"
1Jn 2:7 – "I write no new commandment"
1Jn 2:19 – "no doubt have continued with us"
1Jn 2:21 – "that no lie is of the truth"
1Jn 2:27 – "is truth, and is no lie"
1Jn 3:5 – "and in him is no sin"
1Jn 3:7 – "let no man deceive you"
1Jn 3:15 – "no murderer hath eternal life"
1Jn 4:12 – "No man hath seen God at any time."
1Jn 4:18 – "There is no fear in love"
Rev 2:17 – "which no man knoweth"
Rev 3:7 – "openeth, and no man shutteth"
Rev 3:7 – "shutteth, and no man openeth"
Rev 3:8 – "and no man can shut it"
Rev 3:11 – "that no man take thy crown"
Rev 5:3 – "And no man in heaven"
Rev 5:4 – "no man was found worthy"
Rev 7:9 – "which no man could number"
Rev 13:17 – "that no man might buy or sell"
Rev 14:3 – "no man could learn that song"
Rev 14:5 – "in their mouth was found no guile"
Rev 14:11 – "they have no rest day nor night"
Rev 15:8 – "no man..able to enter..the temple"
Rev 17:12 – "received no kingdom as yet"
Rev 18:7 – "I sit a queen, and am no widow"
Rev 18:11 – "no man buyeth their merchandise"
Rev 18:22 – "no craftsman..found any more"
Rev 19:12 – "name written, that no man knew"
Rev 20:6 – "the second death hath no power"
Rev 20:11 – "was found no place for them"
Rev 21:22 – "And I saw no temple therein"
Rev 21:23 – "the city had no need of the sun"
Rev 21:25 – "there shall be no night there"
Rev 22:5 – "there shall be no night there"
Rev 22:5 – "and they need no candle"

None

"None" (358x) usually appears in the Bible as a pronoun. Standing alone as such, it can represent zero – eg. *"there is none so discreet and wise..."* (Gen 41:39) Such instances will be found in the following list, but as they do not clearly count or modify anything they will not appear in the **Index of Numbered Items** in Section Three of this volume.

"None" can also appear as an adjective counting something, usually in conjunction with the word "other" – eg. *"Thou shalt have none other gods before me."* (Deu 5:7) Because "gods" are being counted (zero of them!), these instances will appear in the **Index of Numbered Items**. Please note however that when the phrase "none other" appears by itself and counts nothing, it has not been included.

Gen 23:6 – "none of us shall withhold"
Gen 39:11 – "none of the men of the house"
Gen 41:8 – "there was none that could interpret"
Gen 41:15 – "there is none that can interpret it"
Gen 41:24 – "none that could declare it to me"
Gen 41:39 – "there is none so discreet and wise"
Exo 8:10 – "there is none like..the LORD"
Exo 9:14 – "there is none like me"
Exo 9:24 – "was none like it in..Egypt"
Exo 11:6 – "as there was none like it"
Exo 12:22 – "none of you shall go out"
Exo 15:26 – "none of these diseases upon thee"
Exo 16:26 – "sabbath, in it there shall be none"
Exo 16:27 – "seventh day..they found none"
Exo 23:15 – "none shall appear before me empty"
Exo 34:20 – "none shall appear before me empty"
Lev 18:6 – "None..approach to any..near of kin"
Lev 21:1 – "none be defiled for the dead"
Lev 22:30 – "leave none of it until the morrow"
Lev 25:26 – "if the man have none to redeem it"
Lev 26:6 – "none shall make you afraid"
Lev 26:17 – "ye shall flee when none pursueth"
Lev 26:36 – "they shall fall when none pursueth"
Lev 26:37 – "when none pursueth"
Lev 27:29 – "None devoted..shall be redeemed"
Num 7:9 – "unto the sons of Kohath he gave none"
Num 9:12 – "leave none of it unto the morning"
Num 21:35 – "until there was none left him alive"
Num 30:8 – "that which..uttered..of none effect"
Num 32:11 – "none of..men that came..of Egypt"
Deu 2:34 – "we left none to remain"
Deu 3:3 – "we smote him until none was left"
Deu 4:35 – "there is none else beside him"
Deu 4:39 – "LORD he is God..there is none else"
Deu 5:7 – "none other gods before me"
Deu 7:15 – "none of the evil diseases of Egypt"
Deu 22:27 – "and there was none to save her"
Deu 28:31 – "thou shalt have none to rescue them"
Deu 28:66 – "shalt have none assurance of thy life"
Deu 32:36 – "and there is none shut up, or left"
Deu 33:26 – "none like unto the God of Jeshurun"
Jos 6:1 – "none went out, and none came in"
Jos 8:22 – "let none of them remain or escape"
Jos 9:23 – "there shall none of you be freed"
Jos 10:21 – "none moved his tongue"
Jos 10:28 – "he let none remain"
Jos 10:30 – "he let none remain in it"
Jos 10:33 – "he had left him none remaining"
Jos 10:37 – "he left none remaining"
Jos 10:39 – "he left none remaining"

Jos 10:40 – "he left none remaining"
Jos 11:8 – "they left them none remaining"
Jos 11:13 – "Israel burned none of them"
Jos 11:22 – "none of the Anakims left in the land"
Jos 13:14 – "unto..Levi he gave none inheritance"
Jos 14:3 – "he gave none inheritance among them"
Jdg 19:28 – "let us be going. But none answered."
Jdg 21:8 – "none to the camp from Jabeshgilead"
Jdg 21:9 – "none of..inhabitants of Jabeshgilead"
Rth 4:4 – "none to redeem it beside thee"
1Sa 2:2 – "There is none holy as the LORD"
1Sa 3:19 – "let none of his words fall to..ground"
1Sa 10:24 – "none like him among all the people?"
1Sa 14:24 – "none of the people tasted any food"
1Sa 21:9 – "There is none like that; give it me"
1Sa 22:8 – "there is none that sheweth me"
2Sa 7:22 – "for there is none like thee"
2Sa 14:6 – "there was none to part them"
2Sa 14:19 – "none can turn to the right hand"
2Sa 14:25 – "was none to be so much praised"
2Sa 18:12 – "Beware that none touch..Absalom"
2Sa 22:42 – "but there was none to save"
1Ki 3:12 – "there was none like thee before thee"
1Ki 8:60 – "God, and that there is none else"
1Ki 10:21 – "vessels of..gold; none were of silver"
1Ki 12:20 – "none that followed..house of David"
1Ki 15:22 – "all Judah; none was exempted"
1Ki 21:25 – "But there was none like unto Ahab"
2Ki 5:16 – "As the LORD liveth..I will receive none"
2Ki 6:12 – "None, my lord, O king: but Elisha"
2Ki 9:10 – "there shall be none to bury her"
2Ki 9:15 – "let none go forth nor escape"
2Ki 10:11 – "until he left him none remaining"
2Ki 10:19 – "let none be wanting"
2Ki 10:23 – "none of the servants of the LORD"
2Ki 10:25 – "Go in..slay..let none come forth"
2Ki 17:18 – "none left but the tribe of Judah only"
2Ki 18:5 – "none like him among all the kings"
2Ki 24:14 – "none remained, save the poorest"
1Ch 15:2 – "None ought to carry the ark of God"
1Ch 17:20 – "O LORD, there is none like thee"
1Ch 23:17 – "Eliezer had none other sons"
1Ch 29:15 – "and there is none abiding"
2Ch 1:12 – "as none of the kings have had"
2Ch 9:11 – "there were none such seen before"
2Ch 9:20 – "drinking vessels..none were of silver"
2Ch 10:16 – "none inheritance in the son of Jesse"
2Ch 16:1 – "let none go out or come in to Asa"
2Ch 20:6 – "none is able to withstand thee?"
2Ch 20:24 – "they were dead..and none escaped"

2Ch 23:6 – "let none..into the house of the LORD"
2Ch 23:19 – "none which..unclean..should enter"
Ezr 8:15 – "found there none of the sons of Levi"
Neh 4:23 – "none of us put off our clothes"
Est 1:8 – "the drinking..none did compel"
Est 4:2 – "none might enter..with sackcloth"
Job 1:8 – "Job..none like him in the earth"
Job 2:3 – "Job..none like him in the earth"
Job 2:13 – "and none spake a word unto him"
Job 3:9 – "let it look for light, but have none"
Job 10:7 – "none..can deliver out of thine hand"
Job 11:19 – "none shall make thee afraid"
Job 18:15 – "because it is none of his"
Job 20:21 – "shall none of his meat be left"
Job 29:12 – "had none to help him"
Job 32:12 – "none of you that convinced Job"
Job 35:10 – "But none saith, Where is God"
Job 35:12 – "they cry, but none giveth answer"
Job 41:10 – "None..so fierce that dare stir him up"
Psa 7:2 – "while there is none to deliver"
Psa 10:15 – "seek..wickedness till thou find none"
Psa 14:1 – "there is none that doeth good"
Psa 14:3 – "there is none that doeth good"
Psa 18:41 – "there was none to save them"
Psa 22:11 – "for there is none to help"
Psa 22:29 – "none can keep alive his own soul"
Psa 25:3 – "none that wait on thee be ashamed"
Psa 33:10 – "devices of the people of none effect"
Psa 34:22 – "none..that trust in him..be desolate"
Psa 37:31 – "none of his steps shall slide"
Psa 49:7 – "None..can..redeem his brother"
Psa 50:22 – "and there be none to deliver"
Psa 53:1 – "there is none that doeth good"
Psa 53:3 – "there is none that doeth good"
Psa 69:20 – "I for some to take pity, but..none"
Psa 69:20 – "Looked..for comforters, but..none"
Psa 69:25 – "let none dwell in their tents"
Psa 71:11 – "for there is none to deliver him"
Psa 73:25 – "none upon earth that I desire"
Psa 76:5 – "none of the men..found their hands"
Psa 79:3 – "there was none to bury them"
Psa 81:11 – "and Israel would none of me"
Psa 86:8 – "none like unto thee, O LORD"
Psa 107:12 – "and there was none to help"
Psa 109:12 – "none to extend mercy unto him"
Psa 139:16 – "all my members..none of them"
Pro 1:25 – "and would none of my reproof"
Pro 1:30 – "They would none of my counsel"
Pro 2:19 – "None that go unto her return again"
Pro 3:31 – "choose none of his ways"
Son 4:2 – "sheep..none is barren among them"
Isa 1:31 – "burn..and none shall quench them"
Isa 5:27 – "None shall be weary nor stumble"
Isa 5:27 – "none shall slumber nor sleep"
Isa 5:29 – "and none shall deliver it"
Isa 10:14 – "none that moved the wing"
Isa 14:6 – "is persecuted, and none hindereth"
Isa 14:31 – "none shall be alone"
Isa 17:2 – "none shall make them afraid"
Isa 22:22 – "open, and none shall shut"
Isa 22:22 – "shall shut, and none shall open"

Isa 34:10 – "none shall pass through it for ever"
Isa 34:12 – "the nobles..but none shall be there"
Isa 34:16 – "none shall want her mate"
Isa 41:17 – "seek water, and there is none"
Isa 41:26 – "there is none that sheweth"
Isa 41:26 – "there is none that declareth"
Isa 41:26 – "there is none that heareth"
Isa 42:22 – "for a prey, and none delivereth"
Isa 42:22 – "for a spoil, and none saith, Restore"
Isa 43:13 – "none that can deliver out of my hand"
Isa 44:19 – "And none considereth in his heart"
Isa 45:5 – "I am the LORD..there is none else"
Isa 45:6 – "there is none beside me"
Isa 45:6 – "I am the LORD..there is none else"
Isa 45:14 – "God is in thee..there is none else"
Isa 45:18 – "I am the LORD..there is none else"
Isa 45:21 – "a Saviour; there is none beside me"
Isa 45:22 – "I am God, and there is none else"
Isa 46:9 – "God, and there is none else"
Isa 46:9 – "I am God, and there is none like me"
Isa 47:8 – "I am, and none else beside me"
Isa 47:10 – "thou hast said, None seeth me"
Isa 47:10 – "I am, and none else beside me"
Isa 47:15 – "none shall save thee"
Isa 50:2 – "was there none to answer?"
Isa 51:18 – "There is none to guide her"
Isa 57:1 – "men..taken away, none considering"
Isa 59:4 – "None calleth for justice"
Isa 59:11 – "look for judgment, but there is none"
Isa 63:3 – "people there was none with me"
Isa 63:5 – "there was none to uphold"
Isa 64:7 – "none that calleth upon thy name"
Isa 66:4 – "I called, none did answer"
Jer 4:4 – "fury..burn that none can quench it"
Jer 4:22 – "they have none understanding"
Jer 7:33 – "none shall fray them away"
Jer 9:10 – "none can pass through them"
Jer 9:12 – "that none passeth through?"
Jer 9:22 – "and none shall gather them"
Jer 10:6 – "is none like unto thee, O LORD"
Jer 10:7 – "there is none like unto thee"
Jer 10:20 – "none to stretch forth my tent"
Jer 13:19 – "cities..shut up..none shall open them"
Jer 14:16 – "shall have none to bury them"
Jer 21:12 – "burn that none can quench it"
Jer 23:14 – "none..return from his wickedness"
Jer 30:7 – "day is great, so that none is like it"
Jer 30:10 – "and none shall make him afraid"
Jer 30:13 – "There is none to plead thy cause"
Jer 34:9 – "none should serve himself of them"
Jer 34:10 – "none should serve themselves"
Jer 35:14 – "wine..unto this day they drink none"
Jer 36:30 – "none to sit upon the throne of David"
Jer 42:17 – "none of them shall remain or escape"
Jer 44:7 – "to leave you none to remain"
Jer 44:14 – "none of the remnant of Judah"
Jer 44:14 – "none shall return but..shall escape"
Jer 46:27 – "none shall make him afraid"
Jer 48:33 – "none shall tread with shouting"
Jer 49:5 – "none shall gather up him"
Jer 50:3 – "none shall dwell therein"

Jer 50:9 – "none shall return in vain"
Jer 50:20 – "iniquity..sought..shall be none"
Jer 50:29 – "let none thereof escape"
Jer 50:32 – "none shall raise him up"
Jer 51:62 – "none shall remain in it"
Lam 1:2 – "among..lovers..none to comfort"
Lam 1:4 – "none come to the solemn feasts"
Lam 1:7 – "none did help her"
Lam 1:17 – "there is none to comfort her"
Lam 1:21 – "there is none to comfort me"
Lam 2:22 – "none escaped nor remained"
Lam 5:8 – "there is none that doth deliver"
Eze 7:11 – "none of them shall remain"
Eze 7:14 – "but none goeth to the battle"
Eze 7:25 – "seek peace..there shall be none"
Eze 12:28 – "none of my words be prolonged"
Eze 16:5 – "None eye pitied thee"
Eze 16:34 – "none followeth thee..whoredoms"
Eze 18:7 – "spoiled none by violence"
Eze 22:30 – "sought for a man..found none"
Eze 31:14 – "none of..trees..exalt themselves"
Eze 33:16 – "None of his sins..be mentioned"
Eze 33:28 – "that none shall pass through"
Eze 34:6 – "none did search or seek after them"
Eze 34:28 – "none shall make them afraid"
Eze 39:26 – "and none made them afraid"
Eze 39:28 – "left none of them any more"
Dan 1:19 – "was found none like Daniel"
Dan 2:11 – "none other that can shew it"
Dan 4:35 – "none can stay his hand"
Dan 6:4 – "find none occasion nor fault"
Dan 8:7 – "none that could deliver the ram"
Dan 8:27 – "but none understood it"
Dan 10:21 – "none that holdeth with me"
Dan 11:16 – "none shall stand before him"
Dan 11:45 – "and none shall help him"
Dan 12:10 – "none of the wicked..understand"
Hos 2:10 – "none shall deliver her"
Hos 5:14 – "and none shall rescue him"
Hos 7:7 – "none among them that calleth"
Hos 11:7 – "none at all would exalt him"
Hos 12:8 – "shall find none iniquity in me"
Joe 2:27 – "I am the LORD..and none else"
Amo 5:2 – "there is none to raise her up"
Amo 5:6 – "none to quench it in Bethel"
Oba 1:7 – "is none understanding in him"
Mic 2:5 – "none that shall cast a cord by lot"
Mic 3:11 – "none evil can come upon us"
Mic 4:4 – "none shall make them afraid"
Mic 5:8 – "and none can deliver"
Mic 7:2 – "there is none upright among men"
Nah 2:8 – "but none shall look back"
Nah 2:9 – "is none end of the store and glory"
Nah 2:11 – "and none made them afraid?"
Nah 3:3 – "there is none end of their corpses"
Zep 2:15 – "there is none beside me"
Zep 3:6 – "that none passeth by"
Zep 3:6 – "that there is none inhabitant"
Zep 3:13 – "and none shall make them afraid"
Zec 7:10 – "let none of you imagine evil"
Zec 8:17 – "let none of you imagine evil"

Mal 2:15 – "let none deal treacherously"
Mat 12:43 – "seeking rest, and findeth none"
Mat 15:6 – "commandment..of none effect"
Mat 19:17 – "there is none good but one"
Mat 26:60 – "But found none"
Mat 26:60 – "witnesses..yet found they none"
Mar 7:13 – "word of God of none effect"
Mar 10:18 – "there is none good but one"
Mar 12:31 – "none other commandment greater"
Mar 12:32 – "one God; and there is none other"
Mar 14:55 – "sought for witness..found none"
Luk 1:61 – "none of thy kindred..by this name"
Luk 3:11 – "2 coats..impart to him that hath none"
Luk 4:26 – "unto none of them was Elias sent"
Luk 4:27 – "lepers..none of them was cleansed"
Luk 11:24 – "seeking rest; and finding none"
Luk 13:6 – "sought fruit thereon..found none"
Luk 13:7 – "seeking fruit..and find none"
Luk 14:24 – "none of those men..bidden"
Luk 18:19 – "none is good, save one, that is, God"
Luk 18:34 – "understood none of these things"
Joh 6:22 – "there was none other boat there"
Joh 7:19 – "none of you keepeth the law?"
Joh 8:10 – "saw none but the woman"
Joh 15:24 – "works which none other man did"
Joh 16:5 – "and none of you asketh me"
Joh 17:12 – "and none of them is lost"
Joh 18:9 – "gavest me have I lost none"
Joh 21:12 – "none of the disciples..ask him"
Act 3:6 – "Silver and gold have I none"
Act 4:12 – "none other name under heaven"
Act 7:5 – "gave him none inheritance in it"
Act 8:16 – "he was fallen upon none of them"
Act 8:24 – "none of these things..upon me"
Act 11:19 – "to none but unto the Jews only"
Act 18:17 – "Gallio cared for none of those"
Act 20:24 – "none of these things move me"
Act 24:23 – "forbid none of his acquaintance"
Act 25:11 – "if there be none of these things"
Act 25:18 – "they brought none accusation"
Act 26:22 – "saying none other things"
Act 26:26 – "none of these things are hidden"
Rom 3:10 – "There is none righteous"
Rom 3:11 – "none that understandeth"
Rom 3:11 – "none that seeketh after God"
Rom 3:12 – "none that doeth good"
Rom 4:14 – "promise made of none effect"
Rom 8:9 – "he is none of his"
Rom 9:6 – "word of God..taken none effect"
Rom 14:7 – "none of us liveth to himself"
1Co 1:14 – "I baptized none of you"
1Co 1:17 – "cross of Christ..of none effect"
1Co 2:8 – "none of the princes of this world"
1Co 7:29 – "have wives..as though..had none"
1Co 8:4 – "is none other God but one"
1Co 9:15 – "I have used none of these things"
1Co 10:32 – "Give none offence..to the Jews"
1Co 14:10 – "voices..none..w/o signification"
2Co 1:13 – "we write none other things"
Gal 1:19 – "other of the apostles saw I none"
Gal 3:17 – "make the promise of none effect"

Gal 5:10 – "will be none otherwise minded"
1Th 5:15 – "none render evil for evil"
1Ti 5:14 – "give none occasion to the adversary"
1Pe 4:15 – "none of you suffer as a murderer"

1Jn 2:10 – "none occasion of stumbling in him"
Rev 2:10 – "Fear none of those things"
Rev 2:24 – "put upon you none other burden"

No One

In modern usage the phrase "no one" generally refers to an absence of people and is a synonym to the word "nobody." However, in Scripture this phrase only occurs twice and both times carries the idea of "not one" or zero.

Isa 34:16 – "no one of these shall fail"
1Co 4:6 – "that no one of you be puffed up"

Nothing

Nothing (225x) is a pronoun that can convey the concept of zero, but in Scripture it is usually a vague term that simply refers to the absence or unimportance of a thing (see "nought" and "naught"). No where in Scripture is the word "nothing" used to count an item. Consult a concordance if further study is desired.

Nought (or Naught)

"Nought" (36x) and "naught" (3x) generally convey the meaning of the word "nothing." In some contexts it refers to nothing as in a thing that is non-existent – eg. nothing is there. In other contexts it refers to the unimportance or diminished aspect of a thing – eg. you may think it was a big deal, but it really was nothing.

In general usage a nought can actually refer to the symbol zero. In England and in many British Commonwealth countries, the game of Tic-Tac-Toe or X's & O's is referred to as Noughts & Crosses.

Scripture uses the words "naught" and "nought" in an ambiguous fashion synonymous with the word "nothing." In almost every case, nought will be found at the end of a prepositional phrase and is never clearly used as an adjective counting anything. For these reasons we have not listed the instances of "nought" and "naught" in the Bible and suggest you consult a concordance for further study.

Not One

The phrase "not one" appears forty times in Scripture. In ten of these occurrences the words may appear next to each other, but the word "not" fails to join with the word "one" to actually modify anything. For instance, in Malachi 2:10 we are told, *"hath not one God created us?"* "Not" modifies hath – it fails to impact "one God" in any way. Colossian 3:9 commands us to, *"Lie not one to another."* Such instances are not included below.

Thirty times however this phrase does carry the idea of zero. In each occurence, the phrase "not one" could be replaced by the word zero. Even though this might render the sentence grammatically incorrect, the sense of the passage is clearly that of zero items.

Exo 8:31 – "flies..there remained not one"
Exo 9:6 – "cattle..died not one"
Exo 9:7 – "was not one of the cattle..dead"
Exo 10:19 – "not one locust in all..of Egypt"
Exo 12:30 – "house where..was not one dead"
Num 31:49 – "there lacketh not one man of us"
Deu 1:35 – "not one of these men..see that..land"
Deu 2:36 – "there was not one city too strong"
Jos 23:14 – "that not one thing hath failed"
Jos 23:14 – "and not one thing hath failed"

1Sa 14:45 – "there shall not one hair..fall"
2Sa 13:30 – "king's sons..not one of them left"
2Sa 14:11 – "there shall not one hair..fall"
2Sa 17:13 – "until there be not one small stone"
2Sa 17:22 – "there lacked not one of them"
1Ki 16:11 – "left him not one that pisseth"
1Ki 18:40 – "prophets..let not one of them escape"
Job 14:4 – "clean..out of an unclean? not one"
Psa 14:3 – "none that doeth good, no, not one"
Psa 34:20 – "his bones: not one of them is broken"

Psa 53:3 – "none that doeth good, no, not one"
Psa 105:37 – "there was not one feeble person"
Psa 106:11 – "there was not one of them left"
Son 6:6 – "sheep..not one barren among them"
Isa 33:20 – "not one of the stakes..be removed"

Isa 40:26 – "strong in power; not one faileth"
Luk 12:6 – "sparrows..not one..is forgotten"
Rom 3:10 – "There is none righteous, no, not one"
Rom 3:12 – "none that doeth good, no, not one"
1Co 6:5 – "wise man among you? no, not one"

Fractions
Numbers between Zero and One

The Bible is rich in fractions, ranging from 1/1000th to 99/100ths. In this section each fraction will be listed in one or more of the following ways depending upon the context. Remember that these four methods of expressing fractional numbers are in fact interchangeable:

1) **Fraction** – as in 1/10 or one-tenth
2) **Decimal** – as in .10
3) **Percentage** – as in 10%
4) **Degrees** – as in 36 degrees

A circle has 360 degrees; one tenth of a circle would then be 36 degrees. Interestingly enough, a prophetic year in scripture is 360 days. Many students of the word believe that the actual length of a solar year may have been 360 days prior to Noah's flood. Regardless of the implications of a world-wide cataclysmic flood, the reality today is that we have a solar year lasting roughly 365.24 days

Verses and references in italics are where the number is not explicitly stated, but inferred.

.1% – one one-thousandeth (1/1000)

Job 9:3 – "he cannot answer him 1 of a 1000"
Job 33:23 – "one among 1000, to shew unto man"
Ecc 7:28 – "one man among a thousand"

.2% – one five-hundredth (1/500)

Num 31:28 – "one soul of five hundred"

.5% – one two-hundredth (1/200)

Ezk 45:15 – "one lamb out of..two hundred"

1% – one one-hundredth (1/100)

Num 18:26 – "heave offering..10th part of the tithe"
Neh 5:11 – "Restore..the 100th part of the money"
Neh 10:38 – "Levites shall bring..tithe of the tithes"
Mat 18:12 – "100 sheep, and one..gone astray"

2% – one-fiftieth (1/50)

Num 31:30 – "one portion of fifty"
Num 31:47 – "one portion of 50..unto the Levites"

2.78% – 1/36th – 10 degrees

2Ki 20:9 – "the shadow go forward 10 degrees"
2Ki 20:9 – "or go back ten degrees?"
2Ki 20:10 – "shadow to go down 10 degrees"
2Ki 20:10 – "shadow return backward 10 degrees"
2Ki 20:11 – "Isaiah..brought..shadow 10 degrees"
1Ch 15:18 – "their brethren of the second degree"
Isa 38:8 – "the sun returned ten degrees"

5% – one-twentieth (1/20)

Lev 6:20 – "1/10..ephah..½ of it in the morning"
Lev 6:20 – "1/10..ephah.. ½ thereof at night"

8.33% – one-twelfth (1/12)

Mat 26:14 – "one of the twelve..Judas Iscariot"
Mat 26:47 – "Judas, one of the twelve, came"
Joh 6:70 – "chosen you 12, and one..is a devil"
Joh 6:71 – "Judas Iscariot..one of the twelve"

10% – one-tenth (1/10)

➢   See **Tithe** in Section Three

Gen. 28:22 – "I will surely give the tenth"
Exo. 16:36 – "an omer is the 10th part of an ephah"
Exo 29:40 – "with the..lamb a tenth deal of flour"
Lev 5:11 – "tenth part of an ephah"
Lev 6:20 – "tenth part of an ephah"
Lev 14:21 – "one tenth deal of fine flour...with oil"
Lev 27:32 – "the 10th shall be holy unto the LORD"
Num 5:15 – "tenth part of an ephah of barley"
Num 15:4 – "meat offering of a tenth deal of flour"
Num 18:26 – "heave offering..10th part of the tithe"
Num 28:5 – "tenth part of an ephah of flour"
Num 28:13 – "a several tenth deal flour"
Num 28:21 – "A several tenth deal...for every lamb"
Num 28:29 – "A several tenth deal unto one lamb"
Num 29:4 – "one tenth deal for one lamb"
Num 29:10 – "A several tenth deal for one lamb"
Num 29:15 – "a several tenth deal to each lamb"
1Sa 8:15 – "he will take the tenth of your seed"
1Sa 8:17 – "He will take the tenth of your sheep"
1Ch 11:15 – "Now three of the thirty"
Neh 5:18 – "once in ten days..all sorts of wine"
Neh 11:1 – "bring one of ten to dwell in Jerusalem"
Isa 6:13 – "in it shall be a tenth, and it shall return"
Ezk 45:11 – "bath..contain..tenth part of an homer"
Ezk 45:11 – "ephah the tenth part of an homer"
Ezk 45:14 – "tenth part of a bath out of the cor"
Amo 5:3 – "went out by a 1000 shall leave 100"
Amo 5:3 – "went out by an 100 shall leave ten"
Heb 7:2 – "To whom..Abraham gave a tenth part"
Heb 7:4 – "Abraham gave the tenth of the spoils"
Rev 11:13 – "earthquake..10th part of the city fell"

14.29% – one-seventh (1/7)

Act 21:8 – "Philip..which was one of the seven"

16.67% – one-sixth (1/6)

Ezk 4:11 – "water by measure..sixth part of an hin"
Ezk 39:2 – "leave but the sixth part of thee"
Ezk 45:13 – "sixth part of an ephah..wheat"
Ezk 45:13 – "sixth part of an ephah..barley"
Ezk 46:14 – "meat offering..sixth part of an ephah"

20% – one-fifth; two-tenths (1/5)

Gen. 41:34 – "to take up the fifth part of the land"
Gen. 47:24 – "shall give the 5th part unto Pharaoh"
Gen. 47:26 – "Pharaoh should have the fifth part"
Lev 5:16 – "shall add the fifth part thereto"
Lev 6:5 – "shall add the fifth part more thereto"
Lev 22:14 – "shall put the 5th part thereof unto it"
Lev 23:13 – "two tenth deals of fine flour"
Lev 23:17 – "two wave loaves of two tenth deals"
Lev 24:5 – "two tenth deals shall be in one cake"
Lev 27:13 – "redeem it..add a fifth part thereof"
Lev 27:15 – "redeem his house...add the fifth part"
Lev 27:19 – "fifth part of the money"
Lev 27:27 – "shall add a fifth part"
Lev 27:31 – "add thereto the fifth part"
Num 5:7 – "add unto it the fifth part thereof"
Num 15:6 – "meat offering...2/10 deals of flour"
Num 28:9 – "2/10 deals of flour...meat offering"
Num 28:12 – "two tenth deals of flour"
Num 28:20 – "two tenth deals for a ram"
Num 28:28 – "flour..2/10 deals unto one ram"
Num 29:3 – "flour..oil..two tenth deals for a ram"
Num 29:9 – "two tenth deals to one ram"
Num 29:14 – "two tenth deals to each ram"
1Ki 6:31 – "lintels..posts..a fifth part of the wall"

25% – one-quarter; one-fourth (1/4)

Exo 29:40 – "¼ part of an hin of beaten oil"
Exo 29:40 – "¼ part of an hin of wine"
Lev 23:13 – "offering..wine, the ¼ part of an hin"
Num 15:4 – "the fourth part of an hin of oil"
Num 15:5 – "the fourth part of an hin of wine"
Num 23:10 – "Who can count..the ¼ part of Israel"
Num 28:5 – "fourth part of an hin of beaten oil"
Num 28:7 – "¼ part of an hin for the one lamb"
Num 28:14 – "fourth part of an hin unto a lamb"
Num 34:3 – "your south quarter..Zin..salt sea"
Deu 22:12 – "fringes..4 quarters of thy vesture"
Jos 18:14 – "this was the west quarter"
Jos 18:15 – "the south quarter was from"
1Sa 9:8 – "I have..¼ part of a shekel of silver"
1Ki 6:33 – "posts of olive tree..¼ part of the wall"
2Ki 6:25 – "fourth part of a cab's of dove dung"
1Ch 9:24 – "In 4 quarters were the porters"
Neh 9:3 – "read in the book.. ¼ part of the day"
Neh 9:3 – "¼ part they confessed..worshipped"
Isa 47:15 – "shall wander every 1 to his quarter"
Mar 1:45 – "they came to him from every quarter"
Act 9:32 – "passed throughout all quarters"
Act 16:3 – "Jews which were in those quarters"
Act 28:7 – "In..same quarters were possessions"
Rev 6:8 – "Death..Hell..over the ¼ part of..earth"

30% – three-tenths (3/10)

Lev 14:10 – "three tenth deals of fine flour"
Num 15:9 – "meat offering of 3/10 deals of flour"

Num 28:12 – "three tenth deals of flour"
Num 28:20 – "three tenth deals...for a bullock"
Num 28:28 – "flour..3/10 deals unto one bullock"
Num 29:3 – "flour..oil..three tenth deals..bullock"
Num 29:9 – "three tenth deals to a bullock"
Num 29:14 – "3/10 deals unto every bullock"

33% – one-third (1/3)

Num 15:6 – "meat offering.. ⅓ part of an hin of oil"
Num 15:7 – "drink offering..⅓part of an hin of oil"
Num 28:14 – "third part of an hin unto a ram"
2Sa 18:2 – "⅓ part of the people under..Joab"
2Sa 18:2 – "⅓ part under the hand of Abishai"
2Sa 18:2 – "⅓ part under the hand of Ittai"
2Ki 11:5 – "A third part..keepers of the watch"
2Ki 11:6 – "a third part shall be at the gate of Sur"
2Ki 11:6 – "a ⅓ part at the gate behind the guard"
2Ch 23:4 – "⅓ part..shall be porters of the doors"
2Ch 23:5 – "⅓ part shall be at the king's house"
2Ch 23:5 – "⅓ part at the gate of the foundation"
Neh 10:32 – "charge ourselves..⅓ part of a shekel"
Ezk 5:2 – "burn..third part in the midst of the city"
Ezk 5:2 – "third part..smith about it with a knife"
Ezk 5:2 – "third part..scatter in the wind"
Ezk 5:12 – "third part..die with..pestilence"
Ezk 5:12 – "third part..fall by the sword"
Ezk 5:12 – "third part into all the winds"
Ezk 46:14 – "the third part of an hin of oil"
Zec 13:8 – "the third shall be left therein"
Zec 13:9 – "I will bring the ⅓ part through..fire"
Rev 8:7 – "the third part of trees was burnt up"
Rev 8:8 – "the third part of the sea became blood"
Rev 8:9 – "the third part of the creatures..sea"
Rev 8:9 – "third part of the ships were destroyed"
Rev 8:10 – "great star..third part of the rivers"
Rev 8:11 – "third part of the waters..wormwood"
Rev 8:12 – "third part of the sun was smitten"
Rev 8:12 – "third part of the moon..was darkened"
Rev 8:12 – "third part of the stars..was darkened"
Rev 8:12 – "the third part of them was darkened"
Rev 8:12 – "day shone not for a third part of it"
Rev 9:15 – "for to slay the third part of men"
Rev 9:18 – "third part of men killed"
Rev 12:4 – "tail drew the third part of the stars"

40% – four-tenths (4/10)

Hag 2:16 – "50 vessels..there were but twenty"

50% – one-half (1/2)

Gen. 15:10 – "divided them in the midst"
Gen. 24:22 – "golden earring..½ a shekel weight"
Exo 24:6 – "half of the blood..in basons"
Exo 24:6 – "half of the blood he sprinkled"
Exo 26:12 – "the half curtain that remaineth"

Exo 30:13 – "give, every one..half a shekel"
Exo 30:13 – "½ shekel..the offering of the LORD"
Exo 30:15 – "poor..not give less than ½ a shekel"
Exo 30:23 – "of sweet cinnamon half so much"
Exo 38:26 – "a bekah..that is, half a shekel"
Lev 6:20 – "offering.. ½ of it in the morning"
Lev 6:20 – "offering.. and ½ thereof at night"
Num 12:12 – "as one dead..flesh is ½ consumed"
Num 15:9 – "flour mingled with half an hin of oil"
Num 15:10 – "drink offering half an hin of wine"
Num 28:14 – "half an hin of wine unto a bullock"
Num 31:27 – "divide the prey into two parts"
Num 31:30 – "of the children of Israel's half"
Num 31:36 – "the half..of them that went to war"
Num 31:42 – "the children of Israel's half"
Num 31:43 – "half..pertained unto..congregation"
Num 31:33 – "half the tribe of Manesseh"
Num 34:14 – "half the tribe of Manessah"
Deu 3:13 – "the half tribe of Manessah"
Deu 3:16 – "Gilead..unto Arnon half the valley"
Deu 29:8 – "to the half tribe of Manasseh"
Jos 1:12 – "and to half the tribe of Manasseh"
Jos 4:12 – "half the tribe of Manasseh..armed"
Jos 8:33 – "half..mount Gerazim..half..mount Ebal"
Jos 12:5 – "And reigned..unto..half Gilead"
Jos 12:6 – "possession..the half tribe of Manasseh"
Jos 13:7 – "divide this land..½ tribe of Manasseh"
Jos 13:25 – "½the land of the children of Ammon"
Jos 13:29 – "inheritance..½ tribe of Manasseh"
Jos 13:29 – "possession of the ½ tribe..Manasseh"
Jos 13:31 – "And ½ Gilead..pertaining..Manasseh"
Jos 13:31 – "even to the ½ of..children of Machir"
Jos 18:7 – "half the tribe of Manasseh"
Jos 21:6 – "half tribe of Manasseh"
Jos 21:7 – "half tribe of Manasseh"
Jos 21:25 – "half tribe of Manasseh"
Jos 21:27 – "out of the other ½tribe of Manasseh"
Jos 22:1 – "Joshua called..the ½tribe of Manasseh"
Jos 22:7 – "to..½ tribe..Moses had given..Bashan"
Jos 22:7 – "unto the other ½ thereof gave Joshua"
Jos 22:9 – "the half tribe of Manasseh returned"
Jos 22:10 – "½ tribe of Manasseh built..an altar"
Jos 22:11 – "Israel heard..½ tribe..built an altar"
Jos 22:13 – "the half tribe of of Manasseh"
Jos 22:15 – "the half tribe of of Manasseh"
Jos 22:21 – "the ½ tribe of of Manasseh answered"
1Sa 14:14 – "½ acre..yoke of oxen might plow"
2Sa 10:4 – "shave off the ½ of their beards"
2Sa 18:3 – "neither if half of us die, will they care"
2Sa 19:40 – "half the people of Israel"
1Ki 3:25 – "give ½ to the one, and ½ to the other"
1Ki 7:35 – "top of..base..compass of ½ cubit high"
1Ki 10:7 – "the half was not told me: thy wisdom"
1Ki 16:9 – "Zimri, captain of half his chariots"
1Ki 16:21 – "people of Israel divided into two parts"
1Ki 16:21 – "half of the people followed Tibni"
1Ki 16:21 – "half followed Omri"
1Ch 2:52 – "half of the Manahethites"
1Ch 2:54 – "half of the Manahethites"
1Ch 5:18 – "half the tribe of Manasseh"
1Ch 5:23 – "of the half tribe of Manasseh"

1Ch 5:26 – "the half tribe of Manasseh"
1Ch 6:61 – "were cities given out of the half tribe"
1Ch 6:61 – "out of the ½ tribe of Manasseh"
1Ch 6:70 – "And out of the half tribe of Manasseh"
1Ch 6:71 – "out of the family of the half tribe"
1Ch 12:31 – "of the half tribe of Manasseh 18,000"
1Ch 12:37 – "Ruebenites..Gadites..½ Manasseh"
1Ch 26:32 – "the half tribe of Manasseh"
1Ch 27:20 – "of the ½ tribe..Joel..son of Pedaiah"
1Ch 27:21 – "Of the ½ tribe..in Gilead, Iddo"
2Ch 9:6 – "the ½ of the greatness of thy wisdom"
Neh 3:9 – "Rephaiah..ruler of..½ part..Jerusalem"
Neh 3:12 – "Shallum..ruler of..½ part..Jerusalem"
Neh 3:16 – "Nehemiah..ruler of..½ part..Bethzur"
Neh 3:17 – "Hashabiah..ruler of..½ part..Keilah"
Neh 3:18 – "Bevai..ruler of the ½ part of Keilah"
Neh 4:16 – "½ of my servants wrought in..work"
Neh 4:16 – "other half..held both the spears"
Neh 4:21 – "half of them held the spears"
Neh 12:32 – "Hoshaiah, and ½..princes of Judah"
Neh 12:38 – "the ½ of the people upon the wall"
Neh 12:40 – "I, and the ½ of the rulers with me"
Neh 13:24 – "children spake ½ in..speech..Ashdod"
Est 1:4 – "shewed..his glorious kingdom..180 days"
Est 5:3 – "given thee to the ½ of the kingdom"
Est 5:6 – "even to the ½ of the kingdom"
Est 7:2 – "even to the ½ of the kingdom"
Psa 55:23 – "shall not live out half their days"
Ezk 16:51 – "Samaria commited ½ thy sins"
Ezk 43:17 – "settle..border about it..half a cubit"
Hag 2:16 – "heap of 20 measures..were but ten"
Zec 14:2 – "half of the city..go forth into captivity"
Zec 14:4 – "½of the mountain..toward the north"
Zec 14:4 – "half of it toward the south"
Zec 14:8 – "waters..half..toward the former sea"
Zec 14:8 – "waters..half..toward the hinder sea"
Mar 6:23 – "unto the half of my kingdom"

Luk 17:34 – "two men in one bed..one taken"
Luk 17:35 – "Two women grinding..one..taken"
Luk 17:36 – "Two men..in the field..one..taken"
Luk 19:8 – "the half of my goods..to the poor"
Rev 8:1 – "silence in heaven..space of ½ an hour"

67% – two-thirds (2/3)

Zec 13:8 – "two parts therein shall be cut off"

80% – four-fifths (4/5)

Gen. 47:24 – "four parts shall be your own"

83.33% – five-sixths; ten-twelfths (5/6 or 10/12)

2Sa 19:43 – "Israel..We have ten parts in the king"

90% – nine-tenths (9/10)

Neh 11:1 – "nine parts to dwell in other cities"
Luk 17:17 – "ten cleansed..where are the nine?"

99% – ninety-nine one-hundredths (99/100)

Mat 18:12 – "100 sheep..leave the 99"

One

One is the most common number found in the Bible. In Bible numerology one is generally considered to be the number of unity or beginnings.   As there is one God, one is considered by some to be the number of God. This section includes:

a)	Articles – A, An & The	g)	Once
b)	1 – One (cardinal number)	h)	Ones
c)	1st – First (ordinal number)	i)	Several (as in "a several")
d)	Firstborn	j)	Single & Singleness
e)	Firstfruits	k)	Singleness
f)	Firstlings	l)	Mixed Numbers – 1⅓ & 1½

Articles "A," "An" & "The"

Countless examples could be provided throughout Scripture where all three definite articles could be interpreted as denoting the number one.   Because the majority of these examples however would be up for debate as to just how specifically they were intended to convey the number one, they have not been included in this volume. The purpose of this volume is to record the clear rather than to interpret the unclear or debateable. For this reason, a concordance should be consulted if further study on how these three definite articles are used to count things throughout Scripture.

1 – One

For "not one" used in the sense of none or zero, see **ZERO**

Gen 1:9 – "waters..gathered..unto one place"
Gen 2:21 – "sleep..upon Adam..took one of his ribs"
Gen 2:24 – "they shall be one flesh"
Gen 3:6 – "tree to be desired to make one wise"
Gen 3:22 – "the man is become as one of us"
Gen 4:14 – "every 1 that findeth me shall slay me"
Gen 4:19 – "the name of the one was Adah"
Gen 10:5 – "isles..divided..every 1 after his tongue"
Gen 10:8 – "Nimrod..he began to be a mighty one"
Gen 10:25 – "sons..name of the one was Peleg"
Gen 11:1 – "whole earth was of one language"
Gen 11:1 – "whole earth was of..one speech"
Gen 11:3 – "And they said one to another"
Gen 11:6 – "Behold, the people is one"
Gen 11:6 – "they have all one language"
Gen 11:7 – "not understand one another's speech"
Gen 13:11 – "separated..one from the other"
Gen 14:13 – "And there came 1 that had escaped"
Gen 15:3 – "one born in my house is mine heir"
Gen 15:10 – "laid each piece one against another"
Gen 19:9 – "This one fellow came in to sojourn"
Gen 19:14 – "But he seemed as one that mocked"
Gen 19:20 – "city is near..it is a little one"
Gen 19:20 – "(is it not a little one?)"
Gen 21:15 – "cast the child under 1 of the shrubs"
Gen 22:2 – "offering upon one of the mountains"
Gen 24:41 – "if they give not thee one"
Gen 25:23 – "the one people shall be stronger"
Gen 26:10 – "one of the people might"
Gen 26:26 – "Ahuzzath one of his friends"
Gen 26:31 – "sware one to another"
Gen 27:29 – "cursed be every 1 that curseth thee"
Gen 27:38 – "Hast thou but one blessing"
Gen 27:45 – "deprived also of you both in one day"
Gen 30:33 – "every 1 that is not speckled..spotted"
Gen 30:35 – "every one that had some white in it"
Gen 31:49 – "when we are absent 1 from another"
Gen 32:8 – "If Esau come to the one company"
Gen 33:13 – "overdrive them one day, all..will die"
Gen 34:14 – "our sister to 1 that is uncircumcised"
Gen 34:16 – "dwell with you..become one people"
Gen 34:22 – "consent..to be one people"
Gen 37:19 – "they said one to another, Behold"
Gen 38:28 – "the one put out his hand"
Gen 40:5 – "dreamed a dream both..in one night"
Gen 41:5 – "7 ears of corn came upon on 1 stalk"
Gen 41:11 – "we dreamed a dream in one night"
Gen 41:22 – "7 ears came up in one stalk"
Gen 41:25 – "The dream of Pharaoh is one"
Gen 41:26 – "the dream is one"

Gen 41:38 – "Can we find such a one as this is"
Gen 42:1 – "Why do ye look one upon another?"
Gen 42:11 – "We are all one man's sons"
Gen 42:13 – "the sons of one man in..Canaan"
Gen 42:13 – "youngest..w/ our father, and 1 is not"
Gen 42:16 – "Send one of you..fetch your brother"
Gen 42:19 – "If ye be true..let 1 of your brethren"
Gen 42:21 – "they said one to another"
Gen 42:27 – "And as one of them opened his sack"
Gen 42:28 – "afraid, saying one to another"
Gen 42:32 – "twelve brethren..one is not"
Gen 42:33 – "leave one of your brethren"
Gen 43:33 – "the men marveled one at another"
Gen 44:20 – "a child of his old age, a little one"
Gen 44:28 – "and the one went out from me"
Gen 47:21 – "one end of the borders of Egypt"
Gen 48:1 – "one told Joseph..thy father is sick"
Gen 48:2 – "one told Jacob..Joseph cometh"
Gen 48:22 – "I have given to thee 1 portion above"
Gen 49:16 – "Dan shall judge..as one of the tribes"
Gen 49:28 – "every one according to his blessing"
Exo 1:15 – "midwives..name of the 1 was Shiphrah"
Exo 2:6 – "This is one of the Hebrews' children"
Exo 2:11 – "he spied..an Hebrew, 1 of his brethren"
Exo 6:25 – "Eleazer..1 of the daughters of Putiel"
Exo 10:23 – "They saw not one another"
Exo 11:1 – "one plague more upon Pharaoh"
Exo 12:30 – "not a house where..was not 1 dead"
Exo 12:46 – "In one house shall it be eaten"
Exo 12:48 – "as one that is born in the land"
Exo 12:49 – "1 law..homeborn, & unto..stranger"
Exo 14:7 – "captains over every one of them"
Exo 14:20 – "1 came not near..other all the night"
Exo 14:28 – "remained not so much as 1 of them"
Exo 16:15 – "they said one to another"
Exo 16:22 – "two omers for one man"
Exo 17:12 – "Aaron and Hur..the 1 on the 1 side"
Exo 18:3 – "2 sons..name of the 1 was Gershom"
Exo 18:16 – "I judge between one and another"
Exo 21:18 – "if men strive..and one smite another"
Exo 21:35 – "if one man's ox hurt another"
Exo 23:29 – "I will not drive them out..in one year"
Exo 24:3 – "all the people answered with 1 voice"
Exo 25:12 – "two rings shall be in the 1 side of it"
Exo 25:19 – "make one cherub on the one end"
Exo 25:20 – "their faces shall look one to another"
Exo 25:32 – "branches..candlestick out of..1 side"
Exo 25:33 – "with a knop & a flower in 1 branch"
Exo 25:36 – "shall be 1 beaten work of pure gold"
Exo 26:2 – "length of one curtain..28 cubits"

Exo 26:2 – "breadth of one curtain..4 cubits"
Exo 26:2 – "every 1 of the curtains..one measure"
Exo 26:3 – "curtains..coupled..one to another"
Exo 26:3 – "other 5 curtains..coupled 1 to another"
Exo 26:4 – "loops of blue upon..the one curtain"
Exo 26:5 – "Fifty loops..make in the one curtain"
Exo 26:5 – "loops may take hold one of another"
Exo 26:6 – "it shall be one tabernacle"
Exo 26:8 – "length of 1 curtain shall be 30 cubits"
Exo 26:8 – "breadth of one curtain four cubits"
Exo 26:8 – "11 curtains shall be all of 1 measure"
Exo 26:10 – "on the edge of the one curtain"
Exo 26:11 – "couple..tent together..may be one"
Exo 26:13 – "a cubit on the one side"
Exo 26:16 – "the breadth of one board"
Exo 26:17 – "Two tenons..in one board"
Exo 26:17 – "set in order one against another"
Exo 26:19 – "two sockets under one board"
Exo 26:21 – "two sockets under one board"
Exo 26:24 – "above the head of it unto one ring"
Exo 26:25 – "two sockets under one board"
Exo 26:26 – "boards..one side of the tabernacle"
Exo 27:9 – "hangings..100 cubits long for one side"
Exo 27:14 – "hangings of one side of the gate"
Exo 28:10 – "Six of their names..one stone"
Exo 28:21 – "every 1 with his name shall they be"
Exo 29:1 – "Take 1 young bullock, and two rams"
Exo 29:3 – "put them into one basket"
Exo 29:15 – "Thou shalt also take one ram"
Exo 29:23 – "one loaf of bread"
Exo 29:23 – "one cake of oiled bread"
Exo 29:23 – "one wafer out of the basket"
Exo 29:39 – "one lamb..offer in the morning"
Exo 29:40 – "with the one lamb..flour..oil..wine"
Exo 30:13 – "give every one..half a shekel"
Exo 30:14 – "Every one that passeth among them"
Exo 31:14 – "sabbath..every one that defileth it"
Exo 32:15 – "tables..written..on the one side"
Exo 33:7 – "every one which sought the LORD"
Exo 34:15 – "one call thee, and thou eat"
Exo 35:21 – "every one whose heart stirred him"
Exo 35:21 – "every 1 whom..spirit made willing"
Exo 35:24 – "Every one that did offer an offering"
Exo 36:2 – "every one whose heart stirred him"
Exo 36:9 – "length of one curtain..28 cubits"
Exo 36:9 – "breadth of one curtain..4 cubits"
Exo 36:9 – "the curtains were all of one size"
Exo 36:10 – "coupled..5 curtains one to another"
Exo 36:10 – "5 curtains..coupled one to another"
Exo 36:11 – "loops of blue on..edge of 1 curtain"
Exo 36:12 – "Fifty loops made he in one curtain"
Exo 36:12 – "the loops held 1 curtain to another"
Exo 36:13 – "coupled the curtains 1 unto another"
Exo 36:13 – "so it became one tabernacle"
Exo 36:15 – "length of one curtain was 30 cubits"
Exo 36:15 – "4 cubits was the breadth of 1 curtain"
Exo 36:15 – "the eleven curtains were of one size"
Exo 36:18 – "couple the tent..that it might be one"
Exo 36:22 – "One board had two tenons"
Exo 36:22 – "equally distant one from another"
Exo 36:24 – "2 sockets..for his 2 tenons"

Exo 36:26 – "two sockets under one board"
Exo 36:29 – "coupled together..to one ring"
Exo 36:31 – "boards of the 1 side of the tabernacle"
Exo 36:33 – "boards from the 1 end to the other"
Exo 37:3 – "even two rings upon the one side"
Exo 37:7 – "beaten out of one piece made he them"
Exo 37:8 – "One cherub on the end on this side"
Exo 37:9 – "their faces one to another"
Exo 37:18 – "three branches..out of the one side"
Exo 37:19 – "fashion of almonds in one branch"
Exo 37:22 – "one beaten work of pure gold"
Exo 38:14 – "hangings of the one side of the gate"
Exo 38:26 – "half a shekel..for every 1 that went"
Exo 39:14 – "signet, every one with his name"
Lev 4:27 – "if any one of the common people sin"
Lev 5:4 – "shall be guilty in one of these"
Lev 5:5 – "guilty in one of these things"
Lev 5:7 – "turtledoves..one for a sin offering"
Lev 5:13 – "that he hath sinned in one of these"
Lev 6:18 – "every one that toucheth them..holy"
Lev 7:7 – "offering..there is one law for them"
Lev 7:10 – "sons of Aaron..one as much as another"
Lev 7:14 – "one out of the whole oblation"
Lev 8:26 – "he took one unleavened cake"
Lev 8:26 – "he took..one wafer"
Lev 11:26 – "every 1 that toucheth them..unclean"
Lev 12:8 – "the one for the burnt offering"
Lev 13:2 – "unto one of his sons the priests"
Lev 14:5 – "one of the birds be killed"
Lev 14:10 – "and one ewe lamb"
Lev 14:10 – "on the eighth day..one log of oil"
Lev 14:12 – "preist shall take one he lamb"
Lev 14:21 – "one lamb for a trespass offering"
Lev 14:22 – "one shall be a sin offering"
Lev 14:30 – "one of the turtledoves..pigeons"
Lev 14:31 – "one for a sin offering"
Lev 14:50 – "shall kill one of the birds"
Lev 15:15 – "one for a sin offering"
Lev 15:30 – "one for a sin offering"
Lev 16:5 – "one ram for a burnt offering"
Lev 16:8 – "one lot for the LORD..other..scapegoat"
Lev 16:27 – "1 carry forth..burn..skins..flesh..dung"
Lev 16:29 – "1 of your own country, or a stranger"
Lev 17:15 – "1 of your own country, or a stranger"
Lev 18:30 – "any 1 of these abominable customs"
Lev 19:8 – "every 1 that it shall bear his iniquity"
Lev 19:11 – "neither lie one to another"
Lev 19:34 – "strangers..as one born among you"
Lev 20:9 – "every 1 that curseth his father..mother"
Lev 22:28 – "and her young both in one day"
Lev 23:18 – "ye shall offer..one young bullock"
Lev 23:19 – "sacrifice one kid of the goats"
Lev 24:5 – "two tenth deals shall be in one cake"
Lev 24:22 – "1 manner of a law...for the stranger"
Lev 24:22 – "one of your own country"
Lev 25:14 – "ye shall not oppress one another"
Lev 25:17 – "Ye shall not..oppress one another"
Lev 25:46 – "ye shall not rule one over another"
Lev 25:48 – "one of his brethren may redeem him"
Lev 26:26 – "10 women..bake..bread in one oven"
Lev 26:37 – "they shall fall one upon another"

Num 1:4 – "every 1 head of..house of his fathers"
Num 1:44 – "12 men..each one was for the house"
Num 2:34 – "every one after their families"
Num 4:19 – "appoint them every 1 to his service"
Num 4:30 – "every 1 that entereth into the service"
Num 4:35 – "every 1 that entereth into the service"
Num 4:39 – "every 1 that entereth into the service"
Num 4:43 – "every 1 that entereth into the service"
Num 4:47 – "every 1 that entereth into the service"
Num 4:49 – "every 1 that entereth into the service"
Num 5:2 – "every one that hath an issue"
Num 6:11 – "offer the one for a sin offering"
Num 6:14 – "one he lamb..burnt offering"
Num 6:14 – "one ewe lamb...for a sin offering"
Num 6:14 – "1 ram w/out blemish..peace offerings"
Num 6:19 – "1 unleavened cake out of the basket"
Num 6:19 – "one unleavened wafer..Nazarite"
Num 7:3 – "for each one an ox"
Num 7:13 – "one silver charger"
Num 7:13 – "one silver bowl"
Num 7:14 – "one spoon of ten shekels"
Num 7:15 – "One young bullock"
Num 7:15 – "one ram"
Num 7:15 – "one lamb of the first year"
Num 7:16 – "One kid of the goats"
Num 7:19 – "one silver charger"
Num 7:19 – "one silver bowl"
Num 7:20 – "one spoon..gold..10 shekels"
Num 7:21– "One young bullock"
Num 7:21 – "one ram"
Num 7:21 – "one lamb of the first year"
Num 7:22 – "One kid of the goats"
Num 7:25 – "one silver charger"
Num 7:25 – "one silver bowl"
Num 7:26 – "one golden spoon..10 shekels"
Num 7:27 – "One young bullock"
Num 7:27 – "one ram"
Num 7:27 – "one lamb of the first year"
Num 7:28 – "One kid of the goats"
Num 7:31 – "one silver charger"
Num 7:31 – "one silver bowl"
Num 7:32 – "one golden spoon..10 shekels"
Num 7:33 – "One young bullock"
Num 7:33 – "one ram"
Num 7:33 – "one lamb of the first year"
Num 7:34 – "One kid of the goats"
Num 7:37 – "one silver charger"
Num 7:37 – "one silver bowl"
Num 7:38 – "one golden spoon..10 shekels"
Num 7:39 – "One young bullock"
Num 7:39 – "one ram"
Num 7:39 – "one lamb of the first year"
Num 7:40 – "One kid of the goats"
Num 7:43 – "one silver charger"
Num 7:44 – "one golden spoon..10 shekels"
Num 7:45 – "One young bullock"
Num 7:45 – "one ram"
Num 7:45 – "one lamb of the first year"
Num 7:46 – "One kid of the goats"
Num 7:49 – "one silver charger"
Num 7:49 – "one silver bowl"

Num 7:50 – "one golden spoon..10 shekels"
Num 7:51 – "One young bullock"
Num 7:51 – "one ram"
Num 7:51 – "one lamb of the first year"
Num 7:52 – "One kid of the goats"
Num 7:55 – "one silver charger"
Num 7:55 – "one silver bowl"
Num 7:56 – "one golden spoon..10 shekels"
Num 7:57 – "One young bullock"
Num 7:57 – "one ram"
Num 7:57 – "one lamb of the first year"
Num 7:58 – "One kid of the goats"
Num 7:61 – "one silver charger"
Num 7:61 – "one silver bowl"
Num 7:62 – "one golden spoon..10 shekels"
Num 7:63 – "One young bullock"
Num 7:63 – "one ram"
Num 7:63 – "one lamb of the first year"
Num 7:64 – "One kid of the goats"
Num 7:67 – "one silver charger"
Num 7:67 – "one silver bowl"
Num 7:68 – "one golden spoon..10 shekels"
Num 7:69 – "One young bullock"
Num 7:69 – "one ram"
Num 7:69 – "one lamb of the first year"
Num 7:70 – "One kid of the goats"
Num 7:73 – "one silver charger"
Num 7:73 – "one silver bowl"
Num 7:74 – "one golden spoon..10 shekels"
Num 7:75 – "One young bullock"
Num 7:75 – "one ram"
Num 7:75 – "one lamb of the first year"
Num 7:76 – "One kid of the goats"
Num 7:79 – "one silver charger"
Num 7:79 – "one silver bowl"
Num 7:80 – "one golden spoon..10 shekels"
Num 7:81 – "One young bullock"
Num 7:81 – "one ram"
Num 7:81 – "one lamb of the first year"
Num 7:82 – "One kid of the goats"
Num 7:89 – "heard the voice of one speaking"
Num 8:12 – "offer the one for a sin offering"
Num 9:14 – "one ordinance..stranger..born..land"
Num 10:4 – "blow but with one trumpet"
Num 11:19 – "ye shall not eat 1 day, nor two days"
Num 11:26 – "the name of the one was Eldad"
Num 11:28 – "Joshua..one of his young men"
Num 12:12 – "Let her not be as one dead"
Num 13:2 – "every one a ruler among them"
Num 13:23 – "Eschol..branch..1 cluster of grapes"
Num 14:4 – "said one to another..make a captain"
Num 14:15 – "if thou..kill all this people as 1 man"
Num 15:5 – "wine for a drink offering..for 1 lamb"
Num 15:11 – "Thus shall it be done for 1 bullock"
Num 15:11 – "for one ram, or for a lamb, or a kid"
Num 15:12 – "every 1 according to their number"
Num 15:15 – "One ordinance shall be both for you"
Num 15:16 – "1 law & 1 manner shall be for you"
Num 15:24 – "1 young bullock for..burnt offering"
Num 15:24 – "1 kid of the goats for a sin offering"
Num 15:29 – "one law..him..sinneth..ignorance"

Num 16:3 – "all the congregation are holy, every 1"
Num 16:15 – "I have not taken one ass from them"
Num 16:15 – "neither have I hurt one of them"
Num 16:22 – "1 man sin..wroth..all congregation"
Num 17:2 – "take every one of them a rod"
Num 17:3 – "1 rod..for the head..house of..fathers"
Num 17:6 – "every one of..princes gave him a rod"
Num 17:6 – "a rod apiece, for each prince one"
Num 18:11 – "every one that is clean in thy house"
Num 18:13 – "every 1 that is clean in thine house"
Num 19:3 – "red heifer..one shall slay her"
Num 19:5 – "one shall burn the heifer in his sight"
Num 19:16 – "whosoever toucheth 1 that is slain"
Num 19:18 – "him that touched..1 slain, or 1 dead"
Num 21:8 – "every one that is bitten"
Num 25:5 – "Slay ye every one his men..Baalpeor"
Num 25:6 – "one of the children of Israel"
Num 26:54 – "to every 1 shall his inheritance be"
Num 28:4 – "one lamb shalt thou offer...morning"
Num 28:7 – "fourth part of an hin for the 1 lamb"
Num 28:11 – "1 ram, seven lambs of the first year"
Num 28:12 – "flour..oil..for one bullock"
Num 28:12 – "flour..oil..for one ram"
Num 28:13 – "flour..oil..unto one lamb"
Num 28:15 – "1 kid of the goats for a sin offering"
Num 28:19 – "two young bullocks, and one ram"
Num 28:22 – "one goat for a sin offering"
Num 28:27 – "burnt offering..one ram"
Num 28:28 – "meat offering..one bullock..one ram"
Num 28:29 – "several tenth deal unto one lamb"
Num 28:30 – "one kid..goats to make atonement"
Num 29:2 – "burnt offering..one young bullock
Num 29:2 – "burnt offering..one ram"
Num 29:4 – "one tenth deal for one lamb"
Num 29:5 – "one kid of the goats for a sin offering"
Num 29:8 – "burnt offering..one young bullock
Num 29:8 – "burnt offering..one ram"
Num 29:9 – "two tenth deals to one ram"
Num 29:10 – "A several tenth deal for one lamb"
Num 29:11 – "1 kid of the goats for a sin offering"
Num 29:16 – "1 kid of the goats for a sin offering"
Num 29:19 – "1 kid of the goats for a sin offering"
Num 29:22 – "one goat for a sin offering"
Num 29:25 – "1 kid of the goats for a sin offering"
Num 29:28 – "one goat for a sin offering"
Num 29:31 – "one goat for a sin offering"
Num 29:34 – " one goat for a sin offering"
Num 29:36 – "burnt offering..1 bullock, one ram"
Num 29:38 – "one goat for a sin offering"
Num 34:18 – "one prince..every tribe..divide..land"
Num 35:8 – "every 1..give..cities unto the Levites"
Num 35:15 – "one that killeth..person unawares"
Num 35:30 – "1 witness..not testify..cause..to die"
Num 36:7 – "every one of the children of Israel"
Num 36:8 – "wife unto one of the family..tribe"
Num 36:9 – "inheritance remove..1 tribe..another"
Num 36:9 – "every 1 of..tribes..keep..inheritance"
Deu 1:22 – "ye came near unto me every 1 of you"
Deu 1:23 – "twelve men of you, one of a tribe"
Deu 4:4 – "alive every one of you this day"
Deu 4:32 – "one side of heaven unto the other"

Deu 4:42 – "fleeing unto one of these cities"
Deu 6:4 – "the LORD our God is one LORD"
Deu 12:14 – "choose in one of thy tribes"
Deu 13:7 – "one end of the earth..unto the other"
Deu 13:12 – "If..shalt hear say in one of thy cities"
Deu 15:7 – "a poor man of one of thy brethren"
Deu 17:6 – "mouth..1 witness..not be put to death"
Deu 17:15 – "God..choose: 1..among thy brethren"
Deu 18:10 – "1..maketh..son..daughter..pass..fire"
Deu 19:5 – "he shall flee unto one of those cities"
Deu 19:11 – "fleeth into one of these cities"
Deu 19:15 – "1 witness..not rise up against a man"
Deu 21:1 – "If one be found slain in the land"
Deu 21:15 – "man have 2 wives, 1 beloved..hated"
Deu 22:12 – "fringes upon..4 quarters of..vesture"
Deu 23:16 – "dwell..in one of thy gates"
Deu 24:5 – "he shall be free at home one year"
Deu 25:5 – "brethren dwell together..one..die"
Deu 25:11 – "men strive..one with another"
Deu 25:11 – "wife of the one draweth near"
Deu 28:7 – "shall come out against thee one way"
Deu 28:25 – "thou..go out one way against them"
Deu 28:57 – "And toward her young one"
Deu 28:64 – "scatter..from..one end of the earth"
Deu 32:30 – "How should one chase a thousand"
Deu 33:3 – "every one shall receive of thy words"
Deu 33:8 – "Thummim..Urim be w/ thy holy one"
Jos 9:2 – "fight w/ Joshua & Israel, w/ one accord"
Jos 10:2 – "Gibeon..great city..one of..royal cities"
Jos 10:42 – "did Joshua take at one time"
Jos 12:9 – "The king of Jericho, one"
Jos 12:9 – "king of Ai, which is beside Bethel, one"
Jos 12:10 – "The king of Jerusalem, one"
Jos 12:10 – "the king of Hebron, one"
Jos 12:11 – "The king of Jarmuth, one"
Jos 12:11 – "the king of Lachish, one"
Jos 12:12 – "The king of Eglon, one"
Jos 12:12 – "the king of Gezer, one"
Jos 12:13 – "The king of Debir, one"
Jos 12:13 – "the king of Geder, one"
Jos 12:14 – "The king of Hormah, one"
Jos 12:14 – "the king of Arad, one"
Jos 12:15 – "The king of Libnah, one"
Jos 12:15 – "the king of Adullam, one"
Jos 12:16 – "The king of Makkedah, one"
Jos 12:16 – "the king of Bethel, one"
Jos 12:17 – "The king of Tappuah, one"
Jos 12:17 – "the king of Hepher, one"
Jos 12:18 – "The king of Aphek, one"
Jos 12:18 – "the king of Lasharon, one"
Jos 12:19 – "The king of Madon, one"
Jos 12:19 – "the king of Hazor, one"
Jos 12:20 – "The king of Shimronmeron, one"
Jos 12:20 – "the king of Achshaph, one"
Jos 12:21 – "The king of Taanach, one"
Jos 12:21 – "the king of Megiddo, one"
Jos 12:22 – "The king of Kedesh, one"
Jos 12:22 – "the king of Jokneam of Carmel, one"
Jos 12:23 – "The king of Dor in..coast of Dor, one"
Jos 12:23 – "the king of the nations of Gilgal, one"
Jos 12:24 – "The king of Tirzah, one"

Jos 17:14 – "Why hast thou given me..one lot"
Jos 17:14 – "Why has thou given me..one portion"
Jos 17:17 – "thou shalt not have one lot only"
Jos 20:4 – "one of those cities"
Jos 21:42 – "cities..every one with their suburbs"
Jos 22:14 – "princes..each one..head of the house"
Jos 23:10 – "One man of you shall chase a 1000"
Jdg 6:16 – "smite the Midianites as one man"
Jdg 6:29 – "said one..Who hath done this"
Jdg 6:31 – "one hath cast down his altar"
Jdg 7:5 – "Every one that lappeth of the water"
Jdg 7:5 – "every one that boweth down..to drink"
Jdg 8:18 – "each 1 resembled..children of a king"
Jdg 9:2 – "or that one reign over you"
Jdg 9:5 – "slew his brethren..upon 1 stone"
Jdg 9:18 – "slain..sons, 70 persons, upon 1 stone"
Jdg 10:18 – "people..princes..said one to another"
Jdg 11:35 – "thou art 1 of them that trouble me"
Jdg 12:7 – "buried in one of the cities of Gilead"
Jdg 16:5 – "give..every 1 of us 1100 pieces..silver"
Jdg 16:29 – "one with his right hand"
Jdg 17:5 – "1 of his sons, who became his priest"
Jdg 17:11 – "young man..unto him as 1 of his sons"
Jdg 18:19 – "better..priest unto..1 man, or..a tribe"
Jdg 19:13 – "draw near to one of these places"
Jdg 20:1 – "congregation..gathered..as one man"
Jdg 20:8 – "all the people arose as one man"
Jdg 20:11 – "men of Israel..knit together as 1 man"
Jdg 20:16 – "every 1..sling stones..hair breadth"
Jdg 20:31 – "one goeth up to the house of God"
Jdg 21:3 – "to day one tribe lacking in Israel?"
Jdg 21:6 – "one tribe cut off from Israel this day"
Jdg 21:8 – "What one is there..came not up"
Rut 1:4 – "the name of the one was Orpah"
Rut 2:13 – "like unto one of thine handmaidens"
Rut 2:20 – "near of kin..one of our next kinsmen"
Rut 3:14 – "she rose up before 1..know another"
Rut 4:1 – "Ho, such a one! turn aside, sit down"
1Sa 1:2 – "the name of the one was Hannah"
1Sa 1:24 – "3 bullocks..one ephah of flour"
1Sa 2:25 – "If one man sin against another"
1Sa 2:34 – "in one day they shall die both of them"
1Sa 2:36 – "every one that is left in thine house"
1Sa 2:36 – "into one of the priests' offices"
1Sa 3:11 – "ears of every one..heareth it..tingle"
1Sa 6:4 – "one plague..on you all..on your lords"
1Sa 6:17 – "golden emerods..for Ashdod one"
1Sa 6:17 – "golden emerods..for Gaza one"
1Sa 6:17 – "golden emerods..for Askelon one"
1Sa 6:17 – "golden emerods..for Gath one"
1Sa 6:17 – "golden emerods..for Ekron one"
1Sa 9:3 – "Take now 1 of the servants with thee"
1Sa 10:3 – "one carrying three kids"
1Sa 10:11 – "the people said one to another"
1Sa 10:12 – "one of..same place answered & said"
1Sa 11:7 – "the came out with one consent"
1Sa 13:1 – "Saul reigned one year"
1Sa 13:17 – "1 company turned..way..to Ophrah"
1Sa 14:4 – "a sharp rock on the one side"
1Sa 14:4 – "rock..the name of the one was Bozez"
1Sa 14:5 – "forefront of..one..situate northward"

1Sa 14:16 – "went on beating down one another"
1Sa 14:28 – "than answered one of the people"
1Sa 14:40 – "Be ye on one side..I and Jonathan"
1Sa 16:18 – "Then answered one of the servants"
1Sa 17:3 – "Philistines stood..on the one side"
1Sa 17:7 – "one bearing a shield went before"
1Sa 17:36 – "Philistine shall be as one of them"
1Sa 18:7 – "women answered one another"
1Sa 18:21 – "my son in law in the 1 of the twain"
1Sa 19:22 – "one said, Behold, they be at Naioth"
1Sa 20:15 – "every one from the face of the earth"
1Sa 20:41 – "they kissed one another"
1Sa 20:41 – "wept one with another, until David"
1Sa 21:11 – "did they not sing one to another"
1Sa 22:2 – "every one that was in distress"
1Sa 22:2 – "and every one that was in debt"
1Sa 22:2 – "and every one that was discontented"
1Sa 22:7 – "son of Jesse give every one of you"
1Sa 22:20 – "one of the sons of Ahimelech"
1Sa 25:14 – "one of the young men told Abigail"
1Sa 26:15 – "came one of the people in to destroy"
1Sa 26:20 – "when one doth hunt a partridge"
1Sa 26:22 – "one of the young men come over"
1Sa 27:1 – "I shall now perish one day by..Saul"
1Sa 29:5 – "David..whom they sang 1 to another"
2Sa 1:15 – "David called one of the young men"
2Sa 2:13 – "one on the one side of the pool"
2Sa 2:16 – "caught every 1 his fellow by the head"
2Sa 2:21 – "lay thee hold on 1 of the young men"
2Sa 2:25 – "became 1 troop, and stood..top..hill"
2Sa 2:27 – "gone up every one from following"
2Sa 3:13 – "but one thing I require of thee"
2Sa 3:29 – "house of Joab one that hath an issue"
2Sa 4:2 – "the name of the one was Baanah"
2Sa 4:10 – "one told me, saying..Saul is dead"
2Sa 6:19 – "to every one a cake of bread"
2Sa 6:19 – "departed every one to his house"
2Sa 6:20 – "as one of the vain fellows"
2Sa 7:23 – "what one nation in the earth is like"
2Sa 8:2 – "with one full line to keep alive"
2Sa 9:11 – "as one of the king's sons"
2Sa 11:3 – "And one said, Is not this Bathsheba"
2Sa 11:25 – "sword devoureth one as well as"
2Sa 12:1 – "2 men in one city; the 1 rich..poor"
2Sa 12:3 – "nothing, save one little ewe lamb"
2Sa 13:13 – "shalt be as one of the fools in Israel"
2Sa 14:6 – "the one smote the other..slew him"
2Sa 14:12 – "speak one word unto my lord"
2Sa 14:13 – "speak this thing as one..faulty"
2Sa 14:27 – "unto Absalom..was born..1 daughter"
2Sa 15:2 – "servant is of one of..tribes of Israel"
2Sa 15:31 – "one told David, saying"
2Sa 17:12 – "shall not be left so much as one"
2Sa 18:17 – "all Israel fled every one to his tent"
2Sa 19:7 – "there will not tarry one with thee"
2Sa 19:14 – "even as the heart of one man"
2Sa 20:11 – "one of Joab's men stood by him"
2Sa 20:12 – "every one that came by..stood still"
2Sa 20:19 – "I am one of them that are peaceable"
2Sa 23:8 – "spear against 800..he slew at 1 time"
2Sa 23:9 – "Eleazer..one of the 3 mighty men"

2Sa 23:15 – "Oh that one would give me drink"
2Sa 23:24 – "Asahel..was one of the thirty"
2Sa 24:12 – "3 things; choose thee one of them"
1Ki 1:48 – "God..hath given 1 to sit on my throne"
1Ki 2:16 – "I ask one petition of thee"
1Ki 2:20 – "I desire one small petition"
1Ki 3:17 – "And the one woman said"
I Ki 3:17 – "I and this woman dwell in one house"
1Ki 3:23 – "the one saith, This is my son"
1Ki 3:25 – "Divide..child..give half to the one"
1Ki 4:22 – "Solomon's provision for one day"
1Ki 6:24 – "5 cubits was the one wing..cherub"
1Ki 6:24 – "uttermost part of the one wing"
1Ki 6:25 – "cherubims..1 measure and 1 size"
1Ki 6:26 – "height of the 1 cherub was 10 cubits"
1Ki 6:27 – "wing of the one touched the one wall"
1Ki 6:27 – "their wings touched one another"
1Ki 6:34 – "2 leaves of the one door were folding"
1Ki 7:7 – "covered with cedar..1 side..to the other"
1Ki 7:16 – "height of the 1 chapiter was 5 cubits"
1Ki 7:17 – "seven for the one chapiter"
1Ki 7:18 – "2 rows round about upon..1 network"
1Ki 7:23 – "molten sea, 10 cubits from..one brim"
1Ki 7:27 – "four cubits was the length of one base"
1Ki 7:34 – "to the four corners of the one base"
1Ki 7:37 – "ten bases: all of them had one casting"
1Ki 7:37 – "ten bases..one measure, and one size"
1Ki 7:38 – "one laver contained forty baths"
1Ki 7:38 – "upon every 1 of the 10 bases 1 laver"
1Ki 7:42 – "2 rows..pomegranates for 1 network"
1Ki 7:44 – "one sea, and 12 oxen under the sea"
1Ki 8:56 – "hath not failed one word of..promise"
1Ki 9:8 – "every one that passeth by..astonished"
1Ki 10:14 – "weight of gold..to Solomon in 1 year"
1Ki 10:16 – "600 shekels of gold went to 1 target"
1Ki 10:17 – "3 pound of gold went to one shield"
1Ki 10:20 – "12 lions stood there on one side"
1Ki 11:13 – "will give one tribe to thy son"
1Ki 11:32 – "he shall have 1 tribe for..David's sake"
1Ki 11:36 – "unto his son will I give one tribe"
1Ki 12:29 – "he set the one in Bethel"
1Ki 12:30 – "people..worship before the one"
1Ki 13:33 – "he became one of the priests"
1Ki 16:11 – "left him not 1..pisseth against a wall"
1Ki 18:6 – "Ahab went one way by himself"
1Ki 18:23 – "choose one bullock for themselves"
1Ki 18:25 – "Choose you 1 bullock for yourselves"
1Ki 18:40 – "prophets..let not one of them escape"
1Ki 19:2 – "make not thy life as..one of them"
1Ki 20:20 – "they slew every one his man"
1Ki 20:29 – "pitched one over against the other"
1Ki 20:29 – "slew..100,000 footmen in one day"
1Ki 22:8 – "There is yet one man, Micaiah"
1Ki 22:13 – "prophets declare good..w/ 1 mouth"
1Ki 22:13 – "be like the word of one of them"
1Ki 22:20 – "And one said on this manner"
1Ki 22:28 – "Hearken, O people, every one of you"
1Ki 22:38 – "And one washed the chariot"
2Ki 3:11 – "one of the king of Israel's servants"
2Ki 3:23 – "they have smitten one another"
2Ki 4:22 – "Send me..one of the young men"

2Ki 4:22 – "Send me..one of the asses"
2Ki 4:39 – "one went out into the field"
2Ki 5:4 – "one went in, and told his lord"
2Ki 6:3 – "And one said, Be content"
2Ki 6:5 – "But as one was felling a beam"
2Ki 6:12 – "And one of his servants said"
2Ki 7:3 – "they said one to another"
2Ki 7:6 – "they said one to another"
2Ki 7:8 – "went into one tent and did eat..drink"
2Ki 7:9 – "they said one to another"
2Ki 7:13 – "And one of his servants answered"
2Ki 8:26 – "Ahaziah..reigned one year"
2Ki 9:1 – "Elisha..called one of the children"
2Ki 9:11 – "Jehu came..and one said unto him"
2Ki 9:18 – "there went one on horseback"
2Ki 10:21 – "house of Baal..full..1 end to another"
2Ki 12:4 – "money of every one that passeth"
2Ki 12:9 – "on the right side as one cometh"
2Ki 14:8 – "let us look one another in the face"
2Ki 14:11 – "Jehoash..Amaziah..looked 1 another"
2Ki 17:27 – "Carry thither one of the priests"
2Ki 17:28 – "one of the priests..came and dwelt"
2Ki 18:24 – "turn away the face of one captain"
2Ki 18:31 – "every one of his fig tree"
2Ki 18:31 – "drink ye every one the waters"
2Ki 19:22 – "even against the Holy One of Israel"
2Ki 21:16 – "shed innocent blood..from one end"
2Ki 23:35 – "every one according to his taxation"
2Ki 25:16 – "two pillars, one sea, and the bases"
2Ki 25:17 – "height of the one pillar was 18 cubits"
1Ch 1:19 – "the name of the one was Peleg"
1Ch 9:31 – "Mattithiah, one of the Levites"
1Ch 10:13 – "counsel of one..had a familiar spirit"
1Ch 11:11 – "lifted..spear against 300..at one time"
1Ch 11:12 – "Eleazer..one of the 3 mighties"
1Ch 11:17 – "Oh that one would give me drink"
1Ch 12:14 – "one of the least was over an 100"
1Ch 12:38 – "the rest of Israel were of one heart"
1Ch 16:3 – "he dealt to every one of Israel"
1Ch 16:3 – "to every one a loaf of bread"
1Ch 16:20 – "from 1 kingdom to another people"
1Ch 17:5 – "from one tabernacle to another"
1Ch 17:21 – "what one nation in the earth is like"
1Ch 21:10 – "I offer thee 3 things: choose thee 1"
1Ch 23:11 – "they were in one reckoning"
1Ch 24:5 – "divided by lot, one sort with another"
1Ch 24:6 – "Shemaiah..one of the Levites"
1Ch 24:6 – "one principal household..for Eleazar"
1Ch 24:6 – "one taken for Ithamar"
1Ch 26:12 – "porters.. wards one against another"
1Ch 27:18 – "Elihu, one of the brethren of David"
2Ch 3:11 – "one wing of the one cherub"
2Ch 3:12 – "And one wing of the other cherub"
2Ch 3:17 – "pillars before..temple..1 on the right"
2Ch 4:15 – "One sea, and twelve oxen under it."
2Ch 5:13 – "trumpeters and singers were as one"
2Ch 5:13 – "to make one sound to be heard"
2Ch 6:29 – "every one shall know his own sore"
2Ch 7:21 – "astonishment..every 1 that passeth by"
2Ch 9:13 – "gold..Solomon in 1 year..666 talents"
2Ch 9:15 – "600 shekels of..gold..to one target"

2Ch 9:16 – "300 shekels of gold..to one shield"
2Ch 9:19 – "12 lions stood there on the one side"
2Ch 18:7 – "There is yet one man..but I hate him"
2Ch 18:8 – "king of Israel called for 1 of..officers"
2Ch 18:12 – "declare good to..king with 1 assent"
2Ch 18:12 – "like one of theirs, and speak..good"
2Ch 18:19 – "one spake saying after this manner"
2Ch 20:23 – "every one helped to destroy another"
2Ch 22:2 – "Ahaziah..reigned 1 year in Jerusalem"
2Ch 25:17 – "Come..see one another in the face"
2Ch 25:21 – "Joash..saw one another..he..Amaziah"
2Ch 26:11 – "Hananiah, one of the king's captains"
2Ch 28:6 – "Pekah..slew..120,000 in one day"
2Ch 30:12 – "one heart to do the commandments"
2Ch 30:17 – "killing of the passover for every one"
2Ch 30:18 – "The good LORD pardon every one"
2Ch 31:16 – "every one that entered..house..LORD"
2Ch 32:12 – "Ye shall worship before one altar"
2Ch 35:24 – "buried in one of the sepulchres"
Ezr 2:1 – "Judah, every one unto his city"
Ezr 3:1 – "gathered..together as one man"
Ezr 3:5 – "every one that willingly offered"
Ezr 5:14 – "delivered unto one..Sheshbazzar"
Ezr 6:5 – "every one to his place"
Ezr 8:34 – "By number & by weight of every one"
Ezr 9:4 – "every one that trembled..words of God"
Ezr 9:11 – "abominations.. one end to another"
Ezr 10:2 – "Jehiel, one of the sons of Elam"
Ezr 10:13 – "neither..a work of one day or two"
Neh 1:2 – "Hanani, one of my brethren"
Neh 3:8 – "Hanaiah..son of one of..apothecaries"
Neh 3:28 – "every one over against his house"
Neh 4:15 – "to the wall, every one unto his work"
Neh 4:17 – "those that laded, every one..wrought"
Neh 4:17 – "one of his hands wrought in the work"
Neh 4:18 – "builders, every one had his sword"
Neh 4:19 – "separated..wall, one far from another"
Neh 4:22 – "Let every one with his servant lodge"
Neh 4:23 – "every one put them off for washing"
Neh 5:7 – "exact usury, every one of his brother"
Neh 5:18 – "prepared for me daily was one ox"
Neh 6:2 – "let us meet..in some one of the villages"
Neh 7:3 – "every one in his watch"
Neh 7:3 – "every one to be over against his house"
Neh 7:6 – "every one unto his city"
Neh 7:63 – "took one of the daughters of Barzillai"
Neh 8:1 – "people gathered..as one man"
Neh 8:16 – "made themselves booths, every one"
Neh 10:28 – "every one having knowledge"
Neh 11:3 – "Judah dwelt every 1 in his possession"
Neh 11:14 – "Zabdiel..son of one of the great men"
Neh 11:20 – "every one in his inheritance"
Neh 12:31 – "whereof one went on the right hand"
Neh 13:10 – "were fled every one to his field"
Neh 13:28 – "one of the sons of Joiada"
Neh 13:30 – "priests..Levites, every one..business"
Est 1:7 – "vessels being diverse one from another"
Est 3:13 – "to kill..all Jews..in one day"
Est 4:5 – "Hatach, one of the king's chamberlains"
Est 4:11 – "there is one law..to put him to death"
Est 6:9 – "one of the king's most noble princes"

Est 7:9 – "Harbonah, one of the chamberlains"
Est 8:12 – "Upon one day in all of the provinces"
Est 9:19 – "sending portions one to another"
Est 9:22 – "sending portions one to another"
Job 1:1 – "one that feared God, and eschewed evil"
Job 1:4 – "feasted in..houses, every one his day"
Job 1:8 – "one that feareth God..escheweth evil"
Job 2:3 – "one that feareth God..escheweth evil"
Job 2:10 – "speakest as one of the foolish women"
Job 2:11 – "every one from his own place"
Job 2:12 – "rent every one his mantle"
Job 5:2 – "envy slayeth the silly one"
Job 6:10 – "not concealed..words of the Holy One"
Job 6:26 – "speeches of one that is desperate"
Job 9:3 – "he cannot answer him 1 of a 1000"
Job 9:22 – "This is one thing"
Job 12:4 – "I am as one mocked of his neighbour"
Job 13:9 – "or as one man mocketh another"
Job 14:3 – "open thine eyes upon such an one"
Job 16:21 – "O that one might plead for a man"
Job 17:10 – "I cannot find 1 wise man among you"
Job 19:11 – "he counteth me..as 1 of his enemies"
Job 21:23 – "One dieth in his full strength"
Job 23:13 – "But he is in one mind"
Job 24:6 – "They reap every one his corn"
Job 24:17 – "if one know them"
Job 29:25 – "as one that comforteth the mourners"
Job 31:15 – "did not one fashion us in the womb?"
Job 31:35 – "Oh that one would hear me!"
Job 33:23 – "one among 1000, to shew unto man"
Job 40:11 – "behold every one that is proud"
Job 40:12 – "Look on every one that is proud"
Job 41:9 – "shall not one be cast down at the sight"
Job 41:16 – "One is so near to another, that no air"
Job 41:17 – "They are joined one to another"
Job 41:32 – "1 would think the deep to be hoary"
Job 42:11 – "every one an earring of gold"
Psa 12:2 – "speak every one with his neighbour"
Psa 16:10 – "Holy One to see corruption"
Psa 27:4 – "One thing have I desired of the LORD"
Psa 29:9 – "in his temple doeth every one speak"
Psa 32:6 – "every one that is godly pray"
Psa 35:14 – "as one that mourneth for his mother"
Psa 49:16 – "when one is made rich"
Psa 50:21 – "altogether such an one as thyself"
Psa 53:3 – "Every one of them is gone back"
Psa 58:8 – "let every one of them pass away"
Psa 63:11 – "every one that sweareth by him"
Psa 64:6 – "inward thought of every one of them"
Psa 68:21 – "scalp of such an one as goeth on"
Psa 68:30 – "every one submit himself w/..silver"
Psa 71:18 – "power to every one that is to come"
Psa 71:22 – "O thou Holy One of Israel"
Psa 73:20 – "As a dream when one awaketh"
Psa 75:7 – "he putteth down one, and setteth up"
Psa 78:41 – "limited the Holy One of Israel"
Psa 78:65 – "LORD awaked as one out of sleep"
Psa 82:7 – "fall like one of the princes"
Psa 83:5 – "consulted together with one consent"
Psa 84:7 – "every one of them in Zion appeareth"
Psa 89:10 – "breakest Rahab..as one that is slain"

Psa 89:18 – "the Holy One of Israel is our king"
Psa 89:19 – "spakest in a vision to thy holy one"
Psa 89:19 – "have laid help upon 1 that is mighty"
Psa 89:19 – "I have exalted one chosen out of"
Psa 105:13 – "they went from 1 nation..another"
Psa 105:13 – "from 1 kingdom to another people"
Psa 105:37 – "there was not one feeble person"
Psa 106:11 – "there was not one of them left"
Psa 115:8 – "so is every one that trusteth in them"
Psa 119:160 – "every 1..thy righteous judgments"
Psa 119:162 – "as one that findeth great spoil"
Psa 128:1 – "Blessed is every one that feareth"
Psa 135:18 – "every one that trusteth in them"
Psa 137:3 – "Sing us one of the songs of Zion."
Psa 141:7 – "as when 1 cutteth & cleaveth wood"
Psa 145:4 – "1 generation shall praise thy works"
Pro 1:14 – "let us all have one purse"
Pro 1:19 – "the ways of every one that is greedy"
Pro 3:18 – "happy is every one that retaineth her"
Pro 6:11 – "poverty come as one that travelleth"
Pro 6:28 – "Can one go upon hot coals"
Pro 8:30 – "as one brought up with him"
Pro 15:12 – "scorner loveth not 1 that reproveth"
Pro 16:5 – "every one that is proud in heart"
Pro 17:14 – "as when one letteth out water"
Pro 19:25 – "reprove 1 that hath understanding"
Pro 20:6 – "proclaim every every 1 his..goodness"
Pro 21:5 – "every one that is hasty only to want"
Pro 22:26 – "one of them that strike hands"
Pro 24:34 – "poverty come as one that travelleth"
Pro 26:17 – "like 1 that taketh a dog by the ears"
Ecc 1:4 – "One generation passeth away"
Ecc 2:14 – "one event happeneth to them all"
Ecc 3:19 – "even one thing befalleth them"
Ecc 3:19 – "as the one dieth, do dieth the other"
Ecc 3:19 – "they all have one breath"
Ecc 3:20 – "All go unto one place"
Ecc 4:8 – "There is one alone..not a second"
Ecc 4:9 – "Two are better than one"
Ecc 4:10 – "if they fall, the one will lift up"
Ecc 4:11 – "how can one be warm alone?"
Ecc 4:12 – "if one prevail against him"
Ecc 5:18 – "it is good..for one to eat and drink"
Ecc 6:6 – "do not all go to one place?"
Ecc 7:1 – "than the day of one's birth"
Ecc 7:14 – "one over against the other"
Ecc 7:27 – "counting one by one"
Ecc 7:28 – "one man among 1000 have I found"
Ecc 8:9 – "time wherein one man ruleth over"
Ecc 9:2 – "there is one event to the righteous"
Ecc 9:3 – "there is one event unto all"
Ecc 9:18 – "one sinner destroyeth much good"
Ecc 10:3 – "saith to every one that he is a fool"
Ecc 10:15 – "labour..wearieth every one of them"
Ecc 12:11 – "which are given from one shepherd"
Son 1:7 – "should I be as one that turneth aside"
Son 2:10 – "Rise up, my love, my fair one"
Son 2:13 – "Arise, my love, my fair one, and come"
Son 4:2 – "sheep..everyone bear twins"
Son 4:9 – "ravished my heart w/ 1 of thine eyes"
Son 4:9 – "ravished..with one chain of thy neck"

Son 6:6 – "sheep..every one beareth twins"
Son 6:9 – "My dove, my undefiled is but one"
Son 6:9 – "she is the only one of her mother"
Son 6:9 – "she is the choice one"
Son 8:10 – "then was I..as one that found favour"
Son 8:11 – "every one for the fruit thereof"
Isa 1:4 – " provoked the Holy One of Israel"
Isa 1:23 – "every one loveth gifts"
Isa 1:24 – "the Mighty One of Israel"
Isa 2:12 – "every one that is proud and lofty"
Isa 2:12 – "upon every one that is lifted up"
Isa 2:20 – "idols..made each one for..to worship"
Isa 3:5 – "people..oppressed, every 1 by another"
Isa 3:5 – "oppressed..every one by his neighbour"
Isa 4:1 – "seven women shall take hold of 1 man"
Isa 4:3 – "every 1 that is written among the living"
Isa 5:10 – "10 acres of vineyard shall yield 1 bath"
Isa 5:19 – "the counsel of the Holy One of Israel"
Isa 5:24 – "despised the word of the Holy One"
Isa 5:30 – "if 1 look unto..land, behold darkness"
Isa 6:2 – "seraphims: each one had six wings"
Isa 6:3 – "and one cried..Holy, holy, holy"
Isa 6:6 – "then flew one of the seraphims"
Isa 7:22 – "butter and honey shall every one eat"
Isa 9:14 – "the LORD will cut off..in one day"
Isa 9:17 – "every 1 is an hypocrite & an evildoer"
Isa 10:14 – "as one gathereth eggs that are left"
Isa 10:17 – "Israel..his Holy One for a flame"
Isa 10:17 – "burn..devour..thorns..briers in 1 day"
Isa 10:20 – "the LORD, the Holy One of Israel"
Isa 10:34 – "Lebanon shall fall by a mighty one"
Isa 12:6 – "great is the Holy One of Israel"
Isa 13:8 – "they shall be amazed one at another"
Isa 13:14 – "flee every one into his own land"
Isa 13:15 – "Every 1 that is found..thrust through"
Isa 13:15 – "every 1..joined unto them shall fall"
Isa 14:18 – "every one in his own house"
Isa 14:32 – "What shall one then answer"
Isa 15:3 – "every one shall howl, weeping"
Isa 16:7 – "Moab, every one shall howl"
Isa 17:7 – "eyes..respect to the Holy One of Israel"
Isa 19:2 – "fight every one against his brother"
Isa 19:2 – "fight..every one against his neighbour"
Isa 19:17 – "every 1 that maketh mention..afraid"
Isa 19:18 – "one..called, The city of destruction"
Isa 19:20 – "send them a savior, and a great one"
Isa 23:15 – "70 years, acc. to the days of one king"
Isa 27:12 – "ye shall be gathered 1 by 1..Israel"
Isa 28:2 – "LORD hath a mighty and strong one"
Isa 29:4 – "as of one that hath a familiar spirit"
Isa 29:11 – "men deliver to one that is learned"
Isa 29:19 – "shall rejoice in the Holy One of Israel"
Isa 29:20 – "the terrible one is brought to nought"
Isa 29:23 – "sanctify the Holy One of Jacob"
Isa 30:11 – "cause the Holy One of Israel to cease"
Isa 30:12 – "thus saith the Holy One of Israel"
Isa 30:15 – "the LORD GOD, the Holy One of Israel"
Isa 30:17 – "1000 shall flee at the rebuke of one"
Isa 30:29 – "as when one goeth with a pipe"
Isa 30:29 – "to the mighty One of Israel"
Isa 31:1 – "they look not unto the Holy One"

Isa 34:15 – "vultures..every one with her mate"
Isa 36:9 – "turn away the face of one captain"
Isa 36:16 – "eat ye every one of his vine"
Isa 36:16 – "eat ye..every one of his fig tree"
Isa 36:16 – "drink ye every one the waters"
Isa 37:23 – "even against the Holy One of Israel"
Isa 40:25 – "shall I be equal? saith the Holy One"
Isa 41:6 – "helped every one his neighbour"
Isa 41:6 – "every one said to his brother"
Isa 41:14 – "thy redeemer, the Holy One"
Isa 41:16 – "glory in the Holy One of Israel"
Isa 41:20 – "Holy One of Israel hath created it"
Isa 41:25 – "I have raised up one from the north"
Isa 41:27 – "give to Jerusalem one that bringeth"
Isa 43:3 – "I am the LORD thy God, the Holy One"
Isa 43:7 – "every one that is called by my name"
Isa 43:14 – "your redeemer, the Holy One"
Isa 43:15 – "I am the LORD, your Holy One"
Isa 44:5 – "One shall say, I am the LORD's"
Isa 45:11 – "saith the LORD, the Holy One"
Isa 45:24 – "Surely, shall one say"
Isa 46:7 – "one shall cry unto him"
Isa 47:4 – "LORD of hosts..Holy One of Israel"
Isa 47:9 – "two things shall come..in one day"
Isa 47:15 – "wander every one to his quarter"
Isa 48:17 – "thy redeemer, the Holy One of Israel"
Isa 49:7 – "Redeemer of Israel, and his Holy One"
Isa 49:7 – "Holy One of Israel..shall choose thee"
Isa 49:26 – "Redeemer, the mighy One of Jacob"
Isa 53:6 – "turned every one to his own way"
Isa 54:5 – "thy Redeemer the Holy One of Israel"
Isa 55:1 – "Ho, every one that thirsteth, come ye"
Isa 55:5 – "Holy One of Israel..hath glorified thee"
Isa 56:6 – "every one that keepth the Sabbath"
Isa 56:11 – "own way, every one for his gain"
Isa 57:2 – "each one walking in his uprightness"
Isa 57:15 – "high and lofty One that inhabiteth"
Isa 60:9 – "to the Holy One of Israel"
Isa 60:14 – "The Zion of the Holy One of Israel"
Isa 60:16 – "the mighty One of Jacob"
Isa 60:22 – "a little one shall become a thousand"
Isa 60:22 – "a small one a strong nation"
Isa 65:8 – "new wine..one saith, Destroy it not"
Isa 66:8 – "Shall the earth..bring forth in one day?"
Isa 66:13 – "As one whom his mother comforteth"
Isa 66:17 – "behind one tree in the midst"
Isa 66:23 – "from one new moon to another"
Isa 66:23 – "from one sabbath to another"
Jer 1:15 – "set every one on his throne"
Jer 3:14 – "I will take you one of a city"
Jer 5:6 – "every one that goeth out..torn..pieces"
Jer 5:8 – "every 1 neighed after..neighbour's wife"
Jer 6:3 – "they shall feed every one in his place"
Jer 6:13 – "every one is given to coveteousness"
Jer 6:13 – "every one dealeth falsely"
Jer 8:6 – "every one turned to his course"
Jer 8:10 – "every one..is given to coveteousness"
Jer 8:10 – "every one dealeth falsely"
Jer 9:4 – "Take ye heed every 1 of his neighbour"
Jer 9:5 – "will deceive every one his neighbour"
Jer 9:8 – "1 speaketh peaceably to his neighbour"

Jer 9:20 – "every one her neighbour lamentation"
Jer 10:3 – "one cutteth a tree out of the forest"
Jer 11:8 – "walked every one..imagination..heart"
Jer 12:12 – "devour from the one end of the land"
Jer 13:14 – "I will dash them one against another"
Jer 15:10 – "every one of them doth curse me"
Jer 16:12 – "every one after..imagination..heart"
Jer 18:11 – "return ye now every one..evil way"
Jer 18:12 – "we will every one do..evil heart"
Jer 18:16 – "hissing: every one that passeth"
Jer 19:8 – "every one that passeth thereby"
Jer 19:9 – "eat every one the flesh of his friend"
Jer 19:11 – "as one breaketh a potter's vessel"
Jer 20:7 – "every one mocketh me"
Jer 20:11 – "LORD is with me..mighty terrible one"
Jer 22:7 – "destroyers..every one w/ his weapons"
Jer 23:17 – "every 1..walketh..imagination..heart"
Jer 23:30 – "stealeth my words every one"
Jer 23:35 – "say every one to his neighbour"
Jer 23:35 – "say..every one to his brother"
Jer 24:2 – "One basket had very good figs"
Jer 25:5 – "Turn ye again now every one"
Jer 25:26 – "kings of the north..one with another"
Jer 25:33 – "slain of the LORD..from one end"
Jer 30:14 – "with the chastisement of a cruel one"
Jer 30:16 – "adversaries..every one..into captivity"
Jer 31:30 – "every 1 shall die for his own iniquity"
Jer 32:19 – "to give every 1 according to his ways"
Jer 32:39 – "And I will give them one heart"
Jer 32:39 – "And I will give them..one way"
Jer 34:10 – "every 1..let his manservant..go free"
Jer 34:10 – "every one his maidservant go free"
Jer 34:17 – "liberty, every one to his brother"
Jer 35:2 – "Go..into one of the chambers"
Jer 36:7 – "return every one from his evil way"
Jer 36:16 – "they were afraid both one and other"
Jer 38:7 – "Ebedmelech..one of the eunuchs"
Jer 46:16 – "one fell upon another"
Jer 49:17 – "every one that goeth by..astonished"
Jer 50:13 – "every one..by Babylon..astonished"
Jer 50:16 – "they..turn every one to his people"
Jer 50:16 – "they..flee every one to his own land"
Jer 50:29 – "against the Holy One of Israel"
Jer 50:42 – "every one put in array..to the battle"
Jer 51:5 – "against the Holy One of Israel"
Jer 51:9 – "let us go every 1 into his own country"
Jer 51:31 – "One post shall run to meet another"
Jer 51:31 – "one messenger to meet another"
Jer 51:31 – "his city is taken at one end"
Jer 51:46 – "a rumour shall both come one year"
Jer 51:56 – "every one of their bows is broken"
Jer 52:20 – "two pillars, one sea"
Jer 52:21 – "height of one pillar was 18 cubits"
Jer 52:22 – "height of the 1 chapiter was 5 cubits"
Ezk 1:6 – "every one had four faces"
Ezk 1:6 – "every one had four wings"
Ezk 1:9 – "wings were joined one to another"
Ezk 1:9 – "they went every one straight forward"
Ezk 1:11 – "two wings of every one were joined"
Ezk 1:11 – "wings..joined one to another"
Ezk 1:12 – "went every one straight forward"

Ezk 1:15 – "one wheel upon the earth"
Ezk 1:16 – "wheels..they four had one likeness"
Ezk 1:23 – "wings straight, the one toward..other"
Ezk 1:23 – "every one had two, which covered"
Ezk 1:23 – "every one had two, which covered"
Ezk 1:28 – "I heard a voice of one that spake"
Ezk 3:13 – "the wings..touched one another"
Ezk 4:8 – "not turn thee from one side to another"
Ezk 4:9 – "put them in one vessel"
Ezk 4:17 – "be astonied one with another"
Ezk 7:16 – "mourning, every one for his iniquity"
Ezk 9:2 – "one man..clothed with linen..inkhorn"
Ezk 10:7 – "one cherub stretched forth his hand"
Ezk 10:9 – "one wheel by one cherub"
Ezk 10:10 – "they four had one likeness"
Ezk 10:14 – "every one had four faces"
Ezk 10:19 – "every 1 stood at the door..east gate"
Ezk 10:21 – "Every one had four faces apiece"
Ezk 10:21 – "and every one four wings"
Ezk 10:22 – "went every one straight forward"
Ezk 11:5 – "I know the things..every one of them"
Ezk 11:19 – "I will give them one heart"
Ezk 13:10 – "no peace; and one built up a wall"
Ezk 14:7 – "every one of the house of Israel"
Ezk 15:7 – "they shall go out from one fire"
Ezk 16:15 – "fornications on every 1 that passed"
Ezk 16:25 – "opened thy feet to every one"
Ezk 16:44 – "every one that useth proverbs"
Ezk 17:22 – "I will crop off..a tender one"
Ezk 18:10 – "doeth the like to any one"
Ezk 18:30 – "every one according to his ways"
Ezk 19:3 – "brought up one of her young whelps"
Ezk 20:39 – "serve ye every one his idols"
Ezk 21:16 – "Go thee one way or the other"
Ezk 21:19 – "shall come forth out of one land"
Ezk 22:6 – "princes of Israel, every one"
Ezk 22:11 – "one hath committed abominations"
Ezk 23:2 – "two women..daughters of one mother"
Ezk 23:13 – "they took both one way"
Ezk 24:23 – "and mourn one toward another"
Ezk 31:11 – "into the hand of the mighty one"
Ezk 33:20 – "I will judge you every one"
Ezk 33:21 – "one..escaped out of Jerusalem"
Ezk 33:24 – "saying, Abraham was one, and he"
Ezk 33:26 – "defile every one..neighbour's wife"
Ezk 33:30 – "speak one to another"
Ezk 33:30 – "every one to his brother saying"
Ezk 33:32 – "song of one..hath a pleasant voice"
Ezk 34:23 – "set up one shepherd over them"
Ezk 37:16 – "son of man, take thee one stick"
Ezk 37:17 – "join them 1 to another into 1 stick"
Ezk 37:17 – "they shall become one in thy hand"
Ezk 37:19 – "make them one stick"
Ezk 37:19 – "they shall be one in mine hand"
Ezk 37:22 – "make them one nation in the land"
Ezk 37:22 – "one king shall be king to them all"
Ezk 37:24 – "they all shall have one shepherd"
Ezk 39:7 – "the Holy One of Israel"
Ezk 40:5 – "breadth of the building, one reed"
Ezk 40:5 – "the building..the height, one reed"
Ezk 40:6 – "gate, which was one reed broad"

Ezk 40:6 – "other threshold..one reed broad"
Ezk 40:7 – "every little chamber..one reed long"
Ezk 40:7 – "every little chamber..one reed broad"
Ezk 40:7 – "gate by the porch..one reed"
Ezk 40:8 – "porch of the gate w/in was one reed"
Ezk 40:10 – "they three were of one measure"
Ezk 40:10 – "the posts had one measure"
Ezk 40:12 – "space..little chambers..one cubit"
Ezk 40:12 – "space was one cubit on that side"
Ezk 40:13 – "the roof of one little chamber"
Ezk 40:26 – "palm trees, one on this side"
Ezk 40:40 – "as one goeth up to the entry"
Ezk 40:42 – "tables..burnt offering..one cubit high"
Ezk 40:44 – "chambers of..singers..one at the side"
Ezk 40:49 – "pillars by the posts..one on this side"
Ezk 41:1 – "posts, six cubits broad..one side"
Ezk 41:2 – "sides..door..5 cubits..one side"
Ezk 41:6 – "side chambers..one over another"
Ezk 41:11 – "one door toward the north"
Ezk 41:15 – "galleries thereof on the one side"
Ezk 41:19 – "face of a man..on the one side"
Ezk 41:21 – "appearance of the one as the..other"
Ezk 41:24 – "two leaves for the one door"
Ezk 41:26 – "windows..palm trees on the 1 side"
Ezk 42:4 – "before the chambers..a way of 1 cubit"
Ezk 42:9 – "as one goeth..from the utter court"
Ezk 42:12 – "a door..as one entereth into them"
Ezk 43:14 – "ground..settle..breadth..one cubit"
Ezk 43:14 – "ground..settle..breadth..one cubit"
Ezk 45:7 – "portion..for the prince on..one side"
Ezk 45:7 – "over against one of the portions"
Ezk 45:11 – "ephah and the bath..of one measure"
Ezk 45:15 – "one lamb out of..two hundred"
Ezk 45:20 – "every one that erreth"
Ezk 46:12 – "one shall then open him the gate"
Ezk 46:12 – "one shall shut the gate"
Ezk 46:17 – "gift..inheritance to one..his servants"
Ezk 46:22 – "four corners were of one measure"
Ezk 47:7 – "many trees on..one side..on the other"
Ezk 47:14 – "inherit it, one as well as another"
Ezk 48:1 – "as one goeth to Hamath"
Ezk 48:8 – "in length as one of the other parts"
Ezk 48:21 – "for the prince, on the one side"
Ezk 48:31 – "one gate of Reuben"
Ezk 48:31 – "one gate of Judah"
Ezk 48:31 – "one gate of Levi"
Ezk 48:32 – "one gate of Joseph"
Ezk 48:32 – "one gate of Benjamin"
Ezk 48:32 – "one gate of Dan"
Ezk 48:33 – "one gate of Simeon"
Ezk 48:33 – "one gate of Issachar"
Ezk 48:33 – "one gate of Zebulun"
Ezk 48:34 – "one gate of Gad"
Ezk 48:34 – "one gate of Asher"
Ezk 48:34 – "one gate of Naphtali"
Dan 2:9 – "there is but one decree for you"
Dan 2:43 – "shall not cleave one to another"
Dan 3:19 – "heat..furnace one seven times more"
Dan 4:13 – "an holy one came down from heaven"
Dan 4:19 – "Daniel..was astonied for one hour"
Dan 4:23 – "holy one coming down from heaven"

Dan 5:6 – "his knees smote one against another"
Dan 7:3 – "great beasts..diverse one from another"
Dan 7:5 – "it raised up itself on one side"
Dan 7:13 – "night visions..1 like the Son of man"
Dan 7:16 – "came near unto 1 of them..stood by"
Dan 8:3 – "horns were high; but one was higher"
Dan 8:9 – "out of one of them came..little horn"
Dan 8:13 – "Then I heard one saint speaking"
Dan 9:27 – "confirm the covenant..for one week"
Dan 10:13 – "Michael, one of the chief princes"
Dan 10:16 – "one like..similitude..sons of men"
Dan 10:18 – "one like the appearance of a man"
Dan 11:5 – "one of his princes"
Dan 11:7 – "one stand up in his estate"
Dan 11:10 – "one shall certainly come"
Dan 11:27 – "they shall speak lies at one table"
Dan 12:1 – "every one..found written in the book"
Dan 12:5 – "one on this side of the bank"
Dan 12:6 – "And one said to the man"
Hos 1:11 – "appoint themselves one head"
Hos 4:3 – "every one that dwelleth..shall languish"
Hos 11:9 – "the Holy One in the midst of thee"
Joe 2:7 – "march every one on his ways"
Joe 2:8 – "Neither shall one thrust another"
Joe 2:8 – "shall walk every one in his path"
Amo 3:5 – "shall one take up a snare"
Amo 4:7 – "I caused it to rain upon one city"
Amo 4:7 – "one piece was rained upon"
Amo 4:8 – "cities wandered unto 1 city, to drink"
Amo 6:9 – "ten men in one house"
Amo 6:12 – "will one plow there with oxen"
Amo 8:8 – "every one mourn..dwelleth therein?"
Oba 9 – "every one of the mount of Esau"
Oba 11 – "even thou wast as one of them"
Jon 1:7 – "said every one to his fellow"
Jon 3:8 – "turn every one from his evil way"
Mic 2:4 – "shall one take up a parable"
Mic 4:5 – "walk every one in the name of his god"
Nah 1:11 – "There is one come out of thee"
Nah 2:4 – "chariots..justle one against another"
Hab 1:12 – "O LORD my God, mine Holy One?"
Hab 3:3 – "the Holy One from mount Paran"
Zep 2:11 – "every one from his place"
Zep 2:15 – "every one that passeth..shall hiss"
Zep 3:9 – "to serve him with one consent"
Hag 2:12 – "If one bear holy flesh in the skirt"
Hag 2:13 – "If one that is unclean by a dead body"
Hag 2:16 – "Since those days..when one came"
Hag 2:16 – "when one came to the pressfat"
Hag 2:22 – "every 1 by the sword of his brother"
Zec 3:9 – "upon one stone shall be seven eyes"
Zec 3:9 – "I remove the iniquity..in one day"
Zec 4:3 – "two olive trees..one upon the right"
Zec 5:3 – "every one that stealeth shall be cut off"
Zec 5:3 – "every one that sweareth..cut off"
Zec 8:10 – "every one against his neighbour"
Zec 8:21 – "inhabitants of one city..to another"
Zec 10:1 – "to every one grass in the field"
Zec 11:6 – "every one into his neighbour's hand"
Zec 11:7 – "the one I called Beauty"
Zec 11:8 – "Three shepherds..cut off in 1 month"

Zec 11:9 – "eat every one the flesh of another"
Zec 11:16 – "neither shall seek the young one"
Zec 12:10 – "as one mourneth for his only son"
Zec 12:10 – "as one that is in bitterness"
Zec 13:4 – "ashamed every one of his vision"
Zec 13:6 – "And one shall say unto him"
Zec 14:7 – "one day which shall be known"
Zec 14:9 – "one LORD, and his name one"
Zec 14:13 – "shall lay hold every one on the hand"
Zec 14:16 – "every 1 that is left of all the nations"
Mal 2:3 – "one shall take you away with it"
Mal 2:10 – "Have we not all one father?"
Mal 2:10 – "hath not one God created us?"
Mal 2:15 – "And did not he make one?"
Mal 2:15 – "And wherefore one?"
Mal 2:16 – "1 covereth violence with his garment"
Mal 2:17 – "Every one that doeth evil is good"
Mal 3:16 – "spake often one to another"
Mat 3:3 – "voice of one crying in the wilderness"
Mat 5:18 – "one jot or one tittle..no wise pass"
Mat 5:19 – "break one of..least commandments"
Mat 5:29 – "one of thy members should perish"
Mat 5:30 – "one of thy members should perish"
Mat 5:36 – "canst not make 1 hair white or black"
Mat 6:24 – "masters..hate the one..love the other"
Mat 6:24 – "masters..hold to..one..despise..other"
Mat 6:27 – "add one cubit unto his stature?"
Mat 6:29 – "not arrayed like one of these"
Mat 7:8 – "every one that asketh receiveth"
Mat 7:21 – "Not every one that saith..Lord, Lord"
Mat 7:26 – "every one that heareth these sayings"
Mat 7:29 – "as one having authority"
Mat 10:29 – "sparrows..one of them shall not fall"
Mat 10:42 – "one of these little ones..cold water"
Mat 12:6 – "one greater than the temple"
Mat 12:11 – "man that shall have one sheep"
Mat 12:22 – "one possessed with a devil"
Mat 12:29 – "can one enter..strong man's house"
Mat 12:47 – "Then one said unto him, Behold"
Mat 13:19 – "When any one heareth the word"
Mat 13:19 – "then cometh the wicked one"
Mat 13:38 – "children of the wicked one"
Mat 13:46 – "found one pearl of great price"
Mat 16:14 – "Jeremias, or one of the prophets"
Mat 17:4 – "three tabernacles, one for thee"
Mat 17:4 – "three tabernacles..one for Moses"
Mat 17:4 – "three tabernacles..and one for Elias"
Mat 18:5 – "receive one such child in my name"
Mat 18:6 – "offend one of these little ones"
Mat 18:9 – "to enter into life with one eye"
Mat 18:10 – "despise not one of these little ones"
Mat 18:12 – "100 sheep, and one..be gone astray"
Mat 18:14 – "that one of these little ones..perish"
Mat 18:9 – "enter into life with one eye"
Mat 18:12 – "100 sheep, and one..gone astray"
Mat 18:14 – "1 of these little ones should perish"
Mat 18:16 – "take with thee one or two more"
Mat 18:24 – "one..brought..owed..10,000 talents"
Mat 18:28 – "1..fellowservants..owed..100 pence"
Mat 18:35 – "forgive not every one his brother"
Mat 19:5 – "they twain shall be one flesh?"

Mat 19:6 – "no more twain, but one flesh"
Mat 19:16 – "one came and said unto him"
Mat 19:17 – "there is none good, but one"
Mat 19:29 – "every 1 that hath forsaken houses"
Mat 20:12 – "have wrought but one hour"
Mat 20:13 – "But he answered one of them"
Mat 20:21 – "one on thy right hand..other..left"
Mat 21:24 – "I also will ask you one thing"
Mat 21:35 – "took his servants, and beat one"
Mat 22:5 – "went their ways, one to his farm"
Mat 22:35 – "one of them, which was a lawyer"
Mat 23:4 – "not move them w/ one..their fingers"
Mat 23:8 – "one is your Master, even Christ"
Mat 23:9 – "1 is your Father, which is in heaven"
Mat 23:10 – "one is your Master, even Christ"
Mat 23:15 – "sea and land to make one proselyte"
Mat 24:2 – "not be left..one stone upon another"
Mat 24:10 – "and shall betray one another"
Mat 24:10 – "and shall hate one another"
Mat 24:31 – "from one end of heaven to another"
Mat 24:40 – "two..in the field..one shall be taken"
Mat 24:41 – "Two..grinding..one shall be taken"
Mat 25:15 – "unto one he gave five talents"
Mat 25:15 – "talents..to another one"
Mat 25:18 – "he that had received one"
Mat 25:24 – "which had received the one talent"
Mat 25:29 – "unto every one that hath..be given"
Mat 25:32 – "separate them one from another"
Mat 25:40 – "done it unto one of the least"
Mat 25:45 – "did it not to one of the least"
Mat 26:14 – "one of the twelve..Judas Iscariot"
Mat 26:21 – "one of you shall betray me"
Mat 26:22 – "began every one of them to say"
Mat 26:40 – "watch with me one hour?"
Mat 26:47 – "Judas, one of the twelve, came"
Mat 26:51 – "one of them..drew his sword"
Mat 26:73 – "thou also art one of them"
Mat 27:38 – "two thieves..one on the right"
Mat 27:48 – "one of them..took a spunge"
Mar 1:3 – "voice of one crying..wilderness"
Mar 1:7 – "cometh one mightier than I"
Mar 1:22 – "taught them as one..had authority"
Mar 1:24 – "the Holy One of God"
Mar 2:3 – "bringing one sick of the palsy"
Mar 4:41 – "feared..and said one to another"
Mar 5:22 – "one of the rulers of the synagogue"
Mar 6:15 – "or as one of the prophets"
Mar 7:14 – "Hearken unto me every one of you"
Mar 7:32 – "they bring unto him one..was deaf"
Mar 8:14 – "neither..in the ship..one loaf"
Mar 8:28 – "One of the prophets"
Mar 9:5 – "tabernacles; one for thee"
Mar 9:5 – "tabernacles..one for Moses"
Mar 9:5 – "tabernacles..and one for Elias"
Mar 9:10 – "questioning one with another"
Mar 9:17 – "one of the multitude answered"
Mar 9:26 – "he was as one dead"
Mar 9:37 – "receive one of such children"
Mar 9:38 – "we saw one casting out devils"
Mar 9:42 – "offend one of these little ones"
Mar 9:47 – "into the kingdom of God with 1 eye"

Mar 9:49 – "every one shall be salted with fire"
Mar 9:50 – "have peace one with another"
Mar 10:8 – "they twain shall be one flesh"
Mar 10:8 – "no more twain, but one flesh"
Mar 10:17 – "there came one running"
Mar 10:18 – "none good but one, that is God"
Mar 10:21 – "One thing thou lackest"
Mar 10:37 – "sit, one on thy right hand"
Mar 11:29 – "I will ask of you one question"
Mar 12:6 – "having one son, his wellbeloved"
Mar 12:28 – "And one of the scribes came"
Mar 12:29 – "The Lord our God is one Lord"
Mar 12:32 – "for there is one God"
Mar 13:1 – "one of his disciples saith unto him"
Mar 13:2 – "not be left one stone upon another"
Mar 14:10 – "Judas Iscariot, one of the twelve"
Mar 14:18 – "One of you..shall betray me"
Mar 14:19 – "say unto him one by one, is it I?"
Mar 14:20 – "It is one of the twelve"
Mar 14:37 – "couldest..not watch one hour?"
Mar 14:43 – "Judas, one of the twelve"
Mar 14:47 – "And one of them that stood by"
Mar 14:66 – "there cometh one of the maids"
Mar 14:69 – "This is one of them."
Mar 14:70 – "Surely thou are one of them"
Mar 15:6 – "released unto them one prisoner"
Mar 15:7 – "there was one named Barabbas"
Mar 15:21 – "compel one Simon a Cyrenian"
Mar 15:27 – "two thieves; one on his right"
Mar 15:36 – "one ran, and filled a spunge"
Luk 2:3 – "taxed, every one into his own city"
Luk 2:15 – "the shepherds said one to another"
Luk 2:36 – "there was one Anna, a prophetess"
Luk 3:4 – "voice of one crying in the wilderness"
Luk 3:16 – "one mightier than I cometh"
Luk 4:34 – "Jesus..the Holy One of God"
Luk 4:40 – "laid his hands on every one of them"
Luk 5:3 – "he entered into one of the ships"
Luk 6:9 – "I will ask you one thing"
Luk 6:11 – "communed one with another"
Luk 6:29 – "smiteth thee on the one cheek"
Luk 6:40 – "but every one that is perfect"
Luk 7:8 – "I say unto one, Go, and he goeth"
Luk 7:32 – "children..calling one to another"
Luk 7:36 – "one of the Pharisees desired him"
Luk 7:41 – "debtors..the one owed 500 pence"
Luk 8:25 – "saying one to another"
Luk 8:42 – "he had one only daughter"
Luk 8:49 – "there cometh one from the ruler"
Luk 9:8 – "one of the old prophets was risen"
Luk 9:19 – "one of the old prophets is risen"
Luk 9:33 – "three tabernacles; one for thee"
Luk 9:33 – "three tabernacles..one for Moses"
Luk 9:33 – "three tabernacles..one for Elias"
Luk 9:43 – "they wondered every one"
Luk 9:49 – "we saw one casting out devils"
Luk 10:42 – "one thing is needful"
Luk 11:1 – "one of his disciples said"
Luk 11:4 – "every one that is indebted to us"
Luk 11:10 – "every one that asketh receiveth"
Luk 11:45 – "answered one of the lawyers"

Luk 11:46 – "burdens with one of your fingers"
Luk 12:1 – "they trode one upon another"
Luk 12:13 – "one of the company said unto him"
Luk 12:25 – "add to his stature one cubit"
Luk 12:27 – "not arrayed like one of these"
Luk 12:52 – "shall be five in one house divided"
Luk 13:10 – "teaching in one of the synagogues"
Luk 13:15 – "doth not each one of you"
Luk 13:23 – "Then said one unto him, Lord"
Luk 14:1 – "house of one of the chief Pharisees"
Luk 14:15 – "one of them that sat at meat"
Luk 14:18 – "with one consent..make excuse"
Luk 15:4 – "an 100 sheep, if he lose one"
Luk 15:7 – "one sinner that repenteth"
Luk 15:8 – "pieces or silver, if she lose one"
Luk 15:10 – "one sinner that repententh"
Luk 15:19 – "make me as one of thy..servants"
Luk 15:26 – "he called one of the servants"
Luk 16:5 – "called every one of his..debtors"
Luk 16:13 – "masters..he will hate the one"
Luk 16:13 – "masters..he will hold to the one"
Luk 16:17 – "one tittle of the law to fail"
Luk 16:30 – "if one went..from the dead"
Luk 16:31- "though one rose from the dead"
Luk 17:2 – "offend one of these little ones"
Luk 17:15 – "And one of them..was healed"
Luk 17:22 – "one of the days of the Son of man"
Luk 17:24 – "out of the one part under heaven"
Luk 17:34 – "two men in one bed..one taken"
Luk 17:35 – "Two women grinding..one..taken"
Luk 17:36 – "Two men..in the field..one..taken"
Luk 18:10 – "Two men..one a Pharisee"
Luk 18:14 – "every one that exalteth himself"
Luk 18:19 – "none is good, save one, that is, God"
Luk 18:22 – "Yet lackest thou one thing"
Luk 19:26 – "unto every one which hath"
Luk 19:44 – "shall not leave in thee one stone"
Luk 20:1 – "on one of those days, as he taught"
Luk 20:3 – "I will also ask you one thing"
Luk 21:6 – "not be left one stone upon another"
Luk 22:36 – "hath no sword..buy one"
Luk 22:50 – "And one of them smote the servant"
Luk 22:59 – "about the space of one hour after"
Luk 23:14 – "as one that perverteth the people"
Luk 23:17 – "release one of them at the feast"
Luk 23:26 – "laid hold upon one Simon..Cyrenian"
Luk 23:33 – "malefactors, one on the right hand"
Luk 23:39 – "one of the malefactors..railed"
Luk 24:17 – "communications..one to another"
Luk 24:18 – "one of them..name was Cleopas"
Luk 24:32 – "they said one to another"
Joh 1:23 – "I am the voice of one crying"
Joh 1:26 – "there standeth one among you"
Joh 1:40 – "One of the two which heard John"
Joh 3:8 – "every one that is born of the Spirit"
Joh 3:20 – "every one that doeth evil hateth..light"
Joh 4:33 – "said the disciples one to another"
Joh 4:37 – "One soweth, and another reapeth."
Joh 5:44 – "which receive honour one of another"
Joh 5:45 – "one that accuseth you, even Moses"
Joh 6:7 – "that every one..may take a little"

Joh 6:22 – "none other boat..save that one"
Joh 6:40 – "every one which seeth the Son"
Joh 6:70 – "chosen you 12, and one..is a devil"
Joh 6:71 – "Judas Iscariot..one of the twelve"
Joh 7:21 – "I have done one work..ye all marvel"
Joh 7:50 – "Nicodemus..being one of them"
Joh 8:9 – "convicted..went out one by one"
Joh 8:18 – "I am one that bear witness"
Joh 8:41 – "we have one Father, even God"
Joh 8:50 – "there is one that seeketh and judgeth"
Joh 9:25 – "one thing I know..blind, now I see"
Joh 9:32 – "eyes of one that was born blind"
Joh 10:16 – "there shall be one fold"
Joh 10:16 – "there shall be..one shepherd"
Joh 10:30 – "I and my Father are one."
Joh 11:49 – "one of them, named Caiaphas"
Joh 11:50 – "expedient..that one man should die"
Joh 11:52 – "gather..into one the children of God"
Joh 12:2 – "one of them that sat at the table"
Joh 12:4 – "Then saith one of his disciples"
Joh 12:48 – "hath one that judgeth him"
Joh 13:14 – "ought to wash one another's feet"
Joh 13:21 – "one of you shall betray me"
Joh 13:22 – "disciples looked one on another"
Joh 13:23 – "on Jesus' bosom one of his disciples"
Joh 13:34 – "That ye love one another"
Joh 13:34 – "that ye also love one another"
Joh 13:35 – "if ye have love one to another"
Joh 15:12 – "That ye love one another"
Joh 15:17 – "that ye love one another"
Joh 17:11 – "that they may be one as we are"
Joh 17:21 – "That they all may be one"
Joh 17:21 – "that they also may be one in us"
Joh 17:22 – "that they may be one..as we are one"
Joh 17:23 – "they may be made perfect in one"
Joh 18:14 – "one man should die for the people"
Joh 18:17 – "one of this man's disciples"
Joh 18:22 – "one of the officers..struck Jesus"
Joh 18:25 – "also one of his disciples"
Joh 18:26 – "One of the servants of..high priest"
Joh 18:37 – "Every one that is of the truth"
Joh 18:39 – "release unto you one at the passover"
Joh 19:18 – "on either side one..Jesus in the midst"
Joh 19:34 – "one of the soldiers with a spear"
Joh 20:12 – "angels..one at..head..other at the feet"
Joh 20:24 – "Thomas, one of the twelve"
Joh 21:25 – "many other things..written every 1"
Act 1:14 – "all continued with one accord"
Act 1:22 – "must one be ordained to be a witness"
Act 2:1 – "all with one accord in one place"
Act 2:7 – "marvelled, saying one to another"
Act 2:12 – "saying one to another, What meaneth"
Act 2:27 – "thine Holy One to see corruption"
Act 2:38 – "Repent, and be baptized every one"
Act 2:46 – "continuing daily with one accord"
Act 3:14 – "denied the Holy One and the Just"
Act 3:26 – "turning away every one of you"
Act 4:24 – "lifted up their voice..with one accord"
Act 4:32 – "were of one heart and of one soul"
Act 5:12 – "all with 1 accord in Solomon's porch"
Act 5:16 – "they were healed every one"

Act 5:25 – "then came one and told them"
Act 5:34 – "stood there up one in the council"
Act 7:24 – "seeing one of them suffer wrong"
Act 7:26 – "would have set them at one again"
Act 7:26 – "why do ye wrong one to another?"
Act 7:52 – "the coming of the Just One"
Act 7:57 – "ran upon him with one accord"
Act 8:6 – "with one accord gave heed unto..Philip"
Act 8:9 – "giving out..himself was some great one"
Act 9:11 – "enquire..for one called Saul"
Act 9:43 – "many days in Joppa with one Simon"
Act 10:2 – "devout man, one that feared God"
Act 10:5 – "call for one Simon..surname is Peter"
Act 10:6 – "lodgeth with one Simon a tanner"
Act 10:22 – "just man, and one that feareth God"
Act 10:28 – "or come unto one of another nation"
Act 10:32 – "the house of one Simon a tanner"
Act 11:28 – "stood up one of them named Agabus"
Act 12:10 – "passed on through one street"
Act 12:20 – "they came with one accord to him"
Act 13:25 – "there cometh one after me"
Act 13:35 – "thine Holy One to see corruption"
Act 15:25 – "being assembled with one accord"
Act 15:39 – "departed..one from the other'
Act 16:26 – "every one's bands were loosed"
Act 17:7 – "there is another king, one Jesus"
Act 17:26 – "hath made of one blood all nations"
Act 17:27 – "he be not far from every one of us"
Act 18:7 – "Justus, one that worshipped God"
Act 18:12 – "with one accord against Paul"
Act 19:9 – "daily in the school of one Tyrannus"
Act 19:14 – "sons of one Sceva, a Jew"
Act 19:29 – "they rushed with one accord"
Act 19:32 – "Some therefore cried one thing"
Act 19:34 – "all with one voice..cried out"
Act 19:38 – "let the implead one another"
Act 20:31 – "to warn every one night and day"
Act 21:6 – "taken our leave one of another"
Act 21:7 – "abode with them one day"
Act 21:8 – "Philip..which was one of the seven"
Act 21:16 – "brought with them one Mnason"
Act 21:26 – "offered for every one of them"
Act 21:34 – "And some cried one thing"
Act 22:12 – "And one Ananias, a devout man"
Act 22:14 – "see that Just One..hear the voice"
Act 23:6 – "Paul perceived..one part..Sadducees"
Act 23:17 – "Paul called one of the centurions"
Act 24:21 – "Except it be for this one voice"
Act 25:19 – "superstitions, and of one Jesus"
Act 27:1 – "prisoners unto one named Julius"
Act 27:2 – "one Aristarchus..being with us"
Act 28:2 – "received us every one..rain..cold"
Act 28:13 – "after one day the south wind blew"
Act 28:25 – "Paul had spoken one word"
Rom 1:16 – "salvation to every one that believeth"
Rom 1:27 – "burned in..lust one toward another"
Rom 2:15 – "or else excusing one another"
Rom 2:28 – "not a Jew, which is one outwardly"
Rom 2:29 – "is a Jew, which is one inwardly"
Rom 3:30 – "it is one God, which shall justify"
Rom 5:7 – "for a righteous man will one die"

Rom 5:12 – "by one man sin entered into..world"
Rom 5:15 – "the offence of one many be dead"
Rom 5:15 – "grace, which is by one man, Jesus"
Rom 5:16 – "by one that sinned"
Rom 5:16 – "was by one to condemnation"
Rom 5:17 – "by one man's offence death reigned"
Rom 5:17 – "death reigned by one"
Rom 5:17 – "shall reign in life by one"
Rom 5:18 – "by the offence of 1 judgement came"
Rom 5:18 – "righteousness of 1 the free gift came"
Rom 5:19 – "by one man's disobedience"
Rom 5:19 – "obedience of 1..many be..righteous"
Rom 9:10 – "Rebeca..conceived by 1, even..Isaac"
Rom 9:21 – "one vessel unto honour..dishonour"
Rom 10:4 – "righteousness to every 1..believeth"
Rom 12:4 – "we have many members in one body"
Rom 12:5 – "being many, are one body in Christ"
Rom 12:5 – "every one members one of another"
Rom 12:10 – "kindly affectioned one to another"
Rom 12:10 – "in honour preferring one another"
Rom 12:16 – "same mind one toward another"
Rom 13:8 – "Owe no man..but to love 1 another"
Rom 14:2 – "one believeth..he may eat all things"
Rom 14:5 – "One man esteemeth one day"
Rom 14:12 – "every one of us shall give account"
Rom 14:13 – "not therefore judge one another"
Rom 14:19 – "one may edify another"
Rom 15:2 – "every one of us please his neighbour"
Rom 15:5 – "likeminded one toward another"
Rom 15:6 – "That ye may have one mind"
Rom 15:6 – "and one mouth glorify God"
Rom 15:7 – "receive ye one another"
Rom 15:14 – "able also to admonish one another"
Rom 16:16 – "Salute one another"
1Co 1:12 – "every one of you saith"
1Co 3:4 – "while one saith, I am of Paul"
1Co 3:8 – "the that planteth..watereth are one"
1Co 4:6 – "no one of you be puffed up"
1Co 4:6 – "puffed up for one against another"
1Co 5:1 – "that one should have..father's wife"
1Co 5:5 – "deliver such an one unto Satan"
1Co 5:11 – "with such an one no not to eat"
1Co 6:7 – "ye go to law one with another"
1Co 6:16 – "joined to an harlot is one body"
1Co 6:16 – "two saith he, shall be one flesh"
1Co 6:17 – "joined unto the Lord is one spirit"
1Co 7:5 – "Defraud ye not one the other"
1Co 7:7 – "one after this manner"
1Co 7:17 – "as the Lord hath called every man"
1Co 7:25 – "as one that hath obtained mercy"
1Co 8:4 – "there is none other God but one"
1Co 8:6 – "to us there is but one God"
1Co 8:6 – "and one Lord Jesus Christ"
1Co 9:24 – "run..race..one receiveth the prize"
1Co 9:26 – "not as one that beateth the air"
1Co 10:8 – "and fell in one day 23,000"
1Co 10:17 – "we being many are one bread"
1Co 10:17 – "we being many are..one body"
1Co 10:17 – "all partakers of that one bread"
1Co 11:5 – "even all one as if she were shaven"
1Co 11:20 – "come together..into one place"

1Co 11:21 – "every one taketh before other"
1Co 11:21 – "one is hungry..another is drunken"
1Co 11:33 – "tarry one for another"
1Co 12:8 – "to one is given by the Spirit"
1Co 12:11 – "worketh that one..selfsame Spirit"
1Co 12:12 – "For as the body is one"
1Co 12:12 – "all the members of that one body"
1Co 12:12 – "being many, are one body"
1Co 12:13 – "by one Spirit are we all baptized"
1Co 12:13 – "are we all baptized into one body"
1Co 12:13 – "been made to drink into one Spirit"
1Co 12:14 – "body is not one member, but many"
1Co 12:18 – "members every one..in the body"
1Co 12:19 – "And if they were all one member"
1Co 12:20 – "many members, yet but one body"
1Co 12:25 – "the same care one for another"
1Co 12:26 – "one member suffer, all..suffer"
1Co 12:26 – "1 member be honoured, all..rejoice"
1Co 14:23 – "whole church..into one place"
1Co 14:24 – "come in one that believeth not"
1Co 14:24 – "come in..one unlearned"
1Co 14:26 – "every one of you hath a psalm"
1Co 14:27 – "and let one interpret"
1Co 14:31 – "ye may all prophesy one by one"
1Co 15:8 – "as of one born out of due time"
1Co 15:39 – "one kind of flesh of men"
1Co 15:40 – "the glory of the celestial is one"
1Co 15:41 – "There is one glory of the sun"
1Co 15:41 – "one star differeth from another"
1Co 16:2 – "let every one of you lay by him"
1Co 16:16 – "every one that helpeth with us"
1Co 16:20 – "Greet ye one another..holy kiss"
2Co 2:7 – "one..swallowed up with..sorrow"
2Co 2:16 – "to the one..savour of death"
2Co 5:10 – "every one may receive the things"
2Co 5:14 – "one died for all, then were all dead"
2Co 10:11 – "Let such an one think this"
2Co 11:2 – "I have espoused you to one husband"
2Co 11:24 – "5 times received..40 stripes save 1"
2Co 12:2 – "such an one caught up to..heaven"
2Co 12:5 – "Of such an one will I glory"
2Co 13:11 – "be of one mind, live in peace"
2Co 13:12 – "Greet one another..holy kiss"
Gal 3:10 – "Cursed is every one..continueth not"
Gal 3:13 – "Cursed is every one..hangeth..tree"
Gal 3:16 – "seeds, as of many; but as of one"
Gal 3:20 – "mediator is not a mediator of one"
Gal 3:20 – "but God is one"
Gal 3:28 – "ye are all one in Christ Jesus"
Gal 4:22 – "two sons, the one by a bondmaid"
Gal 4:24 – "two covenants; the one..Sinai"
Gal 5:13 – "by love serve one another"
Gal 5:14 – "the law is fulfilled in one word"
Gal 5:15 – "if ye bite and devour one another"
Gal 5:15 – "be not consumed one of another"
Gal 5:17 – "are contrary the one to the other"
Gal 5:26 – "provoking one another"
Gal 5:26 – "envying one another"
Gal 6:1 – "restore such an one in the spirit"
Gal 6:2 – "Bear ye one another's burdens"
Eph 1:10 – "gather together in one all things"

Eph 2:14 – "who hath made both one"
Eph 2:15 – "make..of twain one new man"
Eph 2:16 – "both unto God in one body"
Eph 2:18 – "both have access by one Spirit"
Eph 4:2 – "forbearing one another in love"
Eph 4:4 – "There is one body"
Eph 4:4 – "There is..one Spirit"
Eph 4:4 – "one hope of your calling"
Eph 4:5 – "One Lord, one faith, one baptism"
Eph 4:6 – "One God and Father of all"
Eph 4:7 – "unto every one of us..grace"
Eph 4:25 – "we are members one of another"
Eph 4:32 – "be ye kind one to another"
Eph 4:32 – "forgiving one another, as God"
Eph 5:21 – "Submitting..one to another"
Eph 5:31 – "they two shall be one flesh"
Eph 5:33 – "let every one..so love his wife"
Phi 1:16 – "one preach Christ of contention"
Phi 1:27 – "stand fast in one spirit"
Phi 1:27 – "stand fast..with one mind"
Phi 2:2 – "being of one accord, of one mind"
Phi 3:13 – "this one thing I do, forgetting"
Col 3:9 – "Lie not one to another"
Col 3:13 – "Forbearing one another"
Col 3:13 – "and forgiving one another"
Col 3:15 – "ye are called in one body"
Col 3:16 – "admonishing one another"
Col 4:9 – "Onesimus..who is one of you"
Col 4:12 – "Epaphras, who is one of you"
1Th 1:11 – "charged every one of you"
1Th 3:12 – "abound in love one..another"
1Th 4:4 – "every one of you should know"
1Th 4:9 – "taught of God to love one another"
1Th 4:18 – "comfort one another"
1Th 5:11 – "edify one another"
2Th 1:3 – "charity of every one of you all"
1Ti 2:5 – "For there is one God"
1Ti 2:5 – "one mediator between God..man"
1Ti 3:2 – "bishop..husband of one wife"
1Ti 3:4 – "One that ruleth well his own house"
1Ti 3:12 – "deacons..husbands of one wife"
1Ti 5:9 – "having been the wife of one man"
1Ti 5:21 – "w/o preferring one before another"
2Ti 2:19 – "every one that nameth..Christ"
Tit 1:6 – "the husband of one wife"
Tit 1:12 – "One of themselves..a prophet"
Tit 3:3 – "hateful, and hating one another"
Phm 9 – "such an one as Paul the aged"
Heb 2:6 – "one in a certain place testified"
Heb 2:11 – "both..are sanctified..all of one"
Heb 3:13 – "exhort one another daily"
Heb 5:12 – "need that one teach you again"
Heb 5:13 – "every one that useth milk"
Heb 6:11 – "every one of you do shew..diligence"
Heb 10:12 – "offered one sacrifice for sins"
Heb 10:14 – "by one offering..hath perfected
Heb 10:24 – "let us consider one another"
Heb 10:25 – "exhorting one another..so much"
Heb 11:12 – "sprang there even of one"
Heb 12:16 – "Esau..for one morsel of meat"
Heb 13:14 – "continuing city..seek one to come"

Jam 2:10 – "offend in one point..guilty of all"
Jam 2:16 – "one of you say unto them, Depart"
Jam 2:19 – "believest that there is one God"
Jam 4:11 – "Speak not evil one of another"
Jam 4:12 – "There is one lawgiver"
Jam 5:9 – "Grudge no one against another"
Jam 5:16 – "Confess your faults one to another"
Jam 5:16 – "pray one for another"
Jam 5:19 – "err from..truth, and one convert him"
1Pe 1:22 – "see that ye love one another"
1Pe 3:8 – "be ye all of one mind"
1Pe 3:8 – "having compassion one of another"
1Pe 4:9 – "Use hospitality one to another"
1Pe 4:10 – "minister the same one to another"
1Pe 5:5 – "be subject one to another"
1Pe 5:14 – "Greet ye one another"
2Pe 3:8 – "be not ignorant of this one thing"
2Pe 3:8 – "one day..as a 1000 years"
2Pe 3:8 – "a 1000 years as one day"
1Jn 1:7 – "fellowship one with another"
1Jn 2:13 – "have overcome the wicked one"
1Jn 2:14 – "have overcome the wicked one"
1Jn 2:20 – "an unction from the Holy One"
1Jn 2:29 – "every one that doeth righteousness"
1Jn 3:11 – "we should love one another"
1Jn 3:12 – "who was of that wicked one"
1Jn 3:23 – "and love one another"
1Jn 4:7 – "let us love one another"
1Jn 4:7 – "every one that loveth..born of God"
1Jn 4:11 – "ought also to love one another"
1Jn 4:12 – "If we love one another"

1Jn 5:1 – "every one that loveth him"
1Jn 5:7 – "these three are one"
1Jn 5:8 – "these three agree in one"
1Jn 5:18 – "wicked one toucheth him not"
2Jn 5 – "that we love one another"
Rev 1:13 – "one like unto the Son of man"
Rev 2:23 – "unto every one of you..works"
Rev 4:2 – "one sat on the throne"
Rev 5:5 – "one of the elders saith"
Rev 5:8 – "having every one of them harps"
Rev 6:1 – "Lamb opened one of the seals"
Rev 6:1 – "one of the 4 beasts..Come and see"
Rev 6:4 – "they should kill one another"
Rev 6:11 – "robes..given..every one of them"
Rev 7:13 – "one of the elders answered"
Rev 9:12 – "One woe is past"
Rev 11:10 – "shall send gifts one to another"
Rev 13:3 – "I saw one of his heads..wounded"
Rev 14:14 – "one sat like unto the Son of man"
Rev 15:7 – "one of the 4 beasts gave..vials"
Rev 17:1 – "there came one of the seven angels"
Rev 17:10 – "7 kings; 5 are fallen, and one is"
Rev 17:12 – "receive power as kings one hour"
Rev 17:13 – "These have one mind"
Rev 18:8 – "her plagues come in one day"
Rev 18:10 – "in one hour is thy judgment come"
Rev 18:17 – "in one hour..riches..come to nought"
Rev 18:19 – "in one hour is she made desolate"
Rev 21:9 – "one of the seven angels"
Rev 21:21 – "every..gate was of one pearl"

1st – First

Many times the word first refers to a day, month or year – in such cases you will be prompted to see the **DATES** section of this volume

Gen 1:5 – "evening..morning..the first day"
Gen 2:11 – "name of the first is Pison"
Gen 8:5 – "first day" – see *DATES*
Gen 8:13 – "first day" – see *DATES*
Gen 13:4 – "altar..made there at the first"
Gen 25:25 – "the first came out red..hairy"
Gen 26:1 – "famine..beside the first famine"
Gen 28:19 – "name..was called Luz at the first"
Gen 38:28 – "scarlet thread..came out first"
Gen 41:20 – "did eat up the first seven fat kine"
Gen 43:18 – "money..in our sacks at the 1st time"
Gen 43:20 – "came..the first time to buy food"
Exo 4:8 – "listen to the voice of the first sign"
Exo 12:2 – "it shall be the first month..to you"
Exo 12:5 – Passover lamb – "male of the 1st year"
Exo 12:15 – "first day ye shall put away leaven"
Exo 12:15 – "leavened bread..1st day..7th day"
Exo 12:16 – "1st day..an holy convocation"
Exo 12:18 – "first month" – see *DATES*
Exo 22:29 – "offer the first of thy ripe fruits"

Exo 23:19 – "the first of the firstfruits of thy land"
Exo 28:17 – "first row..sardius, a topaz"
Exo 28:17 – "a carbuncle..the first row"
Exo 29:38 – "offer..two lambs of the first year"
Exo 34:1 – "Hew..2 tables of stone like the first"
Exo 34:1 – "words that were in the first tables"
Exo 34:4 – "he hewed 2 tables..like unto the first"
Exo 34:26 – "first of..firstfruits..bring unto..God"
Exo 39:10 – "first row..sardius..topaz..carbuncle"
Exo 39:10 – "this was the first row"
Exo 40:2 – "first day..first month" – see *DATES*
Exo 40:17 – "first mont..first day" – see *DATES*
Lev 4:21 – "as he burned the first bullock"
Lev 5:8 – "shall offer..the sin offering first"
Lev 9:3 – "calf..lamb..both of the first year"
Lev 9:15 – "goat..offered..for sin, as the first"
Lev 12:6 – "lamb of the first year..burnt offering"
Lev 14:10 – "ewe lamb of the first year"
Lev 23:5 – "first month" – see *DATES*
Lev 23:7 – "first day...holy convocation"

Lev 23:12 – "he lamb..of the first year"
Lev 23:18 – "seven lambs..of the first year"
Lev 23:19 – "two lambs of the first year"
Lev 23:24 – "first day" – see *DATES*
Lev 23:35 – "first day..an holy convocation"
Lev 23:39 – "first day shall be a sabbath"
Lev 23:40 – "first day...boughs of goodly trees"
Num 1:1 – "first day" – see *DATES*
Num 1:18 – "first day" – see *DATES*
Num 2:9 – "Judah..shall first set forth"
Num 6:12 – "a lamb of the first year"
Num 6:14 – "one he lamb of the first year"
Num 6:14 – "one ewe lamb of the first year"
Num 7:12 – "offered..the first day..Judah"
Num 7:15 – "one lamb of the first year"
Num 7:17 – "five lambs of the first year"
Num 7:21 – "one lamb of the first year"
Num 7:23 – "five lambs of the first year"
Num 7:27 – "one lamb of the first year"
Num 7:29 – "five lambs of the first year"
Num 7:33 – "one lamb of the first year"
Num 7:35 – "five lambs of the first year"
Num 7:39 – "one lamb of the first year"
Num 7:41 – "five lambs of the first year"
Num 7:45 – "one lamb of the first year"
Num 7:47 – "five lambs of the first year"
Num 7:51 – "one lamb of the first year"
Num 7:53 – "five lambs of the first year"
Num 7:57 – "one lamb of the first year"
Num 7:59 – "five lambs of the first year"
Num 7:63 – "one lamb of the first year"
Num 7:65 – "five lambs of the first year"
Num 7:69 – "one lamb of the first year"
Num 7:71 – "five lambs of the first year"
Num 7:75 – "one lamb of the first year"
Num 7:77 – "five lambs of the first year"
Num 7:81 – "one lamb of the first year"
Num 7:83 – "five lambs of the first year"
Num 7:87 – "the lambs of the first year twelve"
Num 7:88 – the lambs of the first year sixty"
Num 9:1 – "first month" – see *DATES*
Num 9:5 – "first month" – see *DATES*
Num 10:13 – "they first took their journey"
Num 10:14 – "In the first place..standard..Judah"
Num 15:20 – "offer..cake of the 1st of your dough"
Num 15:21 – "first of your dough ye shall give"
Num 15:27 – "she goat of the first year"
Num 18:13 – "whatsoever is first ripe in the land"
Num 20:1 – "Israel.. desert of Zin in the 1st month"
Num 24:20 – "Amalek was the first of the nations"
Num 28:3 – "two lambs of the first year"
Num 28:9 – "two lambs of the first year"
Num 28:11 – "one ram, 7 lambs of the first year"
Num 28:16 – "first month" – see *DATES*
Num 28:18 – "first day..an holy convocation"
Num 28:19 – "seven lambs of the first year"
Num 28:27 – "seven lambs of the first year"
Num 29:1 – "first day" – see *DATES*
Num 29:2 – "seven lambs of the first year"
Num 29:8 – "seven lambs of the first year"
Num 29:13 – "fourteen lambs of the first year"

Num 29:17 – "fourteen lambs of the first year"
Num 29:20 – "14 lambs of the first year"
Num 29:23 – "14 lambs of the first year"
Num 29:26 – "fourteen lambs of the first year"
Num 29:29 – "14 lambs of the first year"
Num 29:32 – "14 lambs of the first year"
Num 29:36 – "seven lambs of the first year"
Num 33:3 – "first month..first month" – see *DATES*
Num 33:38 – "first day" – see *DATES*
Deu 1:3 – "first day" – see *DATES*
Deu 9:18 – "fell down..as at the first"
Deu 9:25 – "as I fell down at the first"
Deu 10:1 – "two tables of stone like unto the first"
Deu 10:2 – "write..words..in the first tables"
Deu 10:3 – "two tables of stone like unto the first"
Deu 10:4 – "wrote..according to the first writing"
Deu 10:10 – "stayed..mount, acc. to the 1st time"
Deu 11:14 – "give..the 1st rain and the latter rain"
Deu 13:9 – "thine hand shall be first upon him"
Deu 16:4 – "sacrificedst the first day at even"
Deu 17:7 – "hands of..witnesses..first upon him"
Deu 18:4 – "first of the fleece of they sheep"
Deu 26:2 – "take..first of all the fruit of the earth"
Deu 33:21 – "provided the first part for himself"
Jos 4:19 – "first month" – see *DATES*
Jos 8:5 – "when..come out against us, as at the 1st"
Jos 8:6 – "They flee before us, as at the first"
Jos 21:10 – "theirs was the first lot"
Jdg 1:1 – "against the Canaanites first, to fight"
Jdg 18:29 – "name of..city was Laish at the first"
Jdg 20:18 – "Which of us..go up first to the battle"
Jdg 20:18 – "LORD said, Judah shall go up first"
Jdg 20:22 – "put themselves in array the first day"
Jdg 20:32 – "smitten..before us, as at the first"
Jdg 20:39 – "smitten down..as in the first battle"
1Sa 14:14 – "first slaughter..was about 20 men"
1Sa 14:35 – "first altar..he built unto the LORD"
2Sa 3:13 – "except thou first bring Michal"
2Sa 17:9 – "some of them..overthrown at the first"
2Sa 19:20 – "I am come the first this day"
2Sa 19:43 – "our advice should not be first had"
2Sa 21:9 – "in the first days...barley harvest"
2Sa 23:19 – "attained not unto the first three"
2Sa 23:23 – "attained not to the first three"
1Ki 17:13 – "make..a little cake first, and bring"
1Ki 18:25 – "Choose you 1 bullock..dress it first"
1Ki 20:9 – "All..thou didst send forth..at the 1st"
1Ki 20:17 – "young men..princes..went out first"
1Ch 9:2 – "first inhabitants..the priests, Levites"
1Ch 11:6 – "smiteth..Jebusites first shall be chief"
1Ch 11:6 – "So Joab..went up first, and was chief."
1Ch 11:21 – "he attained not to the first three"
1Ch 11:25 – "but attained not to the first three"
1Ch 12:9 – "Ezer the first"
1Ch 12:15 – "went over Jordan in the first month"
1Ch 15:13 – "For because ye did it not at the first"
1Ch 16:7 – "David delivered first this psalm"
1Ch 23:19 – "sons of Hebron; Jeriah the first"
1Ch 23:20 – "sons of Uzziel; Micah the first"
1Ch 24:7 – "the first lot came forth to Jehoiarib"
1Ch 24:21 – "sons of Rehabiah, the first..Isshiah"

1Ch 24:23 – "sons of Hebron; Jeriah the first"
1Ch 25:9 – "first lot..for Asaph to Joseph"
1Ch 27:2 – "1st course..1st month..Joshobeam"
1Ch 27:3 – "chief..of the host for the first month"
1Ch 29:29 – "acts of David the king, first and last"
2Ch 3:3 – "length by cubits after the 1st measure"
2Ch 9:29 – "acts of Solomon, first and last"
2Ch 12:15 – "acts of Rehoboam, first and last"
2Ch 16:11 – "acts of Asa, first and last"
2Ch 17:3 – "Jehoshaphat..walked in the first ways"
2Ch 20:34 – "acts of Jehoshaphat, first and last"
2Ch 25:26 – "acts of Amaziah, first and last"
2Ch 26:22 – "acts of Uzziah, first and last"
2Ch 28:26 – Ahaz – "rest of his acts..first and last"
2Ch 29:3 – "first year..first month" – see *DATES*
2Ch 29:17 – "1st day..1st month" – see *DATES*
2Ch 29:17 – "16th day..1st month" – see *DATES*
2Ch 35:1 – "first month" – see *DATES*
2Ch 35:27 – Josiah – "And his deeds, first and last"
2Ch 36:22 – "first year of Cyrus king of Persia"
Ezr 1:1 – "in first year of Cyrus king of Persia"
Ezr 3:6 – "first day" – see *DATES*
Ezr 3:12 – "1st house, when..foundation..was laid"
Ezr 5:13 – "1st year of Cyrus.. a decree to build"
Ezr 6:3 – "1st year of Cyrus.. a decree concerning"
Ezr 6:19 – "first month" – see *DATES*
Ezr 7:9 – "1st day..1st month..1st day" – see *DATES*
Ezr 8:31 – "first month" – see *DATES*
Ezr 10:16 – "first day" – see *DATES*
Ezr 10:17 – "first day..first month" – see *DATES*
Neh 7:5 – "register.. them..came up at the 1st"
Neh 8:2 – "first day" – see *DATES*
Neh 8:18 – "day by day, from the 1st unto the last"
Est 1:14 – "which sat first in the kingdom"
Est 3:7 – "first month" – see *DATES*
Est 3:12 – "first month" – see *DATES*
Job 15:7 – "Art thou the first man that was born?"
Job 42:14 – "name of the first, Jemima"
Pro 18:17 – "he that is first in his own cause"
Isa 1:26 – "restore thy judges as at the first"
Isa 9:1 – "when at the first he lightly afflicted"
Isa 41:4 – "the LORD, the first, and with the last"
Isa 41:27 – "The first shall say to Zion"
Isa 43:27 – "Thy first father hath sinned"
Isa 44:6 – "I am the first, and I am the last"
Isa 48:12 – "I am the first, I also am the last"
Isa 60:9 – "the ships of Tarshish first"
Jer 4:31 – "bringeth forth her first child"
Jer 7:12 – "where I set my name at the first"
Jer 16:18 – "And first I will recompense..iniquity"
Jer 24:2 – "like the figs that are first ripe"
Jer 25:1 – "first year of Nebuchadrezzar..Babylon"
Jer 33:7 – "build them, as at the first"
Jer 33:11 – "return the captivity..as at the first"
Jer 36:28 – "former words that were in..1st roll"
Jer 50:17 – "1st the king of Assyria hath devoured"
Jer 52:31 – "Evil-merodach..first year of his reign"
Ezk 10:14 – "first face was the face of a cherub"
Ezk 26:1 – "first day" – see *DATES*
Ezk 29:17 – "first month..first day" – see *DATES*
Ezk 30:20 – "first month" – see *DATES*

Ezk 31:1 – "first day" – see *DATES*
Ezk 32:1 – "first day" – see *DATES*
Ezk 40:21 – "arches..after the measure of..1st gate"
Ezk 44:30 – "first of all the firstfruits of all things"
Ezk 44:30 – "give unto..priests..1st of your dough"
Ezk 45:18 – "first month..first day" – see *DATES*
Ezk 45:21 – "first month" – see *DATES*
Ezk 46:13 – "lamb of the 1st year without blemish"
Dan 1:21 – "unto the first year of king Cyrus"
Dan 6:2 – "of whom Daniel was the first"
Dan 7:1 – "In the first year of Belshazzar"
Dan 7:4 – "The first was like a lion"
Dan 7:8 – "three of the first horns plucked up"
Dan 7:24 – "he shall be diverse from the first"
Dan 8:1 – "which appeared unto me at the first"
Dan 8:21 – "Grecia..great horn..is the first king"
Dan 9:1 – "In the first year of Darius"
Dan 9:2 – "In the first year of his reign"
Dan 10:4 – "in the 24th day of the first month"
Dan 10:12 – "from the first day..set thine heart"
Dan 11:1 – "in the first year of Darius the Mede"
Hos 2:7 – "go and return to my first husband"
Hos 9:10 – "in the fig tree at her first time"
Joe 2:23 – "the latter rain in the first month"
Amo 6:7 – "go captive with the 1st that go captive"
Mic 4:8 – "even the first dominion"
Hag 1:1 – "first day" – see *DATES*
Hag 2:3 – "saw this house in her first glory?"
Zec 6:2 – "In the first chariot were red horses"
Zec 12:7 – "save the tents of Judah first"
Zec 14:10 – "the place of the first gate"
Mat 5:24 – "first be reconciled to thy brother"
Mat 6:33 – "seek ye first the kingdom of God"
Mat 7:5 – "first cast out the beam..thine own eye"
Mat 8:21 – "suffer me first to go and bury"
Mat 10:2 – "twelve apostles..The first, Simon"
Mat 12:29 – "except he first bind the strong man?"
Mat 12:45 – "last state..worse than the first"
Mat 13:30 – "Gather ye together first the tares"
Mat 17:10 – "that Elias must first come?"
Mat 17:11 – "Elias truly shall first come"
Mat 17:27 – "take up the fish that first cometh up"
Mat 19:30 – "many that are first shall be last"
Mat 19:30 – "the last shall be first"
Mat 20:8 – "from the last unto the first"
Mat 20:10 – "But when the first came"
Mat 20:16 – "last shall be first, and the first last"
Mat 21:28 – "man had two sons..came to the first"
Mat 21:31 – "They say unto him, The first"
Mat 21:36 – "other servants more than the first"
Mat 22:25 – "the first, when he..married a wife"
Mat 22:38 – "the first and great commandment"
Mat 23:26 – "blind Pharisee, cleanse first"
Mat 26:17 – "first day..feast of unleavened bread"
Mat 27:64 – "error shall be worse than the first"
Mat 28:1 – "began to dawn toward the first day"
Mar 3:7 – "he will first bind the strong man"
Mar 4:28 – "earth..fruit..first the blade"
Mar 7:27 – "Let the children first be filled"
Mar 9:11 – "Elias must come first?"
Mar 9:12 – "Elias verily cometh first"

Mar 9:35 – "If any man desire to be first"
Mar 10:31 – "many that are first shall be last"
Mar 10:31 – "and the last first"
Mar 12:20 – "and the first took a wife"
Mar 12:28 – "the first commandment of all?"
Mar 12:29 – "The first of all the commandments"
Mar 12:30 – "this is the first commandment"
Mar 13:10 – "gospel must first be published"
Mar 14:12 – "first day of unleavened bread"
Mar 16:2 – "first day of the week..sepulchre"
Mar 16:9 – "Jesus was risen..first day of the week"
Mar 16:9 – "he appeared first to Mary Magdalene"
Luk 1:3 – "all things from the very first"
Luk 2:2 – "this taxing was first made..Cyrenius"
Luk 6:1 – "on the second Sabbath after the first"
Luk 6:42 – "hypocrite, cast out first the beam"
Luk 9:59 – "suffer me first to go and bury"
Luk 9:61 – "but let me first go bid them farewell"
Luk 10:5 – "first say, Peace be to this house"
Luk 11:26 – "state of that man..worse than the 1st"
Luk 11:38 – "had not first washed before dinner"
Luk 12:1 – "began to say unto his disciples first"
Luk 13:30 – "last which shall be first"
Luk 14:18 – "The first said unto him"
Luk 14:28 – "sitteth not down 1st..counteth..cost"
Luk 14:31 – "sitteth not down first..consulteth"
Luk 16:5 – "called..debtors..said unto the first"
Luk 17:25 – "But first must he suffer many things"
Luk 19:16 – "Then came the first, saying"
Luk 20:29 – "the first took a wife"
Luk 21:9 – "these things must first come to pass"
Luk 24:1 – "Now upon the first day of the week"
Joh 1:41 – "first findeth his own brother Simon"
Joh 5:4 – "first..stepped in was made whole"
Joh 8:7 – "let him first cast a stone at her"
Joh 10:40 – "Jordan..where John first baptized"
Joh 12:16 – "things understood not..at the first"
Joh 18:13 – "led him away to Annas first"
Joh 19:32 – "brake the legs of the first"
Joh 19:39 – "Nicodemus, which at the first came"
Joh 20:1 – "first day of the week cometh Mary"
Joh 20:4 – "came first to the sepulcher"
Joh 20:8 – "disciple, which came 1st to..sepulchre"
Joh 20:19 – "evening, being the 1st day of..week"
Act 3:26 – "Unto you first God, having raised up"
Act 7:12 – "he sent out our fathers first"
Act 11:26 – "called Christians first in Antioch"
Act 12:10 – "past the first and second ward"
Act 13:24 – "When John had first preached"
Act 13:46 – "word of God..first..spoken to you"
Act 15:14 – "God at the first did visit..Gentiles"
Act 20:7 – "1st day of the week..to break bread"
Act 20:18 – "from the 1st day..I came into Asia"
Act 26:4 – "at first among mine own nation"
Act 26:20 – "shewed 1st unto them of Damascus"
Act 26:23 – "first that should rise from..dead"
Act 27:43 – "cast themselves first into the sea"
Rom 1:8 – "First, I thank my God"
Rom 1:16 – "to the Jew first, & also to the Greek"
Rom 2:9 – "Jew first, and also of the Gentile"
Rom 2:10 – Jew first, and also to the Gentile"

Rom 10:19 – "First Moses saith, I will provoke"
Rom 11:35 – "who hath first given to him"
Rom 15:24 – "if first I be somewhat filled"
1Co 11:18 – "first of all, when ye come together"
1Co 12:28 – "set some in the church, 1st apostles"
1Co 14:30 – "let the first hold his peace"
1Co 15:3 – "delivered unto you first of all"
1Co 15:45 – "the first man Adam"
1Co 15:46 – "that was not first which is spiritual"
1Co 15:47 – "first man is of the earth, earthy"
1Co 16:2 – "Upon the first day of the week"
2Co 8:5 – "but first gave their own selves"
2Co 8:12 – "if there be first a willing mind"
Gal 4:13 – "gospel unto you at the first"
Eph 1:12 – "who first trusted in Christ"
Eph 4:9 – "descended first into..lower parts"
Eph 6:2 – "first commandment with promise"
Phi 1:5 – "from the first day until now"
1Th 4:16 – "dead in Christ shall rise first"
2Th 2:3 – "there come a falling away first"
1Ti 1:16 – "that in me first Jesus Christ"
1Ti 2:1 – "first of all, supplications, prayers"
1Ti 2:13 – "Adam was first formed, then Eve"
1Ti 3:10 – "let these also first be proved"
1Ti 5:4 – "learn first to shew piety at home"
1Ti 5:12 – "have cast off their first faith"
2Ti 1:5 – "faith..first in they grandmother"
2Ti 2:6 – "husbandman..first partaker..fruits"
2Ti 4:16 – "At my first answer not man"
Tit 3:10 – "after the 1st and 2nd admonition"
Heb 2:3 – "at the first began to be spoken"
Heb 4:6 – "to whom it was first preached"
Heb 5:12 – "1st principles of the oracles of God"
Heb 7:2 – "first being by interpretation"
Heb 7:27 – "sacrifice, first for his own sins"
Heb 8:7 – "if the 1st covenant had been faultless"
Heb 8:13 – "new covenant..made the 1st old"
Heb 9:1 – "first covenant had also ordinances"
Heb 9:2 – "tabernacle made; the first, wherein"
Heb 9:6 – "went always into the first tabernacle"
Heb 9:8 – "while..1st tabernacle was..standing"
Heb 9:15 – "transgressions..under..1st testament"
Heb 9:18 – "neither..1st testament was dedicated"
Heb10:9 – "He taketh away the first"
Jam 3:17 – "wisdom..from above is first pure"
1Pe 4:17 – "judgment..if it first begin at us"
2Pet 1:20 – "Knowing this first..no prophecy"
2Pet 3:3 – "Knowing this first..scoffers"
1Jn 4:19 – "because he first loved us"
Jud 6 – "angels which kept not their first estate"
Rev 1:5 – "Jesus..the first begotten of the dead"
Rev 1:11 – "Alpha and Omega, the 1st and..last"
Rev 1:17 – "I am the first and the last"
Rev 2:4 – "thou hast left thy first love"
Rev 2:5 – "repent, and do the first works"
Rev 2:8 – "saith the first and the last"
Rev 2:19 – "the last to be more than the first"
Rev 4:1 – "1st voice which I heard..as..a trumpet"
Rev 4:7 – "first beast was like a lion"
Rev 8:7 – "The first angel sounded"
Rev 13:12 – "exerciseth..power of the 1st beast"

Rev 13:12 – "causeth..to worship the 1st beast"
Rev 16:2 – "first went..poured out his vial"
Rev 20:5 – "This is the first resurrection."
Rev 20:6 – "hath part in the first resurrection"
Rev 21:1 – "1st heaven and..1st earth passed away"
Rev 21:19 – "The first foundation was jasper"
Rev 22:13 – "Alpha and Omega..1st and the last"

Firstborn

Gen 10:15 – "Canaan begat Sidon his firstborn"
Gen 19:31 – "firstborn said unto the younger"
Gen 19:33 – "firstborn went in..lay w/ her father"
Gen 19:34 – "firstborn said unto the younger"
Gen 19:37 – "And the firstborn bare a son"
Gen 22:21 – "Huz his firstborn, and Buz"
Gen 25:13 – "the firstborn of Ishmael, Nebajoth"
Gen 27:19 – "I am Esau thy firstborn"
Gen 27:32 – "I am thy son, thy firstborn Esau"
Gen 29:26 – "to give..younger before..firstborn"
Gen 35:23 – "Reuben, Jacob's firstborn"
Gen 36:15 – "Eliphaz the firstborn son of Esau"
Gen 38:6 – "Judah took a wife for Er his firstborn"
Gen 38:7 – "Er, Judah's firstborn, was wicked"
Gen 41:51 – "called..name of..firstborn Manasseh"
Gen 43:33 – "the firstborn acc. to his birthright"
Gen 46:8 – "Reuben, Jacob's firstborn"
Gen 48:14 – "for Manasseh was the firstborn"
Gen 48:18 – "for this is the firstborn"
Gen 49:3 – "Reuben, thou art my firstborn"
Exo 4:22 – "Israel is my son, even my firstborn"
Exo 4:23 – "I will slay thy son, even thy firstborn"
Exo 6:14 – "sons of Reuben the firstborn of Israel"
Exo 11:5 – "firstborn in..land of Egypt shall die"
Exo 11:5 – "from the firstborn of Pharaoh"
Exo 11:5 – "firstborn of the maidservant.. the mill"
Exo 11:5 – "and all the firstborn of beasts"
Exo 12:12 – "smite all..firstborn in..land of Egypt"
Exo 12:29 – "all the firstborn in the land of Egypt"
Exo 12:29 – "firstborn of Pharaoh..on his throne"
Exo 12:29 – "unto the firstborn of the captive"
Exo 12:29 – "and all the firstborn of cattle"
Exo 13:2 – "Sanctify unto me all the firstborn"
Exo 13:13 – "all the firstborn of man..redeem"
Exo 13:15 – "LORD slew all..firstborn..of Egypt"
Exo 13:15 – "LORD slew..the firstborn of man"
Exo 13:15 – "LORD slew..the firstborn of beast"
Exo 13:15 – "firstborn of my children I redeem"
Exo 22:29 – "firstborn of thy sons..give unto me"
Exo 34:20 – "All the firstborn of thy sons..redeem"
Num 3:2 – "sons of Aaron; Nadab the firstborn"
Num 3:12 – "Levites..instead of all the firstborn"
Num 3:13 – "Because all the firstborn are mine"
Num 3:13 – "I smote all the firstborn in..Egypt"
Num 3:13 – "I hallowed unto me all the firstborn"
Num 3:40 – "Number all the firstborn of..males"
Num 3:41 – "Levites..instead of all the firstborn"
Num 3:42 – "all the firstborn among the children"
Num 3:43 – "And all..firstborn males by..names"
Num 3:45 – "Levites instead of all the firstborn"

Num 3:46 – "273 of the firstborn..of Israel"
Num 3:50 – "firstborn of the children of Israel"
Num 8:16 – "instead of the firstborn of..Israel"
Num 8:17 – "all..firstborn of the children of Israel"
Num 8:17 – "smote every firstborn..land of Egypt"
Num 8:18 – "Levites for all the firstborn..of Israel"
Num 18:15 – "firstborn of man shalt..redeem"
Num 33:4 – "Egyptians buried all their firstborn"
Deu 21:15 – "firstborn son be hers that was hated"
Deu 21:16 – "beloved firstborn before..son..hated"
Deu 21:16 – "which is indeed the firstborn"
Deu 21:17 – "son of the hated for the firstborn"
Deu 21:17 – "the right of the firstborn is his"
Deu 25:6 – "firstborn which she beareth..succeed"
Jos 6:26 – "lay..foundation thereof in his firstborn"
Jos 17:1 – "Manasseh..the firstborn of Joseph"
Jos 17:1 – "Machir the firstborn of Manasseh"
Jdg 8:20 – "And he said unto Jether his firstborn"
1Sa 8:2 – "the name of his firstborn was Joel"
1Sa 14:49 – "Saul..daughters..the firstborn Merab"
1Sa 17:13 – "sons of Jesse..Eliab the firstborn"
2Sa 3:2 – "David..his firstborn was Amnon"
1Ki 16:34 – "Hiel..Bethelite..Abiram his firstborn"
1Ch 1:13 – "And Canaan begat Zidon his firstborn"
1Ch 1:29 – "The firstborn of Ishmael, Nebaioth"
1Ch 2:3 – "Er, the firstborn of Judah, was evil"
1Ch 2:13 – "And Jesse begat his firstborn Eliab"
1Ch 2:25 – "Jerahmeel the firstborn of Hezron"
1Ch 2:25 – "sons of Jerahmeel..Ram the firstborn"
1Ch 2:27 – "sons of Ram..firstborn of Jerahmeel"
1Ch 2:42 – "sons of Caleb..Mesha his firstborn"
1Ch 2:50 – "Hur, the firstborn of Ephratah"
1Ch 3:1 – "sons of David..the firstborn Amnon"
1Ch 3:15 – "sons of Josiah..the firstborn Johanan"
1Ch 4:4 – "Hur, the firstborn of Ephratah"
1Ch 5:1 – "sons of Reuben the firstborn of Israel"
1Ch 5:1 – "Rueben..for he was the firstborn"
1Ch 5:3 – "Reuben the firstborn of Israel were"
1Ch 6:28 – "sons of Samuel; the firstborn Vashni"
1Ch 8:1 – "Benjamin begat Bela his firstborn"
1Ch 8:30 – "And his firstborn son Abdon"
1Ch 8:39 – "the sons of Eshek..Ulam his firstborn"
1Ch 9:5 – "of the Shilonites; Asaiah the firstborn"
1Ch 9:31 – "Mattithiah.. the firstborn of Shallum"
1Ch 9:36 – "And his firstborn son Abdon"
1Ch 26:2 – "of Meshelemiah..Zechariah..firstborn"
1Ch 26:4 – "of Obededom..Shemaiah..firstborn"
1Ch 26:10 – "though..not the firstborn..the chief"
2Ch 21:3 – "kingdom..to Jehoram; b/c..firstborn"
Neh 10:36 – "firstborn of our sons..our cattle"
Job 18:13 – "firstborn of death..devour..strength"
Psa 78:51 – "And smote all the firstborn in Egypt"
Psa 89:27 – "Also I will make him my firstborn"
Psa 105:36 – "smote also all the firstborn in..land"
Psa 135:8 – "Who smote the firstborn of Egypt"
Psa 136:10 – "smote Egypt in their firstborn"
Isa 14:30 – "firstborn of the poor shall feed"
Jer 31:9 – "Ephraim is my firstborn"
Mic 6:7 – "give my firstborn for my transgression"
Zec 12:10 – "as one..in bitterness for his firstborn"
Mat 1:25 – "she..brought forth her firstborn son"

Luk 2:7 – "she brought forth her firstborn son"
Rom 8:29 – "the firstborn among many brethren"
Col 1:15 – "the firstborn of every creature"
Col 1:18 – "firstborn from the dead"
Heb 11:28 – "lest he that destroyed the firstborn"
Heb 12:23 – "general assembly..church..firstborn"

Firstfruits

Exo 23:16 – "the firstfruits of thy labours"
Exo 23:19 – "first of the firstfruits of thy land"
Exo 34:22 – "the firstfruits of wheat harvest"
Exo 34:26 – "first of the firstfruits of thy land"
Lev 2:12 – "the oblation of the firstfruits"
Lev 2:14 – "a meat offering of thy firstfruits"
Lev 2:14 – "the meat offering of thy firstfruits"
Lev 23:10 – "bring a sheaf of the firstfruits"
Lev 23:17 – "the firstfruits unto the LORD"
Lev 23:20 – "bread of..firstfruits..wave offering"
Num 18:12 – "firstfruits of them..they shall offer"
Num 28:26 – "Also in the day of the firstfruits"
Deu 18:4 – "firstfruit also of thy corn..wine..oil"
Deu 26:10 – "brought the firstfruits of the land"
2Ki 4:42 – "brought the man..bread of..firstfruits"
2Ch 31:5 – "firstfruits of corn, wine..oil..honey"
Neh 10:35 – "bring the firstfruits of our ground"
Neh 10:35 – "the firstfruits of all fruit of all trees"
Neh 10:37 – "bring the firstfruits of our dough"
Neh 12:44 – "chambers..for the firstfruits"
Neh 13:31 – "wood offering..& for the firstfruits"
Pro 3:9 – "Honour the LORD..with the firstfruits"
Jer 2:3 – "Israel..the firstfruits of his increase"
Eze 20:40 – "require..firstfruits of your oblations"
Eze 44:30 – "first of all the firstfruits of all things"
Eze 48:14 – "nor alienate..firstfruits of the land"
Rom 8:23 – "which have..firstfruits of the Spirit"
Rom 11:16 – "if..firstfruit be holy..lump is..holy"
Rom 16:5 – "Epaenetus..the firstfruits of Achaia"
1Co 15:20 – "the firstfruits of them that slept"
1Co 15:23 – "his own order: Christ the firstfruits"
1Co 16:15 – "Stephanas..firstfruits of Achaia"
Jas 1:18 – "be a kind of firstfruits of his creatures"
Rev 14:4 – "firstfruits unto God and to the Lamb"

Firstlings

Gen 4:4 – "Abel..brought..firstlings of his flock"
Exo 13:12 – "every firstling..cometh of a beast"
Exo 13:13 – "every firstling of an ass..redeem"
Exo 34:19 – "every firstling..cattle..ox..sheep"
Exo 34:20 – "firstling of an ass thou shalt redeem"
Lev 27:26 – "Only the firstling of the beasts"
Lev 27:26 – "should be the LORD'S firstling"
Num 3:41 – "all the firstlings among the cattle"
Num 18:15 – "firstling of unclean beasts..redeem"
Num 18:17 – "firstling of a cow..shalt not redeem"
Num 18:17 – "firstling..a sheep..shalt not redeem"
Num 18:17 – "firstling of a goat..shalt not redeem"

Deu 12:6 – "firstlings of your herds..your flocks"
Deu 12:17 – "firstlings of thy herds or of thy flock"
Deu 14:23 – "firstlings of thy herds..thy flocks"
Deu 15:19 – "firstling males that come of thy herd"
Deu 15:19 – "do no work w/ the firstling..bullock"
Deu 15:19 – "nor shear the firstling of thy sheep"
Deu 33:17 – "glory is like..firstling of his bullock"
Neh 10:36 – "firstlings of our herds..our flocks"

Once *(as in One Time)*

Once may be used in the sense of immediately (eg. *"consume them at once"* – Deu 7:22). Occurrences such as these are not included.

Gen 18:32 – "I will speak yet but this once"
Exo 10:17 – "forgive..my sin only this once"
Exo 30:10 – "upon the horns of it once in a year"
Exo 30:10 – "once in the year..make atonement"
Lev 16:34 – "atonement..for all..sins once a year"
Num 13:30 – "Caleb..go up at once, and possess it"
Jos 6:3 – "go round about the city once"
Jos 6:11 – "the city..going about it once"
Jos 6:14 – "2nd day they compassed the city once"
Jdg 6:39 – "I will speak but this once"
Jdg 6:39 – "I pray thee, but this once"
Jdg 16:18 – "Come up this once"
Jdg 16:28 – "I pray thee, only this once, O God"
Jdg 16:28 – "that I may be at once avenged"
1Ki 10:22 – "once in three years came the navy"
2Ki 6:10 – "saved himself..not once nor twice"
2Ch 9:21 – "every 3 years once came..ships"
Neh 5:18 – "once in 10 days store..of wine"
Neh 13:20 – "merchants..lodged..once or twice"
Job 33:14 – "God speaketh once, yea twice"
Job 40:5 – "Once have I spoken..will not answer"
Psa 62:11 – "God hath spoken once; twice have I"
Psa 76:7 – "who may stand.. once thou art angry?"
Psa 89:35 – "Once have I sworn by my holiness"
Jer 13:27 – "made clean? when shall it once be?"
Jer 16:21 – "I will this once cause them to know"
Hag 2:6 – "Yet once, it is a little while"
Luk 13:25 – "When once the master..is risen up"
Luk 23:18 – "they cried out all at once"
Rom 6:10 – "he died unto sin once"
Rom 7:9 – "I was alive without the law once"
1Co 15:6 – "seen of above 500 brethren at once"
2Co 11:25 – "once was I stoned"
Gal 1:23 – "faith which once he destroyed"
Eph 5:3 – "not be named once among you"
Heb 6:4 – "those who were once enlightened"
Heb 7:27 – "this he did once, when he offered"
Heb 9:7 – "high priest alone once every year"
Heb 9:12 – "entered in once into the holy place"
Heb 9:26 – "now once in the end of the world"
Heb 9:27 – "appointed unto men once to die"
Heb 9:28 – "Christ was once offered to bear"
Heb 10:2 – "the worshippers once purged"
Heb 10:10 – "body of Jesus Christ once for all"

Heb 12:26 – "once more I shake not the earth"
Heb 12:27 – "this word, Yet once more"
1Pe 3:18 – "Christ..once suffered for sins"
1Pe 3:20 – "once the longsuffering of God"
Jud 3 – "faith which was once delivered"
Jud 5 – "though ye once knew this"

Ones

Listed at the end of Section One under the heading, **Indefinite Numbers**.

Several

We usually define "several" as being two or three or view it as an indeterminate number similar to phrases such as "a few" or "a couple." In the Bible however, the phrase "a several" is used as a synonym for the number one. In comparing the following two verses found in the same context, you will note how "one" and "a several" are used interchangeably:

Num 29:4 – "one tenth deal for one lamb"
Num 29:10 – "A several tenth deal for one lamb"

This phrase is found seven times in Scripture. Five times it means "one" (Num 28:13, 21, 29; 29:10, 15) and twice it is found as the adjective "separate" as in "severed" (2Ki 15:5 & 2Ch 28:21).

Single

Mat 6:22 – "if therefore thine eye be single"
Luk 11:34 – "when thine eye is single"

Singleness

Act 2:46 – "with gladness & singleness of heart"
Eph 6:5 – "in singleness of..heart, as unto Christ"
Col 3:22 – "but in singleness of heart, fearing God"

1⅓

1Sa 27:7 – "David dwelt..a full year and 4 months"

1½

Exo 25:10 – "ark..1½ cubit the breadth thereof"
Exo 25:10 – "ark.. 1½ cubit the height thereof"
Exo 25:17 – "mercy seat..1½ cubit the breadth"
Exo 25:23 – "table..shittim wood..1½ cubit..height"
Exo 26:16 – "1½ cubit..the breadth of one board"
Exo 36:21 – "breadth of a board was 1½ cubit"
Exo 37:1 – "made the ark..1½ cubit the breadth"
Exo 37:1 – "made the ard..1½ cubit the height"
Exo 37:6 – "mercy seat.. 1½ cubit the breadth"
Exo 37:10 – "table..shittim wood..1½ cubit..height"
Hos 3:2 – "homer of barley, & an ½ homer"
Act 18:11 – "continued there a year & 6 months"

Two

After one, two is the most common number found in the Bible. In Bible numerology two is is the number of union, division and witnessing.

This section includes:

a)	2 – Two (cardinal number)		h)	Secondarily	
b)	2nd – Second (ordinal number)		i)	Twain	
c)	Both		j)	Twice	
d)	Couple		k)	Twin	
e)	Deuteronomy		l)	Twoedged	
f)	Double		m)	Twofold	
f)	Doubletongued		n)	Mixed Numbers – 2½	
g)	Pair				

2 – Two

Gen 1:16 – "God made two great lights"
Gen 4:19 – "Lamech took unto him two wives"
Gen 6:19 – "two of every sort..bring into the ark"

Gen 6:20 – "two of every sort..come unto thee"
Gen 7:2 – "of beasts that are not clean by two"
Gen 7:9 – "There went in 2 and 2 unto Noah"

Gen 7:15 – "went in unto Noah..2 and 2"
Gen 9:22 – "Ham..told his two brethren without"
Gen 10:25 – "unto Eber were born two sons"
Gen 11:10 – "begat Arphaxad 2 years after..flood"
Gen 19:1 – "came two angels to Sodom at even"
Gen 19:8 – "Behold now, I have two daughters"
Gen 19:15 – "take thy wife, & thy two daughters"
Gen 19:16 – "upon the hand of his two daughters"
Gen 19:30 – "mountain..his 2 daughters with him"
Gen 19:30 – "in a cave, he and his two daughters"
Gen 22:3 – "Abraham..took two of his young men"
Gen 24:22 – "two bracelets for her hands"
Gen 25:23 – "two nations are in thy womb"
Gen 25:23 – "two manner of people shall be"
Gen 27:9 – "fetch..two good kids of the goats"
Gen 27:36 – "supplanted me these two times"
Gen 29:16 – "Laban had two daughters"
Gen 31:33 – "into the two maidservants' tents"
Gen 31:41 – "served..14 years for thy 2 daughters"
Gen 32:7 – "divided the people..into two bands"
Gen 32:10 – "now I am become two bands"
Gen 32:22 – "rose up..and took his two wives"
Gen 32:22 – "rose up..took..his 2 womenservants"
Gen 33:1 – "Esau came..unto the two handmaids"
Gen 34:25 – "two of the sons of Jacob..slew..males"
Gen 40:2 – "Pharaoh was wroth..2 of his officers"
Gen 41:1 – "came to pass..end of two full years"
Gen 41:50 – "unto Joseph were born two sons"
Gen 42:37 – "Reuben spake..Slay my two sons"
Gen 44:27 – "my wife bare me two sons"
Gen 45:6 – "these two years hath the famine been"
Gen 46:27 – "sons of Joseph..born..were 2 souls"
Gen 48:1 – "Joseph..with him his two sons"
Gen 48:5 – "thy two sons..shall be mine"
Gen 49:14 – "Issachar..ass..between two burdens"
Exo 2:13 – "2nd day..two men..strove together"
Exo 4:9 – "will not believe also these two signs"
Exo 12:7 – "blood, strike it on the 2 side posts"
Exo 12:22 – "strike the lintel and the 2 side posts"
Exo 12:23 – "the lintel, and on the 2 side posts"
Exo 16:22 – "gathered..two omers for one man"
Exo 16:29 – "giveth you..the bread of two days"
Exo 18:3 – Zipporah – "her two sons"
Exo 18:6 – "thy wife, and her two sons with her"
Exo 21:21 – "if he continue a day or two"
Exo 25:12 – "two rings shall be in the one side"
Exo 25:12 – "two rings in the other side of it"
Exo 25:18 – "make two cherubims of gold"
Exo 25:18 – "in the two ends of the mercy seat"
Exo 25:19 – "the cherbims on the 2 ends thereof"
Exo 25:22 – "from between the two cherubims"
Exo 25:23 – "table..two cubits..length thereof"
Exo 25:35 – "a knop under two branches"
Exo 25:35 – "and a knop under two branches"
Exo 25:35 – "and a knop under two branches"
Exo 26:17 – "2 tenons shall there be in one board"
Exo 26:19 – "two sockets..for his two tenons"
Exo 26:19 – "two sockets under another board"
Exo 26:19 – "under another board..his 2 tenons"
Exo 26:21 – "two sockets under one board"
Exo 26:21 – "two sockets under another board"

Exo 26:23 – "two boards..for..corners..tabernacle"
Exo 26:23 – "corners of..tabernacle in the 2 sides"
Exo 26:24 – "they shall be for the two corners"
Exo 26:25 – "two sockets under one board"
Exo 26:25 – "two sockets under another board"
Exo 26:27 – "for the two sides westward"
Exo 27:7 – "staves shall be upon the two sides"
Exo 28:7 – "shall have two shoulderpieces"
Exo 28:7 – "joined at the two edges thereof"
Exo 28:9 – "thou shalt take two onyx stones"
Exo 28:11 – "shalt thou engrave the two stones"
Exo 28:12 – "put the 2 stones upon the shoulders"
Exo 28:12 – "upon his 2 shoulders for a memorial"
Exo 28:14 – "two chains of pure gold at the ends"
Exo 28:23 – "make upon the breastplate 2 rings"
Exo 28:23 – "put the two rings on the two ends"
Exo 28:24 – "the two wreathen chains of gold"
Exo 28:24 – "chains of gold in the two rings"
Exo 28:25 – "other two ends of of the..chains"
Exo 28:25 – "ends of the two wreathen chains"
Exo 28:25 – "shalt thou fasten in the two ouches"
Exo 28:26 – "make two rings of gold"
Exo 28:26 – "upon the 2 ends of the breastplate"
Exo 28:27 – "two other rings of gold"
Exo 28:27 – "put them on the 2 sides of the ephod"
Exo 29:1 – "Take one young bullock, and 2 rams"
Exo 29:3 – "with the bullock and the two rams"
Exo 29:13 – "the caul..and the two kidneys"
Exo 29:22 – "the caul..and the two kidneys"
Exo 29:38 – "offer..two lambs of the first year"
Exo 30:2 – "two cubits..the height thereof"
Exo 30:4 – "2 golden rings..under the crown of it"
Exo 30:4 – "by the two corners thereof"
Exo 30:4 – "upon the two sides of it"
Exo 31:18 – "gave..Moses..2 tables of testimony"
Exo 32:15 – "two tables of the testimony"
Exo 34:1 – "Hew thee 2 tables of stone like the 1st"
Exo 34:4 – "he hewed 2 tables..like unto the first"
Exo 34:4 – "took in his hand the 2 tables of stone"
Exo 34:29 – "came..with the 2 tables of testimony"
Exo 36:22 – "one board had two tenons"
Exo 36:24 – "2 sockets under 1 board..2 tenons"
Exo 36:24 – "2 sockets..another board..2 tenons"
Exo 36:26 – "two sockets under one board"
Exo 36:26 – "two sockets under another board"
Exo 36:28 – "2 boards..for..corners..in the 2 sides"
Exo 36:30 – "under every board two sockets"
Exo 37:3 – "even two rings upon the one side"
Exo 37:3 – "two rings upon the other side of it"
Exo 37:7 – "he made two cherubims of gold"
Exo 37:7 – "cherubims..on the 2 ends..mercy seat"
Exo 37:8 – "cherbuims on the two ends thereof"
Exo 37:10 – "table..two cubits was the length"
Exo 37:21 – "knop under 2 branches of the same"
Exo 37:21 – "knop under 2 branches of the same"
Exo 37:21 – "knop under 2 branches of the same"
Exo 37:25 – "incense altar..2 cubits..the height"
Exo 37:27 – "two rings of gold..under the crown"
Exo 37:27 – "two corners of it, upon the 2 sides"
Exo 39:4 – "by the two edges was it coupled"
Exo 39:16 – "they made two ouches of gold"

Exo 39:16 – "they made..two gold rings"
Exo 39:16 – "put the two rings in the two ends"
Exo 39:17 – "two wreathen chains..in the 2 rings"
Exo 39:18 – "two ends of the 2 wreathen chains"
Exo 39:18 – "they fastened in the two ouches"
Exo 39:19 – "they made two rings of gold"
Exo 39:19 – "the two ends of the breastplate"
Exo 39:20 – "they made two other golden rings"
Exo 39:20 – "two sides of the ephod underneath"
Lev 3:4 – "And the two kidneys, and the fat"
Lev 3:10 – "And the two kidneys, and the fat"
Lev 3:15 – "And the two kidneys, and the fat"
Lev 4:9 – "And the two kidneys, and the fat"
Lev 5:7 – "bring for his trespass..two turtledoves"
Lev 5:7 – "for his trespass..two young pigeons"
Lev 5:11 – "not able to bring two turtledoves"
Lev 5:11 – "not able to bring..two young pigeons"
Lev 7:4 – "And the two kidneys, and the fat"
Lev 8:2 – "anointing oil..a bullock..two rams"
Lev 8:16 – "the two kidneys, and their fat"
Lev 8:25 – "the two kidneys, and their fat"
Lev 12:5 – "a maid child..unclean two weeks"
Lev 12:8 – "she shall bring two turtles"
Lev 12:8 – "she shall bring..two young pigeons"
Lev 14:4 – "two birds alive and clean"
Lev 14:10 – "take two he lambs without blemish"
Lev 14:22 – "two turtledoves, or 2 young pigeons"
Lev 14:49 – "to cleanse the house two birds"
Lev 15:14 – "two turtledoves, or 2 young pigeons"
Lev 15:29 – "two turtledoves, or 2 young pigeons"
Lev 16:1 – "after the death of the 2 sons of Aaron"
Lev 16:5 – "two kids of the goats...sin offering"
Lev 16:7 – "2 goats..present them before..LORD"
Lev 16:8 – "Aaron shall cast lots upon the 2 goats"
Lev 23:17 – "out of..habitations two wave loaves"
Lev 23:18 – "offer with the bread..two rams"
Lev 23:19 – "sacrifice..two lambs of the first year"
Lev 23:20 – "wave offering..with the two lambs"
Lev 24:6 – "two rows, six on a row..pure table"
Num 6:10 – "two turtles, or two young pigeons"
Num 7:3 – "a wagon for two of the princes"
Num 7:7 – "two wagons and four oxen..Gershon"
Num 7:17 – "peace offerings, two oxen"
Num 7:23 – "peace offerings, two oxen"
Num 7:29 – "peace offerings, two oxen"
Num 7:35 – "peace offerings, two oxen"
Num 7:41 – "peace offerings, two oxen"
Num 7:47 – "peace offerings, two oxen"
Num 7:53 – "peace offerings, two oxen"
Num 7:59 – "peace offerings, two oxen"
Num 7:65 – "peace offerings, two oxen"
Num 7:71 – "peace offerings, two oxen"
Num 7:77 – "peace offerings, two oxen"
Num 7:83 – "peace offerings, two oxen"
Num 7:89 – "between the two cherubims"
Num 9:22 – "whether..two days..a month..a year"
Num 10:2 – "Make thee two trumpets of silver"
Num 11:19 – "ye shall not eat one day, nor 2 days"
Num 11:26 – "remained 2 of the men in the camp"
Num 11:31 – "quails..as it were two cubits high"
Num 13:23 – "bare it between two upon a staff"

Num 22:22 – "upon his ass..2 servants..with him"
Num 28:3 – "two lambs of the first year"
Num 28:9 – "two lambs of the first year"
Num 28:11 – "burnt offering..two young bullocks"
Num 28:19 – "two young bullocks, and one ram"
Num 28:27 – "burnt offering..2 young bullocks"
Num 29:13 – "burnt offering..two rams"
Num 29:14 – "to each ram of the two rams"
Num 29:17 – "second day ye shall offer..2 rams"
Num 29:20 – "And on the third day..two rams"
Num 29:23 – "And on the fourth day..two rams"
Num 29:26 – "And on the fifth day..two rams"
Num 29:29 – "And on the sixth day..two rams"
Num 29:32 – "And on the seventh day..two rams"
Num 31:27 – "divide the prey into two parts"
Deu 3:8 – "the two kings of the Amorites"
Deu 3:21 – "God hath done unto these two kings"
Deu 4:13 – "10 commandments..2 tables of stone"
Deu 4:47 – "land of..2 kings of the Amorites"
Deu 5:22 – "wrote them in two tables of stone"
Deu 9:10 – "2 tables..written with..finger of God"
Deu 9:11 – "two tables of stone..of the covenant"
Deu 9:15 – "two tables..were in my two hands"
Deu 9:17 – "2 tables..cast them out of my 2 hands"
Deu 10:1 – "two tables of stone like unto the first"
Deu 10:3 – "two tables of stone like unto the first"
Deu 10:3 – "two tables in mine hand"
Deu 14:6 – "cleaveth the cleft into two claws"
Deu 17:6 – "mouth of 2 witnesses, or 3 witnesses"
Deu 18:3 – "unto the priest..2 cheeks, and..maw"
Deu 19:15 – "mouth of 2 witnesses..established"
Deu 21:15 – "man have 2 wives..beloved..hated"
Deut 32:30 – "and two put ten thousand to flight"
Jos 2:1 – "Joshua..sent ..two men to spy..Jericho"
Jos 2:4 – "woman took the 2 men, and hid them"
Jos 2:10 – "what ye did unto the 2 kings..Amorites"
Jos 2:23 – "the 2 men returned..came to Joshua"
Jos 6:22 – "2 men that had spied out the country"
Jos 9:10 – "all..he did to..2 kings of the Amorites"
Jos 14:4 – "the children of Joseph were two tribes"
Jos 15:60 – "two cities with their villages"
Jos 21:16 – "nine cities out of those two tribes"
Jos 21:25 – "out of..half..Manasseh..two cities"
Jos 21:27 – "unto..Gershon..two cities"
Jos 21:16 – "nine cities out of these two tribes"
Jos 24:12 – "two kings of the Amorites"
Jdg 3:16 – "Ehud made..a dagger..had two edges"
Jdg 5:30 – "to every man a damsel or two"
Jdg 7:25 – "took two princes of the Midianites"
Jdg 8:12 – "took the two kings of Midian"
Jdg 9:44 – "2 other companies ran upon..people"
Jdg 11:37 – "alone two months..bewail..virginity"
Jdg 11:38 – "he sent her away for two months"
Jdg 11:39 – "at the end of 2 months..she returned"
Jdg 15:4 – "firebrand in..midst between two tails"
Jdg 15:13 – "bound him with two new cords"
Jdg 16:3 – "Samson..took the doors..and..2 posts"
Jdg 16:28 – "avenged of..Philistines for my 2 eyes"
Jdg 16:29 – "Samson took hold..2 middle pillars"
Jdg 19:10 – "there were with him 2 asses saddled"
Rut 1:1 – "he, and his wife, and his two sons"

Rut 1:2 – "his two sons Mahlon and Chilion"
Rut 1:3 – "she was left, and her two sons"
Rut 1:5 – "woman was left of her two sons"
Rut 1:7 – "her two daughters in law with her"
Rut 1:8 – "Naomi said unto..2 daughters in law"
Rut 1:19 – "2 went until they came to Bethlehem"
Rut 4:11 – "Rachel..Leah, which two did build"
1Sa 1:2 – "he had two wives..Hannah..Peninnah"
1Sa 1:3 – "two sons of Eli, Hophni and Phinnehas"
1Sa 2:21 – "Hannah..3 sons and two daughters"
1Sa 2:34 – "come upon thy two sons..in one day"
1Sa 4:4 – "2 sons of Eli..were there with the ark"
1Sa 4:11 – "two sons of Eli..were slain."
1Sa 4:17 – "thy two sons also..are dead"
1Sa 6:7 – "make a new cart, and take 2 milch kine"
1Sa 6:10 – "the men did so; and took 2 milch kine"
1Sa 10:2 – "two men by Rachel's sepulcher"
1Sa 10:4 – "will salute thee..give thee 2 loaves"
1Sa 11:11 – "so that 2 of them..not left together"
1Sa 13:1 – "when he..reigned 2 years over Israel"
1Sa 14:49 – "Saul..his 2 daughters..Merab..Michal"
1Sa 23:18 – "2 made a covenant..David..Jonathan"
1Sa 25:18 – "Abigail..took..two bottles of wine"
1Sa 27:3 – "David..his 2 wives, Ahinoam..Abigail"
1Sa 28:8 – "Saul..and two men with him"
1Sa 30:5 – "David's 2 wives were taken captives"
1Sa 30:12 – "gave him..figs..2 clusters of raisins"
1Sa 30:18 – "David rescued his two wives"
2Sa 1:1 – "David had abode two days in Ziklag"
2Sa 2:2 – "David..and his two wives"
2Sa 2:10 – "Ishbosheth..reigned two years"
2Sa 4:2 – "Saul's son had 2 men..captains..bands"
2Sa 8:2 – "with 2 lines measured..to put to death"
2Sa 12:1 – "two men in one city..one rich..poor"
2Sa 13:23 – "2 full years, Absalom..sheepshearers"
2Sa 14:6 – "thy handmaid had two sons"
2Sa 14:6 – "they two strove together in the field"
2Sa 14:28 – "Absalom dwelt 2..years in Jerusalem"
2Sa 15:27 – "return into..city..your 2 sons w/ you"
2Sa 15:36 – "two sons, Ahimaaz..Jonathan"
2Sa 18:24 – "David sat between the two gates"
2Sa 21:8 – "king took the two sons of Rizpah"
2Sa 23:20 – "Benaiah..slew 2 lionlike men..Moab"
1Ki 2:5 – "what Joab..did to the two captains"
1Ki 2:32 – "who fell upon 2 men more righteous"
1Ki 2:39 – "2 of the servants of Shimei ran away"
1Ki 3:16 – "came..two women, that were harlots"
1Ki 3:18 – "save we two in the house"
1Ki 3:25 – "Divide..living child in 2, and give half"
1Ki 5:12 – "Hiram and Solomon..2 made a league"
1Ki 5:14 – "month..in Lebanon..2 months at home"
1Ki 6:23 – "two cherubims of olive tree"
1Ki 6:32 – "two doors also were of olive tree"
1Ki 6:34 – "two doors were of fir tree"
1Ki 6:34 – "2 leaves of the one door were folding"
1Ki 6:34 – "2 leaves of the other door..folding"
1Ki 7:15 – "two pillars of brass"
1Ki 7:16 – "made two chapiters of molten brass"
1Ki 7:18 – "made the pillars..2 rows round about"
1Ki 7:20 – "the chapiters upon the two pillars"
1Ki 7:24 – "the knops were cast in two rows"

1Ki 7:41 – "2 pillars..the 2 bowls of the chapiters"
1Ki 7:41 – "were on the top of the two pillars"
1Ki 7:41 – "two networks, to cover the two bowls"
1Ki 7:42 – "400 pomegranates for the 2 networks"
1Ki 7:42 – "even two rows of pomegranates"
1Ki 7:42 – "to cover the 2 bowls of the chapiters"
1Ki 8:7 – "cherubims spread forth their 2 wings"
1Ki 8:9 – "nothing in..ark save..2 tables of stone"
1Ki 9:10 – "when Solomon had built the 2 houses"
1Ki 10:19 – "two lions stood beside the stays"
1Ki 11:29 – "they two were alone in the field"
1Ki 12:28 – "the king..made two calves of gold"
1Ki 15:25 – "Nadab..reigned over Israel two years"
1Ki 16:8 – "Elah..reign over Israel..two years"
1Ki 16:21 – "people of Israel divided into 2 parts"
1Ki 16:24 – "bought..Samaria..for 2 talents..silver"
1Ki 17:12 – "I am gathering two sticks"
1Ki 18:21 – "How long halt..between 2 opinions?"
1Ki 18:23 – "Let them..give us two bullocks"
1Ki 18:32 – "trench..contain 2 measures of seed"
1Ki 20:27 – "Israel..like two little flocks of kids"
1Ki 21:10 – "set 2 men, sons of Belial before him"
1Ki 21:13 – "came in 2 men, children of Belial"
1Ki 22:51 – "Ahaziah..reigned 2 years over Israel"
2Ki 1:14 – "two captains of the former fifties"
2Ki 2:6 – "Elijah..And they two went on."
2Ki 2:7 – "they two stood by Jordan"
2Ki 2:8 – "they two went over on dry ground"
2Ki 2:12 – "his own clothes..rent them in 2 pieces"
2Ki 2:24 – "came..2 she bears out of the wood"
2Ki 4:1 – "take..my two sons to be bondmen"
2Ki 5:17 – "given..two mule's burden of earth?"
2Ki 5:22 – "two young men..sons of the prophets"
2Ki 5:22 – "talent of silver..2 changes of garments"
2Ki 5:23 – "Namaan said..take two talents"
2Ki 5:23 – "bound 2 talents of silver in two bags"
2Ki 5:23 – "two changes of garments"
2Ki 5:23 – "laid them upon two of his servants"
2Ki 7:1 – "two measures of barley for a shekel"
2Ki 7:14 – "They took..two chariot horses"
2Ki 7:16 – "two measures of barley for a shekel"
2Ki 7:18 – "Two measures of barley for a shekel"
2Ki 9:32 – "looked out to him 2 or 3 eunuchs"
2Ki 10:4 – "two kings stood not before him"
2Ki 10:8 – 70 heads – "Lay ye them in two heaps"
2Ki 11:7 – "two parts of all you that go forth"
2Ki 15:23 – "Pekahiah..reigned two years"
2Ki 17:16 – "made..molten images, even 2 calves"
2Ki 21:5 – "built altars..in the 2 courts of..house"
2Ki 21:19 – "Amon..reigned 2 years in Jerusalem"
2Ki 23:12 – "altars..in the 2 courts..king..brake"
2Ki 25:4 – "men of war fled..between two walls"
2Ki 25:16 – "two pillars, one sea, and the bases"
1Ch 1:19 – "And unto Eber were born two sons"
1Ch 4:5 – "Ashur..two wives, Helah and Naarah"
1Ch 11:21 – "more honourable than the two"
1Ch 11:22 – "Benaiah..slew 2 lionlike men Moab"
1Ch 26:17 – "Levites..toward Asuppim 2 and 2"
1Ch 26:18 – "At Parbar westward..two at Parbar"
2Ch 3:10 – "in the most holy house..2 cherubims"
2Ch 3:15 – "he made before the house two pillars"

2Ch 4:3 – "two rows of oxen were cast"
2Ch 4:12 – "the two pillars and the pommels"
2Ch 4:12 – "chapiters..on the top of the 2 pillars"
2Ch 4:12 – "two wreaths to cover the 2 pommels"
2Ch 4:13 – "400 pomegranates on the 2 wreaths"
2Ch 4:13 – "2 rows..pomegranates..each wreath"
2Ch 4:13 – "cover the 2 pommels of the chapiters"
2Ch 5:10 – "nothing in the ark save the 2 tables"
2Ch 9:18 – "two lions standing by the stays"
2Ch 21:19 – "end of 2 years..bowels fell out"
2Ch 24:3 – "Jehoiada took for him two wives"
2Ch 33:5 – "built altars..in the two courts"
2Ch 33:21 – "Amon..reigned 2 years in Jerusalem"
Ezr 8:27 – "2 vessels..copper..precious as gold"
Ezr 10:13 – "neither is this a work of 1 day or 2"
Neh 12:31 – "2 great companies..that gave thanks"
Neh 12:40 – "two companies..that gave thanks"
Est 2:21 – "2..chamberlains, Bigthan and Teresh"
Est 6:2 – "two of the king's chamberlains"
Est 9:27 – "keep these two days"
Job 13:20 – "Only do not two things unto me"
Job 42:7 – "wrath..against thee..thy 2 friends"
Psa 149:6 – "a twoedged sword in their hand"
Pro 5:4 – "her end is..sharp as a twoedged sword"
Pro 30:7 – "Two things have I required of thee"
Pro 30:15 – "The horseleach hath two daughters"
Ecc 4:9 – "Two are better than one"
Ecc 4:11 – "if two lie together..they have heat"
Ecc 4:12 – "if 1 prevail against..2 shall withstand"
Son 4:5 – "two breasts..like two young roes"
Son 6:13 – "the company of two armies"
Son 7:3 – "two breasts..like two young roes"
Isa 7:4 – "two tails of these smoking firebrands"
Isa 7:21 – "a man shall nourish..two sheep"
Isa 17:6 – "2 or 3 berries..top..uppermost bough"
Isa 22:11 – "a ditch between the two walls"
Isa 45:1 – "open before him the two leaved gates"
Isa 47:9 – "two things shall come..in one day"
Isa 51:19 – "These two things are come unto thee"
Jer 2:13 – "my people have committed two evils"
Jer 3:14 – "I will take you..two of a family"
Jer 24:1 – "behold, two baskets of figs"
Jer 28:3 – "Within two full years..vessels"
Jer 28:11 – "within the space of two full years"
Jer 33:24 – "two families..the LORD hath chosen"
Jer 39:4 – "fled..by the gate betwixt the two walls"
Jer 52:7 – "men of war fled..gate between..2 walls"
Jer 52:20 – "The two pillars, one sea"
Ezk 1:11 – "two wings of every one were joined"
Ezk 1:11 – "two covered their bodies"
Ezk 1:23 – "every one had two, which covered"
Ezk 1:23 – "every one had two, which covered"
Ezk 21:19 – "appoint thee two ways"
Ezk 21:21 – "at the head of the two ways"
Ezk 23:2 – "two women..daughters of one mother"
Ezk 35:10 – "These two nations..shall be mine"
Ezk 35:10 – "these two countries shall be mine"
Ezk 37:22 – "they shall no more be two nations"
Ezk 37:22 – "no more..divided into two kingdoms"
Ezk 40:9 – "the posts thereof, two cubits"
Ezk 40:39 – "in the porch..2 tables on this side"

Ezk 40:39 – "in the porch..2 tables on that side"
Ezk 40:40 – "at the side without..were 2 tables"
Ezk 40:40 – "on the other side..were 2 tables"
Ezk 41:3 – "the post of the door, two cubits"
Ezk 41:18 – "every cherub had two faces"
Ezk 41:22 – "altar..length thereof two cubits"
Ezk 41:23 – "temple and..sanctuary had 2 doors"
Ezk 41:24 – "the doors had two leaves apiece"
Ezk 41:24 – "the doors had..two turning leaves"
Ezk 41:24 – "two leaves for the one door"
Ezk 41:24 – "two leaves for the other door"
Ezk 41:22 – "altar of wood..length..two cubits"
Ezk 43:14 – "ground..to lower settle..2 cubits"
Ezk 46:19 – "place on the two sides westward"
Ezk 47:13 – "Joseph shall have two portions"
Dan 8:3 – "a ram which had two horns"
Dan 8:3 – "the two horns were high"
Dan 8:6 – "came to the ram that had two horns"
Dan 8:7 – "moved with choler..brake his 2 horns"
Dan 8:20 – "ram..having two horns..kings"
Dan 12:5 – "behold, there stood other two"
Hos 6:2 – "After two days will he revive us"
Hos 10:10 – "bind themselves in their 2 furrows"
Amo 1:1 – "two years before the earthquake"
Amo 3:3 – "Can two walk together..agreed?"
Amo 3:12 – "out of the mouth of the lion two legs"
Amo 4:8 – "So two or three cities wandered"
Zec 4:3 – "two olive trees by it"
Zec 4:11 – "What are these two olive trees"
Zec 4:12 – "What be these two olive branches"
Zec 4:12 – "through the two golden pipes?"
Zec 4:14 – "These are the two anointed ones"
Zec 5:9 – "two women..wind was in their wings"
Zec 6:1 – "4 chariots..from between 2 mountains"
Zec 11:7 – "I took unto me two staves"
Zec 13:8 – "two parts therein shall be cut off"
Mat 2:16 – "children..from 2 years old and under"
Mat 4:18 – "two brethren, Simon..Andrew"
Mat 4:21 – "other two brethren, James..John"
Mat 6:24 – "No man can serve two masters"
Mat 8:28 – "met him two possessed with devils"
Mat 9:27 – "two blind men followed him"
Mat 10:10 – "Nor scrip..neither two coats"
Mat 10:29 – "are not 2 sparrows sold..farthing?"
Mat 11:2 – "he sent two of his disciples"
Mat 14:17 – "five loaves, and two fishes"
Mat 14:19 – "five loaves, and two fishes"
Mat 18:8 – "two hands or two feet..cast..fire"
Mat 18:9 – "having two eyes..hell fire"
Mat 18:16 – "take with thee one or two more"
Mat 18:16 – "mouth or two or three witnesses"
Mat 18:19 – "if two of you shall agree on earth"
Mat 18:20 – "two or three..gathered..in my name"
Mat 20:21 – "Grant that these my two sons"
Mat 20:24 – "indignation against the 2 brethren"
Mat 20:30 – "2 blind men sitting by the way side"
Mat 21:1 – "then sent Jesus two disciples"
Mat 21:28 – "a certain man had two sons"
Mat 22:40 – "on..two commandments hang..law"
Mat 24:40 – "Then shall two be in the field"

Mat 24:41 – "Two women shall be grinding"
Mat 25:15 – "talents, to another two"
Mat 25:17 – "likewise he that had received two"
Mat 25:17 – "he also gained other two"
Mat 25:22 – "He..that had received two talents"
Mat 25:22 – "deliveredst unto me two talents"
Mat 25:22 – "I have gained two other talents"
Mat 26:2 – "after two days..feast of the passover"
Mat 26:37 – "with him Peter..two sons..Zebedee"
Mat 26:60 – "At the last came 2 false witnesses."
Mat 27:38 – "two thieves..one on the right"
Mar 6:7 – "send them forth by two and two"
Mar 6:9 – "not put on two coats"
Mar 6:38 – "How many loaves..Five, and 2 fishes"
Mar 6:41 – "taken the 5 loaves and the 2 fishes"
Mar 6:41 – "2 fishes divided he among them all"
Mar 9:43 – "having two hands to go into hell"
Mar 9:45 – "having two feet to be cast into hell"
Mar 9:47 – "having two eyes..cast into hell fire"
Mar 11:1 – "sendeth forth two of his disciples"
Mar 11:4 – "place where two ways met"
Mar 12:42 – "poor widow..threw in two mites"
Mar 14:1 – "After two days was..the passover"
Mar 14:13 – "he sendeth forth 2 of his disciples"
Mar 15:27 – "two thieves; one on his right"
Mar 16:12 – "appeared in another form unto two"
Luk 2:24 – "sacrifice..or two young pigeons"
Luk 3:11 – "He that hath two coats..impart to him"
Luk 5:2 – "two ships standing by the lake"
Luk 7:19 – "John..two of his disciples"
Luk 7:41 – "certain creditor which had 2 debtors"
Luk 9:3 – "neither have two coats apiece"
Luk 9:13 – "We have..but 5 loaves..2 fishes"
Luk 9:16 – "he took the 5 loaves and the 2 fishes"
Luk 9:30 – "there talked with him two men"
Luk 9:32 – "two men that stood with him"
Luk 10:1 – "the Lord..sent them two and two"
Luk 10:35 – "he took out two pence"
Luk 12:6 – "5 sparrows sold for 2 farthings"
Luk 12:52 – "divided, three against two"
Luk 12:52 – "divided..two against three"
Luk 15:11 – "certain man had two sons"
Luk 16:13 – "No servant can serve 2 masters"
Luk 17:34 – "two men in one bed..one taken"
Luk 17:35 – "Two women grinding..one..taken"
Luk 17:36 – "Two men..in the field..one..taken"
Luk 18:10 – "Two men..one a Pharisee"
Luk 19:29 – "he sent two of his disciples"
Luk 21:2 – "poor widow casting in..two mites"
Luk 22:38 – "Lord..here are two swords"
Luk 23:32 – "also two other, malefactors"

Luk 24:4 – "2 men stood by..in shining garments"
Luk 24:13 – "two of them..same day..Emmaus"
Joh 1:35 – "John stood, and two of his disciples"
Joh 1:37 – "the two disciples heard him speak"
Joh 1:40 – "One of the two which heard John"
Joh 2:6 – "waterpots..two or three firkins apiece"
Joh 4:40 – "and he abode there two days"
Joh 4:43 – "after two days he departed thence"
Joh 6:9 – "lad here, which hath..two small fishes"
Joh 8:17 – "the testimony of two men is true"
Joh 11:6 – "abode two days..in the same place"
Joh 19:18 – "crucified him, and 2 other with him"
Joh 20:12 – "two angels in white sitting"
Joh 21:2 – "and two other of his disciples"
Act 1:10 – "two men stood..in white apparel"
Act 1:23 – "they appointed two..Joseph..Matthias"
Act 1:24 – "whether of these 2 thou hast chosen"
Act 7:29 – "Moses..begat two sons"
Act 9:38 – "they sent unto him two men"
Act 10:7 – "called two of his household servants"
Act 12:6 – "Peter..sleeping between two soldiers"
Act 12:6 – "Peter..bound with two chains"
Act 19:10 – "continued by the space of two years"
Act 19:22 – "sent into Macedonia two of them"
Act 19:34 – "the space of two hours cried out"
Act 21:33 – "to be bound with two chains"
Act 23:23 – "called unto him two centurions"
Act 24:27 – "after two years Porcius Festus"
Act 27:41 – "a place where two seas met"
Act 28:30 – "Paul dwelt two whole years..house"
1Co 6:16 – "two saith he, shall be one flesh"
1Co 14:27 – "speak..tongue..let it be by two"
1Co 14:29 – "Let the prophets speak two or three"
2Co 13:1 – "mouth of 2..3 witnesses..established"
Gal 4:22 – "two sons, the one by a bondmaid"
Gal 4:24 – "two covenants; the one..Sinai"
Eph 5:31 – "they two shall be one flesh"
Phi 1:23 – "I am in a strait betwixt two"
1Ti 5:19 – "but before 2 or 3 witnesses"
Heb 4:12 – "word of God..twoedged sword"
Heb 6:18 – "That by two immutable things"
Heb 10:28 – "w/o mercy under 2 or 3 witnesses"
Rev 1:16 – "mouth..sharp twoedged sword"
Rev 2:12 – "the sharp sword with two edges"
Rev 9:12 – "behold, there come two woes more"
Rev 11:3 – "power unto my two witnesses"
Rev 11:4 – "These are the two olive trees"
Rev 11:4 – "These are..the two candlesticks"
Rev 11:10 – "these two prophets tormented them"
Rev 12:14 – "to the woman..2 wings..great eagle"
Rev 13:11 – "another beast..two horns like..lamb"

2nd – Second

Gen 1:8 – "evening..morning..the second day"
Gen 2:13 – "name of the second river is Gihon"
Gen 6:16 – "2nd and 3rd stories shalt thou make"
Gen 7:11 – "second month" – see *DATES*

Gen 8:14 – "second month" – see *DATES*
Gen 22:15 – "angel..called..Abraham..the 2nd time"
Gen 30:7 – "Bilhah..bare Jacob a second son"
Gen 30:12 – "Zilpah..bare Jacob a second son"

Gen 32:19 – "commanded he the 2nd, and the 3rd"
Gen 41:5 – "dreamed the second time"
Gen 41:43 – "made him to ride in the 2nd chariot"
Gen 41:52 – "name of the 2nd called he Ephraim"
Gen 43:10 – "we had returned this 2nd time"
Gen 47:18 – "then came unto him the 2nd year"
Exo 2:13 – "2nd day..two men..strove together"
Exo 16:1 – "second month" – see *DATES*
Exo 26:4 – "in the coupling of the second"
Exo 26:5 – "that is in the coupling of the second"
Exo 26:10 – "edge..curtain that coupleth the 2nd"
Exo 26:20 – "2nd side of the tabernacle"
Exo 28:18 – "2nd row..emerald..sapphire"
Exo 36:11 – "another curtain..coupling of the 2nd"
Exo 36:12 – "curtain..in the coupling of the 2nd"
Exo 36:17 – "edge of the curtain..coupleth the 2nd"
Exo 39:11 – "2nd row..emerald..sapphire"
Exo 40;17 – "second year" – see *DATES*
Lev 5:10 – "offer the second for a burnt offering"
Lev 13:58 – "shall be washed the 2nd time..clean"
Num 1:1 – "2nd month..2nd year" – see *DATES*
Num 1:18 – "second month" – see *DATES*
Num 2:16 – "camp of Reuben..second rank"
Num 7:18 – "second day..prince of Issachar"
Num 9:1 – "second year" – see *DATES*
Num 9:11 – "second month" – see *DATES*
Num 10:6 – "blow an alarm the second time"
Num 10:11 – "2nd month..2nd year" – see *DATES*
Num 29:17 – "2nd day ye shall offer..two rams"
Jos 5:2 – "circumcise..Israel the 2nd time"
Jos 6:14 – "2nd day they compassed the city once"
Jos 10:32 – "Lachish..Israel..took it on the 2nd day"
Jos 19:1 – "second lot came forth to Simeon"
Jdg 6:25 – "take the 2nd bullock..offer..sacrifice"
Jdg 6:28 – "2nd bullock was offered upon the altar"
Jdg 20:24 – "Israel came..Benjamin the 2nd day"
Jdg 20:25 – "Benjamin..against them..2nd day"
1Sa 8:2 – "name of his second, Abiah"
1Sa 20:27 – "on the morrow..the 2nd day"
1Sa 20:34 – "Jonathan..eat no meat the 2nd day"
1Sa 26:8 – "I will not smite him the second time"
2Sa 3:3 – "And his second, Chileab, of Abigail"
2Sa 14:29 – "he sent again the second time"
1Ki 6:1 – "second month" – see *DATES*
1Ki 9:2 – "LORD appeared to Solomon..2nd time"
1Ki 15:25 – "Nadab..began to reign..the 2nd year"
1Ki 18:34 – "Do it the second time."
1Ki 18:34 – "And they did it the second time."
1Ki 19:7 – "angel of the LORD came..the 2nd time"
2Ki 1:17 – "in the second year of Jehoram"
2Ki 9:19 – "he sent out a second on horseback"
2Ki 10:6 – "wrote a letter the second time"
2Ki 14:1 – "In the second year of Joash"
2Ki 15:32 – "In the second year of Pekah"
2Ki 19:29 – "in the 2nd year that which springeth"
2Ki 23:4 – "priests of the second order"
2Ki 25:17 – "second pillar with wreathen work"
2Ki 25:18 – "Zephaniah the second priest"
1Ch 2:13 – "Jesse begat..Abinadab the second"
1Ch 3:1 – "the second Daniel, of Abigail"
1Ch 3:15 – "sons of Josiah..the 2nd Jehoiakim"

1Ch 7:15 – "Machir..wife..2nd was Zelophehad"
1Ch 8:1 – "Benjamin's begat..Ashbel the second"
1Ch 8:39 – "sons of Eshek..Jenush the second"
1Ch 12:9 – "Ezer the first, Obadiah the 2nd"
1Ch 15:18 – "their brethren of the 2nd degree"
1Ch 23:11 – "Zizah the second"
1Ch 23:19 – "sons of Hebron..Amariah the 2nd"
1Ch 23:20 – "sons of Uzziel..Jesiah the second"
1Ch 24:7 – "the second to Jedaiah"
1Ch 24:23 – "sons of Hebron..Amariah the 2nd"
1Ch 25:9 – "first lot..the second to Gedaliah"
1Ch 26:2 – "sons of Meshelemiah..Jediael the 2nd"
1Ch 26:4 – "sons of Obededom..Jehozabad the 2nd"
1Ch 26:11 – "Hilkiah the second"
1Ch 27:4 – "course of..2nd month..Dodai..24,000"
1Ch 29:22 – "made Solomon..king the 2nd time"
2Ch 3:2 – "2nd day..2nd month" – see *DATES*
2Ch 27:5 – "did..pay..both the 2nd year, and the 3rd"
2Ch 30:2 – "keep the passover in the 2nd month"
2Ch 30:13 – "feast..unleavened bread..2nd month"
2Ch 30:15 – "second month" – see *DATES*
2Ch 35:24 – "servants..put him in the 2nd chariot"
Ezr 1:10 – "silver basons of a second sort 410"
Ezr 3:8 – "2nd year..2nd month" – see *DATES*
Ezr 4:24 – "work..ceased..the 2nd year..of Darius"
Neh 8:13 – "2nd day were gathered..chief fathers"
Neh 11:9 – "Judah.. was second over the city"
Neh 11:17 – "Bakbukiah..2nd among his brethren"
Est 2:14 – "she returned into the second house"
Est 2:19 – "virgins..gathered together the 2nd time"
Est 7:2 – "king said..unto Esther on the 2nd day"
Est 9:29 – "to confirm this 2nd letter of Purim"
Job 42:14 – "name of the second, Kezia"
Ecc 4:8 – "There is one alone..not a second"
Ecc 4:15 – "second child..stand up in his stead"
Isa 11:11 – "the 2nd time to recover the remnant"
Isa 37:30 – "2nd year..which springeth of the same"
Jer 1:13 – "word of the LORD came..the 2nd time"
Jer 13:3 – "word of the LORD came..the 2nd time"
Jer 33:1 – "word of the LORD came..the 2nd time"
Jer 41:4 – "the 2nd day after he had slain Gedaliah"
Jer 52:22 – "second pillar..and the pomegranates"
Jer 52:24 – "Zephaniah the second priest"
Ezk 10:14 – "second face was the face of a man"
Ezk 43:22 – "2nd day..offer a kid of the goats"
Dan 2:1 – "2nd year..reign of Nebuchadnezzar"
Dan 7:5 – "another beast, a second, like to a bear"
Jon 3:1 – "word of the LORD came..the 2nd time"
Nah 1:9 – "affliction shall not rise up..2nd time"
Zep 1:10 – "cry from..fish gate..howling from..2nd"
Hag 1:1 – "second year" – see *DATES*
Hag 1:15 – "second year" – see *DATES*
Hag 2:10 – "second year" – see *DATES*
Zec 1:1 – "second year" – see *DATES*
Zec 1:7 – "second year" – see *DATES*
Zec 6:2 – "in the second chariot black horses"
Mat 21:30 – "came to the 2nd, and said likewise"
Mat 22:26 – "Likewise the second also"
Mat 22:39 – "the second is like unto it"
Mat 26:42 – "away again the 2nd time, and prayed"
Mar 12:21 – "And the second took her"

Mar 12:31 – "And the second is like, namely"
Mar 14:72 – "the second time the cock crew"
Luk 6:1 – "on the second Sabbath after the first"
Luk 12:38 – "if he shall come in the second watch"
Luk 19:18 – "the second came, saying"
Luk 20:30 – "the second took her to wife"
Joh 3:4 – "the 2nd time into his mother's womb"
Joh 4:54 – "that second miracle that Jesus did"
Joh 21:16 – "saith to him again the second time"
Act 7:13 – "at the 2nd time Joseph..made known"
Act 10:15 – "voice spake..again the second time"
Act 12:10 – "past the first and second ward"
Act 13:33 – "as it is written in the second psalm"
1Co 15:47 – "the second man is the Lord"
2Co 1:15 – "that ye might have a second benefit"
2Co 13:2 – "as if I were present, the second time"
Tit 3:10 – "after the 1st and 2nd admonition"
Heb 8:7 – "no place..sought for the second"
Heb 9:3 – "after the second veil, the tabernacle"
Heb 9:7 – "into the second went the high priest"
Heb 9:28 – "appear the 2nd time without sin"
Heb 10:9 – "that he may establish the second"
2Pet 3:1 – "This second epistle, beloved, I..write"
Rev 2:11 – "not be hurt of the second death"
Rev 4:7 – "second beast like a calf"
Rev 6:3 – "when he had opened the second seal"
Rev 6:3 – "I heard the second beast say"
Rev 8:8 – "And the second angel sounded"
Rev 11:14 – "The second woe is past"
Rev 16:3 – "second angel poured out his vial"
Rev 20:6 – "on such the 2nd death hath no power"
Rev 20:14 – "This is the second death."
Rev 21:8 – "fire..brimstone..which is the 2nd death"
Rev 21:19 – "the second, sapphire"

Secondarily

1Co 12:28 – "set some..secondarily prophets"

Both

The word "both" is found 361 times in Scripture. Because "both" is a term of comparison, it is often used as a synonym for the word "two."

On some occasions "both" describes two of the same thing (*"both the daughters of Lot"* – Gen. 19:36), but more often than not it compares two different things (*"we have both straw and provender"* – Gen 24:25). Comparing different things makes it impossible to record "both" in the *Index of Numbered Items* as the items are not being individually counted but compared with something else.

Because of the difficulties in dealing with the word "both" in a consistent manner, they are not recorded in this volume. For futher study of "both," please consult a standard concordance.

Couple

"Couple" appears in Scripture as both a verb (*"five curtains shall be coupled together"* – Exo. 26:3) and as a pronoun that can be synonymous with the number two. Compare the following two verses:

*"And her husband arose..having his servant with him, and **a couple of asses**"* – Jdg 19:3

*"the man would not tarry..and there were with him **two asses** saddled"* – Jdg 19:10

Jud 19:3 – "a couple of asses"
2Sa 13:6 – "make me a couple of cakes"
2Sa 16:1 – "a couple of asses saddled"
Isa 21:7 - "chariot with a couple of horsemen"
Isa 21:9 – "a couple of horsemen"

Deuteronomy

The name of the fifth book of the Bible carries the meaning of "second law."

Double

Gen 41:32 – "dream..doubled unto Pharaoh twice"
Gen 43:12 – "take double money in your hand"
Gen 43:15 – "took double money in their hand"
Exo 22:4 – "theft..he shall restore double"
Exo 22:7 – "if..thief be found, let him pay double"
Exo 26:9 – "and shalt double the sixth curtain"
Exo 28:16 – "Foursquare..being doubled"
Exo 39:9 – "they made the breastplate double"
Exo 39:9 – "span..length..breadth..being doubled"
Deu 15:18 – "worth a double hired servant"
Deu 21:17 – "a double portion of all that he hath"
2Ki 2:9 – "double portion of thy spirit..upon me"
1Ch 12:33 – "Zebulun..were not of double heart"
Job 11:6 – "secrets of wisdom..they are double"
Job 41:3 – "come to him with his double bridle"
Psa 12:2 – "with a double heart to they speak"
Isa 40:2 – "received of the LORD's hand..double"
Isa 61:7 – "For your shame ye shall have double"
Isa 61:7 – "they shall possess the double"
Jer 16:18 – "I will recompense..their sin double"
Jer 17:18 – "destroy them w/ double destruction"
Ezk 21:14 – "let the sword be double the 3rd time"
Zec 9:12 – "I will render double unto thee"
1Ti 5:17 – "elders..worthy of double honour"
Jam 1:8 – "double minded man is unstable"
Jam 4:8 – "purify your hearts, ye double minded"
Rev 18:6 – "Reward her..double unto her"

Rev 18:6 – "double according to her works"
Rev 18:6 – "in the cup..fill to her double"

Doubletongued

1Ti 3:8 – "deacons..grave, not doubletongued"

Pair

Amo 2:6 – "sold..the poor for a pair of shoes"
Amo 8:6 – "buy..the needy for a pair of shoes"
Luk 2:24 – "sacrifice..A pair of turtledoves"
Rev 6:5 – "had a pair of balances in his hand"

Twain

1Sa 18:21 – "be my son in law in..one of the twain"
2Ki 4:33 – "shut the door upon them twain"
Isa 6:2 – "wings; with twain he covered his face"
Isa 6:2 – "wings..with twain he covered his feet"
Isa 6:2 – "wings..with twain he did fly"
Jer 34:18 – "cut the calf in twain..passed between"
Ezk 21:19 – "both twain shall come forth"
Mat 5:41 – "compel..go a mile, go with him twain"
Mat 19:5 – "they twain shall be one flesh?"
Mat 19:6 – "no more twain, but one flesh"
Mat 21:31 – "Whether of them twain did the will"
Mat 27:21 – "Whether of the twain..Barabbas"
Mat 27:51 – "veil of the temple was rent in twain"
Mar 10:8 – "they twain shall be one flesh"
Mar 10:8 – "no more twain, but one flesh"
Mar 15:38 – "veil..rent in twain"
Eph 2:15 – "make..of twain one new man"

Twice

Gen 41:32 – "dream..doubled unto Pharaoh twice"
Exo 16:5 – "6th day..twice as much as they gather"
Exo 16:22 – "6th day they gathered twice as much"
Num 20:11 – "Moses..smote the rock twice"
1Sa 18:11 – "David..out of his presence twice"
1Ki 11:9 – "LORD God..appeared unto him twice"
2Ki 6:10 – "saved himself..not once nor twice"
Neh 13:20 – "merchants..lodged..once or twice"
Job 33:14 – "God speaketh once, yea twice"

Job 40:5 – "twice; but I will proceed no further"
Job 42:10 – "LORD gave Job twice as much"
Psa 62:11 – "God..spoken once; twice..I heard"
Ecc 6:6 – "though he live 1000 years twice told"
Mark 14:30 – "before the cock crow twice"
Mar 14:72 – "Before the cock crow twice"
Luk 18:12 – "I fast twice in the week"
Jud 12 – "twice dead, plucked up by the roots"

Twins

Gen 25:24 – "there were twins in her womb"
Gen 38:27 – "behold, twins were in her womb"
Son 4:2 – "sheep..every one bear twins"
Son 4:5 – "breasts..2 young roes that are twins"
Son 6:6 – "sheep..every one beareth twins"
Son 7:3 – "breasts..2 young roes that are twins"

Twoedged

See also "Two" & "Edges"

Heb 4:12 – "word of God..twoedged sword"
Rev 1:16 – "mouth..sharp twoedged sword"

Twofold

Mat 23:15 – "twofold more the child of hell"

2½

Many references are made in Scripture to the two tribes (Reuben & Gad) and the half tribe of Manasseh on the east side of Jordan – only two are mentioned directly as such below, but many other indirect references also exist in Scripture.

Exo 25:10 – "ark..shittim wood: 2½ cubits..length"
Exo 25:17 – "mercy seat..gold: 2½ cubits..length"
Exo 37:1 – "ark..2½ cubits was the length of it"
Exo 37:6 – "mercy seat..2½ cubits the length"
Num 34:15 – "2 tribes..½ tribe..this side Jordan"
Jos 14:3 – "inheritance of 2 tribes and an ½ tribe"

Three

In Bible numerology three is is the number of God or divine completeness. As well as God himself being a trinity, virtually everything in God's creation can also be found in trinities where one thing can often be found with three parts or aspects. Some also consider the number three to point to the resurrection.

This section includes:

a)	3 – Three (cardinal number)		d)	Threefold
b)	3rd – Third (ordinal number)		e)	Thrice
c)	Thirdly		f)	Mixed Numbers – 3½

3 – Three

Gen 6:10 – "Noah begat three sons"
Gen 7:13 – "Noah..the three wives of his sons"
Gen 9:19 – "These are the three sons of Noah"
Gen 15:9 – "Take me an heifer of 3 years old"
Gen 15:9 – "a she goat of three years old"
Gen 15:9 – "a ram of three years old"
Gen 18:2 – "three men stood by him"
Gen 18:6 – "Make ready..3 measures of fine meal"
Gen 29:2 – "three flocks of sheep lying by it"
Gen 29:34 – "I have born him three sons"
Gen 30:36 – "3 days' journey..himself and Jacob"
Gen 38:24 – "3 months after..it was told Judah"
Gen 40:10 – "in the vine were three branches"
Gen 40:12 – "The three branches are three days"
Gen 40:13 – "within 3 days shall Pharaoh lift up"
Gen 40:16 – "I had 3 white baskets on my head"
Gen 40:18 – "The three baskets are three days"
Gen 40:19 – "within 3 days shall Pharaoh lift up"
Gen 42:17 – "together into ward three days"
Exo 2:2 – "goodly child, she hid him 3 months"
Exo 3:18 – "3 days' journey into the wilderness"
Exo 5:3 – "three days' journey into the desert"
Exo 8:27 – "go 3 days' journey into..wilderness"
Exo 10:22 – "darkness in..land of Egypt 3 days"
Exo 10:23 – "saw not one another..for 3 days"
Exo 15:22 – "3 days in the wilderness..no water"
Exo 21:11 – "if he do not these three unto her"
Exo 23:14 – "3 times..keep a feast..in the year"
Exo 23:17 – "3 times in..year..all..males..appear"
Exo 25:32 – "three branches..one side"
Exo 25:32 – "three branches..out of the other side"
Exo 25:33 – "3 bowls made like unto almonds"
Exo 25:33 – "three bowls made like almonds"
Exo 27:1 – "height thereof shall be 3 cubits"
Exo 27:14 – "their pillars 3, and their sockets 3"
Exo 27:15 – "their pillars 3, and their sockets 3"
Exo 37:18 – "three branches..out of the one side"
Exo 37:18 – "three branches..out of the other side"
Exo 37:19 – "Three bowls made after the fashion"
Exo 37:19 – "three bowls made like almonds"
Exo 38:1 – "altar..three cubits the height"
Exo 38:14 – "their pillars 3, and their sockets 3"
Exo 38:15 – "their pillars 3, and their sockets 3"
Lev 19:23 – "fruit..3 years..be uncircumcised"

Lev 25:21 – "bring forth fruit for three years"
Lev 27:6 – "estimation..three shekels of silver'
Num 10:33 – "departed..mount..3 days journey"
Num 10:33 – "ark..before them..3 days journey"
Num 12:4 – "Come out ye three"
Num 12:4 – "And they three came out."
Num 22:28 – "smitten me these three times"
Num 22:32 – "smitten thine ass these 3 times"
Num 22:33 – "ass..turned from me these 3 times"
Num 24:10 – "blessed them these three times"
Num 33:8 – "3 days' journey..wilderness..Etham"
Num 35:14 – "three cities on this side Jordan"
Num 35:14 – "three cities..in the land of Canaan"
Deu 4:41 – "severed three cities..this side Jordan"
Deu 14:28 – "end of 3 years..bring..all the tithe"
Deu 16:16 – "3 times in a year..thy males appear"
Deu 17:6 – "mouth of 2 witnesses, or 3 witnesses"
Deu 19:2 – "separate 3 cities.. midst of thy land"
Deu 19:3 – "3 parts, that every slayer may flee"
Deu 19:7 – "Thou shalt separate 3 cities for thee."
Deu 19:9 – "cities more for thee beside these 3"
Deu 19:15 – "mouth of 3 witnesses..established"
Jos 1:11 – "within 3 days..pass over this Jordan"
Jos 2:16 – "hide yourselves there three days"
Jos 2:22 – "abode there three days"
Jos 3:2 – "after 3 days..officers..through the host"
Jos 9:16 – "at the end of 3 days..made a league"
Jos 15:14 – "Caleb drove thence..3 sons of Anak"
Jos 17:11 – "Manasseth had..three countries"
Jos 18:4 – "from among you 3 men for each tribe"
Jos 21:32 – " out of the tribe of Naphtali..3 cities"
Jdg 1:20 – "he expelled thence the 3 sons of Anak"
Jdg 7:16 – "divided..300 men into 3 companies"
Jdg 7:20 – "three companies blew the trumpets"
Jdg 9:22 – "Abimelech..reigned 3 years..Israel"
Jdg 9:43 – "divided them into three companies"
Jdg 14:14 – "could not in 3 days expound..riddle"
Jdg 16:15 – "hast mocked me these three times"
Jdg 19:4 – "he abode with him three days"
1Sa 1:24 – "three bullocks..one ephah of flour"
1Sa 2:13 – "fleshhook of three teeth in his hand"
1Sa 2:21 – "three sons and two daughters"
1Sa 9:20 – "asses that were lost three days ago"
1Sa 10:3 – "three men going up to God to Bethel"

1Sa 10:3 – "one carrying three kids"
1Sa 10:3 – "another carrying 3 loaves of bread"
1Sa 11:11 – "Saul put the people in 3 companies"
1Sa 13:17 – "spoilers..Philistines in 3 companies"
1Sa 17:13 – "3 eldest sons of Jesse..followed Saul"
1Sa 17:13 – "names..3 sons that went to battle"
1Sa 17:14 – "the three eldest followed Saul"
1Sa 20:19 – "when thou hast stayed three days"
1Sa 20:20 – "I will shoot three arrows"
1Sa 20:41 – "David..bowed himself three times"
1Sa 21:5 – "women..kept from us..these 3 days"
1Sa 30:12 – "nor drunk..water 3 days..3 nights"
1Sa 30:13 – "three days agone I fell sick"
1Sa 31:6 – "So Saul died, and his three sons"
1Sa 31:8 – "found Saul and his three sons fallen"
2Sa 2:18 – "three sons of Zeruiah"
2Sa 6:11 – "ark..house of Obededom..3 months"
2Sa 13:38 – "Absalom fled..Geshur..there 3 years"
2Sa 14:27 – "unto Absalom..were born 3 sons"
2Sa 18:14 – "Joab..3 darts..thrust..heart..Absalom"
2Sa 20:4 – "Assemble..men of Judah w/in 3 days"
2Sa 21:1 – "famine in the days of David 3 years"
2Sa 23:9 – "Eleazer...one of the three mighty men"
2Sa 23:13 – "3 of..30 chief went down..to David"
2Sa 23:16 – "three mighty men brake through"
2Sa 23:17 – "These things did..three mighty men."
2Sa 23:18 – "Abishai..was chief among the three"
2Sa 23:18 – "Abishai..had..name among the three"
2Sa 23:19 – "Was he not most honourable of 3?"
2Sa 23:19 – "he attained not unto the first three"
2Sa 23:22 – "Benaiah..name among 3 mighty men"
2Sa 23:23 – "he attained not to the first three"
2Sa 24:12 – "saith the LORD, I offer thee 3 things"
2Sa 24:13 – "flee 3 months before thine enemies"
2Sa 24:13 – "there be three days' pestilence"
1Ki 2:39 – "end of 3 years..servants..ran away"
1Ki 6:36 – "built..inner court with 3 rows..stone"
1Ki 7:4 – "windows in three rows"
1Ki 7:4 – "light was against light in three ranks"
1Ki 7:5 – "light was against light in three ranks"
1Ki 7:12 – "three rows of hewed stones"
1Ki 7:25 – "three looking toward the north"
1Ki 7:25 – "three looking toward the west"
1Ki 7:25 – "three looking toward the south"
1Ki 7:25 – "three looking toward the east"
1Ki 7:27 – "three cubits was the height thereof"
1Ki 9:25 – "3 times in the year did Solomon offer"
1Ki 10:17 – "3 pound of gold went to one shield"
1Ki 10:22 – "once in three years came the navy"
1Ki 12:5 – "Depart..for 3 days, then come again"
1Ki 15:2 – "Three years reigned he in Jerusalem"
1Ki 17:21 – "stretched..upon the child 3 times"
1Ki 22:1 – "3 years without war..Syria and Israel"
2Ki 2:17 – "sought 3 days, but found him not"
2Ki 3:10 – "LORD hath called these 3 kings"
2Ki 3:13 – "LORD hath called these 3 kings"
2Ki 9:32 – "looked out to him 2 or 3 eunuchs"
2Ki 13:25 – "Three times did Joash beat him"
2Ki 17:5 – "king of Assyria..beseiged it 3 years"
2Ki 18:10 – "at the end of 3 years they took it"
2Ki 23:31 – "Jehoahaz..reigned 3 months"

2Ki 24:1 – "Jehoiakim became his servant 3 years"
2Ki 24:8 – "Jehoicahin..reigned..three months"
2Ki 25:17 – "height of the chapiter three cubits"
2Ki 25:18 – "three keepers of the door"
1Ch 2:3 – "the sons of Judah..which 3 were born"
1Ch 2:16 – "Abishai..Joab..Asahel, three"
1Ch 3:23 – "And the sons of Neariah..three"
1Ch 7:6 – "The sons of Benjamin..three"
1Ch 10:6 – "So Saul died, and his three sons"
1Ch 11:12 – "Eleazer..one of the 3 mighties"
1Ch 11:15 – "3 of the thirty captains went down"
1Ch 11:18 – "three brake through the host"
1Ch 11:19 – "These things did these 3 mightiest"
1Ch 11:20 – "Abishai..was chief of the three"
1Ch 11:20 – "Abishai..had a name among the 3"
1Ch 11:21 – "Of the 3, he was more honorable"
1Ch 11:21 – "he attained not to the first three"
1Ch 11:24 – "Benaiah..name among..3 mighties"
1Ch 11:25 – "but attained not to the first three"
1Ch 12:39 – "they were with David three days"
1Ch 13:14 – "ark..remained..Obededom..3 months"
1Ch 21:10 – "offer thee 3 things: choose thee one"
1Ch 21:12 – "Either three years' famine"
1Ch 21:12 – "3 months..destroyed before thy foes"
1Ch 21:12 – "3 days the sword of the LORD"
1Ch 23:8 – "The sons of Laadan..three"
1Ch 23:9 – "The sons of Shimei..three"
1Ch 23:23 – "The sons of Mushi..three"
1Ch 25:5 – "Heman 14 sons & 3 daughters"
2Ch 4:4 – "three looking toward the north"
2Ch 4:4 – "three looking toward the west"
2Ch 4:4 – "three looking toward the south"
2Ch 4:4 – "three looking toward the east"
2Ch 6:13 – "brasen scaffold..3 cubits high"
2Ch 8:13 – "3 times in the year"
2Ch 9:21 – "every 3 years once came..ships"
2Ch 10:5 – "Come again unto me after three days."
2Ch 11:17 – "made Rehoboam..strong, 3 years"
2Ch 11:17 – "3 years..walked in the way of David"
2Ch 13:2 – "He reigned 3 years in Jerusalem"
2Ch 20:25 – "three days in gathering of the spoil"
2Ch 31:16 – "geneology..males, from 3 years old"
2Ch 36:2 – "Jehoahaz..reigned 3 months"
Ezr 6:4 – "3 rows of great stones"
Ezr 8:15 – "there abode we in tents three days"
Ezr 8:32 – "came to Jerusalem..abode..3 days"
Ezr 10:8 – "whosoever..not come within 3 days"
Ezr 10:9 – "men..gathered..within 3 days"
Neh 2:11 – "came to Jerusalem..was there 3 days"
Est 4:16 – "neither eat nor drink three days"
Job 1:2 – "born unto him 7 sons and 3 daughters"
Job 1:4 – "called for their three sisters"
Job 1:17 – "The Chaldeans made out three bands"
Job 2:11 – "Now when Job's three friends heard"
Job 32:1 – "So these 3 men ceased to answer Job"
Job 32:3 – "against his 3 friends..wrath kindled"
Job 32:5 – "no answer in..mouth of these 3 men"
Job 42:13 – "He had also 7 sons and 3 daughters."
Pro 30:15 – "three things that are never satisfied"
Pro 30:18 – three things..too wonderful for me"
Pro 30:21 – "For 3 things the earth is disquieted"

Pro 30:29 – "There be three things which go well"
Isa 15:5 – "an heifer of three years old"
Isa 16:14 – "Within 3 years..Moab..contemned"
Isa 17:6 – "2 or 3 berries..top..uppermost bough"
Isa 20:3 – "Isaiah..walked naked..barefoot 3 years"
Jer 36:23 – "when Jehudi had read 3 or 4 leaves"
Jer 48:34 – "as an heifer of three years old"
Jer 52:24 – "captain..took..3 keepers of the door"
Ezk 14:14 – "Though these three men..were in it"
Ezk 14:16 – "Though these three men were in it"
Ezk 14:18 – "Though these three men were in it"
Ezk 40:10 – "little chambers..eastward were 3"
Ezk 40:10 – "chambers..three on that side"
Ezk 40:10 – "they three were of one measure"
Ezk 40:21 – "little chambers..three on this side"
Ezk 40:21 – "little chambers..three on that side"
Ezk 40:48 – "breadth of..gate..3 cubits..this side"
Ezk 40:48 – "breadth of..gate..3 cubits..that side"
Ezk 41:6 – "side chambers were three"
Ezk 41:16 – "galleries round about on..3 stories"
Ezk 41:22 – "altar of wood was 3 cubits high"
Ezk 42:3 – "gallery against gallery in 3 stories"
Ezk 42:6 – "they were in 3 stories..had not pillars"
Ezk 48:31 – "three gates northward"
Ezk 48:32 – "east side..and three gates"
Ezk 48:33 – "south side..and three gates"
Ezk 48:34 – "west side..with their three gates"
Dan 1:5 – "so nourishing them three years"
Dan 3:23 – "these three men, Shadrach"
Dan 3:24 – "Did not we cast three men bound"
Dan 6:2 – "And over these three presidents"
Dan 6:10 – "upon his knees three times a day"
Dan 6:13 – "maketh his petition three times a day"
Dan 7:5 – "it had three ribs in the mouth of it"
Dan 7:8 – "three of the first horns plucked up"
Dan 7:20 – "before whom three fell"
Dan 7:24 – "he shall subdue three kings"
Dan 10:2 – "I Daniel was mourning 3 full weeks"
Dan 10:3 – "till three whole weeks were fulfilled"
Dan 11:2 – "stand up yet three kings in Persia"
Amo 1:3 – "3 transgressions of Damascus, & for 4"
Amo 1:6 – "3 transgressions of Gaza, and for 4"
Amo 1:9 – "3 transgressions of Tyrus, and for 4"
Amo 1:11 – "3 transgressions of Edom, and for 4"
Amo 1:13 – "3 transgressions of..Ammon, & for 4"
Amo 2:1 – "3 transgressions of Moab, and for 4"
Amo 2:4 – "3 transgressions of Judah, and for 4"
Amo 2:6 – "3 transgressions of Israel, and for 4"
Amo 4:4 – "your tithes after three years"
Amo 4:7 – "yet three months to the harvest"
Amo 4:8 – "So two or three cities wandered"
Jon 1:17 – "belly of the fish 3 days and 3 nights"
Jon 3:3 – "Nineveh..city of three days' journey"
Zec 11:8 – "3 shepherds..cut off in one month"
Mat 12:40 – "3 days and 3 nights..whale's belly"
Mat 12:40 – "Son of man..3 days and 3 nights"
Mat 13:33 – "leaven..hid in 3 measures of meal"
Mat 15:32 – "continue with me now three days"
Mat 17:4 – "three tabernacles, one for thee"

Mat 18:16 – "mouth or two or three witnesses"
Mat 18:20 – "where 2 or 3 are gathered"
Mat 26:61 – "destroy..temple..build it in 3 days"
Mat 27:40 – "temple, and buildest it in 3 days"
Mat 27:63 – "After three days I will rise again"
Mar 8:2 – "three days, and have nothing to eat"
Mar 8:31 – "killed, and after 3 days rise again"
Mar 9:5 – "let us make three tabernacles"
Mar 14:58 – "within three days I will build"
Mar 15:29 – "buildest it in three days"
Luk 1:56 – "Mary abode with her about 3 months"
Luk 2:46 – "after three days they found him"
Luk 9:33 – "three tabernacles; one for thee"
Luk 10:36 – "Which..of these 3..was neighbour"
Luk 11:5 – "Friend, lend me three loaves"
Luk 12:52 – "divided, three against two"
Luk 12:52 – "divided..two against three"
Luk 13:7 – "three years I come seeking fruit"
Luk 13:21 – "hid in three measures of meal"
Joh 2:6 – "waterpots..two or three firkins apiece"
Joh 2:19 – "in 3 days I will raise it up again"
Joh 2:20 – "will thou rear it up in three days?"
Act 5:7 – "about the space of three hours"
Act 7:20 – "in his father's house three months"
Act 9:9 – "three days without sight"
Act 10:19 – "Behold, three men seek thee."
Act 11:10 – "this was done three times"
Act 11:11 – "3 men already come unto the house"
Act 17:2 – "three sabbath days reasoned"
Act 19:8 – "3 months, disputing and persuading"
Act 20:3 – "And there abode three months"
Act 20:31 – "three years I ceased not to warn"
Act 25:1 – "Festus..after three days he ascended"
Act 28:7 – "Publius..lodged us three days"
Act 28:11 – "after 3 months..departed in a ship"
Act 28:12 – "Syracuse, we tarried there 3 days"
Act 28:15 – "Appii forum, and The three taverns"
Act 28:17 – "after 3 days, Paul called..the Jews"
1Co 13:13 – "faith, hope, charity, these three"
1Co 14:27 – "speak..tongue..at the most by three"
1Co 14:29 – "Let the prophets speak two or three"
2Co 13:1 – "mouth of 2 or 3 witnesses"
1Ti 5:19 – "but before 2 or 3 witnesses"
Heb 10:28 – "w/o mercy under 2 or 3 witnesses"
Heb 11:23 – "Moses..hid 3 months of his parents"
1Jn 5:7 – "three that bear record in heaven"
1Jn 5:7 – "these three are one"
1Jn 5:8 – "three that bear witness in earth"
1Jn 5:8 – "these three agree in one"
Rev 6:6 – "three measures of barley..a penny"
Rev 8:13 – "trumpet of the three angels"
Rev 9:18 – "By these three was..men killed"
Rev 16:13 – "three unclean spirits like frogs"
Rev 16:19 – "great city was divided into 3 parts"
Rev 21:13 – "On the east three gates"
Rev 21:13 – "on the north three gates"
Rev 21:13 – "on the south three gates"
Rev 21:13 – "on the west three gates"

3rd – Third

This section lists "third" as an ordinal number (as in first, second, third...). See the fraction **one-third** for those occurances in Scripture where "third" is used as a fraction. In almost all cases, when the word "third" is found in the sense of the fraction "one-third," it will appear as "third part" – see the word **Part** in the *Index of Numbered Items*.

Gen 1:13 – "evening..morning..the third day"
Gen 2:14 – "name of the third river is Hiddekel"
Gen 6:16 – "2nd and 3rd stories shalt thou make"
Gen 22:4 – "third day Abraham..saw the place"
Gen 31:22 – "told Laban on the 3rd day..Jacob..fled"
Gen 32:19 – "commanded he the 2nd, and the 3rd"
Gen 34:25 – "third day, when they were sore"
Gen 40:20 – "the 3rd day..was Pharaoh's birthday"
Gen 42:18 – "Joseph said unto them the third day"
Gen 50:23 – "Ephraim's children..3rd generation"
Exo 19:1 – "In the 3rd month..gone forth..of Egypt"
Exo 19:11 – "be ready against the third day"
Exo 19:11 – "3rd day the LORD will come down"
Exo 19:15 – "Be ready against the third day"
Exo 19:16 – "it came to pass on the third day"
Exo 20:5 – "visiting..iniquity..the 3rd..generation"
Exo 28:19 – "third row a ligure..agate..amethyst"
Exo 34:7 – "visiting the inquity..unto the third"
Exo 39:12 – "third row..ligure..agate..amethyst"
Lev 7:17 – "remainder..on the 3rd day..be burnt"
Lev 7:18 – "be eaten at all on the third day"
Lev 19:6 – "remain until the 3rd day..burnt"
Lev 19:7 – "eaten..on the 3rd day, it is abominable"
Num 2:24 – "camp of Ephraim..third rank"
Num 7:24 – "third day..Zebulun did offer"
Num 14:18 – "iniquity..3rd and 4th generation"
Num 19:12 – "purify himself..on the 3rd day"
Num 19:12 – "purify not himself the third day"
Num 19:19 – "sprinkle upon..unclean on..3rd day"
Num 29:20 – "And on the third day...two rams"
Num 31:19 – "purify..yourselves..on the third day"
Deu 5:9 – "visiting..iniquity..3rd and 4th generation"
Deu 23:8 – "enter..congregation..in..3rd generation"
Deu 26:12 – "tithes of thine increase the 3rd year"
Jos 9:17 – "came unto their cities on the third day"
Jos 19:10 – "the 3rd lot..children of Zebulun"
Jdg 20:30 – "Israel..against..Benjamin on..3rd day"
1Sa 3:8 – "LORD called Samuel again the 3rd time"
1Sa 17:13 – "sons of Jesse..the third Shammah"
1Sa 19:21 – "Saul sent messengers..the 3rd time"
1Sa 20:5 – "hide myself in..field unto the 3rd day"
1Sa 20:12 – "Jonathan..sounded my father..3rd day"
1Sa 30:1 – "David..men..to Ziklag on the third day"
2Sa 1:2 – "It came even to pass on the third day"
2Sa 3:3 – "the third, Absalom the son of Maacah"
1Ki 3:18 – "third day after that I was delivered"
1Ki 6:6 – "chamber..third was 7 cubits broad"
1Ki 6:8 – "middle chamber..into the third"
1Ki 12:12 – "Jeroboam..people came the 3rd day"
1Ki 12:12 – "Come to me again the third day."
1Ki 15:28 – "in the 3rd year..did Baasha slay him"
1Ki 15:33 – "In the 3rd year of Asa..began Baasha"
1Ki 18:1 – "word of..LORD..to Elijah in..3rd year"
1Ki 18:34 – "Do it the third time"
1Ki 18:34 – "And they did it the third time"

1Ki 22:2 – "third year..Jehoshaphat..came down"
2Ki 1:13 – "captain of the third 50 with his 50"
2Ki 1:13 – "And the third captain of fifty"
2Ki 18:1 – "3rd year of Hoshea..Hezekiah..began"
2Ki 19:29 – "3rd year sow ye, and reap, and plant"
2Ki 20:5 – "I will heal thee: on the third day"
2Ki 20:8 – "go up into..house of..LORD the 3rd day"
1Ch 2:13 – "Jesse begat..Shimma the third"
1Ch 3:2 – "The 3rd, Absalom the son of Maachah"
1Ch 3:15 – "sons of Josiah..the 3rd Zedekiah"
1Ch 8:1 – "Aharah the third"
1Ch 8:39 – "sons of Eshek..Eliphelet the third"
1Ch 12:9 – "Eliab the third"
1Ch 23:19 – "sons of Hebron..Jahaziel the third"
1Ch 24:8 – "The third to Harim"
1Ch 24:23 – "sons of Hebron..Jahaziel the third"
1Ch 25:10 – "Zaccur..sons..brethren..12"
1Ch 26:2 – "sons..Zebadiah the third"
1Ch 26:4 – "sons of Obededom..Joah the third"
1Ch 26:11 – "Tebaliah the third"
1Ch 27:5 – "3rd month was Benaiah..24,000"
2Ch 10:12 – "came to Rehoboam on the 3rd day"
2Ch 10:12 – "Come again to me on the third day."
2Ch 15:10 – "third month" – see *DATES*
2Ch 17:7 – "in the third year of his reign"
2Ch 27:5 – "Ammon gave..2nd year, and the 3rd"
2Ch 31:7 – "3rd month..began to lay..foundation"
Ezr 6:15 – "3rd day of the month Adar"
Est 1:3 – "third year of his reign"
Est 5:1 – "it came to pass on the third day"
Est 8:9 – "third month" – see *DATES*
Job 42:14 – "name of the third, Keren-happuch"
Isa 19:24 – "Israel.. third with Egypt and..Assyria"
Isa 37:30 – "in the 3rd year sow ye, and reap"
Jer 38:14 – "3rd entry..in the house of the LORD"
Ezk 10:14 – "third the face of a lion"
Ezk 21:14 – "let the sword be double the 3rd time"
Ezk 31:1 – "third month" – see *DATES*
Dan 1:1 – "third year of the reign of Jehoiakim"
Dan 2:39 – "another third kingdom of brass"
Dan 5:7 – "shall be the third ruler in the kingdom"
Dan 5:16 – "be the third ruler in the kingdom"
Dan 5:29 – "he should be the third ruler"
Dan 8:1 – "3rd year of the reign of king Belshazzar"
Dan 10:1 – "In the 3rd year of Cyrus king of Persia"
Hos 6:2 – "in the third day he will raise us up"
Zec 6:3 – "in the third chariot white horses"
Zec 13:8 – "the third shall be left therein"
Zec 13:9 – "bring the third part through the fire"
Mat 16:21 – "be raised again the third day"
Mat 17:23 – "third day he shall be raised again"
Mat 20:3 – "he went out about the third hour"
Mat 20:19 – "crucify him..third day..rise again"
Mat 22:26 – "and the third, unto the seventh"
Mat 26:44 – "went away..prayed the third time"

Mat 27:64 – "be made sure unto the third day"
Mar 9:31 – "killed, he shall rise the third day"
Mar 10:34 – "the third day he shall rise again"
Mar 12:21 – "and the third likewise"
Mar 14:41 – "he cometh the third time"
Mar 15:25 – "it was the 3rd hour..crucified him"
Luk 9:22 – "slain, and be raised the third day"
Luk 12:38 – "or come in the third watch"
Luk 13:32 – "third day I shall be perfected"
Luk 18:33 – "third day he shall rise again"
Luk 20:12 – "again he sent a third..wounded him"
Luk 20:31 – "And the third took her"
Luk 23:22 – "he said unto them the third time"
Luk 24:7 – "the third day rise again"
Luk 24:21 – "to day is the third day"
Luk 24:46 – "rise from the dead the third day"
Joh 2:1 – "third day..marriage in Cana"
Joh 21:14 – "third time that Jesus shewed himself"
Joh 21:17 – "saith unto him the third time"
Joh 21:17 – "said unto him the third time"
Act 2:15 – "not drunken..but the third hour"
Act 10:40 – "God raised him up the third day"
Act 20:9 – "fell down from the third loft..dead"
Act 23:23 – "to go to Caesarea..at the third hour"
Act 27:19 – "the 3rd day we cast out..the tackling"
1Co 15:4 – "he rose again the third day"
2Co 12:2 – "caught up to the third heaven"
2Co 12:14 – "third time I am ready to come"
2Co 13:1 – "This is the third time I am coming"
Rev 4:7 – "third beast had a face as a man"
Rev 6:5 – "when he had opened the third seal"
Rev 6:5 – "I heard the third beast say"
Rev 8:10 – "And the third angel sounded"
Rev 11:14 – "the third woe cometh quickly"
Rev 14:9 – "the third angel followed them"
Rev 16:4 – "third angel poured out his vial"
Rev 21:19 – "the third, a chalcedony"

Thirdly

1Co 12:28 – "set some..thirdly teachers"

Threefold

Ecc 4:12 - "a threefold cord is not quickly broken"

Thrice

See also "three times"

Exo 34:23 – "Thrice in..year..appear before..LORD"
Exo 34:24 – "appear before..LORD..thrice in..year"
2Ki 13:18 – "And he smote thrice, and stayed."
2Ki 13:19 – "thou shalt smite Syria but thrice"
Mat 26:34 – "thou shalt deny me thrice"
Mat 26:75 – "thou shalt deny me thrice"
Mar 14:30 – "thou shalt deny me thrice"
Mar 14:72 – "thou shalt deny me thrice"
Luk 22:34 – "thrice deny..thou knowest me"
Luk 22:61 – "thou shalt deny me thrice"
Joh 13:38 – "till thou has denied me thrice"
Act 10:16 – "This was done thrice"
2Co 11:25 – "Thrice was I beaten with rods"
2Co 11:25 – "thrice I suffered shipwreck"
2Co 12:8 – "I besought the Lord thrice"

3½

Dan 7:25 – "a time & times & the dividing of time"
Dan 12:7 – "time, times, and an half"
Luk 4:25 – "heaven shut up 3 years and 6 months"
Jam 5:17 – "Elias..prayed..rained not..3 yrs & 6 mos"
Rev 11:9 – "see their dead bodies 3 days & an ½"
Rev 11:11 – "after 3½ days..Spirit..entered..them"
Rev 12:14 – "nourished for a time..times..½ a time"

Four

In Bible numerology four is is the number of the earth, creation, the world & worldliness.

This section includes:

a)   4 – Four (cardinal number)
b)   4th – Fourth (ordinal number)
c)   Fourfold
d)   Fourfooted
e)   Foursquare

4 - Four

Gen 2:10 – "river..Eden..became into four heads"
Gen 14:9 – Battle of Siddim – "4 kings with 5"
Gen. 47:24 – "four parts shall be your own"
Exo 22:1 – "If a man steal..restore..four sheep"
Exo 25:12 – "thou shalt cast four rings of gold"
Exo 25:12 – "put them in the four corners thereof"
Exo 25:26 – "make for it four rings of gold"
Exo 25:26 – "put the rings in the four corners"
Exo 25:26 – table – "four feet thereof"
Exo 25:34 – "four bowls made like unto almonds"
Exo 26:2 – "breadth of one curtain four cubits"
Exo 26:8 – "breadth of one curtain four cubits"
Exo 26:32 – "hang it upon 4 pillars..shittim wood"
Exo 26:32 – "upon the four sockets of silver"
Exo 27:2 – "horns of it upon the 4 corners thereof"
Exo 27:4 – "upon the net..make four brasen rings"
Exo 27:4 – "rings in the four corners thereof"
Exo 27:16 – "their pillars 4, and their sockets 4"
Exo 28:17 – breastplate – "four rows of stones"
Exo 36:9 – "breadth of one curtain..4 cubits"
Exo 36:15 – "4 cubits..the breadth of 1 curtain"
Exo 36:36 – "four pillars of shittim wood"
Exo 36:36 – "he cast for them 4 sockets of silver"
Exo 37:3 – "cast for it four rings of gold"
Exo 37:3 – "to be set by the four corners of it"
Exo 37:13 – "he cast for it four rings of gold"
Exo 37:13 – "put the rings upon the four corners"
Exo 37:13 – "corners that were in the four feet"
Exo 37:20 – "four bowls made like almonds"
Exo 38:2 – "horns thereof on the four corners"
Exo 38:5 – "four rings for the four ends"
Exo 38:19 – "And their pillars were four"
Exo 38:19 – "their sockets of brass four"
Exo 39:10 – "they set it in four rows of stones"
Lev 11:20 – "fowls..going upon all four [feet]"
Lev 11:21 – "flying creeping thing..upon all 4"
Lev 11:23 – "flying creeping things..have four feet"
Lev 11:27 – "beasts that go on all four [feet]"
Lev 11:42 – "whatsoever goeth upon all 4 [feet]"
Num 7:7 – "two wagons and four oxen"
Num 7:8 – "four wagons and eight oxen"
Deu 3:11 – "Og..bedstead..length..four cubits"
Deu 22:12 – "fringes..four quarters of thy vesture"
Jos 19:7 – "four cities and their villages"
Jos 21:18 – "four cities"
Jos 21:22 – "four cities"
Jos 21:24 – "four cities"
Jos 21:29 – "four cities"
Jos 21:31 – "four cities"
Jos 21:35 – "four cities"
Jos 21:37 – "four cities"
Jos 21:39 – "four cities"
Jdg 9:34 – "against Shechem in four companies"
Jdg 11:40 – "lament..daughter..Jephthath..4 days"
Jdg 19:2 – "concubine..was there 4 whole months"
Jdg 20:47 – "abode in..rock Rimmon four months"
2Sa 12:6 – "he shall restore the lamb fourfold"
2Sa 21:22 – "These four..born to the giant in Gath"
1Ki 7:2 – "four rows of cedar pillars"

1Ki 7:19 – "chapiters..of lily work..four cubits"
1Ki 7:27 – "four cubits was the length of one base"
1Ki 7:27 – "four cubits was the breadth thereof"
1Ki 7:30 – "every base had four brazen wheels"
1Ki 7:30 – "four corners thereof had undersetters"
1Ki 7:32 – "under the borders were four wheels"
1Ki 7:34 – "4 undersetters..4 corners of 1 base"
1Ki 7:38 – "and every laver was four cubits"
1Ki 18:33 – "Fill 4 barrels with water, and pour it"
2Ki 7:3 – "four leprous men at..the gate"
1Ch 3:5 – "Shimea..Shobab..Nathan..Solomon, 4"
1Ch 7:1 – "sons of Issachar were..four"
1Ch 9:24 – "In 4 quarters were the porters"
1Ch 9:26 – "4 chief porters..in their set office"
1Ch 21:20 – "Ornan..his four sons..hid themselves"
1Ch 23:10 – "These four were the sons of Shimei."
1Ch 23:12 – "The sons of Kohath...four"
1Ch 26:17 – "northward four a day"
1Ch 26:17 – "southward four a day"
1Ch 26:17 – "toward Asuppim two and two"
1Ch 26:18 – "four at the causeway"
Neh 6:4 – "they sent unto me four times"
Job 1:19 – "great wind..smote the four corners"
Job 42:16 – "Job..saw..even four generations"
Pro 30:15 – "four things say not, It is enough"
Pro 30:18 – "four which I know not"
Pro 30:21 – "four which it cannot bear"
Pro 30:24 – "four things..little upon the earth"
Pro 30:29 – "four are comely in going"
Isa 11:12 – "gather..Judah from..4 corners..earth"
Isa 17:6 – "4 or 5 in the outmost fruitful branches"
Jer 15:3 – "I will appoint over them four kinds"
Jer 36:23 – "when Jehudi had read 3 or 4 leaves"
Jer 49:36 – "upon Elam..4 winds from..4 quarters"
Jer 52:21 – "pillars..thickness..was four fingers"
Ezk 1:5 – "the likeness of four living creatures"
Ezk 1:6 – "every one had four faces"
Ezk 1:6 – "every one had four wings"
Ezk 1:8 – "hands of a man..on their 4 sides"
Ezk 1:8 – "they 4 had their faces and their wings"
Ezk 1:10 – "they four had the face of a man"
Ezk 1:10 – "they four had the face of an ox"
Ezk 1:10 – "they four also had the face of an eagle"
Ezk 1:15 – "living creatures, with his four faces"
Ezk 1:16 – "wheels..they four had one likeness"
Ezk 1:17 – "they went upon their four sides"
Ezk 1:18 – "rings..full of eyes round about them 4"
Ezk 7:2 – "end is come upon the 4 corners of..land"
Ezk 10:9 – "the four wheels by the cherubim"
Ezk 10:10 – "they four had one likeness"
Ezk 10:11 – "they went upon their four sides"
Ezk 10:12 – "even the wheels that they four had"
Ezk 10:14 – "every one had four faces"
Ezk 10:21 – "Every one had four faces apiece"
Ezk 10:21 – "and every one four wings"
Ezk 14:21 – "when I send my sore four judgments"
Ezk 37:9 – "Come from the four winds, O breath"
Ezk 40:41 – "Four tables were on this side"
Ezk 40:41 – "four tables were on that side"

Ezk 40:42 – "four tables were of hewn stone"
Ezk 41:5 – "breadth..side chamber..four cubits"
Ezk 42:20 – "He measured it by the four sides"
Ezk 43:14 – "lesser settle..to..greater..4 cubits"
Ezk 43:15 – "So the altar shall be four cubits"
Ezk 43:15 – "altar and upward shall be 4 horns"
Ezk 43:16 – "altar..four squares" (12x12 cubits)
Ezk 43:17 – "settle..four squares" (14x14 cubits)
Ezk 43:20 – "blood..put it on the four horns"
Ezk 43:20 – "blood..put it..on the for corners"
Ezk 45:19 – "blood..sin offering..upon..4 corners"
Ezk 46:21 – "pass by the 4 corners of the court"
Ezk 46:22 – "4 corners of the court..were courts"
Ezk 46:22 – "these 4 corners were of 1 measure"
Ezk 46:23 – "row..buildings..round about them 4"
Dan 1:17 – "As for these four children"
Dan 3:25 – "Lo, I see four men loose"
Dan 7:2 – "4 winds of the heaven strove upon..sea"
Dan 7:3 – "four great beasts came up from the sea"
Dan 7:6 – "leopard..upon the back of it four wings"
Dan 7:6 – "leopard..the beast had also four heads"
Dan 7:17 – "These great beasts, which are four"
Dan 7:17 – "These great beasts..are four kings"
Dan 8:8 – "horn..broken..came up 4 notable ones"
Dan 8:8 – "toward the four winds of heaven"
Dan 8:22 – "whereas four stood up for it"
Dan 8:22 – "four kingdoms shall stand up for it"
Dan 11:4 – "divided toward..4 winds of heaven"
Amo 1:3 – "3 transgressions of Damascus, & for 4"
Amo 1:6 – "3 transgressions of Gaza, and for 4"
Amo 1:9 – "3 transgressions of Tyrus, and for 4"
Amo 1:11 – "3 transgressions of Edom, and for 4"
Amo 1:13 – "3 transgressions of..Ammon, & for 4"
Amo 2:1 – "3 transgressions of Moab, and for 4"
Amo 2:4 – "3 transgressions of Judah, and for 4"
Amo 2:6 – "3 transgressions of Israel, and for 4"
Zec 1:18 – "and saw, and behold four horns"
Zec 1:20 – "the LORD shewed me four carpenters"

Zech 2:6 – "as the four winds of the heaven"
Zec 6:1 – "4 chariots..from between 2 mountains"
Zec 6:5 – "These are the 4 spirits of the heavens"
Mat 24:31 – "gather..elect from the four winds"
Mar 2:3 – "one sick..which was borne of four"
Mar 13:27 – "gather..elect from the four winds"
Joh 4:35 – "four months..then cometh harvest?"
Joh 11:17 – "lain in the grave four days already"
Joh 11:39 – "he hath been dead four days"
Joh 19:23 – "took his garments, and made 4 parts"
Act 10:11 – "great sheet knit at the four corners"
Act 10:12 – "all manner of fourfooted beasts"
Act 10:30 – "Four days ago I was fasting"
Act 11:5 – "let down from heaven by 4 corners"
Act 11:6 – "saw fourfooted beasts of the earth"
Acts 12:4 – "four quaternions of soliders"
Act 21:9 – "same man had 4 daughters, virgins"
Act 21:23 – "four men which have a vow on them"
Act 27:29 – "cast four anchors out of the stern"
Rev 4:6 – "midst of the throne..were 4 beasts"
Rev 4:8 – "four beasts had each..six wings"
Rev 5:6 – "in the midst..of the four beasts"
Rev 5:8 – "4 beasts..fell down before the Lamb"
Rev 5:14 – "And the 4 beasts said, Amen."
Rev 6:1 – "one of the four beasts saying"
Rev 6:6 – "voice in the midst of the 4 beasts"
Rev 7:1 – "After these things I saw 4 angels"
Rev 7:1 – "standing on..4 corners of the earth"
Rev 7:1 – "holding the four winds of the earth"
Rev 7:2 – "loud voice to the four angels"
Rev 7:11 – "about the elders and the 4 beasts"
Rev 9:13 – "voice from the four horns..altar"
Rev 9:14 – "Loose the four angels..in..Euphrates"
Rev 9:15 – "And the four angels were loosed"
Rev 14:3 – "sung..new song..before..the 4 beasts"
Rev 15:7 – "one of the 4 beasts gave..vials"
Rev 19:4 – "four beasts fell down..worshipped"
Rev 20:8 – "nations..in the 4 quarters of..earth"

4th – Fourth

This section lists "fourth" as an ordinal number (as in first, second, third, fourth...). See the fraction **one-fourth** for those occurances in Scripture where "fourth" is used as a fraction. In almost all cases, when the word "fourth" is found in the sense of the fraction *one-fourth*, it will appear as "fourth part" – see the word **Part** in the *Index of Numbered Items*.

Gen 1:19 – "evening..morning..the fourth day"
Gen 2:14 – "And the fourth river is Euphrates."
Gen 15:16 – "in..4th generation they shall come"
Exo 20:5 – "visiting the iniquity..4th..generation"
Exo 29:20 – "fourth row a beryl..onyx..jasper"
Exo 34:7 – "visiting..inquity..to the 4th generation"
Exo 39:13 – "fourth row..beryl..onyx..jasper"
Lev 19:24 – "4th year all the fruit..shall be holy"
Num 7:30 – "on the fourth day Elizur..did offer"
Num 14:18 – "visiting..iniquity..3rd..4th generation"
Num 29:23 – "And on the fourth day...two rams"
Deu 5:9 – "visiting..iniquity..3rd..4th generation"

Jos 19:17 – "the 4th lot came out to Issachar"
Jdg 19:5 – "on the 4th day..rose up to depart"
2Sa 3:4 – "And the 4th, Adonijah..son of Haggith"
1Ki 6:1 – "in the fourth year of Solomon's reign"
1Ki 6:37 – "In..4th year was the foundation..laid"
1Ki 22:41 – "Jehoshaphat..began to reign..4th year"
2Ki 10:30 – "children of the 4th generation..throne"
2Ki 15:12 – "sons..sit..throne..unto..4th generation"
2Ki 18:9 – "4th year..Hezekiah..Shalmaneser..came"
2Ki 25:3 – "fourth month" – see *DATES*
1Ch 2:14 – "Nethaneel the fourth"
1 Ch 3:2 – "the 4th, Adonijah, the son of Haggith"

1Ch 3:15 – "sons of Josiah..the fourth Shallum"
1Ch 8:2 – "Nohah the fourth"
1Ch 12:10 – "Mismanah the fourth"
1Ch 23:19 – "sons of Hebron..Jekameam the 4th"
1Ch 24:8 – "the fourth to Seorim"
1Ch 24:23 – "sons of Hebron..Jekameam the 4th"
1Ch 25:11 – "The fourth lot to Izri"
1Ch 26:2 – "sons of Meshelemiah..Jathniel the 4th"
1Ch 26:4 – "sons of Obededom..Sacar the fourth"
1Ch 26:11 –"Zechariah the fourth..sons..of Hosah"
1Ch 27:7 – "4th captain for..4th month was Asahel"
2Ch 3:2 – "fourth year" – see *DATES*
2Ch 20:26 – "4th day..assembled..valley..Berachah"
Ezr 8:33 – "on the 4th day..vessels weighed"
Jer 25:1 – "the 4th year of Jehoiakim..son of Josiah"
Jer 28:1 – "fourth year" – see *DATES*
Jer 36:1 – "the 4th year of Jehoiakim..son of Josiah"
Jer 39:2 – "fourth month" – see *DATES*
Jer 45:1 – "the 4th year of Jehoiakim..son of Josiah"
Jer 46:2 – "the 4th year of Jehoiakim..son of Josiah"
Jer 51:59 – "Zedekiah..4th year of his reign"
Jer 52:6 – "fourth month" – see *DATES*
Ezk 1:1- "fourth month" – see *DATES*
Ezk 10:14 – "fourth the face of an eagle"
Dan 2:40 – "4th kingdom shall be strong as iron"
Dan 3:25 – "the fourth is like the Son of God"
Dan 7:7 – "fourth beast, dreadful and terrible"
Dan 7:19 – "I would know..truth of the 4th beast"
Dan 7:23 – "4th beast shall be the fourth kingdom"
Dan 11:2 – "4th shall be far richer than they all"
Zec 6:3 – "in the 4th chariot grisled and bay"
Zec 7:1 – "fourth month..fourth day" – see *DATES*
Zec 8:19 – "The fast of the fourth month"
Mat 14:25 – "in the fourth watch of the night"
Mar 6:48 – "4th watch of the night..upon the sea"
Rev 4:7 – "fourth beast was like a flying eagle"
Rev 6:7 – "when he had opened the fourth seal"
Rev 6:7 – "the voice of the fourth beast say"
Rev 8:12 – "And the fourth angel sounded"
Rev 16:8 – "fourth angel poured out his vial"

Rev 21:19 – "the fourth, an emerald"

Fourfold

2Sa 12:6 – "he shall restore the lamb fourfold"
Luk 19:8 – "I restore him fourfold"

Fourfooted

See also "four feet" under **Foot**

Act 10:12 – "all manner of fourfooted beasts"
Act 11:6 – "saw fourfooted beasts of the earth"
Rom 1:23 – "fourfooted beasts..creeping things"

Foursquare

Exo 27:1 – "the altar shall be foursquare"
Exo 28:16 – "Foursquare it shall..being doubled"
Exo 30:2 – ""foursquare shall it be"
Exo 37:25 – "incense altar..it was foursquare"
Exo 38:1 – "altar..burnt offering..was foursquare"
Exo 39:9 – "It was foursquare..the breastplate"
1Ki 7:31 – "borders, foursquare, not round"
Ezk 40:47 – "the court, an 100 cubits..foursquare"
Ezk 48:20 –"the holy oblation foursquare"
Rev 21:16 – "the city lieth foursquare"

Five

In Bible numerology five is often associated with death and its opposite grace.

This section includes:

   a)   5 – Five (cardinal number)
   b)   5th – Fifth (ordinal number)
   c)   Fivefold

5 - Five

Gen 14:9 – "four kings with five"
Gen 18:28 – "shall lack 5 of the 50 righteous"
Gen 18:28 – "destroy all the city for lack of five?"

Gen 43:34 – "Benjamin's mess..5 times so much"
Gen 45:6 – "5 years..neither be earing nor harvest"
Gen 45:11 – "yet there are five years of famine"

Gen 45:22 – "to Benjamin..five changes of raiment"
Gen 47:2 – "took some of his brethren..5 men"
Exo 22:1 – "If a man steal..shall restore five oxen"
Exo 26:3 – "The five curtains shall be coupled"
Exo 26:3 – "other five curtains shall be coupled"
Exo 26:9 – "couple five curtains by themselves"
Exo 26:26 – "bars of shittim wood; five"
Exo 26:27 – "5 bars..boards of the other side"
Exo 26:27 – "5 bars for the boards of the side"
Exo 26:37 – "five pillars of shittim wood"
Exo 26:37 – "cast five sockets of brass for them"
Exo 27:1 – "altar of shittim wood, 5 cubits long"
Exo 27:1 – "altar..five cubits broad"
Exo 27:18 – "the court..the height five cubits"
Exo 36:10 – "coupled the 5 curtains 1 to another"
Exo 36:10 – "other five curtains he coupled"
Exo 36:16 – "coupled five curtains by themselves"
Exo 36:31 – "bars..shittim wood..5 for the 1 side"
Exo 36:32 – "five bars for..the other side"
Exo 36:32 – "five bars for the boards..westward"
Exo 36:38 – "five pillars of it with their hooks"
Exo 36:38 – "their five sockets were of brass"
Exo 38:1 – "altar..five cubits was the length"
Exo 38:1 – "altar..five cubits the breadth"
Exo 38:18 – "hanging for the gate..height..5 cubits"
Lev 26:8 – "five of you shall chase an 100"
Lev 27:5 – "from five years old even unto twenty"
Lev 27:6 – "a month old even unto five years old"
Lev 27:6 – "estimation shall be...five shekels"
Num 3:47 – "five shekels apiece by the poll"
Num 7:17 – "five rams..offering of Nashon"
Num 7:17 – "five he goats..offering of Nashon"
Num 7:17 – "five lambs of the first year"
Num 7:23 – "five rams..offering of Nethaneel"
Num 7:23 – "five he goats..offering of Nethaneel"
Num 7:23 – "five lambs of the first year"
Num 7:29 – "five rams..offering of Eliab"
Num 7:29 – "five he goats..offering of Eliab"
Num 7:29 – "five lambs of the first year"
Num 7:35 – "five rams..offering of Elizur"
Num 7:35 – "five he goats..offering of Elizur"
Num 7:35 – "five lambs of the first year"
Num 7:41 – "five rams..offering of Shelumiel"
Num 7:41 – "five he goats..offering of Shelumiel"
Num 7:41 – "five lambs of the first year"
Num 7:47 – "five rams..offering of Eliasaph"
Num 7:47 – "five he goats..offering of Eliasaph"
Num 7:47 – "five lambs of the first year"
Num 7:53 – "five rams..offering of Elishama"
Num 7:53 – "five he goats..offering of Elishama"
Num 7:53 – "five lambs of the first year"
Num 7:59 – "five rams..offering of Gamaliel"
Num 7:59 – "five he goats..offering of Gamaliel"
Num 7:59 – "five lambs of the first year"
Num 7:65 – "five rams..offering of Abidan"
Num 7:65 – "five he goats..offering of Abidan"
Num 7:65 – "five lambs of the first year"
Num 7:71 – "five rams..offering of Ahiezer"
Num 7:71 – "five he goats..offering of Ahiezer"
Num 7:71 – "five lambs of the first year"
Num 7:77 – "five rams..offering of Pagiel"

Num 7:77 – "five he goats..offering of Pagiel"
Num 7:77 – "five lambs of the first year"
Num 7:83 – "five rams..offering of Ahira"
Num 7:83 – "five he goats..offering of Ahira"
Num 7:83 – "five lambs of the first year"
Num 11:19 – "nor 5 days, neither 10..nor 20"
Num 18:16 – "estimation..five shekels"
Num 31:8 – "five kings of Midian"
Jos 10:5 – "five kings of the Amorites"
Jos 10:16 – "five kings fled..hid..in a cave"
Jos 10:17 – "five kings are found hid in a cave"
Jos 10:22 – "bring out those 5 kings unto me"
Jos 10:23 – "brought forth those five kings"
Jos 10:26 – "Joshua..hanged them on 5 trees"
Jos 13:3 – "five lords of the Philistines"
Jdg 3:3 – "five lords of the Philistines"
Jdg 18:2 – "Dan sent..5 men from their coasts"
Jdg 18:7 – "5 men departed, and came to Laish"
Jdg 18:14 – "Then answered the five men"
Jdg 18:17 – "5 men that went to spy out the land"
1Sa 6:4 – "trespass offering...5 golden emerods"
1Sa 6:4 – "trespass offering...five golden mice"
1Sa 6:16 – "five lords of the Philistines"
1Sa 6:18 – "cities..belonging to the five lords"
1Sa 17:40 – "5 smooth stones out of the brook"
1Sa 21:3 – "give me five loaves of bread"
1Sa 25:18 – "Abigail made haste..took..5 sheep"
1Sa 25:18 – "Abigail..took..5 measures of..corn"
1Sa 25:42 – "Abigail..five damsels of hers"
2Sa 4:4 – "had a son..lame..five years old"
2Sa 21:8 – "king took...the five sons of Michal"
1Ki 6:6 – "nethermost chamber..5 cubits broad"
1Ki 6:10 – "chambers..five cubits high"
1Ki 6:24 – "five cubits..one wing of the cherub"
1Ki 6:24 – "five cubits the other wing..cherub"
1Ki 7:16 – "height of..chapiter was five cubits"
1Ki 7:16 – "height..other chapiter was 5 cubits"
1Ki 7:23 – "molten sea..height.. was five cubits"
1Ki 7:39 – "five bases..right side of the house"
1Ki 7:39 – "five on the left side of the house"
1Ki 7:49 – "candlesticks..five on the right side"
1Ki 7:49 – "candlesticks..five on the left"
2Ki 6:25 – "dove's dung for five pieces of silver"
2Ki 7:13 – "five of the horses that remain"
2Ki 13:19 – "shouldest..smitten 5 or 6 times"
2Ki 25:19 – "five men..in the king's presence"
1Ch 2:4 – "All the sons of Judah were five."
1Ch 2:6 – "sons of Zerah..five of them in all"
1Ch 3:20 – "Hasubah..Ohel..five"
1Ch 4:32 – "villages were..five cities"
1Ch 7:3 – "and the sons of Izrahiah..five"
1Ch 7:7 – "And the sons of Bela..five"
1Ch 11:23 – "slew an Egyptian..5 cubits high"
2Ch 3:11 – "one wing..was five cubits"
2Ch 3:11 – "other wing was likewise 5 cubits"
2Ch 3:12 – "wing of..other cherub was 5 cubits"
2Ch 3:12 – "the other wing was five cubits also"
2Ch 3:15 – "chapiter..on the top..was 5 cubits"
2Ch 4:2 – "molten sea..five cubits the height "
2Ch 4:6 – "ten lavers..five on the right hand"
2Ch 4:6 – "ten lavers..five on the left"

2Ch 4:7 – "ten candlsticks..five on the right"
2Ch 4:8 – "ten tables..five on the right side"
2Ch 4:8 – "ten tables..five on the left"
2Ch 6:13 – "brazen scaffold, of 5 cubits long"
2Ch 6:13 – "brazen scaffold..5 cubits broad"
Isa 17:6 – "4 or 5 in the outmost..branches"
Isa 19:18 – "five cities in the land of Egypt"
Isa 30:17 – "at the rebuke of five shall ye flee"
Jer 52:22 – "height of one chapiter was 5 cubits"
Ezk 40:7 – "between the..chambers were 5 cubits"
Ezk 40:30 – "arches..5 cubits broad"
Ezk 40:48 – "each post..5 cubits on this side"
Ezk 40:48 – "each post..5 cubits on that side"
Ezk 41:2 – "sides..door..5 cubits..one side"
Ezk 41:2 – "sides..door..5 cubits..other side"
Ezk 41:9 – "thickness of the wall..5 cubits"
Ezk 41:11 – "breadth..5 cubits round about"
Ezk 41:12 – "wall..five cubits thick"
Mat 14:17 – "five loaves, and two fishes"
Mat 14:19 – "five loaves, and the two fishes"
Mat 16:9 – "five loaves of the five thousand"
Mat 25:2 – "five of them were wise"
Mat 25:2 – "five were foolish"
Mat 25:15 – "unto one he gave five talents"
Mat 25:16 – "he that had received the 5 talents"
Mat 25:16 – "made them other five talents"
Mat 25:20 – "he that had received five talents"

2Ch 4:7 – "ten candlsticks..five on the left"
Mat 25:20 – "brought other five talents"
Mat 25:20 – "deliveredst unto me five talents"
Mat 25:20 – "I have gained..five talents more"
Mar 6:38 – "How many loaves..Five, and 2 fishes"
Mar 6:41 – "taken the 5 loaves and the 2 fishes"
Mar 8:19 – "When I brake the five loaves"
Luk 1:24 – "Elisabeth..hid herself five months"
Luk 9:13 – "We have..but 5 loaves..2 fishes"
Luk 9:16 – "he took the 5 loaves and the 2 fishes"
Luk 12:6 – "5 sparrows sold for 2 farthings"
Luk 12:52 – "shall be five in one house divided"
Luk 14:19 – "I have bought five yoke of oxen"
Luk 16:28 – "for I have five brethren"
Luk 19:18 – "thy pound hath gained five pounds"
Luk 19:19 – "Be thou also over five cities"
Joh 4:18 – "thou hast had five husbands"
Joh 5:2 – "Bethesda, having five porches"
Joh 6:9 – "lad here, which hath five barley loaves"
Joh 6:13 – "fragments of the five barley loaves"
Act 20:6 – "came unto them to Troas in 5 days"
Act 24:1 – "after 5 days Ananias..descended"
1Co 14:19 – "speak 5 words with..understanding"
2Co 11:24 – "5 times received..40 stripes save 1"
Rev 9:5 – "should be tormented five months"
Rev 9:10 – "power was to hurt men 5 months"
Rev 17:10 – "7 kings; 5 are fallen, and one is"

5th – Fifth

This section lists "fifth" as an ordinal number (as in third, fourth, fifth...). See the fraction **One-fifth** for those occurances in Scripture where "fifth" is used as a fraction. In almost all cases, when the word "fifth" is found in the sense of the fraction one-fifth, it will appear as "fifth part" – see the word **Part** in the *Index of Numbered Items*.

Gen 1:23 – "evening..morning..the fifth day"
Gen 30:17 – "Leah..bare Jacob the fifth son"
Lev 19:25 – "fifth year..eat of the fruit thereof"
Num 7:36 – "fifth day Shelumiel..did offer"
Num 29:26 – "And on the fifth day...two rams"
Num 33:38 – "fifth month" – see *DATES*
Jos 19:24 – "5th lot came out for..tribe of..Asher"
Jdg 19:8 – "arose early.. on the 5th day to depart"
2Sa 2:23 – "Abner..smote him under the fifth rib"
2Sa 3:4 – "the fifth, Shephatiah..son of Abital"
2Sa 3:27 – "Joab..smote..under fifth the fifth rib"
2Sa 4:6 – "smote ..under the 5th rib..Rechab"
2Sa 20:10 – "Joab..smote him..in the fifth rib"
1Ki 14:25 – "in the 5th year of..Rehoboam"
2Ki 8:16 – "in the 5th year..Jehoram began..reign"
2Ki 25:8 – "fifth month" – see *DATES*
1Ch 2:14 – "Nethaneel the 4th , Raddai the fifth."
1Ch 3:3 – "The fifth, Shephatiah of Abital"
1Ch 8:2 – "Nohah the fourth, Rapha the fifth."
1Ch 12:10 – "Mishmannah..4th, Jeremiah the 5th"
1Ch 24:9 – "The fifth to Malchijah"
1Ch 25:12 – "The fifth to Nethaniah"
1Ch 26:3 – "Elam the fifth, Jehohanan the sixth"

1Ch 26:4 – "sons of Obededom..Nethaneel the 5th"
1Ch 27:8 – "5th captain for..5th month..Shamhuth"
2Ch 12:2 – "in the 5th year of..Rehoboam"
Ezr 7:8 – "fifth month" – see *DATES*
Ezr 7:9 – "fifth month" – see *DATES*
Neh 6:5 – "Then sent Sanballat..the fifth time"
Jer 1:3 – "fifth month" – see *DATES*
Jer 28:1 – "fifth month" – see *DATES*
Jer 36:9 – "fifth year" – see *DATES*
Jer 52:12 – "fifth month" – see *DATES*
Ezk 1:1 – "fifth day" – see *DATES*
Ezk 1:2 – "fifth day..fifth year" – see *DATES*
Ezk 8:1 – "fifth day" – see *DATES*
Ezk 20:1 – "fifth month" – see *DATES*
Ezk 33:21 – "fifth day" – see *DATES*
Zec 7:3 – "Should I weep in the fifth month"
Zec 7:5 – "fasted..in the 5th and 7th month"
Zec 8:19 – "the fast of the fifth"
Rev 6:9 – "when he had opened the fifth seal"
Rev 9:1 – "And the fifth angel sounded"
Rev 16:10 – "fifth angel poured out his vial"
Rev 21:20 – "The fifth, sadonyx"

Fivefold

Luk 19:18 – "thy pound hath gained five pounds"

Six

In Bible numerology six is usually considered to be the number of man and the manifestation of sin.

This section includes:

a)   6 – Six (cardinal number)
b)   6th – Sixth (ordinal number)
c)   Mixed Numbers – 6½

6 – Six

Gen 30:20 – "I have born him six sons"
Gen 31:41 – "served..six years for thy cattle"
Exo 16:26 – "Six days ye shall gather it"
Exo 20:9 – "Six days shalt thou labour"
Exo 20:11 – "in six days the LORD made heaven"
Exo 21:2 – "servant, six years he shall serve"
Exo 23:10 – "six years thou shalt sow thy land"
Exo 23:12 – "Six days thou shalt do thy work"
Exo 24:16 – "Sinai..cloud covered it six days"
Exo 25:32 – "six branches..of the candlestick"
Exo 25:33 – "six branches..out of the candlestick"
Exo 25:35 – "six branches..out of the candlestick"
Exo 26:9 – "couple..six curtains by themselves"
Exo 26:22 – "thou shalt make six boards"
Exo 28:10 – "Six of their names..one stone"
Exo 28:10 – "other six names..other stone"
Exo 31:15 – "Six days may work be done"
Exo 31:17 – "in six days the LORD made heaven"
Exo 34:21 – "Six days thou shalt work"
Exo 35:2 – "Six days shall work be done"
Exo 36:16 – "six curtains by themselves"
Exo 36:27 – "tabernacle..he made six boards"
Exo 37:18 – "six branches going out of the sides"
Exo 37:19 – "six branches..of the candlestick"
Exo 37:21 – "six branches going out of it"
Lev 23:3 – "six days shall work be done"
Lev 24:6 – "set them in two rows, six on a row"
Lev 25:3 – "Six years thou shalt sow thy field"
Lev 25:3 – "six years..prune thy vineyard"
Num 7:3 – "offering..six covered wagons"
Num 35:6 – "six cities for refuge..flee thither"
Num 35:13 – "six cities shall ye have for refuge"
Num 35:15 – "six cities shall be a refuge"
Deu 5:13 – "six days..do all thy work"
Deu 15:12 – "thy brother..serve thee six years"
Deu 15:18 – "hired servant..serving thee 6 years"
Deu 16:8 – "Six days..eat unleavened bread"
Jos 6:3 – "Thus shalt thou do six days."
Jos 6:14 – "compassed the city..they did six days"

Jos 15:59 – "six cities with their villages"
Jos 15:62 – "six cities with their villages"
Jdg 12:7 – "Jephthah judged Israel six years"
Rut 3:15 – "he measured six measures of barley"
Rut 3:17 – "six measures of barley gave he me"
2Sa 6:13 – "gone 6 paces..sacrificed oxen..fatlings"
2Sa 21:20 – "on every hand six fingers"
2Sa 21:20 – "and on every foot six toes"
1Ki 6:6 – "chamber was..six cubits broad"
1Ki 10:19 – "The throne had six steps"
1Ki 10:20 – "12 lions stood.. upon the six steps"
1Ki 11:16 – "six months did Joab remain there"
1Ki 16:23 – "Omri..six years reigned he in Tirzah"
2Ki 11:3 – "he was with her hid..six years"
2Ki 13:19 – "shouldest have smitten 5 or 6 times"
2Ki 15:8 – "Zachariah..reign over Israel..6 months"
1Ch 3:4 – "six were born unto him in Hebron"
1Ch 3:22 – "And the sons of Shechaniah..six"
1Ch 4:27 – "Shimei had 16 sons & six daughters"
1Ch 8:38 – "And Azel had six sons"
1Ch 9:44 – "And Azel had six sons"
1Ch 20:6 – "fingers..six on each hand"
1Ch 20:6 – "toes..six on each foot"
1Ch 25:3 – "sons of Jeduthun..six"
1Ch 26:17 – "Eastward were six Levites"
2Ch 9:18 – "there were six steps to the throne"
2Ch 9:19 – "and the other upon the six steps"
2Ch 22:12 – "hid in the house of God 6 years"
Neh 5:18 – "prepared..daily..six choice sheep"
Est 2:12 – "6 months with oil of myrrh"
Est 2:12 – "6 months with sweet odours"
Job 5:19 – "delivereth thee in 6 troubles"
Pro 6:16 – "these six things doth the LORD hate"
Isa 6:2 – "seraphims: each one had six wings"
Jer 34:14 – "served thee 6 years..let him go free"
Ezk 9:2 – "six men..from..way of the higher gate"
Ezk 40:5 – "a measuring reed of six cubits long"
Ezk 40:12 – "little chambers..6 cubits..this side"
Ezk 40:12 – "little chambers..6 cubits..that side"

Ezk 41:1 – "posts, six cubits broad..one side"
Ezk 41:1 – "posts..six cubits broad..other side"
Ezk 41:3 – "measured..the door, six cubits"
Ezk 41:5 – "wall of the house, six cubits"
Ezk 41:8 – "a full reed of six great cubits"
Ezk 46:1 – "gate..shut the six working days"
Ezk 46:4 – "burnt offering..shall be six lambs"
Ezk 46:6 – "day of the new moon..six lambs"

Dan 3:1 – "image of gold..breadth..six cubits"
Mat 17:1 – "after six days Jesus taketh Peter"
Mar 9:2 – "And after six days..was transfigured"
Luk 13:14 – "6 days in which men ought to work"
Joh 2:6 – "set there six waterpots of stone"
Joh 12:1 – "Jesus six days before..passover"
Act 11:12 – "six brethren accompanied me"
Rev 4:8 – "four beasts had each..six wings"

6th – Sixth

This section lists "sixth" as an ordinal number (as in fourth, fifth, sixth...). See the fraction **one-sixth** for those occurances in Scripture where "sixth" is used as a fraction. In all of the occurences where the word "sixth" is found in the sense of the fraction *one-sixth*, it will appear as "sixth part" – see the word **Part** in the *Index of Numbered Items.*

Gen 1:31 – "evening..morning..the sixth day"
Gen 30:19 – "Leah..bare Jacob the sixth son"
Exo 16:5 – "on the 6th day..twice as much"
Exo 16:22 – "6th day..gathered twice as much"
Exo 16:29 – "giveth..6th day the bread of 2 days"
Exo 26:9 – "and shalt double the sixth curtain"
Lev 25:21 – "blessing upon you in the sixth year"
Num 7:42 – "sixth day..children of Gad, offered"
Num 29:29 – "And on the sixth day..two rams"
Jos 19:32 – "The 6th lot came out to..Naphtali"
2Sa 3:5 – "the sixth, Ithream, by Eglah"
2Ki 18:10 – "even in the 6th year of Hezekiah"
1Ch 2:15 – "Ozem the sixth"
1Ch 3:3 – "the sixth, Ithream by Eglah"
1Ch 12:11 – "Attai the 6th"
1Ch 24:9 – "the sixth to Mijamin"
1Ch 25:13 – "The sixth to Bukkiah"
1Ch 26:3 – "Jehohanan the sixth"
1Ch 26:5 – "Ammiel the sixth"
1Ch 27:9 – "6th captain for..6th month was Ira"
Ezr 6:15 – "house finished..6th year..of Darius"
Neh 3:30 – "Hanun the sixth son of Zalaph"

Ezk 8:1 – "sixth year..sixth month" – see *DATES*
Hag 1:1 – "sixth month" – see *DATES*
Hag 1:15 – "sixth month" – see *DATES*
Mat 20:5 – "went out about the 6th and 9th hour"
Mat 27:45 – "from the sixth hour..darkness"
Mar 15:33 – "sixth hour was come..darkness"
Luk 1:26 – "in the sixth month..Gabriel was sent"
Luk 1:36 – "this is the sixth month with her"
Luk 23:44 – "it was about the sixth hour"
Joh 4:6 – "and it was about the sixth hour"
Joh 19:14 – "preparation..about the 6th hour"
Act 10:9 – "to pray about the 6th hour"
Rev 6:12 – "when he had opened the sixth seal"
Rev 9:13 – "And the sixth angel sounded"
Rev 9:14 – "Saying to the sixth angel"
Rev 16:12 – "sixth angel poured out his vial"
Rev 21:20 – "the sixth, sardius"

6 ½

1Sa 17:4 – Goliath – *"height was 6 cubits and a span"*

Seven

In Bible numerology seven is usually considered to be the number of completion or spiritual perfection. When God acts in the affairs of men, he will often do it in sets of seven – eg. seven days in a week.

This section includes:

a)	7 – Seven (cardinal number)		d)	Sevens
b)	7th – Seven (ordinal number)		e)	Mixed Numbers – 7½
c)	Sevenfold			

7 – Seven

Gen 7:4 – "yet 7 days, and I will cause it to rain"
Gen 7:10 – "after 7 days..waters of the flood"
Gen 8:10 – "stayed yet other seven days"
Gen 8:12 – "stayed yet other seven days"
Gen 21:28 – "Abraham set seven ewe lambs"
Gen 21:29 – "What mean these 7 ewe lambs"
Gen 21:30 – "these 7 ewe lambs..take of my hand"
Gen 29:18 – "I will serve thee 7 years for Rachel"
Gen 29:20 – "Jacob served 7 years for Rachel"
Gen 29:27 – "serve with me yet 7 other years"
Gen 29:30 – "served with him yet 7 other years"
Gen 31:23 – "pursued after him 7 days' journey"
Gen 33:3 – "bowed himself to the ground 7 times"
Gen 41:2 – "out of the river, 7 well favoured kine"
Gen 41:3 – "7 other kine camp up"
Gen 41:4 – "did eat up the 7 well favoured..kine"
Gen 41:5 – "7 ears of corn came upon on 1 stalk"
Gen 41:6 – "7 thin ears and blasted with..wind"
Gen 41:7 – "the 7 thin ears devoured..7..full ears"
Gen 41:18 – "up out of the river seven kine"
Gen 41:19 – "behold, seven other kine came up"
Gen 41:20 – "did eat up the first seven fat kine"
Gen 41:22 – "behold, seven ears came up"
Gen 41:23 – "behold, seven ears, withered, thin"
Gen 41:24 – "thin ears devoured the 7 good ears"
Gen 41:26 – "the 7 good kine are 7 years"
Gen 41:26 – "the 7 good ears are 7 years"
Gen 41:27 – "7 thin..ill favoured kine..are 7 years"
Gen 41:27 – "7 empty ears..be 7 years..famine"
Gen 41:29 – "there come 7 years of great plenty"
Gen 41:30 – "arise after them 7 years of famine"
Gen 41:34 – "Egypt in the 7 plenteous years"
Gen 41:36 – "food..for store..against the 7 years"
Gen 41:47 – "in the 7 plenteous years"
Gen 41:48 – "gathered up all..food of the 7 years"
Gen 41:53 – "7 years of plenteousness.. ended"
Gen 41:54 – "7 years of dearth began to come"
Gen 46:25 – "sons of Bilhah..all the souls were 7"
Gen 50:10 – "a mourning for his father 7 days"
Exo 2:16 – "priest of Midian had 7 daughters"
Exo 7:25 – "7 days were fulfilled..smitten river"
Exo 12:15 – "7 days shall..eat unleavened bread"
Exo 12:19 – "7 days shall..be no leaven found"
Exo 13:6 – "7 days..shalt eat unleavened bread"
Exo 13:7 – "Unleavened bread..be eaten 7 days"
Exo 22:30 – "seven days it shall be with his dam"
Exo 23:15 – "shalt eat unleavened bread 7 days"
Exo 25:37 – "shalt make the 7 lamps thereof"
Exo 29:30 – "priest..shall put them on seven days"
Exo 29:35 – "7 days shalt thou consecrate them"
Exo 29:37 – "7 days..shalt make an atonement"
Exo 34:18 – "Seven days..eat unleavened bread"
Exo 37:23 – "he made his seven lamps..snuffers"
Lev 1:6 – "sprinkle of the blood seven times"
Lev 4:17 – "sprinkle of it seven times"
Lev 8:11 – "sprinkled..upon the altar 7 times"
Lev 8:33 – "not go out..tabernacle..in seven days"
Lev 8:33 – "for 7 days shall he consecrate you"
Lev 8:35 – "abide at the door..day & night 7 days"

Lev 12:2 – "she shall be unclean seven days"
Lev 13:4 – "shut up him that hath..plague 7 days"
Lev 13:5 – "priest shall shut him up 7 days more"
Lev 13:21 – "priest shall shut him up seven days"
Lev 13:26 – "priest shall shut him up seven days"
Lev 13:31 – "shut up..plague of the scall 7 days"
Lev 13:33 – "him that hath the scall 7 days more"
Lev 13:50 – "shut up it that hath..plague 7 days"
Lev 13:54 – "shut it up seven days more"
Lev 14:7 – "sprinkle..cleansed..leprosy 7 times"
Lev 14:8 – "tarry abroad out of his tent 7 days"
Lev 14:16 – "oil..seven times before the LORD"
Lev 14:27 – "oil..seven times before the LORD"
Lev 14:38 – "shut up the house seven days"
Lev 14:51 – "shall sprinkle the house seven times"
Lev 15:13 – "number to himself 7 days..cleansing"
Lev 15:19 – "she shall be put apart seven days"
Lev 15:24 – "he shall be unclean seven days"
Lev 15:28 – "she shall number to herself 7 days"
Lev 16:14 – "sprinkle of the blood..seven times"
Lev 16:19 – "sprinkle of the blood..seven times"
Lev 22:27 – "it shall be 7 days under the dam"
Lev 23:6 – "7 days ye must eat unleavened bread"
Lev 23:8 – "offering made by fire..seven days"
Lev 23:15 – "seven sabbaths shall be complete"
Lev 23:18 – "offer with the bread seven lambs"
Lev 23:34 – "feast of tabernacles..seven days"
Lev 23:36 – "seven days ye shall offer an offering"
Lev 23:39 – "keep a feast unto the LORD 7 days"
Lev 23:40 – "rejoice before the LORD..seven days"
Lev 23:41 – "keep it a feast unto the LORD 7 days"
Lev 23:42 – "Ye shall dwell in booths seven days"
Lev 25:8 – "seven sabbaths of years"
Lev 25:8 – "seven times seven years"
Lev 25:8 – "space of the seven sabbaths of years"
Lev 26:18 – "seven times more for your sins"
Lev 26:21 – "seven times more plagues"
Lev 26:24 – "seven times for your sins"
Lev 26:28 – "seven times for your sins"
Num 8:2 – "seven lamps shall give light"
Num 12:14 – "should she not be ashamed 7 days?"
Num 12:14 – "shut out from the camp seven days"
Num 12:15 – "Miriam..shut out..seven days"
Num 13:22 – "Hebron..built 7 years before Zoan"
Num 19:4 – "sprinkle of her blood...seven times"
Num 19:11 – "toucheth..body..unclean 7 days"
Num 19:14 – "man dieth in a tent..unclean 7 days"
Num 19:16 – "toucheth..body..unclean 7 days"
Num 23:1 – "Balaam said..Build me here 7 altars"
Num 23:1 – "prepare me here seven oxen..7 rams"
Num 23:4 – "I have prepared seven altars"
Num 23:14 – "top of Pisgah, and built 7 altars"
Num 23:29 – "Build me here seven altars..."
Num 23:29 – "prepare me..7 bullocks & 7 rams"
Num 28:11 – "one ram, 7 lambs of the first year"
Num 28:17 – "7 days..unleavened bread be eaten"
Num 28:19 – "seven lambs of the first year"
Num 28:21 – "throughout the seven lambs"
Num 28:24 – "throughout the seven days"

Num 28:27 – "burnt offering..7 lambs of..1st year"
Num 28:29 – "throughout the seven lambs"
Num 29:2 – "7 lambs of the 1st year w/o blemish"
Num 29:4 – "throughout the seven lambs"
Num 29:8 – "seven lambs of the first year"
Num 29:10 – "throughout the seven lambs"
Num 29:12 – "keep a feast unto the LORD 7 days"
Num 29:32 – "on the seventh day seven bullocks"
Num 29:36 – "7 lambs of the 1st year w/o blemish"
Num 31:19 – "abide without the camp seven days"
Deu 7:1 – "7 nations greater..mightier than thou"
Deu 15:1 – "end of every 7 years...make a release"
Deu 16:3 – "7 days shalt..eat unleavened bread"
Deu 16:4 – "no unleavened bread..7 days"
Deu 16:9 – "7 weeks shalt thou number unto thee"
Deu 16:9 – "number..7 weeks..sickle to the corn"
Deu 16:13 – "observe..feast of tabernacles 7 days"
Deu 16:15 – "Seven days..keep a solemn feast"
Deu 28:7 – "flee before thee seven ways"
Deu 28:25 – "thou shalt..flee 7 ways before them"
Deu 31:10 – "end of every 7 years..year of release"
Jos 6:4 – "7 priests..bear before..ark 7 trumpets"
Jos 6:4 – "7th day..compass the city 7 times"
Jos 6:6 – "7 priests bear 7 trumpets..rams' horns"
Jos 6:8 – "7 priests bearing..7 trumpets..horns"
Jos 6:13 – "7 priests bearing 7 trumpets..horns"
Jos 6:15 – "compassed..city..same manner 7 times"
Jos 6:15 – "that day..compassed the city 7 times"
Jos 18:2 – "7 tribes..not yet received..inheritance"
Jos 18:5 – "divide it into seven parts"
Jos 18:6 – "describe the land into seven parts"
Jos 18:9 – "by cities into 7 parts in a book"
Jdg 6:1 – "delivered..into..hand of Midian 7 years"
Jdg 6:25 – "even the second bullock of 7 years old"
Jdg 12:9 – "And he judged Israel seven years."
Jdg 14:12 – "seven days of the feast"
Jdg 14:17 – "she wept before him the 7 days"
Jdg 16:7 – "If they bind me with 7 green withs"
Jdg 16:8 – "Philistines brought..7 green withs"
Jdg 16:13 – "weavest the 7 locks of my head"
Jdg 16:19 – "shave off the 7 locks of his head"
Rut 4:15 – "which is better to thee than 7 sons"
1Sa 2:5 – "the barren hath borne seven"
1Sa 6:1 – "ark..in..country of the Philistines 7 mos."
1Sa 11:3 – "Give us seven days respite"
1Sa 13:8 – "And he tarried seven days"
1Sa 16:10 – "Jesse..7..sons..pass before Samuel"
1Sa 31:13 – "bones..buried them..fasted 7 days"
2Sa 21:6 – "Let 7 men of his sons be delivered"
2Sa 21:9 – "they fell all 7 together..put to death"
2Sa 24:13 – "Shall seven years of famine come"
1Ki 2:11 – "seven years reigned he in Hebron"
1Ki 6:6 – "nethermost chamber..7 cubits broad"
1Ki 6:38 – "So he was seven years in building it."
1Ki 7:17 – "seven for the one chapiter"
1Ki 7:17 – "seven for the other chapiter"
1Ki 8:65 – "7 days and 7 days, even 14 days"
1Ki 16:15 – "did Zimri reign 7 days in Tirzah"
1Ki 18:43 – "And he said, Go again seven times"
1Ki 20:29 – "pitched 1 over against..other 7 days"
2Ki 3:9 – "fetched a compass of 7 days journey"

2Ki 4:35 – "the child sneezed seven times"
2Ki 5:10 – "Go and wash in the Jordan 7 times"
2Ki 5:14 – "dipped himself seven times in Jordan"
2Ki 8:1 – "famine..upon the land seven years"
2Ki 8:2 – "sojourned..land of..Philistines 7 years"
2Ki 8:3 – "came to pass at the seven years' end"
2Ki 11:21 – "Seven years old was Jehoash..began"
1Ch 3:24 – "the sons of Elioenai were..seven"
1Ch 5:13 – "And their brethren..seven"
1Ch 9:25 – "come after 7 days from time to time"
1Ch 10:12 – "buried their bones..fasted 7 days"
1Ch 15:26 – "offered 7 bullocks and 7 rams"
1Ch 29:27 – "7 years reigned he in Hebron"
2Ch 7:8 – "Solomon kept the feast 7 days"
2Ch 7:9 – "dedication of the altar seven days"
2Ch 7:9 – "kept..the feast seven days"
2Ch 13:9 – "consecrate himself with..seven rams"
2Ch 24:1 – "Joash was 7 years old..began to reign"
2Ch 29:21 – "brought 7 bullocks..for a sin offering"
2Ch 29:21 – "brought..7 rams..for a sin offering"
2Ch 29:21 – "brought..7 lambs..for a sin offering"
2Ch 29:21 – "brought..7 he goats..for..sin offering"
2Ch 30:21 – "kept feast..unleavened bread 7 days"
2Ch 30:22 – "did eat throughout the feast 7 days"
2Ch 30:23 – "took counsel to keep other 7 days"
2Ch 30:23 – "kept other 7 days with gladness"
2Ch 35:17 – "kept..feast..unleavened bread 7 days"
Ezr 6:22 – "feast of unleavened bread 7 days"
Ezr 7:14 – "the king, and of his seven counselors"
Neh 8:18 – "they kept the feast seven days"
Est 1:5 – "king made a feast..seven days"
Est 1:10 – "7 chamberlains..served..Ahasuerus"
Est 1:14 – "seven princes of Media and Persia"
Est 2:9 – "seven maidens..meet to be given her"
Job 1:2 – "born unto him 7 sons and 3 daughters"
Job 2:13 – "upon the ground 7 days and 7 nights"
Job 5:19 – "delivereth thee in 6 troubles: yea, in 7"
Job 42:8 – "take unto you..7 bullocks & 7 rams"
Job 42:13 – "He had also 7 sons and 3 daughters."
Psa 12:6 – "in a furnace of earth, purified 7 times"
Psa 119:164 – "7 times a day do I praise thee"
Pro 6:16 – "yea, seven are an abomination"
Pro 9:1 – "Wisdom..hath hewn out her 7 pillars"
Pro 24:16 – "a just man falleth seven times..riseth"
Pro 26:16 – "seven men that can render a reason"
Pro 26:25 – "seven abominations in his heart"
Ecc 11:2 – "Give a portion to 7, and also to 8"
Isa 4:1 – "7 women shall take hold of one man"
Isa 11:15 – "shall smite it in the seven streams"
Isa 30:26 – "the sun..as the light of seven days"
Jer 15:9 – "She that hath borne 7 languisheth"
Jer 34:14 – "end of 7 years let ye go every man"
Jer 52:25 – "7 men..near the king's person"
Ezk 3:15 – "astonished among them seven days"
Ezk 3:16 – "the end of 7 days..word of the LORD"
Ezk 39:9 – "shall burn them with fire seven years"
Ezk 39:12 – "seven months..be burying of them"
Ezk 39:14 – "end of 7 months shall they search"
Ezk 40:22 – "went up unto it by seven steps"
Ezk 40:26 – "seven steps to go up to it"
Ezk 41:3 – "breadth of the door, seven cubits"

Ezk 43:25 – "7 days..prepare..a goat..sin offering"
Ezk 43:26 – "7 days..purge the altar and purify it"
Ezk 44:26 – "after he is cleansed..reckon..7 days"
Ezk 45:21 – "the passover, a feast of seven days"
Dan 3:19 – "heat the furnace one 7 times more"
Dan 4:16 – "let seven times pass over him"
Dan 4:23 – "till seven times pass over him"
Dan 4:25 – "seven times shall pass over thee"
Dan 4:32 – "seven times shall pass over thee"
Dan 9:25 – "commandment..Messiah..7 weeks"
Amo 5:8 – "Seek him that maketh the 7 stars"
Mic 5:5 – "raise against him seven shepherds"
Zec 3:9 – "upon one stone shall be seven eyes"
Zec 4:2 – "candlestick..his seven lamps thereon"
Zec 4:2 – "seven pipes to the seven lamps"
Zec 4:10 – "Zerubbabel with those seven"
Mat 12:45 – "seven other spirits more wicked"
Mat 15:34 – "how many loaves..Seven"
Mat 15:36 – "he took the seven loaves"
Mat 15:37 – "broken meat..left seven baskets full"
Mat 16:10 – "seven loaves of the four thousand"
Mat 18:21 – "how oft..forgive..till seven times?"
Mat 18:22 – "I say not..Until seven times"
Mat 22:25 – "there were with us seven brethren"
Matt 22:28 – "whose wife shall be of the seven?"
Mar 8:5 – "How many loaves have ye?..Seven"
Mar 8:6 – "he took the 7 loaves..gave thanks"
Mar 8:8 – "broken meat that was left 7 baskets"
Mar 8:20 – "when the seven among 4,000"
Mar 8:20 – "how many baskets..Seven"
Mar 12:20 – "there were seven brethren"
Mar 12:22 – "And the seven had her"
Mar 12:23 – "for the seven had her to wife"
Mar 16:9 – "Mary..out of whom..cast 7 devils"
Luk 2:36 – "Anna..seven years from her virginity"
Luk 8:2 – "Mary..out of whom went 7 devils"
Luk 11:26 – "seven other spirits more wicked"
Luk 17:4 – "trespass against thee 7 times"
Luk 17:4 – "seven times in a day turn again"
Luk 20:29 – "there were therefore 7 brethren"
Luk 20:31 – "in like manner the seven also"
Luk 20:33 – "for seven had her to wife"
Act 6:3 – "seven men of honest report"
Act 13:19 – "destroyed 7 nations in..Chanaan"
Act 19:14 – "there were seven sons of one Sceva"
Act 20:6 – "where we abode seven days"
Act 21:4 – "we tarried there seven days"
Act 21:8 – "Philip..which was one of the seven"
Act 21:27 – "when the 7 days were almost ended"
Act 28:14 – "found brethren..tarry..7 days"
Heb 11:30 – "walls..compassed about 7 days"

Ezk 45:23 – "7 days of the feast..prepare..offering"
Ezk 45:23 – "burnt offering..7 bullocks & 7 rams"
Ezk 45:23 – "burnt offering..daily the seven days"
Ezk 45:25 – "in the feast of the seven days"
Rev 1:4 – "John to the seven churches..in Asia"
Rev 1:4 – "the seven Spirits..before his throne"
Rev 1:11 – "send it unto the seven churches"
Rev 1:12 – "I saw seven golden candlesticks"
Rev 1:13 – "in the midst of the 7 candlesticks"
Rev 1:16 – "had in his right hand seven stars"
Rev 1:20 – "The mystery of the seven starts"
Rev 1:20 – "The mystery of..the 7..candlesticks"
Rev 1:20 – "7 stars..are angels of the 7 churches"
Rev 1:20 – "7 candlesticks..are the 7 churches"
Rev 2:1 – "holdeth the 7 stars in his right hand"
Rev 2:1 – "in the midst of..7 golden candlesticks"
Rev 3:1 – "he that hath the 7 Spirits of God"
Rev 3:1 – "saith he that hath..the seven stars"
Rev 4:5 – "7 lamps of fire..are the 7 Spirits"
Rev 5:1 – "a book written..with 7 seals"
Rev 5:5 – "to loose the seven seals thereof"
Rev 5:6 – "Lamb as..slain, having 7 horns"
Rev 5:6 – "7 eyes, which are the 7 Spirits"
Rev 8:2 – "And I saw the seven angels"
Rev 8:2 – "to them were given 7 trumpets"
Rev 8:6 – "7 angels which had the 7 trumpets"
Rev 10:3 – "7 thunders uttered their voices"
Rev 10:4 – "when the 7 thunders had uttered"
Rev 10:4 – "things..the 7 thunders uttered"
Rev 12:3 – "great red dragon, having 7 heads"
Rev 12:3 – "dragon..7 crowns upon his heads"
Rev 13:1 – "beast..having seven heads"
Rev 15:1 – "another sign in heaven..7 angels"
Rev 15:1 – "angels having the seven last plagues"
Rev 15:6 – "the 7 angels came out of the temple"
Rev 15:6 – "angels..having the seven plagues"
Rev 15:7 – "beasts gave unto the 7 angels..vials"
Rev 15:7 – "seven golden vials full..wrath of God"
Rev 15:8 – "the 7 plagues of the 7 angels"
Rev 16:1 – "great voice..saying to the 7 angels"
Rev 17:1 – "there came one of the seven angels"
Rev 17:1 – "angels which had the seven vials"
Rev 17:3 – "beast..having 7 heads and 10 horns"
Rev 17:7 – "beast..hath..7 heads and ten horns"
Rev 17:9 – "the 7 heads are 7 mountains"
Rev 17:10 – "7 kings; 5 are fallen, and one is"
Rev 17:11 – "beast..is the 8th, and is of the seven"
Rev 21:9 – "came unto me one of the 7 angels"
Rev 21:9 – "angels which had the seven vials"
Rev 21:9 – "vials full of the 7 last plagues"

7th – Seventh

Gen 2:2 – "On the 7th day God ended his work"
Gen 2:2 – "rested on the 7th day from all his work"
Gen 2:3 – "God blessed the 7th day..sanctified it"
Gen 8:4 – "seventh month" – see *DATES*

Exo 12:15 – "leavened bread..1st day..7th day"
Exo 12:16 – "in the 7th day..an holy convocation"
Exo 13:6 – "7th day shall be a feast to the LORD"
Exo 16:26 – "7th day, which is the sabbath"

Exo 16:27 – "went..some..on the 7ᵗʰ day..to gather"
Exo 16:29 – "no man..out of his place on..7ᵗʰ day"
Exo 16:30 – "So the people rested on the 7ᵗʰ day"
Exo 20:10 – "7ᵗʰ day is the Sabbath of the LORD"
Exo 20:11 – "LORD..rested the seventh day"
Exo 21:2 – "in the 7ᵗʰ..out free for nothing"
Exo 23:11 – "But the 7ᵗʰ year thou shalt let it rest"
Exo 23:12 – "on the 7ᵗʰ day thou shalt rest"
Exo 24:16 – "7ᵗʰ day he called unto Moses..cloud"
Exo 31:15 – "the seventh is the Sabbath of rest"
Exo 31:17 – "on the seventh day he rested"
Exo 34:21 – "on the seventh day thou shalt rest"
Exo 35:2 – "on the seventh day..an holy day"
Lev 13:5 – "priest shall look on him the 7ᵗʰ day"
Lev 13:6 – "priest..look on him again the 7ᵗʰ day"
Lev 13:27 – "priest..look upon him the 7ᵗʰ day"
Lev 13:32 – "in the seventh day..priest shall look"
Lev 13:34 – "in the seventh day..priest shall look"
Lev 13:51 – "look on the plague on the 7ᵗʰ day"
Lev 14:9 – "seventh day..shall shave all his hair"
Lev 14:39 – "come again the seventh day"
Lev 16:29 – "seventh month" – see *DATES*
Lev 23:3 – "the seventh day is the sabbath of rest"
Lev 23:8 – "seventh day is an holy convocation"
Lev 23:16 – "morrow after the seventh sabbath"
Lev 23:24 – "seventh month" – see *DATES*
Lev 23:27 – "seventh month" – see *DATES*
Lev 23:34 – "seventh month" – see *DATES*
Lev 23:39 – "seventh month" – see *DATES*
Lev 23:41 – " ye shall celebrate it in the 7ᵗʰ month"
Lev 25:4 – "7ᵗʰ year shall be a sabbath of rest"
Lev 25:9 – "seventh month" – see *DATES*
Lev 25:20 – "What shall we eat the seventh year?"
Num 6:9 – "shave his head...seventh day"
Num 7:48 – "seventh day"
Num 19:12 – "shall purify himself..on the 7ᵗʰ day"
Num 19:12 – "the 7ᵗʰ day he shall not be clean"
Num 19:19 – "sprinkle..the unclean..on..7ᵗʰ day"
Num 19:19 – "the 7ᵗʰ day he shall purify himself"
Num 28:25 – "the seventh day..holy convocation"
Num 29:1 – "seventh month" – see *DATES*
Num 29:7 – "seventh month" – see *DATES*
Num 29:12 – "seventh month" – see *DATES*
Num 29:32 – "And on the seventh day..two rams"
Num 31:19 – "purify..yourselves..on the 7ᵗʰ day"
Num 31:24 – "wash your clothes on the 7ᵗʰ day"
Deu 5:14 – "7ᵗʰ day is the sabbath of the LORD"
Deu 15:9 – "The seventh year, the year of release"
Deu 15:12 – "in the seventh year..let him go free"
Deu 16:8 – "7ᵗʰ day shall be a solemn assembly"
Jos 6:4 – "the 7ᵗʰ day..compass the city 7 times"
Jos 6:15 – "on the 7ᵗʰ day..they rose early"
Jos 6:16 – "7ᵗʰ time..priests blew w/ the trumpets"
Jos 19:40 – "7ᵗʰ lot came out for..Dan"
Jdg 14:15 – "on the 7ᵗʰ day...Entice thy husband"
Jdg 14:17 – "on the 7ᵗʰ day, that he told her"
Jdg 14:18 – "men of the city said..on the 7ᵗʰ day"
2Sa 12:18 – "seventh day, that the child died"
1Ki 8:2 – "Ethanim, which is the seventh month"
1Ki 18:44 – "And it came to pass at the 7ᵗʰ time"
1Ki 20:29 – "in the 7ᵗʰ day the battle was joined"

2Ki 11:4 – "7ᵗʰ year Jehoiada sent and fetched"
2Ki 12:1 – "In the 7ᵗʰ year of Jehu Jehoash began"
2Ki 18:9 – "in..7ᵗʰ year of Hoseha's son of Elah"
2Ki 25:8 – "seventh day" – see *DATES*
2Ki 25:25 – "7ᵗʰ month..Ishmael..smote Gedaliah"
1Ch 2:15 – "David the seventh"
1Ch 12:11 – "Eliel the seventh"
1Ch 24:10 – "The seventh to Hakkoz"
1Ch 25:14 – "The seventh to Jesharelah""
1Ch 26:3 – "Elioenai the seventh"
1Ch 26:5 – "Issachar the seventh"
1Ch 27:10 – "The 7ᵗʰ captain for the 7ᵗʰ month"
2Ch 5:3 – "feast which was in the 7ᵗʰ month"
2Ch 7:10 – "23ʳᵈ day of..7ᵗʰ month..sent..people"
2Ch 23:1 – "in the 7ᵗʰ year Jehoiada strengthened"
2Ch 31:7 – "foundation..finished..in the 7ᵗʰ month"
Ezr 3:1 – "when the 7ᵗʰ month was come"
Ezr 3:6 – "seventh month" – see *DATES*
Ezr 7:7 – "in the 7ᵗʰ year of Artaxerxes the king"
Ezr 7:8 – "which was in the 7ᵗʰ year of the king"
Neh 7:73 – "when the 7ᵗʰ month came"
Neh 8:2 – "seventh month" – see *DATES*
Neh 8:14 – "booths in the feast of the 7ᵗʰ month"
Neh 10:31 – "that we would leave the 7ᵗʰ year"
Est 1:10 – "on the 7ᵗʰ day..heart of the king..merry"
Est 2:16 – "seventh year" – see *DATES*
Jer 28:17 – "Hananiah..died..same year..7ᵗʰ month"
Jer 41:1 – "7ᵗʰ month..Ishmael..son of Nethaniah"
Jer 52:28 – "carried away captive: in the 7ᵗʰ year"
Ezk 20:1 – "seventh year" – see *DATES*
Ezk 30:20 – "seventh day" – see *DATES*
Ezk 45:20 – "shalt do the 7ᵗʰ day of the month"
Ezk 45:25 – "seventh month" – see *DATES*
Hag 2:1 – "seventh month" – see *DATES*
Zec 7:5 – "fasted..mourned in the 5ᵗʰ & 7ᵗʰ month"
Zec 8:19 – "and the fast of the seventh"
Matt 22:26 – "and the third, unto the seventh"
Joh 4:52 – "at the 7ᵗʰ hour the fever left him"
Heb 4:4 – "For he spake..of the seventh day"
Heb 4:4 – "God did rest the seventh day"
Jud 14 – "Enoch also, the 7ᵗʰ from Adam"
Rev 8:1 – "when he had opened the 7ᵗʰ seal"
Rev 10:7 – "the voice of the seventh angel"
Rev 11:15 – "And the seventh angel sounded"
Rev 16:17 – "seventh angel poured out his vial"
Rev 21:20 – "the seventh, chrysolyte"

Sevenfold

Gen 4:15 – "vengeance..taken on him sevenfold"
Gen 4:24 – "If Cain shall be avenged sevenfold"
Psa 79:12 – "render..our neighbours sevenfold"
Pro 6:31 – "if..found, he shall restore sevenfold"
Isa 30:26 – "light of the sun shall be sevenfold"

Sevens

Listed at the end of Section One under the heading, **Indefinite Numbers**.

7½

2Sa 2:11 – "David..king..Hebron..7 years & 6 mos."
2Sa 5:5 – "Hebron..reigned..7 years & 6 months"
1Ch 3:4 – "Hebron..reigned 7 years & 6 months"

Eight

Eight in the Bible is the number of new beginnings, a new creation and the new birth. The "eighth day of the week" is of course the first day of a new week – hence the concept of new beginnings.

8 - Eight

Gen 17:12 – "he..8 days old shall be circumcised"
Gen 21:4 – "Abraham circumcised..Isaac..8 days"
Gen 22:23 – "these 8 Milcah did bear to Nahor"
Exo 26:25 – "shall be 8 boards and their sockets"
Exo 36:30 – "there were eight boards"
Num 7:8 – "four wagons and eight oxen"
Num 29:29 – "on the sixth day eight bullocks"
Jdg 3:8 – "served Cushanrishathaim eight years"
Jdg 12:14 – Abdon – "he judged Israel eight years"
1Sa17:12 – "Jesse..had eight sons"
1Ki 7:10 – "foundation..great stones..of 8 cubits"
2Ki 8:17 – "reigned 8 years in Jerusalem"
2Ki 22:1 – "Josiah was 8 years old..began to reign"
1Ch 24:4 – "eight among the sons of Ithamar"
2Ch 21:5 – "Jehoram..8 years in Jerusalem"
2Ch 21:20 – "reigned in Jerusalem 8 years"

2Ch 29:17 – "the house of the LORD in 8 days"
2Ch 34:1 – "Josiah was 8 years old..began..reign"
2Ch 36:9 – "Jehoiachin..8 years old..began..reign"
Ecc 11:2 – "Give a portion to 7, and also to 8"
Jer 41:15 – "escaped from Johanan with 8 men"
Ezk 40:9 – "porch of the gate, eight cubits"
Ezk 40:31 – "the going up to it had eight steps"
Ezk 40:34 – "the going up to it had eight steps"
Ezk 40:37 – "the going up to it had eight steps"
Ezk 40:41 – "eight tables..slew..sacrifices"
Mic 5:5 – "raise against him...eight principal men"
Luk 2:21 – "when eight days were accomplished"
Luk 9:28 – "eight days after these sayings"
Joh 20:26 – "after 8 days..disciples were within"
Act 9:33 – "Aenas, which had kept his bed 8 years"
1Pe 3:20 – "eight souls were saved by water"

8th – Eighth

Exo 22:30 – "on the 8th day thou shalt give it me"
Lev 9:1 – "on the eighth day"
Lev 12:3 – "in the eighth day..circumcised"
Lev 14:10 – "on the 8th day he shall take..lambs"
Lev 14:23 – "eighth day for his cleansing"
Lev 15:14 – "eighth day..turtledoves..pigeons"
Lev 15:29 – "8th day..take unto her two turtles"
Lev 22:27 – "from the 8th day..it shall be accepted"
Lev 23:36 – "8th day shall be an holy convocation"
Lev 23:39 – "eighth day shall be a sabbath"
Lev 25:22 – "ye shall sow the eighth year"
Num 6:10 – "eighth day he shall bring 2 turtles"
Num 7:54 – "eighth day offered..Manasseh"
Num 29:35 – "8th day..have a solemn assembly"
1Ki 6:38 – "the month Bul, which is the 8th month"
1Ki 8:66 – "On..8th day he sent the people away"
1Ki 12:32 – "eighth month" – see *DATES*
1Ki 12:33 – "eighth month" – see *DATES*

2Ki 24:12 – "king of Babylon took him in..8th year"
1Ch 12:12 – "Johanan the eighth"
1Ch 24:10 – "the eighth to Abijah"
1Ch 25:15 – "The eighth to Jeshaiah, he, his sons"
1Ch 26:5 – "Peulthai the eighth"
1Ch 27:11 – "8th captain for..8th month..Sibbecai"
2Ch 7:9 – "8th day..made a solemn assembly"
2Ch 29:17 – "eighth day" – see *DATES*
2Ch 34:3 – "8th year..began to seek..God"
Neh 8:18 – "the 8th day was a solemn assembly"
Ezk 43:27 – "8th day..make your burnt offerings"
Zec 1:1 – "eighth month" – see *DATES*
Luk 1:59 – "on the 8th day..came to circumcise"
Act 7:8 – "Isaac..circumcised him the 8th day"
Phil 3:5 – "circumcised the 8th day"
2Pet 2:5 – "saved Noah the eighth person"
Rev 17:11 – "beast..is the 8th, and is of the seven"
Rev 21:20 – "the eighth, beryl"

Nine

In Bible numerology nine is considered the number of fruitfulness. The primary reason for this concept revolves around the nine aspects of the fruit of the Spirit in Galatians chapter five.

This section includes:

a)   9 – Nine (cardinal number)
b)   9th – Ninth (ordinal number)
c)   Mixed Numbers 9½ and 9⅔

9 – Nine

Num 29:26 – "And on the fifth day nine bullocks"
Deu 3:11 – "Og..bedstead..9 cubits was the length"
Jos 15:44 – "nine cities with their villages"
Jos 15:54 – "nine cities with their villages"
Jos 21:16 – "nine cities out of those two tribes"
2Ki 17:1 – "Hoshea..reign..nine years"
1Ch 3:8 – "Elishama..Eliada..nine"
Neh 11:1 – "nine parts to dwell in other cities"
Luk 17:17 – "but where are the nine?"

9th – Ninth

Lev 23:32 – "Sabbath..9th day of the month"
Lev 25:22 – "eat yet of old fruit until the 9th year"
Num 7:60 – "ninth day..Benjamin, offered"
2Ki 17:6 – "9th year of Hoshea..king..took Samaria"
2Ki 18:10 – "9th year of Hoshea's king of Israel"
2Ki 25:1 – "ninth year" – see *DATES*
2Ki 25:3 – "ninth year" – see *DATES*
1Ch 12:12 – "Elzabad the 9th"
1Ch 24:11 – "The ninth to Jeshuah"
1Ch 25:16 – "The 9th to Mattaniah..sons..12"
1Ch 27:12 – "9th captain for..9th month..Abiezer"
Ezr 10:9 – "ninth month" – see *DATES*
Jer 36:9 – "ninth month" – see *DATES*
Jer 36:22 – "king sat..winterhouse in..9th month"
Jer 39:1 – "ninth year" – see *DATES*

Jer 39:2 – "ninth day" – see *DATES*
Jer 52:4 – "ninth year" – see *DATES*
Jer 52:6 – "ninth day" – see *DATES*
Ezk 24:1 – "ninth year" – see *DATES*
Hag 2:10 – "ninth month" – see *DATES*
Hag 2:18 – "ninth month" – see *DATES*
Zec 7:1 – "ninth month" – see *DATES*
Mat 20:5 – "went out about the 6th and 9th hour"
Mat 27:45 – "over all the land unto the 9th hour"
Mat 27:46 – "about the ninth hour Jesus cried"
Mar 15:33 – "darkness..whole land..9th hour"
Mar 15:34 – "ninth hour Jesus cried"
Luk 23:44 – "darkness over..earth..until 9th hour"
Act 3:1 – "the hour of prayer, being the 9th hour"
Act 10:3 – "in a vision..about the 9th hour"
Act 10:30 – "at the 9th hour I prayed in my house"
Rev 21:20 – "the ninth, a topaz"

9½

Num 34:13 – "land..to give unto the 9½ tribe(s)"
Jos 13:7 – "divide this land unto the 9½ tribe(s)"
Jos 14:2 – "inheritance..for the 9½ tribe(s)"

9⅔

2Sa 24:8 – "came to Jerusalem..9 mos. & 20 days"

Ten

Ten in Scripture is often associated with the Gentiles. Others find numerological applications in kingship, the Bible itself, as well as in law, government and responsibility.

This section includes:

a)   10 – Ten (cardinal number)
b)   10th – Tenth (ordinal number)
c)   Tenfold
d)   Tens

10 – Ten

Gen 16:3 – "Abram..dwelt 10 years in..Canaan"
Gen 18:32 – "Peradventure ten shall be found"
Gen 18:32 – "I will not destroy it for ten's sake"
Gen 24:10 – "servant took 10 camels..his master"
Gen 24:22 – "bracelets..10 shekels weight of gold"
Gen 24:55 – "a few days, at the least ten"
Gen 31:7 – "changed my wages ten times"
Gen 31:41 – hast changed my wages ten times"
Gen 32:15 – "10 bulls, 20 she asses, and 10 foals"
Gen 42:3 – "Joseph's ten brethren went..Egypt"
Gen 45:23 – "10 asses laden..good things of Egypt"
Gen 45:23 – "10 she asses laden w/ corn & bread"
Exo 26:1 – "make..tabernacle with ten curtains"
Exo 26:16 – "Ten cubits..the length of a board"
Exo 27:12 – "their pillars 10, and their sockets 10"
Exo 34:28 – "upon the tables..10 commandments"
Exo 36:8 – "ten curtains of fine twined linen"
Exo 36:21 – "length of a board was ten cubits"
Exo 38:12 – "west side..their pillars ten"
Exo 38:12 – "west side..their sockets ten"
Lev 26:26 – "10 women..bake..bread in one oven"
Lev 27:5 – "estimation shall be..ten shekels"
Lev 27:7 – "estimation shall be...ten shekels"
Num 7:14 – "One spoon of ten shekels of gold"
Num 7:20 – "One spoon of gold of 10 shekels"
Num 7:26 – "One golden spoon of 10 shekels"
Num 7:32 – "One golden spoon of 10 shekels"
Num 7:38 – "One golden spoon of 10 shekels"
Num 7:44 – "One golden spoon of 10 shekels"
Num 7:50 – "One golden spoon of 10 shekels"
Num 7:56 – "One golden spoon of 10 shekels"
Num 7:62 – "One golden spoon of 10 shekels"
Num 7:68 – "One golden spoon of 10 shekels"
Num 7:74 – "One golden spoon of 10 shekels"
Num 7:80 – "One golden spoon of 10 shekels"
Num 7:86 – "spoons..incense..10 shekels apiece"
Num 11:19 – "nor 5 days..10 days, nor 20 days"
Num 11:32 – "quails..gathered..ten homers"
Num 14:22 – "tempted me now these ten times"
Num 29:23 – "And on the fourth day ten bullocks"
Deu 4:13 – "ten commandments..2 tables of stone"
Deu 10:4 – "the first writing..10 commandments"
Jos 15:57 – "ten cities with their villages"
Jos 17:5 – "there fell ten portions to Manasseh"
Jos 21:5 – "children of Kohath had..ten cities"
Jos 21:26 – "All the cities were 10..of Kohath"
Jos 22:14 – "And with him ten princes"
Jdg 6:27 – "Gideon took ten men of his servants"
Jdg 12:11 – "Elon..judged Israel ten years"
Jdg 17:10 – "I will give thee 10 shekels of silver"
Jdg 20:10 – "we will take ten men of an hundred"
Rut 1:4 – "they dwelled there about ten years"
Rut 4:2 – "took ten men of the elders of the city"
1Sa 1:8 – "am not I better to thee than ten sons?"
1Sa 17:17 – "Take now..these ten loaves"
1Sa 17:18 – "And carry these ten cheeses"
1Sa 25:5 – "David sent out ten young men"
1Sa 25:38 – "10 days after..LORD smote Nabal"
2Sa 15:16 – "10 women, which were concubines"

2Sa 18:11 – "given thee ten shekels of silver"
2Sa 18:15 – "ten young men..bare Joab's armour"
2Sa 19:43 – "We have ten parts in the king"
2Sa 20:3 – "ten women his concubines"
1Ki 4:23 – "Ten fat oxen"
1Ki 6:3 – "And the porch..10 cubits..the breadth"
1Ki 6:23 – "two cherubims..each ten cubits high"
1Ki 6:24 – "1 wing unto..the other were 10 cubits"
1Ki 6:25 – "the other cherub was ten cubits"
1Ki 6:26 – "height of the 1 cherub was 10 cubits"
1Ki 7:10 – "foundation..great stones..of 10 cubits"
1Ki 7:23 – "molten sea, 10 cubits from the 1 brim"
1Ki 7:24 – "knops compassing it, ten in a cubit"
1Ki 7:27 – "he made ten bases of brass"
1Ki 7:37 – "After this manner..made the 10 bases"
1Ki 7:38 – "Then made he ten lavers of brass"
1Ki 7:38 – "upon every 1 of the 10 bases 1 laver"
1Ki 7:43 – "the 10 bases, & 10 lavers on the bases"
1Ki 11:31 – "said to Jeroboam, Take..ten pieces"
1Ki 11:31 – "will give ten tribes to thee"
1Ki 11:35 – "will give it unto thee, even ten tribes"
1Ki 14:3 – "take with thee 10 loaves & cracknels"
2Ki 5:5 – "took with him ten talents of silver"
2Ki 5:5 – "took with him..ten changes of raiment"
2Ki 13:7 – "50 horsemen, and 10 chariots"
2Ki 15:17 – "Menahem..reigned 10 years..Samaria"
2Ki 20:9 – "shall..shadow go forward 10 degrees"
2Ki 20:9 – "or go back ten degrees?"
2Ki 20:10 – "light thing..to go down 10 degrees"
2Ki 20:10 – "shadow return backward 10 degrees"
2Ki 20:11 – "Isaiah..brought..shadow 10 degrees"
2Ki 25:25 – "Ishmael..10 men..smote Gedaliah"
1Ch 6:61 – "the sons of Kohath..by lot, 10 cities"
2Ch 4:1 – "altar of brass..10 cubits the height"
2Ch 4:2 – "molten sea of ten cubits..brim to brim"
2Ch 4:3 – "oxen..10 in a cubit, compassing the sea"
2Ch 4:6 – "He made also ten lavers"
2Ch 4:7 – "he made 10 candlesticks of gold"
2Ch 4:8 – "made also ten tables..in the temple"
2Ch 14:1 – "Asa..reigned..land was quiet 10 years"
Ezr 8:24 – "Sherebiah, Hasabiah..ten..brethren"
Neh 4:12 – "they said unto us ten times"
Neh 5:18 – "once in 10 days store..all sorts..wine"
Est 9:10 – "The ten sons of Haman..slew they"
Est 9:12 – "the ten sons of Haman"
Est 9:13 – "let Haman's ten sons be hanged"
Est 9:14 – "they hanged Haman's ten sons"
Job 19:3 – "ten times have ye reproached me"
Psa 33:2 – "psaltery and..instrument of 10 strings"
Psa 92:3 – "Upon an instrument of ten strings"
Psa 144:9 – "an instrument of ten strings"
Ecc 7:19 – "ten mighty men which are in the city"
Isa 5:10 – "10 acres of vineyard..yield one bath"
Isa 38:8 – "sun dial of Ahaz, 10 degrees backward"
Isa 38:8 – "the sun returned ten degrees"
Jer 41:1 – "Ishmael..ten men with him"
Jer 41:2 – "then arose Ishmael..ten men..with him"
Jer 41:8 – "ten men..found..said unto Ishmael"
Jer 42:7 – "after 10 days..word of the LORD came"

Ezk 40:11 – "breadth..entry of the gate, 10 cubits"
Ezk 41:2 – "breadth of the door was 10 cubits"
Ezk 42:4 – "a walk of 10 cubits breadth inward"
Ezk 45:14 – "which is an homer of ten baths"
Ezk 45:14 – "for ten baths are an homer"
Dan 1:12 – "prove thy servants..ten days"
Dan 1:14 – "proved them ten days"
Dan 1:15 – "at the end of ten days..countenances"
Dan 1:20 – "10 times better than..the magicians"
Dan 7:7 – "fourth beast..it had ten horns"
Dan 7:20 – "the ten horns that were in his head"
Dan 7:24 – "ten horns..are ten kings"
Amo 5:3 – "went out by an 100 shall leave ten"
Amo 6:9 – "if there remain ten men in one house"
Hag 2:16 – "heap of 20 measures..were but ten"
Zec 5:2 – "flying roll..breadth thereof 10 cubits"
Zec 8:23 – "ten men shall take hold"
Mat 4:25 – "Decapolis" = ten cities
Mat 20:24 – "when the ten heard it..indignation"
Mat 25:1 – "heaven likened unto ten virgins"
Mat 25:28 – "unto him which hath 10 talents"

Mar 5:20 – "Decapolis" = ten cities
Mar 10:41 – "the ten heard it..displeased"
Luk 14:19 – "I have bought five yoke of oxen"
Luk 15:8 – "woman having ten pieces of silver"
Luk 17:12 – "ten men that were lepers"
Luk 17:17 – "Were there not ten cleansed?"
Luk 19:13 – "he called his ten servants"
Luk 19:13 – "delivered them ten pounds"
Luk 19:16 – "thy pound hath gained ten pounds"
Luk 19:17 – "have..authority over ten cities"
Luk 19:24 – "give it to him that hath ten pounds"
Luk 19:25 – "Lord, he hath ten pounds"
Act 25:6 – "tarried..more than 10 days"
Rev 2:10 – "have tribulation ten days"
Rev 12:3 – "red dragon, having..ten horns"
Rev 13:1 – "beast rise up..having..ten horns"
Rev 13:1 – "beast..upon his horns ten crowns"
Rev 17:3 – "beast..having 7 heads and 10 horns"
Rev 17:7 – "beast..hath..7 heads and ten horns"
Rev 17:12 – "the ten horns..are ten kings"
Rev 17:16 – "the ten horns..hate the whore

10th – Tenth

This section lists "tenth" as an ordinal number (as in ninth, tenth, eleventh...). See the fraction **one-tenth** for those occurances in Scripture where "tenth" is used as a fraction. In most of the occurences where the word "tenth" is found in the sense of the fraction *one-tenth*, it will appear as "tenth part" or "tenth deal(s)" – see the words **Part** and **Deal** in the *Index of Numbered Items*.

The term "tenth" also presents a unique situation in Scripture with relation to the doctrine of tithing where God requests that 10%, or one-tenth of one's income be given to him in several Old Testament contexts. Although this is a concept better dealt with in the section covering the fraction one-tenth, we wish to notify the reader of this special case where:

1) The phrase "the tenth" appears referring to the tithe – e.g. Gen28:22;
2) The word "tithe" itself literally means one-tenth. For more study please consult the word "tithe" and its forms in a standard concordance.

Gen 8:5 – "tenth month" – see *DATES*
Exo 12:3 – "tenth day of this month..take..a lamb"
Lev 16:29 – "tenth day" – see *DATES*
Lev 23:27 – "tenth day" – see *DATES*
Lev 25:9 – "tenth day" – see *DATES*
Num 7:66 – "On the tenth day..Dan, offered"
Num 29:7 – "tenth day" – see *DATES*
Deu 23:2 – "bastard..not enter..10th generation"
Deu 23:3 – "Ammonite..Moabite..10th generation"
Jos 4:19 – "tenth day" – see *DATES*
2Ki 25:1 – "tenth month..tenth day" – see *DATES*
1Ch 12:13 – "Jeremiah the 10th"
1Ch 24:11 – "the tenth to Shechaniah"
1Ch 25:17 – "The tenth to Shimei"
1Ch 27:13 – "10th captain for the 10th month"
Ezr 10:16 – "tenth month" – see *DATES*
Est 2:16 – "tenth month" – see *DATES*
Jer 32:1 – "10th year of Zedekiah king of Judah"
Jer 39:1 – "tenth month" – see *DATES*
Jer 52:4 – "tenth month..tenth day" – see *DATES*

Jer 52:12 – "tenth day" – see *DATES*
Ezk 20:1 – "tenth day" – see *DATES*
Ezk 24:1 – "tenth month..tenth day" – see *DATES*
Ezk 29:1 – "tenth year..tenth month" – see *DATES*
Ezk 33:21 – "tenth month" – see *DATES*
Ezk 40:1 – tenth day" – see *DATES*
Zec 8:19 – "and the fast of the tenth"
Joh 1:39 – "for it was about the tenth hour"
Rev 21:20 – "the tenth, a chrysoprasus"

Tenfold

Luk 19:16 – "thy pound hath gained ten pounds"

Tens

Listed at the end of Section One under the heading, **Indefinite Numbers.**

Eleven

The number eleven in Scripture is most commonly associated with judgment and disorder.

11 – Eleven

Gen 32:22 – "rose up that night, and..his 11 sons"
Gen 37:9 – "eleven stars made obeisance to me"
Exo 26:7 – "eleven curtains thou shalt make"
Exo 26:8 – "11 curtains..be all of one measure"
Exo 36:14 – "eleven curtains he made them"
Exo 36:15 – "the eleven curtains were of one size"
Num 29:20 – "And on the third day 11 bullocks"
Deu 1:2 – "There are eleven days' journey"
Jos 15:51 – Judah – "11 cities with their villages"
2Ki 23:36 – "Jehoiakim..reigned 11 years"
2Ki 24:18 – "Zedekiah..reigned 11 years"
2Ch 36:5 – "Jehoiakim..reigned 11 years"
2Ch 36:11 – "Zedekiah..reigned 11 years"
Jer 52:1 – "Zedekiah..reigned 11 years"
Ezk 40:49 – "the porch..breadth eleven cubits"
Mat 28:16 – "eleven disciples went away"
Mar 16:14 – "he appeared unto the eleven"
Luk 24:9 – "told all these things unto the eleven"
Luk 24:33 – "found the eleven gathered together"
Act 1:26 – "was numbered with the 11 apostles"
Act 2:14 – "Peter, standing up with the eleven"

11th – Eleventh

Num 7:72 – "eleventh day" – Asher's offering
Deu 1:3 – "eleventh month" – see *DATES*
1Ki 6:38 – "eleventh year" – see *DATES*
2Ki 9:29 – "11th year of Joram..began Ahaziah"
2Ki 25:2 – "city was besieged unto the 11th year"
1Ch 12:13 – "Machbanai the eleventh"
1Ch 24:12 – "The eleventh to Eliashib"
1Ch 25:18 – "The eleventh to Azareel"
1Ch 27:14 – "The 11th captain for the 11th month"
Jer 1:3 – "eleventh year" – see *DATES*
Jer 39:2 – "eleventh year" – see *DATES*
Jer 52:5 – "city was besieged unto the 11th year"
Ezk 26:1 – "eleventh year" – see *DATES*
Ezk 30:20 – "eleventh year" – see *DATES*
Ezk 31:1 – "eleventh year" – see *DATES*
Zec 1:7 – "eleventh month" – see *DATES*
Mat 20:6 – "about the 11th hour he went out"
Mat 20:9 – "were hired about the 11th hour"
Rev 21:20 – "the eleventh, a jacinth"

Twelve

The number twelve is the number of the nation Israel, government perfection and Christ's kingdom.

This section includes:

a)   12 – Twelve (cardinal number)
b)   12th – Twelfth (ordinal number)
c)   Noon – Also Noonday, Noontide and Midday
d)   Midnight

12 – Twelve

Gen 14:4 – "12 years they served Chedorlaomer"
Gen 17:20 – "Ishmael..12 princes shall he beget"
Gen 25:16 – "Ishmael..12 princes"
Gen 35:22 – "Now the sons of Jacob were twelve"
Gen 42:13 – "Thy servants are 12 brethren"
Gen 42:32 – "12 brethren, sons of our father"
Gen 49:28 – "these are the 12 tribes of Israel"
Exo 15:27 – "Elim, where were 12 wells of water"
Exo 24:4 – "12 pillars according to the 12 tribes"
Exo 28:21 – "stones shall be with the names..12"
Exo 28:21 – "according to the twelve tribes"
Exo 39:14 – "stones..12 according to their names"
Exo 39:14 – "according to the twelve tribes"
Lev 24:5 – "fine flour, and bake 12 cakes thereof"

Num 1:44 – "princes of Israel being twelve men"
Num 7:3 – "twelve oxen" – offerings of the tribes
Num 7:84 – "twelve chargers of silver"
Num 7:84 – "twelve silver bowls"
Num 7:84 – "twelve spoons of gold"
Num 7:86 – "golden spoons were twelve"
Num 7:87 – "twelve bullocks"
Num 7:87 – "the rams twelve"
Num 7:87 – "the lambs of the first year twelve"
Num 7:87 – "kids..goats for sin offering twelve"
Num 17:2 – "the house of their fathers 12 rods"
Num 17:6 – "their fathers' houses, even 12 rods"
Num 29:17 – "2nd day..offer 12 young bullocks"
Num 33:9 – "in Elim were 12 fountains of water"
Deu 1:23 – "twelve men of you, one of a tribe"
Jos 3:12 – "twelve men out of the tribes of Israel"

Jos 4:2 – "twelve men out of the people"
Jos 4:3 – "out of the midst of Jordan..12 stones"
Jos 4:4 – "Joshua called the twelve men"
Jos 4:8 – "12 stones out of the midst of Jordan"
Jos 4:9 – "set up 12 stones in the midst of Jordan"
Jos 4:20 – "12 stones..they took out of Jordan"
Jos 18:24 – "twelve cities with their villages"
Jos 19:15 – "twelve cities with their villages"
Jos 21:7 – "Merari by their families..12 cities"
Jos 21:40 – "Merari..by their lot 12 cities"
Jud 19:29 – "knife.. divided her..into 12 pieces"
2Sa 2:15 – "arose..by number 12 of Benjamin"
2Sa 2:15 – "and 12 of the servants of David"
1Ki 4:7 – "Solomon had 12 officers over all Israel"
1Ki 7:15 – "pillars..line of 12 cubits did compass"
1Ki 7:25 – "It stood upon twelve oxen"
1Ki 7:44 – "one sea, and 12 oxen under the sea"
1Ki 10:20 – "12 lions stood there on..the six steps"
1Ki 11:30 – "Ahijah..rent it in twelve pieces"
1Ki 16:23 – "Omri..reign over Israel, 12 years"
1Ki 18:31 – "Elijah took 12 stones"
1Ki 19:19 – "Elisha..plowing w/ 12 yoke of oxen"
2Ki 3:1 – "Jehoram..reigned twelve years"
2Ki 21:1 – "Manasseh..12 years old..began..reign"
1Ch 6:63 – "unto the sons of Merari..12 cities"
1Ch 20:6 – "fingers and toes were 24"
1Ch 25:9 – "2nd to Gedaliah..his brethren..sons..12"
1Ch 25:10 – "3rd to Zaccur..sons..brethren..12"
1Ch 25:11 – "4th to Izri..sons..brethren, were 12"
1Ch 25:12 – "5th to Nethaniah..sons..brethren..12"
1Ch 25:13 – "6th to Bukkiah..sons..brethren..12"
1Ch 25:14 – "7th to Jesharelah..sons..brethren..12"
1Ch 25:15 – "8th to Jeshaiah..sons..brethren..12"
1Ch 25:16 – "9th to Mattaniah..sons..brethren..12"
1Ch 25:17 – "10th to Shimei..sons..brethren..12"
1Ch 25:18 – "11th to Azareel..sons..brethren..12"
1Ch 25:19 – "12th to Hashabiah..sons..brethren..12"
1Ch 25:20 – "13th to Shubael..sons..brethren..12"
1Ch 25:21 – "14th to Mattithiah..sons..brethren..12"
1Ch 25:22 – "15th to Jeremoth..sons..brethren..12"
1Ch 25:23 – "16th to Hananiah..sons..brethren..12"
1Ch 25:24 – "17th to Joshbekashah..sons..12"
1Ch 25:25 – "18th to Hanani..sons..brethren..12"
1Ch 25:26 – "19th to Mallothi..sons..brethren..12"
1Ch 25:27 – "20th to Eliathah..sons..brethren..12"
1Ch 25:28 – "21st to Hothir..sons..brethren..12"
1Ch 25:29 – "22nd to Giddalti..sons..brethren..12"
1Ch 25:30 – "23rd to Mahazioth..sons..brethren..12"
1Ch 25:31 – "24th to Romamtiezer..sons..12"
2Ch 4:4 – "It stood upon twelve oxen"
2Ch 4:15 – "One sea, and twelve oxen under it."
2Ch 9:19 – "12 lions stood there on the one side"
2Ch 33:1 – "Manasseh..12 years old..began..reign"
Ezr 6:17 – "dedication of this house..12 he goats"
Ezr 8:24 – "I separated 12 of the chief..priests"
Ezr 8:35 – "burnt offerings..12 bullocks for..Israel"
Ezr 8:35 – "burnt offerings..12 he goats"
Neh 5:14 – "20th..unto the 32nd..that is, 12 years"
Est 2:12 – "12 months..the manner of the women"
Job 3:6 – "the number of the months"
Jer 52:20 – "12 brasen bulls..under the bases"

Jer 52:21 – "fillet of 12 cubits did compass it"
Ezk 43:16 – "altar shall be twelve cubits long"
Ezk 43:16 – "altar shall be..twelve broad"
Ezk 47:13 – "inherit the land acc. to..12 tribes"
Dan 4:29 – "At the end of twelve months"
Mat 9:20 – "woman..with..issue of blood 12 years"
Mat 10:1 – "called unto him his 12 disciples"
Mat 10:2 – "names of the 12 apostles are these"
Mat 10:5 – "These 12 Jesus sent forth..saying, Go"
Mat 11:1 – "commanding his 12 disciples"
Mat 14:20 – "fragments..remained 12 baskets full"
Mat 19:28 – "ye also shall sit upon 12 thrones"
Mat 19:28 – "ye also..judging..12 tribes of Israel"
Mat 20:17 – "Jesus..took the 12 disciples apart"
Mat 26:14 – "one of the twelve..Judas Iscariot"
Mat 26:20 – "he sat down with the twelve"
Mat 26:47 – "Judas, one of the twelve, came"
Mat 26:53 – "more than twelve legions of angels?"
Mar 3:14 – "And he ordained twelve"
Mar 4:10 – "they that were about him with the 12"
Mar 5:25 – "woman..issue of blood 12 years"
Mar 5:42 – "damsel arose..age of 12 years"
Mar 6:7 – "he called unto him the twelve"
Mar 6:43 – "twelve baskets full of fragments"
Mar 8:19 – "how many baskets..Twelve"
Mar 9:35 – "sat down, and called the twelve"
Mar 10:32 – "And he took again the twelve"
Mar 11:11 – "unto Bethany with the twelve"
Mar 14:10 – "Judas Iscariot, one of the twelve"
Mar 14:17 – "he cometh with the twelve"
Mar 14:20 – "It is one of the twelve"
Mar 14:43 – "Judas, one of the twelve"
Luk 2:42 – "when he was twelve years old"
Luk 6:13 – "disciples..chose twelve..apostles"
Luk 8:1 – "and the twelve were with him"
Luk 8:42 – "daughter, about 12 years of age"
Luk 8:43 – "issue of blood 12 years"
Luk 9:1 – "Then he called his 12 disciples"
Luk 9:12 – "then came the 12, and said"
Luk 9:17 – "fragments that remained..12 baskets"
Luk 18:31 – "he took unto him the twelve"
Luk 22:3 – "Judas..being of the number of the 12"
Luk 22:14 – "sat down..12 apostles with him"
Luk 22:30 – "judging the 12 tribes of Israel"
Luk 22:47 – "Judas, one of the 12..to kiss him"
Joh 6:13 – "gathered them..filled 12 baskets"
Joh 6:67 – "then said Jesus unto the twelve"
Joh 6:70 – "chosen you 12, and one..is a devil"
Joh 6:71 – "Judas Iscariot..one of the twelve"
Joh 11:9 – "Are there not 12 hours in the day?"
Joh 20:24 – "Thomas, one of the twelve"
Act 6:2 – "Then the 12 called the multitude"
Act 7:8 – "Jacob begat the twelve patriarchs"
Act 19:7 – "all the men were about twelve"
Act 24:11 – "12 days since I went up to Jerusalem"
Act 26:7 – "Unto which promise our 12 tribes"
1Co 15:5 – "seen of Cephas, then of the twelve"
Jam 1:1 – "to the 12 tribes scattered abroad"
Rev 12:1 – "upon her head a crown of 12 stars"
Rev 21:12 – "a wall..had twelve gates"
Rev 21:12 – "and at the gates twelve angels"

Rev 21:12 – "names of the twelves tribes"
Rev 21:14 – "wall of the city had 12 foundations"
Rev 21:14 – "names of the 12 apostles"
Rev 21:21 – "And the 12 gates were 12 pearls"
Rev 22:2 – "tree of life..12 manner of fruits"

12th – Twelfth

Num 7:78 – "twelfth day..Naphtali offered"
1Ki 19:19 – "12 yoke oxen and he with the 12th"
2Ki 8:25 – "12th year of Joram..Ahaziah..to reign"
2Ki 17:1 – "In..12th year of Ahaz..began Hoshea"
2Ki 25:27 – "twelfth month" – see *DATES*
1Ch 24:12 – "the twelfth to Jakim"
1Ch 25:19 – "the twelfth to Hashabiah"
1Ch 27:15 – "the 12th captain for the 12th month"
2Ch 34:3 – "12th year he began to purge Judah"
Ezr 8:31 – "twelfth day" – see *DATES*
Est 3:7 – "12th year..12th month" – see *DATES*
Est 3:13 – "twelfth month" – see *DATES*
Est 8:12 – "twelfth month" – see *DATES*
Est 9:1 – "twelfth month" – see *DATES*
Jer 52:31 – "twelfth month" – see *DATES*
Ezk 29:1 – "twelfth day" – see *DATES*
Ezk 32:1 – "12th year..12th month" – see *DATES*
Ezk 32:17 – "twelfth year" – see *DATES*
Ezk 33:21 – "twelfth year" – see *DATES*
Rev 21:20 – "the twelfth, an amethyst"

Noon, Noonday, Noontide & Midday – 12:00 pm

Gen 43:16 – "shall dine with me at noon"
Gen 43:25 – "Joseph came at noon"
Deu 28:29 – "tho shalt grope at noonday"
2Sa 4:5 – "Ishbosheth..lay on a bed at noon"
1Ki 18:29 – "when midday was past"

1Ki 18:26 – "called on..Baal..until noon"
1Ki 18:27 – "at noon..Elijah mocked them"
1Ki 20:16 – "And they went out at noon."
2Ki 4:20 – "he sat on her knees till noon"
Neh 8:3 – "from the morning until midday"
Job 5:14 – "grope in the noonday"
Job 11:17 – "clearer than the noonday"
Psa 37:6 – "thy judgment as the noonday"
Psa 55:17 – "Evening, morning, and at noon"
Psa 91:6 – "destruction..wasteth at noonday"
Son 1:7 – "makest thy flock to rest at noon"
Isa 16:3 – "in the midst of the noonday"
Isa 58:10 – "thy darkness be as the noonday"
Isa 59:10 – "we stumble at noonday"
Jer 6:4 – "arise, and let us go up at noon"
Jer 15:8 – "I have brought..a spoiler at noonday"
Jer 20:16 – "the shouting at noontide"
Amo 8:9 – "the sun to go down at noon"
Zep 2:4 – "drive out Ashdod at the noon day"
Act 22:6 – "nigh unto Damascus about noon"
Act 26:13 – "at midday, O king, I saw"

Midnight – 12:00 am

Exo 11:4 – "About midnight will I go out"
Exo 12:29 – "at midnight the LORD smote"
Jdg 16:3 – "Samson lay till midnight"
Jdg 16:3 – "Samson..arose at midgnight"
Rut 3:8 – "at midnight..the man was afraid"
1Ki 3:20 – "she arose at midnight..took my son"
Job 34:20 – "people shall be troubled at midnight"
Psa 119:62 – "At midnight I will rise..give thanks"
Mat 25:6 – "at midnight, there was a cry made"
Mar 13:35 – "at even, or at midnight"
Luk 11:5 – "shall go unto him at midnight"
Act 16:25 – "at midnight Paul and Silas prayed"
Act 20:7 – "continued his speech until midnight"
Act 27:27 – "about midnight..shipmen deemed"

Thirteen

The number thirteen in Bible numerology is associated with rebellion and the Antichrist.

This will be the last number treated to its own separate heading and comments. The remainder of the numbers in Section One will follow on in normal concordance style.

13 – Thirteen

Gen 17:25 – "Ishmael..13 years old..circumcised"
Num 29:13 – "burnt offering...13 young bullocks"
Num 29:14 – "every bullock of the 13 bullocks"
Jos 6:14-15 – 13 times around Jericho (6x1 + 7)
Jos 19:6 – "thirteen cities and their villages"
Jos 21:4 – "Kohathites..thirteen cities"

Jos 21:6 – "children of Gershon..13 cities"
Jos 21:19 – "children of Aaron..13 cities"
Jos 21:33 – "All the cities of the Gershonites..13"
1Ki 7:1 – "building his own house 13 years"
1Ch 6:60 – "All their cities..were thirteen cities"
1Ch 6:62 – "to the sons of Gershom..13 cities"
1Ch 26:11 – "all the sons..brethren of Hosah..13"
Ezk 40:11 – "length of the gate, thirteen cubits"

13th – Thirteen

Gen 14:4 – "in the 13th year they rebelled"
1Ch 24:13 – "The thirteenth to Huppah"
1Ch 25:20 – "The thirteenth to Shubael"
Est 3:12 – "thirteenth day" – see *DATES*

Est 3:13 – "thirteenth day" – see *DATES*
Est 9:1 – "thirteenth day" – see *DATES*
Est 9:17 – "thirteenth day" – see *DATES*
Est 9:18 – "thirteenth day" – see *DATES*
Jer 1:2 – "Josiah..13th year of his reign"
Jer 25:3 – "From the 13th year of Josiah"

14 – Fourteen

Gen 31:41 – "I served thee14 years"
Gen 46:22 – "sons of Rachel..the souls were 14"
Lev 12:4 – "she shall be unclean two weeks"
Num 29:13 – "fourteen lambs of the first year"
Num 29:15 – "each lamb of the fourteen lambs"
Num 29:17 – "14 lambs of the 1st year w/o spot"
Num 29:20 – "14 lambs of..1st year w/o blemish"
Num 29:23 – "14 lambs of..1st year w/o blemish"
Num 29:26 – "14 lambs of..1st year without spot"
Num 29:29 – "14 lambs of..1st year w/o blemish"
Num 29:32 – "14 lambs of..1st year w/o blemish"
Jos 15:36 – "fourteen cities with their villages"
Jos 18:28 – "14 cities w/ their villages..Benjamin"
1Ki 8:65 – "7 days and 7 days, even 14 days"
1Ch 25:5 – "God gave to Heman 14 sons"
2Ch 13:21 – "Abijah..married 14 wives"
Ezk 43:17 – "the settle shall be 14 cubits long"
Ezk 43:17 – "the settle shall be..14 broad"
Mat 1:17 – "Abraham to David are 14 generations"
Mat 1:17 – "David..into Babylon..14 generations"
Mat 1:17 – "Babylon unto Christ..14 generations"
2Co 12:2 – "a man in Christ above 14 years ago"
Gal 2:1 – "Then 14 years after..again to Jerusalem"

Ezk 40:1 – "14th year after..city was smitten"
Exk 45:21 – "fourteenth day" – see *DATES*
Act 27:27 – "14th night..up and down in Adria"
Act 27:33 – "14th day that ye..continued fasting"

15 – Fifteen

Gen 7:20 – "15 cubits upward..waters prevail"
Exo 27:14 – "hangings of one side..15 cubits"
Exo 27:15 – "the other side..hangings 15 cubits"
Exo 38:14 – "hangings of the gate were 15 cubits"
Exo 38:15 – "other side of..court gate..15 cubits"
Lev 27:7 – "estimation shall be fifteen shekels"
2Sa 9:10 – "Ziba had 15 sons and 20 servants"
2Sa 19:17 – "Ziba..his 15 sons..his 20 servants"
1Ki 7:3 – "45 pillars, fifteen in a row"
2Ki 14:17 – "Amaziah..after..Jehoash..15 years"
2Ki 20:6 – "I will add unto thy days 15 years"
2Ch 25:25 – "Amaziah..lived after..Joash..15 years"
Isa 38:5 – "I will add unto thy days 15 years"
Ezk 45:12 – "20..25 shekels, 15 shekels..maneh"
Hos 3:2 – "I bought her..for 15 pieces of silver"
Joh 11:18 – "Bethany..unto Jerusalem..15 furlongs"
Act 27:28 – "sounded again..found it 15 fathoms"
Gal 1:18 – "Peter, and abode with him 15 days"

14th – Fourteeneth

Gen 14:5 – "in the 14th year came Chedorlaomer"
Exo 12:6 – "fourteenth day" – see *DATES*
Exo 12:18 – "fourteenth day" – see *DATES*
Lev 23:5 – "fourteenth day" – see *DATES*
Num 9:3 – "fourteenth day" – see *DATES*
Num 9:5 – "fourteenth day" – see *DATES*
Num 9:11 – "fourteenth day" – see *DATES*
Num 28:16 – "fourteenth day" – see *DATES*
Jos 5:10 – "kept the passover on the 14th day"
2Ki 18:13 – "in the 14th year of..Hezekiah"
1Ch 24:13 – "the fourteenth to Jeshebeab"
1Ch 25:21 – "the fourteenth to Mattithiah"
2Ch 30:15 – "fourteenth day" – see *DATES*
2Ch 35:1 – "fourteenth day" – see *DATES*
Ezr 6:19 – "fourteenth day" – see *DATES*
Est 9:15 – "fourteenth day" – see *DATES*
Est 9:17 – "fourteenth day" – see *DATES*
Est 9:18 – "fourteenth day" – see *DATES*
Est 9:19 – "fourteenth day" – see *DATES*
Est 9:21 – "fourteenth day" – see *DATES*
Isa 36:1 – "in the 14th year of..Hezekiah"

15th – Fifteenth

Exo 16:1 – "fifteenth day" – see *DATES*
Lev 23:6 – "fifteenth day" – see *DATES*
Lev 23:34 – "fifteenth day" – see *DATES*
Lev 23:39 – "fifteenth day" – see *DATES*
Num 28:17 – "fifteenth day" – see *DATES*
Num 29:12 – "fifteenth day" – see *DATES*
Num 33:3 – "fifteenth day" – see *DATES*
1Ki 12:32 – "fifteenth day" – see *DATES*
1Ki 12:33 – "fifteenth day" – see *DATES*
2Ki 14:23 – "In the 15th year of Amaziah"
1Ch 24:14 – "The fifteenth to Bilgah"
1Ch 25:22 – "The fifteenth to Jeremoth"
2Ch 15:10 – "fifteenth year" – see *DATES*
Est 9:18 – "fifteenth day" – see *DATES*
Est 9:21 – "fifteenth day" – see *DATES*
Ezk 32:17 – "fifteenth day" – see *DATES*
Ezk 45:25 – "fifteenth day" – see *DATES*
Luk 3:1 – "in the 15th year of..Tiberius Caesar"

16 – Sixteen

Gen 46:18 – "sons of Zilpah..even 16 souls"
Exo 26:25 – "eight boards..sixteen sockets"
Exo 36:30 – "sockets were 16 sockets of silver"
Jos 15:41 – "sixteen cities with their villages"
Jos 19:22 – "sixteen cities with their villages"
2Ki 13:10 – "Jehoash..reigned 16 years"
2Ki 14:21 – "Azariah..16 years old..made..king"
2Ki 15:2 – "16 years old..when he began to reign"
2Ki 15:33 – "reigned 16 years in Jerusalem"
2Ki 16:2 – "Ahaz..reigned 16 years in Jerusalem"
1Ch 4:27 – "Shimei had 16 sons & six daughters"
1Ch 24:4 – "sons of Eliazar..16 chief men"
2Ch 13:21 – "Abijah begat 22 sons..16 daughters"
2Ch 26:1 – "Uzziah, who was 16 years old"
2Ch 26:3 – "16 years old was Uzziah..began..reign"
2Ch 27:1 – "Jotham..reigned 16 years..Jerusalem"
2Ch 27:8 – "reigned 16 years in Jerusalem"
2Ch 28:1 – "Ahaz..reigned 16 years in Jerusalem"

16th – Sixteenth

1Ch 24:14 – "the sixteenth to Immer"
1Ch 25:23 – "the sixteenth to Hananiah"
2Ch 29:17 – "sixteenth day" – see *DATES*

17 - Seventeen

Gen 37:2 – "Joseph being 17 years old"
Gen 47:28 – "Jacob lived in..Egypt 17 years"
1Ki 14:21 – "Rehoboam.. 17 years in Jerusalem"
2Ki 13:1 – "Jehoahaz..reigned 17 years"
2Ch 12:13 – "Rehoboam..17 years in Jerusalem"
Jer 32:9 – "money, even 17 shekels of silver"

17th – Seventeenth

Gen 7:11 – "seventeenth day" – see *DATES*
Gen 8:4 – "seventeenth day" – see *DATES*
1Ki 22:51 – "Ahaziah..began to reign..17th year"
2Ki 16:1 – "17th year of Pekah..Ahaz..began"
1Ch 24:15 – "The seventeenth to Hezir"
1Ch 25:24 – "The seventeenth to Joshbekashah"

18 – Eighteen

Jdg 3:14 – "served Eglon..king of Moab 18 years"
Jdg 10:8 – "vexed and oppressed..Israel: 18 years"
1Ki 7:15 – "two pillars of brass, of 18 cubits high"
2Ki 24:8 – "Jehoiachin..18 years old..began..reign"
2Ki 25:17 – "height of the 1 pillar was 18 cubits"
1Ch 26:9 – "Meshelemiah..sons & brethren..18"
2Ch 11:21 – "Rehoboam..took 18 wives"
Ezr 8:18 – "sons of Mahli..sons & his brethren, 18"

Jer 52:21 – "height of one pillar was 18 cubits"
Luk 13:4 – "Or those 18..tower in Siloam fell"
Luk 13:11 – "woman..spirit of infirmity 18 years"
Luk 13:16 – "Satan hath bound, lo, these 18 years"

18th – Eighteenth

1Ki 15:1 – "in the 18th year of Jeroboam"
2Ki 3:1 – "Jehoram..began to reign..18th year"
2Ki 22:3 – "in the 18th year of king Josiah"
2Ki 23:23 – "in the 18th year of king Josiah"
1Ch 24:15 – "the eighteenth to Aphses"
1Ch 25:25 – "the eighteenth to Hanani"
2Ch 13:1 – "in the 18th year of king Jeroboam"
2Ch 34:8 – "in the 18th year of his reign"
2Ch 35:19 – "18th year of..Josiah..passover kept"
Jer 32:1 – "the 18th year of Nebuchadrezzar"
Jer 52:29 – "the 18th year of Nebuchadrezzar"

19 – Nineteen

Jos 19:38 – "19 cities with their villages"
2Sa 2:30 – "lacked of David's servants 19 men"

19th – Nineteenth

2Ki 25:8 – "the 19th year of..Nebuchadnezzar"
1Ch 24:16 – "The nineteenth to Pethahiah"
1Ch 25:26 – "The nineteenth to Mallothi"
Jer 52:12 – "nineteenth year" – see *DATES*

20 – Twenty

Gen 18:31 – "Peradventure there..be 20 found"
Gen 18:31 – "I will not destroy it for 20's sake"
Gen 31:38 – "This 20 years have I been with thee"
Gen 31:41 – "I have been 20 years in thy house"
Gen 32:14 – Jacob's present – "20 he goats"
Gen 32:14 – Jacob's present – "20 rams"
Gen 32:15 – Jacob's present – "20 she asses"
Gen 37:28 – "sold Joseph..for 20 pieces of silver"
Exo 26:18 – "20 boards on the south side"
Exo 26:19 – "sockets of silver under..20 boards"
Exo 26:20 – "north side..twenty boards"
Exo 27:10 – "20 pillars thereof..their 20 sockets"
Exo 27:11 – "his 20 pillars and their 20 sockets"
Exo 27:16 – "an hanging of 20 cubits"
Exo 30:13 – "a shekel is twenty gerahs"
Exo 30:14 – "from twenty years old and above"
Exo 36:23 – "twenty boards for the south side"
Exo 36:24 – "40 sockets..under the 20 boards"
Exo 36:25 – "other side..he made 20 boards"
Exo 38:10 – "Their pillars were twenty"
Exo 38:10 – "their brasen sockets twenty"
Exo 38:11 – "north side..pillars were twenty"
Exo 38:11 – "north side..sockets of brass twenty"

Exo 38:18 – "hanging for..gate..20 cubits..length"
Exo 38:26 – "numbered, from 20 years old"
Lev 27:3 – "estimation..from twenty years old"
Lev 27:5 – estimation "unto twenty years old"
Lev 27:5 – "estimation shall be..twenty shekels"
Lev 27:25 – "twenty gerahs shall be the shekel"
Num 1:3 – "twenty years old and upward"
Num 1:18 – "twenty years old and upward"
Num 1:20 – "Reuben..20 years old and upward"
Num 1:22 – "Simeon..20 years old and upward"
Num 1:24 – "Gad..twenty years old and upward"
Num 1:26 – "Judah..twenty years old and upward"
Num 1:28 – "Issachar..20 years old and upward"
Num 1:30 – "Zebulun..20 years old and upward"
Num 1:32 – "Ephraim..20 years old and upward"
Num 1:34 – "Mannaseh..20 years old and upward"
Num 1:36 – "Benjamin..20 years old and upward"
Num 1:38 – "Dan..twenty years old and upward"
Num 1:40 – "Asher..twenty years old and upward"
Num 1:42 – "Naphtali..20 years old and upward"
Num 1:45 – "Israel..twenty years old and upward"
Num 3:47 – "the shekel is twenty gerahs"
Num 11:19 – "nor 5 days..10 days, nor 20 days"
Num 14:29 – "20 years old..upward..murmured"
Num 18:16 – "shekel..which is twenty gerahs"
Num 26:2 – "sum..from 20 years old..upward"
Num 26:4 – "sum..from 20 years old..upward"
Num 32:11 – "none..from 20 years old..see..land"
Jdg 4:3 – "20 years he mightily oppressed"
Jdg 11:33 – "he smote..even twenty cities"
Jdg 15:20 – "he judged Israel..twenty years"
Jdg 16:31 – "And he judged Israel 20 years."
1Sa 7:2 – "ark abode in Kirjath-jearim..20 years"
1Sa 14:14 – "first slaughter..was about 20 men"
2Sa 3:20 – "Abner came to David..20 men w/ him"
2Sa 9:10 – "Ziba had 15 sons and 20 servants"
2Sa 19:17 – "Ziba..his 15 sons & his 20 servants"
1Ki 4:23 – "twenty oxen out of the pastures"
1Ki 5:11 – "20 measures of pure oil"
1Ki 6:2 – "house..breadth thereof 20 cubits"
1Ki 6:3 – "porch..temple..20 cubits..length"
1Ki 6:16 – "20 cubits on the sides of the house"
1Ki 6:20 – "oracle..20 cubits in length"
1Ki 6:20 – "oracle..20 cubits in breadth"
1Ki 6:20 – "oracle..20 cubits in height thereof"
1Ki 9:10 – "20 years..Solomon..built..2 houses"
1Ki 9:11 – "Solomon gave Hiram 20 cities"
2Ki 4:42 – "brought the man of God..20 loaves"
2Ki 15:27 – "Pekah..reigned twenty years"
2Ki 16:2 – "20 years old..Ahaz..began to reign"
1Ch 23:24 – "sons of Levi..20 years and upward"
1Ch 23:27 – "numbered from 20 years old"
1Ch 27:23 – "number of them 20 years old..under"
2Ch 3:3 – "house of God..breadth 20 cubits"
2Ch 3:4 – "porch..length of it was..20 cubits"
2Ch 3:8 – "most holy house..length..20 cubits"
2Ch 3:8 – "most holy house..breadth..20 cubits"
2Ch 3:11 – "wings of..cherubims..20 cubits long"
2Ch 3:13 – "wings..spread..forth 20 cubits"
2Ch 4:1 – "altar of brass..20 cubits the length"
2Ch 4:1 – "altar of brass..20 cubits the breadth"

2Ch 8:1 – "20 years..Solomon had built"
2Ch 25:5 – "numbered..20 years old and above"
2Ch 28:1 – "Ahaz was 20 years old..began..reign"
2Ch 31:17 – "Levites from 20 years old..upward"
Ezr 3:8 – "Levites, from 20 years old and upward"
Ezr 8:19 – "sons of Merari..brethren..sons, 20"
Ezr 8:27 – "20 basons of gold, of a 1000 drams"
Ezk 4:10 – "thy meat..by weight, 20 shekels a day"
Ezk 40:49 – "length of the porch was 20 cubits"
Ezk 41:2 – "the door..the breadth, 20 cubits"
Ezk 41:4 – "length..20 cubits..most holy place"
Ezk 41:4 – "breadth..20 cubits..most holy place"
Ezk 41:10 – "between..chambers..20 cubits"
Ezk 42:3 – "20 cubits..were for the inner court"
Ezk 45:5 – "Levites..possession for 20 chambers"
Ezk 45:12 – "the shekel shall be twenty gerahs"
Ezk 45:12 – "20..25 shekels, 15 shekels..maneh"
Hag 2:16 – "heap of 20 measures..were but 10"
Hag 2:16 – "draw out 50 vessels..were but 20"
Zec 5:2 – "flying roll; the length..20 cubits"
Act 27:28 – "sounded, and found it 20 fathoms"

20th – Twentieth

Num 10:11 – "twentieth day" – see *DATES*
1Ki 15:9 – "in the 20th year of Jeroboam"
2Ki 15:30 – "a conspiracy..20th year of Jotham"
1Ch 24:16 – "the twentieth to Jehezekel"
1Ch 25:27 – "The twentieth to Eliathah"
Ezr 10:9 – "twentieth day" – see *DATES*
Neh 1:1 – "20th year, as I was in Shushan"
Neh 2:1 – "in the 20th year of Artaxerxes"
Neh 5:14 – "20th..unto..32nd year of Artaxerxes"

21

2Ki 24:18 – "Zedekiah..21 years old..began..reign"
2Ch 36:11 – "Zedekiah..21 years old..began..reign"
Jer 52:1 – "Zedekiah..21 years old..began to reign"
Dan 10:13 – "prince..Persia withstood me 21 days"

21st

Exo 12:18 – "one and twentieth day" – see *DATES*
1Ch 24:17 – "The one and twentieth to Jachin"
1Ch 25:28 – "The one and twentieth to Hothir"
Hag 2:1 – "one and twentieth day" – see *DATES*

22

Jos 19:30 – "22 cities with their villages"
Jdg 10:3 – "Jair..judged Israel 22 years"
1Ki 14:20 – "days..Jeroboam reigned..22 years"
1Ki 16:29 – "Ahab..reigned..in Samaria 22 years"
2Ki 8:26 – "22 years old..Ahaziah..began..reign"
2Ki 21:19 – "Amon..22 years old..began to reign"

1Ch 12:28 – "Zadok..father's house..22 captains"
2Ch 13:21 – "Abija..begat 22 sons & 16 daughters"
2Ch 33:21 – "Amon..22 years old..began to reign"

22nd

1Ch 24:17 – "the two and twentieth to Gamul"
1Ch 25:29 – "the two and twentieth to Giddalti"

23

Jdg 10:2 – "he judged Israel 23 years"
2Ki 23:31 – "Jehoahaz..23 years old..began..reign"
1Ch 2:22 – "Segub..who had 23 cities in..Gilead"
2Ch 36:2 – "Jehoahaz..23 years old..began..reign"

23rd

2Ki 12:6 – "in the 23rd year of king Jehoash"
2Ki 13:1 – "23rd year of Joash..Jehoahaz..began"
1Ch 24:18 – "The 23rd to Delaiah"
1Ch 25:30 – "The 23rd to Mahazioth"
2Ch 7:10 – "three and twentieth day" – see *DATES*
Est 8:9 – "three and twentieth day" – see *DATES*
Jer 25:3 – "Josiah..that is the 23rd year"
Jer 52:30 – "23rd year of Nebuchadrezzar"

24

Num 7:88 – "peace offerings..24 bullocks"
2Sa 21:20 – "fingers...toes...24 in number"
1Ki 15:33 – "Baasha..reign over Israel..24 years"
1Ki 19:19 – "Elisha..plowing with 12 yoke of oxen"
1Ch 20:6 – "fingers and toes were 24"
Rev 4:4 – "round about throne..were 24 seats"
Rev 4:4 – "I saw 24 elders sitting"
Rev 4:10 – "The 24 elders fall down before him"
Rev 5:8 – "and 24 elders fell down before..Lamb"
Rev 5:14 – "the 24 elders fell down..worshipped"
Rev 11:16 – "the 24 elders..fell upon their faces"
Rev 19:4 – "the 24 elders..fell down..worshipped"

24th

1Ch 24:18 – "the four and twentieth to Maaziah"
1Ch 25:31 – "the 24th to Romamtiezer"
Neh 9:1 – "in the 24th day of this month..fasting"
Dan 10:4 – "four and twentieth day" – see *DATES*
Hag 1:5 – "four and twentieth day" – see *DATES*
Hag 2:10 – "four and twentieth day" – see *DATES*
Hag 2:18 – "four and twentieth day" – see *DATES*
Hag 2:20 – "four and twentieth day" – see *DATES*
Zec 1:7 – "four and twentieth day" – see *DATES*

25

Num 8:24 – "Levites: from 25 years old"
1Ki 22:42 – "Jehoshaphat..reigned 25 years"
2Ki 14:2 – "He was 25 years old..began to reign"
2Ki 15:33 – "25 years old..began to reign"
2Ki 18:2 – "25 years old..began to reign"
2Ki 23:36 – "Jehoiakim..25 years old..began..reign"
2Ch 20:31 – "Jehoshaphat reigned..25 years"
2Ch 25:1 – "Amaziah..25 years old..began..reign"
2Ch 27:1 – "Jotham..25 years old..began to reign"
2Ch 27:8 – "was 25 years old..began to reign"
2Ch 29:1 – "Hezekiah began..reign..25 years old"
2Ch 36:5 – "Jehoiakim..25 years old..began..reign"
Ezk 8:16 – "25 men..worshipped the sun"
Ezk 11:1 – "at the door of the gate 25 men"
Ezk 40:13 – "gate..breadth was 25 cubits"
Ezk 40:21 – "arches..breadth 25 cubits"
Ezk 40:25 – "arches..breadth 25 cubits"
Ezk 40:29 – "arches..25 cubits broad"
Ezk 40:30 – "arches..25 cubits long"
Ezk 40:33 – "arches..25 cubits broad"
Ezk 40:36 – "arches..breadth 25 cubits"
Ezk 45:12 – "20..25 shekels, 15 shekels..maneh"
Joh 6:19 – "rowed about 25 or 30 furlongs"

25th

Neh 6:15 – "wall..finished in the 25th day of..Elul"
Jer 52:31 – "five and twentieth day" – see *DATES*
Ezk 40:1 – "five and twentieth year" – see *DATES*

26

None – this is the first cardinal number not to appear in the King James Bible.

26th

1Ki 16:8 – "In the 26th year of Asa..began Elah"

27

None

27th

1Ki 16:10 – "Zimri..smote..in the 27th year of Asa"
1Ki 16:15 – "27th year of Asa..did Zimri reign"
2Ki 15:1 – "27th year of Jeroboam..began Azariah"

28

Exo 26:2 – "length of one curtain..28 cubits"
Exo 36:9 – "length of one curtain..28 cubits"
2Ki 10:36 – "Jehu reigned over Israel..28 years"
2Ch 11:21 – "begat 28 sons and 60 daughters"
Ezr 8:11 – "sons of Bebai..28 males"

28th

None – this is the first ordinal number not to appear in the King James Bible.

29

Gen 11:24 – "Nahor lived 29 years ..begat Terah"
Exo 38:24 – "gold..29 talents, and 730 shekels"
➤ *Thus, 87,730 shekels or 29.24 talents*
Jos 15:32 – "cities are 29, with their villages"
2Ki 14:2 – "reigned 29 years in Jerusalem"
2Ki 18:2 – "reigned 29 years in Jerusalem"
2Ch 25:1 – "Amaziah..reigned 29 years"
2Ch 29:1 – "Hezekiah..reigned 29 years"
Ezr 1:9 – "1000 chargers of silver, 29 knives"

29.24

Exo 38:24 – "gold..29 talents, and 730 shekels"
➤ *Thus, 87,730 shekels or 29.24 talents*

30

Gen 6:15 – "the ark..the height of it 30 cubits"
Gen 11:14 – "Salah lived 30 years..begat Eber"
Gen 11:18 – "Peleg lived 30 years..begat Reu"
Gen 11:22 – "Serug lived 30 years..begat Nahor"
Gen 18:30 – "Peradventure..30 be found there"
Gen 18:30 – "I will not do it, if I find 30 there"
Gen 32:15 – Jacbo's present – "30 milch camels"
Gen 41:46 – "Joseph was 30 years old..stood"
Exo 21:32 – "he shall give..30 shekels of silver"
Exo 26:8 – "length of one curtain..30 cubits"
Exo 36:15 – "length of one curtain..30 cubits"
Lev 27:4 – "estimation shall be thirty shekels"
Num 4:3 –"30 years old and upward..until 50"
Num 4:23 – "30 years old and upward..until 50"
Num 4:35 – "30 years old and upward..until 50"
Num 4:39 – "30 years old and upward..until 50"
Num 4:43 – "30 years old and upward..until 50"
Num 4:47 – "30 years old and upward..until 50"
Num 11:19-20 – "even a whole month" - implied
Num 20:29 – "mourned for Aaron 30 days"
Deu 34:8 – "Israel wept for Moses..thirty days"
Jdg 10:4 – "he had 30 sons"
Jdg 10:4 – "sons that rode on 30 ass colts"

Jdg 10:4 – "they had 30 cities"
Jdg 12:9 – "he had 30 sons, and 30 daughters"
Jdg 12:9 – "took in 30 daughters..for his sons"
Jdg 12:14 – "he had 40 sons and 30 nephews"
Jdg 14:11 – "30 companions to be with him"
Jdg 14:12 – "I will give you 30 sheets"
Jdg 14:12 – "give you..30 change of garments"
Jdg 14:13 – "give me 30 sheets"
Jdg 14:13 – "give me..30 change of garments"
Jdg 14:19 – "to Ashkelon, and slew 30 men"
Jdg 20:31 – "began to smite..about 30 men"
Jdg 20:39 – "began to smite..about 30 persons"
1Sa 9:22 – "were bidden..about thirty persons"
2Sa 5:4 – "David..30 years old..began to reign"
2Sa 23:13 – "three of the 30 chief went down"
2Sa 23:23 – "more honourable than the 30"
2Sa 23:24 – "Asahel...was one of the thirty"
1Ki 4:22 – "provision..30 measures..fine flour"
1Ki 6:2 – "house..for the LORD..height..30 cubits"
1Ki 7:2 – "house..of Lebanon..height..30 cubits"
1Ki 7:6 – "porch of pillars..breadth..30 cubits"
1Ki 7:23 – "molten sea..line of 30 cubits"
2Ki 18:14 – "king..appointed..30 talents..gold"
1Ch 11:15 – "three of the thirty captains"
1Ch 11:25 – "he was honourable among the 30"
1Ch 11:42 – "Adina..and thirty with him"
1Ch 12:4 – "Ismaiah..mighty man among the 30"
1Ch 12:4 – "Ismaiah..mighty..over the thirty"
1Ch 23:3 – "Levites.. from the age of 30 years"
1Ch 27:6 – "Benaiah..mighty among the 30
1Ch 27:6 – "Benaiah..above the thirty"
2Ch 4:2 – "molten sea..a line of 30 cubits"
Ezr 1:9 – "thirty chargers of gold"
Ezr 1:10 – "thirty basons of gold"
Est 4:11 – "not been called..these 30 days"
Jer 38:10 – "Take..thirty men with thee"
Ezk 40:17 – "30 chambers..upon the pavement"
Ezk 41:6 – "side chambers..thirty in order"
Ezk 46:22 – "courts..40 cubits long..30 broad"
Dan 6:7 – "petition of any God..man for 30 days"
Dan 6:12 – "petition of any God..man..30 days"
Zec 11:12 – "my price thirty pieces of silver"
Zec 11:13 – "And I took the 30 pieces of silver"
Mat 13:23 – "beareth fruit..some thirty"
Mat 26:15 – "covenanted..30 pieces of silver"
Mat 27:3 – "brought again the 30 pieces of silver"
Mat 27:9 – "they took the 30 pieces of silver"
Mar 4:8 – "yield fruit..increased..some thirty"
Luk 3:23 – "Jesus..about 30 years of age"
Joh 6:19 – "rowed about 25 or 30 furlongs"
Rev 8:1 – "silence in heaven..space of ½ an hour"

30-fold – Thirtyfold

Mat 13:8 – "brought forth fruit, some 30-fold"
Mat 13:23 – "beareth fruit..some thirty"
Mar 4:8 – "yield fruit..increased..some thirty"
Mar 4:20 – "bring forth fruit, some thirtyfold"

31

Jos 12:24 – "all the kings thirty and one"
2Ki 22:1 – "Josiah..reigned 31 years in Jerusalem"
2Ch 34:1 – "Josiah..reigned in Jerusalem 31 years"

31st

1Ki 16:23 – "In the 31st year of Asa..began Omri"

32

Gen 11:20 – "Reu lived 32 years..begat Serug"
Num 31:40 – "the LORD's tribute was 32 persons"
1Ki 20:1 – "Benhadad..gathered..32 kings"
1Ki 20:16 – "drinking..drunk..he and the..32 kings"
1Ki 22:31 – "king..commanded his 32 captains"
2Ki 8:17 – "32 years old ..when he began to reign"
2Ch 21:5 – "Jehoram..32 years old..began to reign"
2Ch 21:20 – "32 years old..began to reign"

32nd

Neh 5:14 – "20th year..unto..32nd year..Artaxerxes"
Neh 13:6 – "in..32nd year of Artaxerxes..came I"

33

Gen 46:15 – "sons of Leah..all the souls..were 33"
Lev 12:4 – "the blood of her purifying 33 days"
2Sa 5:5 – "reigned 33 years over all Israel"
1Ki 2:11 – "33 years reigned he in Jerusalem"
1Ch 3:4 – "in Jerusalem he reigned 33 years"
1Ch 29:27 – "33 years reigned he in Jerusalem"

34

Gen 11:16 – "Eber lived 34 years..begat Peleg"

35

Gen 11:12 – "Arphaxad..35 years..begat Salah"
1Ki 22:42 – "Jehoshaphat was 35 years old..reign"
2Ch 3:15 – "two pillars of 35 cubits high"
2Ch 20:31 – "Jehoshaphat..35 years old..reign"

35th

2Ch 15:19 – "no more war..the 35th year of..Asa"

36

Jos 7:5 – "men of Ai smote of them about 36 men"

36th

2Ch 16:1 – "In the 36th year of the reign of Asa"

37

2Sa 23:39 – David's mighty men – "37 in all"

37th

2Ki 13:10 – "In the 37th year of Joash king"
2Ki 25:27 – "37th year" – see *DATES*
Jer 52:31 – "37th year" – see *DATES*

38

Deu 2:14 – "Kadeshbarnea..Zered, was 38 years"
Joh 5:5 – "certain man..had an infirmity 38 years"

38th

1Ki 16:29 – "in the 38th year of Asa..began Ahab"
2Ki 15:8 – "38th year of Azariah..Zachariah..reign"

39

2Co 11:24 – "5 times received..40 stripes save 1"

39th

2Ki 15:13 – "Shallum..in the 39th year of Uzziah"
2Ki 15:17 – "39th year..Azariah..began Menahem"
2Ch 16:12 – "Asa..39th year..diseased in his feet"

40

Gen 7:4 – "rain..40 days & 40 nights"
Gen 7:12 – "rain..earth 40 days & 40 nights"
Gen 7:17 – "flood was 40 days upon the earth"
Gen 8:6 – "end of 40 days..Noah opened..window"
Gen 18:29 – "Peradventure there..be 40 found"
Gen 18:29 – "I will not destroy it for forty's sake"
Gen 25:20 – "Isaac..40 years old..took Rebekkah"
Gen 26:34 – "Esau was 40 years old..took to wife"
Gen 32:15 – "40 kine, and 10 bulls"

Gen 50:3 – "40 days were fulfilled for him"
Exo 16:35 – "Israel did eat manna 40 years"
Exo 24:18 – "Moses..in..mount..40 days..40 nights"
Exo 26:19 – "make 40 sockets of silver"
Exo 26:21 – "And their 40 sockets of silver"
Exo 34:28 – "with the LORD 40 days & 40 nights"
Exo 36:24 – "40 sockets..under the 20 boards"
Exo 36:26 – "their forty sockets of silver"
Lev 12:2-4 – 7 + 33 days separation for man child
Num 13:25 – "searching..the land after 40 days"
Num 14:33 – "in the wilderness forty years"
Num 14:34 – "even 40 days, each day for a year"
Num 14:34 – "bear your iniquities, even 40 years"
Num 32:13 – "LORD's anger..wilderness 40 years"
Deu 2:7 – "40 years..God hath been with thee"
Deu 8:2 – "God, led thee these forty years"
Deu 8:4 – "raiment waxed not old..these 40 years"
Deu 9:9 – "40 days and 40 nights"
Deu 9:11 – "40 days and 40 nights"
Deu 9:18 – "40 days and 40 nights"
Deu 9:25 – "40 days and 40 nights"
Deu 10:10 – "40 days and 40 nights"
Deu 25:3 – "40 stripes he may give..not exceed"
Deu 29:5 – "led you 40 years in the wilderness"
Jos 5:6 – "walked forty years in the wilderness"
Jos 14:7 – "40 years old..when Moses..sent me"
Jdg 3:11 – "the land had rest forty years"
Jdg 5:31 – "And the land had rest forty years."
Jdg 8:28 – "country..quietness 40 years..Gideon"
Jdg 12:14 – "he had 40 sons and 30 nephews"
Jdg 13:1 – "delivered..hand..Philistines 40 years"
1Sa 4:18 – "he had judged Israel forty years"
1Sa 17:16 – "Philistine..presented..40 days"
2Sa 2:10 – "Ishbosheth..40 years old..began..reign"
2Sa 5:4 – "David..reigned 40 years"
2Sa 15:7 – "after 40 years, that Absalom said"
1Ki 2:11 – "David reigned over Israel..40 years"
1Ki 6:17 – "the house..was 40 cubits long"
1Ki 7:38 – "one laver contained forty baths"
1Ki 11:42 – "Solomon reigned..forty years"
1Ki 19:8 – "strength..meat..40 days and 40 nights"
2Ki 8:9 – "every good thing..40 camels' burden"
2Ki 12:1 – "Jehoash..40 years reigned..Jerusalem"
1Ch 29:27 – "reigned over Israel..40 years"
2Ch 9:30 – "Solomon reigned in..forty years"
2Ch 24:1 – "Joash..reigned 40 years in Jerusalem"
Neh 5:15 – "taken of them..40 shekels of silver"
Neh 9:21 – "40 years didst thou sustain them"
Psa 95:10 – "40 years long was I grieved w/ this"
Ezk 4:6 – "bear..iniquity..house of Judah 40 days"
Ezk 29:11 – "neither..be inhabited 40 years"
Ezk 29:12 – "cities..laid waste..desolate 40 years"
Ezk 29:13 – " end of 40 years..gather Egyptians"
Ezk 41:2 – "the door..length thereof 40 cubits"
Ezk 46:22 – "courts..40 cubits long and 30 broad"
Amo 2:10 – "led you 40 years through..wilderness"
Amo 5:25 – "offerings in the wilderness 40 years"
Jon 3:4 – "40 days..Nineveh shall be overthrown"
Mat 4:2 – "fasted 40 days and 40 nights"
Mar 1:13 – "in the wilderness 40 days, tempted"
Luk 4:2 – "forty days tempted of the devil"

Act 1:3 – "being seen of them 40 days"
Act 4:22 – "man was above 40 years old"
Act 7:23 – "when he was full 40 years old"
Act 7:30 – "when 40 years were expired"
Act 7:36 – "in the wilderness 40 years"
Act 7:42 – "sacrifices by the space of 40 years"
Act 13:18 – "40 years suffered he their manners"
Act 13:21 – "a king..Saul..by the space of 40 years"
Act 23:13 – "more than 40..made this conspiracy"
Act 23:21 – "forty men..bound themselves"
2Co 11:24 – "5 times received..40 stripes save 1"
Heb 3:9 – "saw my works forty years"
Heb 3:17 – "with whom he was grieved 40 years"

40ᵗʰ

Num 33:38 – "fortieth year" – see *DATES*
Deu 1:3 – "fortieth year" – see *DATES*
1Ch 26:31 – "40ᵗʰ year of the reign of David"

41

1Ki 14:21 – "Rehoboam was 41 years old..reign"
1Ki 15:10 – "41 years reigned he in Jerusalem"
2Ki 14:23 – "Jeroboam..reigned 41 years"
2Ch 12:13 – "Rehoboam was 41 years old..reign"

41ˢᵗ

2Ch 16:13 – "Asa..died in..41ˢᵗ year of his reign"

42

Num 35:6 – "to them ye shall add 42 cities"
2Ki 2:24 – "2 she bears..tare 42 children of them"
2Ki 10:14 – "slew them at the pit..even 42 men"
2Ch 22:2 – "42 years old..Ahaziah..began to reign"
Ezr 2:24 – "The children of Azmaveth, 42"
Neh 7:28 – "The men of Bethazmaveth, 42"
Rev 11:2 – "holy city..tread under..42 months"
Rev 13:5 – "power was given..him..42 months"

43

First number that is completely missing in the King James Bible.

45

Gen 18:28 – "shall lack 5 of the 50 righteous"
Gen 18:28 – "If I find..45, I will not destroy it"
Jos 14:10 – "LORD..kept me alive..these 45 years"
1Ki 7:3 – "beams, that lay on 45 pillars"

46

Joh 2:47 – "46 years was this temple in building"

48

Num 35:7 – "give to the Levites..48 cities"
Jos 21:41 – "All the cities of the Levites..were 48"

49

Lev 23:15 – "seven sabbaths shall be complete"
Lev 25:8 – "seven sabbaths of years"
Lev 25:8 – "seven times seven years"
Lev 25:8 – "space of the seven sabbaths of years"
Lev 25:8 – "7 sabbaths..be unto thee 49 years"
Deu 16:9 – "7 weeks shalt thou number unto thee"
Deu 16:9 – "number the 7 weeks..sickle to the corn"
Dan 9:25 – "unto the Messiah..seven weeks"

50

Gen 6:15 – "the ark..breadth of it 50 cubits"
Gen 18:24 – "50 righteous within the city"
Gen 18:24 – "spare the place for the 50 righteous"
Gen 18:26 – "If I find in Sodom 50 righteous"
Gen 18:28 – "shall lack 5 of the 50 righteous"
Exo 26:5 – "Fifty loops..make in the one curtain"
Exo 26:5 – "fifty loops..in the edge of the curtain"
Exo 26:6 – "shalt make fifty taches of gold"
Exo 26:10 – "50 loops on the edge of the 1 curtain"
Exo 26:10 – "50 loops in the edge of the curtain"
Exo 26:11 – "thou shalt make fifty taches of brass"
Exo 27:12 – "hangings of fifty cubits"
Exo 27:13 – "breadth of the court..east..50 cubits"
Exo 27:18 – "the courth..breadth fifty everywhere"
Exo 36:12 – "Fifty loops made he in one curtain"
Exo 36:12 – "fifty loops..in the edge of the curtain"
Exo 36:13 – "he made fifty taches of gold"
Exo 36:17 – "fifty loops upon..edge of the curtain"
Exo 36:17 – "fifty loops made he upon the edge"
Exo 36:18 – "he made fifty taches of brass"
Exo 38:12 – "west side were hangings..50 cubits"
Exo 38:13 – "east side eastward 50 cubits"
Lev 23:16 – "morrow after the seventh sabbath"
Lev 23:16 – "shall ye number fifty days"
Lev 27:3 – "estimation shall be fifty shekels"
Lev 27:16 – "homer..seed..valued 50 shekels"
Num 4:3 – "From 30 years old..until 50 years old"
Num 4:23 – "30 years old..until 50 years old"
Num 4:30 – "30 years old..until 50 years old"
Num 4:35 – "30 years old..until 50 years old"
Num 4:39 – "30 years old..until 50 years old"
Num 4:43 – "30 years old..until 50 years old"
Num 4:47 – "30 years old..until 50 years old"
Num 8:25 – "from..50 years..cease waiting"
Num 31:30 – "take one portion of fifty"

Num 31:47 – "Moses took one portion of fifty"
Deu 22:29 – "unto the damsel's father 50 shekels"
Jos 7:21 – "spoils..wedge of gold of 50 shekels"
2Sa 15:1 – "Absalom..50 men to run before him"
2Sa 24:24 – "threshingfloor..oxen for 50 shekels"
1Ki 1:5 – "Adonijah..fifty men to run before him"
1Ki 7:2 – "house of the forest..breadth..50 cubits"
1Ki 7:6 – "porch of pillars..length..50 cubits"
1Ki 18:4 – "took 100 prophets..hid them by 50"
1Ki 18:13 – "how I hid 100 men ..by 50 in a cave"
2Ki 1:9 – "king sent..a captain of 50 with his 50"
2Ki 1:10 – "Elijah answered the captain of 50"
2Ki 1:10 – "let fire..consume thee and thy 50"
2Ki 1:10 – "came..fire..consumed him and his 50"
2Ki 1:11 – "another captain of 50 with his 50"
2Ki 1:12 – "let fire..consume thee and thy 50"
2Ki 1:12 – "fire..consumed him and his 50"
2Ki 1:13 – "captain of the third 50 with his 50"
2Ki 1:13 – "And the third captain of fifty"
2Ki 1:13 – "let..the life of these 50 thy servants"
2Ki 2:7 – "50 men of the sons of the prophets"
2Ki 2:16 – "be with thy servants 50 strong men"
2Ki 2:17 – "They sent therefore 50 men"
2Ki 13:7 – "50 horsemen, and 10 chariots"
2Ki 15:20 – "of each man 50 shekels of silver"
2Ki 15:25 – "with him 50 men of the Gileadites"
2Ch 3:9 – "weight..nails was 50 shekels of gold"
Ezr 8:6 – "sons also of Adin..50 males"
Neh 7:70 – "gave to the treasure..50 basons"
Est 5:14 – "gallows be made of 50 cubits hight"
Est 7:9 – "gallows 50 cubits high, which Haman"
Isa 3:3 – "captain of 50, and the honourable man"
Ezk 40:15 – "gate..unto..porch..were 50 cubits"
Ezk 40:21 – "arches..length thereof..50 cubits"
Ezk 40:25 – "arches..length was 50 cubits"
Ezk 40:29 – "arches..it was 50 cubits long"
Ezk 40:33 – "arches..it was 50 cubits long"
Ezk 40:36 – "arches..length was 50 cubits"
Ezk 42:2 – "Before..north door..breadth..50 cubits"
Ezk 42:7 – "wall..length thereof was 50 cubits"
Ezk 42:8 – "length of the chambers..was 50 cubits"
Ezk 45:2 – "50 cubits round about..suburbs"
Hag 2:16 – "draw out 50 vessels..were but 20"
Luk 7:41 – "one owed 500 pence..the other 50"
Luk 16:6 – "sit down quickly, and write 50"
Joh 8:57 – "Thou are not yet 50 years old"

50th

Lev 25:10 – "ye shall hallow the fiftieth year"
Lev 25:11 – "A jubile shall..50th year be unto you"
2Ki 15:23 – "50th year of Azariah..Pekahiah..began"

50's   Fifties

Listed at the end of Section One under the heading,
Indefinite Numbers.

52

2Ki 15:2 – "he reigned 52 years in Jerusalem"
2Ch 26:3 – "Uzziah..reigned 52 years..Jerusalem"
Ezr 2:29 – "The children of Nebo, 52"
Neh 6:15 – "wall was finished..in 52 days"
Neh 7:33 – "The men of the other Nebo, 52"

52nd

2Ki 15:27 – "52nd year of Azariah..Pekah..began"

55

2Ki 21:1 – "Manasseh..reigned 55 years"
2Ch 33:1 – "Manasseh..reigned 55 years"

56

Ezr 2:22 – "The men of Netophah, 56"

60

Gen 25:26 – "Isaac..60 years old when she bare"
Lev 27:3 – "estimation..unto sixty years old"
Lev 27:7 – estimation "be from sixty years old"
Num 7:88 – "the rams sixty"
Num 7:88 – the he goats sixty"
Num 7:88 – "the lambs of the first year sixty"
Deu 3:4 – "we took all his cities..60 cities..Og"
Jos 13:30 – "Bashan..all the towns of Jair..60 cities"
1Ki 4:13 – "60 great cities w/ walls & brazen bars"
1Ki 4:22 – "Solomon's..60 measures of meal"
1Ki 6:2 – "house..for the LORD..length..60 cubits"
2Ki 25:19 – "60 men of the people of the land"
1Ch 2:21 – "Hezron..married when..60 years old"
1Ch 2:23 – "60 cities..belonged to..sons of Machir"
2Ch 3:3 – "house of God..length..60 cubits"
2Ch 11:21 – "Rehoboam..took..60 concubines"
2Ch 11:21 – "Rehoboam..begat..60 daughters"
Ezr 6:3 – "house of God..height thereof 60 cubits"
Ezr 6:3 – "house of God..breadth..60 cubits"
Ezr 8:13 – "last sons of Adonikam..60 males"
Son 3:7 – "bed..60 valiant men are about it"
Son 6:8 – "There are threescore queens"
Jer 52:25 – "60 men of the people of the land"
Ezk 40:14 – "He made also posts of 60 cubits"
Dan 3:1 – "image of gold..height was 60 cubits"
Mat 13:23 – "beareth fruit..some sixty"
Luk 24:13 – "Emmaus..Jerusalem..60 furlongs"
1Ti 5:9 – "not a widow..under 60 years old"

60-fold – Sixtyfold

Mat 13:8 – "brought forth fruit, some 60-fold"
Mat 13:23 – "beareth fruit..some sixty"
Mar 4:8 – "yield fruit..increased..some sixty"
Mar 4:20 – "bring forth fruit..some sixty"

61

Num 31:39 – "asses..the LORD's tribute was 61"

62

1Ch 26:8 – "these of the sons of Obededom..62"
Dan 5:31 – "Darius..Median..about 62 years old"
Dan 9:25 – "commandment..Messiah..62 weeks"
Dan 9:26 – "after 62 weeks..Messiah be cut off"

65

Gen 5:15 – "Mahalaleel lived 65 years and begat"
Gen 5:21 – "Enoch lived 65 years, and begat"
Isa 7:8 – "w/in 65 years shall Ephraim be broken"

66

Gen 46:26 – "All the souls..into Egypt..66"
Lev 12:5 – "continue...blood...purifying 66 days"

67

Neh 7:72 – "people gave..67 priests garments"

68

1Ch 16:38 – "Obededom with their brethren, 68"

70

Gen 5:12 – "Cainan lived 70 years, and begat"
Gen 11:26 – "Terah lived 70 years..begat Abrahm"
Gen 46:27 – "all..souls of the house of Jacob..70"
Gen 50:3 – "mourned for him 70 days"
Exo 1:5 – "souls..of the loins of Jacob..70 souls"
Exo 15:27 – "Elim..70 palm trees"
Exo 24:1 – "seventy of the elders of Israel"
Exo 24:9 – "seventy of the elders of Israel"
Exo 38:29 – "brass..70 talents, and 2,400 shekels"
    ➢ *Thus, 212,400 shekels or 70.8 talents*
Num 7:13 – "silver bowl of 70 shekels"
Num 7:19 – "silver bowl of 70 shekels"

Num 7:25 – "silver bowl of 70 shekels"
Num 7:31 – "silver bowl of 70 shekels"
Num 7:37 – "silver bowl of 70 shekels"
Num 7:43 – "silver bowl of 70 shekels"
Num 7:49 – "silver bowl of 70 shekels"
Num 7:55 – "silver bowl of 70 shekels"
Num 7:61 – "silver bowl of 70 shekels"
Num 7:67 – "silver bowl of 70 shekels"
Num 7:73 – "silver bowl of 70 shekels"
Num 7:79 – "silver bowl of 70 shekels"
Num 7:85 – "30 shekels, each bowl seventy"
Num 11:16 – "seventy men of the elders of Israel"
Num 11:24 – "gathered the 70 men of the elders"
Num 11:25 – "spirit..gave it unto the 70 elders"
Num 33:9 – "Elim..70 palm trees"
Deu 10:22 – "down into Egypt with 70 persons"
Jdg 1:7 – "70 kings..thumbs..great toes cut off"
Jdg 8:30 – "Gideon had 70 sons of his body"
Jdg 9:2 – "sons of Jerubbaal..70 persons"
Jdg 9:4 – "they gave him 70 pieces of silver"
Jdg 9:5 – "slew.. sons of Jerubbaal..70 persons"
Jdg 9:18 – "slain..70 persons, upon one stone"
Jdg 9:24 – "cruelty..to the 70 sons of Jerubbaal"
Jdg 9:56 – "Abimelech..slaying his 70 brethren"
Jdg 12:14 – "40 sons..rode..70 ass colts"
2Ki 10:1 – "Ahab had 70 sons in Samaria"
2Ki 10:6 – "the king's sons, being 70 persons"
2Ki 10:7 – "slew 70 persons, and put their heads"
2Ch 29:32 – "congregation brought..70 bullocks"
2Ch 36:21 – "she kept Sabbath, to fulfil 70 years"
Ezr 8:7 – "sons of Elam..70 males"
Ezr 8:14 – "sons also of Bigvai..70 males"
Psa 90:10 – "days of our years are 70"
Isa 23:15 – "Tyre shall be forgotten 70 years"
Isa 23:15 – "after..70 years..Tyre sing as an harlot"
Isa 23:17 – "after..70 years..LORD will visit Tyre"
Jer 25:11 – "serve the king of Babylon 70 years"
Jer 25:12 – "when 70 years are accomplished'
Jer 29:10 – "after 70 years be accomplished"
Ezk 8:11 – "70 men of the ancients of ..Israel"
Ezk 41:12 – "building..west..70 cubits broad"
Dan 9:2 – "70 years..desolations of Jerusalem"
Dan 9:24 – "70 weeks are determined"
Zec 1:12 – "had indignation these 70 years"
Zec 7:5 – "fasted..mourned..those 70 years"
Luk 10:1 – "the Lord appointed other 70 also"
Luk 10:17 – "the 70 returned again with joy"
Act 23:23 – "to Caesarea..horsemen 70"

70.8

Exo 38:29 – "brass..70 talents, and 2,400 shekels"
  ➢ *Thus, 212,400 shekels or 70.8 talents*

72

Num 31:38 – "beeves..the LORD's tribute was 72"
2Ki 25:19 – number slain by Nebuchadnezzar

74

Ezr 2:40 – "Levites..children of Jesuha..74"
Neh 7:43 – "Levites..children of Jeshua..74"

75

Gen 12:4 – "Abram..75 years old..departed..Haran"
Act 7:14 – "Joseph..all his kindred, 75 souls"

77

Jdg 8:14 – "Succoth..princes..elders..77 men"
Ezr 8:35 – "burnt offerings..77 lambs"

77-fold – Seventy-seven Fold

Gen 4:24 – "avenged..truly Lamech 77-fold"

80

Exo 7:7 – "Moses..80 years old..spake..Pharaoh"
Lev 12:5 – 2 weeks + 66 days – lady's purification
Jdg 3:30 – "Moab subdued..land had rest 80 years"
2Sa 19:32 – "Barzillai..very aged..80 years old"
2Sa 19:35 – "I am this day fourscore years old"
2Ki 6:25 – "ass's head..sold for 80 pieces of silver"
2Ki 10:24 – "Jehu appointed 80 men without"
1Ch 15:9 – "sons of Hebron..brethren..80"
2Ch 26:17 – "Azariah..80 priests of the LORD"
Ezr 8:8 – "sons of Shephatiah..80 males"
Psa 90:10 – "reason of strength they be 80 years"
Son 6:8 – "There are..fourscore concubines"
Jer 41:5 – "80 men..beards shaven..clothes rent"
Luk 16:7 – "Take thy bill, and write 80"

83

Exo 7:7 – "Aaron 83 years old..unto Pharaoh"

84

Luk 2:37 – "she was a widow of about 84 years"

85

Jos 14:10 – "lo, I am this day 85 years old"
1Sa 22:18 – "slew..85 persons..did wear..ephod"

86

Gen 16:16 – "Abram..86 years old..Hagar bare"

90

Gen 5:9 – "Enos lived 90 years, and begat Cainan"
Gen 17:17 – "Sarah, that is 90 years old, bear?"
Ezk 41:12 – "building..length thereof 90 cubits"

95

Ezr 2:20 – "The children of Gibbar, 95"
Neh 7:25 – "The children of Gibeon, 95"

96

Ezr 8:35 – "burnt offerings..96 rams"
Jer 52:23 – "96 pomegranates on a side"

98

1Sa 4:15 – "Now Eli was 98 years old"
Ezr 2:16 – "The children of Ater of Hezekiah, 98"
Neh 7:21 – "The children of Ater of Hezekiah, 98"

99

Gen 17:1 – "Abram..99 years old..LORD appeared"
Gen 17:24 – "Abraham..99 years old..circumcised"
Mat 18:12 – "100 sheep..leave the 99"
Mat 18:13 – "the 99 which went not go astray"
Luk 15:4 – "doth not leave the 99 in..wilderness"
Luk 15:7 – "99 just persons..need no repentance"

100

Gen 11:10 – "Shem..100 years..begat Arphaxad"
Gen 17:17 – "child..born unto him..100 years old?"
Gen 21:5 – "Abraham..100 years old..Isaac..born"
Gen 33:19 – "bought..a field..100 pieces of money"
Exo 27:9 – "hangings for..court..100 cubits long"
Exo 27:11 – "hangings of 100 cubits long"
Exo 27:18 – "length of the court..be 100 cubits"
Exo 38:9 – "the hangings of the court..100 cubits"
Exo 38:11 – "north side the hangings..100 cubits"
Exo 38:25 – "silver..100 talents, & 1,775 shekels"
  ➢ *Thus, 301,775 shekels or 100.59 talents*
Exo 38:27 – "of the 100 talents..cast the sockets"
Exo 38:27 – "100 sockets of the 100 talents"
Lev 26:8 – "five of you shall chase an 100"
Lev 26:8 – "100 of you shall put 10,000 to flight"
Deu 22:19 – "amerce him in 100 shekels of silver"

Jos 24:32 – "Jacob bought..for 100 pieces..silver"
Jdg 7:19 – "Gideon and the 100 men..with him"
Jdg 20:10 – "we will take ten men of an hundred"
Jdg 20:10 – "an hundred of a thousand"
1Sa 18:25 – "an 100 foreskins of the Philistines"
1Sa 25:18 – "Abigail..took..100 clusters of raisins"
2Sa 3:14 – "an 100 foreskins of the Philistines"
2Sa 8:4 – "reserved of them for an 100 chariots"
2Sa 16:1 – "Ziba..with..100 bunches of raisins"
2Sa 16:1 – "Ziba..with..100 of summer fruits"
1Ki 4:23 – "100 sheep, beside harts"
1Ki 7:2 – "house..of Lebanon..length..100 cubits"
1Ki 18:4 – "Obadiah took 100 prophets..hid them"
1Ki 18:13 – "how I hid 100 men..by 50 in a cave"
2Ki 4:43 – "should I set this before 100 men?"
2Ki 23:33 – "a tribute of 100 talents of silver"
1Ch 12:14 – "one of the least was over an 100"
1Ch 18:4 – "David..reserved of them 100 chariots"
1Ch 21:3 – "LORD make his people 100 times"
2Ch 3:16 – "made 100 pomegranates..chains"
2Ch 4:8 – "he made 100 basons of gold"
2Ch 25:6 – "hired..men..for 100 talents of silver"
2Ch 25:9 – "what shall we do for the 100 talents"
2Ch 27:5 – "Ammon gave..100 talents of silver"
2Ch 29:32 – "congregation brought..100 rams"
2Ch 36:3 – "condemned..land..100 talents..silver"
2Ch 36:9 – "Jeohiachin..reigned 3 months..10 days"
Ezr 2:69 – "They gave..100 priests' garments"
Ezr 6:17 – "offered at..dedication..100 bullocks"
Ezr 7:22 – "Unto 100 talents of silver"
Ezr 7:22 – "and to 100 measures of wheat"
Ezr 7:22 – "and to 100 baths of wine"
Ezr 7:22 – "and to 100 baths of oil, and salt"
Ezr 8:26 – "weighed..silver vessels 100 talents"
Ezr 8:26 – "weighed..of gold 100 talents"
Pro 17:10 – "more than 100 stripes into a fool"
Ecc 6:3 – "if a man beget 100 children"
Ecc 8:12 – "Though a sinner do evil 100 times"
Isa 65:20 – "child shall die an 100 years old"
Isa 65:20 – "sinner..100 years old..be accursed"
Jer 52:23 – "pomegranates..an 100 round about"
Ezk 40:19 – "100 cubits eastward and northward"
Ezk 40:23 – "from gate to gate 100 cubits"
Ezk 40:27 – "from gate to gate..100 cubits"
Ezk 40:47 – "the court, 100 cubits long"
Ezk 40:47 – "the court..100 cubits broad"
Ezk 41:13 – "the house, an 100 cubits long"
Ezk 41:13 – "building..walls..100 cubits long"
Ezk 41:14 – "breadth..house..east, an 100 cubits"
Ezk 41:15 – "length of the building..100 cubits"
Ezk 42:2 – "Before..length..100 cubits..north door"
Ezk 42:8 – "before the temple were an 100 cubits"
Amo 5:3 – "went out by a 1000 shall leave 100"
Amo 5:3 – "went out by an 100 shall leave ten"
Mat 18:12 – "100 sheep, and one..gone astray"
Mat 18:28 – "fellowservants..owed..100 pence"
Luk 15:4 – "an 100 sheep, if he lose one"
Luk 16:6 – "An 100 measures of oil"
Luk 16:7 – "An 100 measures of wheat"
Joh 19:39 – "myrrh..aloes..100 pound weight"
Rom 4:19 – "when he was about an 100 years old"

100's – Hundreds

Listed at the end of Section One under the heading, **Indefinite Numbers.**

Centurion – Leader of 100 Men

Appears 24x as *centurion, centurions,* and *centurion's* – see a standard concordance

100-fold – Hundredfold

Gen 26:12 – "Isaac sowed..received..100 fold"
2Sa 24:3 – "God add unto thy people..100 fold"
Mat 13:8 – "brought forth fruit, some an 100 fold"
Mat 13:23 – "beareth fruit..some an 100 fold"
Mat 19:29 – "receive 100-fold..everlasting life"
Mar 4:8 – "yield fruit..increased..some an 100"
Mar 4:20 – "bring forth fruit..some an 100"
Mar 10:30 – "shall receive an hundredfold now"
Luk 8:8 – "fell on good ground..bare fruit 100 fold"

100.59

Exo 38:25 – "silver..100 talents, & 1,775 shekels"
   ➢ *Thus, 301,775 shekels or 100.59 talents*

105

Gen 5:6 – "Seth lived 105 years and begat"

110

Gen 50:22 – "Joseph lived an 110 years"
Gen 50:26 – "Joseph died, being an 110 years old"
Jos 24:29 – "Joshua..died being an 110 years old"
Jdg 2:8 – "Joshua..died being an 110 years old"
Ezr 8:12 – "sons of Azgad..110 males"

112

1Ch 15:10 – "sons of Uzziel..112"
Ezr 2:18 – "The children of Jorah, 112."
Neh 7:24 – "The children of Hariph, 112."

119

Gen 11:25 – "Nahor lived after..Terah 119 years"

120

Gen 6:3 – "his days shall be 120 years"
Num 7:86 – "gold..spoons was 120 shekels"
Deu 31:2 – "I am an 120 years old this day"
Deu 34:7 – "Moses..120 years old when he died"
1Ki 9:14 – "Hiram sent..king 120 talents of gold"
1Ki 10:10 – "she gave..king an 120 talents of gold"
1Ch 15:5 – "Of the sons of Kohath..an 120"
2Ch 3:4 – "porch..cubits..height was 120"
2Ch 5:12 – "120 priests sounding with trumpets"
2Ch 9:9 – "gave the king 120 talents of gold"
Dan 6:1 – "Darius set over..kingdom 120 princes"
Act 1:15 – "number of the names..about an 120"

122

Ezr 2:27 – "The men of Michmas, 122"
Neh 7:31 – "The men of Michmas, 122"

123

Num 33:39 – "Aaron..123 years old when he died"
Ezr 2:21 – "The children of Bethlehem, 123"
Neh 7:32 – "The men of Bethel and Ai, 123

127

Gen 23:1 – "Sarah was 127 years old"
Est 1:1 – "Ahasuerus..reigned..over 127 provinces"
Est 8:9 – "India unto Ethiopia, an 127 provinces"
Est 9:30 – "sent..letters..unto all..127 provinces"

128

Ezr 2:23 – "The men of Anathoth, 128"
Ezr 2:41 – "singers: the children of Asaph, 128"
Neh 7:27 – "The men of Anathoth, 128"
Neh 11:14 – "brethren, mighty men..valour, 128"

130

Gen 5:3 – "Adam lived 130 years..begat"
Gen 47:9 – "year of my pilgrimage are 130 years"
Num 7:13 – "charger..weight..130 shekels"
Num 7:19 – "charger..weight..130 shekels"
Num 7:25 – "charger..weight..130 shekels"
Num 7:31 – "charger..weight..130 shekels"
Num 7:37 – "charger..weight..130 shekels"
Num 7:43 – "charger..weight..130 shekels"
Num 7:49 – "charger..weight..130 shekels"
Num 7:55 – "charger..weight..130 shekels"
Num 7:61 – "charger..weight..130 shekels"
Num 7:67 – "charger..weight..130 shekels"

Num 7:73 – "charger..weight..130 shekels"
Num 7:79 – "charger..weight..130 shekels"
Num 7:85 – "each charger..weighing 130 shekels"
1Ch 15:7 – "Of the sons of Gershom..130"
2Ch 24:15 – "Jehoiada..130 years old..he died"

133

Exo 6:18 – "years of the life of Kohath..133 years"

137

Gen 25:17 – "life of Ishmael..137 years"
Exo 6:16 – "years of the life of Levi..137 years"
Exo 6:20 – "years of the life of Amram..137 years"

138

Neh 7:45 – "porters..children of Shallum..138"

139

Ezr 2:42 – "The children of the porters..in all 139"

140

Job 42:16 – "After this lived Job 140 years"

144

Rev 21:17 – "measured the wall..144 cubits"

147

Gen 47:28 – "whole age of Jacob was 147 years"

148

Neh 7:44 – "singers: the children of Asaph, 148"

150

Gen 7:24 – "waters prevailed..150 days"
Gen 8:3 – "end of the 150 days..waters..abated"
1Ki 10:29 – "skekels of silver..horse for an 150"
1Ch 8:40 – "sons of Ulam..mighty men..an 150"
2Ch 1:17 – "shekels of silver..horse for an 150"
Ezr 8:3 – "sons of Shechaniah..males 150"
Neh 5:17 – "at my table 150 of the Jews & rulers"

153

Joh 21:11 – "net..full of great fishes, an 153"

156

Ezr 2:30 – "The children of Magbish, 156"

160

Ezr 8:10 – "sons of Shelomith..160 males"

162

Gen 5:18 – "Jared lived 162 years and begat"

172

Neh 11:19 – "porters..kept the gates, were 172"

175

Gen 25:7 – "Abraham's life..175 years"

180

Gen 35:28 – "days of Isaac were 180 years"
Est 1:4 – "shewed..glorious kingdom..180 days"

182

Gen 5:28 – "Lamech lived 182 years, and begat"

187

Gen 5:25 – "Methuselah lived 187 years, & begat"

188

Neh 7:26 – "men of Bethlehem..Netophah, 188"

195

2Co 11:24 – "5 times received..40 stripes save 1"

200

Gen 11:23 – "Serug lived after..Nahor 200 years"
Gen 32:14 – "200 she goats..200 ewes"
Jos 7:21 – "I saw..200 shekels of silver..took them"
Jdg 17:4 – "200 shekels..made..a graven image"
1Sa 18:27 – "slew of the Philistines 200 men"
1Sa 25:13 – "and 200 abode by the stuff"
1Sa 25:18 – "Abigail..took 200 loaves"
1Sa 25:18 – "Abigail..took..200 cakes of figs"
1Sa 30:10 – "for 200 abode behind"
1Sa 30:21 – "200 men, which we so faint"
2Sa 14:26 – "weighed the hair..at 200 shekels"
2Sa 15:11 – "w/ Absalom..200 men..of Jerusalem"
2Sa 16:1 – "Ziba..met him..200 loaves of bread"
1Ki 7:20 – "the pomegranates were 200 in rows"
1Ki 10:16 – "Solomon made 200 targets of..gold"
1Ch 12:32 – "Issachar..heads of them were 200"
1Ch 15:8 – "Of the sons of Elizaphan..200"
2Ch 9:15 – "Solomon made 200 targets of..gold"
2Ch 29:32 – "congregation brought..200 lambs"
Ezr 2:65 – "200 singing men and singing women"
Ezr 6:17 – "dedication of this house..200 rams"
Ezr 8:4 – "sons of Pahathmoab..200 males"
Son 8:12 – "those that keep the fruit thereof 200"
Ezk 45:15 – "one lamb out of..two hundred"
Mar 6:37 – "buy 200 pennyworth of bread"
Joh 6:7 – "200 pennyworth..bread..not sufficient"
Joh 21:8 – "not far from land..200 cubits"
Act 23:23 – "Make ready 200 soldiers..Caesarea"
Act 23:23 – "to Caesarea..spearmen 200"

205

Gen 11:32 – "days of Terah were 205 years"

207

Gen 11:21 – "Reu..after he begat Serug 207 years"

209

Gen 11:19 – "Peleg..after he begat Reu 209 years"

212

1Ch 9:22 – "porters in the gates were 212"

218

Ezr 8:9 – "sons of Joab..218 males"

220

1Ch 15:6 – "Of the sons of Merari..220"
Ezr 8:20 – "of the Nethinims..220 Nethinims"

223

Ezr 2:19 – "The children of Hashum, 223."
Ezr 2:28 – "The men of Bethel and Ai, 223."

232

1Ki 20:15 – "numbered the young men..232"

242

Neh 11:13 – "brethren, chief of the fathers, 242"

245

Ezr 2:66 – "their mules, 245"
Neh 7:67 – "245 singing men and singing women"
Neh 7:68 – "their mules, 245"

250

Exo 30:23 – "spices..cinnamon..250 shekels"
Exo 30:23 – "spices..calamus 250 shekels"
Num 16:2 – "250 princes of the assembly"
Num 16:17 – "every man his censer, 250 censers"
Num 16:35 – "fire..consumed..250 men..incense"
Num 26:10 – "Korah...fire devoured 250 men"
2Ch 8:10 – "Solomon's officers..250..bare rule"
Ezk 48:17 – "suburbs..toward the north 250"
Ezk 48:17 – "suburbs..toward the south 250"
Ezk 48:17 – "suburbs..toward the east 250"
Ezk 48:17 – "suburbs..toward the west 250"

273

Num 3:46 – *firstborn of Israel minus all of the Levites*
  ➢ *22,273 – 22,000 = 273*

276

Act 27:37 – "we were in all in the ship 276 souls"

284

Neh 11:18 – "Levites in the holy city were 284"

288

1Ch 25:7 – "brethren..instructed in the songs..288"

290

2Sa 24:8 – 9 mos & 20 days to number Israel

300

Gen 5:22 – "Enoch walked with God..300 years"
Gen 6:15 – "length of the ark shall be 300 cubits"
Gen 45:22 – "to Benjamin..300 pieces of silver"
Jdg 7:6 – "putting..hand to their mouth..300 men"
Jdg 7:7 – "By..300 men that lapped will I save you"
Jdg 7:8 – "he..retained those 300 men"
Jdg 7:16 – "divided the 300 men into 3 companies"
Jdg 7:22 – "And the 300 blew the trumpets"
Jdg 8:4 – "300 men..faint, yet pursuing them"
Jdg 11:26 – "Israel..coasts of Arnon, 300 years"
Jdg 15:4 – "Samson went and caught 300 foxes"
2Sa 21:16 – "Ishbibenob..spear..300 shekels"
2Sa 23:18 – "Abishai..spear against 300..slew"
1Ki 10:17 – "he made 300 shields of beaten gold"
1Ki 11:3 – "he had 700 wives..300 concubines"
2Ki 18:14 – "king..appointed..300 talents..silver"
1Ch 11:11 – "his spear against 300..at one time"
1Ch 11:20 – "Abishai..his spear against 300"
2Ch 9:16 – "300 shields made he of beaten gold"
2Ch 9:16 – "300 shekels of gold went to 1 shield"
2Ch 14:9 – "Zerah the Ethiopian w/..300 chariots"
2Ch 35:8 – "for the passover offerings..300 oxen"
Ezr 8:5 – "sons of Shechaniah..300 males"
Est 9:15 – "Jews..in Shushan..slew 300 men"
Mar 14:5 – "sold for more than 300 pence"
Joh 12:5 – "this ointment sold for 300 pence"

318

Gen 14:14 – "he armed his trained servants..318"

320

Ezr 2:32 – "The children of Harim, 320."
Neh 7:35 – "The children of Harim, 320."

323

Ezr 2:17 – "The children of Bezai, 323"

324

Neh 7:23 – "The children of Bezai, 324."

328

Neh 7:22 – "The children of Hashum, 328."

345

Ezr 2:34 – "The children of Jericho, 345."
Neh 7:36 – "The children of Jericho, 345."

350

Gen 9:28 – "Noah lived after the flood 350 years."

360

2Sa 2:31 – "Abner's men..360 men died"

365

Gen 5:23 – "days of Enoch were 365 years"

372

Ezr 2:4 – "The children of Shephatiah. 372."
Neh 7:9 – "The children of Shephatiah, 372."

390

Ezk 4:5 – "years of their iniquity..390 days"
Ezk 4:9 – "lie upon thy side, 390 days"

392

Ezr 2:58 – "All the Nethinims..392"
Neh 7:60 – "All the Nethinims..392"

400

Gen 15:13 – "they shall afflict them 400 years"
Gen 23:15 – "land..worth 400 shekels of silver"
Gen 23:16 – "Abraham..weighed..400 shekels"
Gen 32:6 – "Esau..cometh..400 men with him"
Gen 33:1 – "Esau came, and with him 400 men"
Jdg 21:12 – "four hundred young virgins"
1Sa 22:2 – "were with him about 400 men"
1Sa 25:13 – "up after David about 400 men"
1Sa 30:10 – "David pursued, he and 400 men"
1Sa 30:17 – "400 young men..rode..camels..fled"
1Ki 7:42 – "400 pomegranates..two networks"
1Ki 18:19 – "the prophets of the groves 400"

1Ki 22:6 – "gathered..prophets..about 400 men"
2Ki 14:13 – "brake down the wall..400 cubits"
2Ch 4:13 – "400 pomegranates..two wreaths"
2Ch 18:5 – "gathered..of prophets 400 men"
2Ch 25:23 – "brake down the wall..400 cubits"
Ezr 6:17 – "dedication..house of God..400 lambs"
Act 5:36 – "Theudas..number of men, about 400"
Act 7:6 – "entreat them evil 400 years"

403

Gen 11:13 – "lived after he begat Salah 403 years"
Gen 11:15 – "Salah..after..begat Eber 403 years"

410

Ezr 1:10 – "silver basons of a 2nd sort 410"

420

1Ki 9:28 – "fetched from thence gold, 420 talents"

430

Gen 11:17 – "Eber lived after..Peleg 430 years"
Exo 12:40 – "sojourning..in Egypt, was 430 years"
Exo 12:41 – "end of the 430 years..selfsame day"
Gal 3:17 – "the law, which was 430 years after"

435

Ezr 2:67 – "Their camels, 435"
Neh 7:69 – "Their camels, 435"

450

1Ki 18:19 – "the prophets of Baal 450"
1Ki 18:22 – "Baal's prophets are 450 men"
2Ch 8:18 – "450 talents of gold..to king Solomon"
Act 13:20 – "judges about the space of 450 years"

454

Ezr 2:15 – "The children of Adin, 454"

468

Neh 11:6 – "sons of Perez..were 468"

480th

1Ki 6:1 – "the 480th year..come out..Egypt"

490

Mat 18:22 – "but, Until seventy times seven"

500

Gen 5:32 – "Noah..500 years old..begat Shem"
Gen 11:11 – "Shem..after..Arphaxad 500 years"
Exo 30:23 – "spices..myrrh 500 shekels"
Exo 30:24 – "And of cassia 500 shekels"
1Ch 4:42 – "sons of Simeon, 500 men"
2Ch 35:9 – "for passover offerings..500 oxen"
Est 9:6 – "in Shushan..Jews slew..500 men"
Est 9:12 – "Jews have..destroyed 500 men"
Job 1:3 – "His substance..500 yoke of oxen"
Job 1:3 – "His substance..500 she asses"
Ezk 42:16 – "east side..500 reeds"
Ezk 42:17 – "north side..500 reeds"
Ezk 42:18 – "south side..500 reeds"
Ezk 42:19 – "west side..500 reeds"
Ezk 42:20 – "wall round about, 500 reeds long"
Ezk 42:20 – "wall round about..500 reeds broad"
Ezk 45:2 – "for the sanctuary 500 in length"
Ezk 45:2 – "for the sanctuary..500 in breadth"
Luk 7:41 – "one owed 500 pence..the other 50"
1Co 15:6 – "seen of above 500 brethren at once"

530

Neh 7:70 – "gave..530 priests' garments"

550

1Ki 9:23 – "550, which bare rule over the people"

595

Gen 5:30 – "Lamech lived after..Noah 595 years"

600

Gen 7:6 – "Noah..600 years old when the flood"
Exo 14:7 – "he took 600 chosen chariots"
Jdg 3:31 – "Shamgar..slew..Philistines 600 men"
Jdg 18:11 – "Danites..600 men..weapons of war"
Jdg 18:16 – "600 men..with their weapons"
Jdg 18:17 – "600 men..with weapons of war"
Jdg 20:47 – "600 men..fled to the wilderness"
1Sa 13:15 – "Saul numbered..about 600 men"

1Sa 14:2 – "Saul..with him were about 600 men"
1Sa 17:7 – "spear's head weighed 600 shekels"
1Sa 23:13 – "David and his men..were about 600"
1Sa 27:2 – "David arose..with the 600 men"
1Sa 30:9 – "David went, he and the 600 men"
2Sa 15:18 – "600 men which came after him"
1Ki 10:16 – "600 shekels of gold..to one target"
1Ki 10:29 – "chariot..for 600 shekels of silver"
1Ch 21:25 – "David gave..600 shekels of gold"
2Ch 1:17 – "a chariot for 600 shekels of silver"
2Ch 3:8 – "overlaid..with fine gold..600 talents"
2Ch 9:15 – "600 shekels of..gold..to one target"
2Ch 29:33 – "consecrated things..600 oxen"

621

Ezr 2:26 – "children of Ramah and Gaba, 621"
Neh 7:30 – "The men of Ramah and Geba, 621"

623

Ezr 2:11 –"The children of Bebai, 623"

628

Neh 7:16 – "The children of Bebai, 628"

642

Ezr 2:10 –"The children of Bani, 642"
Neh 7:62 – "The children of Delaiah..642"

648

Neh 7:15 – "The children of Binnui, 648"

650

Ezr 8:26 – "I..weighed..650 talents of silver"

652

Ezr 2:60 – "The children of Delaiah..652"
Neh 7:10 – "The children of Arah, 652"

655

Neh 7:20 – "The children of Adin, 655"

666

1Ki 10:14 – "gold..to Solomon..1 year..666 talents"
2Ch 9:13 – "gold..to Solomon..1 year..666 talents"
Ezr 2:13 – "The children of Adonikam, 666"
Rev 13:18 – "count the number of the beast..666"

667

Neh 7:18 – "The children of Adonikam, 667"

675

Num 31:37 – "LORD's tribute of..sheep was 675"

690

1Ch 9:6 – "And the sons of Zerah..690"

700

Jdg 20:15 – "children..Benjamin..700 chosen men"
Jdg 20:16 – "700 chosen men..could sling stones"
2Sa 8:4 – "David took..700 horsemen"
2Sa 10:18 – "David slew the men of 700 chariots"
1Ki 11:3 – "And he had 700 wives, princesses"
2Ki 3:26 – "king of Moab..took..700 men"
2Ch 15:11 – "offered..of the spoil..700 oxen"

721

Neh 7:37 – "children of Lod, Hadid, and Ono, 721"

725

Ezr 2:33 – "The children of Lod..725"

730

Exo 38:24 – "gold..29 talents, and 730 shekels"
  ➢   *Thus, 87,730 shekels or 29.24 talents*

736

Ezr 2:66 – "Their horses *were* 736"
Neh 7:68 – "Their horses, 736"

743

Ezr 2:25 – "The children of Kirjatharim..743"
Neh 7:29 – "The men of Kirjathjearim..743"

745

Jer 52:30 – "carried away captive..745 persons"

760

Ezr 2:9 – "The children of Zaccai, 760"
Neh 7:14 – "The children of Zaccai, 760"

775

Ezr 2:5 – "The children of Arah, 775"

777

Gen 5:31 – "the days of Lamech were 777 years"

782

Gen 5:26 – "Methuselah..after..Lamech 782 years"

800

Gen 5:4 – "days of Adam after..Seth..800 years"
Gen 5:19 – "Jared lived after..Enoch..800 years"
2Sa 23:8 – "Adino..against 800 whom he slew"

807

Gen 5:7 – "Seth lived after..Enos 807 years"

815

Gen 5:10 – "Enos lived after..Cainan..815 years"

822

Neh 11:12 – "brethren that did the work..822"

830

Gen 5:16 – "Mahalaleel..after..Jared 830 years"

832

Jer 52:29 – "carried away captive..832 persons"

840

Gen 5:13 – "Cainan..after..Mahalaleel..840 years"

845

Neh 7:13 – "The children of Zattu, 845"

895

Gen 5:17 – "days of Mahalaleel were 895 years"

900

Jdg 4:3 – "900 chariots..iron..mightily oppressed"
Jdg 4:13 – "Sisera gathered..900 chariots of iron"

905

Gen 5:11 – "the days of Enos were 905 years"

910

Gen 5:14 – "the days of Cainan were 910 years"

912

Gen 5:8 – "the days of Seth were 912 years"

928

Neh 11:8 – "after him Gabbai, Sallai, 928"

930

Gen 5:5 – "all the days..Adam..930 years"

945

Ezr 2:8 – "The children of Zattu, 945"

950

Gen 9:29 – "days of Noah were 950 years"

956

1Ch 9:9 – "And their brethren..956"

962

Gen 5:20 – "days of Jared were 962 years"

969

Gen 5:27 – "days of Methuselah..969 years"

973

Ezr 2:36 – "priests: the children of Jedaiah, 973"
Neh 7:39 – "priests: the children of Jedaiah..973"

1,000

Gen 20:16 – "given..brother 1000 pieces of silver"
Num 31:4 – "of every tribe a thousand"
Num 31:5 – "were delivered..1000 of every tribe"
Num 31:6 – "to the war, 1000 of every tribe"
Num 35:4 – "suburbs..from the wall..1000 cubits"
Deu 1:11 – "make you a 1000 times so many"
Deu 7:9 – "commandments to a 1000 generations"
Deu 32:30 – "How should one chase a thousand"
Jos 23:10 – "One man of you shall chase a 1000"
Jdg 9:49 – "died..about 1000 men and woman"
Jdg 15:15 – "jawbone of an ass..slew 1000 men"
Jdg 15:16 – "jaw of an ass have I slain 1000 men"
Jdg 20:10 – "take..an hundred of a thousand"
Jdg 20:10 – "a thousand out of ten thousand"
1Sa 13:2 – "1000 were with Jonathan in Gibeah"
1Sa 17:18 – "cheeses unto..captain of their 1000"
1Sa 18:13 – "Saul..made him..captain over a 1000"
1Sa 25:2 – "man in Maon..had..1000 goats"
2Sa 8:4 – "David took from him a 1000 chariots"
2Sa 10:6 – "and of king Maacah 1000 men"
2Sa 18:12 – "Though I..receive 1000 shekels"
2Sa 19:17 – "there were a 1000 men of Benjamin"
1Ki 3:4 – "1000 burnt offerings did Solomon offer"
2Ki 15:19 – "gave Pul 1000 talents of silver"
2Ki 24:16 – "craftsmen & smiths 1000..Babylon"
1Ch 12:14 – "the greatest over a thousand"
1Ch 12:34 – "And of Naphtali a 1000 captains"
1Ch 16:15 – "commanded to a 1000 generations"
1Ch 18:4 – "David took from him 1000 chariots"
1Ch 19:6 – "children of Ammon sent 1000 talents"
1Ch 29:21 – "sacrificed..even a thousand bullocks"

1Ch 29:21 – "sacrificed..1000 rams"
1Ch 29:21 – "sacrificed..1000 lambs"
2Ch 1:6 – "Solomon..offered 1000 burnt offerings"
2Ch 30:24 – "Hezekiah..did give..1000 bullocks"
2Ch 30:24 – "princes gave..1000 bullocks"
Ezr 1:9 – "1000 chargers of silver"
Ezr 1:10 – "basons of gold..other vessels 1000"
Ezr 8:27 – "20 basons of gold, of a 1000 drams"
Neh 3:13 – "repaired Hanun..1000 cubits..wall"
Neh 7:70 – "to the treasure..1000 drams of gold"
Job 1:3 – "His substance..500 yoke of oxen"
Job 9:3 – "he cannot answer him 1 of a 1000"
Job 33:23 – "one among 1000, to shew unto man"
Job 42:12 – "later end of Job..1000 yoke of oxen"
Job 42:12 – "later end of Job..1000 she asses"
Psa 50:10 – "cattle upon a 1000 hills"
Psa 84:10 – "a day in thy courts..better than 1000"
Psa 90:4 – "For 1000 years..are but as yesterday"
Psa 91:7 – "1000 shall fall at they side"
Psa 105:8 – "commanded to 1000 generations"
Ecc 6:6 – "though he live 1000 years twice told"
Ecc 7:28 – "one man among 1000 have I found"
Son 4:4 – "whereon they hang a 1000 bucklers"
Son 8:11 – "was to bring 1000 pieces of silver"
Son 8:12 – "O Solomon, must have a 1000"
Isa 7:23 – "were 1000 vines at a 1000 silverings"
Isa 30:17 – "1000 shall flee at the rebuke of one"
Isa 60:22 – "a little one shall become a thousand"
Ezk 47:3 – "he measured a 1000 cubits..ancles"
Ezk 47:4 – "he measured a 1000..to the knees"
Ezk 47:4 – "he measured a 1000..to the loins"
Ezk 47:5 – "he measured a 1000..was a river"
Dan 5:1 – "Belshazzar..feast to a 1000..lords"
Dan 5:1 – "drank wine before the 1000"
Amo 5:3 – "went out by a 1000 shall leave 100"
2Pe 3:8 – "one day..as a 1000 years"
2Pe 3:8 – "a 1000 years as one day"
Rev 20:2 – "Satan..bound him 1000 years"
Rev 20:3 – "till the 1000 years should be fulfilled"
Rev 20:4 – "lived..reigned with Christ 1000 years"
Rev 20:5 – "rest of the dead lived not..1000 years"
Rev 20:6 – "shall reign with him 1000 years"
Rev 20:7 – "1000 years are expired..Satan..loosed"

1,000's – Thousands

Listed at the end of Section One under the heading, **Indefinite Numbers**.

1,005

1Ki 4:32 – "his songs were 1005"

1,017

Ezr 2:39 – "The children of Harim, 1017"
Neh 7:42 – "The children of Harim, 1017"

1,052

Ezr 2:37 – "The children of Immer, 1052"
Neh 7:40 – "The children of Immer, 1052"

1,100

Jdg 16:5 – "every one of us 1100 pieces..silver"
Jdg 17:2 – "1100 shekels of silver..were taken"
Jdg 17:3 – "restored the 1100 shekels of silver"

1,200

2Ch 12:3 – "1200 chariots..out of Egypt"

1,222

Ezr 2:12 – "The children of Azgad, 1222"

1,247

Ezr 2:38 – "The children of Pashur, 1247"
Neh 7:41 – "The children of Pashur, 1247"

1,254

Ezr 2:7 – "The children of Elam, 1254"
Ezr 2:31 – "children of the other Elam, 1254"
Neh 7:12 – "The children of Elam, 1254"
Neh 7:34 – "children of the other Elam, 1254"

1,260

Rev 11:3 – "my witnesses..prophesy 1260 days"
Rev 12:6 – "should feed her there 1260 days"

1,290

Dan 12:11 – "there shall be 1290 days"

1,335

Dan 12:12 – "Blessed..cometh to the 1335 days"

1,365

Num 3:50 – "Of the firstborn..1365 shekels"

1,400

1Ki 10:26 – "Solomon..had 1400 chariots"
2Ch 1:14 – "Solomon..had 1400 chariots"

1,600

Rev 14:20 – "blood..space of 1600 furlongs"

1,700

Jdg 8:26 – "earrings..1700 shekels of gold"
1Ch 26:30 – "Hebronites..1700, were officers"

1,760

1Ch 9:13 – "brethren..of their fathers, 1760"

1,775

Exo 38:25 – "silver..100 talents..1775 shekels"
  ➢ *Thus, 301,775 shekels or 100.59 talents*
Exo 38:28 – "of the 1775 shekels..made hooks"

2,000

Num 35:5 – "measure..city..east side 2000 cubits"
Num 35:5 – "measure..city..south..2000 cubits"
Num 35:5 – "measure..city..west side 2000 cubits"
Num 35:5 – "measure..city..north..2000 cubits"
Jos 3:4 – "space between you and it..2000 cubits"
Jos 7:3 – "about *2000* or 3000 men go..smite Ai"
Jdg 20:45 – "unto Gidom, and slew 2,000 men"
1Sa 13:2 – "2000 were with Saul in Michmash"
1Ki 7:26 – "it contained 2000 baths"
2Ki 18:23 – "I will deliver thee 2000 horses"
1Ch 5:21 – "they took away..of asses 2000"
Neh 7:72 – "people gave..2000 pound of silver"
Ecc 6:6 – "though he live 1000 years twice told"
Isa 36:8 – "I will give thee 2000 horses"
Mar 5:13 – "swine..they were about 2000"

2,056

Ezr 2:14 – "The children of Bigvai, 2056"

2,067

Neh 7:19 – "The children of Bigvai, 2067"

2,172

Ezr 2:3 – "The children of Parosh, 2172"
Neh 7:8 – "The children of Parosh, 2172"

2,200

Neh 7:71 – "fathers gave..2200 pound of silver"

2,300

Dan 8:14 – "Unto 2300 days..sanctuary..cleansed"

2,322

Neh 7:17 – "The children of Azgad, 2322"

2,400

Exo 38:29 – "brass..70 talents..2400 shekels"
   ➢   *Thus, 212,400 shekels or 70.8 talents*
Num 7:85 – "all the silver vessels..2400 shekels"

2,600

2Ch 26:12 – "chief of the fathers..were 2600"
2Ch 35:8 – "passover offerings 2,600 small cattle"

2,630

Num 4:40 – "those..numbered..were 2630"

2,700

1Ch 26:32 – "2700 chief fathers..made rulers"

2,750

Num 4:36 – "those..numbered..were 2750"

2,812

Ezr 2:6 – "children of Pahathmoab..2812"

2,818

Neh 7:11 – "children of Pahathmoab..2818"

3,000

Exo 32:28 – "fell of the people..about 3000 men"
Jos 7:3 – "about *2000* or 3000 men..smite Ai"
Jos 7:4 – "went up..about 3000 men"
Jdg 15:11 – "3000 men of Judah..to Samson"
Jdg 16:27 – "upon..roof about 3000 men..women"
1Sa 13:2 – "Saul chose him 3000 men of Israel"
1Sa 24:2 – "Saul took 3000 chosen men..of..Israel"
1Sa 25:2 – "man in Maon..had 3000 sheep"
1Sa 26:2 – "Saul arose..3000 chosen men of Israel"
1Ki 4:32 – "And he spake 3000 proverbs"
1Ch 12:29 – "kindred of Saul, 3000"
1Ch 29:4 – "Even 3000 talents of gold..of Ophir"
2Ch 4:5 – "it received and held 3000 baths"
2Ch 25:13 – "smote 3000..took much spoil"
2Ch 29:33 – "consecrated things..3000 sheep"
2Ch 35:7 – "passover offerings..3000 bullocks"
Job 1:3 – "His substance..3000 camels"
Act 2:41 – "added unto them about 3000 souls"

3,023

Jer 52:28 – "away captive..3023 Jews"

3,200

Num 4:44 – "those that were numbered..3200"

3,300

1Ki 5:16 – "3300 which ruled over the people"

3,600

2Ch 2:2 – "Solomon told out..3600 to oversee"
2Ch 2:18 – "3600 overseers to set..people a work"

3,630

Ezr 2:35 – "The children of Senaah, 3630"

3,700

1Ch 12:27 – "Jehoiada..Aaronites..were 3700"

3,930

Neh 7:38 – "The children of Senaah, 3930"

4,000

1Sa 4:2 – "Philistines..slew..about 4000 men"
1Ch 23:5 – "Moreover 4000 were porters"
1Ch 23:5 – "4000 praised..with instruments"
2Ch 9:25 – "Solomon had 4000 stalls for horses"
Mat 15:38 – "they that did eat were 4000 men"
Mat 16:10 – "seven loaves of the four thousand"
Mar 8:9 – "they that had eaten were about 4000"
Mar 8:20 – "when the seven among 4000"
Act 21:38 – "into the wilderness 4000 men"

4,500

Ezk 48:16 – "north side 4500"
Ezk 48:16 – "south side 4500"
Ezk 48:16 – "east side 4500"
Ezk 48:16 – "west side 4500"
Ezk 48:30 – "on the north side, 4500 measures"
Ezk 48:32 – "And at the east side, 4500"
Ezk 48:33 – "at the south side, 4500 measures"
Ezk 48:34 – "At the west side, 4500"

4,600

1Ch 12:26 – "Of the children of Levi 4600"
Jer 52:30 – "away captive..4600 persons"

5,000

Jos 8:12 – "about 5000 men..ambush..Bethel..Ai"
Jdg 20:45 – "gleaned..in the highways 5000 men"
1Sa 17:5 – "weight..was 5000 shekels of brass"
1Ch 29:7 – "gave..of gold 5000 talents"
2Ch 35:9 – "passover offerings 5000 small cattle"
Ezr 2:69 – "They gave..5000 pound of silver"
Ezk 45:6 – "appoint..of the city..5000 broad"
Ezk 48:15 – "5000, that are left..profane place"
Mat 14:21 – "they..had eaten..about 5000 men"
Mat 16:9 – "five loaves of the five thousand"
Mar 6:44 – "eat of the loaves..about 5000 men"
Mar 8:19 – "the five loaves among 5000"
Luk 9:14 – "For they were about 5000 men."
Joh 6:10 – "men sat down..about 5000"
Act 4:4 – "number of the men was about 5000"

5,400

Ezr 1:11 – "all the vessels..gold..silver were 5400"

6,000

1Sa 13:5 – "Philistines..6000 horsemen"
2Ki 5:5 – "took with him..6000 pieces of gold"

1Ch 23:4 – "6000 were officers and judges"
Job 42:12 – "later end of Job..6000 camels"

6,200

Num 3:34– "numbered of them..6200"

6,720

Ezr 2:67 – "their asses 6720"
Neh 7:69 – "6720 asses"

6,800

1Ch 12:24 – "Judah..6800, ready armed to..war"

7,000

1Ki 19:18 – "Yet I have left me 7000 in Israel"
1Ki 20:15 – "numbered the people..Israel..7000"
2Ki 24:16 – "all the men of might, even 7000"
1Ch 18:14 – "David took..7000 horsemen"
1Ch 19:18 – "David slew of..Syrians 7000 men"
1Ch 29:4 – "7000 talents of refined silver"
2Ch 15:11 – "offered..of the spoil..7000 sheep"
2Ch 30:24 – "Hezekiah..did give..7000 sheep"
Job 1:3 – "His substance also was 7000 sheep"
Rom 11:4 – "7000 men..have not bowed the knee"
Rev 11:13 – "in..earthquake..slain of men 7000"

7,100

1Ch 12:25 –"Simeon..men..for the war, 7100"

7,337

Ezr 2:65 – "their servants and their maids, 7337"
Neh 7:67 – "manservants..maidservants..7337"

7,500

Num 3:22 – "males..month old..upward..7500"

7,700

2Ch 17:11 – "Arabians brought him..7700 rams"
2Ch 17:11 – "Arabians brought..7700 he goats"

8,580

Num 4:48 – "numbered of them..8580"

8,600

Num 3:28 – "males..month old..upward..8600"

10,000

Lev 26:8 – "100 of you shall put 10,000 to flight"
Deut 32:30 – "and two put ten thousand to flight"
Jdg 1:4 – "Judah..slew..in Bezek 10,000 men"
Jdg 3:29 – "slew of Moab..about 10,000 men"
Jdg 4:6 – "10,000 men of..Naphtali..Zebulun"
Jdg 4:10 – "Barak..went up with 10,000 men"
Jdg 4:14 – "Barak went down..and 10,000 men"
Jdg 7:3 – "fearful..return..there remained 10,000"
Jdg 20:10 – "a thousand out of ten thousand"
Jdg 20:34 – "against Gibeah 10,000 chosen men"
1Sa 15:4 – "Saul gathered..10,000 men of Judah"
2Sa 18:3 – "thou art worth 10,000 of us"
1Ki 5:14 – "sent..to Lebanon, 10,000 a month"
2Ki 13:7 – "leave..to Jehoahaz..10,000 footmen"
2Ki 14:7 – "slew of Edom..valley of salt 10,000"
2Ki 24:14 – "carried away..10,000 captives"
1Ch 29:7 – "gave..of gold..10,000 drams"
1Ch 29:7 – "gave..of silver 10,000 talents"
2Ch 25:11 – "smote,,children of Seir 10,000"
2Ch 25:12 – "And other 10,000 left alive"
2Ch 27:5 – "gave..10,000 measures of wheat"
2Ch 27:5 – "Ammon gave..10,000 of barley"
2Ch 30:24 – "princes gave..10,000 sheep"
Est 3:9 – "I will pay 10,000 talents of silver"
Psa 91:7 – "shall fall..10,000 at thy right side"
Son 5:10 – "my beloved..chiefest among 10,000"
Ezk 45:1 – "holy portion..breadth..10,000"
Ezk 45:3 – "breadth of 10,000..most holy place"
Ezk 45:5 – "the 10,000 of breadth..Levites..have"
Ezk 48:9 – "oblation..10,000 in breadth"
Ezk 48:10 – "oblation..west 10,000 in breadth"
Ezk 48:10 – "oblation..east 10,000 in breadth"
Ezk 48:13 – "Levites..have 10,000 in breadth"
Ezk 48:13 – "the breadth 10,000"
Ezk 48:18 – "holy portion..10,000 eastward"
Ezk 48:18 – "holy portion..10,000 westward"
Mat 18:24 – "owed him 10,000 talents"
Luk 14:31 – "whether he be able with 10,000"
1Co 4:15 – "10,000 instructors in Christ"
1Co 14:19 – "10,000 words in..unknown tongue"

10,000's – Ten Thousands

Listed at the end of Section One under the heading, **Indefinite Numbers**.

12,000

Num 12:5 – "of Israel..12,000 armed for war"
Jos 8:25 – "fell that day..12,000..of Ai"
Jdg 21:10 – "congregation sent..12,000 men"
2Sa 10:6 – "and of Ishtob 12,000 men"
2Sa 17:1 – "Let me now choose out 12,000 men"
1Ki 4:26 – "Solomon had..12,000 horsemen"
1Ki 10:26 – "Solomon..had..12,000 horsemen"
2Ch 1:14 – "Solomon..had..12,000 horsemen"
2Ch 9:25 – "Solomon had..12,000 horsemen"
Psa 60 title – "smote of Edom..12,000"
Rev 7:5 – "of Juda were sealed 12,000"
Rev 7:5 – "of Reuben were sealed 12,000"
Rev 7:5 – "of Gad were sealed 12,000"
Rev 7:6 – "of Aser were sealed 12,000"
Rev 7:6 – "of Nepthalim were sealed 12,000"
Rev 7:6 – "of Manassas were sealed 12,000"
Rev 7:7 – "of Simeon were sealed 12,000"
Rev 7:7 – "of Levi were sealed 12,000"
Rev 7:7 – "of Issachar were sealed 12,000"
Rev 7:8 – "of Zabulon were sealed 12,000"
Rev 7:8 – "of Joseph were sealed 12,000"
Rev 7:8 – "of Benjamin were sealed 12,000"
Rev 21:16 – "the city..12,000 furlongs"

14,000

Job 42:12 – "later end of Job..had 14,000 sheep"

14,700

Num 16:49 – "died in the plague..14,700"

15,000

Jdg 8:10 – "Zebah..Zalumnna..15,000 men"

16,000

Num 31:40 – "And the persons were 16,000"
Num 31:46 – "And 16,000 persons;"

16,750

Num 31:52 – "gold..offering..16,750 shekels"

17,200

1Ch 7:11 – "men of valour..17,200 soldiers"

18,000

Jdg 20:25 – "Benjamin..destroyed..18,000 men"
Jdg 20:44 – "fell of Benjamin 18,000 men"
2Sa 8:13 – "David..smiting..Syrians..18,000 men"
1Ch 12:31 – "of the half tribe of Manasseh 18,000"
1Ch 18:12 – "Abishai..slew..Edomites..18,000"
1Ch 29:7 – "of brass 18,000 talents"
Ezk 48:35 – "round about 18,000 measures"

20,000

2Sa 8:4 – "700 horsemen and 20,000 footmen"
2Sa 10:6 – "Syrians of Zoba, 20,000 footment"
2Sa 18:7 – "great slaugher that day..20,000 men"
1Ki 5:11 – "Solomon..20,000 measures..wheat"
1Ch 18:4 – "David took..20,000 footmen"
2Ch 2:10 – "20,000 measures of beaten wheat"
2Ch 2:10 – "20,000 measures of barley"
2Ch 2:10 – "20,000 baths of wine"
2Ch 2:10 – "20,000 baths of oil"
Neh 7:71 – "fathers gave..20,000 drams of gold"
Neh 7:72 – "people gave..20,000 drams of gold"
Psa 68:17 – "The chariots of God are 20,000"
Luk 14:31 – "meet him that cometh..with 20,000"

20,200

1Ch 7:9 – "mighty men of valour, was 20,200"

20,800

1Ch 12:30 – "the children of Ephraim 20,800"

22,000

Num 3:39 – "males from a month old..22,000"
Jdg 7:3 – "fearful..there returned..22,000"
Jdg 20:21 – "Benjamin..destroyed..22,000 men"
2Sa 8:5 – "David slew of..Syrians 22,000 men"
1Ki 8:63 – "Solomon offered..22,00 oxen"
1Ch 17:15 – "David slew..Syrians 22,000 men"
2Ch 7:5 – "Solomon..a sacrifice of 22,000 oxen"

22,034

1Ch 7:7 – "mighty men of valour..22,034"

20,800

1Ch 12:30 – "of Ephraim 20,800, mighty men"

22,200

Num 26:14 – "Simeonites, 22,200"

22,273

Num 3:43 – "firstborn males..22,273"

22,600

1Ch 7:2 – "And the sons of Tola..22,600"

23,000

Num 26:62 – "23,000..month old..upward"
1Co 10:8 – "fornication..fell in one day 23,000"

24,000

Num 25:9 – "died in the plague were 24,000"
1Ch 23:4 – "24,000..the work of the house"
1Ch 27:1 – "of every course were 24,000"
1Ch 27:2 – "1st course..Jashobeam..24,000"
1Ch 27:4 – "of the 2nd month..Dodai..24,000"
1Ch 27:5 – "3rd month was Benaiah..24,000"
1Ch 27:7 – "4th month..Asahel.. 24,000"
1Ch 27:8 – "5th month..Shamhuth..24,000"
1Ch 27:9 – "6th month was Ira..24,000"
1Ch 27:10 –7th month..Helez..24,000"
1Ch 27:11 – "8th month..Sibbecai..24,000"
1Ch 27:12 – "9th month..Abiezer..24,000"
1Ch 27:13 – "10th month..Maharai..24,000"
1Ch 27:14 – "11th month..Benaiah..24,000"
1Ch 27:15 – "..12th month..Heldai..24,000"
Mat 26:53 – "more than twelve legions of angels?"

25,000

Jdg 20:46 – "fell..of Benjamin..25,000 men"
Ezk 45:1 – "holy portion..length of 25,000 reeds"
Ezk 45:3 – "length..25,000..sanctuary..holy place"
Ezk 45:5 – "the 25,000 of length..Levites..have"
Ezk 45:6 – "appoint..of the city..25,000 long"
Ezk 48:8 – "border..Judah..25,000 reeds..breadth"
Ezk 48:9 – "oblation..25,000 in length"
Ezk 48:10 – "oblation..north 25,000 in length"
Ezk 48:10 – "oblation..south 25,000 in length"
Ezk 48:13 – "Levites shall have 25,000 in length"
Ezk 48:13 – "all the length shall be 25,000"
Ezk 48:15 – "against the 25,000..profane place"
Ezk 48:20 – "oblation..25,000 by 25,000"
Ezk 48:21 – "over against the 25,000..oblation"
Ezk 48:21 – "25,000 toward the west border"

25,100

Jdg 20:35 – "LORD smote Benjamin..25,100 men"

26,000

Jdg 20:15 – "children of Benjamin..26,000 men"
1Ch 7:40 – "children of Asher..26,000 men"

26,700

Jdg 20:15 – *total forces of Benjamin in Gibeah*

27,000

1Ki 20:30 – "Aphek..a wall fell upon 27,000..men"

28,600

1Ch 12:35 – "of the Danites expert in war 28,600"

30,000

Jos 8:3 – "30,000 mighty men of valour"
1Sa 4:10 – "fell of Israel 30,000 footmen"
1Sa 11:8 – "the men of Judah 30,000"
1Sa 13:5 – "Philistines..30,000 chariots"
2Sa 6:1 – "chosen men of Israel, 30,000"
1Ki 5:13 – "Solomon..levy was 30,000 men"
2Ch 35:7 – "of the..lambs and kids..30,000"

30,500

Num 31:39 – "And the asses were 30,500"
Num 31:45 – "And 30,000 asses and 500."

32,000

Num 31:35 – "32,000 persons in all..women"
1Ch 19:7 – "hired 32,000 chariots..Ammon"

32,200

Num 1:35 – "numbered..Manasseh..32,200"
Num 2:21 – "numbered of them..32,200"

32,500

Num 26:37 – "Ephraim..numbered..32,500"

35,400

Num 1:37 – "numbered..Benjamin..35,400"
Num 2:23 – "numbered of them..35,400"

36,000

Num 31:38 – "And the beeves were 36,000"
Num 31:44 – "And 36,000 beeves."
1Ch 7:4 – "soldiers for war, 36,000 men"

37,000

1Ch 12:34 – "And of Naphtali..37,000"

38,000

1Ch 23:3 – "Levites were numbered..38,000"

40,000

Jos 4:13 – "About 40,000 prepared for war"
Jdg 5:8 – "spear seen among 40,000 in Israel?"
2Sa 10:18 – "David slew..40,000 horsemen"
1Ki 4:26 – "Solomon..40,000 stalls of horses"
1Ch 12:36 – "of Asher..expert in war, 40,000"
1Ch 19:18 – "slew..Syrians..40,000 footmen"

40,500

Num 1:33 – "numbered..Ephraim..40,500"
Num 2:19 – "numbered of them..40,500"
Num 26:18 – "Gad..numbered..40,500"

41,500

Num 1:41 – "numbered..Asher..41,500"
Num 2:28 – "numbered of them..41,500"

42,000

Jdg 12:6 – "fell..of the Ephramites 42,000"

42,360

Ezr 2:64 – "whole congregation..was 42,360"
Neh 7:66 – "whole congregation..was 42,360"

43,730

Num 26:7 – "Reubenites..numbered..43,730"

44,760

1Ch 5:18 – "44,760 that went out to the war"

45,400

Num 26:50 – "Napthali..numbered..45,400"

45,600

Num 26:41 – "Benjamin..numbered..45,600"

45,650

Num 1:25 – "numbered..of Gad, were 45,650"
Num 2:15 – "numbered of them, were 45,650"

46,500

Num 1:21 – "numbered..of Rueben, were 46,500"
Num 2:11 – "numbered thereof, were 46,500"

50,000

1Ch 5:21 – "took away..of their camels 50,000"
1Ch 12:33 – "Of Zebulun..to battle..50,000"
Act 19:19 – "books..price..50,000 pieces of silver"

50,070

1Sa 6:19 – "smote..of Bethshemesh...50,070 men"

52,700

Num 26:34 – "of Manasseh..numbered..52,700"

53,400

Num 1:43 – "numbered..of Naphtali, were 53,400"
Num 2:30 – "numbered of them, were 53,400"
Num 26:47 – "Asher..numbered..were 53,400"

54,400

Num 1:29 – "numbered..of Issachar..54,400"
Num 2:6 – "numbered thereof, were 54,400"

57,400

Num 1:31 – "numbered..of Zebulun, were 57,400"
Num 2:8 – "numbered thereof, were 57,400"

59,300

Num 1:23 – "numbere..of Simeon, were 59,300"
Num 2:13 – "numbered of them, were 59,300"

60,000

2Ch 12:3 – "1200 chariots & 60,000 horsemen"

60,500

Num 26:27 – "Zebulunites..numbered..60,500"

61,000

Num 31:34 – "And 61,000 asses."
Ezr 2:69 – "They gave..61,000 drams of gold"

62,700

Num 1:39 – "numbered..of Dan, were 62,700"
Num 2:26 – "numbered of there, were 62,700"

64,300

Num 26:25 – "Issachar..numbered..them, 64,300"

64,400

Num 26:43 – "numbered of them, were 64,400"

70,000

2Sa 24:15 – "pestilence..there died..70,000 men"
1Ki 5:15 – "Solomon had 70,000..bare burdens"
1Ch 21:14 – "pestilence..fell of Israel 70,000 men"
2Ch 2:2 – "Solomon..70,000 men to bear burdens"
2Ch 2:18 – "70,000 of them..bearers of burdens"

72,000

Num 31:33 – "And 72,000 beeves,"

74,600

Num 1:27 – "numbered..of Judah, were 74,600"
Num 2:4 – "numbered of them, were 74,600"

76,500

Num 26:22 – "Judah..numbered of them, 76,500"

80,000

1Ki 5:15 – "Solomon had..80,000 hewers"
2Ch 2:2 – "Solomon told out..80,000 to hew"
2Ch 2:18 – "80,000 to be hewers in..mountains"

87,000

1Ch 7:5 – "valiant men of might..87,000"

87,730

Exo 38:24 – "gold..29 talents, and 730 shekels"
> ➢ *Thus, 87,730 shekels or 29.24 talents*

100,000

1Ki 20:29 – "slew of the Syrians 100,000 footmen"
2Ki 3:4 – "Mesha..rendered..100,000 lambs"
2Ki 3:4 – "Mesha..rendered..100,000 rams"
1Ch 5:21 – "took away..of men an 100,000"
1Ch 22:14 – "prepared..an 100,000 talents of gold"
1Ch 29:7 – "house of God..100,000 talents of iron"
2Ch 25:6 – "He hired also 100,000 mighty men"

108,100

Num 2:24 – "camp of Ephraim were an 108,100"

120,000

Jdg 8:10 – "fell 120,000 men that drew sword"
1Ki 8:63 – "Solomon offered..an 120,000 sheep"
1Ch 12:37 – "other side of Jordan..an 120,000"
2Ch 7:5 – "Solomon offered..an 120,000 sheep"
2Ch 28:6 – "Pekah..slew..120,000..valiant men"
Jon 4:11 – "120,000 persons that cannot discern"

144,000

Rev 7:4 – "sealed..144,000 of all..Israel"
Rev 14:1 – "Lamb..and with him an 144,000"
Rev 14:3 – "learn that song but the 144,000"

151,450

Num 2:16 – "camp of Reuben were an 151,450"

153,600

2Ch 2:17 – "strangers..in the land..153,600"

157,600

Num 2:31 – "camp of Dan were an 157,600"

180,000

1Ki 12:21 – "Rehoboam..180,000 chosen men"
2Ch 11:1 – "Rehoboam..180,000 chosen men"
2Ch 17:18 – "Jehozabad, & with him an 180,000"

185,000

2Ki 19:35 – "angel..smote..Assyrians..185,000"
Isa 37:36 – "angel..smote..Assyrians..185,000"

186,400

Num 2:9 – "camp of Judah were an 186,400"

200,000

1Sa 15:4 – "Saul..numbered..200,000 footmen"
2Ch 17:16 – "Amasiah..200,000 mighty men"
2Ch 17:17 – "Eliada..w/ him armed men..200,000"
2Ch 28:8 – "Israel carried away captive..200,000"

212,400

Exo 38:29 – "brass..70 talents, and 2,400 shekels"
> ➢ *Thus, 212,400 shekels or 70.8 talents*

250,000

1Ch 5:21 – "they took away..of sheep 250,000"

280,000

2Ch 14:8 – "Asa..army of men..Benjamin..280,000"
2Ch 17:15 – "Jehohanan..with him 280,000"

300,000

1Sa 11:8 – "the children of Israel were 300,000"
2Ch 14:8 – "Asa..army of men..Judah..300,000"
2Ch 17:14 – "Adnah..mighty men..300,000"
2Ch 25:5 – "found them 300,000 choice men"

301,775

Exo 38:25 – "silver..100 talents, and 1,775 shekels"
> ➤   Thus, 301,775 shekels or 100.59 talents

307,500

2Ch 26:13 – "an army, 307,500, that made war"

337,500

Num 31:36 – "the half..was..337,500 sheep"
Num 31:43 – "the half..was 337,500 sheep"

400,000

Jdg 20:2 – "400,000 footmen that drew sword"
Jdg 20:17 – "400,000 men that drew sword"
2Ch 13:3 – "Abijah..an army..400,000 chosen men"

470,000

1Ch 21:5 – "Joab..sum..Judah was 470,000 men"

500,000

2Sa 24:9 – "Joab..sum..men of Judah..500,000"
2Ch 13:17 – "slain of Israel 500,000 chosen men"

600,000

Exo 12:37 – "Israel..600,000 on foot..men"
Num 11:21 – "Moses..600,000 footmen"

601,730

Num 26:51 – "numbered of..Israel, 201, 730"

603,550

Exo 38:26 – "half a shekel..for 603,550 men"
Num 1:46 – "all..that were numbered..603,550"
Num 2:32 – "numbered of..Israel..603,550"

675,000

Num 31:32 – "booty…was 675,000 sheep"

800,000

2Sa 24:9 – "Joab..sum..Israel 800,000 valiant men"
2Ch 13:3 – "Jeroboam..800,000 chosen men"

1,000,000

1Ch 22:14 – "prepared 1000 1000 talents..silver"
2Ch 14:9 – "Ethiopian..an host of a 1000 1000"

1,000,000's – Millions

Listed at the end of Section One under the heading, **Indefinite Numbers**.

1,100,000

1Ch 21:5 – "all they of Israel..1,100,000 men"

1,160,00

2Ch 17:14-18 – total of Jehoshphat's army under five captains from Judah and Benjamin

100,000,000

Dan 7:10 – "10,000 times 10,000 stood before"

1,000,000,000's – Billions

Listed at the end of Section One under the heading, **Indefinite Numbers**.

Indefinite Numbers

This section deals with all of the numbers in Scripture that are non-specific or ambiguous. Comments on each word will underscore how the word was recorded in Scripture with respect to the parts of speech it represents.

This section covers:

1)	A Couple	8)	7's/Sevens
2)	Few	9)	50's/Fifties
3)	Many	10)	1000's/Thousands
4)	Much	11)	10,000's/Ten Thousands
5)	Several	12)	1,000,000's/Millions
6)	Some	13)	1,000,000,000's/Billions
7)	1's/Ones	14)	Infinite and/or Uncountable

A Couple

Comparing Judges 19:3 & 10, "a couple" would appear to equal two.

Jud 19:3 – "a couple of asses"
2Sa 13:6 – "make me a couple of cakes"
2Sa 16:1 – "a couple of asses saddled"
Isa 21:7 - "a chariot with a couple of horsemen"
Isa 21:9 – "a couple of horsemen"

Few

Few is generally an indefinite number. In a number of references however, the identity of the term "few" is either alluded to or directly identified in the context or seen by comparing scripture with scripture. The following verses note those instances. Observe that some of these are metaphorical.

Gen 24:44 – ten or more
Gen 29:20 – 2520 (7 years)
Gen 47:9 – 46,800 (130 years)
1Sa 14:6 – two
1Pe 3:21 - eight

Actual instances of the word "few" in Scripture:

Gen 24:55 – "a few days, at the least ten"
Gen 27:44 – "And tarry with him a few days"
Gen 29:20 – "7 years..seemed..but a few days"
Gen 34:30 – "and I being few in number"
Gen 47:9 – "few and evil..days..of my life been"
Lev 25:52 – "few years unto the year of jubilee"
Lev 26:22 – " make you few in number"
Num 9:20 – "cloud..a few days upon..tabernacle"
Num 13:18 – "the people..few or many"
Num 26:54 – "to few..give the less inheritance"
Num 26:56 – "lot..divided between many and few"
Num 35:8 – "from them that have few..give few"
Deu 4:27 – "ye shall be left few in number"
Deu 26:5 – "Egypt..sojourned there with a few"
Deu 28:62 – "And ye shall be left few in number"
Deu 33:6 –"Reuben..let not his men be few."
Jos 7:3 – "smite Ai..for they are but few"
1Sa 14:6 – "LORD to save by many or by few"
1Sa 17:28 – "with whom..left those few sheep"

2Ki 4:3 – "vessels; borrow not a few"
1Ch 16:19 – "When ye were but few"
1Ch 16:19 – "even a few, and strangers in it"
2Ch 29:34 – "But the priests were too few"
Neh 2:12 – "I and some few men with me"
Neh 7:4 – "but the people were few therein"
Job 10:20 – "Are not my days few?"
Job 14:1 – "Man..is of few days"
Job 16:22 – "When a few years are come"
Psa 105:12 – "but a few men in number"
Psa 109:8 – "Let his days be few"
Ecc 5:2 – "therefore let thy words be few"
Ecc 9:14 – "a little city, and few men within it"
Ecc 12:3 – "grinders cease because they are few"
Isa 10:7 – "cut off nations not a few"
Isa 10:19 – "trees of his forest shall be few"
Isa 24:6 – "earth..burned, and few men left"
Jer 30:19 – "and they shall not be few"
Jer 42:2 – "we are left but a few of many"

Ezk 5:3 – "take thereof a few in number"
Ezk 12:16 – "I will leave a few men of them"
Dan 11:20 – "within few days..be destroyed"
Mat 7:14 – "and few there be that find it"
Mat 9:37 – "but the labourers are few"
Mat 15:34 – "and a few little fishes"
Mat 20:16 – "many be called, but few chosen"
Mat 22:14 – "many are called, but few are chosen"
Mat 25:21 – "been faithful over a few things"
Mat 25:23 – "been faithful over a few things"
Mar 6:5 – "laid his hands upon a few sick folk"
Mar 8:7 – "they had a few small fishes"

Luk 10:2 – "but the labourers are few"
Luk 12:48 – "shall be beaten with few stripes"
Luk 13:23 – "are there few that be saved?"
Act 17:4 – "of the chief women not a few"
Act 17:12 – "and of men, not a few"
Act 24:4 – "hear us..a few words.
Eph 3:3 – "as I wrote afore in few words"
Heb 12:10 – "for a few days chastened us"
Heb 13:22 – "I have written..you in few words"
1Pe 3:20 – "few, that is, eight souls were saved"
Rev 2:14 – "I have a few things against thee"
Rev 2:20 – "I have a few things against thee"
Rev 3:4 – "a few names even in Sardis"

Many

Many is generally an indefinite number. In a number of references however, the identity of the term "many" is either alluded to or directly identified in the context, or by comparing scripture with scripture. The following verses note those instances.

Deu 25:3 – more than forty
1Ki 18:1 – 1260 (3½ years)
Est 1:4 - 180

Actual instances of the word "many" in Scripture:

Gen 17:4 – "a father of many nations"
Gen17:5 – "a father of many nations"
Gen 21:34 – "sojourned in the..land many days"
Gen 37:3 – "made him a coat of many colours"
Gen 37:23 – "his coat of many colours"
Gen 37:32 – "sent the coat of many colours"
Gen 37:34 – "mourned for his son many days"
Exo 5:5 – "the people of the land now are many"
Exo 19:21 – "people..many of them perish"
Exo 23:2 – "decline after many to wrest judgment"
Exo 35:22 – "as many as were willing hearted"
Lev 15:25 – "issue of her blood many days"
Lev 25:51 – "If there be yet many years"
Num 9:19 – "cloud tarried long..many days"
Num 10:36 – "unto the many thousands of Israel"
Num 13:18 – "people that dwelleth..few or many"
Num 22:3 – "people, because they were many"
Num 24:7 – "his seed shall be in many waters"
Num 26:54 – "To many..give the more inheritance"
Num 26:56 – "divided between many and few"
Num 35:8 – "cities..have many ye shall give many"
Deu 1:46 – "ye abode in Kadesh many days"
Deu 2:1 – " compassed mount Seir many days"
Deu 2:10 – "Emims..people great, and many"
Deu 2:21 – "A people great, and many"
Deu 3:5 – "All these cities..a great many"
Deu 7:1 – "cast out many nations before thee"
Deu 15:6 – "thou shalt lend unto many nations"
Deu 25:3 – "beat him..with many stripes"
Deu 28:12 – "thou shalt lend unto many nations"
Deu 31:17 – "many evils & troubles..befall them"
Deu 31:21 – "many evils & troubles are befallen"
Deu 32:7 – "the years of many generations"
Jos 11:4 – "horses and chariots very many"

Jos 22:3 – "these many days unto this day"
Jdg 3:1 – "many of Israel as had not known"
Jdg 7:2 – "people..with thee are too many"
Jdg 7:4 – "The people are yet too many"
Jdg 8:30 – "And Gideon..had many wives"
Jdg 9:40 – "and many were overthrown"
Jdg 16:24 – "destroyer..which slew many of us"
1Sa 2:5 – "she that hath many children"
1Sa 6:19 – "LORD had smitten many..people"
1Sa 14:6 – "to save by many or by few"
1Sa 25:10 – "be many servants now a days"
2Sa 1:4 – "many of the people also are fallen"
2Sa 2:23 – "many..came..to where Asahel fell"
2Sa 12:2 – "exceeding many flocks and herds"
2Sa 22:17 – "he drew me out of many waters"
2Sa 23:20 – "Benaiah..had done many acts"
1Ki 2:38 – "Shimei dwelt in Jerusalem many days"
1Ki 4:20 – "Judah and Israel were many"
1Ki 7:47 – "vessels..were exceeding many"
1Ki 11:1 – "Solomon loved many strange women"
1Ki 17:15 – "he, and her house..eat many days"
1Ki 18:1 – "And it came to pass after many days"
1Ki 18:25 – "prophets of Baal..ye are many"
2Ki 9:22 – "Jezebel and her witchcrafts..so many"
1Ch 4:27 – "his brethren had not many children"
1Ch 5:22 – "For there fell down many slain"
1Ch 7:4 – "for they had many wives and sons"
1Ch 7:22 – "And Ephraim..mourned many days"
1Ch 8:40 – "sons of Ulam had many sons"
1Ch 11:22 – "Benaiah..had done many acts"
1Ch 23:11 – "Jeush & Beriah had not many sons"
1Ch 23:17 – "sons of Rehabiah were very many"
1Ch 28:5 – "LORD hath given me many sons"
2Ch 11:23 – "And he desired many wives."

2Ch 14:11 – "to help, whether with many"
2Ch 16:8 – "very many chariots and horsemen"
2Ch 26:10 – "digged many wells"
2Ch 29:31 – "as many as were of a free heart"
2Ch 30:17 – "many in the congregation"
2Ch 30:18 – "even many of Ephraim & Manasseh"
2Ch 32:23 – "many brought gifts unto the LORD"
Ezr 3:12 – "many of the priests and Levites"
Ezr 5:11 – "house..builded these many years ago"
Ezr 10:13 – "But the people are many"
Neh 5:2 – "our sons, and our daughters, are many"
Neh 6:17 – "nobles of Judah sent many letters"
Neh 6:18 – "many in Judah sworn unto him"
Neh 7:2 – "and feared God above many"
Neh 9:28 – "many times didst thou deliver"
Neh 9:30 – "many years didst thou forbear them"
Neh 13:26 – "many nations..no king like him"
Est 1:4 – "shewed..riches..many days, even 180"
Est 2:8 – "many maidens were gathered together"
Est 4:3 – "many lay in sackcloth and ashes"
Est 8:17 – "many of the people..became Jews"
Job 4:3 – "thou hast instructed many"
Job 11:19 – "many shall make suit unto thee"
Job 16:2 – "I have heard many such things"
Job 23:14 – "many such things are with him"
Job 41:3 – "make many supplications unto thee"
Psa 3:1 – "many are they that rise up against me"
Psa 3:2 – "Many there be which say"
Psa 4:6 – "There be many that say"
Psa 18:16 – "he drew me out of many waters"
Psa 22:12 – "Many bulls have compassed me"
Psa 25:19 – "enemies; for they are many"
Psa 29:3 – "LORD is upon many waters"
Psa 31:13 – "heard the slander of many"
Psa 32:10 – "Many sorrows..to the wicked"
Psa 34:12 – "What man..loveth many days"
Psa 34:19 – "Many..afflictions of the righteous"
Psa 37:16 – "the riches of many wicked"
Psa 40:3 – "many shall see it, and fear"
Psa 40:5 – "Many..are thy wonderful works "
Psa 55:18 – "for there were many with me"
Psa 56:2 – "they be many that fight against me"
Psa 61:6 – "his years as many generations"
Psa 71:7 – "I am as a wonder unto many"
Psa 78:38 – "many a time turned he his anger"
Psa 93:4 – "the noise of many waters"
Psa 106:43 – "Many times did he deliver them"
Psa 110:6 – "the heads over many countries"
Psa 119:157 – "Many..my persecutors..enemies"
Psa 129:1 – "Many a time have they afflicted me"
Psa 129:2 – "Many a time have they afflicted me"
Pro 4:10 – "years of thy life shall be many"
Pro 6:35 – "though thou givest many gifts"
Pro 7:26 – "she hath cast down many wounded"
Prov 7:26 – "many strong men..slain by her"
Pro 10:21 – "lips of the righteous feed many"
Pro 14:20 – "but the rich hath many friends"
Pro 19:4 – "Wealth maketh many friends
Pro 19:6 – "Many will intreat..the prince"
Pro 19:21 – "many devices in a man's heart"

Pro 28:2 – "many are the princes thereof"
Pro 28:27 – "hideth his eyes..many a curse"
Pro 29:26 – "Many seek the ruler's favour"
Pro 31:29 – "Many daughters..done virtuously"
Ecc 5:7 – "many words..divers vanities"
Ecc 6:3 – "If a man..live many years"
Ecc 6:3 – "the days of his years be many"
Ecc 6:11 – "many things that increase vanity"
Ecc 7:29 – "sought out many inventions"
Ecc 11:1 – "shalt find it after many days"
Ecc 11:8 – "But if a man live many years"
Ecc 11:8 – "days of darkness..shall be many"
Ecc 12:9 – "set in order many proverbs"
Ecc 12:12 – "making many books..is no end"
Son 8:7 – "Many waters cannot quench love"
Isa 1:15 – "when ye make many prayers"
Isa 2:3 – "many people shall go and say"
Isa 2:4 – "and shall rebuke many people"
Isa 5:9 – "many houses shall be desolate"
Isa 8:7 – "waters..strong and many"
Isa 8:15 – "many among them shall stumble"
Isa 17:12 – "the multitude of many people"
Isa 17:13 – "like the rushing of many waters"
Isa 22:9 – "breaches of the city..are many"
Isa 23:16 – "harlot..sing many songs"
Isa 24:22 – "after many days shall..be visited"
Isa 31:1 – "trust in chariots, b/c they are many"
Isa 32:10 – "Many days & years..ye be troubled"
Isa 42:20 – "Seeing many things"
Isa 52:14 – "As many were astonied at thee"
Isa 52:15 – "So shall he sprinkle many nations"
Isa 53:11 – "my righteous servant justify many"
Isa 53:12 – "he bare the sin of many"
Isa 58:12 – "foundations of many generations"
Isa 60:15 – "a joy of many generations"
Isa 61:4 – "desolations of many generations"
Isa 66:16 – "slain of the LORD shall be many"
Jer 3:1 – "played the harlot with many lovers"
Jer 5:6 – "their transgressions are many"
Jer 11:15 – "wrought lewdness with many"
Jer 12:10 – "Many pastors have destroyed"
Jer 13:6 – "came to pass after many days"
Jer 14:7 – "our backslidings are many"
Jer 16:16 – "will I send for many hunters"
Jer 20:10 – "I heard the defaming of many"
Jer 22:8 – "many nations shall pass by this city"
Jer 25:14 – "many nations and great kings"
Jer 27:7 – "many nations and great kings"
Jer 28:8 – "prophets.. against many countries"
Jer 32:14 – "that they may continue many days"
Jer 35:7 – "live many days in the land"
Jer 36:32 – "added..unto them many like words"
Jer 37:16 – "Jeremiah..remained..many days"
Jer 42:2 – "we are left but a few of many"
Jer 46:11 – "in vain shalt..use many medicines"
Jer 46:16 – "He made many to fall"
Jer 50:41 – "many kings shall be raised up"
Jer 51:13 – "that dwellest upon many waters"
Lam 1:22 – "for my sighs are many"
Ezk 3:6 – "Not to many..of a strange speech"
Ezk 12:27 – "vision..is for many days to come"

Ezk 16:41 – "in the sight of many women"
Ezk 17:7 – "eagle with..many feathers"
Ezk 17:9 – "many people to pluck it up"
Ezk 17:17 – "to cut off many persons"
Ezk 19:10 – "by reason of many waters"
Ezk 22:25 – "made her many widows"
Ezk 26:3 – "cause many nations to come up"
Ezk 27:3 – "merchant of the people for many isles"
Ezk 27:15 – "many isles were the merchandise"
Ezk 27:33 – "thou filledst many people"
Ezk 32:3 – "a company of many people"
Ezk 32:9 – "vex the hearts of many people"
Ezk 32:10 – "I will make many people amazed"
Ezk 33:24 – "but we are many"
Ezk 37:2 – "very many in the open valley"
Ezk 38:6 – "Gomer..many people with thee"
Ezk 38:8 – "After many days..shalt be visited"
Ezk 38:8 – "out of many people"
Ezk 38:9 – "many people with thee"
Ezk 38:15 – "many people with thee"
Ezk 38:17 – "prophesied..many years"
Ezk 38:22 – "upon..many people..with him"
Ezk 38:23 – "known in the eyes of many nations"
Ezk 39:27 – "in the sight of many nations"
Ezk 43:2 – "like a noise of many waters"
Ezk 47:7 – "very many trees on the one side"
Ezk 47:10 – "fish of the..sea, exceeding many"
Dan 2:48 – "gave him many great gifts"
Dan 8:25 – "by peace shall destroy many"
Dan 8:26 – "the vision..shall be for many days"
Dan 9:27 – "covenant with many for one week"
Dan 10:14 – "for yet the vision is for many days"
Dan 11:12 – "he shall cast down many 10,000's"
Dan 11:14 – "many stand up against the king"
Dan 11:18 – "the isles, and shall take many"
Dan 11:26 – "and many shall fall down slain"
Dan 11:33 – "the people shall instruct many
Dan 11:33 – "they shall fall..many days"
Dan 11:34 – "many shall cleave..with flatteries"
Dan 11:39 – "cause them to rule over many"
Dan 11:40 – "king of the north..with many ships"
Dan 11:41 – "many countries..be overthrown"
Dan 11:44 – "and utterly to make away many"
Dan 12:2 – "many of them..sleep in the dust"
Dan 12:3 – "that turn many to righteousness"
Dan 12:4 – "many shall run to and fro"
Dan 12:10 – "Many shall be purified"
Hos 3:3 – "abide for me many days"
Hos 3:4 – "children of Israel..abide many days"
Hos 8:11 – "Ephraim..made many altars to sin"
Joe 2:2 – "the years of many generations"
Amo 8:3 – "many dead bodies in every place"
Mic 4:2 – "And many nations shall come"
Mic 4:3 – "judge among many people"
Mic 4:11 – "many nations..against thee"
Mic 4:13 – "shalt beat in pieces many people"
Mic 5:7 – "in the midst of many people"
Mic 5:8 – "in the midst of many people"
Nah 1:12 – "they be quiet, and likewise many"
Nah 3:15 – "thyself many as the cankerworm"

Nah 3:15 – "make thyself many as the locusts"
Hab 2:8 – "thou hast spoiled many nations"
Hab 2:10 – "by cutting off many people"
Zec 2:11 – "many nations..joined to the LORD"
Zec 7:3 – "as I have done these so many years"
Zec 8:20 – "the inhabitants of many cities"
Zec 8:22 – "many people and strong nations"
Mal 2:6 – "did turn many away from iniquity"
Mal 2:8 – "ye have caused many to stumble"
Mat 3:7 – "many of the Pharisees & Sadducees"
Mat 7:13 – "many there be which go in thereat"
Mat 7:22 – "Many will say to me in that day"
Mat 7:22 – "in thy name..many wonderful works"
Mat 8:11 – "many..from the east and west"
Mat 8:16 – "many..were possessed with devils"
Mat 8:30 – "an herd of many swine feeding"
Mat 9:10 – "many publicans and sinners"
Mat 10:31 – "more value than many sparrows"
Mat 13:3 – "many things unto them in parables"
Mat 13:17 – "many prophets and righteous men"
Mat 13:58 – "he did not many mighty works"
Mat 14:36 – "as many as touched..made..whole"
Mat 15:30 – "dumb, maimed, and many others"
Mat 16:21 – "suffer many things of the elders"
Mat 19:30 – "many that are first shall be last"
Mat 20:16 – "many be called, but few chosen"
Mat 20:28 – "give his life a ransom for many"
Mat 22:9 – "as many as ye shall find, bid"
Mat 22:10 – "gathered..as many as they found"
Mat 22:14 – "many are called, but few..chosen"
Mat 24:5 – "For many shall come in my name"
Mat 24:5 – "saying, I am Christ..deceive many"
Mat 24:10 – "And then shall many be offended"
Mat 24:11 – "false prophets..shall deceive many"
Mat 24:12 – "love of many shall wax cold"
Mat 25:21 – "make thee ruler over many things"
Mat 25:23 – "make thee ruler over many things"
Mat 26:28 – "blood..which is shed for many"
Mat 26:60 – "though many false witnesses came"
Mat 27:19 – "I have suffered many things"
Mat 27:52 – "many bodies of the saints..arose"
Mat 27:53 – "graves..appeared unto many"
Mat 27:55 – "many women..beholding afar off"
Mar 1:34 – "he healed many that were sick"
Mar 2:2 – "many were gathered together"
Mar 2:15 – "many publicans and sinners sat also"
Mar 2:15 – "for there were many..followed him"
Mar 3:10 – "For he had healed many"
Mar 3:10 – "as many as had plagues"
Mar 4:2 – "taught them many things by parables"
Mar 4:33 – "And with many such parables spake"
Mar 5:9 – "My name is Legion: for we are many"
Mar 5:26 – "suffered many things"
Mar 5:26 – "suffered..of many physicians"
Mar 6:2 – "many hearing him were astonished"
Mar 6:13 – "And they cast out many devils"
Mar 6:13 – "anointed with oil many..sick"
Mar 6:20 – "For Herod..did many things"
Mar 6:31 – "many coming and going"
Mar 6:33 – "the people..many knew him"
Mar 6:34 – "began to teach them many things"

Mar 6:56 – "as many as touched..made whole"
Mar 7:4 – "And many other things there be"
Mar 7:8 – "many other such like things ye do"
Mar 7:13 – "and many such like things do ye"
Mar 8:31 – "Son of man..suffer many things"
Mar 9:12 – "he must suffer many things"
Mar 9:26 – "many said, He is dead"
Mar 10:31 – "many that are first shall be last"
Mar 10:45 – "his life a ransom for many"
Mar 10:48 – "And many charged him"
Mar 11:8 – "many spread their garments"
Mar 12:5 – "and many others; beating some"
Mar 12:41 – "many..rich cast in much"
Mar 13:6 – "many shall come in my name"
Mar 14:24 – "blood..which is shed for many"
Mar 14:56 – "many bare false witness against"
Mar 15:3 – "priests accused him of many things"
Mar 15:4 – "many things they witness against"
Mar 15:41 – "many other women which came"
Luk 1:1 – "many have taken in hand"
Luk 1:14 – "many shall rejoice at his birth"
Luk 1:16 – "many of the children of Israel"
Luk 2:34 – "fall & rising again of many in Israel"
Luk 2:35 – "thoughts of many hearts..revealed"
Luk 3:18 – "many other things..preached he"
Luk 4:25 – "many widows were in Israel"
Luk 4:27 – "many lepers were in Israel"
Luk 4:41 – "devils also came out of many"
Luk 7:11 – "many of his disciples went with him"
Luk 7:21 – "cured many of their infirmities"
Luk 7:47 – "Her sins, which are many"
Luk 8:3 – "Joanna..Susanna, and many others"
Luk 8:30 – "many devils were entered into him"
Luk 8:32 – "herd of many swine feeding"
Luk 9:22 – "Son of man must suffer many things"
Luk 10:24 – "many prophets..kings have desired"
Luk 10:41 – "troubled about many things"
Luk 11:8 – "give him as many as he needeth"
Luk 11:53 – "provoke him..speak of many things"
Luk 12:7 – "more value than many sparrows"
Luk 12:19 – "goods laid up for many years"
Luk 12:47 – "be beaten with many stripes"
Luk 13:24 – "for many..will seek to enter in"
Luk 14:16 – "great supper, and bade many"
Luk 15:13 – "And not many days after"
Luk 15:29 – "these many years do I serve"
Luk 17:25 – "first must he suffer many things"
Luk 21:8 – "many shall come in my name"
Luk 22:65 – "many other things..spake they"
Luk 23:8 – "he had heard many things of him"
Luk 23:9 – "questioned..him in many words"
Joh 1:12 – "But as many as received him"
Joh 2:12 – "continued there not many days"
Joh 2:23 – "many believed in his name"
Joh 4:39 – "many of the Samaritans..believed"
Joh 4:41 – "And many more believed"
Joh 6:9 – "but what are they among so many"
Joh 6:60 – "Many therefore of his disciples"
Joh 6:66 – "many of his disciples went back"
Joh 7:31 – "many of the people believed"
Joh 7:40 – "Many of the people therefore"

Joh 8:26 – "I have many things to say..judge"
Joh 8:30 – "many believed on him"
Joh 10:20 – "And many of them said"
Joh 10:32 – "Many good works have I shewed"
Joh 10:41 – "And many resorted unto him"
Joh 10:42 – "And many believed on him there"
Joh 11:19 – "And many of the Jews came"
Joh 11:45 – "many of the Jews..came to Mary"
Joh 11:47 – "this man doeth many miracles"
Joh 11:55 – "many went out of the country"
Joh 12:11 – "many of the Jews went away"
Joh 12:37 – "he had done so many miracles"
Joh 12:42 – "also many believed on him"
Joh 14:2 – "Father's house..many mansions"
Joh 16:12 – "yet many things to say unto you"
Joh 17:2 – "life to as many as thou hast given"
Joh 19:20 – "then read many of the Jews"
Joh 20:30 – "many other signs truly did Jesus"
Joh 21:11 – "fishes.. there were so many"
Joh 21:25 – "many other things..Jesus did"
Act 1:3 – "alive..by many infallible proofs"
Act 1:5 – "baptized..not many days hence"
Act 2:39 – "as many as the Lord..shall call"
Act 2:40 – "And with many other words"
Act 2:43 – "many wonders & signs were done"
Act 3:24 – "as many as have spoken"
Act 4:4 – "many of them which heard..word"
Act 4:6 – "as many as were of the kindred"
Act 4:34 – "as many as were possessors"
Act 5:11 – "as many as heard these things"
Act 5:12 – "many signs and wonders wrought"
Act 5:36 – "as many as obeyed him..scattered"
Act 5:37 – "as many as obeyed him..dispersed"
Act 8:7 – "unclean spirits..came out of many"
Act 8:25 – "preached..gospel in many villages"
Act 9:13 – "I have heard by many of this man"
Act 9:23 – "after that many days..fulfilled"
Act 9:42 – "many believed in the Lord"
Act 9:43 – "tarried many days in Joppa"
Act 10:27 – "many that were come together"
Act 10:45 – "as many as came with Peter"
Act 12:12 – "many were gathered..praying"
Act 13:31 – "seen many days of them"
Act 13:43 – "many of the Jews &..proselytes"
Act 13:48 – "as many as were ordained to..life"
Act 14:21 – "preached..and had taught many"
Act 15:32 – "exhorted..with many words"
Act 15:35 – "Paul..Barnabas..with many others"
Act 16:18 – "And this did she many days."
Act 16:23 – "had laid many stripes upon them"
Act 17:12 – "Therefore many of them believed"
Act 18:8 – "many..Corinthians hearing believed"
Act 19:18 – "And many that believed came"
Act 19:19 – "Many..which used curious arts"
Act 20:8 – "many lights in the upper chamber"
Act 20:19 – "Serving the Lord..with many tears"
Act 21:10 – "as we tarried there many days"
Act 21:20 – "many 1000's of Jews..believe"
Act 24:10 – "hast been of many years a judge"
Act 24:17 – "Now after many years I came"
Act 25:7 – "laid many and grievous complaints"

Act 25:14 – "they had been there many days"
Act 26:9 – "do many things contrary to..Jesus"
Act 26:10 – "many of the saints did I shut up"
Act 27:7 – "we had sailed slowly many days"
Act 27:20 – "neither sun nor stars in many days"
Act 28:10 – "honoured us with many honours"
Act 28:23 – "came many to..his lodging"
Rom 2:12 – "as many as have sinned w/o law"
Rom 4:17 – "a father of many nations"
Rom 4:18 – "the father of many nations"
Rom 5:15 – "offence of one many be dead"
Rom 5:15 – "grace.. abounded unto many"
Rom 5:16 – "gift is of many offences"
Rom 5:19 – "shall many be made righteous"
Rom 6:3 – "many of us..baptized into Jesus"
Rom 8:14 – "as many as are led by the Spirit"
Rom 8:29 – "firstborn among many brethren"
Rom 12:4 – "many members in one body"
Rom 12:5 – "we, being many, are one body"
Rom 15:23 – "great desire these many years"
Rom 16:2 – "hath been a succourer of many"
1Co 1:26 – "not many wise men after the flesh
1Co 1:26 – "not many mighty..are called"
1Co 1:26 – "not many noble, are called"
1Co 4:15 – "yet have ye not many fathers"
1Co 8:5 – "there be gods many..lords many"
1Co 10:5 – "with many..God was not..pleased"
1Co 10:17 – "we being many are one bread"
1Co 10:33 – "seeking..the profit of many"
1Co 11:30 – "many are weak and sickly"
1Co 12:12 – "body is 1..hath many members"
1Co 12:12 – " being many, are one body"
1Co 12:14 – "body..not 1 member, but many"
1Co 12:20 – "many members, yet but 1 body"
1Co 14:10 – "many kinds of voices in..world"
1Co 16:9 – "there are many adversaries"
2Co 1:11 – "by the means of many persons"
2Co 1:11 – "thanks may be given by many"
2Co 2:4 – "wrote unto you with many tears"
2Co 2:6 – "punishment..inflicted of many"
2Co 2:17 – "many, which corrupt the word"
2Co 4:15 – "the thanksgiving of many"
2Co 6:10 – "yet making many rich"
2Co 8:22 – "proved diligent in many things"
2Co 9:2 – "zeal hath provoked very many"
2Co 9:12 – "many thanksgivings unto God"
2Co 11:18 – "many glory after the flesh"
2Co 12:21 – "many which have sinned"

Gal 1:14 – "above many my equals"
Gal 3:4 – "suffered so many things in vain"
Gal 3:10 – "many as are of the works..law"
Gal 3:16 – "And to seeds, as of many"
Gal 3:27 – "as many,,as have been baptized"
Gal 4:27 – "desolate hath many more children"
Gal 6:12 – " many..make a fair shew"
Gal 6:16 – "many as walk according to this rule"
Phi 1:14 – "many of the brethren in the Lord"
Phi 3:15 – "as many as be perfect"
Phi 3:18 – "many walk..enemies of the cross"
Col 2:1 – "many as have not seen my face"
1Ti 6:1 – "as many servants..under the yoke"
1Ti 6:9 – "into many foolish and hurtful lusts"
1Ti 6:10 – "pierced..with many sorrows"
1Ti 6:12 – "profession before many witnesses"
2Ti 1:18 – "many things he ministered"
2Ti 2:2 – "heard of me among many witnesses"
Tit 1:10 – "many unruly..talkers..deceivers"
Heb 2:10 – "bringing many sons unto glory"
Heb 5:11 – "we have many things to say"
Heb 7:23 – " they truly were many priests"
Heb 9:28 – "to bear the sins of many"
Heb 11:12 – "so many as the stars of the sky"
Heb 12:15 – "bitterness..many be defiled"
Jam 3:1 – "brethren, be not many masters"
Jam 3:2 – "For in many things we offend all."
2Pe 2:2 – "many shall follow their..ways"
1 Jo 2:18 – "now are there many antichrists"
1Jo 4:1 – "many false prophets are gone out"
2Jo 1:7 – "many deceivers..into the world,"
2Jo 1:12 – "many things to write unto you"
3Jo 1:13 – "I had many things to write"
Rev 1:15 – "voice as,,sound of many waters"
Rev 2:24 – "many as have not this doctrine"
Rev 3:19 – "As many as I love, I rebuke"
Rev 5:11 – "heard the voice of many angels"
Rev 8:11 – "many men died of the waters"
Rev 9:9 – "sound..many horses running"
Rev 10:11 – "many peoples..nations
Rev 10:11 – "many..tongues..kings"
Rev 13:15 – "many..not worship..the beast"
Rev 14:2 – "as the voice of many waters"
Rev 17:1 – "great whore..upon many waters"
Rev 18:17 – "as many as trade by sea"
Rev 19:6 – "as the voice of many waters"
Rev 19:12 – "on his head were many crowns"

Much

As an adjective, "much" usually means *a large, indeterminate amount.*   Out of the 276 references in the Bible to the word "much," few actually count any objects in a specific, albeit indefinite way.   The majority of the references to "much" describe an ambiguous amount of something.

Several

Today "several" means *more than two, but not many*. In all twelve Bible references however, "several" carries the alternative definition of *separate, distinct or different*. There are no instances in Scripture where the word "several" counts anything.

Some

The term "some" will be one of three parts of speech:

1) An adjective describing *an unspecified amount or number* – eg. "I will give you some money"
2) A pronoun representing *an unspecified amount or number* – eg. "If you want money, I will give you some."
3) An adverb meaning *somewhat or to some extent* – eg. "The rules change some."

For the purposes of this volume, we are interested in the term "some" where it is used as an adjective describing unspecified numbers of things. Where "some" describes a vague amount (*"some of the blood"*) or a specific, but undetermined object (*"some pit"*), nothing is actually being counted.

Because of the inherently vague aspects of this term, there will be a wide divergence of opinion as to whether a specific instance of the term "some" is actually counting something or not. For this reason we have not included any references to "some" and suggest the reader consult a standard concordance if there is further interest in this term.

1's / Ones

Num 32:24 – "Build you cities for your little ones"
Num 32:26 – "Our little ones..in..cities of Gilead"
Deu 1:39 – "little ones..ye said should be a prey"
Deu 2:34 – "destroyed..men..women..little ones"
Deu 20:14 – "little ones..cattle..spoil..unto thyself"
Deu 22:6 – "whether they be young ones, or eggs"
Deu 29:11 – "Your little ones, your wives..."
Jos 1:14 – "wives, your little ones, and your cattle"
Jos 8:35 – "women..little ones, and the strangers"
2Sa 15:22 – "the little ones that were with him"
Job 39:16 – "hardened against her young ones"
Psa 10:10 – "the poor my fall by his strong ones"
Psa 83:3 – "consulted against they hidden ones"
Pro 7:7 – "And beheld among the simple ones"
Isa 10:16 – "send among his fat ones leanness"
Isa 10:33 – "high ones of stature..hewn down"
Isa 11:17 – "young ones shall lie down together"
Isa 13:1 – "commanded my sanctified ones"
Isa 13:1 – "I have also called my mighty ones"
Isa 14:9 – "even all the chief ones of the earth"
Isa 25:5 – "the branch of the terrible ones"
Isa 29:5 – "the multitude of the terrible ones"
Isa 32:11 – "be troubled, ye careless ones"
Jer 2:33 – "taught the wicked ones thy ways"
Jer 8:16 – "the neighing of his strong ones"
Jer 14:3 – "sent their little ones to the waters"
Jer 48:4 – "Moab is destroyed; her little ones"
Jer 48:45 – "crown..head of the tumultuous ones"
Lam 4:3 – "give suck to their young ones"
Dan 4:17 – "demand by the word of the holy ones"
Dan 8:8 – "horn..broken..came up 4 notable ones"
Dan 11:17 – "upright ones with him"
Joe 3:11 – "cause thy mighty ones to come down"
Mat 10:42 – "one of these little ones..cold water"

Mat 18:6 – "offend one of these little ones"
Mat 18:10 – "despise not one of these little ones"
Mat 18:14 – "that one of these little ones..perish"
Mar 9:42 – "offend one of these little ones"
Mar 10:42 – "Gentiles..their great ones exercise"

7's / Sevens

Gen 7:2 – "clean beast..take to thee by sevens"
Gen 7:3 – "fowls also of the air by sevens"

10's / Tens

Exo 18:21 – "rulers of tens"
Exo 18:25 – "rulers of tens"
Deu 1:15 – "captains over tens"

50's / Fifties

Exo 18:21 – "rulers of fifties"
Exo 18:25 – "rulers of fifties"
Deu 1:15 – "captains over fifties"
1Sa 8:12 – "will appoint him...captains over 50's"
2Ki 1:14 – "captains of..former 50's w/ their 50's"
Mar 6:40 – "sat..by ranks, by 100's, and by 50's"
Luk 9:14 – "Make them sit down by 50's"

100's / Hundreds

Exo 18:21 – "rulers of hundreds"
Exo 18:25 – "rulers of hundreds"

Num 31:14 – "captains over hundreds"
Num 31:48 – "captains of hundreds"
Num 31:52 – "offering…of the captains of 100's"
Num 31:54 – "captains of thousands and 100's"
Deu 1:15 – "captains over hundreds"
1Sa 22:7 – "captains of hundreds"
1Sa 29:2 – "lords..Philistines passed on by 100's"
2Sa 18:1 – "set captains of 1000's and..of 100's
2Sa 18:4 – "people came..by 100's and by 1000's"
2Ki 11:4 – "Jehoiada..fetched..rulers over 100's"
2Ki 11:9 – "And the captains over the 100's did"
2Ki 11:10 – "to the captains over 100's"
2Ki 11:19 – "he took the rulers over 100's"
1Ch 13:1 – "consulted..captains of 1000's & 100's"
1Ch 26:26 – "captains over 1000's and 100's"
1Ch 27:1 – "captains of thousands and hundreds"
1Ch 28:1 – "captains over the hundreds"
1Ch 29:6 – "the captains of 1000's and of 100's"
2Ch 1:2 – "spake..to captains of 1000's & of 100's"
2Ch 23:1 – "Jehoiada..took the captains of 100's"
2Ch 23:9 – "delivered to the captains of 100's"
2Ch 23:14 – "brought out the captains of 100's"
2Ch 23:20 – "he took the captains of 100's"
2Ch 25:5 – "made them..captains over 100's"
Mar 6:40 – "sat..by ranks, by 100's, and by 50's"

1000's / Thousands

Exo 18:21 – "rulers of thousands"
Exo 18:25 – "rulers of thousands"
Exo 20:6 – "mercy unto 1000's..that love me"
Exo 34:7 – "keeping mercy for 1000's"
Num 1:16 – "princes..of the 1000's in Israel"
Num 10:4 – "heads of the thousands of Israel"
Num 10:36 – "O LORD..many 1000's of Israel"
Num 31:5 – "delivered out of the 1000's of Israel"
Num 31:14 – "captains over thousands"
Num 31:48 – "officers which were over 1000's"
Num 31:48 – "the captains of thousands"
Num 31:52 – "offering…of the captains of 1000's"
Num 31:54 – "captains of 1000's and hundreds"
Deu 1:15 – "captains over thousands"
Deu 5:10 – "mercy unto 1000's..that love me"
Deu 33:17 – "they are the 1000's of Manasseh"
Jos 22:14 – "among the 1000's of Israel"
Jos 22:21 – "the heads of the 1000's of Israel"
Jos 22:30 – "princes..heads of the 1000's of Israel"
1Sa 8:12 – "will appoint him captains over 1000's"
1Sa 10:19 – "present yourselves..by your 1000's"
1Sa 18:7 – "Saul hath slain his 1000's"
1Sa 18:8 – "to me they have ascribed but 1000's"
1Sa 21:11 – "Saul hath slain his 1000's"
1Sa 22:7 – "make you all captains of 1000's"
1Sa 29:2 – "Philistines passed on by..1000's"
1Sa 29:5 – "Saul slew his thousands"
2Sa 18:1 – "set captains of 1000's and..of 100's
2Sa 18:4 – "people came..by 100's and by 1000's"
1Ch 12:20 – "captains of the 1000's..of Manasseh"
1Ch 13:1 – "consulted..captains of 1000's & 100's"
1Ch 15:25 – "captains over 1000's..bring..the ark"

1Ch 26:26 – "captains over 1000's and 100's"
1Ch 27:1 – "captains of thousands and 100's"
1Ch 28:1 – "the captains over the thousands"
1Ch 29:6 – "the captains of 1000's and of 100's"
2Ch 1:2 – "spake..to captains of 1000's & of 100's"
2Ch 17:14 – "Of Judah, the captains of 1000's"
2Ch 25:5 – "made them captains over 1000's"
Psa 68:17 – "even thousands of angels"
Psa 119:72 – "law..is better..than 1000's of gold"
Psa 144:13 – "our sheep may bring forth 1000's"
Mic 5:2 – "little among the 1000's of Judah"
Mic 6:7 – "LORD be pleased with 1000's of rams"
Act 21:20 – "how many 1000's of Jews..zealous"

10,000's / Ten Thousands

Deu 33:2 – "from Sinai..with 10,000's of saints"
Deu 33:17 – "they are the 10,000's of Ephraim"
1Sa 18:7 – "and David his 10,000's"
1Sa 18:8 – "have ascribed unto David 10,000's"
1Sa 21:11 – "and David his 10,000's"
1Sa 29:5 – "and David his 10,000's"
Psa 3:6 – "will not be afraid of 10,000's of people"
Psa 144:13 – "sheep may bring forth..10,000's"
Dan 11:12 – "shall cast down many 10,000's"
Mic 6:7 – "pleased..with 10,000's of rivers of oil?"
Jud 14 – "Lord cometh with 10,000's of his saints"

1,000,000's / Millions

Dan 7:10 – "thousand thousands ministered unto him"

1,000,000,000's / Billions

Gen 24:60 – "be thou the mother of thousands of millions"

Short of infinity, this is the largest, specific number mentioned in Scripture

Infinite and/or Uncountable

Gen 13:16 – "seed as the dust of the earth"
Gen 13:16 – "if a man can number the dust..then shall also thy seed be numbered"
Gen 15:5 – "tell the stars, if..able to number them"
Gen 15:5 – "the stars..So shall thy seed be"
Gen 16:10 – "I will multiply thy seed exceedingly"
Gen 16:10 – "seed..not..numbered for multitude"
Gen 17:2 – "will multiply thy seed exceedingly"
Gen 17:20 – "Ishmael..multiply him exceedingly"
Gen 22:17 – "multiply thy seed as the stars"
Gen 22:17 – "multiply thy seed..as the sand"
Gen 24:60 – "the mother of thousands of millions"
Gen 26:4 – "seed..multiply as the stars of heaven"

Gen 32:12 – "thy seed as the sand of the sea,
   which cannot be numbered"
Gen 41:49 – "corn as the sand of the sea"
Gen 41:49 – "corn..until he left numbering"
Gen 41:49 – "corn..it was without number"
Deu 1:10 – "as the stars of heaven for multitude"
Deu 28:62 – "as the stars of heaven for multitude"
Jos 11:4 – "as the sand that is on the sea shore"
Jdg 6:5 – "they and their camels..w/o number"
Jdg 7:12 – "camels..w/o number, as the sand"
2Sa 17:11 – "as the sand that is by the sea"
1Ki 3:8 – "people..cannot be numbered..counted"
1Ki 4:29 – "wisdom..understanding..as the sand"
1Ki 4:29 – "heart..as the sand"
1Ki 8:5 – "sheep..oxen..not be told nor numbered"
2Ki 25:16 – "brass of all..vessels was w/o weight"
1Ch 22:3 – "brass in abundance without weight"
1Ch 22:14 – "brass and iron without weight"
1Ch 22:16 – "gold..silver.. there is no number"
1Ch 22:16 – "brass..iron, there is no number"
1Ch 27:23 – "Israel like..the stars of the heavens"
2Ch 1:9 – "people like..dust of..earth in multitude"
2Ch 4:18 – "weight..brass could not be found out"
2Ch 5:6 – "not be told..numbered for multitude"
Ezr 7:22 – "salt w/o prescribing how much"
Neh 9:23 – "their children..as the stars of heaven"
Job 5:9 – "marvelous things without number"
Job 5:25 – "seed..great..as the grass of the earth"
Job 9:10 – "doeth..wonders without number"
Job 21:33 – "man.. are innumerable before him"
Job 29:18 – "I shall multiply my days as the sand"
Job 34:24 – "break in pieces..men w/o number"
Job 36:26 – "number of his years be searched"
Job 38:37 – "Who can number the clouds"
Job 39:2 – "Canst thou number the months"
Psa 40:5 – "thy..works..cannot be reckoned up"
Psa 40:5 – "works..more than can be numbered"
Psa 40:12 – "innumerable evils..compassed me"

Psa 40:12 – "iniquities..more than..hairs of..head"
Psa 69:4 – "They that hate me..more than..hairs of"
Psa 78:27 – "rained flesh also upon them as dust"
Psa 78:27 – "feathered fowls like..sand of the sea"
Psa 102:27 – "thy years shall have no end"
Psa 104:25 – "are things creeping innumerable"
Psa 105:34 – "locusts..caterpillars..w/o number"
Psa 139:18 – "count..more in number than..sand"
Psa 147:4 – "He telleth the number of the stars"
Son 6:8 – "There are..virgins without number"
Isa 9:7 – "increase of his government..be no end"
Isa 10:22 – "people Israel be as..sand of the sea"
Isa 65:22 – "as..days of a tree..days of my people"
Jer 2:32 – "forgotten me days w/o number"
Jer 15:8 – "widows increased..above..sands..seas"
Jer 15:13 – "treasures will I give..without price"
Jer 33:22 – "host of heaven cannot be numbered"
Jer 33:22 – "neither the sand of the sea measured"
Jer 33:22 – "so will I multiply the seed of David"
Jer 46:23 – "the grasshoppers..innumerable"
Jer 52:20 – "brass.vessels..was without weight"
Hos 1:10 – "Israel..as the sand of the sea..cannot
   be measured nor numbered"
Joe 1:6 – "a nation is come up..without number"
Nah 3:3 – "multitude..slain..great number..corpses"
Nah 3:3 – "there is none end of their corpses"
Nah 3:9 – "Ethiopia..Egypt..strength..was infinite"
Nah 3:16 – "multiplied..merchants above..stars"
Hab 1:9 – "shall gather the captivity as the sand"
Rom 9:27 – "children..Israel..as the sand of..sea"
Heb 11:12 – "as the stars of the sky in multitude"
Heb 11:12 – "as the sand.. innumerable"
Heb 12:22 – "an innumerable company of angels"
Rev 5:11 – "number of then was 10,000 times
   10,000 and 1000's of 1000's"
Rev 7:9 – "great multitude..no man could number"
Rev 20:8 – "number of whom is as the sand"

DIRECTORY OF BIBLE DATES
SECTION TWO

Section Two includes Bible numbers that are attached to the dates found in Scripture. They are most easily identified because they are counting a specific day, month and in some cases year.

This section is divided into two parts:

    1)   **Dates With Respect to a Generic Yearly Calendar** – as such all of these dates will only have a **month** and **day** associated with them

    2)   **Dates With Respect to Some Beginning Point** – each will have a **year**, a **month** and in most cases (but not all) a **day** associated with them. Each entry will list the reference, the beginning point from which the date is determined and a brief description of what the date refers to.

Each component of each date can also be found in the *Dictionary of Items Counted* under the three entries: **Days**, **Months** and **Years**.

Part A – Dates With Respect to a Generic Yearly Calendar

1ˢᵗ month, 1ˢᵗ day

Ezr 10:17 – Ezra finishes matter of strange wives
Ezk 45:18 – Millennial temple cleansed

1ˢᵗ month, 10ᵗʰ day

Exo. 12:3 – Passover – "take..every man a lamb"
Jos 4:19 – Israelites over Jordan to Promised Land

1ˢᵗ month, 14ᵗʰ day

Exo. 12:6 – Passover lamb was to be killed
Exo. 12:18 – at even, feast of unleavened begins
Lev 23:5 – "the LORD'S Passover"
Num 28:16 – "is the passover of the LORD"
2Ch 35:1 – "they killed the passover"
Ezr 6:19 – "children of..captivity kept..passover"
Ezk 45:21 – Passover in the Millennial kingdom

1ˢᵗ month, 15ᵗʰ day

Lev 23:6 – "feast of unleavened bread unto..LORD"
Num 28:17 – "feast: 7 days..unleavened bread"
Num 33:3 – departure of Israel from Ramses

1ˢᵗ month, 21ˢᵗ day

Exo. 12:18 – feast of unleavened bread ends

1ˢᵗ month, 24ᵗʰ day

Dan 10:4 – Daniel's vision next to Hiddekel

2ⁿᵈ month, 14ᵗʰ day

Num 9:11 – Passover kept by some a month late
2Ch 30:15 – Hezekiah's great passover

7ᵗʰ month, 1ˢᵗ day

Lev 23:24 – Feast of Trumpets began w/ trumpets
Num 29:1 – "day of blowing..trumpets unto you"
Neh 8:2 – Ezra read the law before God's people

7ᵗʰ month, 9ᵗʰ day

Lev 23:32 – fasting begins for Day of Atonement

7ᵗʰ month, 10ᵗʰ day

Lev 16:29 – Day of Atonement
Lev 23:27 – Day of Atonement
Lev 25:9 – trumpet sound to mark year of Jubilee
Num 29:7 – "holy convocation..affict your souls"

7ᵗʰ month, 15ᵗʰ day

Lev 23:34 – beginning of Feast of Tabernacles
Lev 23:39 – beginning of Feast of Tabernacles

Num 29:12 – "keep a feast unto the LORD 7 days"
Ezk 45:25 – Millennial kingdom "feast of..7 days"

7ᵗʰ month, 23ʳᵈ day

2Ch 7:10 – end of Solomon's feast of dedication

7ᵗʰ month, 24ᵗʰ day

Neh 9:1 – Israel before Ezra with fasting

8ᵗʰ month, 15ᵗʰ day

1Ki 12:32 – Jeroboam's feast to the two calves
1Ki 12:33 – Jeroboam's feast to the two calves

9ᵗʰ month, 20ᵗʰ day

Ezr 10:9 – Ezra deals w/ problem of strange wives

10ᵗʰ month, 1ˢᵗ day

Ezr 10:16 – examining matter of the strange wives

12ᵗʰ month, 14ᵗʰ day

Est 9:19 – first celebration of Feast of Purim

12ᵗʰ month, 14ᵗʰ & 15ᵗʰ days

Est 9:21 – establishment of days of Purim

Part B – Dates With Respect to a Starting Point

1ˢᵗ year, 1ˢᵗ month, 1ˢᵗ day

2Ch 29:3 – reign of Hezekiah
  ➢ Hezekiah reopens and repairs temple
2Ch 29:17 – reign of Hezekiah
  ➢ Hezekiah reopens and repairs temple

1ˢᵗ year, 1ˢᵗ month, 8ᵗʰ day

2Ch 29:17 – reign of Hezekiah
  ➢ priests cleanse as far as temple porch

1ˢᵗ year, 1ˢᵗ month, 16ᵗʰ day

2Ch 29:17 – reign of Hezekiah
  ➢ priests finish cleansing temple complex

1ˢᵗ Year, 2ⁿᵈ month, 15ᵗʰ day

Exo. 16:1 – after the Jews left Egypt
  ➢ arrival in the wilderness of Sin

1ˢᵗ year, 7ᵗʰ month, 1ˢᵗ day

Ezr 3:6 – return from Babylonian captivity
  ➢ "began they to offer burnt offerings"

2ⁿᵈ Year, 1ˢᵗ month

Num 9:1 – after the Jews left Egypt
  ➢ "LORD spoke unto Moses in..Sinai"

2ⁿᵈ Year, 1ˢᵗ month, 1ˢᵗ day

Exo 40:2 – after the Jews left Egypt
  ➢ command to set up the tabernacle
Exo 40:17 – after the Jews left Egypt
  ➢ "the tabernacle was reared up"

2ⁿᵈ Year, 1ˢᵗ month, 14ᵗʰ day

Num 9:3 – after the Jews left Egypt
  ➢ command to keep the very first Passover
Num 9:5 – after the Jews left Egypt
  ➢ Israel kept the very first Passover

2ⁿᵈ year, 2ⁿᵈ month

Ezr 3:8 – return from Babylonian captivity
  ➢ began construction of the temple

2ⁿᵈ year, 2ⁿᵈ month, 1ˢᵗ day

Num 1:1 – after the Jews left Egypt
  ➢ introduction to book of Numbers

Num 1:18 – after the Jews left Egypt
  ➤ assembly of the nation of Israel

2ⁿᵈ year, 2ⁿᵈ month, 20ᵗʰ day

Num 10:11 – after the Jews left Egypt
  ➤ Israel journeys from Sinai to Paran

2ⁿᵈ year, 6ᵗʰ month, 1ˢᵗ day

Hag 1:1 – reign of Darius
  ➤ beginning of Haggai's prophecy

2ⁿᵈ year, 6ᵗʰ month, 24ᵗʰ day

Hag 1:15 – reign of Darius
  ➤ work began on Zerubbabel's temple

2ⁿᵈ year, 7ᵗʰ month, 21ˢᵗ day

Hag 2:1 – reign of Darius
  ➤ Haggai's second prophecy

2ⁿᵈ year, 8ᵗʰ month

Zec 1:1 – reign of Darius
  ➤ beginning of Zechariah's prophecy

2ⁿᵈ year, 9ᵗʰ month, 24ᵗʰ day

Hag 2:10 – reign of Darius
  ➤ Haggai's third prophecy
Hag 2:18 – reign of Darius
  ➤ foundation of temple laid
Hag 2:20 – reign of Darius
  ➤ Haggai's fourth prophecy

2ⁿᵈ year, 11ᵗʰ month, 24ᵗʰ day

Zec 1:7 – reign of Darius
  ➤ Zechariah's second prophecy

4ᵗʰ year, 2ⁿᵈ month

1Ki 6:1 – reign of Solomon
  ➤ Solomon began building the temple

4ᵗʰ year, 2ⁿᵈ month, 2ⁿᵈ day

2Ch 3:2 – reign of Solomon
  ➤ Solomon began building the temple

4ᵗʰ year, 5ᵗʰ month

Jer 28:1 – reign of Zedekiah
  ➤ Jeremiah and the false prophet Hananiah

4ᵗʰ year, 7ᵗʰ month

Jer 28:17 – reign of Zedekiah
  ➤ death of false prophet Hananiah

4ᵗʰ year, 9ᵗʰ month, 4ᵗʰ day

Zec 7:1 – reign of Darius
  ➤ "word of the LORD came unto Zechariah"

5ᵗʰ year, 4ᵗʰ month, 5ᵗʰ day

Ezk 1:2 – Jehoiachin's Babylonian captivity
  ➤ beginning of Ezekiel's visions

5ᵗʰ year, 9ᵗʰ month

Jer 36:9 – reign of Jehoiakim
  ➤ fast proclaimed, Baruch reads God's law
Jer 36:22 – reign of Jehoiakim
  ➤ king destroys scroll with penknife

6ᵗʰ year, 6ᵗʰ month, 5ᵗʰ day

Ezk 8:1 – Babylonian captivity
  ➤ Ezekiel's vision of idolatry in the temple

7ᵗʰ year, 1ˢᵗ month, 1ˢᵗ day

Ezr 7:9 – reign of Artaxerxes
  ➤ Ezra departed Babylon for Jerusalem

7ᵗʰ year, 1ˢᵗ month, 12ᵗʰ day

Ezr 8:31 – reign of Artaxerxes
  ➤ Ezra departs from the river of Ahava

7th year, 5th month, 1st day

Ezr 7:8 – reign of Artaxerxes
> Ezra arrives in Jerusalem
Ezr 7:9 – reign of Artaxerxes
> Ezra arrives in Jerusalem

7th year, 5th month, 10th day

Ezk 20:1 – Babylonian captivity
> God's word to Ezekiel

7th year, 10th month

Est 2:16 – reign of Ahasuerus
> Esther taken in before King Ahasuerus

9th year, 10th month

Jer 39:1 – reign of Zedekiah
> "Nebuchadnezzar besieged Jerusalem

9th year, 10th month, 10th day

2Ki 25:1 – reign of Zedekiah
> Nebuchadnezzar against Jerusalem
Jer 52:4 – reign of Zedekiah
> Nebuchadnezzar against Jerusalem
Ezk 24:1 – Babylonian captivity
> word from God about the boiling pot

11th year, 1st month, 1st day

Ezk 26:1 – Babylonian captivity
> word from God to Ezekiel about Tyrus

11th year, 1st month, 7th day

Ezk 30:20 – Babylonian captivity
> word from God to Ezekiel about Pharaoh

11th year, 3rd month, 1st day

Ezk 31:1 – Babylonian captivity
> word from God about the Assyrians

11th year, 4th month, 9th day

2Ki 25:2-3 – reign of Zedekiah
> famine reached climax; Jerusalem broken up

Jer 39:1 – reign of Zedekiah
> city of Jerusalem broken up by the siege
Jer 52:5-6 – reign of Zedekiah
> city of Jerusalem broken up by the siege

11th year, 5th month

Jer 1:3 – reign of Zedekiah
> "carrying away of Jerusalem captive"

11th year, 5th month, 7th day

2Ki 25:8 – reign of Zedekiah
> Nebuzaradan burnt Jerusalem

11th year, 8th month

1Ki 6:38 – reign of Solomon
> Solomon finished building the temple

12th year, 1st month thru 12th month

Est 3:7 – reign of Ahasuerus
> "they cast Pur..the lot, before Haman"

12th year, 1st month thru 12th month

Est 3:7 – reign of Ahasuerus
> "they cast Pur..the lot, before Haman"

12th year, 10th month, 5th day

Ezk 33:21 – Babylonian captivity
> Ezekiel hears about the fall of Jerusalem

12th year, 12th month, 1st day

Ezk 32:1 – Babylonian captivity
> word from God to Ezekiel about Pharaoh

12th year, 12th month, 15th day

Ezk 32:17 – Babylonian captivity
> word from God to Ezekiel about Egypt

13th year, 1st month, 13th day

Est 3:12 – reign of Ahasuerus
> Haman's edict to kill Jews written

13th year, 3rd month, 23rd day

Est 8:9 – reign of Ahasuerus
> Jews permitted to defend themselves

13th year, 12th month, 13th day

Est 3:13 – reign of Ahasuerus
> day the Jews were to be destroyed
Est 8:12 – reign of Ahasuerus
> day the Jews were to be destroyed
Est 9:1 – reign of Ahasuerus
> the Jews stand against their enemies
Est 9:17 – reign of Ahasuerus
> Jews in provinces stood for their lives
Est 9:18 – reign of Ahasuerus
> Jews in Shushan fought their enemies

13th year, 12th month, 14th day

Est 9:15 – reign of Ahasuerus
> Jews in Shushan slew 300 men
Est 9:17 – reign of Ahasuerus
> Jews in the provinces rested and feasted
Est 9:18 – reign of Ahasuerus
> Jews in Shushan fought their enemies

13th year, 12th month, 15th day

Est 9:18 – reign of Ahasuerus
> Jews in Shushan rested and feasted

15th year, 4th month

2Ch 15:10 – reign of Asa
> offering made in Jerusalem

18th year, 10th month, 12th day

Ezk 29:1 – Babylonian captivity
> word from God to Ezekiel about Egypt

19th year, 5th month, 10th day

Jer 52:12 – reign of Nebuchadrezzar
> Nebuzaradan razes Jerusalem with fire

25th year, 1st month, 10th day

Ezk 40:1 – Babylonian captivity
> word from God about millennial temple

27th year, 1st month, 1st day

Ezk 29:17 – Babylonian captivity
> word from God about Nebuchadnezzar

30th year, 4th month, 5th day

Ezk 1:1 – in the life of Ezekiel
> Ezekiel's first vision

37th year, 12th month, 25th day

Jer 52:31 – captivity of King Jehoiachin in Babylon
> released from prison by Evilmerodach

37th year, 12th month, 27th day

2Ki 25:27 – captivity of Jehoiachin in Babylon
> released from prison by Evilmerodach

40th year, 5th month, 1st day

Num 33:38 – after the Jews left Egypt
> death of Aaron at Mt. Hor

40th year, 11th month, 1st day

Deu 1:3 – after the Jews left Egypt
> book of Deuteronomy begins

480th year

1Ki 6:1 – after the Jews left Egypt
> Solomon commenced building the temple

600th year, 2nd month, 17th day

Gen. 7:11 – in the life of Noah
> rain began; fountains of deep broken up

600th year, 7th month, 17th day

Gen. 8:4 – in the life of Noah
> "ark rested..upon the mountains of Aarat"

600th year, 10th month, 1st day

Gen 8:5 – in the life of Noah
> "were the tops of the mountains seen"

113

601st year, 1st month, 1st day

Gen. 8:13 – in the life of Noah
  ➢ waters of the flood dried up; ark opened

601st year, 2nd month, 27th day

Gen 8:14 – in the life of Noah
  ➢ "was the earth dried"

INDEX OF NUMBERED ITEMS
SECTION THREE

Section Three includes Bible numbers that are indexed according to the thing or item being counted. Please note carefully the following tips that will assist you in finding the headings and entries you are searching for:

> ➤ All item headings are listed in alphabetical order.

> ➤ Generally speaking nouns are listed alone without identifying adjectives – eg. **talker** instead of "unruly talkers" or **tree** instead of "apple tree" or "willow tree"

> ➤ Each item heading is listed in its singular form. For instance, regardless of how many **men** are being counted, they are all listed under the singular heading of **Man**. This may be significant for two reasons:

> > 1) Always look for the heading under the singular form of the word you are searching for – e.g. "loaves" will be under **Loaf**.
> > 2) The difference in spelling between the singular and the plural may affect the alphabetical order of a heading – e.g. "brethren" actually appears under **Brother** and there are a number of headings between BRE and BRO. If you have difficulty locating a heading that you are confident in finding in this volume, this will be the most common reason. Be sure you are looking for the properly spelled, singular form of the word.

> ➤ Larger item headings are often further broken down into subsections for ease of searching.

> ➤ The entries under each heading are organized chronologically, by book of the Bible.

> ➤ Cardinal & ordinal numbers along with zero, fractions and indefinite numbers, all appear together under each heading according to the items that they are counting.

> ➤ *Whenever an entry appears in italics*, there is no explicit reference to that item heading by name in the verse, but is implied or named in a nearby verse

> ➤ There may be more than one heading for the same word where the meanings are significantly different – eg. **Sea** appears twice: one heading is for the *ocean* and the other is for the *laver* in the earthly tabernacle.

Abomination

Pro 26:25 – "seven abominations in his heart"

Accord

Jos 9:2 – "to fight with Joshua..with one accord"
Act 1:14 – "all continued with one accord"
Act 2:1 – "all with one accord in one place"
Act 2:46 – "continuing daily with one accord"
Act 4:24 – "lifted up their voice..with one accord"
Act 5:12 – "all w/ one accord in Solomon's porch"
Act 7:57 – "ran upon him with one accord"
Act 8:6 – "with one accord gave heed unto..Philip"
Act 12:20 – "they came with one accord to him"
Act 15:25 – "being assembled with one accord"
Act 18:12 – "with one accord against Paul"
Act 19:29 – "they rushed with one accord"

Phi 2:2 – "being of one accord, of one mind"

Accusation

Act 25:18 – "they brought none accusation"

Acquaintance

Act 24:23 – "forbid none of his acquaintance"

Acre

1Sa 14:14 – "1/2 acre of land..oxen might plow"
Isa 5:10 – "10 acres of vineyard shall yield 1 bath"

Act

2Sa 23:20 – "Benaiah..had done many acts"
1Ch 11:22 – "Benaiah..had done many acts"
1Ch 29:29 – "acts of David the king, first and last"
2Ch 9:29 – "acts of Solomon, first and last"
2Ch 12:15 – "acts of Rehoboam, first and last"
2Ch 16:11 – "acts of Asa, first and last"
2Ch 20:34 – "acts of Jehoshaphat, first and last"
2Ch 25:26 – "acts of Amaziah, first and last"
2Ch 26:22 – "acts of Uzziah, first and last"
2Ch 28:26 – "rest of his acts..first and last"

Admonition

Tit 3:10 – "after the 1st and 2nd admonition"

Adulteress

Rom 7:3 – "so that she is no adulteress"

Adversary

Jer 30:16 – "adversaries..every one..into captivity"
1Co 16:9 – "there are many adversaries"

Affliction

Psa 34:19 – "Many..afflictions of the righteous"

Air

Job 41:16 – "no air can come between them"

Altar

Num 23:1 – "Balaam..Build me here 7 altars..."
Num 23:4 – "I have prepared seven altars"
Num 23:14 – "top of Pisgah, and built 7 altars"
Num 23:29 – "Build me here seven altars..."
Num 23:29 – "prepare me..7 bullocks and 7 rams"
1Sa 14:35 – "1st altar that he built unto the LORD"
2Ch 32:12 – "Ye shall worship before one altar"
Hos 8:11 – "Ephraim..made many altars to sin"

Ananias

Act 22:12 – "And one Ananias, a devout man"

Anchor

Act 27:29 – "cast four anchors out of the stern"

Angel

Gen 19:1 – "came two angels to Sodom at even"
Psa 68:17 – "even thousands of angels"
Joh 20:12 – "two angels in white sitting"
Joh 20:12 – "angels..one at the head..other at..feet"
Heb 12:22 – "an innumerable company of angels"
Rev 5:11 – "heard the voice of many angels"
Rev 7:1 – "After these things I saw 4 angels"
Rev 7:2 – "loud voice to the four angels"
Rev 8:2 – "And I saw the seven angels"
Rev 8:6 – "7 angels which had the 7 trumpets"
Rev 8:7 – "The first angel sounded"
Rev 8:8 – "And the second angel sounded"
Rev 8:10 – "And the third angel sounded"
Rev 8:12 – "And the fourth angel sounded"
Rev 8:13 – "trumpet of the three angels"
Rev 9:1 – "And the fifth angel sounded"
Rev 9:13 – "And the sixth angel sounded"
Rev 9:14 – "Saying to the sixth angel"
Rev 9:14 – "Loose the four angels..in..Euphrates"
Rev 9:15 – "And the four angels were loosed"
Rev 10:7 – "the voice of the seventh angel"
Rev 11:15 – "And the seventh angel sounded"
Rev 14:9 – "the third angel followed them"
Rev 15:1 – "another sign in heaven..7 angels"
Rev 15:6 – "the 7 angels came out of the temple"
Rev 15:7 – "beasts gave unto the 7 angels..vials"
Rev 15:8 – "the 7 plagues of the 7 angels"
Rev 16:1 – "great voice..saying to the 7 angels"
Rev 16:2 – "first went..poured out his vial"
Rev 16:3 – "second angel poured out his vial"
Rev 16:4 – "third angel poured out his vial"
Rev 16:8 – "fourth angel poured out his vial"
Rev 16:10 – "fifth angel poured out his vial"
Rev 16:12 – "sixth angel poured out his vial"
Rev 16:17 – "seventh angel poured out his vial"
Rev 17:1 – "there came one of the seven angels"
Rev 21:9 – "came unto me one of the 7 angels"
Rev 21:12 – "and at the gates twelve angels"

Anna

Luk 2:36 – "there was one Anna, a prophetess"

Another

Gen 11:7 – "understand one another's speech"
Exo 10:23 – "They saw not one another"
Lev 25:14 – "ye shall not oppress one another"
Lev 25:17 – "Ye shall not..oppress one another"
1Sa 14:16 – "beating down one another"
1Sa 18:7 – "the women answered one another"

1Sa 20:41 – "and they kissed one another"
1Ki 6:27 – "their wings touched one another"
2Ki 3:23 – "have smitten one another"
2Ki 14:8 – "let us look one another in the face"
2Ki 14:11 – "looked one another in the face"
2Ch 25:17 – "let us see one another in the face"
2Ch 25:21 – "saw one another in the face"
Eze 3:13 – "wings..touched one another"
Mat 24:10 – "and shall betray one another"
Mat 24:10 – "and shall hate one another"
Joh 13:14 – "ought to wash one another's feet"
Joh 13:34 – "That ye love one another"
Joh 13:34 – "that ye also love one another"
Joh 15:12 – "That ye love one another"
Joh 15:17 – "that ye love one another"
Act 19:38 – "let them implead one another"
Rom 2:15 – "accusing..excusing one another"
Rom 12:10 – "kindly affectioned one to another"
Rom 12:10 – "in honour preferring one another"
Rom 13:8 – "but to love one another"
Rom 13:8 – "he that loveth another..fulfilled..law"
Rom 14:13 – "Let us not..judge one another"
Rom 15:7 – "Wherefore receive ye one another"
Rom 15:14 – "able..to admonish one another"
Rom 16:16 – "Salute one another..holy kiss."
1Co 16:20 – "Greet ye one another..holy kiss."
2Co 13:12 – "Greet one another..holy kiss."
Gal 5:13 – "but by love serve one another"
Gal 5:15 – "if ye bite and devour one another"
Gal 5:26 – "provoking one another"
Gal 5:26 – "envying one another"
Gal 6:2 – "Bear ye one another's burdens"
Eph 4:2 – "forbearing one another in love"
Eph 4:32 – "forgiving one another"
Col 3:13 – "Forbearing one another"
Col 3:13 – "and forgiving one another"
Col 3:16 – "admonishing one another"
1Th 4:9 – "taught of God to love one another"
1Th 4:18 – "Wherefore comfort one another"
1Th 5:11 – "edify one another"
Tit 3:3 – "hateful, *and* hating one another"
Heb 3:13 – "But exhort one another daily"
Heb 10:24 – "let us consider one another"
Heb 10:25 – "but exhorting one another"
1Pe 1:22 – "love one another with a pure heart"
1Pe 5:14 – "Greet ye one another with a kiss"
1Jn 3:11 – "that we should love one another"
1Jn 3:23 – "love one another"
1Jn 4:7 – "Beloved, let us love one another"
1Jn 4:11 – "we ought also to love one another"
1Jn 4:12 – "If we love one another"
2Jn 1:5 – "that we love one another"
Rev 6:4 – "that they should kill one another"

Answer

Job 19:16 – "and he gave me no answer"
Job 32:3 – "three friends..had found no answer"
Job 32:5 – "no answer..of these three men"
Son 5:6 – "but he gave me no answer"

Mic 3:7 – "for there is no answer of God"
Joh 19:9 – "But Jesus gave him no answer."
2Ti 4:16 – "At my first answer no man"

Antichrist

1 Jo 2:18 – "now are there many antichrists"

Apothecary

Neh 3:8 – "Hanaiah..son of 1 of the apothecaries"

Apostle

Mat 10:2 – "twelve apostles..The first, Simon"
Mat 10:2 – "names of the 12 apostles are these"
Luk 6:13 – "disciples..chose twelve..apostles"
Luk 22:14 – "sat down..12 apostles with him"
Act 1:26 – "was numbered with the 11 apostles"
Gal 1:19 – "other of the apostles saw I none"
Rev 21:14 – "names of the 12 apostles"

Aristarchus

Act 27:2 – "one Aristarchus..being with us"

Army

Son 6:13 – "the company of two armies"

Arrow

1Sa 20:20 – "I will shoot three arrows"
Jer 50:14 – "against Babylon..spare no arrows"

Ass

Gen 32:15 – "20 she asses"
Gen 45:23 – "10 asses laden..good things of Egypt"
Gen 45:23 – "10 she asses laden with corn..bread"
Exo 13:13 – "every firstling of an ass..redeem"
Exo 34:20 – "the firstling of an ass..redeem"
Num 16:15 – "I have not taken one ass from them"
Num 31:34 – "And 61,000 asses."
Num 31:39 – "And the asses were 30,500"
Num 31:39 – "asses..the LORD's tribute was 61"
Num 31:45 – "And 30,000 asses and 500"
Jud 19:3 – "a couple of asses"
Jdg 19:10 – "there were w/ him two asses saddled"
2Sa 16:1 – "a couple of asses saddled"
2Ki 4:22 – "Send me..one of the asses"
1Ch 5:21 – "they took away..of asses 2000"

Ezr 2:67 – "their asses 6720"
Neh 7:69 – "6,720 asses"
Job 1:3 – "His substance..500 she asses"
Job 42:12 – "later end of Job..1000 she asses"

Assent

2Ch 18:12 – "declare good to the king w/ 1 assent"

Backsliding

Jer 14:7 – "our backslidings are many"

Bag

2Ki 5:23 – "bound 2 talents of silver in 2 bags"

Balances

Rev 6:5 – "had a pair of balances in his hand"

Balm

Jer 8:22 – "Is there no balm in Gilead"

Band

Gen 32:7 – "Jacob..divided..into two bands"
Gen 32:10 – "now I am become two bands"
Job 1:17 – "The Chaldeans made out three bands"
Psa 73:4 – "no bands in their death"

Baptism

Eph 4:5 – "One Lord, one faith, one baptism"

Bar

Exo 26:26 – "bars..shittim wood; 5 for the boards"
Exo 26:27 – "5 bars for the boards..the other side"
Exo 26:27 – "5 bars for the boards of the side"
Exo 36:31 – "bars of shittim wood..5 for the 1 side"
Exo 36:32 – "five bars for..the other side"
Exo 36:32 – "five bars for the boards..westward"

Barrel

1Ki 18:33 – "Fill 4 barrels with water, and pour it"

Base

1Ki 7:27 – "he made ten bases of brass"
1Ki 7:27 – "four cubits was the length of one base"
1Ki 7:34 – "to the four corners of the one base"
1Ki 7:37 – "After this manner..made the 10 bases"
1Ki 7:38 – "upon every 1 of the 10 bases 1 laver"
1Ki 7:43 – "10 bases, and 10 lavers on the bases"
1Ki 7:39 – "5 bases on the right side of the house"
1Ki 7:39 – *"five on the left side of the house"*

Basket

Gen 40:16 – "I had 3 white baskets on my head"
Gen 40:18 – "The three baskets are three days"
Exo 29:3 – "put them into one basket"
Jer 24:1 – "behold, two baskets of figs"
Jer 24:2 – "One basket had very good figs"
Mat 14:20 – "fragments..remained 12 baskets full"
Mat 15:37 – "broken meat..left seven baskets full"
Mar 6:43 – "twelve baskets full of fragments"
Mar 8:8 – "broken meat that was left 7 baskets"
Mar 8:19 – "how many baskets..Twelve"
Mar 8:20 – "how many baskets..Seven"
Luk 9:17 – "fragments that remained..12 baskets"
Joh 6:13 – "gathered them..filled 12 baskets"

Bason

2Ch 4:8 – "he made 100 basons of gold"
Ezr 1:10 – "30 basons of gold"
Ezr 1:10 – "silver basons of a 2nd sort 410"
Ezr 8:27 – "20 basons of gold, of a 1000 drams"
Neh 7:70 – "gave to the treasure..50 basons"

Bath

1Ki 7:26 – "it contained 2000 baths"
1Ki 7:38 – "one laver contained forty baths"
2Ch 2:10 – "I will give..20,000 baths of wine"
2Ch 2:10 – "I will give..20,000 baths of oil"
2Ch 4:5 – "received..held 3000 baths"
Ezr 7:22 – "to 100 baths of wine"
Ezr 7:22 – "to 100 baths of oil"
Isa 5:10 – "10 acres of vineyard shall yield 1 bath"
Ezk 45:14 – "which is an homer of ten baths"
Ezk 45:14 – "for ten baths are an homer"

Battle

Jdg 20:39 – "smitten down..as in the first battle"

Bear

2Ki 2:24 – "came..two she bears out of the wood"

Beard

2Sa 10:4 – "shave off the ½ of their beards"

Beast

Gen 7:2 – "of beasts that are not clean by two"
Gen 7:2 – "clean beast..take to thee by sevens"
Exo 11:5 – "and all the firstborn of beasts"
Exo 13:12 – "every firstling that cometh of a beast"
Exo 13:15 – "LORD slew..the firstborn of beast"
Lev 27:26 – "Only the firstling of the beasts"
Num 18:15 – "firstling of unclean beasts..redeem"
Dan 7:3 – "four great beasts came up from the sea"
Dan 7:3 – "great beasts..diverse one from another"
Dan 7:4 – "The first was like a lion"
Dan 7:5 – "another beast, a second, like to a bear"
Dan 7:7 – "fourth beast, dreadful and terrible"
Dan 7:17 – "These great beasts, which are four"
Dan 7:19 – "I would know..truth of the 4th beast"
Dan 7:23 – "4th beast shall be the fourth kingdom"
Dan 8:4 – "no beasts might stand before him"
Rev 4:6 – "midst of the throne..were 4 beasts"
Rev 4:7 – "first beast was like a lion"
Rev 4:7 – "second beast like a calf"
Rev 4:7 – "third beast had a face as a man"
Rev 4:7 – "fourth beast was like a flying eagle"
Rev 4:8 – "four beasts had each..six wings"
Rev 5:6 – "in the midst..of the four beasts"
Rev 5:8 – "4 beasts..fell down before the Lamb"
Rev 5:14 – "And the 4 beasts said, Amen."
Rev 6:1 – "one of the 4 beasts..Come and see"
Rev 6:3 – "I heard the second beast say"
Rev 6:5 – "I heard the third beast say"
Rev 6:6 – "voice in the midst of the 4 beasts"
Rev 6:7 – "the voice of the fourth beast say"
Rev 7:11 – "about the elders and the 4 beasts"
Rev 13:12 – "exerciseth..power of the 1st beast"
Rev 13:12 – "causeth..to worship the 1st beast"
Rev 14:3 – "sung..new song..before..the 4 beasts"
Rev 15:7 – "one of the 4 beasts gave..vials"
Rev 19:4 – "four beasts fell down..worshipped"

Beauty

Isa 53:2 – "no beauty that we..desire him"

Bed

Luk 17:34 – "two men in one bed..one taken"

Begotten

Rev 1:5 – "Jesus..the first begotten of the dead"

Beeve

Num 31:33 – "And 72,000 beeves"
Num 31:38 – "And the beeves were 36,000"
Num 31:38 – "beeves..the LORD's tribute was 72"
Num 31:44 – "And 36,000 beeves"

Benefit

2Co 1:15 – "that ye might have a second benefit"

Berry

Isa 17:6 – "2 or 3 berries..top..uppermost bough"
Isa 17:6 – "4 or 5 in the outmost fruitful branches"

Bird

Lev 14:4 – "two birds alive and clean"
Lev 14:5 – "one of the birds be killed"
Lev 14:49 – "to cleanse the house two birds"
Lev 14:50 – "shall kill one of the birds"

Blemish

Lev 22:21 – "shall be no blemish therein"
Num 19:2 – "heifer..wherein is no blemish"
2Sa 14:25 – "there was no blemish in him"
Dan 1:4 – "Children in whom was no blemish"

Blessing

Gen 27:38 – "Hast thou but one blessing"

Blood

Exo 22:2 – "no blood be shed for him"
Exo 24:6 – "half of the blood..in basons"
Exo 24:6 – "half of the blood he sprinkled"
Act 17:26 – "hath made of one blood all nations"

Board

Exo 26:16 – "the breadth of one board"
Exo 26:17 – "Two tenons..in one board"
Exo 26:18 – "20 boards on the south side"

Exo 26:19 – "sockets of silver under..20 boards"
Exo 26:19 – "two sockets under one board"
Exo 26:20 – "north side..twenty boards"
Exo 26:21 – "two sockets under one board"
Exo 26:22 – "westward thou shalt make 6 boards"
Exo 26:23 – "2 boards..for the corners..tabernacle"
Exo 26:25 – "they shall be 8 boards..their sockets"
Exo 26:25 – "two sockets under one board"
Exo 36:22 – "one board had two tenons"
Exo 36:23 – "twenty boards for the south side"
Exo 36:24 – "And 40 sockets..under the 20 boards"
Exo 36:25 – "other side..tabernacle..20 boards"
Exo 36:26 – "two sockets under one board"
Exo 36:27 – "tabernacle westward..made 6 boards"
Exo 36:28 – "2 boards..the corners..in the 2 sides"
Exo 36:30 – "there were eight boards"

Boat

Joh 6:22 – "there was none other boat there"
Joh 6:22 – "none other boat..save that one"

Body

Num 6:6 – "he shall come at no dead body"
Amo 8:3 – "many dead bodies in every place"
Mat 27:52 – "many bodies of the saints..arose"
Rom 12:4 – "we have many members in one body"
Rom 12:5 – "we, being many, are 1 body in Christ"
1Co 6:16 – "joined to an harlot is one body"
1Co 10:17 – "we being many are..one body"
1Co 12:12 – "For as the body is one"
1Co 12:12 – "all the members of that one body"
1Co 12:12 – "being many, are one body"
1Co 12:13 – "are we all baptized into one body"
1Co 12:20 – "many members, yet but one body"
Eph 2:16 – "both unto God in one body"
Eph 4:4 – "There is one body"
Col 3:15 – "ye are called in one body"

Bondman

1Ki 9:22 – "did Solomon make no bondmen"

Bone

Psa 34:20 – "bones: not one of them is broken"
Ezk 37:2 – "very many in the open valley"

Book

Ecc 12:12 – "making many books..is no end"

Bottle

1Sa 25:18 – "Abigail..haste..two bottles of wine"

Bow

Jer 51:56 – "every one of their bows is broken"

Bowl

Exo 25:33 – "3 bowls made like unto almonds"
Exo 25:33 – "three bowls made like almonds"
Exo 25:34 – "four bowls made like unto almonds"
Exo 37:19 – "Three bowls made after the fashion"
Exo 37:19 – "three bowls made like almonds"
Exo 37:20 – "four bowls made like almonds"
Num 7:13 – "one silver bowl"
Num 7:19 – "one silver bowl"
Num 7:25 – "one silver bowl"
Num 7:31 – "one silver bowl"
Num 7:37 – "one silver bowl"
Num 7:49 – "one silver bowl"
Num 7:55 – "one silver bowl"
Num 7:61 – "one silver bowl"
Num 7:67 – "one silver bowl"
Num 7:73 – "one silver bowl"
Num 7:79 – "one silver bowl"
Num 7:84 – "twelve silver bowls"
1Ki 7:41 – "2 pillars..the 2 bowls of the chapiters"
1Ki 7:41 – "two networks, to cover the two bowls"
1Ki 7:42 – "to cover the 2 bowls of the chapiters"

Bracelet

Gen 24:22 – "two bracelets for her hands"

Branch

Gen 40:10 – "in the vine were three branches"
Gen 40:12 – "The three branches are three days"
Exo 25:32 – "six branches..candlestick"
Exo 25:32 – "three branches..one side"
Exo 25:32 – "three branches..out of the other side"
Exo 25:33 – "with a knop and a flower in 1 branch"
Exo 25:33 – "six branches..out of the candlestick"
Exo 25:35 – "a knop under two branches"
Exo 25:35 – "and a knop under two branches"
Exo 25:35 – "and a knop under two branches"
Exo 25:35 – "six branches..out of the candlestick"
Exo 37:18 – "six branches going out of the sides"
Exo 37:18 – "three branches..out of the one side"
Exo 37:18 – "three branches..out of the other side"
Exo 37:19 – "fashion of almonds in one branch"
Exo 37:19 – "six branches..out of the candlestick"
Exo 37:21 – "knop under 2 branches of the same"

Exo 37:21 – "knop under 2 branches of the same"
Exo 37:21 – "knop under 2 branches of the same"
Exo 37:21 – "six branches going out of it"
Ezk 17:22 – "I will crop off..a tender one"
Zec 4:12 – "What be these two olive branches"

Brass

2Ki 25:16 – "brass of..vessels was without weight"
1Ch 22:3 – "brass in abundance without weight"
1Ch 22:14 – "brass and iron without weight"
1Ch 22:16 – "brass..iron, there is no number"
2Ch 4:18 – "weight of..brass could not be found"
Jer 52:20 – "brass..vessels was without weight"

Breach

Neh 6:1 – "wall..there was no breach left therein"
Isa 22:9 – "breaches of the city..are many"

Bread   *(see also **Loaf**)*

Gen 47:13 – "there was no bread in all the land"
Exo 13:3 – "shall no leavened bread be eaten"
Exo 13:7 – "shall no leavened bread be seen"
Num 21:5 – "for there is no bread"
Deu 16:3 – "Thou shalt eat no leavened bread"
Deu 16:4 – "no leavened bread seen with thee"
1Sa 21:4 – "There is no common bread"
1Sa 21:6 – "no bread there but the showbread"
1Sa 30:12 – "he had eaten no bread"
1Ki 13:9 – "Eat no bread, nor drink water"
1Ki 13:17 – "Thou shalt eat no bread"
1Ki 21:4 – "And Ahab..would eat no bread"
1Ki 21:5 – "so sad, that thou eatest no bread?"
2Ki 25:3 – "there was no bread for the people"
Ezr 10:6 – "he did eat no bread, nor drink water"
Jer 52:6 – "famine..there was no bread"
Dan 10:3 – "I ate no pleasant bread"
Mat 16:7 – "we have taken no bread"
Mat 16:8 – "ye have brought no bread"
Mar 6:8 – "no scrip, no bread, no money"
Mar 8:16 – "because we have no bread"
Mar 8:17 – "because ye have no bread?"
1Co 10:17 – "we being many are one bread"
1Co 10:17 – "all partakers of that one bread"

Breast

Son 4:5 – "2 breasts..like 2 young roes..are twins"
Son 7:3 – "2 breasts..like 2 young roes..are twins"
Son 8:8 – "sister..who hath no breasts"

Breath

1Ki 17:17 – "there was no breath left in him"
Ecc 3:19 – "they all have one breath"
Jer 10:14 – "there is no breath in them"
Jer 51:17 – "there is no breath in them"
Eze 37:8 – "there was no breath in them"
Hab 2:19 – "there is no breath at all"

Bridle

Job 41:3 – "come to him with his double bridle"

Brightness

Amo 5:20 – "day of the LORD..no brightness"

Brim

1Ki 7:23 – "molten sea, 10 cubits from the 1 brim"

Brother/Brethren

Gen 9:22 – "Ham..told his two brethren without"
Gen 42:3 – "Joseph's ten brethren went..Egypt"
Gen 42:13 – "Thy servants are 12 brethren"
Gen 42:18 – "If..true men, let one of your brethren"
Gen 42:32 – "12 brethren, sons of our father"
Gen 42:32 – "twelve brethren..one is not"
Gen 42:33 – "leave one of your brethren"
Gen 47:2 – "took..of his brethren, even 5 men"
Exo 2:11 – "spied..an Hebrew, one of his brethren"
Lev 25:48 – "one of his brethren may redeem him"
Num 27:10 – "if he have no brethren"
Num 27:11 – "if his father have no brethren"
Deu 15:7 – "a poor man of one of thy brethren"
Jdg 9:56 – "Abimelech..in slaying his 70 brethren"
Neh 1:2 – "Hanani, one of my brethren"
Neh 11:12 – "brethren..did the work..were 822"
Neh 11:13 – "brethren, chief of the fathers, 242"
Neh 11:14 – "brethren, mighty men of valour, 128"
Mat 4:18 – "two brethren, Simon..Andrew"
Mat 4:21 – "other two brethren, James..John"
Mat 20:24 – "indignation against the 2 brethren"
Mat 22:25 – "there were with us seven brethren"
Mat 22:25 – "the first, when he had married a wife"
Mat 22:26 – "Likewise the second also"
Matt 22:26 – "and the third, unto the seventh"
Matt 22:28 – "whose wife shall be of the seven?"
Mat 25:40 – "done it unto one of the least"
Mat 25:45 – "did it not to one of the least"
Mar 12:20 – "there were seven brethren"
Mar 12:20 – "and the first took a wife"
Mar 12:21 – "And the second took her"

Mar 12:21 – "and the third likewise"
Mar 12:22 – "And the seven had her"
Mar 12:23 – "for the seven had her to wife"
Luk 16:28 – "for I have five brethren"
Luk 20:29 – "there were therefore 7 brethren"
Luk 20:29 – "the first took a wife"
Luk 20:30 – "the second took her to wife"
Luk 20:31 – "And the third took her"
Luk 20:31 – "in like manner the seven also"
Luk 20:33 – "for seven had her to wife"
Act 11:12 – "six brethren accompanied me"
Rom 8:29 – "the firstborn among many brethren"
Phi 1:14 – "many of the brethren in the Lord"
1Co 15:6 – "seen of above 500 brethren at once"

Buckler

Son 4:4 – "whereon they hang a 1000 bucklers"

Bull

Gen 32:15 – "10 bulls"
Psa 22:12 – "Many bulls have compassed me"
Jer 52:20 – "twelve brasen bulls"

Bullock

0 *Bullocks*

Psa 50:9 – "take no bullock out of thy house"

1 *Bullock*

Exo 29:1 – "Take one young bullock, and 2 rams"
Lev 4:21 – "as he burned the first bullock"
Lev 23:18 – "offer w/ the bread..1 young bullock"
Num 7:15 – "One young bullock"
Num 7:21– "One young bullock"
Num 7:27 – "One young bullock"
Num 7:33 – "One young bullock"
Num 7:39 – "One young bullock"
Num 7:45 – "One young bullock"
Num 7:51 – "One young bullock"
Num 7:57 – "One young bullock"
Num 7:63 – "One young bullock"
Num 7:69 – "One young bullock"
Num 7:75 – "One young bullock"
Num 7:81 – "One young bullock"
Num 15:11 – "Thus shall it be done for 1 bullock"
Num 15:24 – "1 young bullock for a burnt offering"
Num 28:12 – "flour..oil..for one bullock"
Num 28:28 – "meat offering..one bullock..one ram"
Num 29:2 – "burnt offering..one..bullock..one ram"
Num 29:36 – "burnt offering..one bullock, 1 ram"
Deu 15:19 – "do no work w the firstling..bullock"
Deu 33:17 – "glory..like the firstling of his bullock"

1Ki 18:23 – "choose one bullock for themselves"
1Ki 18:25 – "Choose you 1 bullock for yourselves"
1Ch 29:21 – "sacrificed..even a thousand bullocks"
Job 42:8 – "take unto you..7 bullocks & 7 rams"
Ezk 45:23 – "burnt offering..7 bullocks & 7 rams"

2-9 *Bullocks*

Num 23:29 – "prepare me..7 bullocks and 7 rams"
Num 28:11 – "two young bullocks"
Num 28:19 – "two young bullocks, and one ram"
Num 28:27 – "burnt offering...two young bullocks"
Num 29:26 – "And on the fifth day nine bullocks"
Num 29:29 – "And on the sixth day eight bullocks"
Num 29:32 – "And on the seventh day 7 bullocks"
Jdg 6:25 – "even the second bullock of 7 years old"
Jdg 6:25 – "take the second bullock..offer..sacrifice"
Jdg 6:28 – "2nd bullock was offered upon the altar"
1Sa 1:24 – "three bullocks..1 ephah of flour"
1Ki 18:23 – "Let them..give us two bullocks"
1Ch 15:26 – "offered 7 bullocks and 7 rams"
2Ch 29:21 – "brought 7 bullocks..for a sin offering"

10-99 *Bullocks*

Num 7:87 – "twelve bullocks"
Num 7:88 – "peace offerings..24 bullocks"
Num 29:13 – "burnt offering...13 young bullocks"
Num 29:14 – "every bullock of the 13 bullocks"
Num 29:17 – "2nd day..offer 12 young bullocks"
Num 29:20 – "And on the third day 11 bullocks"
Num 29:23 – "And on the fourth day ten bullocks"
2Ch 29:32 – "congregation brought..70 bullocks"
Ezr 8:35 – " offerings..12 bullocks for all Israel"

100+ *Bullocks*

2Ch 30:24 – "Hezekiah..did give..1000 bullocks"
2Ch 30:24 – "princes gave..1000 bullocks"
2Ch 35:7 – "passover offerings..3000 bullocks"
Ezr 6:17 – "dedication..house..100 bullocks"

Bunch

2Sa 16:1 – "100 bunches of raisins"
2Sa 16:1 – "and an 100 of summer fruits"

Burden

Gen 49:14 – "Issachar..ass..between two burdens"
Neh 13:19 "there should no burden be brought"
Jer 17:21 – "bear no burden.. sabbath day"
Jer 17:24 – " bring in no burden through..gates"
Act 15:28 – "lay upon you no greater burden"
Rev 2:24 – "put upon you none other burden"

Burial

Ecc 6:3 – "also that he have no burial"

Burning

2Ch 21:19 – "people made no burning for him"

Cake

Exo 29:23 – "one cake of oiled bread"
Lev 8:26 – "one unleavened cake"
Lev 24:5 – "two tenth deals shall be in one cake"
Lev 24:5 – "fine flour, and bake 12 cakes thereof"
Lev 24:6 – "two rows, six on a row"
Num 6:19 – "1 unleavened cake out of the basket"
1Sa 25:18 – "200 cakes of figs"
2Sa 13:6 – "make me a couple of cakes"

Calf

1Ki 12:28 – "the king..made two calves of gold"
1Ki 12:29 – *"he set the one in Bethel"*
1Ki 12:30 – *"people went to worship before the 1"*
2Ki 17:16 – "made..molten images, even 2 calves"

Camel

Gen 24:10 – "servant took ten camels"
Gen 32:15 – "thirty milch camels"
Jdg 6:5 – "they and their camels..w/o number"
Jdg 7:12 – "camels..without number, as the sand"
2Ki 8:9 – "every good thing..40 camels' burden"
1Ch 5:21 – "of their camels 50,000"
Ezr 2:67 – "Their camels, 435"
Neh 7:69 – "Their camels, 435"
Job 1:3 – "His substance..3,000 camels"
Job 42:12 – "later end of Job..6,000 camels"

Candle

Rev 22:5 – "and they need no candle"

Candlestick

1Ki 7:49 – "candlesticks..five on the right side"
1Ki 7:49 – "candlesticks..five on the left"
2Ch 4:7 – "he made 10 candlesticks of gold"
2Ch 4:7 – *"5 on the right hand, and 5 on the left"*
Rev 1:12 – "I saw seven golden candlesticks"
Rev 1:13 – "in the midst of the 7 candlesticks"
Rev 1:20 – "The mystery of..the 7..candlesticks"
Rev 1:20 – "7 candlesticks..are the 7 churches"

Rev 2:1 – "in the midst of..7 golden candlesticks"
Rev 11:4 – "These are..the two candlesticks"

Cane

Isa 43:24 – "bought me no sweet cane"

Captain

1Ki 2:5 – "what Joab..did to the two captains"
1Ki 22:31 – "king..commanded his 32 captains"
2Ki 1:13 – "And the third captain of fifty"
2Ki 1:14 – "two captains of the former fifties"
2Ki 18:24 – "turn away the face of one captain"
1Ch 11:15 – "three of the 30 captains went down"
1Ch 12:28 – "Zadok..father's house..22 captains"
1Ch 12:34 – "And of Naphtali a 1000 captains"
1Ch 27:7 – "4th captain..4th month..Asahel..24,000"
1Ch 27:8 – "5th captain..Shamhuth..24,000"
1Ch 27:9 – "6th captain..6th month was Ira..24,000"
1Ch 27:10 – "7th captain..7th month..Helez..24,000"
1Ch 27:11 – "8th captain..Sibbecai..24,000"
1Ch 27:12 – "9th captain..Abiezer..24,000"
1Ch 27:13 – "10th captain..Maharai..24,000"
1Ch 27:14 – "11th captain..Benaiah..24,000"
1Ch 27:15 – "12th captain..Heldai..24,000"
2Ch 26:11 – "Hananiah, one of the king's captains"
Isa 36:9 – "turn away the face of one captain"

Captive

Exo 12:29 – "unto the firstborn of the captive"
2Ki 24:14 – "carried away..10,000 captives"

Carpenter

Zec 1:20 – "the LORD shewed me four carpenters"

Casting

1Ki 7:37 – "ten bases: all of them had one casting"

Caterpillar

Psa 105:34 – "locusts..caterpillars..w/o number"

Cattle

Exo 9:6 – "cattle..died not one"
Exo 9:7 – "was not one of the cattle..dead"
Exo 12:29 – "and all the firstborn of cattle"
Exo 34:19 – "firstling among thy cattle..ox..sheep"

Num 3:41 – "all the firstlings among the cattle"
2Ch 35:8 – "passover offerings 2,600 small cattle"
2Ch 35:9 – "passover offerings 5000 small cattle"
Neh 10:36 – "firstborn of our sons, & of our cattle"

Cause

2Sa 13:16 – "There is no cause"
Luk 23:22 – "I have found no cause of death"
Act 13:28 – "no cause of death in him"
Act 19:40 – "no cause..may give an account"
Act 28:18 – "there was no cause of death in me"

Censer

Num 16:17 – "every man his censer, 250 censers"

Centurion

Act 23:17 – "Paul called one of the centurions"
Act 23:23 – "called unto him two centurions"

Chain

Exo 28:14 – "two chains of pure gold at the ends"
Exo 28:24 – "the two wreathen chains of gold"
Exo 28:25 – "other two ends of of the..chains"
Exo 28:25 – "ends of the two wreathen chains"
Exo 39:17 – "two wreathen chains..in the 2 rings"
Exo 39:18 – "two ends of the 2 wreathen chains"
Son 4:9 – "ravished..with one chain of thy neck"
Act 12:6 – "Peter..bound with two chains"
Act 21:33 – "to be bound with two chains"

Chamber

1Ki 6:6 – "chamber..third was 7 cubits broad"
1Ki 6:8 – "middle chamber..into the third"
Jer 35:2 – "Go..into one of the chambers"
Ezk 40:10 – "little chambers..eastward..three"
Ezk 40:10 – "chambers..three on that side"
Ezk 40:10 – "they three were of one measure"
Ezk 40:13 – "the roof of one little chamber"
Ezk 40:17 – "30 chambers..upon the pavement"
Ezk 40:21 – "little chambers..three on this side"
Ezk 40:21 – "little chambers..three on that side"
Ezk 40:44 – "chambers of..singers..one at the side"
Ezk 41:6 – "side chambers were three"
Ezk 41:6 – "side chambers..one over another"
Ezk 41:6 – "side chambers..thirty in order"
Ezk 45:5 – "for a possession for 20 chambers"

Chamberlain

Est 1:10 – "7 chamerblains..served..Ahasuerus"
Est 2:21 – "2..chamberlains, Bigthan and Teresh"
Est 4:5 – "Hatach, one of the king's chamberlains"
Est 6:2 – "two of the king's chamberlains"
Est 7:9 – "Harbonah, one of the chamberlains"

Change

Gen 45:22 – "to Benjamin..5 changes of raiment"
Jdg 14:12 – "I will give..30 change of garments"
Jdg 14:13 – "30 sheets..30 change of garments"
2Ki 5:5 – "took with him..ten changes of raiment"
2Ki 5:22 – "talent of silver..2 changes of garments"
2Ki 5:23 – "two changes of garments"
Psa 55:19 – "Because they have no changes"

Chapiter

1Ki 7:16 – "made two chapiters of molten brass"
1Ki 7:16 – "height of the 1 chapiter was 5 cubits"
1Ki 7:17 – "seven for the one chapiter"
Jer 52:22 – "height of the 1 chapiter was 5 cubits"

Charger

Num 7:13 – "one silver charger"
Num 7:19 – "one silver charger"
Num 7:25 – "one silver charger"
Num 7:31 – "one silver charger"
Num 7:37 – "one silver charger"
Num 7:43 – "one silver charger"
Num 7:49 – "one silver charger"
Num 7:55 – "one silver charger"
Num 7:61 – "one silver charger"
Num 7:67 – "one silver charger"
Num 7:73 – "one silver charger"
Num 7:79 – "one silver charger"
Num 7:84 – "twelve chargers of silver"
Ezr 1:9 – "thirty chargers of gold"
Ezr 1:9 – "a thousand chargers of silver"

Chariot

Gen 41:43 – "made him to ride in the 2nd chariot"
Exo 14:6 – "he took 600 chosen chariots"
Jos 11:4 – "horses and chariots very many"
Jdg 4:3 – "900 chariots of iron"
Jdg 4:13 – "Sisera gathered..900 chariots of iron"
1Sa 13:5 – "Philistines...30,000 chariots"
2Sa 8:4 – "David took from him a 1000 chariots"
2Sa 8:4 – "reserved of them for an 100 chariots"
2Sa 10:18 – "David slew the men of 700 chariots"
1Ki 10:26 – "Solomon..had 1400 chariots"

2Ki 13:7 – "50 horsemen, and 10 chariots"
1Ch 18:4 – "David took from him 1000 chariots"
1Ch 18:4 – "David..reserved of them 100 chariots"
1Ch 19:7 – "hired 32,000 chariots..Ammon"
2Ch 1:14 – "Solomon..had 1400 chariots"
2Ch 12:3 – "1200 chariots & 60,000 horsemen"
2Ch 14:9 – "Zerah the Ethiopian..300 chariots"
2Ch 16:8 – "very many chariots and horsemen"
2Ch 35:24 – "servants..put him in the 2nd chariot"
Psa 68:17 – "The chariots of God are 20,000"
Isa 31:1 – "trust in chariots, b/c they are many"
Nah 2:4 – "chariots..justle one against another"
Zec 6:1 – "4 chariots out from..two mountains"
Zec 6:2 – "In the first chariot were red horses"
Zec 6:2 – "in the second chariot black horses"
Zec 6:3 – "in the third chariot white horses"
Zec 6:3 – "in the 4th chariot grisled and bay"

Chastening

Heb 12:11 – "no chastening..seemeth..joyous"

Cheek

Deu 18:3 – "give unto the priest..two cheeks"
Luk 6:29 – "smiteth thee on the one cheek"

Cheese

1Sa 17:18 – "And carry these ten cheeses"

Cherubim *(see Creature as in Living Creature)*

Exo 25:18 – "make two cherubims of gold"
Exo 25:19 – "the cherbims on the 2 ends thereof"
Exo 25:22 – "from between the two cherubims"
Exo 25:19 – "make one cherub on the one end"
Exo 37:8 – "One cherub on the end on this side"
Exo 37:7 – "he made two cherubims of gold"
Num 7:89 – "between the two cherubim"
1Ki 6:23 – "two cherubims of olive tree"
1Ki 6:26 – "height of the 1 cherub was 10 cubits"
2Ch 3:10 – "in the most holy house..2 cherubims"
2Ch 3:11 – "one wing of the one cherub"
Ezk 10:7 – "one cherub stretched forth his hand"
Ezk 10:9 – "one wheel by one cherub"
Ezk 10:12 – "even the wheels that they four had"

Chief

2Sa 23:13 – "three of the 30 chief went down"

Child/Children

Indefinite or 0 *Children*

Gen 11:30 – "But Sarai..had no child"
Gen 16:1 – "wife bare him no children"
Gen 30:1 – "she bare Jacob no children"
Lev 22:13 – "priest's daughter..have no child"
Num 3:4 – "they had no children"
Deu 25:5 – "If brethren..have no child"
1Sa 1:2 – "Hannah had no children"
1Sa 2:5 – "she that hath many children"
2Sa 6:23 – "Therefore Michal..had no child"
2Ki 4:14 – "Verily she hath no child"
1Ch 4:27 – "his brethren had not many children"
1Ch 24:2 - Nadab and Abihu..had no children"
Mat 22:24 – "a man die, having no children"
Mar 12:19 – "brother die..leave no children"
Luk 1:7 – "And they had no child"
Luk 20:31 – "left no children, and died"
Rom 9:27 – "children of Israel..as..sand of the sea"
Gal 4:27 – "desolate hath many more children"

½-10 *Children*

Exo 2:6 – "This is one of the Hebrews' children"
Exo 13:15 – "firstborn of my children I redeem"
Num 25:6 – "one of the children of Israel"
1Ki 3:25 – "give ½ to the one, and ½ to the other"
2Ki 9:1 – "one of the children of the prophets"
Ecc 4:15 – "second child..stand up in his stead"
Jer 4:31 – "bringeth forth her first child"
Jer 15:9 – "She that hath borne 7 languisheth"
Dan 1:17 – "As for these four children"
Mat 18:5 – "receive one such child in my name"
Mar 9:37 – "receive one of such children"
Luk 7:32 – "children..calling one to another"

11-50 *Children*

2Ki 2:24 – "2 she bears..tare 42 children of them"
Ezr 2:24 – "The children of Azmaveth, 42"
Ezr 2:29 – "The children of Nebo, 52"

51-100 *Children*

Ezr 2:16 – "The children of Ater of Hezekiah, 98"
Ezr 2:20 – "The children of Gibbar, 95"
Ezr 2:22 – "The men of Netophah, 56"
Ezr 2:40 – "The Levites..74"
Neh 7:21 – "The children of Ater of Hezekiah, 98"
Neh 7:25 – "The children of Gibeon, 95"
Neh 7:43 – "The Levites..children of Jeshua..74"
Ecc 6:3 – "if a man beget 100 children"

101-500 *Children*

Ezr 2:4 – "The children of Shephatiah, 372"
Ezr 2:15 – "The children of Adin, 454"

Ezr 2:17 – "The children of Bezai, 323"
Ezr 2:18 – "The children of Jorah, 112"
Ezr 2:19 – "The children of Hashum, 223"
Ezr 2:21 – "The children of Bethlehem, 123"
Ezr 2:23 – "The men of Anathoth, 128"
Ezr 2:30 – "The children of Magbish, 156"
Ezr 2:32 – "The children of Harim, 320"
Ezr 2:34 – "The children of Jericho, 345"
Ezr 2:41 – "singers: the children of Asaph, 128"
Ezr 2:42 – "children of the porters.. in all 139"
Ezr 2:58 – "All the Nethinims..children..392"
Neh 7:9 – "The children of Shephatiah, 372"
Neh 7:22 – "The children of Hashum, 328"
Neh 7:23 – "The children of Bezai, 324"
Neh 7:24 – "The children of Hariph, 112"
Neh 7:35 – "The children of Harim, 320"
Neh 7:36 – "The children of Jericho, 345"
Neh 7:44 – "singers: the children of Asaph, 148"
Neh 7:45 – "porters: the children of Shallum..138"
Neh 7:60 – "All the Nethinims..children..392"

500-1000 *Children*

Ezr 2:5 – "The children of Arah, 775"
Ezr 2:8 – "The children of Zattu, 945"
Ezr 2:9 – "The children of Zaccai, 760"
Ezr 2:10 –"The children of Bani, 642"
Ezr 2:11 –"The children of Bebai, 623"
Ezr 2:13 – "The children of Adonikam, 666"
Ezr 2:25 – "The children of Kirjatharim..743"
Ezr 2:26 – "The children of Ramah and Gaba, 621"
Ezr 2:33 – "The children of Lod, Hadid..Ono, 725"
Ezr 2:36 – "priests: the children of Jedaiah, 973"
Ezr 2:60 – "The children of Delaiah..652"
Neh 7:10 – "The children of Arah, 652"
Neh 7:13 – "The children of Zattu, 845"
Neh 7:14 – "The children of Zaccai, 760"
Neh 7:15 – "The children of Binnui, 648"
Neh 7:16 – "The children of Bebai, 628"
Neh 7:18 – "The children of Adonikam, 667"
Neh 7:20 – "The children of Adin, 655"
Neh 7:37 – "children of Lod, Hadid, and Ono, 721"
Neh 7:39 – "priests: the children of Jedaiah..973"
Neh 7:62 – "The children of Delaiah..642"

1001+ *Children*

Ezr 2:3 – "The children of Parosh, 2172"
Ezr 2:6 – "The children of Pahathmoab..2812"
Ezr 2:7 – "The children of Elam, 1254"
Ezr 2:12 –"The children of Azgad, 1222"
Ezr 2:14 – "The children of Bigvai, 2056"
Ezr 2:31 – "The children of the other Elam, 1254"
Ezr 2:35 – "The children of Senaah, 3630"
Ezr 2:37 – "The children of Immer, 1052"
Ezr 2:38 – "The children of Pashur, 1247"
Ezr 2:39 – "The children of Harim, 1017"
Neh 7:8 – "The children of Parosh, 2172"
Neh 7:11 – "The children of Pahathmoab..2818"
Neh 7:12 – "The children of Elam, 1254"

Neh 7:17 – "The children of Azgad, 2322"
Neh 7:19 – "The children of Bigvai, 2067"
Neh 7:34 – "The children of the other Elam, 1254"
Neh 7:38 – "The children of Senaah, 3930"
Neh 7:40 – "The children of Immer, 1052"
Neh 7:41 – "The children of Pashur, 1247"
Neh 7:42 – "The children of Harim, 1017"

Church

Php 4:15 – "no church communicated"
Rev 1:4 – "John to the seven churches..in Asia"
Rev 1:11 – "send it unto the seven churches"
Rev 1:20 – "7 stars..are angels of the 7 churches"
Rev 1:20 – "7 candlesticks..are the 7 churches"

City

Indefinite or O *Cities*

Num 35:8 – "cities..them that have few..give few"
Num 35:8 – "cities..have many ye shall give many"
Deu 2:36 – "there was not one city too strong"
Deu 3:5 – "All these cities..a great many"
1Ki 8:16 – "I chose no city out..of Israel"
2Ch 6:5 – "I chose no city..of Israel"
Psa 107:4 – "they found no city to dwell in"
Isa 25:2 – "palace of strangers to be no city"
Jer 48:8 – "no city shall escape"
Zec 8:20 – "the inhabitants of many cities"
Act 21:39 – "a citizen of no mean city"
Heb 13:14 – "have we no continuing city"

½ *City*

Zec 14:2 – "half of the city..go forth into captivity"

1 *City*

Gen 19:20 – "city is near..it is a little one"
Gen 19:20 – "(is it not a little one?)"
Deu 2:36 – "not one city too strong for us"
Deu 4:42 – "fleeing unto one of these cities"
Deu 13:12 – "hear say in one of thy cities"
Deu 19:5 – "he shall flee unto one of those cities"
Deu 19:11 – "fleeth into one of these cities"
Jos 10:2 – "Gibeon..as one of the royal cities"
Jos 20:4 – "one of those cities..dwell among them"
Jos 21:42 – "cities..every one with their suburbs"
Jdg 12:7 – "buried in one of the cities of Gilead"
2Sa 12:1 – "two men in one city..rich..other poor"
Isa 19:18 – "one..called, The city of destruction"
Amo 4:7 – "I caused it to rain upon one city"
Amo 4:8 – "cities wandered unto one city"
Zec 8:21 – "inhabitants of one city..to another"
Heb 13:14 – "continuing city..seek one to come"

2 *Cities*

Jos 15:60 – "two cities with their villages"
Jos 21:25 – "Tanach..Gathrimmon..two cities"
Jos 21:27 – "Golan..Beeshterah..two cities"
Amo 4:8 – "So two or three cities wandered"

3 *Cities*

Num 35:14 – "three cities on this side Jordan"
Num 35:14 – "three cities..in the land of Canaan"
Deu 4:41 – "severed three cities..this side Jordan"
Deu 19:2 – "separate 3 cities..midst of thy land"
Deu 19:7 – "Thou shalt separate 3 cities for thee."
Deu 19:9 – "add thee cities more..beside these 3"
Jos 21:32 – "ou..of Naphtali..three cities"
Amo 4:8 – "So two or three cities wandered"

4 *Cities*

Jos 19:7 – "four cities and their villages"
Jos 21:18 – "four cities"
Jos 21:22 – "four cities"
Jos 21:24 – "four cities"
Jos 21:29 – "four cities"
Jos 21:31 – "four cities"
Jos 21:35 – "four cities"
Jos 21:37 – "four cities"
Jos 21:39 – "four cities"

5-9 *Cities*

Num 35:6 – "six cities..refuge..for the manslayer"
Num 35:13 – "six cities shall ye have for refuge"
Num 35:15 – "six cities shall be a refuge"
Jos 15:44 – "nine cities with their villages"
Jos 15:54 – "nine cities with their villages"
Jos 15:59 – "six cities with their villages"
Jos 15:62 – "six cities with their villages"
Jos 21:16 – "nine cities"
1Ch 4:32 – "five cities"
Isa 19:18 – "five cities in the land of Egypt"

10 *Cities*

Jos 15:57 – "ten cities with their villages"
Jos 21:5 – "ten cities"
Jos 21:26 – "All their cities were ten"
1Ch 6:61 – "the sons of Kohath..by lot, 10 cities"
Mat 4:25 – "Decapolis" = ten cities
Mar 5:20 – "Decapolis" = ten cities
Mar 7:31 – "Decapolis" = ten cities
Luk 19:17 – "have..authority over ten cities"
Luk 19:19 – "Be thou also over five cities"

11-15 *Cities*

Jos 15:36 – "14 cities with their villages"
Jos 15:51 – "11 cities with their villages"
Jos 18:24 – "12 cities with their villages"

Jos 18:28 – "14 cities with their villages"
Jos 19:6 – "13 cities and their villages"
Jos 19:15 – "12 cities with their villages"
Jos 21:4 – "13 cities"
Jos 21:6 – "13 cities"
Jos 21:7 – "12 cities"
Jos 21:19 – "13 cities"
Jos 21:33 – "All the cities..13"
Jos 21:40 – "by their lot 12 cities"
1Ch 6:60 – "All their cities..13"
1Ch 6:62 – "to the sons of Gershom..13 cities"
1Ch 6:63 – "unto the sons of Merari..12 cities"

16+ *Cities*

Num 35:6 – "ye shall add 42 cities"
Num 35:7 – "give to the Levites..48 cities"
Deu 3:4 – "we took..60 cities..of Og in Bashan"
Jos 13:30 – "Bashan..the towns of Jair..60 cities"
Jos 15:32 – "all the cities are 29"
Jos 15:41 – "16 cities with their villages"
Jos 19:22 – "16 cities with their villages"
Jos 19:30 – "22 cities with their villages"
Jos 19:38 – "19 cities with their villages"
Jos 21:41 – "All the cities..were 48"
Jdg 10:4 – "they had 30 cities..Havothjair"
Jdg 11:33 – "smote..20 cities..Ammon..subdued"
1Ki 4:13 – "Argob..60 great cities with walls..bars"
1Ki 9:11 – "Solomon gave Hiram 20 cities"
1Ch 2:22 – "Segub..who had 23 cities in..Gilead"
1Ch 2:23 – "60 cities..belonged to..sons of Machir"

Claw

Deu 14:6 – "cleaveth the cleft into two claws"

Cloak

Joh 15:22 – "they have no cloke for their sin"

Clothes

Luk 8:27 – "certain man..ware no clothes"

Cluster

Num 13:23 – "Eschol..branch w/ 1 cluster..grapes"
1Sa 25:18 – "Abigail..took..100 clusters..raisins"
1Sa 30:12 – "gave him..figs..2 clusters of raisins"
Mic 7:1 – "there is no cluster to eat"

Coat

Mat 10:10 – "Nor scrip..neither two coats"

Mar 6:9 – "not put on two coats"
Luk 3:11 – "He that hath two coats..impart to him"
Luk 3:11 – "coats..impart to him that hath none"
Luk 9:3 – "neither have two coats apiece"

Color

Gen 37:3 – "made him a coat of many colours"
Gen 37:23 – "his coat of many colours"
Gen 37:32 – "sent the coat of many colours"

Colt

Jdg 10:4 – "sons that rode on 30 ass colts"
Jdg 12:14 – "sons..nephews..rode on..70 ass colts"

Comeliness

Isa 53:2 – "he hath no form nor comeliness"

Comforter

Psa 69:20 – "Looked..for comforters, but..none"
Ecc 4:1 – "and they had no comforter"
Ecc 4:1 – "but they had no comforter"
Lam 1:9 – "she had no comforter"

Commandment

Exo 34:28 – "wrote..tables..10 commandments"
Deu 4:13 – "10 commandments..2 tables of stone"
Deu 10:4 – "the first writing..10 commandments"
Mat 5:19 – "one of these least commandments"
Mat 22:38 – "the first and great commandment"
Mat 22:39 – "the second is like unto it"
Mat 22:40 – "on..two commandments hang..law"
Mar 12:28 – "Which..the 1st commandment of all?"
Mar 12:29 – "The first of all the commandments"
Mar 12:30 – "this is the first commandment"
Mar 12:31 – "And the second is like, namely"
Mar 12:31 – "none other commandment greater"
Act 15:24 – "we gave no such commandment"
1Co 7:25 – "no commandment of the Lord"
Eph 6:2 – "first commandment with promise"
1Co 7:25 – "no commandment of the Lord"

Communication

Eph 4:29 – "Let no corrupt communication"

Company

Gen 32:8 – "If Esau come to the one company"
Jdg 7:16 – "divided..300 men into 3 companies"
Jdg 7:20 – "three companies blew the trumpets"
Jdg 9:34 – "against Shechem in 4 companies"
Jdg 9:43 – "divided them into three companies"
Jdg 9:44 – "2..companies ran upon all the people"
1Sa 11:11 – "Saul put the people in 3 companies"
1Sa 13:17 – "spoilers..Philistines in 3 companies"
1Sa 13:17 – "1 company turned..way..to Ophrah"
Neh 12:31 – "2 great companies..that gave thanks"
Neh 12:31 – "whereof one went on the right hand"
Neh 12:40 – "two companies..that gave thanks"
2Th 3:14 – "have no company with him"

Companion

Jdg 14:11 – "30 companions to be with him"

Compassion

2Ch 36:17 – "no compassion upon..man..maiden"

Complaining

Psa 144:14 – "that there be no complaining"

Compliant

Act 25:7 – "laid many and grievous complaints"

Concubine

1Ki 11:3 – "he had 700 wives..300 concubines"
2Ch 11:21 – "Rehoboam..took..60 concubines"
Son 6:8 – "There are..fourscore concubines"

Condemnation

Rom 8:1 – "therefore now no condemnation"

Confidence

Php 3:3 – "have no confidence in the flesh"

Consent

1Sa 11:7 – "the came out with one consent"

Psa 83:5 – "consulted together with one consent"
Zep 3:9 – "to serve him with one consent"
Luk 14:18 – "with one consent..make excuse"

Cord

Jdg 15:13 – "bound him with two new cords"
Ecc 4:12 – "a threefold cord is not quickly broken"

Corinthian

Act 18:8 – "many..Corinthians hearing believed"

Corn

Gen 41:49 – "corn as the sand of the sea"
Gen 41:49 – "corn..it was without number"
Gen 41:49 – "corn..until he left numbering"

Corner

Exo 25:12 – "put them in the four corners thereof"
Exo 25:26 – "put the rings in the four corners"
Exo 26:24 – "they shall be for the two corners"
Exo 27:2 – "horns of it upon the 4 corners thereof"
Exo 27:4 – "rings in the four corners thereof"
Exo 30:4 – altar – "by the two corners thereof"
Exo 37:3 – "to be set by the four corners of it"
Exo 37:13 – "put the rings upon the four corners"
Exo 37:27 – "2 corners of it, upon the 2 sides"
Exo 38:2 – "horns thereof on the four corners"
1Ki 7:30 – "four corners thereof had undersetters"
1Ki 7:34 – "4 undersetters..4 corners of one base"
Job 1:19 – "wind..smote the 4 corners..house"
Isa 11:12 – "gather..Judah from..4 corners..earth"
Ezk 7:2 – "end..upon the 4 corners of the land"
Ezk 43:20 – "blood..put it..on the for corners"
Ezk 45:19 – "sin offering..upon the 4 corners"
Ezk 46:21 – "pass by the 4 corners of the court"
Ezk 46:22 – "In the 4 corners of the court"
Ezk 46:22 – "these 4 corners were of 1 measure"
Ezk 46:23 – "row of buildings..round..them four"
Act 10:11 – "great sheet knit at the four corners"
Act 11:5 – "let down from heaven by 4 corners"
Rev 7:1 – "standing on..4 corners of the earth"

Corpse

Nah 3:3 – "slain, and a great number of corpses"
Nah 3:3 – "there is none end of their corpses"

Correction

Jer 2:30 – "they received no correction"

Corruption

Act 13:37 – "But he..saw no corruption"

Counsel

Pro 11:14 – "Where no counsel is, the people fall"
Pro 21:30 – "no..counsel..against the LORD"

Counselor

Ezr 7:14 – "the king, and of his seven counselors"

Country

Jos 17:11 – "Manasseh..3 countries"
Psa 110:6 – "the heads over many countries"
Jer 28:8 – "prophets.. against many countries"
Ezk 35:10 – "these two countries shall be mine"
Dan 11:41 – "many countries..be overthrown"

Course

1Ch 27:2 – "1st course..Jashobeam..24,000"

Court

2Ki 21:5 – "he built altars..in the two courts"
2Ki 23:12 – "altars..in the two courts..brake"
2Ch 33:5 – "built altars..in the two courts"

Covenant

Exo 23:32 – "make no covenant with them"
Deu 7:2 – "make no covenant with them"
Gal 4:24 – "two covenants; the one..Sinai"
Heb 8:7 – "if the 1st covenant had been faultless"
Heb 8:13 – "new covenant..made the 1st old"
Heb 9:1 – "first covenant had also ordinances"
Heb 8:7 – "no place..sought for the second"

Covering

Num 19:15 – "vessel, which hath no covering"
Job 24:7 – "they have no covering in the cold"
Job 26:6 – "destruction hath no covering"

Cow

Num 18:17 – "firstling of a cow..shalt not redeem"

Craftsman

Rev 18:22 – "no craftsman..found any more"

Creature *(Living Creatures)*

Ezk 1:5 – "the likeness of four living creatures"
Ezk 1:6 – "every one had four wings"
Ezk 1:6 – "every one had four faces"
Ezk 1:8 – "they 4 had their faces and their wings"
Ezk 1:10 – "they four had the face of a man"
Ezk 1:10 – "they four had the face of an ox"
Ezk 1:10 – "they four also had the face of an eagle"
Ezk 1:23 – "every one had two, which covered"
Ezk 1:23 – "and every one had two, which covered"
Col 1:15 – "the firstborn of every creature"

Crow *(as in the sound of a rooster)*

Mark 14:30 – "before the cock crow twice"
Mar 14:72 – "Before the cock crow twice"

Crown

Rev 12:3 – "dragon..7 crowns upon his heads"
Rev 13:1 – "beast..upon his horns ten crowns"
Rev 19:12 – "on his head were many crowns"

Cubit

½ Cubit

1Ki 7:35 – "top..base..compass of ½ a cubit high"
Ezk 43:17 – "settle..border about it..half a cubit"

1 Cubit

Ezk 40:12 – "space..before..chambers..1 cubit"
Ezk 40:12 – "space was one cubit on that side"
Ezk 40:42 – "tables..burnt offering..one cubit high"
Ezk 42:4 – "before the chambers..a way of 1 cubit"
Ezk 43:14 – "and the breadthone cubit"
Ezk 43:14 – "and the breadthone cubit"
Mat 6:27 – "add one cubit unto his stature?"
Luk 12:25 – "add to his stature one cubit"

1½ Cubits

Exo 25:10 – "ark..1½ cubit the breadth thereof"

Exo 25:10 – "ark.. 1½ cubit the height thereof"
Exo 25:17 – "mercy seat..1½ cubit the breadth"
Exo 25:23 – "table..1½ cubit the height"
Exo 26:16 – "1½ cubit..the breadth of one board"
Exo 36:21 – "breadth of a board was 1½ cubit"
Exo 37:1 – "made the ark..1½ cubit the breadth"
Exo 37:1 – "made the ark..1½ cubit the height"
Exo 37:6 – "mercy seat..1½ cubit the breadth"
Exo 37:10 – "table..1½ cubit the height"
1Ki 7:31 – "mouth of it..a cubit and an half"
1Ki 7:32 – "height of a wheel was 1½ cubit"
Ezk 40:42 – "tables..offering..1½ cubits long"
Ezk 40:42 – "tables..offering..1½ cubits broad"

2 Cubits

Exo 25:23 – "table..two cubits..length thereof"
Exo 30:2 – "two cubits..the height thereof"
Exo 37:10 – "table..two cubits was the length"
Exo 37:25 – "incense altar..two cubits..the height"
Num 11:31 – "quails..as it were two cubits high"
Ezk 40:9 – "the posts thereof, two cubits"
Ezk 41:3 – "the post of the door, two cubits"
Ezk 41:22 – "altar of wood..length..two cubits"
Ezk 43:14 – "ground..to lower settle..2 cubits"

2½ Cubits

Exo 25:10 – "ark..shittim wood: 2½ cubits..length"
Exo 25:17 – "mercy seat..gold: 2½ cubits..length"
Exo 37:1 – "the ark..2½ cubits was the length"
Exo 37:6 – "mercy seat..2½ cubits the length"

3 Cubits

Exo 27:1 – "height thereof shall be 3 cubits"
Exo 38:1 – "altar..three cubits the height"
1Ki 7:27 – "three cubits was the height thereof"
2Ki 25:17 – "height of the chapiter three cubits"
2Ch 6:13 – "brasen scaffold..3 cubits high"
Ezk 40:48 – "breadth of..gate..3 cubits..this side"
Ezk 40:48 – "breadth of..gate..3 cubits..that side"
Ezk 41:22 – "altar of wood was 3 cubits high"

4 Cubits

Exo 26:2 – "breadth of one curtain four cubits"
Exo 26:8 – "breadth of one curtain four cubits"
Exo 36:15 – "4 cubits was..breadth of one curtain"
Exo 36:9 – "breadth of one curtain..4 cubits"
Deu 3:11 – "Og..bedstead..4 cubits the breadth"
1Ki 7:19 – "chapiters..lily work in..porch, 4 cubits"
1Ki 7:27 – "four cubits was the length of one base"
1Ki 7:27 – "four cubits was the breadth thereof"
1Ki 7:38 – "and every laver was four cubits"
Ezk 41:5 – "breadth..side chamber..four cubits"
Ezk 43:14 – "lesser settle..to..greater..4 cubits"
Ezk 43:15 – "So the altar shall be four cubits"

5 *Cubits*

Exo 27:1 – "altar of shittim wood, 5 cubits long"
Exo 27:1 – "altar..five cubits broad"
Exo 27:18 – "the court..the height five cubits"
Exo 38:1 – "altar..five cubits was the length"
Exo 38:1 – "altar..five cubits the breadth"
Exo 38:18 – "hanging for the gate..height..5 cubits"
1Ki 6:6 – "nethermost chamber..5 cubits broad"
1Ki 6:10 – "chambers..five cubits high"
1Ki 6:24 – "five cubits..the one wing of the cherub"
1Ki 6:24 – "five cubits the other wing..cherub"
1Ki 7:16 – "height of the 1 chapiter was 5 cubits"
1Ki 7:16 – "height,,other chapiter was 5 cubits"
1Ki 7:23 – "molten sea..height was five cubits"
1Ch 11:23 – "slew an Egyptian..5 cubits high"
2Ch 3:11 – "one wing..was five cubits"
2Ch 3:11 – "the other wing was likewise 5 cubits"
2Ch 3:12 – "one wing..other cherub was 5 cubits"
2Ch 3:12 – "the other wing was five cubits also"
2Ch 3:15 – "chapiter..on the top of each..5 cubits"
2Ch 4:2 – "molten sea..five cubits the height"
2Ch 6:13 – "brazen scaffold..five cubits long"
2Ch 6:13 – "brazen scaffold..five cubits broad"
Jer 52:22 – "height of the 1 chapiter was 5 cubits"
Ezk 40:7 – "between the little chambers..5 cubits"
Ezk 40:30 – "arches..5 cubits broad"
Ezk 40:48 – "each post..5 cubits on this side"
Ezk 40:48 – "each post..5 cubits on that side"
Ezk 41:2 – "sides..door..5 cubits..one side"
Ezk 41:2 – "sides..door..5 cubits..other side"
Ezk 41:9 – "thickness of the wall..5 cubits"
Ezk 41:11 – "breadth..5 cubits round about"
Ezk 41:12 – "wall..five cubits thick"

6 *Cubits*

1Sa 17:4 – "Goliath..height..6 cubits and a span"
1Ki 6:6 – "chamber..middle was 6 cubits broad"
Ezk 40:5 – "a measuring reed of six cubits long"
Ezk 40:12 – "little chambers..six cubits..this side"
Ezk 40:12 – "little chambers..6 cubits on that side"
Ezk 41:1 – "posts, six cubits broad..one side"
Ezk 41:1 – "posts..six cubits broad..other side"
Ezk 41:3 – "measured..the door, six cubits"
Ezk 41:5 – "wall of the house, six cubits"
Ezk 41:8 – "a full reed of six great cubits"
Dan 3:1 – "image..gold..breadth thereof 6 cubits"

7 *Cubits*

1Ki 6:6 – "chamber..third was 7 cubits broad"
Ezk 41:3 – "breadth of the door, seven cubits"

8 *Cubits*

1Ki 7:10 – "foundation..great stones..of 8 cubits"
Ezk 40:9 – "porch of the gate, eight cubits"

9 *Cubits*

Deu 3:11 – "Og..bedstead..9 cubits was the length"

10 *Cubits*

Exo 26:16 – "Ten cubits..the length of a board"
Exo 36:21 – "length of a board was ten cubits"
1Ki 6:3 – "porch before..temple..10 cubits..breadth"
1Ki 6:23 – "two cherubims..each ten cubits high"
1Ki 6:24 – "1 wing unto..the other were 10 cubits"
1Ki 6:25 – "the other cherub was ten cubits"
1Ki 6:26 – "height of the one cherub..ten cubits"
1Ki 7:10 – "foundation..great stones..of 10 cubits"
1Ki 7:23 – "molten sea, 10 cubits from the 1 brim"
2Ch 4:1 – "altar of brass..10 cubits the height"
2Ch 4:2 – "molten sea of ten cubits..brim to brim"
Ezk 40:11 – "breadth..entry of the gate, 10 cubits"
Ezk 41:2 – "breadth of the door was 10 cubits"
Ezk 42:4 – "a walk of 10 cubits breadth inward"
Zec 5:2 – "flying roll..breadth thereof 10 cubits"

11-19 *Cubits*

Gen 7:20 – "15 cubits upward..waters prevail"
Exo 27:14 – "hangings of one side..15 cubits"
Exo 27:15 – "on..other side..hangings 15 cubits"
Exo 38:14 – "hangings of the gate were 15 cubits"
Exo 38:15 – "other side of..court gate..15 cubits"
1Ki 7:15 – "a line of 12 cubits did compass..them"
1Ki 7:15 – "two pillars of brass, of 18 cubits high"
2Ki 25:17 – "height of the 1 pillar was 18 cubits"
Jer 52:21 – "fillet of 12 cubits did compass it"
Jer 52:21 – "height of one pillar was 18 cubits"
Ezk 40:11 – "length of the gate, thirteen cubits"
Ezk 40:49 – "the porch..breadth eleven cubits"
Ezk 43:16 – "altar shall be 12 cubits long"
Ezk 43:16 – "altar shall be..twelve broad"
Ezk 43:17 – "the settle shall be 14 cubits long"
Ezk 43:17 – "the settle shall be..14 broad"

20 *Cubits*

Exo 27:16 – "an hanging of 20 cubits"
Exo 38:18 – "hanging for..gate..20 cubits..length"
1Ki 6:2 – "house..Solomon..breadth..20 cubits"
1Ki 6:3 – "porch before..temple..20 cubits..length"
1Ki 6:16 – "built 20 cubits on..sides of the house"
1Ki 6:20 – "oracle in..forepart..20 cubits..length"
1Ki 6:20 – "oracle..20 cubits in breadth"
1Ki 6:20 – "oracle..20 cubits in height thereof"
2Ch 3:3 – "house of God..breadth 20 cubits"
2Ch 3:4 – "porch..house..length of it..20 cubits"
2Ch 3:8 – "most holy house..length..20 cubits"
2Ch 3:8 – "most holy house..breadth..20 cubits"
2Ch 3:11 – "wings..cherubims..20 cubits long"
2Ch 3:13 – "wings..spread themselves..20 cubits"
2Ch 4:1 – "altar of brass..20 cubits the length"
2Ch 4:1 – "altar of brass..20 cubits the breadth"
Ezk 40:49 – "length of the porch was 20 cubits"

Ezk 41:2 – "the door..the breadth, 20 cubits"
Ezk 41:4 – "length..20 cubits..most holy place"
Ezk 41:4 – "breadth..20 cubits..most holy place"
Ezk 41:10 – "between..chambers..20 cubits"
Ezk 42:3 – "20 cubits..were for the inner court"
Zec 5:2 – "flying roll; the length..20 cubits"

25 *Cubits*

Ezk 40:13 – "gate..breadth was 25 cubits"
Ezk 40:21 – "arches..breadth 25 cubits"
Ezk 40:25 – "arches..breadth 25 cubits"
Ezk 40:29 – "arches..25 cubits broad"
Ezk 40:30 – "arches..25 cubits long"
Ezk 40:33 – "arches..25 cubits broad"
Ezk 40:36 – "arches..breadth 25 cubits"

26-49 *Cubits*

Gen 6:15 – "the ark..the height of it 30 cubits"
Exo 26:2 – "length of one curtain..28 cubits"
Exo 26:8 – "length of 1 curtain shall be 30 cubits"
Exo 36:9 – "length of one curtain..28 cubits"
Exo 36:15 – "length of one curtain was 30 cubits"
1Ki 6:2 – "house..Solomon..height 30 cubits"
1Ki 6:17 – "the house..was 40 cubits long"
1Ki 7:2 – "house of the forest..height..30 cubits"
1Ki 7:6 – "porch of pillars..breadth..30 cubits"
1Ki 7:23 – "molten sea..30 cubits did compass it"
2Ch 3:15 – "two pillars of 35 cubits high"
2Ch 4:2 – "molten sea..30 cubits did compass it"
Ezk 41:2 – "the door..length thereof 40 cubits"
Ezk 46:22 – "courts..40 cubits long and 30 broad"

50 *Cubits*

Gen 6:15 – "the ark..breadth of it 50 cubits"
Exo 27:12 – "hangings of fifty cubits"
Exo 27:13 – "breadth of the court..east..50 cubits"
Exo 27:18 – "the courth..breadth fifty everywhere"
Exo 38:12 – "west side were hangings..50 cubits"
Exo 38:13 – "east side eastward 50 cubits"
1Ki 7:2 – "house of the forest..breadth..50 cubits"
1Ki 7:6 – "porch of pillars..length..50 cubits"
Est 5:14 – "gallows be made of 50 cubits hight"
Est 7:9 – "gallows 50 cubits high, which Haman"
Ezk 40:15 – "gate..unto..porch..were 50 cubits"
Ezk 40:21 – "arches..length thereof..50 cubits"
Ezk 40:25 – "arches..length was 50 cubits"
Ezk 40:29 – "arches..it was 50 cubits long"
Ezk 40:33 – "arches..it was 50 cubits long"
Ezk 40:36 – "arches..length was 50 cubits"
Ezk 42:2 – "Before..north door..breadth..50 cubits"
Ezk 42:7 – "wall..length thereof was 50 cubits"
Ezk 42:8 – "length of the chambers..was 50 cubits"
Ezk 45:2 – "50 cubits round about..suburbs"

60 *Cubits*

1Ki 6:2 – "house..Solomon..length..60 cubits"

2Ch 3:3 – "house of God..length..60 cubits"
Ezr 6:3 – "house of God..height..60 cubits"
Ezr 6:3 – "house of God..breadth..60 cubits"
Ezk 40:14 – "He made also posts of 60 cubits"
Dan 3:1 – "image of gold..height was 60 cubits"

70 *Cubits*

Ezk 41:12 – "building..west..70 cubits broad"

90 *Cubits*

Ezk 41:12 – "building..length thereof 90 cubits"

100 *Cubits*

Exo 27:9 – "hangings..court..100 cubits long"
Exo 27:11 – "hangings of 100 cubits long"
Exo 27:18 – "length..court shall be 100 cubits"
Exo 38:9 – "the hangings of the court..100 cubits"
Exo 38:11 – "north side the hangings..100 cubits"
1Ki 7:2 – "house of the forest..length..100 cubits"
Ezk 40:19 – "100 cubits eastward and northward"
Ezk 40:23 – "from gate to gate 100 cubits"
Ezk 40:27 – "from gate to gate..100 cubits"
Ezk 40:47 – "the court, an 100 cubits long"
Ezk 40:47 – "the court..and an 100 cubits broad"
Ezk 41:13 – "the house, an 100 cubits long"
Ezk 41:13 – "building..walls..100 cubits long"
Ezk 41:14 – "breadth..house..east, an 100 cubits"
Ezk 41:15 – "length of the building..100 cubits"
Ezk 42:2 – "Before..length..100 cubits..north door"
Ezk 42:8 – "before the temple were an 100 cubits"

101-999 *Cubits*

Gen 6:15 – "the ark..length..300 cubits"
2Ki 14:13 – "brake..wall..Jerusalem..400 cubits"
2Ch 3:4 – *"porch..of the house..height was 120"*
2Ch 25:23 – "brake..wall of Jerusalem..400 cubits"
Joh 21:8 – "not far from land..200 cubits"
Rev 21:17 – "measured the wall..144 cubits"

1000+ *Cubits*

Num 35:4 – "suburbs.. from the wall..1000 cubits"
Num 35:5 – "measure..city..east side 2000 cubits"
Num 35:5 – "measure..city..south side 2000 cubits"
Num 35:5 – "measure..city..west side 2000 cubits"
Num 35:5 – "measure..city..north side 2000 cubits"
Jos 3:4 – "space between you and it..2000 cubits"
Neh 3:13 – "1000 cubits on..wall unto..dung gate"
Ezk 47:3 – "measured a 1000 cubits..to the ancles"
Ezk 47:4 – "measured a 1000..to the knees"
Ezk 47:4 – "measured a 1000..to the loins"
Ezk 47:5 – "measured a 1000..it was a river"

Curse

Pro 28:27 – "hideth his eyes..many a curse"

Curtain

Exo 26:1 – "make the tabernacle with 10 curtains"
Exo 26:2 – "length of one curtain..28 cubits"
Exo 26:2 – "breadth of one curtain..4 cubits"
Exo 26:3 – "The five curtains shall be coupled"
Exo 26:3 – "five curtains..coupled one to another"
Exo 26:4 – "loops of blue upon..the one curtain"
Exo 26:4 – "curtain, in the coupling of the second"
Exo 26:5 – "Fifty loops..make in the one curtain"
Exo 26:5 – "curtain..in the coupling of the second"
Exo 26:7 – "eleven curtains thou shalt make"
Exo 26:8 – "length of 1 curtain shall be 30 cubits"
Exo 26:8 – "breadth of one curtain four cubits"
Exo 26:8 – "11 curtains shall be all of 1 measure"
Exo 26:9 – "couple five curtains by themselves"
Exo 26:9 – "couple..six curtains by themselves"
Exo 26:9 – "and shalt double the sixth curtain"
Exo 26:10 – "on the edge of the one curtain"
Exo 26:10 – "edge of..curtain that coupleth the 2nd"
Exo 26:12 – "the half curtain that remaineth"
Exo 36:8 – "ten curtains of fine twined linen"
Exo 36:9 – "length of one curtain..28 cubits"
Exo 36:9 – "breadth of one curtain..4 cubits"
Exo 36:10 – "coupled the 5 curtains 1 to another"
Exo 36:10 – "five curtains..coupled one to another"
Exo 36:11 – "loops of blue..edge of one curtain"
Exo 36:11 – "another curtain..coupling of the 2nd"
Exo 36:12 – "Fifty loops made he in one curtain"
Exo 36:12 – "loops held one curtain to another"
Exo 36:12 – "curtain..in the coupling of the 2nd"
Exo 36:13 – "coupled the curtains 1 unto another"
Exo 36:14 – "eleven curtains he made them"
Exo 36:15 – "length of one curtain was 30 cubits"
Exo 36:15 – "four cubits..breadth of one curtain"
Exo 36:15 – "the eleven curtains were of one size"
Exo 36:16 – "coupled five curtains by themselves"
Exo 36:16 – "six curtains by themselves"
Exo 36:17 – "edge of the curtain..coupleth the 2nd"

Custom

Lev 18:30 – "one of these abominable customs"
1Co 11:16 – "we have no such custom"

Damage

Dan 6:2 – "the king should have no damage"

Damsel

Jdg 5:30 – "to every man a damsel or two"
1Sa 25:42 – "Abigail..with 5 damsels of hers"

Darkness

Job 34:22 – "There is no darkness"
1Jn 1:5 – "in him is no darkness at all"

Dart

2Sa 18:14 – "Joab..3 darts..thrust..heart..Absalom"

Daughter

Gen 19:8 – "Behold now, I have two daughters"
Gen 19:15 – "take thy wife, and thy two daughters"
Gen 19:16 – "upon the hand of his two daughters"
Gen 19:30 – "mountain..his 2 daughters w/ him"
Gen 19:30 – "in a cave, he and his two daughters"
Gen 29:16 – "Laban had two daughters"
Gen 31:41 – "served..14 years for thy 2 daughters"
Exo 2:16 – "priest of Midian had 7 daughters"
Exo 6:25 – "Eleazer..one of the daughters of Putiel"
Num 27:9 – "And if he have no daughter"
Jdg 12:9 – "he had 30 sons and 30 daughters"
Jdg 12:9 – "took in 30 daughters..for his sons"
1Sa 2:21 – "three sons and two daughters"
1Sa 14:49 – "Saul..daughters..the firstborn Merab"
1Sa 14:49 – "Saul..his 2 daughters..Merab..Michal"
2Sa 14:27 – "unto Absalom..was born..1 daughter"
1Ch 4:27 – "Shimei had 16 sons and six daughters"
1Ch 25:5 – "God gave to Heman..3 daughters"
2Ch 11:21 – "begat 28 sons and 60 daughters"
2Ch 13:21 – "begat 22 sons and 16 daughters"
Neh 5:2 – "our sons, and our daughters, are many"
Neh 7:63 – "took one of the daughters of Barzillai"
Job 1:2 – "born unto him 7 sons and 3 daughters"
Job 42:13 – "He had also 7 sons and 3 daughters."
Job 42:14 – "name of the first, Jemima"
Job 42:14 – "name of the second, Kezia"
Job 42:14 – "name of the third, Keren-happuch"
Pro 30:15 – "The horseleach hath two daughters"
Pro 31:29 – "Many daughters..done virtuously"
Luk 8:42 – "he had one only daughter"
Act 21:9 – "same man had 4 daughters, virgins"

Daughter In Law

Rut 1:7 – "her two daughters in law with her"
Rut 1:8 – "Naomi..unto her two daughters in law"

Day

Indefinite *Days*

Gen 21:34 – "sojourned in the..land many days"
Gen 24:55 – "a few days, at the least ten"
Gen 27:44 – "And tarry with him a few days"
Gen 29:20 – "7 years..seemed..but a few days"
Gen 37:34 – "mourned for his son many days"
Gen 47:9 – "few and evil..days..of my life been"
Lev 15:25 – "issue of her blood many days"
Num 9:19 – "cloud tarried long..many days"
Num 9:20 – "cloud..few days upon the tabernacle"
Deu 1:46 – "ye abode in Kadesh many days"
Deu 2:1 – " compassed mount Seir many days"
Jos 22:3 – "these many days unto this day"
1Ki 2:38 – "Shimei dwelt in Jerusalem many days"
1Ki 17:15 – "he, and her house, did eat many days"
1Ki 18:1 – "And it came to pass after many days"
1Ch 7:22 – "And Ephraim..mourned many days"
Est 1:4 – "shewed..riches..many days, even 180"
Est 8:17 – "many of the people..became Jews"
Job 10:20 – "Are not my days few?"
Job 14:1 – "Man..is of few days"
Job 29:18 – "multiply my days as the sand"
Psa 34:12 – "What man..loveth many days"
Psa 109:8 – "Let his days be few"
Ecc 6:3 – "the days of his years be many"
Ecc 11:1 – "shalt find it after many days"
Ecc 11:8 – "days of darkness..shall be many"
Isa 24:22 – "after many days shall..be visited"
Isa 32:10 – "Many days & years..ye be troubled"
Isa 65:22 – "as..days of a tree..days of my people"
Jer 2:32 – "forgotten me days w/o number"
Jer 13:6 – "came to pass after many days"
Jer 32:14 – "that they may continue many days"
Jer 35:7 – "live many days in the land"
Jer 37:16 – "Jeremiah..remained..many days"
Ezk 12:27 – "vision..is for many days to come"
Ezk 38:8 – "After many days..shalt be visited"
Dan 8:26 – "the vision..shall be for many days
Dan 10:14 – "for yet the vision is for many days"
Dan 11:20 – "w/in few days he shall be destroyed"
Dan 11:33 – "they shall fall..many days"
Hos 3:3 – "abide for me many days"
Hos 3:4 – "children of Israel..abide many days"
Luk 15:13 – "And not many days after"
Joh 2:12 – "continued there not many days"
Act 1:5 – "baptized..not many days hence"
Act 9:23 – "after that many days..fulfilled"
Act 9:43 – "tarried many days in Joppa"
Act 13:31 – "seen many days of them"
Act 16:18 – "And this did she many days."
Act 21:10 – "as we tarried there many days"
Act 25:14 – "they had been there many days"
Act 27:7 – "we had sailed slowly many days"
Act 27:20 – "neither sun nor stars in many days"
Heb 12:10 – "for a few days chastened us"

0 *Days*

Jos 10:14 – "And there was no day like that"
Jer 30:7 – "day is great, so that none is like it"

1 *Day*

Gen 1:5 – "evening..morning..the first day"
Gen 27:45 – "deprived also of you both in one day"
Gen 33:13 – "overdrive them one day, all..will die"
Exo 12:15 – "first day ye shall put away leaven"
Exo 12:15 – "leavened bread..1st day until..7th day"
Exo 12:16 – "1st day..shall be an holy convocation"
Lev 22:28 – "and her young both in one day"
Lev 23:7 – "first day..holy convocation"
Lev 23:35 – "1st day shall be an holy convocation"
Lev 23:39 – "first day shall be a sabbath"
Lev 23:40 – "first day..boughs of goodly trees"
Num 7:12 – "offering the first day..of Judah"
Num 11:19 – "ye shall not eat one day, nor 2 days"
Num 28:18 – "first day..an holy convocation"
Deu 16:4 – "sacrificedst the first day at even"
Jdg 20:22 – "put themselves in array the first day"
1Sa 2:34 – "in one day they shall die both of them"
1Sa 27:1 – "I shall..perish one day by..hand of Saul"
2Sa 21:9 – "in the first days..barley harvest"
1Ki 4:22 – "Solomon's provision for one day"
1Ki 20:29 – "slew..100,000 footmen in one day"
2Ch 28:6 – "Pekah..slew..120,000 in one day"
Ezr 10:13 – "neither is this a work of 1 day or 2"
Neh 5:18 – "once in 10 days..all sorts of wine"
Neh 8:18 – "day by day, from the 1st unto the last"
Est 3:13 – "to kill..all Jews..in one day"
Est 8:12 – "Upon one day in all of the provinces"
Isa 9:14 – "the LORD will cut off..in one day"
Isa 10:17 – "burn..devour..thorns..briers in 1 day"
Isa 47:9 – "two things shall come..in one day"
Isa 66:8 – "Shall the earth..bring forth in one day?"
Dan 10:12 – "from the first day..set thine heart"
Zec 3:9 – "I remove the iniquity..in one day"
Zec 14:7 – "one day which shall be known"
Mat 26:17 – "first day..feast of unleavened bread"
Mat 28:1 – "began to dawn toward the first day"
Mar 14:12 – "first day of unleavened bread"
Mar 16:2 – "first day of the week..sepulchre"
Mar 16:9 – "Jesus was risen..first day of the week"
Luk 17:22 – "one of the days of the Son of man"
Luk 20:1 – "on one of those days, as he taught"
Luk 24:1 – "Now upon the first day of the week"
Joh 20:1 – "first day of the week cometh Mary"
Joh 20:19 – "being the 1st day of the week"
Act 21:7 – "abode with them one day"
Act 20:7 – "1st day of the week..to break bread"
Act 20:18 – "from the 1st day..I came into Asia"
Act 28:13 – "after one day the south wind blew"
Rom 14:5 – "One man esteemeth one day"
1Co 10:8 – "and fell in one day 23,000"
1Co 16:2 – "Upon the first day of the week"
Phi 1:5 – "from the first day until now"
2Pe 3:8 – "one day..as a 1000 years"

2Pe 3:8 – "a 1000 years as one day"
Rev 18:8 – "her plagues come in one day"

2 *Days*

Gen 1:8 – "evening..morning..the second day"
Exo 2:13 – "2nd day..two men..strove together"
Exo 16:29 – "on the 6th day the bread of two days"
Exo 21:21 – "if he continue a day or two"
Num 7:18 – "second day..Issachar, did offer"
Num 9:22 – "two days..a month..a year"
Num 11:19 – "ye shall not eat one day, nor 2 days"
Num 29:17 – "2nd day ye shall offer...two rams"
Jos 6:14 – "2nd day they compassed the city once"
Jos 10:32 – "Lachish..Israel..took it on the 2nd day"
Jdg 20:24 – "Israel came near..Benjamin..2nd day"
Jdg 20:25 – "Benjamin..against them..the 2nd day"
1Sa 20:27 – "on the morrow..the second day"
1Sa 20:34 – "Jonathan..eat no meat the 2nd day"
2Sa 1:1 – "David had abode two days in Ziklag"
Ezr 10:13 – "neither is this a work of 1 day or 2"
Neh 8:13 – "2nd day were gathered..chief fathers"
Est 7:2 – "king said..unto Esther on the 2nd day"
Est 9:27 – "they would keep these two days"
Jer 41:4 – "the 2nd day after he had slain Gedaliah"
Ezk 43:22 – "2nd day..offer a kid of the goats"
Hos 6:2 – "After two days will he revive us"
Mat 26:2 – "after two days..feast of the passover"
Mar 14:1 – "After two days was..the passover"
Joh 4:40 – "and he abode there two days"
Joh 4:43 – "after two days he departed thence"
Joh 11:6 – "abode two days..in the same place"

3 *Days*

Gen 1:13 – "evening..morning..the third day"
Gen 22:4 – "third day Abraham..saw the place"
Gen 30:36 – "set 3 days' journey..himself & Jacob"
Gen 31:22 – "told Laban..3rd day..Jacob was fled"
Gen 34:25 – "third day, when they were sore"
Gen 40:12 – "The three branches are three days"
Gen 40:13 – "within 3 days shall Pharaoh lift up"
Gen 40:18 – "The three baskets are three days"
Gen 40:19 – "within 3 days shall Pharaoh lift up"
Gen 40:20 – "the 3rd day..was Pharaoh's birthday"
Gen 42:17 – "together into ward three days"
Gen 42:18 – "Joseph said unto them the third day"
Exo 3:18 – "3 days' journey into the wilderness"
Exo 5:3 – "three days' journey into the desert"
Exo 8:27 – "go 3 days' journey into..wilderness"
Exo 10:22 – "darkness in..the land of Egypt 3 days"
Exo 10:23 – "They saw not one another..3 days"
Exo 15:22 – "3 days in the wilderness..no water"
Exo 19:11 – "be ready against the third day"
Exo 19:11 – "third day the LORD will come down"
Exo 19:15 – "Be ready against the third day"
Exo 19:16 – "It came to pass on the third day"
Lev 7:17 – "remainder..on..3rd day shall be burnt"
Lev 7:18 – "be eaten at all on the third day"
Lev 19:6 – "remain until..3rd day..burnt in the fire"

Lev 19:7 – "eaten..on the 3rd day, it is abominable"
Num 7:24 – "third day..Zebulun, did offer"
Num 10:33 – "departed..mount..3 days journey"
Num 10:33 – "ark..before them..3 days journey"
Num 19:12 – "purify himself with it..the 3rd day"
Num 19:12 – "if he purify not himself the 3rd day"
Num 19:19 – "sprinkle upon the unclean..3rd day"
Num 29:20 – "And on the third day...two rams"
Num 33:8 – "3 days' journey..wilderness of Etham"
Jos 1:11 – "w/in 3 days ye..pass over this Jordan"
Jos 2:16 – "hide yourselves there three days"
Jos 2:22 – "abode there three days"
Jos 3:2 – "after 3 days...officers went through"
Jos 9:16 – "at the end of three days..they heard"
Jos 9:17 – "came unto their cities on the third day"
Jdg 14:14 – "could not in 3 days expound..riddle"
Jdg 19:4 – "he abode with him three days"
Jdg 20:30 – "Israel..against..Benjamin on..3rd day"
1Sa 9:20 – "asses that were lost three days ago"
1Sa 20:5 – "hide..in the field unto the third day"
1Sa 20:12 – "sounded my father..the third day"
1Sa 20:19 – "when thou hast stayed three days"
1Sa 21:5 – "women..kept from us..these 3 days"
1Sa 30:1 – "David..men..to Ziklag on the third day"
1Sa 30:12 – "nor drunk any water 3 days..3 nights"
1Sa 30:13 – "three days agone I fell sick"
2Sa 1:2 – "It came even to pass on the third day"
2Sa 20:4 – "Assemble..men of Judah w/in 3 days"
2Sa 24:13 – "that there be three days' pestilence"
1Ki 3:18 – "third day after that I was delivered"
1Ki 12:5 – "Depart yet for 3 days..come again"
1Ki 12:12 – "Jeroboam..people came the 3rd day"
1Ki 12:12 – "Come to me again the third day"
2Ki 2:17 – "they sought 3 days, but found him not"
2Ki 20:5 – "I will heal thee: on the third day"
2Ki 20:8 – "go..into the house..LORD the 3rd day?"
1Ch 12:39 – "they were with David three days"
1Ch 21:12 – "or..3 days the sword of the LORD"
2Ch 10:5 – "Come again unto me after three days"
2Ch 10:12 – "people came to Rehoboam..3rd day"
2Ch 10:12 – "Come again to me on the third day"
2Ch 20:25 – "3 days in gathering of the spoil"
Ezr 6:15 – "house..finished..3rd day..month Adar"
Ezr 8:15 – "there abode we in tents three days"
Ezr 8:32 – "came to Jerusalem..abode there 3 days"
Ezr 10:8 – "would not come w/in 3 days"
Ezr 10:9 – "men..gathered..within 3 days"
Neh 2:11 – "I came to Jerusalem..was there 3 days"
Est 4:16 – "neither eat nor drink three days"
Est 5:1 – "it came to pass on the third day"
Hos 6:2 – "in the third day he will raise us up"
Jon 1:17 – "belly of the fish 3 days and 3 nights"
Jon 3:3 – "Nineveh..city of three days' journey"
Mat 12:40 – "3 days and 3 nights..whale's belly"
Mat 12:40 – "Son of man..3 days and 3 nights"
Mat 15:32 – "continue with me now three days"
Mat 16:21 – "be raised again the third day"
Mat 17:23 – "the 3rd day he shall be raised again"
Mat 20:19 – "crucify him..third day..rise again"
Mat 26:61 – "destroy..temple..build it in 3 days"
Mat 27:40 – "temple, and buildest it in three days"

Mat 27:63 – "After three days I will rise again"
Mat 27:64 – "be made sure unto the third day"
Mar 8:2 – "three days, and have nothing to eat"
Mar 8:31 – "killed, and after 3 days rise again"
Mar 9:31 – "killed, he shall rise the third day"
Mar 10:34 – "the third day he shall rise again"
Mar 14:58 – "within three days I will build"
Mar 15:29 – "buildest it in three days"
Luk 2:46 – "after three days they found him"
Luk 9:22 – "slain, and be raised the third day"
Luk 13:32 – "third day I shall be perfected"
Luk 18:33 – "third day he shall rise again"
Luk 20:12 – "again he sent a third..wounded him"
Luk 20:31 – "And the third took her"
Luk 24:7 – "the third day rise again"
Luk 24:21 – "to day is the third day"
Luk 24:46 – "rise from the dead the third day"
Joh 2:1 – "third day..marriage in Cana"
Joh 2:19 – "in 3 days I will raise it up again"
Joh 2:20 – "will thou rear it up in three days?"
Act 9:9 – "three days without sight"
Act 10:40 – "God raised him up the third day"
Act 17:2 – "three sabbath days reasoned"
Act 25:1 – "Festus..after three days he ascended"
Act 27:19 – "the 3rd day we cast out..the tackling"
Act 28:12 – "Syracuse, we tarried there 3 days"
Act 28:17 – "after 3 days, Paul called..the Jews"
Act 28:7 – "Publius..lodged us three days"
1Co 15:4 – "he rose again the third day"

3½ *Days*

Rev 11:9 – "see their dead bodies 3 days & an ½"
Rev 11:11 – "after 3½ days..Spirit..entered..them"

4 *Days*

Gen 1:19 – "evening..morning..the fourth day"
Num 7:30 – "fourth day..Reuben did offer"
Num 29:23 – "And on the fourth day...two rams"
Jdg 11:40 – "lament..daughter..Jephthath..4 days"
Jdg 19:5 – "on the 4th day..rose up to depart"
2Ch 20:26 – "4th day..assembled..valley..Berachah"
Ezr 8:33 – "on the 4th day..vessels weighed"
Joh 11:17 – "lain in the grave four days already"
Joh 11:39 – "he hath been dead four days"
Act 10:30 – "Four days ago I was fasting"

5 *Days*

Gen 1:23 – "evening..morning..the fifth day"
Num 7:36 – "fifth day..Simeon did offer"
Num 11:19 – "nor 5 days, neither 10 days"
Num 29:26 – "And on the fifth day..two rams"
Jdg 19:8 – "arose early..morning on the 5th day"
Act 20:6 – "came unto them to Troas in 5 days"
Act 24:1 – "after 5 days Ananias..descended"

6 *Days*

Gen 1:31 – "evening..morning..the sixth day"
Exo 16:5 – "6th day..twice as much"
Exo 16:22 – "6th day they gathered twice as much"
Exo 16:26 – "Six days ye shall gather it"
Exo 16:29 – "giveth..6th day the bread of two days"
Exo 20:9 – "Six days shalt thou labour"
Exo 20:11 – "in six days the LORD made heaven"
Exo 23:12 – "Six days thou shalt do thy work"
Exo 24:16 – "Sinai..cloud covered it six days"
Exo 31:15 – "Six days may work be done"
Exo 31:17 – "6 days the LORD made heaven..earth"
Exo 34:21 – "Six days thou shalt work"
Exo 35:2 – "Six days shall work be done"
Lev 23:3 – "six days shall work be done"
Num 7:42 – "sixth day..Gad, offered"
Num 29:29 – "And on the sixth day...two rams"
Deu 5:13 – "six days..labour and do all thy work"
Deu 16:8 – "Six days..shalt eat unleavened bread"
Jos 6:3 – "Thus shalt thou do six days."
Jos 6:14 – "compassed..city..so they did six days"
Ezk 46:1 – "gate..shut the six working days"
Mat 17:1 – "after six days Jesus taketh Peter"
Mar 9:2 – "And after six days..was transfigured"
Luk 13:14 – "6 days in which men ought to work"
Joh 12:1 – "Jesus six days before..passover"

7 *Days*

Gen 2:2 – "On the 7th day God ended his work"
Gen 2:2 – "he rested on..7th day from all his work"
Gen 2:3 – "God blessed the 7th day..sanctified it"
Gen 7:4 – "For yet 7 days..I will cause it to rain"
Gen 7:10 – "after 7 days..waters of the flood"
Gen 8:10 – "stayed yet other seven days"
Gen 8:12 – "stayed yet other seven days"
Gen 31:23 – "pursued after him 7 days' journey"
Gen 50:10 – "a mourning for his father 7 days"
Exo 7:25 – "7 days were fulfilled..smitten..river"
Exo 12:15 – "7 days shall ye eat unleavened bread"
Exo 12:15 – "leavened bread..1st day until..7th day"
Exo 12:16 – "in the 7th day..an holy convocation"
Exo 12:19 – "7 days shall..be no leaven found"
Exo 13:6 – "7 days..shalt eat unleavened bread"
Exo 13:6 – "7th day shall be a feast to the LORD"
Exo 13:7 – "Unleavened bread..be eaten 7 days"
Exo 16:26 – "7th day, which is the sabbath"
Exo 16:27 – "went out..on the 7th day..to gather"
Exo 16:29 – "no man go out..on the 7th day"
Exo 16:30 – "So the people rested on the 7th day"
Exo 20:10 – "7th day is the Sabbath of the LORD"
Exo 20:11 – "LORD..rested the seventh day"
Exo 22:30 – "seven days it shall be with his dam"
Exo 23:15 – "shalt eat unleavened bread 7 days"
Exo 24:16 – "7th day he called unto Moses..cloud"
Exo 29:30 – "priest..shall put them on seven days"
Exo 29:35 – "7 days shalt thou consecrate them"
Exo 29:37 – "7 days thou shalt make..atonement"
Exo 31:15 – "the seventh is the Sabbath of rest"

Exo 31:17 – "on the seventh day he rested"
Exo 34:18 – "Seven days..eat unleavened bread"
Exo 34:21 – "on the seventh day thou shalt rest"
Exo 35:2 – "on the seventh day..an holy day"
Lev 8:33 – "not go out..tabernacle..in seven days"
Lev 8:33 – "for 7 days shall he consecrate you"
Lev 8:35 – "abide at the door..day & night 7 days"
Lev 12:2 – "she shall be unclean seven days"
Lev 13:4 – "shut up him that hath..plague 7 days"
Lev 13:5 – "priest shall look on him the 7th day"
Lev 13:5 – "priest shall shut him up 7 days more"
Lev 13:6 – "priest..look on him again the 7th day"
Lev 13:21 – "priest shall shut him up seven days"
Lev 13:26 – "priest shall shut him up seven days"
Lev 13:27 – "priest..look upon him the 7th day"
Lev 13:31 – "shut up..plague of the scall 7 days"
Lev 13:32 – "in the seventh day..priest shall look"
Lev 13:33 – "him that hath the scall 7 days more"
Lev 13:34 – "in the seventh day..priest shall look"
Lev 13:50 – "shut up it that hath..plague 7 days"
Lev 13:51 – "look on the plague on the 7th day"
Lev 13:54 – "shut it up seven days more"
Lev 14:8 – "tarry abroad out of his tent 7 days"
Lev 14:9 – "seventh day..shall shave all his hair"
Lev 14:38 – "shut up the house seven days"
Lev 14:39 – "come again the seventh day"
Lev 15:13 – "number to himself 7 days..cleansing"
Lev 15:19 – "she shall be put apart seven days"
Lev 15:24 – "he shall be unclean seven days"
Lev 15:28 – "she shall number to herself 7 days"
Lev 22:27 – "it shall be seven days under the dam"
Lev 23:3 – "the seventh day is the sabbath of rest"
Lev 23:6 – "7 days ye must eat unleavened bread"
Lev 23:8 – "offering made by fire...seven days"
Lev 23:8 – " seventh day is an holy convocation"
Lev 23:34 – "feast of tabernacles...seven days"
Lev 23:36 – "seven days ye shall offer an offering"
Lev 23:39 – "keep a feast unto the LORD 7 days"
Lev 23:40 – "rejoice before the LORD..7 days"
Lev 23:41 – "keep it a feast unto the LORD 7 days"
Lev 23:42 – "Ye shall dwell in booths seven days"
Num 6:9 – "shave his head...seventh day"
Num 7:48 – "seventh day..Ephraim, offered"
Num 12:14 – "should she not be ashamed 7 days?"
Num 12:14 – "shut out from the camp seven days"
Num 12:15 – "Miriam..shut out..seven days"
Num 19:11 – "toucheth..body..unclean 7 days"
Num 19:12 – "shall purify himself...on the 7th day"
Num 19:12 – "the 7th day he shall not be clean"
Num 19:14 – "man dieth in a tent..unclean 7 days"
Num 19:16 – "toucheth..body..unclean 7 days"
Num 19:19 – "sprinkle..the unclean..on the 7th day"
Num 19:19 – "the 7th day he shall purify himself"
Num 28:17 – "7 days..unleavened bread be eaten"
Num 28:24 – "throughout the seven days"
Num 28:25 – "on the 7th day..holy convocation"
Num 29:12 – "keep a feast unto the LORD 7 days"
Num 29:32 – "And on the seventh day...two rams"
Num 31:19 – "abide without the camp seven days"
Num 31:19 – "purify..yourselves..on the 7th day"
Num 31:24 – "wash your clothes on the 7th day"

Deu 5:14 – "7th day is the sabbath of the LORD"
Deu 16:3 – "7 days shalt..eat unleavened bread"
Deu 16:4 – "no unleavened bread..coast 7 days"
Deu 16:8 – "on the 7th day..a solemn assembly"
Deu 16:13 – "observe..feast of tabernacles 7 days"
Deu 16:15 – "Seven days..keep a solemn feast"
Jos 6:4 – "7th day ye shall compass the city 7 times"
Jos 6:15 – "on the 7th day..they rose early"
Jdg 14:12 – "riddle..seven days of the feast"
Jdg 14:15 – "on the 7th day..Entice thy husband"
Jdg 14:17 – "she wept before him the 7 days"
Jdg 14:17 – "on the 7th day, that he told her"
Jdg 14:18 – "men of the city said..on the 7th day"
1Sa 10:8 – "seven days shalt thou tarry"
1Sa 11:3 – "Give us seven days respite"
1Sa 13:8 – "tarried seven days..Samuel came not"
1Sa 31:13 – "took their bones..fasted 7 days"
2Sa 12:18 – "on the 7th day, that the child died"
1Ki 8:65 – "7 days and 7 days, even 14 days"
1Ki 16:15 – "did Zimri reign 7 days in Tirzah"
1Ki 20:29 – "pitched one..against the other 7 days"
1Ki 20:29 – "in the 7th day the battle was joined"
2Ki 3:9 – "fetched a compass of 7 days journey"
1Ch 9:25 – "come after 7 days from time to time"
1Ch 10:12 – "buried their bones..fasted 7 days"
2Ch 7:8 – "Solomon kept the feast 7 days"
2Ch 7:9 – "dedication of the altar seven days"
2Ch 7:9 – "kept..the feast seven days"
2Ch 30:21 – "kept feast..unleavened bread 7 days"
2Ch 30:22 – "did eat throughout the feast 7 days"
2Ch 30:23 – "took counsel to keep other 7 days"
2Ch 30:23 – "they kept other 7 days with gladness"
2Ch 35:17 – "kept..feast..unleavened bread 7 days"
Ezr 6:22 – "kept..feast of unleavened bread 7 days"
Neh 8:18 – "they kept the feast seven days"
Est 1:5 – "king made a feast..seven days"
Est 1:10 – "on the 7th day..heart of the king..merry"
Job 2:13 – "upon the ground 7 days and 7 nights"
Isa 30:26 – "the sun..as the light of seven days"
Ezk 3:15 – "astonished among them seven days"
Ezk 3:16 – "at..end of 7 days..word of the LORD"
Ezk 43:25 – "7 days..prepare..a goat..sin offering"
Ezk 43:26 – "7 days..purge the altar and purify it"
Ezk 44:26 – "after he is cleansed..reckon..7 days"
Ezk 45:20 – "shalt do the 7th day of the month"
Ezk 45:21 – "the passover, a feast of seven days"
Ezk 45:23 – "7 days of the feast..prepare..offering"
Ezk 45:23 – "burnt offering..daily the seven days"
Ezk 45:25 – "in the feast of the seven days"
Act 20:6 – "where we abode seven days"
Act 21:4 – "we tarried there seven days"
Act 21:27 – "when the 7 days were almost ended"
Act 28:14 – "found brethren..tarry with..7 days"
Heb 4:4 – "For he spake..of the seventh day"
Heb 4:4 – "God did rest the seventh day"
Heb 11:30 – "walls..compassed about 7 days"

8 *Days*

Gen 17:12 – "8 days old shall be circumcised"
Gen 21:4 – "circumcised..Isaac..8 days old"

Exo 22:30 – "on the 8th day thou shalt give it me"
Lev 9:1 – "on the eighth day"
Lev 12:3 – "in the eighth day...circumcised"
Lev 14:10 – "on the 8th day he shall take..lambs"
Lev 14:23 – "eighth day for his cleansing"
Lev 15:14 – "eighth day..turtledoves..pigeons"
Lev 15:29 – "eighth day..take unto her two turtles"
Lev 22:27 – "from the 8th day..it shall be accepted"
Lev 23:36 – "8th day shall be an holy convocation"
Lev 23:39 – "eighth day shall be a sabbath"
Num 6:10 – "eighth day..bring..turtles..pigeons"
Num 7:54 – "eighth day offered..Manasseh"
Num 29:35 – "eighth day..have a solemn assembly"
1Ki 8:66 – "On the 8th day he sent the people away"
2Ch 7:9 – "in the 8th day..made a solemn assembly"
2Ch 29:17 – "sanctified..house of..LORD in 8 days"
Neh 8:18 – "on the 8th day was a solemn assembly"
Ezk 43:27 – "8th day..so forward..burnt offerings"
Luk 1:59 – "on the 8th day..came to circumcise"
Luk 2:21 – "when eight days were accomplished"
Luk 9:28 – "eight days after these sayings"
Joh 20:26 – "after 8 days..disciples were within"
Act 7:8 – "Isaac..circumcised him the 8th day"
Phi 3:5 – "circumcised the eighth day"

9 *Days*

Lev 23:32 – "Sabbath..9th day of..month at even"
Num 7:60 – "ninth day..Benjamin, offered"

10 *Days*

Gen 24:55 – "a few days, at the least ten"
Exo 12:3 – "tenth day of this month..take..a lamb"
Num 7:66 – "tenth day..Dan, offered"
Num 11:19 – "neither 10 days, nor 20 days"
1Sa 25:38 – "10 days after..the LORD smote Nabal"
2Ch 36:9 – "Jehoiachin..reigned 3 months..10 days"
Neh 5:18 – "once in 10 days store..all sorts..wine"
Jer 42:7 – "after 10 days..word of the LORD came"
Dan 1:12 – "prove thy servants..ten days"
Dan 1:14 – "proved them ten days"
Dan 1:15 – "at the end of ten days..countenances"
Act 25:6 – "tarried..more than 10 days"
Rev 2:10 – "have tribulation ten days"

11-19 *Days*

Lev 12:4 – "she shall be unclean two weeks"
Num 7:72 – "eleventh day..Asher, offered"
Num 7:78 – "twelfth day..Naphtali, offered"
Jos 5:10 – "kept..Passover..14th day of the month"
Deu 1:2 – "There are eleven days' journey"
1Ki 8:65 – "7 days and 7 days, even 14 days"
Act 24:11 – "12 days since I went up to Jerusalem"
Act 27:33 – "14th day that ye..continued fasting"
Gal 1:18 – "Peter, and abode with him 15 days"

20-29 *Days*

Num 11:19 – "neither 10 days, nor 20 days"
2Ch 7:10 – "23rd day..7th month..sent..people away"
Neh 6:15 – "wall..finished..25th day of the month"
Neh 9:1 – "in the 24th day of this month..fasting"
Dan 10:2 – "Daniel was mourning three full weeks"
Dan 10:3 – "till three whole weeks were fulfilled"
Dan 10:4 – "in the 24th day of the first month"
Dan 10:13 – "prince..Persia w/stood me 21 days"
Hag 2:20 – "word of the LORD came..24th day"

30-39 *Days*

Lev 12:4 – "in the blood of..purifying 33 days"
Num 11:19-20 – "even a whole month"
Num 20:29 – "mourned for Aaron 30 days"
Deu 34:8 – "wept for Moses in..Moab 30 days"
Est 4:11 – "not..called to come in..these 30 days"
Dan 6:7 – "petition of any God or man for 30 days"
Dan 6:12 – "petition of..God or man w/in 30 days"

40 *Days*

Gen 7:4 – "rain upon..earth 40 days & 40 nights"
Gen 7:12 – "rain..upon..earth 40 days & 40 nights"
Gen 7:17 – "the flood was 40 days upon the earth"
Gen 8:6 – "end of 40 days..Noah opened..window"
Gen 50:3 – "40 days were fulfilled for him"
Exo 24:18 – "Moses..in..mount..40 days..40 nights"
Exo 34:28 – "w/ the LORD 40 days and 40 nights"
Lev 12:2-4 – 7 + 33 days of separation for man child
Num 13:25 – "returned..searching..after 40 days"
Num 14:34 – "even 40 days, each day for a year"
Deu 9:9 – "40 days and 40 nights"
Deu 9:11 – "40 days and 40 nights"
Deu 9:18 – "40 days and 40 nights"
Deu 9:25 – "40 days and 40 nights"
Deu 10:10 – "40 days and 40 nights"
1Sa 17:16 – "presented himself 40 days"
1Ki 19:8 – "40 days and 40 nights"
Ezk 4:6 – "bear..iniquity..house of Judah 40 days"
Jon 3:4 – "40 days..Nineveh shall be overthrown"
Mat 4:2 – "fasted 40 days and 40 nights"
Mar 1:13 – "in the wilderness 40 days, tempted"
Luk 4:2 – "forty days tempted of the devil"
Act 1:3 – "being seen of them 40 days"

41-99 *Days*

Gen 50:3 – "mourned for him 70 days"
Lev 12:5 – "continue..blood..purifying 66 days"
Lev 23:16 – "shall ye number fifty days"
Deu 16:9 – "Seven weeks shalt..number unto thee"
Deu 16:9 – "number the 7 weeks..sickle to the corn"
Neh 6:15 – "wall was finished..in 52 days"

100-999 *Days*

Gen 7:24 – "waters prevailed..150 days"

Gen 8:3 – "end of the 150 days..waters..abated"
2Sa 24:8 – 9 mos & 20 days to number Israel (290)
2Ch 36:9 – "Jeohiachin..reigned 3 months..10 days"
Est 1:4 – "shewed..glorious kingdom..180 days"
Ezk 4:5 – "years of their iniquity..390 days"
Ezk 4:9 – "thou shalt lie upon thy side, 390 days"

1000+ *Days*

Psa 84:10 – "day in thy courts is better than 1000"
Dan 8:14 – "Unto 2,300 days..sanctuary..cleansed"
Dan 12:11 – "there shall be 1290 days"
Dan 12:12 – "Blessed..cometh to the 1335 days"
Rev 11:3 – "my witnesses..prophesy 1260 days"
Rev 12:6 – "should feed here there 1260 days"

Dead

Col 1:18 – "firstborn from the dead"

Deal *(Unit of Measurement)*

Exo 29:40 – "with the..lamb a tenth deal of flour"
Lev 14:10 – "three tenth deals of fine flour"
Lev 14:21 – "one tenth deal of fine flour..with oil"
Lev 23:13 – "meat offering..2/10th deals..fine flour"
Lev 23:17 – "two wave loaves of two tenth deals"
Lev 24:5 – "two tenth deals shall be in one cake"
Num 15:4 – "meat offering of a tenth deal of flour"
Num 15:6 – "meat offering..2/10th deals of flour"
Num 15:9 – "meat offering of 3/10th deals of flour"
Num 28:9 – "2/10th deals of flour...meat offering"
Num 28:12 – "three tenth deals of flour"
Num 28:12 – "two tenth deals of flour"
Num 28:13 – "a several tenth deal flour"
Num 28:20 – "three tenth deals...for a bullock"
Num 28:20 – "two tenth deals for a ram"
Num 28:21 – "A several tenth deal...for every lamb"
Num 28:28 – "flour..3/10th deals unto one bullock"
Num 28:28 – "flour..2/10th deals unto one ram"
Num 28:29 – "A several tenth deal unto one lamb"
Num 29:3 – "flour..oil..three tenth deals..bullock"
Num 29:3 – "flour..oil..two tenth deals for a ram"
Num 29:4 – "one tenth deal for one lamb"
Num 29:9 – "three tenth deals to a bullock"
Num 29:9 – "two tenth deals to one ram"
Num 29:10 – "A several tenth deal for one lamb"
Num 29:14 – "3/10th deals unto every bullock"
Num 29:14 – "two tenth deals to each ram"
Num 29:15 – "a several tenth deal to each lamb"

Dealing

Joh 4:9 – "Jews have no dealings..Samaritans"

Death

Job 18:13 – "firstborn of death shall devour"
Pro 12:28 – "pathway thereof there is no death"
Rev 2:11 – "not be hurt of the second death"
Rev 20:6 – "on such the 2nd death hath no power"
Rev 20:14 – "This is the second death."
Rev 21:8 – "fire..brimstone..which is the 2nd death"

Debtor

Luk 7:41 – "certain creditor which had 2 debtors"
Luk 7:41 – "debtors..the one owed 500 pence"
Luk 16:5 – "called every one of his..debtors"
Luk 16:5 – "called..debtors..said unto the first"

Deceiver

Tit 1:10 – "many unruly..talkers..deceivers"
2Jo 1:7 – "many deceivers..into the world"

Decree

Dan 2:9 – "there is but one decree for you"
Dan 6:15 – " no decree nor statute..be changed"

Deed

Jdg 19:30 – "There was no such deed done"
2Ch 35:27 – Josiah – "And his deeds, first and last"

Deepness

Mat 13:5 – "had no deepness of earth"

Degree

2Ki 20:9 – "the shadow go forward 10 degrees"
2Ki 20:9 – "or go back ten degrees?"
2Ki 20:10 – "shadow to go down 10 degrees"
2Ki 20:10 – "shadow return backward 10 degrees"
2Ki 20:11 – "brought the shadow 10 degrees"
1Ch 15:18 – "their brethren of the second degree"
Isa 38:8 – "sun dial of Ahaz, 10 degrees backward"
Isa 38:8 – "the sun returned ten degrees"

Delight

Deu 21:14 – "if thou have no delight in her"
2Sa 15:26 – "I have no delight in thee"
Pro 18:2 – "fool hath no delight in understanding"
Jer 6:10 – "they have no delight in it"

Deliverer

Jdg 18:28 – "And there was no deliverer"

Depth

Pro 8:24 – "When there were no depths"
Mar 4:5 – "it had no depth of earth"

Destruction

Jer 17:18 – "destroy them w/ double destruction"

Device

Pro 19:21 – "many devices in a man's heart"
Ecc 9:10 – "no..device..in the grave"

Devil

Mar 6:13 – "And they cast out many devils"
Mar 16:9 – "Mary..out of whom..cast 7 devils"
Luk 8:2 – "Mary..out of whom went 7 devils"
Luk 8:30 – "many devils were entered into him"

Dew

2Sa 1:21 – "let there be no dew, neither..rain"

Difference

Eze 22:26 – "no difference..holy..profane"
Act 15:9 – "no difference between us and them"
Rom 3:22 – "for there is no difference"
Rom 10:12 – "no difference..Jew..Greek"

Disciple

Mat 10:1 – "called unto him his 12 disciples"
Mat 11:1 – "commanding his 12 disciples"
Mat 11:2 – "he sent two of his disciples"
Mat 20:17 – "Jesus..took the 12 disciples apart"
Mat 21:1 – "then sent Jesus two disciples"
Mat 28:16 – "eleven disciples went away"
Mar 11:1 – "sendeth forth two of his disciples"
Mar 13:1 – "one of his disciples saith unto him"
Mar 14:13 – "he sendeth forth 2 of his disciples"
Luk 6:13 – "disciples..chose twelve..apostles"
Luk 7:11 – "many of his disciples went with him"
Luk 7:19 – "John..two of his disciples"
Luk 9:1 – "Then he called his 12 disciples"

Luk 11:1 – "one of his disciples said"
Luk 19:29 – "he sent two of his disciples"
Joh 1:35 – "John stood, and two of his disciples"
Joh 1:37 – "the two disciples heard him speak"
Joh 1:40 – "One of the two which heard John"
Joh 4:33 – "said the disciples one to another"
Joh 6:8 – "One of his disciples, Andrew"
Joh 6:60 – "Many therefore of his disciples"
Joh 6:66 – "many of his disciples went back"
Joh 12:4 – "Then saith one of his disciples"
Joh 13:22 – "disciples looked one on another"
Joh 13:23 – "on Jesus' bosom one of his disciples"
Joh 18:17 – "one of this man's disciples"
Joh 18:25 – "also one of his disciples"
Joh 20:8 – "disciple, which came 1st to..sepulchre"
Joh 21:2 – "and two other of his disciples"
Joh 21:12 – "none of the disciples..ask him"

Disease

Exo 15:26 – "none of these diseases upon thee"
Deu 7:15 – "none of the evil diseases of Egypt"

Division

1Co 1:10 – "there be no divisions among you"

Dominion

Mic 4:8 – "even the first dominion"

Door

1Ki 6:32 – "two doors also were of olive tree"
1Ki 6:34 – "two doors were of fir tree"
1Ki 6:34 – "2 leaves of the one door were folding"
Ezk 41:11 – "one door toward the north"
Ezk 41:24 – "two leaves for the one door"
Ezk 41:23 – "temple and..sanctuary had 2 doors"

Doubt

Job 12:2 – "No doubt but ye are the people"
Luk 11:20 – "no doubt the kingdom of God"
Act 28:4 – "No doubt this man is a murderer"
1Jn 2:19 – "no doubt have continued with us"

Dough

Num 15:20 – "offer up a cake of..1st of your dough"
Num 15:21 – "the 1st of your dough ye shall give"
Ezk 44:30 – "give unto..priests..first of your dough"

Dram

1Ch 29:7 – "of gold 5000 talents & 10,000 drams"
Ezr 2:69 – "They gave..61,000 drams of gold"
Ezr 8:27 – "20 basons of gold, of a 1000 drams"
Neh 7:70 – "gave to..treasure..1000 drams of gold"
Neh 7:71 – "gave to..treasure..20,000 drams..gold"
Neh 7:72 – "people gave..20,000 drams of gold"

Dream

Gen 41:25 – "The dream of Pharaoh is one"
Gen 41:26 – "the dream is one"
Gen 41:32 – "dream..doubled unto Pharaoh twice"

Drink

Jdg 13:7 – "drink no wine nor strong drink"
Mat 25:42 – "ye gave me no drink"

Dwellingplace

1Co 4:11 – "and have no certain dwellingplace"

Ear *(as in ears of grain)*

Gen 41:5 – "7 ears of corn came upon on 1 stalk"
Gen 41:6 – "7 thin ears and blasted with..wind"
Gen 41:7 – "the 7 thin ears devoured..7..full ears"
Gen 41:22 – "behold, seven ears came up"
Gen 41:23 – "behold, seven ears, withered, thin"
Gen 41:24 – "thin ears devoured the 7 good ears"
Gen 41:26 – "the 7 good ears are 7 years"
Gen 41:27 – "7 empty ears..be 7 years..famine"

Earth *(Dirt)*

2Ki 5:17 – "given..two mule's burden of earth?"

Earth *(Planet)*

Rev 21:1 – "1st heaven and..1st earth passed away"

Ease

Deu 28:65 – "shalt thou find no ease"

Edge/Twoedged

Exo 28:7 – "joined at the two edges thereof"

Exo 39:4 – "by the two edges was it coupled"
Jdg 3:16 – "Ehud made..dagger..had two edges"
Psa 149:6 – "a twoedged sword in their hand"
Pro 5:4 – "her end is..sharp as a twoedged sword"
Heb 4:12 – "word of God..twoedged sword"
Rev 1:16 – "mouth..sharp twoedged sword"
Rev 2:12 – "the sharp sword with two edges"

Effect

Num 30:8 – "which she uttered..of none effect"
Psa 33:10 – "devices of the people of none effect"
Mat 15:6 – "commandment..of none effect"
Mar 7:13 – "word of God of none effect"
Rom 4:14 – "promise made of none effect"
Rom 9:6 – "word of God..taken none effect"
1Co 1:17 – "cross of Christ..of none effect"
Gal 3:17 – "make the promise of none effect"
Gal 5:4 – "Christ is become of no effect"

Elders

Exo 24:1 – "seventy of the elders of Israel"
Exo 24:9 – "seventy of the elders of Israel"
Num 11:25 – "spirit..gave it unto the 70 elders"
Rev 5:5 – "one of the elders saith"
Rev 5:8 – "having every one of them harps"
Rev 7:13 – "one of the elders answered"
Rev 4:4 – "I saw 24 elders sitting"
Rev 4:10 – "The 24 elders fall down before him"
Rev 5:8 – "and 24 elders fell down before..Lamb"
Rev 5:14 – "the 24 elders fell down..worshipped"
Rev 11:16 – "the 24 elders..fell upon their faces"
Rev 19:4 – "the 24 elders..fell down..worshipped"

Emerod

1Sa 6:4 – "trespass offering..Five golden emerods"

Enchantment

Num 23:23 – "no enchantment against Jacob"

End

Gen 47:21 – "one end of the borders of Egypt"
Exo 25:18 – "in the two ends of the mercy seat"
Exo 25:19 – "make one cherub on the one end"
Exo 28:23 – "put the two rings on the two ends"
Exo 28:26 – "upon the two ends of the breastplate"
Exo 36:33 – "boards from the 1 end to the other"
Exo 37:7 – "cherubims..on the 2 ends..mercy seat"
Exo 37:8 – "cherbuims on the two ends thereof"
Exo 38:5 – "four rings for the four ends"

Exo 39:16 – "put the two rings in the two ends"
Exo 39:18 – "two ends of the 2 wreathen chains"
Exo 39:19 – "the two ends of the breastplate"
Deu 13:7 – "from one end of..earth..unto the other"
Deu 28:64 – "scatter..from..one end of..earth unto"
2Ki 10:21 – "house..full from one end to another"
2Ki 21:16 – "shed innocent blood..from one end"
Ezr 9:11 – "abominations..filled it from one end"
Psa 102:27 – "thy years shall have no end"
Ecc 4:8 – "no end of all his labour"
Ecc 4:16 – "There is no end of all the people"
Ecc 12:12 – "making many books there is no end"
Isa 9:7 – "peace there shall be no end"
Jer 12:12 – "devour from the one end of the land"
Jer 25:33 – "slain of the LORD..from one end"
Jer 51:31 – "his city is taken at one end"
Nah 2:9 – "is none end of the store and glory"
Nah 3:3 – "there is none end of their corpses"
Mat 24:31 – "from one end of heaven to another"
Luk 1:33 – "of his kingdom..shall be no end"

Enemy

Job 19:11 – "he counteth me..as 1 of his enemies"
Psa 25:19 – "enemies; for they are many"
Psa 119:157 – "Many..my persecutors..enemies"

Entry

Jer 38:14 – "3rd entry..in the house of the LORD"

Ephah

1Sa 1:24 – "she took..3 bullocks..1 ephah of flour"

Epistle

2Pet 3:1 – "This second epistle, beloved, I..write"

Escape

Ezr 9:14 – "should be no remnant nor escaping"

Estate

Jud 6 – "angels which kept not their first estate"

Eunuch

2Ki 9:32 – "there looked out..2 or 3 eunuchs"
Jer 38:7 – "Ebedmelech..one of the eunuchs"

Event

Ecc 2:14 – "one event happeneth to them all"
Ecc 9:2 – "there is one event to the righteous"
Ecc 9:3 – "there is one event unto all"

Evil

Deu 31:17 – "many evils & troubles..befall them"
Deu 31:21 – "many evils & troubles are befallen"
Job 5:19 – "there shall no evil touch thee"
Psa 23:4 – "I will fear no evil"
Psa 40:12 – "innumerable evils..compassed me"
Psa 91:10 – "There shall no evil befall thee"
Pro 12:21 – "shall no evil happen to the just"
Jer 2:13 – "my people have committed two evils"
Jer 23:17 – "No evil shall come upon you"
Jer 44:17 – "had we plenty..and saw no evil"
Mic 3:11 – "none evil can come upon us"
Act 23:9 – "We find no evil in this man"
1Co 13:5 – "thinketh no evil"
2Co 13:7 – "I pray to God that ye do no evil"

Ewe

Gen 32:14 – "200 ewe, and twenty rams"

Eye

Jdg 16:28 – "avenged of the Philistines..my 2 eyes"
Job 10:18 – "Oh that..no eye had seen me!"
Job 24:15 – "No eye shall see me"
Son 4:9 – "ravished my heart w/ one of thine eyes"
Isa 59:10 – "we grope as if we had no eyes"
Eze 16:5 – "None eye pitied thee"
Zec 3:9 – "upon one stone shall be seven eyes"
Zec 4:10 – "Zerubbabel with those seven"
Mat 6:22 – "if therefore thine eye be single"
Mat 18:9 – "enter into life with one eye"
Mat 18:9 – "having two eyes..hell fire"
Mar 9:47 – "into the kingdom of God with one eye"
Mar 9:47 – "having two eyes..cast into hell fire"
Rev 5:6 – "7 eyes, which are the 7 Spirits"

Face

Ezk 1:6 – "every one had four faces"
Ezk 1:15 – "living creatures, with his four faces"
Ezk 10:14 – "every one had four faces"
Ezk 10:14 – "first face was the face of a cherub"
Ezk 10:14 – "second face was the face of a man"
Ezk 10:14 – "third the face of a lion"
Ezk 10:14 – "fourth the face of an eagle"
Ezk 10:21 – "Every one had four faces apiece"
Ezk 41:18 – "every cherub had two faces"

Faith

Deu 32:20 – "children in whom is no faith"
Mar 4:40 – "how is it that ye have no faith?"
Eph 4:5 – "One Lord, one faith, one baptism"
1Ti 5:12 – "have cast off their first faith"

Faithfulness

Psa 5:9 – "no faithfulness in their mouth"

Family

Jer 33:24 – "two families..the LORD hath chosen"

Famine

Gen 26:1 – "famine..beside the first famine"
Eze 36:29 – "and lay no famine upon you"

Farthing

Luk 12:6 – "5 sparrows sold for 2 farthings"

Fast

Luk 18:12 – "I fast twice in the week"

Father

1Ch 26:32 – "2700 chief fathers..made rulers"
Isa 43:27 – "Thy first father hath sinned"
Mal 2:10 – "Have we not all one father?"
Joh 8:41 – "we have one Father, even God"
1Co 4:15 – "yet have ye not many fathers"
Eph 4:6 – "One God and Father of all"

Fathom

Act 27:28 – "sounded, and found it 20 fathoms"
Act 27:28 – "sounded again..found it 15 fathoms"

Fault

1Sa 29:3 – "I have found no fault in him"
Luk 23:4 – "I find no fault in this man"
Luk 23:14 – "found no fault in this man"
Joh 18:38 – "Pilate..I find in him no fault at all"
Joh 19:4 – "that I find no fault in him"
Joh 19:6 – "for I find no fault in him"

Favour

Deu 24:1 – "she find no favour in his eyes"
Jos 11:20 – "that they might have no favour"
Pro 21:10 – "findeth no favour in his eyes"

Fear

Psa 36:1 – "there is no fear of God before his eyes"
Psa 53:5 – "great fear, where no fear was"
Rom 3:18 – "no fear of God before their eyes"
1Jn 4:18 – "There is no fear in love"

Feather

Ezk 17:7 – "eagle with..many feathers"

Feller

Isa 14:8 – "no feller is come up against us"

Fellow

Gen 19:9 – "This one fellow came in to sojourn"
2Sa 6:20 – "as one of the vain fellows"

Fellowservant

Mat 18:28 – "one of his fellowservants..owed..100"

Fellowship

Eph 5:11 – "have no fellowship with..darkness"

Fifty

2Ki 1:13 – "again a captain of the third fifty"

Fin

Lev 11:12 – "Whatsoever hath no fins nor scales"

Finger

2Sa 21:20 – "on every hand six fingers"
1Ch 20:6 – "fingers and toes were 24"
1Ch 20:6 – "six on each hand"
Jer 52:21 – "pillars..thickness..was four fingers"
Mat 23:4 – "not move them with 1 of their fingers"

Luk 11:46 – "burdens with one of your fingers"

Fire

Exo 35:3 – "Ye shall kindle no fire"
1Ki 18:23 – "lay it on wood..put no fire under"
1Ki 18:23 – "and put no fire under"
1Ki 18:25 – "but put no fire under"
Ezk 15:7 – "they shall go out from one fire"

Firkin

Joh 2:6 – "waterpots..two or three firkins apiece"

Fish

Ezk 47:10 – "fish of the..sea, exceeding many"
Mat 14:17 – "five loaves, and two fishes"
Mat 14:19 – "five loaves, and two fishes"
Mat 15:34 – "and a few little fishes"
Mat 17:27 – "take up the fish that first cometh up"
Mar 6:38 – "How many loaves..Five, and 2 fishes"
Mar 6:41 – "taken the 5 loaves and the 2 fishes"
Mar 6:41 – "2 fishes divided he among them all"
Mar 8:7 – "they had a few small fishes"
Luk 9:13 – "We have..but 5 loaves..2 fishes"
Luk 9:16 – "he took the 5 loaves and the 2 fishes"
Joh 6:9 – "lad here, which hath..two small fishes"
Joh 21:11 – "net..full of great fishes, an 153"
Joh 21:11 – "fishes.. there were so many"

Firstfruit

Exo 23:19 – "the first of the firstfruits of thy land"
Exo 34:26 – "1st of thy firstfruits..bring unto..God"
Ezk 44:30 – "first of all the firstfruits of all things"

Flesh

Gen 2:24 – "they shall be one flesh"
Jer 12:12 – "no flesh shall have peace"
Mat 19:5 – "they twain shall be one flesh?"
Mat 19:6 – "no more twain, but one flesh"
Mat 24:22 – "there should no flesh be saved"
Mar 10:8 – "they twain shall be one flesh"
Mar 10:8 – "no more twain, but one flesh"
Mar 13:20 – "no flesh should be saved"
Rom 3:20 – "no flesh be justified in his sight"
1Co 1:29 – "That no flesh should glory"
1Co 6:16 – "two saith he, shall be one flesh"
1Co 8:13 – "I will eat no flesh while the world"
Gal 2:16 – "shall no flesh be justified"
Eph 5:31 – "they two shall be one flesh"

Flock

Gen 4:4 – "Abel..brought..firstlings of his flock"
Gen 29:2 – "three flocks of sheep lying by it"
Deu 12:6 – "firstlings of your herds..your flocks"
Deu 12:17 – "the firstlings of thy herds..thy flock"
Deu 14:23 – "the firstlings of thy herds..thy flocks"
2Sa 12:2 – "exceeding many flocks and herds"
1Ki 20:27 – "children of Israel..like 2 little flocks"
Neh 10:36 – "firstlings of our herds..our flocks"

Fly

Exo 8:31 – "swarms of flies..remained not one"

Foal

Gen 32:15 – "20 she asses, and 10 foals"

Fold

Joh 10:16 – "there shall be one fold"

Folk

Mar 6:5 – "laid his hands upon a few sick folk"

Food

Pro 28:3 – "sweeping rain which leaveth no food"

Fool

2Sa 13:13 – "shalt be as one of the fools in Israel"

Foot

Exo 25:26 – "that are on the four feet thereof"
Exo 37:13 – "corners that were in the four feet"
Lev 11:20 – "fowls...going upon all four"
Lev 11:21 – "flying creeping..goeth upon all four"
Lev 11:23 – "flying creeping things..have four feet"
Lev 11:27 – "beasts that go on all four"
Lev 11:42 – "whatsoever goeth upon all four"
Eze 29:11 – "No foot of man shall pass through"
Mat 18:8 – "two hands or two feet..cast..fire"
Mar 9:45 – "having two feet to be cast into hell"
Act 10:12 – "all manner of fourfooted beasts"
Act 11:6 – "saw fourfooted beasts of the earth"
Rom 1:23 – "fourfooted beasts, & creeping things"

Footman

Num 11:21 – "the people are..600,000 footmen"
Jdg 20:2 – "400,000 footmen that drew sword"
1Sa 4:10 – "very great slaughter..30,000 footmen"
1Sa 15:4 – "Saul gathered..200,000 footmen"
2Sa 8:4 – "700 horsemen and 20,000 footmen"
2Sa 10:6 – "Syrians of Zoba, 20,000 footmen"
1Ki 20:29 – "slew of the Syrians 100,000 footmen"
2Ki 13:7 – "leave to Jehoahaz..10,000 footmen"
1Ch 18:4 – "David took..20,000 footmen"
1Ch 19:18 – "David slew..Syrians..40,000 footmen"

Foreskin

1Sa 18:25 – "an 100 foreskins of the Philistines"
2Sa 3:14 – "an 100 foreskins of the Philistines"

Form

Isa 53:2 – "he hath no form nor comeliness"

Foundation

Rev 21:14 – "wall of the city had 12 foundations"
Rev 21:19 – "The first foundation was jasper"
Rev 21:19 – "the second, sapphire"
Rev 21:19 – "the third, a chalcedony"
Rev 21:19 – "the fourth, an emerald"
Rev 21:20 – "The fifth, sadonyx"
Rev 21:20 – "the sixth, sardius"
Rev 21:20 – "the seventh, chrysolyte"
Rev 21:20 – "the eighth, beryl"
Rev 21:20 – "the ninth, a topaz"
Rev 21:20 – "the tenth, a chrysoprasus"
Rev 21:20 – "the eleventh, a jacinth"
Rev 21:20 – "the twelfth, an amethyst"

Fountain

Num 33:9 – "in Elim were 12 fountains of water"
Pro 8:24 – "when there were no fountains"
Jas 3:12 – "no fountain both yield salt..fresh"

Fowl

Gen 7:3 – "fowls also of the air by sevens"
Job 28:7 – "a path which no fowl knoweth"

Fox

Jdg 15:4 – "Samson went and caught 300 foxes"

Friend

Gen 26:26 – "Ahuzzath one of his friends"
Job 2:11 – "Now when Job's three friends heard"
Job 32:3 – "against his 3 friends..wrath kindled"
Job 42:7 – "My wrath..against thee..thy 2 friends"
Pro 14:20 – "but the rich hath many friends"
Pro 19:4 – "Wealth maketh many friends

Friendship

Pro 22:24 – "no friendship with an angry man"

Fruit

> ➢ *See also* **Firstfruit** *under number* **One**

Deu 26:2 – "the first of all the fruit of the earth"
Exo 22:29 – "offer the first of thy ripe fruits"
Hos 9:16 – "Ephraim..shall bear no fruit"
Mat 21:19 – "Let no fruit grow on thee"
Mar 4:7 – "choked it..yielded no fruit"
Luk 8:14 – "bring no fruit to perfection"
Luk 13:6 – "sought fruit thereon..found none"
Luk 13:7 – "seeking fruit..and find none"
Rev 22:2 – "tree of life..12 manner of fruits"

Fuller

Mar 9:3 – "as no fuller on earth can white"

Furlong

Luk 24:13 – "Emmaus..Jerusalem..60 furlongs"
Joh 6:19 – "rowed about 25 or 30 furlongs"
Joh 11:18 – "Bethany..unto Jerusalem..15 furlongs"
Rev 14:20 – "blood..space of 1600 furlongs"
Rev 21:16 – "measured the city..12,000 furlongs"

Furrow

Hos 10:10 – "bind themselves in their 2 furrows"

Gain

Jdg 5:19 – "they took no gain of money"

Galley

Isa 33:21 – "shall go no galley with oars"

Garment

Ezr 2:69 – "They gave..100 priests' garments"
Neh 7:70 – "gave..treasure..530 priests' garments"
Neh 7:72 – "people gave..67 priests garments"

Gate

Deu 23:16 – "He shall dwell..in one of thy gates"
2Sa 18:24 – "David sat between the two gates"
Isa 45:1 – "open before him the two leaved gates"
Ezk 40:21 – "arches..after the measure of..1st gate"
Ezk 48:31 – "three gates northward"
Ezk 48:31 – "one gate of Reuben"
Ezk 48:31 – "one gate of Judah"
Ezk 48:31 – "one gate of Levi"
Ezk 48:32 – "east side..and three gates"
Ezk 48:32 – "one gate of Joseph"
Ezk 48:32 – "one gate of Benjamin"
Ezk 48:32 – "one gate of Dan"
Ezk 48:33 – "south side..and three gates"
Ezk 48:33 – "one gate of Simeon"
Ezk 48:33 – "one gate of Issachar"
Ezk 48:33 – "one gate of Zebulun"
Ezk 48:34 – "west side..with their three gates"
Ezk 48:34 – "one gate of Gad"
Ezk 48:34 – "one gate of Asher"
Ezk 48:34 – "one gate of Naphtali"
Zep 1:10 – "cry from ..fish gate..howling from..2nd"
Zec 14:10 – "the place of the first gate"
Rev 21:13 – "On the east three gates"
Rev 21:13 – "on the north three gates"
Rev 21:13 – "on the south three gates"
Rev 21:13 – "on the west three gates"
Rev 21:12 – "a wall..had twelve gates"
Rev 21:21 – "And the 12 gates were 12 pearls"

Gathering

1Co 16:2 – "be no gatherings when I come"

Generation

Gen 15:16 – "in..4th generation they shall come"
Gen 50:23 – "Ephraim's children of..3rd generation"
Exo 20:5 – "visiting..iniquity..the 3rd..generation"
Exo 20:5 – "visiting..iniquity..the 4th..generation"
Exo 34:7 – "visiting the inquity..unto the third"
Exo 34:7 – "visiting..inquity.. to the 4th generation"
Num 14:18 – "visiting..iniquity..3rd..4th generation"
Deu 5:9 – "visiting..iniquity..3rd and 4th generation"
Deu 7:9 – "commandments to a 1000 generations"
Deu 23:2 – "bastard..not enter..to..10th generation"
Deu 23:3 – "Ammonite..Moabite..10th generation"
Deu 23:8 – "shall enter..in their 3rd generation"
Deu 32:7 – "the years of many generations"
2Ki 10:30 – "4th generation shall sit..throne"

2Ki 15:12 – "sons..sit..throne..unto..4th generation"
1Ch 16:15 – "word..to a 1000 generations"
Job 42:16 – "Job..saw..even four generations"
Psa 61:6 – "his years as many generations"
Psa 105:8 – "word.. to 1000 generations"
Psa 145:4 – "1 generation shall praise thy works"
Ecc 1:4 – "One generation passeth away"
Isa 58:12 – "foundations of many generations"
Isa 60:15 – "a joy of many generations"
Isa 61:4 – "desolations of many generations"
Joe 2:2 – "the years of many generations"
Mat 1:17 – "Abraham to David are 14 generations"
Mat 1:17 – "David..into Babylon..14 generations"
Mat 1:17 – "Babylon unto Christ..14 generations"

Gentile

Mar 10:42 – "Gentiles..their great ones exercise"

Gerah

Exo 30:13 – "a shekel is twenty gerahs"
Ezk 45:12 – "the shekel shall be twenty gerahs"
Lev 27:25 – "twenty gerahs shall be the shekel"
Num 3:47 – "the shekel is twenty gerahs"
Num 18:16 – "shekel..which is twenty gerahs"

Gift

Exo 23:8 – "And thou shalt take no gift"
Pro 6:35 – "though thou givest many gifts"
Dan 2:48 – "gave him many great gifts"
1Co 1:7 – "come behind in no gift"

Gilead

Jos 12:5 – "And reigned..half Gilead"
Jos 13:31 – "And half Gilead, and Ashtaroth"

Gin

Amo 3:5 – "Can a bird fall..where no gin is"

Glory

Hag 2:3 – "saw this house in her first glory?"
1Co 15:40 – "the glory of the celestial is one"
1Co 15:41 – "There is one glory of the sun"
2Co 3:10 – "had no glory in this respect"

Goats

Gen 30:33 – "every one that is not speckled..spotted"
Gen 30:35 – "every one that had some white in it"
Gen 32:14 – "200 she goats, and 20 he goats"
Lev 16:7 – "2 goats & present..before the LORD"
Lev 16:8 – "Aaron shall cast lots upon the 2 goats"
Num 7:17 – "five he goats..offering of Nahshon"
Num 7:23 – "five he goats..offering of Nethaneel"
Num 7:29 – "five he goats..offering of Eliab"
Num 7:35 – "five he goats..offering of Elizur"
Num 7:41 – "five he goats..offering of Shelumiel"
Num 7:47 – "five he goats..offering of Eliasaph"
Num 7:53 – "five he goats..offering of Elishama"
Num 7:59 – "five he goats..offering of Gamaliel"
Num 7:65 – "five he goats..offering of Abidan"
Num 7:71 – "five he goats..offering of Ahiezer"
Num 7:77 – "five he goats..offering of Pagiel"
Num 7:83 – "five he goats..offering of Ahira"
Num 7:88 – the he goats sixty"
Num 18:17 – "firstling of a goat..shalt not redeem"
Num 28:22 – "one goat for a sin offering"
Num 28:30 – "1 kid of the goats..make atonement"
Num 29:11 – "1 kid of the goats for a sin offering"
Num 29:16 – "1 kid of the goats for a sin offering"
Num 29:19 – "1 kid of the goats for a sin offering"
Num 29:22 – "one goat for a sin offering"
Num 29:25 – "1 kid of the goats for a sin offering"
Num 29:28 – "one goat for a sin offering"
Num 29:31 – "one goat for a sin offering"
Num 29:34 – " one goat for a sin offering"
Num 29:38 – "one goat for a sin offering"
2Ch 17:11 – "Arabians brought..7,700 he goats"
2Ch 29:21 – "brought..7 he goats..for a sin offering"
Ezr 6:17 – "offered at the dedication..12 he goats"
Ezr 8:35 – "burnt offerings..12 he goats"

God

1Ki 8:23 – "there is no God like thee"
2Ki 1:16 – "because there is no God in Israel"
2Ki 5:15 – "there is no God in all the earth"
2Ch 6:14 – "there is no God like thee"
Psa 14:1 – " The fool..said..There is no God"
Psa 53:1 – "fool hath said..There is no God"
Isa 43:10 – "before me there was no God"
Isa 44:6 – "beside me there is no God"
Isa 44:8 – "yea, there is no God"
Isa 45:5 – "there is no God beside me"
Isa 45:14 – "is none else, there is no God"
Isa 45:21 – "there is no God else beside me"
Eze 28:9- "thou shalt be a man, and no God"
Dan 3:29 – "no other God that can deliver"
Mal 2:10 – "hath not one God created us?"
Mar 12:32 – "for there is one God"
Rom 3:30 – "it is one God, which shall justify"
1Co 8:4 – "there is none other God but one"
1Co 8:6 – "to us there is but one God"
Eph 4:6 – "One God and Father of all"

1Ti 2:5 – "For there is one God"
Jam 2:19 – "believest that there is one God"

Gods *(as in False Gods)*

Exo 20:3 – "no other gods before me"
Exo 23:13 – "make no mention of..other gods"
Exo 34:14 – "thou shalt worship no other god"
Exo 34:17 – "shalt make thee no molten gods"
Deu 5:7 – "none other gods before me"
Deu 32:12 – "was no strange god with him"
Deu 32:39 – "there is no god with me"
2Ki 19:18 – "for they were no gods"
2Ch 32:15 – "no god.. able to deliver his people"
Psa 81:9 – "no strange god be in thee"
Isa 37:19 – "for they were no gods"
Isa 43:12 – "there was no strange god among you"
Jer 2:11 – "gods, which are yet no gods?"
Jer 5:7 – "sworn by them that are no gods"
Jer 16:20 – "gods..they are no gods?"
Hos 13:4 – "know no god but me"
Act 19:26 – "they be no gods..made with hands"

Gold *(See Pieces, Talents & Shekels)*

2Sa 21:4 – "have no silver nor gold of Saul"
1Ch 22:16 – "Of the gold..there is no number"
Psa 119:72 – "law.. better..than 1000's of gold"
Act 3:6 – "Silver and gold have I none"

Good *(As in Benefit or Righteousness)*

1Ki 22:18 – "prophesy no good concerning me"
Job 9:25 – "days..flee away, they see no good"
Job 9:25 – "days..flee away, they see no good"
Pro 17:20 – "a froward heart findeth no good"
Ecc 3:12 – "there is no good in them"
Ecc 6:6 – "yet hath he seen no good"
Jer 8:15 – "looked for peace, but no good"
Jer 14:19 – "peace, and there is no good"

Goods *(As in Belongings)*

Luk 19:8 – "the half of my goods..to the poor"

Grape

Jer 8:13 – "there shall be no grapes on the vine"

Grass

Jer 14:5 – "because there was no grass"
Jer 14:6 – "because there was no grass"

Grave

Exo 14:11 – "no graves in Egypt"

Greatness

2Ch 9:6 – "the ½ of the greatness of thy wisdom"

Grief

1Sa 25:31 – "this shall be no grief unto thee"

Grinder

Ecc 12:3 – "grinders cease because they are few"

Guide

Pro 6:7 – "having no guide, overseer, or ruler"

Guile

Psa 32:2 – "in whose spirit there is no guile"
Joh 1:47 – "an Israelite..in whom is no guile!"
1Pe 3:10 – "his lips that they speak no guile"
Rev 14:5 – "in their mouth was found no guile"

Hail

Exo 9:26 – "was there no hail"

Hair

Lev 13:21 – "there be no white hairs therein"
Lev 13:26 – "there be no white hair"
Lev 13:31 – "there is no black hair in it"
Lev 13:32 – "there be in it no yellow hair"
1Sa 14:45 – "not 1 hair of his head fall to..ground"
2Sa 14:11 – "not one hair of thy son shall fall"
Ezk 5:2 – "burn..third part in the midst of the city"
Ezk 5:2 – "third part..smith about it with a knife"
Ezk 5:2 – "third part..scatter in the wind"
Ezk 5:3 – "take thereof a few in number"
Mat 5:36 – "canst not make 1 hair white or black"

Hand

Gen 37:22 – "lay no hand upon him"
Gen 41:44 – "shall no man lift up his hand"
Deu 9:15 – "two tables..were in my two hands"
Deu 9:17 – "2 tables..cast them out of my 2 hands"
Neh 4:17 – "one of his hands wrought in the work"
Isa 45:9 – "He hath no hands?"
Lam 4:6 – "no hands stayed on her"
Mat 18:8 – "two hands or two feet..cast..fire"
Mar 9:43 – "having two hands to go into hell"
Luk 22:53 – "stretched forth no hands"

Handmaid

Gen 33:1 – "Esau came..unto the two handmaids"

Handmaidens

Rut 2:13 – "like unto one of thine handmaidens"

Harlot

Gen 38:21 – "There was no harlot in this place"
Gen 38:22 – "there was no harlot in this place"

Harm

2Ki 4:41 – "there was no harm in the pot"
1Ch 16:22 – "do my prophets no harm"
Psa 105:15 – "do my prophets no harm"
Pro 3:30 – "if he have done thee no harm"
Jer 39:12 – "and do him no harm"
Act 16:28 – "Do thyself no harm"
Act 28:5 – "shook off the beast..felt no harm"
Act 28:6 – "saw no harm come to him"

Head

Gen 2:10 – "river..Eden..became into four heads"
1Ch 12:32 – "Issachar...heads of them were 200"
Dan 7:6 – "leopard..the beast had also four heads"
Hos 1:11 – "appoint themselves one head"
Rev 12:3 – "great red dragon, having 7 heads"
Rev 13:1 – "beast..having seven heads"
Rev 13:3 – "one of his heads..wounded to death"
Rev 17:3 – "beast..having 7 heads and 10 horns"
Rev 17:7 – "beast..hath..7 heads and ten horns"
Rev 17:9 – "the 7 heads are 7 mountains"

Healing

Jer 14:19 – "there is no healing for us?"
Nah 3:19 – "is no healing of thy bruise"

Heap

2Ki 10:8 – 70 heads – "Lay ye them in two heaps"

Heart

1Sa 17:32 – "Let no man's heart fail"
1Ch 12:33 – "Zebulun..were not of double heart"
1Ch 12:38 – "all the rest of Israel were of 1 heart"
2Ch 30:12 – "one heart to do the commandments"
Psa 12:2 – "with a double heart to they speak"
Pro 17:16 – "seeing he hath no heart to it"
Jer 32:39 – "And I will give them one heart"
Ezk 11:19 – "I will give them one heart"
Luk 2:35 – "thoughts of many hearts..revealed"
Act 4:32 – "were of one heart and of one soul"

Heat

1Ki 1:1 – "but he gat no heat"

Heaven

2Co 12:2 – "caught up to the third heaven"
Rev 21:1 – "1st heaven and..1st earth passed away"

Heed

2Sa 20:10 – "Amasa took no heed to the sword"
2Ki 10:31 – "Jehu took no heed to walk"
Ecc 7:21 – "take no heed unto all words"

Help

Psa 3:2 – "There is no help for him in God"
Psa 146:3 – "man, in whom there is no help"

Helper

Job 30:13 – "they have no helper"
Psa 72:12 – "him that hath no helper"

Herd

Deu 12:6 – "firstlings of your herds and..flocks"

Deu 12:17 – "the firstlings of thy herds or..flock"
Deu 14:23 – "the firstlings of thy herds and..flocks"
2Sa 12:2 – "exceeding many flocks and herds"
Neh 10:36 – "firstlings of our herds and..flocks"
Hab 3:17 – "shall be no herd in the stalls"

Hill

Psa 50:10 – "cattle upon a 1000 hills"

Hin

Num 15:9 – "flour mingled with half an hin of oil"
Num 15:10 – "drink offering half an hin of wine"
Num 28:14 – "half an hin of wine unto a bullock"
Num 28:14 – "third part of an hin unto a ram"
Num 28:14 – "fourth part of an hin unto a lamb"
Ezk 4:11 – "water by measure..sixth part of an hin"

Hire

Eze 16:41 – "shalt give no hire any more"
Zec 8:10 – "there was no hire for man"

Hold

Mat 26:55 – "and ye laid no hold on me"

Homer

Num 11:32 – "gathered least..ten homers"
Hos 3:2 – "homer of barley..½ homer of barley"

Honour

Joh 4:44 – "a prophet hath no honour"
Act 28:10 – "honoured us with many honours"
1Ti 5:17 – "elders that rule well..double honour"

Hope

Isa 57:10 – "There is no hope"
Jer 2:25 – "There is no hope"
Jer 18:12 – "There is no hope"
Eph 2:12 – "having no hope, and without God"
Eph 4:4 – "one hope of your calling"
1Th 4:13 – "as others which have no hope"

Horn

Ezk 43:15 – "altar and upward shall be 4 horns"
Ezk 43:20 – "blood..put it on the four horns"
Dan 7:7 – "fourth beast..it had ten horns"
Dan 7:8 – "three of the first horns plucked up"
Dan 7:8 – "three of the first horns plucked up"
Dan 7:20 – "the ten horns that were in his head"
Dan 7:20 – "before whom three fell"
Dan 7:24 – "ten horns..are ten kings"
Dan 8:3 – "a ram which had two horns"
Dan 8:3 – "the two horns were high"
Dan 8:3 – "horns were high; but one was higher"
Dan 8:6 – "he came to the ram that had two horns"
Dan 8:7 – "moved with choler..brake his 2 horns"
Dan 8:8 – "horn..broken..came up 4 notable ones"
Dan 8:9 – "out of one of them came..little horn"
Dan 8:20 – "ram..having two horns..kings"
Dan 8:22 – "whereas four stood up for it"
Zec 1:18 – "and saw, and behold four horns"
Rev 5:6 – "Lamb as..slain, having 7 horns"
Rev 9:13 – "voice from the four horns..altar"
Rev 12:3 – "red dragon, having..ten horns"
Rev 13:1 – "beast rise up..having..ten horns"
Rev 13:11 – "another beast..two horns like..lamb"
Rev 17:3 – "beast..having 7 heads and 10 horns"
Rev 17:7 – "beast..hath..7 heads and ten horns"
Rev 17:12 – "the ten horns..are ten kings"
Rev 17:16 – "the ten horns..hate the whore"

Horse

Jos 11:4 – "horses and chariots very many"
2Ki 7:13 – "five of the horses that remain"
2Ki 7:14 – "They took..two chariot horses"
2Ki 18:23 – "I will deliver thee 2000 horses"
Ezr 2:66 – "Their horses *were* 736"
Neh 7:68 – "Their horses, 736"
Isa 36:8 – "I will give thee 2000 horses"
Rev 9:9 – "sound..many horses running"

Horseman

1Sa 13:5 – "Philistines...6000 horsemen"
2Sa 8:4 – "700 horsemen and 20,000 footmen"
2Sa 10:18 – "David slew...40,000 horsemen"
1Ki 4:26 – "Solomon had..12,000 horsemen"
1Ki 10:26 – "Solomon..had..12,000 horsemen"
2Ki 13:7 – "50 horsemen, and 10 chariots"
1Ch 18:14 – "David took..7000 horsemen"
2Ch 1:14 – "Solomon..had..12,000 horsemen"
2Ch 9:25 – "Solomon had..12,000 horsemen"
2Ch 12:3 – "1200 chariots & 60,000 horsemen"
2Ch 16:8 – "very many chariots and horsemen"
Isa 21:7 – "a chariot with a couple of horsemen"
Isa 21:9 – "a couple of horsemen"
Act 23:23 – "to Caesarea, and horsemen 70"

Host

Jer 33:22 – "host of heaven cannot be numbered"

Hour

Dan 4:19 – "Daniel..was astonied for one hour"
Mat 20:3 – "he went out about the third hour"
Mat 20:5 – "he went out about the 6th and 9th hour"
Mat 20:6 – "about the 11th hour he went out"
Mat 20:9 – "were hired about the 11th hour"
Mat 20:12 – "have wrought but one hour"
Mat 26:40 – "could ye not watch..one hour?"
Mat 27:45 – "from the sixth hour..darkness"
Mat 27:45 – "over all the land unto the ninth hour"
Mat 27:46 – "about the ninth hour Jesus cried"
Mar 14:37 – "couldest..not watch one hour?"
Mar 15:25 – "it was the 3rd hour..crucified him"
Mar 15:33 – "sixth hour was come..darkness"
Mar 15:33 – "darkness..whole land..9th hour"
Mar 15:34 – "ninth hour Jesus cried"
Luk 22:59 – "about the space of one hour after"
Luk 23:44 – "it was about the sixth hour"
Luk 23:44 – "darkness over..earth..until 9th hour"
Joh 1:39 – "for it was about the tenth hour"
Joh 4:6 – "and it was about the sixth hour"
Joh 4:52 – "at the 7th hour the fever left him"
Joh 11:9 – "Are there not 12 hours in the day?"
Joh 19:14 – "preparation of the passover..6th hour"
Act 2:15 – "not drunken..but the third hour"
Act 3:1 – "the hour of prayer, being the 9th hour"
Act 5:7 – "about the space of three hours"
Act 10:3 – "in a vision..about the 9th hour"
Act 10:9 – "to pray about the 6th hour"
Act 10:30 – "at the 9th hour I prayed in my house"
Act 19:34 – "the space of two hours cried out"
Act 23:23 – "to go to Caesarea..at the third hour"
Rev 8:1 – "silence in heaven..space of ½ an hour"
Rev 17:12 – "receive power as kings one hour"
Rev 18:10 – "in one hour is thy judgment come"
Rev 18:17 – "in one hour..riches..come to nought"
Rev 18:19 – "in one hour is she made desolate"

House

Exo 12:46 – "In one house shall it be eaten"
1Ki 3:2 – "there was no house built"
1Ki 3:17 – "I and this woman dwell in one house"
1Ki 9:10 – "when Solomon had built the 2 houses"
1Ki 13:8 – "If thou will give me half thine house"
Ezr 3:12 – "1st house, when..foundation..was laid"
Est 2:14 – "she returned into the second house"
Isa 5:9 – "many houses shall be desolate"
Isa 23:1 – "so that there is no house"
Amo 6:9 – "ten men in one house"
Luk 12:52 – "shall be five in one house divided"

Household

1Ch 24:6 – "one principal household..for Eleazar"
1Ch 24:6 – "one taken for Ithamar"

Hunter

Jer 16:16 – "will I send for many hunters"

Hurt

Gen 26:29 – "That thou wilt do us no hurt"
1Sa 20:21 – "peace to thee, and no hurt"
Jer 25:6 – "I will do you no hurt"
Dan 3:25 – "four men..they have no hurt"
Dan 6:22 – "O king, have I done no hurt"

Husband

Lev 21:3 – "sister..which hath had no husband"
Hos 2:7 – "I will go and return to my first husband"
Joh 4:17 – "I have no husband"
Joh 4:17 – "I have no husband"
Joh 4:18 – "thou hast had five husbands"
2Co 11:2 – "I have espoused you to one husband"

Idol

Lev 26:1 – "Ye shall make you no idols"

Ill

Rom 13:10 – "Love worketh no ill"

Incense

Exo 30:9 – "offer no strange incense"
Jer 44:5 – "burn no incense unto..gods"

Inhabitant

1Ch 9:2 – "first inhabitants..the priests, Levites"
Zep 2:5 – "there shall be no inhabitant"

Inheritance

Num 18:20 – "Thou shalt have no inheritance"
Num 18:23 – "Levites..have no inheritance"
Num 18:24 – "Levites..have no inheritance"
Num 26:62 – "there was no inheritance given"

Deu 10:9 – "Levi hath no part nor inheritance"
Deu 12:12 – "no part nor inheritance with you"
Deu 14:27 – "Levite..hath no part nor inheritance"
Deu 14:29 – "Levite..hath no part nor inheritance"
Deu 18:1 – "Levi..no part nor inheritance"
Deu 18:2 – "no inheritance among..brethren"
Jos 13:14 – "unto..Levi he gave none inheritance"
Jos 14:3 – "he gave none inheritance among them"
2Ch 10:16 – "none inheritance in the son of Jesse"
Act 7:5 – "gave him none inheritance in it"

Iniquity

2Ch 19:7 – "there is no iniquity with the LORD"
Psa 40:12 – "iniquities..more than..hairs of..head"
Psa 119:3 – "They also do no iniquity"
Jer 50:20 – "iniquity..sought..shall be none"
Hos 12:8 – "shall find none iniquity in me"
Zep 3:5 – "LORD..he will not do iniquity"

Instructor

1Co 4:15 – "have 10,000 instructors in Christ"

Intercessor

Isa 59:16 – "there was no intercessor"

Interpreter

Gen 40:8 – "dream, and there is no interpreter"
1Co 14:28 – "if there be no interpreter"

Invention

Ecc 7:29 – "sought out many inventions"

Iron

1Ch 22:14 – "brass and iron without weight"
1Ch 22:16 – "brass..iron, there is no number"

Isle

Ezk 27:3 – "merchant of the people for many isles"
Ezk 27:15 – "many isles were the merchandise"
Dan 11:18 – "the isles, and shall take many"

Issue

Mat 22:25 – "seven brethren.. having no issue"

Jesus

Act 17:7 – "there is another king, one Jesus"
Act 25:19 – "superstitions, and of one Jesus"
1Co 8:6 – "and one Lord Jesus Christ"

Jew

Neh 5:16 – "at my table 150 of the Jews & rulers"
Jer 52:28 – "carried away captive..3,023 Jews"
Joh 11:19 – "And many of the Jews came"
Joh 11:45 – "many of the Jews..came to Mary"
Joh 12:11 – "many of the Jews went away"
Joh 19:20 – "then read many of the Jews"
Act 21:20 – "how many 1000's of Jews..zealous"

Jot

Mat 5:18 – "one jot or one tittle..no wise pass"

Joy

Pro 17:21 – "the father of a fool hath no joy
Isa 9:17 – "LORD shall have no joy"

Judge

1Ch 23:4 – "6,000 were officers and judges"
Act 18:15 – "I will be no judge of such matters"

Judgment

Job 19:7 – "but there is no judgment"
Psa 119:160 – "every 1 of..righteous judgments"
Isa 59:8 – "no judgment in their goings"
Isa 59:11 – "look for judgment, but there is none"
Isa 59:15 – "it displeased him..no judgment"
Ezk 14:21 – "when I send my sore four judgments"

Keeper

2Ki 25:18 – "three keepers of the door"
Jer 52:24 – "captain..took..3 keepers of the door"

Kidney

Exo 29:13 – "the caul..and the two kidneys"
Exo 29:22 – "the caul..and the two kidneys"
Lev 3:4 – "and the two kidneys"
Lev 3:10 – "and the two kidneys"
Lev 3:15 – "and the two kidneys"
Lev 4:9 – "And the two kidneys"
Lev 7:4 – "And the two kidneys"
Lev 8:16 – "the two kidneys, and their fat"
Lev 8:25 – "the two kidneys, and their fat"

Kid

Gen 27:9 – "fetch..two good kids of the goats"
Lev 16:5 – "two kids of the goats...sin offering"
Lev 23:19 – "sacrifice one kid of the goats"
Num 7:16 – "One kid of the goats..sin offering"
Num 7:22 – "One kid of the goats..sin offering"
Num 7:28 – "One kid of the goats..sin offering"
Num 7:34 – "One kid of the goats..sin offering"
Num 7:40 – "One kid of the goats..sin offering"
Num 7:46 – "One kid of the goats..sin offering"
Num 7:52 – "One kid of the goats..sin offering"
Num 7:58 – "One kid of the goats..sin offering"
Num 7:64 – "One kid of the goats..sin offering"
Num 7:70 – "One kid of the goats..sin offering"
Num 7:76 – "One kid of the goats..sin offering"
Num 7:82 – "One kid of the goats..sin offering"
Num 7:87 – "kids..goats for sin offering twelve"
Num 15:24 – "1 kid of the goats for a sin offering"
Num 28:15 – "1 kid of the goats for a sin offering"
Num 28:30 – "1 kid of the goats..make atonement"
Num 29:5 – "one kid of the goats for a sin offering"
Num 29:11 – "1 kid of the goats for a sin offering"
Num 29:16 – "1 kid of the goats for a sin offering"
Num 29:19 – "1 kid of the goats for a sin offering"
Num 29:25 – "1 kid of the goats for a sin offering"
1Sa 10:3 – "one carrying three kids"
1Sa 25:2 – "man in Maon..he had...1000 goats"
2Ch 35:7 – "of the flock, lambs and kids..30,000"

Kind

Jer 15:3 – "I will appoint over them four kinds"
1Co 14:10 – "many kinds of voices in..world"
1Co 15:39 – "one kind of flesh of men"

Kindred

Luk 1:61 – "none of thy kindred..by this name"

Kine

Gen 32:15 – "forty kine , and ten bulls"

Gen 41:2 – "out of the river, 7 well favoured kine"
Gen 41:3 – "7 other kine camp up"
Gen 41:4 – "did eat up the 7 well favoured..kine"
Gen 41:18 – "up out of the river seven kine"
Gen 41:19 – "behold, seven other kine came up"
Gen 41:20 – "did eat up the first seven fat kine"
Gen 41:26 – "the 7 good kine are 7 years"
Gen 41:27 – "7 thin and ill favoured kine..7 years"
1Sa 6:7 – "make a new cart..take two milch kine"
1Sa 6:10 – "the men did so..took two milch kine"

King

Indeterminate or 0 *Kings*

Jdg 17:6 – "there was no king in Israel"
Jdg 18:1 – "there was no king in Israel"
Jdg 19:1 – "there was no king in Israel"
Jdg 21:25 – "there was no king in Israel"
1Ki 22:47 – "There was then no king in Edom"
2Ki 23:25 – "like unto him was there no king"
2Ch 1:12 – "as none of the kings have had"
Neh 13:26 – "Solomon..was there no king like him"
Psa 33:16 – "There is no king saved by..an host"
Pro 30:27 – "The locusts have no king"
Jer 50:41 – "many kings shall be raised up"
Dan 2:10 – "there is no king, lord, nor ruler"
Hos 10:3 – "shall say, We have no king"
Mic 4:9 – "is there no king in thee?"
Luk 10:24 – "many prophets..kings have desired"
Joh 19:15 – "We have no king but Caesar"
Rev 10:11 – "many..tongues..kings"

1 *King*

Jos 12:9 – "The king of Jericho, one"
Jos 12:9 – "king of Ai, which is beside Bethel, one"
Jos 12:10 – "The king of Jerusalem, one"
Jos 12:10 – "the king of Hebron, one"
Jos 12:11 – "The king of Jarmuth, one"
Jos 12:11 – "the king of Lachish, one"
Jos 12:12 – "The king of Eglon, one"
Jos 12:12 – "the king of Gezer, one"
Jos 12:13 – "The king of Debir, one"
Jos 12:13 – "the king of Geder, one"
Jos 12:14 – "The king of Hormah, one"
Jos 12:14 – "the king of Arad, one"
Jos 12:15 – "The king of Libnah, one"
Jos 12:15 – "the king of Adullam, one"
Jos 12:16 – "The king of Makkedah, one"
Jos 12:16 – "the king of Bethel, one"
Jos 12:17 – "The king of Tappuah, one"
Jos 12:17 – "the king of Hepher, one"
Jos 12:18 – "The king of Aphek, one"
Jos 12:18 – "the king of Lasharon, one"
Jos 12:19 – "The king of Madon, one"
Jos 12:19 – "the king of Hazor, one"
Jos 12:20 – "The king of Shimronmeron, one"
Jos 12:20 – "the king of Achshaph, one"

Jos 12:21 – "The king of Taanach, one"
Jos 12:21 – "the king of Megiddo, one"
Jos 12:22 – "The king of Kedesh, one"
Jos 12:22 – "the king of Jokneam of Carmel, one"
Jos 12:23 – "king of Dor in the coast of Dor, one"
Jos 12:23 – "the king of the nations of Gilgal, one"
Jos 12:24 – "The king of Tirzah, one"
Isa 23:15 – "70 years, acc. to the days of one king"
Jer 25:26 – "kings of the north..one with another"
Ezk 37:22 – "one king shall be king to them all"
Dan 7:24 – "he shall be diverse from the first"
Rev 17:10 – "7 kings; 5 are fallen, and one is"

2 *Kings*

Deu 3:8 – "the two kings of the Amorites"
Deu 3:21 – "God hath done unto these two kings"
Deu 4:47 – "land of..two kings of the Amorites"
Jos 2:10 – "what ye did unto..2 kings of..Amorites"
Jos 9:10 – "all that he did to..2 kings of..Amorites"
Jos 24:12 – "two kings of the Amorites"
Jdg 8:12 – "2 kings of Midian, Zebah & Zalmunna"
2Ki 10:4 – "two kings stood not before him"

3 *Kings*

2Ki 3:10 – "LORD hath called..3 kings together"
2Ki 3:13 – "LORD hath called..3 kings together"
Dan 7:24 – "he shall subdue three kings"
Dan 11:2 – "stand up yet three kings in Persia"

4 *Kings*

Gen 14:9 – "four kings with five"
Dan 7:17 – "These great beasts..are four kings"
Dan 11:2 – "the 4th shall be far richer than they all"

5 *Kings*

Gen 14:9 – "four kings with five"
Num 31:8 – "five kings of Midian"
Jos 10:5 – "five kings of the Amorites"
Jos 10:16 – "five kings fled..hid..in a cave"
Jos 10:17 – "five kings are found hid in a cave"
Jos 10:22 – "bring out those five kings unto me"
Jos 10:23 – "brought forth those five kings"
Rev 17:10 – "7 kings; 5 are fallen, and one is"

7+ *Kings*

Jos 12:24 – "all the kings 31"
Jdg 1:7 – "70 kings..thumbs..great toes cut off"
1Ki 20:1 – "Benhadad..gathered..32 kings w/ him"
1Ki 20:16 – "drunk..he and the..32 kings"
Dan 7:24 – "ten horns..are ten kings"
Dan 8:21 – "Grecia..great horn..is the first king"
Rev 17:10 – "7 kings; 5 are fallen, and one is"
Rev 17:11 – "beast..is the 8th, and is of the seven"
Rev 17:12 – "the ten horns..are ten kings"

Kingdom

1Ch 16:20 – "from one kingdom to another people"
Est 5:3 – "given thee to the ½ of the kingdom"
Est 5:6 – "even to the ½ of the kingdom"
Est 7:2 – "even to the ½ of the kingdom"
Psa 105:13 – "from 1 kingdom to another people"
Ezk 37:22 – "no more..divided into two kingdoms"
Dan 2:39 – "another third kingdom of brass"
Dan 2:40 – "4th kingdom shall be strong as iron"
Dan 7:23 – "4th beast shall be the fourth kingdom"
Dan 8:22 – "four kingdoms shall stand up for it"
Mar 6:23 – "unto the half of my kingdom"

Kinsman

Num 5:8 – "But if the man have no kinsman"

Kiss

Luk 7:45 – "Thou gavest me no kiss"

Knee

Dan 5:6 – "his knees smote one against another"

Knife

Ezr 1:9 – "this is the number..29 knives"

Knop

1Ki 7:24 – "knops compassing it, ten in a cubit"

Knowledge

Deu 1:39 – "no knowledge between good..evil"
Psa 14:4 – "workers of iniquity no knowledge"
Psa 53:4 – "workers of iniquity no knowledge"
Ecc 9:10 – "no..knowledge..in the grave"
Isa 5:13 – "because they have no knowledge"
Isa 45:20 – "they have no knowledge"
Isa 58:3 – "thou takest no knowledge?"
Jer 4:22 – "to do good they have no knowledge"
Hos 4:1 – "no..knowledge of God in the land"

Labour

Joh 4:38 – "whereon ye bestowed no labour"

Labourer

Mat 9:37 – "but the labourers are few"
Luk 10:2 – "but the labourers are few"

Lack

Exo 16:18 – "he that gathered little had no lack"
2Co 8:15 – "had gathered little had no lack"

Lamb

1 *Lamb*

Exo 29:39 – "one lamb..offer in the morning"
Exo 29:40 – "with the one lamb..flour..oil..wine"
Lev 14:10 – "and one ewe lamb"
Lev 14:12 – "one he lamb"
Lev 14:21 – "one lamb for a trespass offering"
Num 6:14 – "one he lamb..burnt offering"
Num 6:14 – "one ewe lamb...for a sin offering"
Num 7:15 – "one lamb of the first year"
Num 7:21 – "one lamb of the first year"
Num 7:27 – "one lamb of the first year"
Num 7:33 – "one lamb of the first year"
Num 7:39 – "one lamb of the first year"
Num 7:45 – "one lamb of the first year"
Num 7:51 – "one lamb of the first year"
Num 7:57 – "one lamb of the first year"
Num 7:63 – "one lamb of the first year"
Num 7:69 – "one lamb of the first year"
Num 7:75 – "one lamb of the first year"
Num 7:81 – "one lamb of the first year"
Num 15:5 – "wine for a drink offering..for 1 lamb"
Num 28:4 – "one lamb shalt thou offer..morning"
Num 28:7 – "fourth part of an hin for the 1 lamb"
Num 28:13 – "flour..oil..unto one lamb"
Num 28:29 – "several tenth deal unto one lamb"
Num 29:4 – "one tenth deal for one lamb"
Num 29:10 – "A several tenth deal for one lamb"
2Sa 12:3 – "nothing, save one little ewe lamb"
Ezk 45:15 – "one lamb out of..two hundred"

2 *Lambs*

Exo 29:38 – "offer..two lambs of the first year"
Lev 14:10 – "he shall take two he lambs"
Lev 23:19 – "two lambs of the first year"
Lev 23:20 – "with the two lambs"
Num 28:3 – "two lambs of the first year"
Num 28:9 – "two lambs of the first year"
Son 4:2 – "sheep..every one bear twins"
Son 6:6 – "sheep..every one beareth twins"

5 *Lambs*

Num 7:17 – "five lambs of the first year"

Num 7:23 – "five lambs of the first year"
Num 7:29 – "five lambs of the first year"
Num 7:35 – "five lambs of the first year"
Num 7:41 – "five lambs of the first year"
Num 7:47 – "five lambs of the first year"
Num 7:53 – "five lambs of the first year"
Num 7:59 – "five lambs of the first year"
Num 7:65 – "five lambs of the first year"
Num 7:71 – "five lambs of the first year"
Num 7:77 – "five lambs of the first year"
Num 7:83 – "five lambs of the first year"

6 *Lambs*

Ezk 46:4 – "burnt offering..shall be six lambs"
Ezk 46:6 – "day of the new moon..six lambs"

7 *Lambs*

Gen 21:28 – "Abraham set 7 ewe lambs"
Gen 21:29 – "What mean these 7 ewe lambs"
Gen 21:30 – "For these 7 ewe lambs..a witness"
Lev 23:18 – "offer with the bread seven lambs"
Num 28:11 – "one ram, 7 lambs of the first year"
Num 28:19 – "seven lambs of the first year"
Num 28:21 – "throughout the seven lambs"
Num 28:27 – "offering...7 lambs of the first year"
Num 28:29 – "throughout the seven lambs"
Num 29:2 – "7 lambs of the first year w/o blemish"
Num 29:4 – "throughout the seven lambs"
Num 29:8 – "seven lambs of the first year"
Num 29:10 – "throughout the seven lambs"
Num 29:36 – "7 lambs of the 1st year w/o blemish"
2Ch 29:21 – "brought..7 lambs..for a sin offering"

8-99 *Lambs*

Num 7:87 – "the lambs of the first year twelve"
Num 7:88 – the lambs of the first year sixty"
Num 29:13 – "fourteen lambs of the first year"
Num 29:15 – "tenth deal to each..of the 14 lambs"
Num 29:17 – "14 lambs of the 1st year w/o spot"
Num 29:20 – "14 lambs of..1st year w/o blemish"
Num 29:23 – "14 lambs of..1st year w/o blemish"
Num 29:26 – "14 lambs of the 1st year w/o spot"
Num 29:29 – "14 lambs of..1st year w/o blemish"
Num 29:32 – "14 lambs of..1st year w/o blemish"
Ezr 8:35 – "burnt offerings..77 lambs"

100+ *Lambs*

2Ki 3:4 – "Mesha..rendered..100,000 lambs"
1Ch 29:21 – "sacrificed..1000 lambs"
2Ch 29:32 – "congregation brought..200 lambs"
2Ch 35:7 – "of the flock, lambs and kids..30,000"
Ezr 6:17 – "offered at the dedication..100 lambs"
Psa 144:13 – "our sheep may bring forth 1000's"
Psa 144:13 – "our sheep may bring forth..10,000's"

Lamentation

Psa 78:64 – "widows made no lamentation"

Lamp

Exo 25:37 – "thou shalt make the 7 lamps thereof"
Exo 37:23 – "he made his seven lamps..snuffers"
Num 8:2 – "seven lamps shall give light"
Zec 4:2 – "candlestick..his seven lamps thereon"
Zec 4:2 – "seven pipes to the seven lamps"
Rev 4:5 – "7 lamps of fire..are the 7 Spirits"

Land

Jos 13:25 – "½ the land of the children of Ammon"
Ezk 21:19 – "shall come forth out of one land"

Language

Gen 11:1 – "whole earth was of one language"
Gen 11:6 – "they have all one language"
Psa 19:3 – "There is no speech nor language"

Laver

1Ki 7:38 – "Then made he ten lavers of brass"
1Ki 7:38 – "upon every 1 of the 10 bases 1 laver"
1Ki 7:43 – "10 bases, and 10 lavers on the bases"
1Ki 7:38 – "one laver contained forty baths"
2Ch 4:6 – "He made also ten lavers"
2Ch 4:6 – "put 5 on the right hand..5 on the left"

Law

> ➢ **Deuteronomy** = *second law*

Exo 12:49 – "One law..homeborn, and..stranger"
Lev 7:7 – "offering..there is one law for them"
Num 15:16 – "1 law and 1 manner shall be for you"
Num 15:29 – "one law for him that sinneth"
Est 4:11 – "there is one law..to put him to death"
Rom 5:13 – "when there is no law"
Gal 5:23 – "against such there is no law"

Lawgiver

Jam 4:12 – "There is one lawgiver"

Lawyer

Luk 11:45 – "answered one of the lawyers"

League

Jdg 2:2 – "And ye shall make no league"

Leaven

Exo 12:19 – "no leaven found in your houses"
Lev 2:11 – "ye shall burn no leaven"

Leaf

1Ki 6:34 – "2 leaves of the one door were folding"
1Ki 6:34 – "2 leaves of..other door were folding"
Jer 36:23 – "when Jehudi had read 3 or 4 leaves"
Ezk 41:24 – "the doors had two leaves apiece"
Ezk 41:24 – "the doors had..two turning leaves"
Ezk 41:24 – "two leaves for the one door"
Ezk 41:24 – "two leaves for the other door"

Leg

Amo 3:12 – "out of the mouth of the lion two legs"

Legion

Mat 26:53 – "more than twelve legions of angels?"

Leisure

Mar 6:31 – "no leisure so much as to eat"

Leper

Luk 4:27 – "lepers..none of them was cleansed"
Luk 4:27 – "many lepers were in Israel"
Luk 17:12 – "ten men that were lepers"
Luk 17:15 – "And one of them..was healed"
Luk 17:17 – "Were there not ten cleansed?"
Luk 17:17 – "but where are the nine?"

Letter

Neh 6:17 – "nobles of Judah sent many letters"
Est 9:29 – "to confirm this 2nd letter of Purim"

Levite

1Ch 9:31 – "Mattithiah, one of the Levites"
1Ch 26:17 – "Eastward were six Levites"
Ezr 3:12 – "many of the priests and Levites"
Neh 7:43 – "Levites: the children of Jeshua..74"
Neh 11:18 – "All the Levites in..holy city were 284"

Lie

1Jn 2:21 – "that no lie is of the truth"
1Jn 2:27 – "is truth, and is no lie"

Life

Joh 6:53 – "ye have no life in you"

Light

Gen 1:16 – "God made two great lights"
Isa 8:20 – "because there is no light in them"
Isa 30:26 – "the light of the sun shall be sevenfold"
Isa 50:10 – "walketh in darkness..hath no light"
Jer 4:23 – "heavens, and they had no light"
Joh 11:10 – "because there is no light in him"
Act 20:8 – "many lights in the upper chamber"

Likeness

Ezk 10:10 – "they four had one likeness"

Lily

Mat 6:29 – "not arrayed like one of these"

Line

2Sa 8:2 – "w/ 2 lines measured he to put to death"
2Sa 8:2 – "with one full line to keep alive"

Lion

1Ki 10:19 – "two lions stood beside the stays"
1Ki 10:20 – "12 lions stood there on..the six steps"
2Ch 9:18 – "two lions standing by the stays"
2Ch 9:19 – "12 lions stood there on the one side"
Isa 35:9 – "No lion shall be there"

Loaf

Exo 29:23 – "one loaf of bread"
Lev 23:17 – "two wave loaves"
1Sa 10:3 – "another carrying 3 loaves of bread"
1Sa 10:4 – "will salute thee..give thee two loaves"
1Sa 17:17 – "Take..for thy brethren..teb loaves"
1Sa 21:3 – "give me five loaves of bread"
1Sa 25:18 – "Abigail..took 200 loaves"
2Sa 16:1 – "Ziba..met him, w/..200 loaves of bread"
1Ki 14:3 – "take with thee 10 loaves and cracknels"
2Ki 4:42 – "brought..man of God..20 loaves..barley"
Mat 14:17 – "five loaves, and two fishes"
Mat 14:19 – "five loaves, and two fishes"
Mat 15:34 – "how many loaves..Seven"
Mat 15:36 – "he took the seven loaves"
Mat 16:9 – "five loaves of the five thousand"
Mat 16:10 – "seven loaves of the four thousand"
Mar 6:38 – "How many loaves..Five, and 2 fishes"
Mar 6:41 – "taken the 5 loaves and the 2 fishes"
Mar 8:5 – "How many loaves have ye?..Seven"
Mar 8:6 – "he took the 7 loaves..gave thanks"
Mar 8:14 – "neither..in the ship..one loaf"
Mar 8:19 – "When I brake the five loaves"
Mar 8:20 – "when the seven among 4,000"
Luk 9:13 – "We have..but 5 loaves..2 fishes"
Luk 9:16 – "he took the 5 loaves and the 2 fishes"
Luk 11:5 – "Friend, lend me three loaves"
Luk 11:8 – "give him as many as he needeth"
Joh 6:9 – "lad here, which hath five barley loaves"
Joh 6:13 – "fragments of the five barley loaves"

Lock

Jdg 16:13 – "weavest the 7 locks of my head"
Jdg 16:19 – "shave off the 7 locks of his head"

Locust

Exo 10:19 – "remained not one locust"
Psa 105:34 – "locusts..caterpillars..w/o number"

Loft

Act 20:9 – "fell down from the third loft..dead"

Log

Lev 14:10 – "one log of oil"

Loop

Exo 26:5 – "Fifty loops..make in the one curtain"
Exo 26:5 – "fifty loops..in the edge of the curtain"

Exo 26:10 – "50 loops on the edge of the 1 curtain"
Exo 26:10 – "50 loops in the edge of the curtain"
Exo 36:12 – "Fifty loops made he in one curtain"
Exo 36:12 – "fifty loops..in the edge of the curtain"
Exo 36:17 – "fifty loops upon..edge of the curtain"
Exo 36:17 – "fifty loops made he upon the edge"

Lord

Deu 6:4 – "the LORD our God is one LORD"
Jos 13:3 – "five lords of the Philistines"
Jdg 3:3 – "five lords of the Philistines"
1Sa 6:16 – "five lords of the Philistines"
1Sa 6:18 – "cities of the Philistines..five lords"
Dan 2:10 – "there is no king, lord, nor ruler"
Dan 5:1 – "Belshazzar..feast to a 1000 of his lords"
Dan 5:1 – "drank wine before the 1000"
Zec 14:9 – "one LORD, and his name one"
Mar 12:29 – "The Lord our God is one Lord"
1Co 8:5 – "there be gods many..lords many"
1Co 8:6 – "and one Lord Jesus Christ"
Eph 4:5 – "One Lord, one faith, one baptism"

Loss

Act 27:22 – "no loss of any man's life"

Lot

Lev 16:8 – "1 lot for..LORD..other..for..scapegoat"
Jos 17:14 – "Why hast thou given me..one lot"
Jos 17:17 – "thou shalt not have one lot only"
Jos 19:1 – "2ⁿᵈ lot..Simeon"
Jos 19:10 – "3ʳᵈ lot..Zebulun"
Jos 19:17 – "4ᵗʰ lot..Issachar"
Jos 19:24 – "5ᵗʰ lot..Asher"
Jos 19:32 – "6ᵗʰ lot..Naphtali"
Jos 19:40 – "7ᵗʰ lot..Dan"
Jos 21:10 – "theirs was the first lot"
1Ch 24:7 – "the first lot came forth to Jehoiarib"
1Ch 24:7 – "the second to Jedaiah"
1Ch 24:8 – "The third to Harim"
1Ch 24:8 – "the fourth to Seorim"
1Ch 24:9 – "The fifth to Malchijah"
1Ch 24:9 – "the sixth to Mijamin"
1Ch 24:10 – "The seventh to Hakkoz"
1Ch 24:10 – "the eighth to Abijah"
1Ch 24:11 – "The ninth to Jeshuah"
1Ch 24:11 – "the tenth to Shechaniah"
1Ch 24:12 – "The 11ᵗʰ to Eliashib"
1Ch 24:12 – "the 12ᵗʰ to Jakim"
1Ch 24:13 – "The 13ᵗʰ to Huppah"
1Ch 24:13 – "the 14ᵗʰ to Jeshebeab"
1Ch 24:14 – "The 15ᵗʰ to Bilgah"
1Ch 24:14 – "the 16ᵗʰ to Immer"
1Ch 24:15 – "The 17ᵗʰ to Hezir"

1Ch 24:15 – *"the 18th to Aphses"*
1Ch 24:16 – *"The 19th to Pethahiah"*
1Ch 24:16 – *"the 20th to Jehezekel"*
1Ch 24:17 – *"The 21st to Jachin"*
1Ch 24:17 – *"the 22nd to Gamul"*
1Ch 24:18 – *"The 23rd to Delaiah"*
1Ch 24:18 – *"the 24th to Maaziah"*
1Ch 25:9 – *"1st lot came forth for Asaph to Joseph"*
1Ch 25:9 – *"the second to Gedaliah..were 12"*
1Ch 25:10 – *"the third to Zaccur..were 12"*
1Ch 25:11 – *"the fourth to Izri..were 12"*
1Ch 25:12 – *"the fifth to Nethaniah..were 12"*
1Ch 25:13 – *"the sixth to Bukkiah..were 12"*
1Ch 25:14 – *"the seventh to Jesharelah..were 12"*
1Ch 25:15 – *"the eighth to Jeshaiah..were 12"*
1Ch 25:16 – *"the ninth to Mattaniah..were 12"*
1Ch 25:17 – *"the tenth to Shimei..were 12"*
1Ch 25:18 – *"the eleventh to Azareel..were 12"*
1Ch 25:19 – *"the twelfth to Hashabiah..were 12"*
1Ch 25:20 – *"the 13th to Shubael..were 12"*
1Ch 25:21 – *"the 14th to Mattithiah..were 12"*
1Ch 25:22 – *"the 15th to Jeremoth..were 12"*
1Ch 25:23 – *"the 16th to Hananiah..were 12"*
1Ch 25:24 – *"the 17th to Joshbekashah..were 12"*
1Ch 25:25 – *"the 18th to Hanani..were 12"*
1Ch 25:26 – *"the 19th to Mallothi..were 12"*
1Ch 25:27 – *"the 20th to Eliathah..were 12"*
1Ch 25:28 – *"the 21st to Hothir were 12"*
1Ch 25:29 – *"the 22nd to Giddalti were 12"*
1Ch 25:30 – *"the 23rd to Mahazioth..were 12"*
1Ch 25:31 – *"the 24th to Romamtiezer..were 12"*
Eze 24:6 – *"let no lot fall upon it"*

Love

Rev 2:4 – "thou hast left thy first love"

Lover

Jer 3:1 – "played the harlot with many lovers"
Lam 1:2 – "among..lovers..none to comfort"

Lust

1Ti 6:9 – " into many foolish and hurtful lusts"

Machir

Jos 13:31 – "even to..½ of the children of Machir"

Magistrate

Jdg 18:7 – "no magistrate in the land"

Maid

Ezr 2:65 – "their servants and their maids, 7337"
Mar 14:66 – "there cometh one of the maids"

Maiden

Est 2:9 – "seven maidens..meet to be given her"

Maidservant

Neh 7:67 – "manservants..maidservants..7,337"
Est 2:8 – "many maidens were gathered together"

Male

Num 3:40 – "Number all the firstborn..males"
Num 3:43 – "all the firstborn males by..names"
Deu 15:19 – "firstling males that come of thy herd"
Ezr 8:3 – "sons of Shechaniah..males 150"
Ezr 8:4 – "sons of Pahathmoab..200 males"
Ezr 8:5 – "sons of Shechaniah..300 males"
Ezr 8:6 – "sons also of Adin..50 males"
Ezr 8:7 – "sons of Elam..70 males"
Ezr 8:8 – "sons of Shephatiah..80 males"
Ezr 8:9 – "sons of Joab..218 males"
Ezr 8:10 – "sons of Shelomith..160 males"
Ezr 8:11 – "sons of Bebai..28 males"
Ezr 8:12 – "sons of Azgad..110 males"
Ezr 8:13 – "last sons of Adonikam..60 males"
Ezr 8:14 – "sons also of Bigvai..70 males"

Malefactor

Luk 23:32 – "also two other, malefactors"
Luk 23:33 – "malefactors, one on the right hand"
Luk 23:39 – "one of the malefactors..railed"

Man

Indefinite

Deu 33:6 – "Reuben..let not his men be few."
Neh 2:12 – "I and some few men with me"
Job 21:33 – "man..are innumerable before him"
Psa 105:12 – "but a few men in number"
Prov 7:26 – "many strong men..slain by her"
Ecc 9:14 – "a little city, and few men within it"
Isa 24:6 – "earth..burned, and few men left"
Ezk 12:16 – "I will leave a few men of them"
Mat 13:17 – "many prophets and righteous men"
Act 17:12 – "and of men, not a few"
1Co 1:26 – "not many wise men after the flesh
1Co 1:26 – "not many mighty..are called"

1Co 1:26 – *"not many noble, are called"*
Rev 8:11 – *"many men died of the waters"*

0 *Men*

Gen 31:50 – "no man is with us"
Gen 39:11 – "none of the men of the house"
Gen 45:1 – "there stood no man with him"
Exo 2:12 – "he saw that there was no man"
Exo 16:19 – "Let no man leave of it"
Exo 16:29 – "let no man go out of his place"
Exo 22:10 – "no man seeing it"
Exo 33:4 – "no man did put on..ornaments"
Exo 33:20 –"shall no man see me, and live"
Exo 34:3 – "no man shall come up with thee"
Lev 16:17 – "shall be no man in the tabernacle"
Lev 21:21 – "No man that hath a blemish"
Lev 27:26 – "no man shall sanctify it"
Num 5:19 – "If no man have lain with thee"
Num 32:11 – "none of the men..came..of Egypt"
Deu 7:24 – "no man..able to stand before thee"
Deu 11:25 – "no man be able to stand before you"
Deu 24:6 – "No man shall take the..millstone"
Deu 28:26 – "no man shall fray them away"
Deu 28:29 – "no man shall save thee"
Deu 34:6 – "no man knoweth of his sepulcher"
Jos 8:31 – "no man hath lift up any iron"
Jos 23:9 – "no man hath been able to stand"
Jdg 11:39 – "and she knew no man"
Jdg 19:15 – "no man that took them"
Jdg 19:18 – "no man that receiveth me to house"
Jdg 21:12 – "that had known no man"
1Sa 2:9 – "by strength shall no man prevail"
1Sa 11:3 – "if there be no man to save us"
1Sa 14:26 – "no man put his hand to his mouth"
1Sa 21:1 – "alone, and no man with thee?"
1Sa 21:2 – "Let no man know any thing"
1Sa 26:12 – "gat them away, and no man saw"
2Sa 15:3 – "no man deputed of the king"
1Ki 8:46 – "there is no man that sinneth not"
2Ki 7:5 – "there was no man there"
2Ki 7:10 – "there was no man there"
2Ki 23:10 – "no man might make his son"
2Ki 23:18 – "let no man move his bones"
1Ch 16:21 – "suffered no man to do..wrong"
2Ch 6:36 – "there is no man which sinneth not"
Est 5:12 – "queen did let no man come in"
Est 8:8 – "the writing..may no man reverse"
Est 9:2 – "no man could withstand them"
Job 11:3 – "shall no man make thee ashamed?"
Job 15:28 – "houses which no man inhabiteth"
Job 20:21 – "shall no man look for his goods"
Job 24:22 – "and no man is sure of life"
Job 38:26 – "on the earth, where no man is"
Psa 76:5 – "none of the men..found their hands"
Psa 105:14 – "suffered no man to do them wrong"
Psa 142:4 – "no man that would know me"
Psa 143:2 – "shall no man living be justified"
Pro 1:24 – "and no man regarded"
Pro 28:1 – "wicked flee when no man pursueth"
Pro 28:17 – "let no man stay him"

Ecc 3:11 – "no man can find out the work"
Ecc 8:8 – "no man..hath power over the spirit"
Ecc 9:1 – "no man knoweth..love or hatred"
Ecc 9:15 – "no man remembered that..poor man"
Isa 9:19 – "no man shall spare his brother"
Isa 13:14 – "a sheep that no man taketh up"
Isa 24:10 – "that no man may come in"
Isa 33:8 – "he regardeth no man"
Isa 41:28 – "I beheld, and there was no man"
Isa 50:2 – "when I came, was there no man?"
Isa 57:1 – "no man layeth it to heart"
Isa 59:16 – "saw that there was no man"
Isa 60:15 – "no man went through thee"
Jer 2:6 – "land that no man passed through"
Jer 4:25 – "and, lo, there was no man"
Jer 8:6 – "no man repented..wickedness"
Jer 12:11 – "no man layeth it to heart"
Jer 22:30 – "no man of his seed shall prosper"
Jer 30:17 – "Zion, whom no man seeketh after"
Jer 36:19 – "let no man know where ye be"
Jer 38:24 – "Let no man know of these words"
Jer 40:15 – "slay Ishmael..no man shall know"
Jer 41:4 – "slain Gedaliah, and no man knew it"
Jer 44:2 - Jerusalem..no man dwelleth"
Jer 49:18 – "Sodom..no man shall abide there"
Jer 49:33 – "Hazor..no man abide there"
Jer 50:40 – "so shall no man abide there"
Jer 51:43 – "land wherein no man dwelleth"
Lam 4:4 – "bread, and no man breaketh it"
Eze 14:15 – "no man may pass through"
Eze 22:30 – "sought for a man..found none"
Eze 44:2 – "gate..no man shall enter in by it"
Hos 4:4 – "Yet let no man strive"
Nah 3:18 – "and no man gathereth them"
Zep 3:6 – "so that there is no man"
Zec 1:21 – "no man did lift up his head"
Zec 7:14 – "no man passed through"
Mat 6:24 – "No man can serve two masters"
Mat 8:4 – "See thou tell no man"
Mat 8:28 – "that no man might pass by"
Mat 9:16 – "No man putteth a piece of..cloth"
Mat 9:30 – "See that no man know it"
Mat 11:27 – "no man knoweth the Son"
Mat 16:20 – "tell no man that he was..Christ"
Mat 17:8 – "saw no man, save Jesus only"
Mat 17:9 – "Tell the vision to no man"
Mat 20:7 – "Because no man hath hired us"
Mat 22:46 – "And no man was able to answer"
Mat 23:9 – "And call no man your father"
Mat 24:4 – "Take heed that no man deceive you"
Mar 2:21 – "No man also seweth"
Mar 2:22 – "no man putteth new wine"
Mar 3:27 – "No man can enter into"
Mar 5:3 – "no man could bind him"
Mar 5:37 – "suffered no man to follow him"
Mar 5:43 – "that no man should know it"
Mar 7:24 – "would have no man know it"
Mar 7:36 – "that they should tell no man"
Mar 8:30 – "they should tell no man of him"
Mar 9:8 – "they saw no man any more"
Mar 9:9 – "tell no man what..they had seen"

Mar 9:39 – "no man which shall do a miracle"
Mar 10:29 – "no man that hath left house"
Mar 11:14 – "No man eat fruit of thee"
Mar 12:14 – "carest for no man"
Mar 12:34 – "no man after that durst ask"
Mar 13:32 – "day..hour knoweth no man"
Luk 3:14 – "Do violence to no man"
Luk 5:14 – "charged him to tell no man"
Luk 5:36 – "No man putteth a piece"
Luk 5:37 – "And no man putteth new wine"
Luk 5:39 – "No man also having drunk old wine"
Luk 8:16 – "No man..lighted a candle"
Luk 8:51 – "he suffered no man to go in"
Luk 8:56 – "should tell no man what was done"
Luk 9:21 – "to tell no man that thing"
Luk 9:36 – "told no man in those days"
Luk 9:62 – "No man..hand to the plough"
Luk 10:4 – "salute no man by the way"
Luk 10:22 – "no man knoweth who the Son is"
Luk 11:33 – "No man..lighted a candle"
Luk 14:24 – "none of those men..bidden"
Luk 15:16 – "no man gave unto him"
Luk 18:29 – "no man that hath left house"
Joh 1:18 – "No man hath seen God at any time"
Joh 3:2 – "no man can do these miracles"
Joh 3:13 – "And no man hath ascended"
Joh 3:32 – "no man receiveth his testimony"
Joh 4:27 – "no man said, What seekest thou?"
Joh 5:7 – "Sir, I have no man"
Joh 5:22 – "the Father judgeth no man"
Joh 6:44 – "No man can come to me"
Joh 6:65 – "no man can come unto me"
Joh 7:4 – "no man..doeth any thing in secret"
Joh 7:13 – "no man spake openly of him"
Joh 7:27 – "no man knoweth whence he is"
Joh 7:30 – "no man laid hands on him"
Joh 7:44 – "but no man laid hands on him"
Joh 8:10 – "hath no man condemned thee?"
Joh 8:11 – "She said, No man, Lord."
Joh 8:15 – "I judge no man"
Joh 8:20 – "and no man laid hands on him"
Joh 9:4 – "the night cometh..no man can work"
Joh 10:18 – "No man taketh it from me"
Joh 10:29 – "no man is able to pluck them out"
Joh 13:28 – "no man at the table knew"
Joh 14:6 – "no man cometh unto the Father"
Joh 15:13 – "Greater love hath no man"
Joh 15:24 – "works which none other man did"
Joh 16:22 – "your joy no man taketh from you"
Act 1:20 – "and let no man dwell therein"
Act 4:17 – "speak..to no man in this name"
Act 5:13 – "durst no man join himself"
Act 5:23 – "we found no man within"
Act 9:7 – "hearing a voice, but seeing no man"
Act 9:8 – "eyes..opened, he saw no man"
Act 18:10 – "no man shall set on thee..hurt thee"
Act 20:33 – "coveted no man's silver..gold"
Act 23:22 – "see thou tell no man"
Act 25:11 – "no man may deliver me unto them"
Act 28:31 – "no man forbidding him"
Rom 12:17 – "Recompense to no man evil"

Rom 13:8 – "Owe no man any thing"
Rom 14:7 – "no man dieth to himself"
Rom 14:13 – "no man put a stumblingblock"
1Co 2:11 – "things of God knoweth no man"
1Co 2:15 – "he himself is judged of no man"
1Co 3:11 – "other foundation can no man lay"
1Co 3:18 – "Let no man deceive himself."
1Co 3:21 – "let no man glory in men"
1Co 10:24 – "Let no man seek his own"
1Co 12:3 – "no man speaking by the Spirit"
1Co 12:3 – "no man can say that Jesus is the Lord"
1Co 14:2 – "for no man understandeth him"
1Co 16:11 – "Let no man therefore despise"
2Co 5:16 – "know we no man after the flesh"
2Co 7:2 – "we have wronged no man"
2Co 7:2 – "we have corrupted no man"
2Co 7:2 – "we have defrauded no man"
2Co 8:20 – "no man should blame us"
2Co 11:9 – "I was chargeable to no man"
2Co 11:10 – "no man shall stop me"
2Co 11:16 – "Let no man think me a fool"
Gal 3:11 – "no man is justified by the law"
Gal 3:15 – "no man disannulleth, or addeth"
Gal 6:17 – "let no man trouble me"
Eph 5:6 – "Let no man deceive you"
Eph 5:29 – "no man ever yet hated his own flesh"
Php 2:20 – "I have no man likeminded"
Col 2:16 – "Let no man therefore judge you"
Col 2:18 – "Let no man beguile you"
1Th 3:3 – "no man should be moved by these"
1Th 4:6 – "That no man go beyond..defraud"
2Th 2:3 – "Let no man deceive you"
1Ti 4:12 – "Let no man despise thy youth"
1Ti 5:22 – "Lay hands suddenly on no man"
1Ti 6:16 – "light which no man can approach"
1Ti 6:16 – "whom no man hath seen"
2Ti 2:4 – "No man that warreth entangleth"
2Ti 4:16 – "At my first answer no man stood"
Tit 2:15 – "Let no man despise thee."
Tit 3:2 – "To speak evil of no man"
Heb 5:4 – "no man taketh this honour"
Heb 7:13 – "of which no man gave attendance"
Heb 12:14 – "no man shall see the Lord"
Jas 1:13 – "Let no man say when..tempted"
Jas 3:8 – "the tongue can no man tame"
1Jn 3:7 – "let no man deceive you"
1Jn 4:12 – "No man hath seen God at any time."
Rev 2:17 – "which no man knoweth"
Rev 3:7 – "openeth, and no man shutteth"
Rev 3:7 – "shutteth, and no man openeth"
Rev 3:8 – "and no man can shut it"
Rev 3:11 – "that no man take thy crown"
Rev 5:3 – "And no man in heaven"
Rev 5:4 – "no man was found worthy"
Rev 7:9 – "which no man could number"
Rev 13:17 – "that no man might buy or sell"
Rev 14:3 – "no man could learn that song"
Rev 15:8 – "no man..able to enter..the temple"
Rev 18:11 – "no man buyeth their merchandise"
Rev 19:12 – "name written, that no man knew"
Num 31:49 – "there lacketh not one man of us"

Deu 1:35 – "not one of these men..see that..land"
1Co 6:5 – "wise man among you? no, not one"

1 *Man*

Gen 42:11 – "We are all one man's sons"
Gen 42:13 – "the sons of one man in..Canaan"
Exo 13:13 – "all the firstborn of man..redeem"
Exo 13:15 – "LORD slew..the firstborn of man
Exo 16:22 – "two omers for one man"
Exo 21:18 – "if men strive..and one smite another"
Exo 21:35 – "if one man's ox hurt another"
Num 14:15 – "if ..kill all this people as one man"
Num 16:22 – "shall one man sin..wroth with..all"
Num 18:15 – "firstborn of man shalt..redeem"
Num 31:49 – "there lacketh not one man of us"
Deu 1:35 – "not one of these men..see that..land"
Jos 23:10 – "One man of you shall chase a 1000"
Jdg 6:16 – "shalt smite the Midianites as one man"
Jdg 18:19 – "be a priest unto..one man, or..a tribe"
Jdg 20:1 – "congregation was gathered..as 1 man"
Jdg 20:8 – "all the people arose as one man"
Jdg 20:11 – "men of Israel..knit together as 1 man"
1Sa 2:25 – "If one man sin against another"
2Sa 1:15 – "David called one of the young men"
2Sa 2:21 – "lay thee hold on one of the young men"
2Sa 19:14 – "even as the heart of one man"
1Ki 22:8 – "There is yet one man, Micaiah"
2Ki 4:22 – "Send me..one of the young men"
2Ch 18:6 – "There is yet one man..but I hate him"
Ezr 3:1 – "gathered themselves together as 1 man"
Neh 8:1 – "people gathered themselves..as 1 man"
Neh 11:14 – "Zabdiel..son of one of the great men"
Job 13:9 – "or as one man mocketh another"
Job 15:7 – "Art thou the first man that was born?"
Job 17:10 – "I cannot find 1 wise man among you"
Ecc 7:28 – "one man among 1000 have I found"
Ecc 8:9 – "time wherein one man ruleth over"
Isa 4:1 – "7 women shall take hold of one man"
Ezk 9:2 – "one man..clothed with linen..inkhorn"
Luk 17:34 – "two men in one bed..one taken"
Luk 17:36 – "Two men..in the field..one..taken"
Joh 11:50 – "expedient..that one man should die"
Joh 18:14 – "that 1 man should die for the people"
Rom 5:12 – "by one man sin entered into..world"
Rom 5:15 – "grace, which is by one man, Jesus"
Rom 5:17 – "by one man's offence death reigned"
Rom 5:19 – "by one man's disobedience"
1Co 15:45 – "the first man Adam"
1Co 15:47 – "first man is of the earth, earthy"
Eph 2:15 – "make..of twain one new man"
1Ti 5:9 – "having been the wife of one man"

2 *Men*

Gen 22:3 – "Abraham..took two of his young men"
Exo 2:13 – "2nd day..two men..strove together"
Jos 2:1 – "sent..two men to spy secretly..Jericho"
Jos 2:4 – "woman took the 2 men, and hid them"
Jos 2:23 – "the two men returned..came to Joshua"

Jos 6:22 – "2 men that had spied out the country"
1Sa 10:2 – "two men by Rachel's sepulcher"
1Sa 28:8 – "Saul..and two men with him"
2Sa 4:2 – "Saul's son had 2 men..captains of bands"
2Sa 12:1 – "2 men in 1 city; the 1 rich..other poor"
2Sa 23:20 – "Benaiah..slew 2 lionlike men..Moab"
1Ki 2:32 – "who fell upon 2 men more righteous"
1Ki 21:10 – "set 2 men, sons of Belial before him"
1Ki 21:13 – "came in two men, children of Belial"
2Ki 5:22 – "two young men..sons of the prophets"
1Ch 11:22 – "Benaiah..slew 2 lionlike men..Moab"
Mat 9:27 – "two blind men followed him"
Mat 20:30 – "2 blind men sitting by the way side"
Luk 9:30 – "there talked with him two men"
Luk 9:32 – "two men that stood with him"
Luk 17:34 – "two men in one bed..one taken"
Luk 17:36 – "Two men..in the field..one..taken"
Luk 18:10 – "Two men..one a Pharisee"
Luk 24:4 – "2 men stood by..in shining garments"
Joh 8:17 – "the testimony of two men is true"
Act 1:10 – "two men stood..in white apparel"
Act 9:38 – "they sent unto him two men"
1Co 15:47 – "the second man is the Lord"

3 *Men*

Gen 18:2 – "three men stood by him"
Jos 18:4 – "out from among you 3 men..each tribe"
1Sa 10:3 – "three men going up to God to Bethel"
2Sa 23:9 – "Eleazer...one of the three mighty men"
2Sa 23:16 – "the three mighty men brake through"
2Sa 23:17 – "These things did these 3 mighty men"
2Sa 23:22 – "Benaiah..name among 3 mighty men"
Job 32:1 – "So these 3 men ceased to answer Job"
Job 32:5 – "no answer in..mouth of these 3 men"
Ezk 14:14 – "Though these three men..were in it"
Ezk 14:16 – "Though these three men were in it"
Ezk 14:18 – "Though these three men were in it"
Dan 3:23 – "these three men, Shadrach"
Dan 3:24 – "Did not we cast three men bound"
Act 10:19 – "Behold, three men seek thee."
Act 11:11 – "3 men already come unto the house"

4 *Men*

2Ki 7:3 – "4 leprous men at the entering in..gate"
Dan 3:25 – "Lo, I see four men loose"
Dan 3:25 – "the fourth is like the Son of God"
Act 21:23 – "four men which have a vow on them"

5 *Men*

Gen 47:2 – "took..of his brethren, even 5 men"
Jdg 18:2 – "children..Dan..5 men from their coasts"
Jdg 18:7 – "five men departed, and came to Laish"
Jdg 18:14 – "answered..5 men that went to spy"
Jdg 18:17 – "5 men that went to spy out the land"
2Ki 25:19 – "5 men..were in the king's presence"

7-9 *Men*

2Sa 21:6 – "Let 7 men of his sons be delivered"
Pro 26:16 – "7 men that can render a reason"
Jer 41:15 – "escaped from Johanan with 8 men"
Jer 52:25 – "7 men.. were near the king's person"
Ezk 9:2 – "6 men..from the way of the higher gate"
Mic 5:5 – "raise against him...eight principal men"
Act 6:3 – "seven men of honest report"

10 *Men*

Jdg 6:27 – "Gideon took ten men of his servants"
Jdg 20:10 – "we will take ten men of an hundred"
Rut 4:2 – "he took 10 men of the elders of the city"
1Sa 25:5 – "David sent out ten young men"
2Sa 18:15 – "10 young men..bare Joab's armour"
2Ki 25:25 – "Ishmael..10 men with him..smote"
Ecc 7:19 – "ten mighty men which are in the city"
Jer 41:1 – "Ishmael..ten men with him"
Jer 41:2 – "then arose Ishmael..ten men..with him"
Jer 41:8 – "10 men were found..said unto Ishmael"
Amo 6:9 – "if there remain ten men in one house"
Zec 8:23 – "ten men shall take hold"
Luk 17:12 – "ten men that were lepers"

11-19 *Men*

Num 1:44 – "princes of Israel being twelve men"
Deu 1:23 – "twelve men of you, one of a tribe"
Jos 3:12 – "twelve men out of the tribes of Israel"
Jos 4:2 – "twelve men out of the people"
Jos 4:4 – "Joshua called the twelve men"
2Sa 2:30 – "lacked of David's servants 19 men"
1Ch 24:4 – "sons of Eliazar..16 chief men"
Act 19:7 – "all the men were about twelve"

20 -49 *Men*

Jos 7:5 – "men of Ai smote of them about 36 men"
Jdg 14:19 – "to Ashkelon, and slew 30 men"
Jdg 20:31 – "Benjamin.. to smite..about 30 men"
1Sa 14:14 – "first slaughter..was about 20 men"
2Sa 3:20 – "Abner came to David..20 men w/ him"
2Ki 10:14 – "slew them at the pit..even 42 men"
Neh 7:28 – "The men of Bethazmaveth, 42"
Jer 38:10 – "Take from hence 30 men with thee"
Ezk 8:16 – "25 men..worshipped the sun"
Act 23:13 – "more than 40..made this conspiracy"
Act 23:21 – "more than 40 men..bound"

50 *Men*

2Sa 15:1 – "Absalom...50 men to run before him"
1Ki 1:5 – "Adonijah..fifty men to run before him"
1Ki 18:13 – "how I hid 100 men ..by 50 in a cave"
2Ki 2:7 – "50 men of the sons of the prophets"
2Ki 2:16 – "be with thy servants 50 strong men"
2Ki 2:17 – "They sent therefore 50 men"
2Ki 15:25 – "with him 50 men of the Gileadites"

51-99 *Men*

Num 11:16 – "seventy men of the elders of Israel"
Num 11:24 – "gathered the 70 men of the elders"
Jdg 8:14 – "princes of Succoth..elders..77 men"
2Ki 10:24 – "Jehu appointed 80 men without"
2Ki 25:19 – "60 men of the people of the land"
Ezr 2:22 – "The men of Netophah, 56"
Neh 7:33 – "The men of the other Nebo, 52"
Son 3:7 – "60 valiant men are about it"
Jer 41:5 – "80 men..beards shaven..clothes rent"
Jer 52:25 – "60 men of the people of the land"
Ezk 8:11 – "70 men of the ancients of ..Israel"

100-199 *Men*

Jdg 7:19 – "Gideon and the 100 men..with him"
1Ki 18:13 – "how I hid 100 men ..by 50 in a cave"
2Ki 4:43 – "should I set this before 100 men?"
Neh 7:26 – "men of Bethlehem & Netophah, 188"
Neh 7:27 – "The men of Anathoth, 128"
Neh 7:31 – "The men of Michmas, 122"
Neh 7:32 – "The men of Bethel and Ai, 123
Ezr 2:23 – "The men of Anathoth, 128"

200 -299 *Men*

Num 16:35 – "fire..LORD..consumed..250 men"
Num 26:10 – "Korah...fire devoured 250 men"
1Sa 18:27 – "slew of the Philistines 200 men"
1Sa 25:13 – "and 200 abode by the stuff"
1Sa 30:10 – "for 200 abode behind"
1Sa 30:21 – "200 men, which we so faint"
2Sa 15:11 – "w/ Absalom..200 men..of Jerusalem"
1Ki 20:15 – "numbered the young men.. 232"
Ezr 2:65 – "200 singing men and singing women"

300-399 *Men*

Jdg 7:6 – "putting..hand to their mouth..300 men"
Jdg 7:7 – "By the 300 men that lapped will I save"
Jdg 7:8 – "retained those 300 men"
Jdg 7:16 – "divided..300 men into 3 companies"
Jdg 8:4 – "300 men..faint, yet pursuing them"
2Sa 2:31 – "David..smitten..Abner's men..360"
Est 9:15 – "Jews..in Shushan..slew 300 men"

400-499 *Men*

Gen 32:6 – "Esau..cometh..400 men with him"
Gen 33:1 – "Esau came, and with him 400 men"
1Sa 22:2 – "there were with him about 400 men"
1Sa 25:13 – "went up after David about 400 men"
1Sa 30:10 – "David pursued, he and 400 men"
1Sa 30:17 – "400 young men..rode..camels..fled"
1Ki 18:22 – "Baal's prophets are 450 men"
1Ki 22:6 – "gathered..prophets..about 400 men"
2Ch 18:5 – "king..gathered..of prophets 400 men"
Act 5:36 – "a number of men, about 400"

162

500-999 *Men*

Jdg 3:31 – "Shamgar..slew..Philistines 600 men"
Jdg 18:11 – "Danites, out of..Eshtaol, 600 men"
Jdg 18:16 – "600 men appointed with..weapons"
Jdg 18:17 – "600 men appointed with weapons"
Jdg 20:15 – "Gibeah..numbered 700 chosen men"
Jdg 20:16 – "700 chosen men lefthanded..sling"
Jdg 20:47 – "600 men turned & fled to..wilderness"
1Sa 13:15 – "Saul..people..w/ him, about 600 men"
1Sa 14:2 – "Saul..people..w/ him..about 600 men"
1Sa 27:2 – "David..the 600 men that were w/ him"
1Sa 30:9 – "David..the 600 men that were w/ him"
2Sa 15:18 – "600 men which came after him"
2Ki 3:26 – "took w/ him 700 men..drew swords"
1Ch 4:42 – "sons of Simeon, 500 men"
Neh 7:29 – "The men of Kirjathjearim..743"
Neh 7:30 – "The men of Ramah and Geba, 621"
Est 9:6 – "in Shushan..Jews slew..500 men"
Est 9:12 – "Jews have slain & destroyed 500 men"

1000 *Men*

Jdg 9:49 – "Shechem died..1000 men & woman"
Jdg 15:15 – "jawbone of an ass..slew 1000 men"
Jdg 15:16 – "jaw of an ass have I slain 1000 men"
2Sa 10:6 – "and of king Maacah 1000 men"
2Sa 19:17 – "there were a 1000 men of Benjamin"
Ecc 7:28 – "one man among 1000 have I found"

1001-4999 *Men*

Exo 32:28 – "fell of the people..about 3000 men"
Jos 7:3 – "about *2000* or 3000 men go..smite Ai"
Jos 7:4 – "about 3000 men..they fled before..Ai"
Jdg 15:11 – "3000 men of Judah went..to Samson"
Jdg 16:27 – "upon..roof about 3000 men..women"
Jdg 20:45 – "pursued.. Gidom..slew 2,000 men"
1Sa 4:2 – "Philistines..slew..about 4,000 men"
1Sa 13:2 – "Saul chose him 3,000 men of Israel"
1Sa 24:2 – "took 3,000 chosen men..of all Israel"
1Sa 26:2 – "having 3,000 chosen men of Israel"
1Ki 5:16 – *"3,300 which ruled over the people"*
2Ch 2:1 – *"Solomon told out..3,600 to oversee"*
Mat 15:38 – "they that did eat were 4,000 men"
Act 21:38 – "leddest..into..wilderness 4,000 men"

5000-9999 *Men*

Jos 8:12 – "about 5,000 men..ambush..Bethel..Ai"
Jdg 20:45 – "gleaned..in the highways 5,000 men"
2Ki 24:16 – "all the men of might, even 7,000"
1Ch 19:18 – "David slew of the Syrians 7000 men"
Mat 14:21 – "they..had eaten..about 5000 men"
Mar 6:44 – "did eat of the loaves..about 5000 men"
Luk 9:14 – "For they were about 5000 men."
Joh 6:10 – "men sat down..about 5000"
Act 4:4 – "number of the men was about 5000"
Rom 11:4 – "7000 men.. not bowed the knee"
Rev 11:13 – "in..earthquake..slain of men 7000"

10,000 *Men*

Jdg 1:4 – "Judah..slew of..Bezek 10,000 men"
Jdg 3:29 – "slew of Moab..about 10,000 men"
Jdg 4:6 – "10,000 men of.. Naphtali..Zebulun"
Jdg 4:10 – "Barak..went up with 10,000 men"
Jdg 4:14 – "Barak..and 10,000 men after him"
Jdg 20:34 – "against Gibeah 10,000 chosen men"
1Ki 5:14 – *"sent them to Lebanon, 10,000 a month"*

10,001-99,999 *Men*

Jos 8:3 – "30,000 mighty men of valour"
Jdg 8:10 – "15,000 men, all that were left"
Jdg 20:15 – "children of Benjamin..26,000 men"
Jdg 20:21 – "Benjamin..destroyed..22,000 men"
Jdg 20:25 – "Benjamin..destroyed..18,000 men"
Jdg 20:35 – "LORD smote Benjamin..25,100 men"
Jdg 20:44 – "fell of Benjamin 18,000 men"
Jdg 20:46 – "fell..of Benjamin..25,000 men"
Jdg 21:10 – "congregation sent..12,000 men"
1Sa 6:19 – "smote..of Bethshemesh...50,070 men"
2Sa 8:5 – "David slew of the Syrians 22,000 men"
2Sa 8:13 – "David..smiting..Syrians..18,000 men"
2Sa 10:6 – "and of Ishtob 12,000 men"
2Sa 17:1 – "Let me now choose out 12,000 men"
2Sa 18:7 – "great slaugher..of 20,000 men"
2Sa 24:15 – "pestilence..died..people..70,000 men"
1Ki 5:13 – "Solomon..levy was 30,000 men"
1Ki 5:15 – *"Solomon..70,000 that bare burdens"*
1Ki 5:15 – *"Solomon..80,000 hewers ..mountains"*
1Ki 20:30 – "Aphek..wall fell upon 27,000..men"
1Ch 7:4 – "soldiers for war, 36,000 men"
1Ch 7:5 – "Issachar..valiant men..87,000"
1Ch 7:7 – "mighty men of valour..22,034"
1Ch 7:9 – "men of valour, was 20,200"
1Ch 7:11 – "men of valour..17,200 soldiers"
1Ch 7:40 – "children of Asher..26,000 men"
1Ch 12:30 – "Ephraim 20,800, mighty men"
1Ch 17:15 – "David slew..Syrians 22,000 men"
1Ch 21:14 – "fell of Israel 70,000 men"
2Ch 2:2 – "Solomon..70,000 men to bear burdens"
2Ch 2:2 – *"Solomon told out..80,000 to hew"*

100,000+ *Men*

Exo 12:37 – "Israel..600,000 on foot..men"
Exo 38:26 – "half a shekel..for 603,550 men"
Jdg 8:10 – "fell 120,000 men that drew sword"
Jdg 20:17 – "Israel..400,000 men that drew sword"
1Sa 15:4 – "Saul..10,000 men of Judah"
2Sa 24:9 – "in Israel 800,000 valiant men"
2Sa 24:9 – "men of Judah were 500,000"
1Ki 12:21 – "Rehoboam..180,000 chosen men"
1Ch 5:21 – "took away..of men an 100,000"
1Ch 21:5 – "all they of Israel were 1,100,000 men"
1Ch 21:5 – "they of..Judah was 470,000 men"
2Ch 11:1 – "Rehoboam..180,000 chosen men"
2Ch 13:3 – "Abihah..battle..400,000 chosen men"
2Ch 13:3 – "Jeroboam..800,000 chosen men"

2Ch 13:17 – "slain of Israel 500,000 chosen men"
2Ch 14:8 – *Asa..army of men..Judah..300,000*
2Ch 14:8 – *Asa..army of men..Benjamin..280,000*
2Ch 17:14 – "Adnah..mighty men..300,000"
2Ch 17:15 – *Jehohanan..with him 280,000*
2Ch 17:16 – "Amasiah..200,000 mighty men"
2Ch 17:17 – "Eliada..armed men..200,000"
2Ch 17:18 – *Jehozabad..with him an 180,000*
2Ch 25:5 – "found them 300,000 choice men"
2Ch 25:6 – "hired also 100,000 mighty men"
2Ch 28:6 – "Pekah..slew..120,000..valiant men"

Manna

Exo 16:26 – *"sabbath, in it there shall be none"*
Exo 16:27 – *"seventh day..they found none"*

Manner

Gen 25:23 – "two manner of people shall be"
Exo 12:16 – "no manner of work shall be done"
Lev 7:23 – "Ye shall eat no manner of fat"
Lev 7:26 – "ye shall eat no manner of blood"
Lev 17:14 – "eat the blood of no manner of flesh"
Lev 23:31 – "do no manner of work"
Lev 24:22 – "1 manner of a law..for the stranger"
Num 15:16 – "1 law & 1 manner shall be for you"
Num 28:18 – "do no manner of servile work"
Deu 4:15 – "ye saw no manner of similitude"
Dan 6:23 – "no manner of hurt was found"

Manservant/Maidservant

Neh 7:67 – "manservants..maidservants..7,337"

Mansion

Joh 14:2 – "Father's house..many mansions"

Master

1Ki 22:17 – "These have no master"
Mat 6:24 – "No man can serve two masters"
Mat 6:24 – "masters..hate the 1, & love the other"
Mat 6:24 – "masters..hold to the 1..despise..other"
Luk 16:13 – "No servant can serve 2 masters"
Luk 16:13 – "masters..he will hate the one
Luk 16:13 – "masters..he will hold to the one"
Jam 3:1 – "brethren, be not many masters"

Matter

2Sa 18:13 – "no matter hid from the king"

Meal

Hos 8:7 – "the bud shall yield no meal"

Measure

Gen 18:6 – "Make ready..3 measures of fine meal"
Exo 26:2 – "every 1 of the curtains..one measure"
Exo 26:8 – "11 curtains shall be all of 1 measure"
Rut 3:15 – "he measured six measures of barley"
Rut 3:17 – "six measures of barley gave he me"
1Sa 25:18 – "Abigail..took..5 measures of..corn"
1Ki 4:22 – "provision..60 measures of meal"
1Ki 4:22 – "provision..30 measures..fine flour"
1Ki 5:11 – "gave Hiram 20,000 measures...wheat"
1Ki 5:11 – "20 measures of pure oil"
1Ki 6:25 – "cherubims were of 1 measure & 1 size"
1Ki 7:37 – "ten bases..one measure, and one size"
1Ki 18:32 – "trench..contain 2 measures of seed"
2Ki 7:1 – "two measures of barley for a shekel"
2Ki 7:16 – "two measures of barley for a shekel"
2Ki 7:18 – "Two measures of barley for a shekel"
2Ch 2:10 – "20,000 measures of beaten wheat"
2Ch 2:10 – "20,000 measures of barley"
2Ch 3:3 – "length by cubits after the first measure"
2Ch 27:5 – "gave..10,000 measures of wheat"
2Ch 27:5 – *"Ammon gave..10,000 of barley"*
Ezr 7:22 – "to 100 measures of wheat"
Ezk 40:10 – "they three were of one measure"
Ezk 40:10 – "the posts had one measure"
Ezk 45:11 – "ephah and the bath..of one measure"
Ezk 46:22 – "these 4 corners were of 1 measure"
Ezk 48:30 – "on the north side, 4,500 measures"
Ezk 48:32 – *"And at the east side, 4,500"*
Ezk 48:33 – "at the south side, 4,500 measures"
Ezk 48:34 – *"At the west side, 4,500"*
Ezk 48:35 – "round about 18,000 measures"
Hag 2:16 – "heap of 20 measures..were but ten"
Mat 13:33 – "leaven..hid in 3 measures of meal"
Luk 13:21 – "hid in three measures of meal"
Luk 16:6 – "An 100 measures of oil"
Luk 16:6 – *"sit down quickly, and write 50"*
Luk 16:7 – "An 100 measures of wheat"
Luk 16:7 – *"Take thy bill, and write 80"*
Rev 6:6 – "three measures of barley..a penny"

Meat

1Sa 20:34 – "did eat no meat the second day"
Job 20:21 – "shall none of his meat be left"
Hab 3:17 – "the fields shall yield no meat"
Mat 25:42 – "ye gave me no meat"

Mediator

1Ti 2:5 – "one mediator between God..man"

Medicine

Jer 30:13 – "thou hast no healing medicines"
Jer 46:11 – "in vain shalt..use many medicines"

Members

Psa 139:16 – "all my members..none of them"
Mat 5:29 – "one of thy members should perish"
Mat 5:30 – "one of thy members should perish"
Rom 12:4 – "many members in one body"
1Co 12:12 – "body is 1..hath many members"
1Co 12:14 – "body is not one member, but many"
1Co 12:14 – "body..not 1 member, but many"
1Co 12:18 – "members every one..in the body"
1Co 12:19 – "And if they were all one member"
1Co 12:20 – "many members, yet but 1 body"
1Co 12:26 – "one member suffer, all..suffer"
1Co 12:26 – "1 member be honoured, all..rejoice"

Mention

Exo 23:13 – "make no mention of..other gods"
Job 28:18 – "No mention shall be made"

Mercy

Isa 47:6 – "thou didst shew them no mercy"
Jer 6:23 – "cruel, and have no mercy"
Hos 4:1 – "there is no..mercy..in the land"
Jas 2:13 – "that hath shewed no mercy"

Messenger

Jer 51:31 – "one messenger to meet another"

Midwife

Exo 1:15 – "midwives..name of..one was Shiphrah"

Might

Deu 28:32 – "shall be no might in thine hand"

Mighties/Mightiest

1Ch 11:12 – "Eleazer.. one of the 3 mighties"
1Ch 11:19 – "These things did these 3 mightiest"
1Ch 11:24 – "Benaiah..name among..3 mighties"

Mile

Mat 5:41 – "compel..to go a mile, go w/ him twain"

Mind

Job 23:13 – "But he is in one mind"
Rom 15:6 – "That ye may have one mind"
2Co 13:11 – "be of one mind, live in peace"
Phi 1:27 – "stand fast..with one mind"
Phi 2:2 – "being of one accord, of one mind"
Jam 1:8 – "double minded man is unstable"
Jam 4:8 – "purify your hearts, ye double minded"
Rev 17:13 – "These have one mind"

Minute

Rev 8:1 – "silence in heaven..space of ½ an hour"

Miracle

Joh 4:54 – "that second miracle that Jesus did"
Joh 10:41 – "John did no miracle"
Joh 11:47 – "this man doeth many miracles"
Joh 12:37 – "he had done so many miracles"

Mischief

Exo 21:22 – "yet no mischief follow"

Mite

Mar 12:42 – "poor widow..threw in two mites"
Luk 21:2 – "poor widow casting in..two mites"

Mnason

Act 21:16 – "brought with them one Mnason"

Money

Gen 43:12 – "take double money in your hand"
Gen 43:15 – "took double money in their hand"
2Ki 12:7 – "receive no more money"
2Ki 12:8 – "receive no more money"
Isa 55:1 – "he that hath no money; come..buy"
Mar 6:8 – "no scrip, no bread, no money"

Month

> *See the **Directory of Bible Dates***

1 *Month*

Exo 12:2 – "it shall be the first month..to you"
Num 20:1 – "Israel.. desert of Zin in the 1st month"
1Ch 12:15 – "went over Jordan in the first month"
1Ch 27:2 –"1st course for..1st month..Joshobeam"
1Ch 27:3 – "chief..of the host for the first month"
Dan 10:4 – "in the 24th day of the first month"
Joe 2:23 – "the latter rain in the first month"
Zec 11:8 – "Three shepherds..cut off in one month"

2 *Months*

Jdg 11:37 – "alone two months..bewail..virginity"
Jdg 11:38 – "he sent her away for two months"
Jdg 11:39 – "at the end of 2 months..she returned"
1Ki 5:14 – "month..in Lebanon..2 months at home"
1Ch 27:4 – "course of..2nd month..Dodai..24,000"
2Ch 30:2 – "keep the passover in the 2nd month"
2Ch 30:13 – "feast..unleavened bread..2nd month"

3 *Months*

Gen 38:24 – "3 months after..it was told Judah"
Exo 2:2 – "goodly child, she hid him 3 months"
Exo 19:1 – "In the 3rd month..gone forth..of Egypt"
2Sa 6:11 – "ark..house of Obededom..3 months"
2Sa 24:13 – "flee 3 months before thine enemies"
2Ki 23:31 – "Jehoahaz..reigned 3 months"
2Ki 24:8 – "Jehoicahin..reigned..3 months"
1Ch 13:14 – "ark..remained..Obededom..3 months"
1Ch 21:12 – "3 months..destroyed before thy foes"
1Ch 27:5 – "3rd month was Benaiah..24,000"
2Ch 31:7 – "3rd month they began..the foundation"
2Ch 36:2 – "Jehoahaz..3 months in Jerusalem"
2Ch 36:9 – "Jeohiachin..reigned 3 months..10 days"
Amo 4:7 – "yet three months to the harvest"
Luk 1:56 – "Mary abode with her about 3 months"
Act 7:20 – "in his father's house three months"
Act 19:8 – "3 months, disputing and persuading"
Act 20:3 – "And there abode three months"
Act 28:11 – "after 3 months we departed in a ship"
Heb 11:23 – "Moses..hid 3 months of his parents"

3⅓ *Months*

2Ch 36:9 – "Jeohiachin..reigned 3 months..10 days"

4 *Months*

Jdg 19:2 – "concubine..was there 4 whole months"
Jdg 20:47 – "abode in the rock Rimmon 4 months"
1Ch 27:7 – "4th captain..4th month..Asahel..24,000"
Zec 8:19 – "The fast of the fourth month"
Joh 4:35 – "four months..then cometh harvest?"

5 *Months*

1Ch 27:8 – "5th captain..5th month..Shamhuth"
Zec 7:3 – "Should I weep in the fifth month"
Zec 7:5 – "fasted & mourned in the 5th & 7th month"
Zec 8:19 – "the fast of the fifth"
Luk 1:24 – "Elisabeth..hid herself five months"
Rev 9:5 – "should be tormented five months"
Rev 9:10 – "power was to hurt men 5 months"

6 *Months*

1Ki 11:16 – "For 6 months did Joab remain there"
2Ki 15:8 – "Zachariah..reign over Israel..6 months"
1Ch 27:9 – "6th captain..6th month was Ira..24,000"
Est 2:12 – "6 months with oil of myrrh"
Est 2:12 – "6 months with sweet odours"
Luk 1:26 – "in the sixth month..Gabriel was sent"
Luk 1:36 – "this is the sixth month with her"

7 *Months*

Lev 23:41 – " ye shall celebrate it in the 7th month"
1Sa 6:1 – "ark.. in..country of..Philistines 7 months"
1Ki 8:2 – "Ethanim, which is the seventh month"
2Ki 25:25 – "7th month..Ishmael..smote Gedaliah"
1Ch 27:10 – 7th captain..7th month..Helez..24,000"
2Ch 5:3 – "feast which was in the 7th month"
2Ch 7:10 – "23rd day..7th month..sent..people away"
2Ch 31:7 – "foundation..finished..in the 7th month"
Ezr 3:1 – "when the 7th month was come"
Neh 7:73 – "when the 7th month came"
Neh 8:14 – "booths in the feast of the 7th month"
Jer 28:17 – "Hananiah..died..same year..7th month"
Jer 41:1 – "in the 7th month..Ishmael..came"
Ezk 39:12 – "seven months..be burying of them"
Ezk 39:14 – "end of 7 months shall they search"
Zec 7:5 – "fasted & mourned in the 5th & 7th month"
Zec 8:19 – "and the fast of the seventh"

8 *Months*

1Ki 6:38 – "the month Bul, which is the 8th month"
1Ch 27:11 – "8th captain for..8th month..Sibbecai"

9 *Months*

1Ch 27:12 – "9th captain for..9th month..Abiezer"
Jer 36:22 – "king sat..winterhouse in the 9th month"

10 *Months*

1Ch 27:13 – "10th captain..10th month..Maharai"
Zec 8:19 – "and the fast of the tenth"

11 *Months*

1Ch 27:14 – "11th captain..11th month..Benaiah"

12 *Months*

1Ch 27:15 – "12th captain..12th month..Heldai"
Est 2:12 – "12 months..the manner of..women"
Job 3:6 – "the number of the months"
Dan 4:29 – "At the end of twelve months"

16 *Months*

1Sa 27:7 – "David dwelt..a full year and 4 months"

18 *Months*

Act 18:11 – "continued there a year and 6 months"

42 *Months*

Rev 11:2 – "holy city..tread under..42 months"
Rev 13:5 – "power was given..him..42 months"

Moon

Isa 66:23 – "from one new moon to another"

Morsel

Heb 12:16 – "Esau..for one morsel of meat"

Mother

Ezk 23:2 – "two women..daughters of one mother"

Mountain

Gen 22:2 – "offering upon one of the mountains"
Zec 6:1 – "4 chariots..from between 2 mountains"
Zec 14:4 – "half of the mountain..toward the north"
Zec 14:4 – "half of it toward the south"
Rev 17:9 – "the 7 heads are 7 mountains"

Mourning

Eze 24:17 – "make no mourning for the dead"

Mouse

1Sa 6:4 – "trespass offering...five golden mice"

Mouth

1Ki 22:13 – "prophets declare good..with 1 mouth"

Rom 15:6 – "and one mouth glorify God"

Mule

Ezr 2:66 – "their mules, 245"
Neh 7:68 – "their mules, 245"

Murder

Mat 19:18 – "Thou shalt do no murder"

Murderer

1Jn 3:15 – "no murderer hath eternal life"

Name

Exo 28:10 – "Six of their names..one stone"
Exo 28:10 – "other six names..on the other stone"
Job 18:17 – "he shall have no name in the street"
Zec 14:9 – "one LORD, and his name one"
Act 1:15 – "number of the names..about an 120"
Act 4:12 – "none other name under heaven"
Rev 3:4 – "a few names even in Sardis"

Nation

Genesis 17:4 – "a father of many nations"
Gen 17:5 – "a father of many nations"
Gen 25:23 – "two nations are in thy womb"
Num 24:20 – "Amalek was the first of the nations"
Deu 7:1 – "7 nations greater & mightier than thou"
Deu 7:1 – "cast out many nations before thee"
Deu 15:6 – "thou shalt lend unto many nations"
Deu 28:12 – "thou shalt lend unto many nations"
2Sa 7:23 – "what one nation in the earth is like"
1Ch 17:21 – "what one nation in the earth is like"
Neh 13:26 – "many nations..no king like him"
Psa 105:13 – "they went from one nation..another"
Isa 10:7 – "cut off nations not a few"
Isa 52:15 – "So shall he sprinkle many nations"
Jer 22:8 – "many nations shall pass by this city"
Jer 25:14 – "many nations and great kings"
Jer 27:7 – "many nations and great kings"
Ezk 26:3 – "cause many nations to come up"
Ezk 35:10 – "These two nations..shall be mine"
Ezk 37:22 – "I will make them 1 nation in the land"
Ezk 37:22 – "they shall no more be two nations"
Ezk 38:23 – "known in the eyes of many nations"
Ezk 39:27 – "in the sight of many nations"
Joe 1:6 – "a nation is come up..without number"
Mic 4:2 – "And many nations shall come"
Mic 4:11 – "many nations..against thee"
Hab 2:8 – "thou hast spoiled many nations"

Zec 2:11 – "many nations..joined to the LORD"
Zec 8:22 – "many people and strong nations"
Act 13:19 – "destroyed 7 nations in..Chanaan"
Rom 4:17 – "a father of many nations"
Rom 4:18 – "the father of many nations"
Rev 10:11 – "many peoples..nations

Necessity

1Co 7:37 – "no necessity, but hath power"

Need

Pro 31:11 – "he shall have no need of spoil"
Mar 2:17 – "have no need of the physician"
1Co 12:21 – "I have no need of thee"
1Co 12:21 – "I have no need of you"
1Co 12:24 – "our comely parts have no need"
1Th 5:1 – "ye have no need that I write"
Rev 21:23 – "the city had no need of the sun"

Nephew

Jdg 12:14 – "he had 40 sons and 30 nephews"

Nethinim

Ezr 8:20 – "of the Nethinims..220 Nethinims"
Neh 7:60 – "All the Nethinims..children..392"

Network

1Ki 7:18 – "2 rows round..upon the 1 network"
1Ki 7:41 – "2 networks, to cover the two bowls"
1Ki 7:42 – "400 pomegranates for the 2 networks"
1Ki 7:42 – "2 rows of pomegranates for 1 network"

Night

Gen 7:4 – "rain upon the earth 40 days & 40 nights"
Gen 7:12 – "rain..upon..earth 40 days & 40 nights"
Gen 40:5 – "dreamed a dream both..in one night"
Gen 41:11 – "we dreamed a dream in one night"
Exo 24:18 – "Moses..in..mount..40 days..40 nights"
Exo 34:28 – "with the LORD 40 days and 40 nights"
Deu 9:9 – "40 days and 40 nights"
Deu 9:11 – "40 days and 40 nights"
Deu 9:18 – "40 days and 40 nights"
Deu 9:25 – "40 days and 40 nights"
Deu 10:10 – "40 days and 40 nights"
1Sa 30:12 – "nor drunk..water 3 days & 3 nights"
1Ki 19:8 – "40 days and 40 nights unto Horeb"
Job 2:13 – "upon the ground 7 days and 7 nights"

Jon 1:17 – "belly of the fish 3 days and 3 nights"
Mat 4:2 – "fasted 40 days and 40 nights"
Mat 12:40 – "3 days and 3 nights..whale's belly"
Mat 12:40 – "Son of man..3 days and 3 nights"
Act 27:27 – "14th night..up and down in Adria"
Rev 21:25 – "there shall be no night there"
Rev 22:5 – "there shall be no night there"

Noble

Isa 34:12 – "the nobles..but none shall be there"

Number

1Ch 22:16 – "Of the gold..there is no number"

Oath

Zec 8:17 – "love no false oath"

Oblation

Isa 40:20 – "he hath no oblation"

Occasion

Dan 6:4 – "find none occasion nor fault"
1Ti 5:14 – "give none occasion to the adversary"
1Jn 2:10 – "none occasion of stumbling in him"

Offence

Rom 5:16 – "gift is of many offences"
1Co 10:32 – "Give none offence..to the Jews"
2Co 6:3 – "Giving no offence in any thing"

Offering

Lev 2:11 – "No meat offering..shall be made"
Lev 6:20 – "offering..half of it in the morning"
Lev 6:20 – "offering..half thereof at night"
Lev 6:30 – "no sin offering..shall be eaten"
1Ki 3:4 – "1000 burnt offerings did Solomon offer"
2Ch 1:6 – "Solomon..offered 1000 burnt offerings"
Heb 10:14 – "by one offering..hath perfected

Office

1Sa 2:36 – "into one of the priests' offices"

Officer

Gen 40:2 – "Pharaoh was wroth..2 of his officers"
1Ki 4:7 – "Solomon had 12 officers over all Israel"
1Ki 9:23 – *"550, which bare rule over the people"*
1Ch 23:4 – "6,000 were officers and judges"
1Ch 26:30 – "Hebronites..1700 were officers"
2Ch 8:10 – "Solomon's officers, even 250"
Joh 18:22 – "one of the officers..struck Jesus"

Oil

Lev 5:11 – "he shall put no oil upon it"
Num 5:15 – "he shall pour no oil upon it"
Mat 25:3 – "and took no oil with them"

Ointment

Ecc 9:8 – "let thy head lack no ointment"

Olive

Isa 17:6 – "2 or 3 berries..top..uppermost bough"
Isa 17:6 – "4 or 5 in the outmost fruitful branches"

Omer

Exo 16:22 – "gathered..two omers for one man"

One

Zec 4:14 – "These are the two anointed ones"
Mat 10:42 – "one of these little ones..cold water"
Mat 18:6 – "offend one of these little ones"
Mat 18:10 – "despise not one of these little ones"
Mat 18:14 – "that one of these little ones..perish"
Mar 9:42 – "offend one of these little ones"

Onyx

Exo 28:9 – "thou shalt take two onyx stones"

Opening

Job 12:14 – "there can be no opening"

Opinion

1Ki 18:21 – "How long halt..between 2 opinions?"

Oppressor

Zec 9:8 – "no oppressor shall pass through"

Order

2Ki 23:4 – "priests of the second order"

Ordinance

Num 9:14 – "ye shall have one ordinance both"
Num 15:15 – "One ordinance shall be both for you"

Ouch *(as in **Pouch**)*

Exo 28:25 – "shalt thou fasten in the two ouches"
Exo 39:16 – "they made two ouches of gold"
Exo 39:18 – "they fastened in the two ouches"

Oven

Lev 26:26 – "10 women..bake..bread in one oven"

Overseer

Pro 6:7 – "having no guide, overseer, or ruler"

Ox/Oxen

Exo 22:1 – "If a man steal..restore five oxen"
Exo 34:19 – "every firstling..thy cattle..ox..sheep"
Num 7:3 – "offering before the LORD..12 oxen"
Num 7:7 – "two wagons and four oxen..Gershon"
Num 7:8 – "four wagons and eight oxen..Merari"
Num 7:17 – "peace offerings, two oxen..Nahshon"
Num 7:23 – "peace offerings, two oxen..Nethaneel"
Num 7:29 – "peace offerings, two oxen..Eliab"
Num 7:35 – "peace offerings, two oxen..Elizur"
Num 7:41 – "peace offerings, two oxen..Shelumiel"
Num 7:47 – "peace offerings, two oxen..Eliasaph"
Num 7:53 – "peace offerings, two oxen..Elishama"
Num 7:59 – "peace offerings, two oxen..Gamaliel"
Num 7:65 – "peace offerings, two oxen..Abidan"
Num 7:71 – "peace offerings, two oxen..Ahiezer"
Num 7:77 – "peace offerings, two oxen..Pagiel"
Num 7:83 – "peace offerings, two oxen..Ahira"
Num 23:1 – "prepare me here 7 oxen..seven rams"
1Ki 4:23 – "ten fat oxen"
1Ki 4:23 – "20 oxen..of the pastures"
1Ki 7:25 – "it stood upon twelve oxen"
1Ki 7:25 – *"three looking toward the north"*
1Ki 7:25 – *"three looking toward the west"*
1Ki 7:25 – *"three looking toward the south"*

1Ki 7:25 – *"three looking toward the east"*
1Ki 7:44 – "one sea, and twelve oxen under the sea"
1Ki 8:5 – "sheep..oxen..not be told nor numbered"
1Ki 8:63 – "Solomon offered..22,00 oxen"
1Ki 19:19 – "Elisha..plowing with 12 yoke of oxen"
2Ch 4:3 – *"oxen..ten in a cubit, compassing the sea"*
2Ch 4:4 – "It stood upon twelve oxen"
2Ch 4:4 – *"three looking toward the north"*
2Ch 4:4 – *"three looking toward the west"*
2Ch 4:4 – *"three looking toward the south"*
2Ch 4:4 – *"three looking toward the east"*
2Ch 4:15 – "One sea, and twelve oxen under it."
2Ch 7:5 – "Solomon..a sacrifice of 22,000 oxen"
2Ch 15:11 – "offered..of the spoil..700 oxen"
2Ch 29:33 – "consecrated things..600 oxen"
2Ch 35:8 – "for the passover offerings..300 oxen"
2Ch 35:9 – "for passover offerings..500 oxen"
Neh 5:18 – "prepared for me daily was one ox"
Job 1:3 – "His substance..500 yoke of oxen"
Job 42:12 – "later end of Job..1000 yoke of oxen"
Pro 14:4 – "Where no oxen are..crib is clean"

Overseer

2Ch 2:18 – "3,600 overseers..set the people..work"

Pace

2Sa 6:13 – "gone 6 paces..sacrificed oxen..fatlings"

Palm Trees *(see also Trees)*

Num 33:9 – "Elim...70 palm trees"

Parable

Mar 4:33 – "And with many such parables spake"

Part

0 *Parts*

Deu 10:9 – "Levi hath no part nor inheritance"
Deu 12:12 – "no part nor inheritance with you"
Deu 14:27 – "Levite..hath no part nor inheritance"
Deu 14:29 – "Levite..hath no part nor inheritance"
Deu 18:1 – "Levi..no part nor inheritance"
Jos 14:4 – "they gave no part unto the Levites"
Jos 18:7 – "the Levites have no part among you"
Jos 22:25 – "ye have no part in the LORD"
Jos 22:27 – "Ye have no part in the LORD"
2Sa 20:1 – "We have no part in David"
Luk 11:36 – "body..having no part dark"
Joh 13:8 – "thou hast no part with me"

100ᵗʰ Part (1%)

Neh 5:11 – "Restore..the 100th part of the money"

Tenth Part (10%)

Exo. 16:36 – "an omer is the 10th part of an ephah"
Lev 5:11 – "tenth part of an ephah"
Lev 6:20 – "tenth part of an ephah"
Num 5:15 – "tenth part of an ephah of barley"
Num 18:26 – "heave offering..10th part of the tithe"
Num 28:5 – "tenth part of an ephah of flour"
Ezk 45:11 – "bath..contain..tenth part of an homer"
Ezk 45:11 – "ephah the tenth part of an homer"
Ezk 45:14 – "tenth part of a bath out of the cor"
Heb 7:2 – "To whom..Abraham gave a tenth part"
Rev 11:13 – "earthquake..tenth part of the city fell"

Sixth Part (16.7%)

Ezk 39:2 – "leave but the sixth part of thee"
Ezk 45:13 – "sixth part of an ephah..wheat"
Ezk 45:13 – "sixth part of an ephah..barley"
Ezk 46:14 – "meat offering..sixth part of an ephah"

Fifth Part (20%)

Gen. 41:34 – "to take up the fifth part of the land"
Gen. 47:24 – "shall give the 5th part unto Pharaoh"
Gen. 47:26 – "Pharaoh should have the fifth part"
Lev 5:16 – "shall add the fifth part thereto"
Lev 6:5 – "shall add the fifth part more thereto"
Lev 22:14 – "shall put the fifth part thereof unto it"
Lev 27:13 – "redeem it..add a 5th part..estimation"
Lev 27:15 – "redeem his house...add the fifth part"
Lev 27:19 – "fifth part of the money"
Lev 27:27 – "redeem it..add a fifth part"
Lev 27:31 – "add thereto the fifth part"
Num 5:7 – "recompense..trespass..add..fifth part"
1Ki 6:31 – "doors..lintels..posts..a 5th part of..wall"

Fourth Part (25%)

Exo 29:40 – "¼ part of an hin of beaten oil"
Exo 29:40 – "¼ part of an hin of wine"
Lev 23:13 – "offering ..wine, the ¼ part of an hin"
Num 15:4 – "the fourth part of an hin of oil"
Num 15:5 – "the fourth part of an hin of wine"
Num 23:10 – "Who can count..the ¼ part of Israel"
Num 28:5 – "fourth part of an hin of beaten oil"
Num 28:7 – "¼ part of an hin for the one lamb"
1Sa 9:8 – "I have..the ¼part of a shekel of silver"
1Ki 6:33 – "posts of olive tree, a ¼ part of the wall"
2Ki 6:25 – "fourth part of a cab's of dove dung"
Neh 9:3 – "read in the book.. ¼ part of the day"
Neh 9:3 – "another ¼ part..confessed..worshipped"
Rev 6:8 – "Death..Hell..over the ¼ part of the earth"

Third Part (33%)

Num 15:6 – "meat offering.. ⅓ part of an hin of oil"
Num 15:7 – "drink offering.. ⅓ part of an hin of oil"
2Sa 18:2 – "⅓ part of the people under..Joab"
2Sa 18:2 – "⅓ part under the hand of Abishai"
2Sa 18:2 – "⅓ part under the hand of Ittai"
2Ki 11:5 – "A third part..keepers of the watch"
2Ki 11:6 – "a third part shall be at the gate of Sur"
2Ki 11:6 – "a ⅓ part at the gate behind the guard"
2Ch 23:4 – "A ⅓ part..shall be porters of the doors"
2Ch 23:5 – "a ⅓ part shall be at the king's house"
2Ch 23:5 – "a ⅓ part at the gate of the foundation"
Neh 10:32 – "charge ourselves..⅓ part of a shekel"
Ezk 46:14 – "the third part of an hin of oil"
Zec 13:8 – "the third shall be left therein"
Zec 13:9 – "I will bring the ⅓ part through the fire"
Rev 8:7 – "the third part of trees was burnt up"
Rev 8:8 – "the third part of the sea became blood"
Rev 8:9 – "the third part of the creatures..sea"
Rev 8:9 – "third part of the ships were destroyed"
Rev 8:10 – "great star..third part of the rivers"
Rev 8:11 – "third part of the waters..wormwood"
Rev 8:12 – "third part of the sun was smitten"
Rev 8:12 – "third part of the moon..was darkened"
Rev 8:12 – "third part of the stars..was darkened"
Rev 8:12 – "the third part of them was darkened"
Rev 8:12 – "day shone not for a third part of it"
Rev 9:15 – "for to slay the third part of men"
Rev 9:18 – "third part of men killed"
Rev 12:4 – "tail drew the third part of the stars"

Half Part (50%)

Neh 3:9 – "Rephaiah..ruler..½ part..Jerusalem"
Neh 3:12 – "Shallum..ruler..½ part..Jerusalem"
Neh 3:16 – "Nehemiah..ruler..½ part..Bethzur"
Neh 3:17 – "Hashabiah..ruler of the ½ part..Keilah"
Neh 3:18 – "Bevai..ruler of the ½ part of Keilah"

Two Parts of Three (67%)

Zec 13:8 – "two parts therein shall be cut off"

Four Parts of Five (80%)

Gen. 47:24 – "four parts shall be your own"

1 *Part*

Deu 33:21 – "he provided the first part for himself"
Ezk 48:8 – "in length as one of the other parts"
Luk 17:24 – "out of the one part under heaven"
Act 23:6 – "Paul perceived..1 part were Sadducees"

2 *Parts*

Num 31:27 – "divide the prey into two parts"
1Ki 16:21 – "people of Israel divided into 2 parts"
2Ki 11:7 – "2 parts of all you that go forth..sabbath"

Jer 34:18 – "cut..calf..twain..passed between..parts"

3+ *Parts*

Gen. 47:24 – "four parts shall be your own"
Deu 19:3 – "3 parts, that every slayer may flee"
Jos 18:5 – "divide it into seven parts"
Jos 18:6 – "describe the land into seven parts"
Jos 18:9 – "described it by cities into 7 parts"
2Sa 19:43 – "We have ten parts in the king"
Neh 11:1 – "nine parts to dwell in other cities"
Joh 19:23 – "took his garments, and made 4 parts"
Rev 16:19 – "great city was divided into 3 parts"

Partaker

2Ti 2:6 – "husbandman..first partaker..fruits"

Passover

2Ch 35:18 – "And there was no passover"

Pastor

Jer 12:10 – "Many pastors have destroyed"

Pasture

Gen 47:4 – "thy servants have no pasture"
Lam 1:6 – "like harts that find no pasture"
Joe 1:18 – "herds of cattle..have no pasture"

Patriarch

Act 7:8 – "Jacob begat the twelve patriarchs"

Peace

Deu 20:12 – "if it will make no peace with thee"
2Ch 15:5 – "there was no peace to him"
Isa 48:22 – "is no peace..unto the wicked"
Isa 57:21 – "is no peace..to the wicked"
Jer 6:14 – "peace; when there is no peace"
Jer 8:11 – "peace; when there is no peace"
Eze 7:25 – "seek peace..there shall be none"
Eze 13:10 – "Peace; and there was no peace"
Eze 13:16 – "and there is no peace"

Pearl

Mat 13:46 – "found one pearl of great price"

Rev 21:21- "every..gate was of one pearl"
Rev 21:21 – "And the 12 gates were 12 pearls"

Pence

Mat 18:28 – "1..fellowservants..owed..100 pence"
Mar 14:5 – "sold for more than 300 pence"
Luk 7:41 – "one owed 500 pence, and the other 50"
Luk 10:35 – "he took out two pence"
Joh 12:5 – "Why..not..ointment sold for 300 pence"

Pennyworth

Mar 6:37 – "buy 200 pennyworth of bread"
Joh 6:7 – "200 pennyworth of bread..not sufficient"

People

Gen 11:6 – "the people is one"
Gen 25:23 – "the one people shall be stronger"
Gen 34:16 – "dwell with you..become one people"
Gen 34:22 – "consent..to be one people"
Exo 5:5 – "the people of the land now are many"
Exo 19:21 – "people..many of them perish"
Num 13:18 – "the people..few or many"
Num 22:3 – "people, because they were many"
Deu 2:10 – "Emims..people great, and many"
Deu 2:21 – "A people great, and many"
Jdg 7:2 – "people..with thee are too many"
Jdg 7:4 – "The people are yet too many"
1Sal 6:19 – "LORD had smitten many..people"
1Sa 14:24 – "none of the people tasted any food"
2Sa 1:4 – "many of the people also are fallen"
Ezr 10:13 – "But the people are many"
Neh 7:4 – "but the people were few therein"
Neh 12:38 – "the ½ of the people upon the wall"
Isa 2:3 – "many people shall go and say"
Isa 2:4 – "and shall rebuke many people"
Isa 17:12 – "the multitude of many people"
Isa 63:3 – "people there was none with me"
Ezk 17:9 – "many people to pluck it up"
Ezk 27:33 – "thou filledst many people"
Ezk 32:3 – "a company of many people"
Ezk 32:9 – "vex the hearts of many people"
Ezk 32:10 – "I will make many people amazed"
Ezk 38:6 – "Gomer..many people with thee"
Ezk 38:8 – "out of many people"
Ezk 38:9 – "many people with thee"
Ezk 38:15 – "many people with thee"
Ezk 38:22 – "upon..many people..with him"
Mic 4:3 – "judge among many people"
Mic 4:13 – "shalt beat in pieces many people"
Mic 5:7 – "in the midst of many people"
Mic 5:8 – "in the midst of many people"
Hab 2:10 – "by cutting off many people"
Zec 8:22 – "many people and strong nations"
Mar 6:33 – "the people..many knew him"

Joh 7:31 – "many of the people believed"
Joh 7:40 – "Many of the people therefore"
Rom 10:19 – "by them that are no people"
Rev 10:11 – "many peoples..nations"

Persecutor

Psa 119:157 – "Many..my persecutors..enemies"

Person

Exo 12:48 – "no uncircumcised person shall eat"
Num 31:35 – "32,000 persons in all, of women"
Num 31:40 – "And the persons were 16,000"
Num 31:40 – "the LORD's tribute was 32 persons"
Num 31:46 – "And 16,000 persons;"
Deu 10:22 – "down into Egypt with 70 persons"
Jdg 9:2 – "sons of Jerubbaal..are 70 persons"
Jdg 9:5 – "slew.. sons of Jerubbaal..70 persons"
Jdg 9:18 – "slain..70 persons, upon one stone"
Jdg 20:39 – "Benjamin.. to smite..about 30 persons"
1Sa 9:22 – "were bidden..about thirty persons"
1Sa 22:18 – "slew..85 persons..wear a linen ephod"
2Ki 10:6 – "Now the king's sons, being 70 persons"
2Ki 10:7 – "slew 70 persons, and put their heads"
Psa 105:37 – "there was not one feeble person"
Jer 52:28 – "carried away captive..3,023 Jews"
Jer 52:29 – "carried away captive..832 persons"
Jer 52:30 – "carried away captive..745 persons"
Jer 52:30 – "captive..all the persons were 4600"
Ezk 17:17 – "to cut off many persons"
Eze 44:25 – "shall come at no dead person"
Jon 4:11 – "120,000 persons that cannot discern"
Luk 15:7 – "99 just persons..need no repentance"
2Co 1:11 – "by the means of many persons"
2Pet 2:5 – "saved Noah the eighth person"

Petition

1Ki 2:16 – "I ask one petition of thee"
1Ki 2:20 – "I desire one small petition"

Pharisee

Mat 3:7 – "many of the Pharisees & Sadducees"
Luk 7:36 – "one of the Pharisees desired him"
Luk 14:1 – "house of one of the chief Pharisees"
Luk 18:10 – "Two men..one a Pharisee"

Physician

Jer 8:22 – "is there no physician there?"
Mar 5:26 – "suffered..of many physicians"

Piece

Gen 15:10 – "laid each piece one against another"
Gen 20:16 – "given..brother 1000 pieces of silver"
Gen 33:19 – "bought..a field..100 pieces of money"
Gen 37:28 – "sold Joseph..for 20 pieces of silver"
Gen 45:22 – "to Benjamin..300 pieces of silver"
Exo 37:7 – "beaten out of one piece made he them"
Jos 24:32 – "ground.. bought..100 pieces of silver"
Jdg 9:4 – "they gave him 70 pieces of silver"
Jdg 16:5 – "give..every 1 of us 1100 pieces..silver"
Jud 19:29 – "concubine..divided her..into 12 pieces"
1Ki 11:30 – "Ahijah..rent it in twelve pieces"
1Ki 11:31 – "said to Jeroboam, Take thee 10 pieces"
2Ki 2:12 – "his own clothes..rent them in 2 pieces"
2Ki 5:5 – "took with him..6,000 pieces of gold"
2Ki 6:25 – "ass's head..sold for 80 pieces of silver"
2Ki 6:25 – "dove's dung for five pieces of silver"
Son 8:11 – "was to bring 1000 pieces of silver"
Hos 3:2 – "I bought her to me for 15 piees of silver"
Amo 4:7 – "one piece was rained upon"
Zec 11:12 – "my price thirty pieces of silver"
Zec 11:13 – "And I took the 30 pieces of silver"
Mat 26:15 – "they covenanted..30 pieces of silver"
Mat 27:3 – "brought again the 30 pieces of silver"
Mat 27:9 – "they took the 30 pieces of silver"
Luk 15:8 – "woman having ten pieces of silver"
Luk 15:8 – "pieces or silver, if she lose one"
Act 19:19 – "books..price..50,000 pieces of silver"

Pigeon

Lev 5:7 – "two young pigeons..sin..burnt offering"
Lev 5:11 – "not able to bring..two young pigeons"
Lev 12:8 – "2 young pigeons..burnt..sin offering"
Lev 14:22 – "2 young pigeons..sin..burnt offering"
Lev 15:14 – "two young pigeons..unto the priest"
Lev 15:29 – "two young pigeons..unto the priest"
Num 6:10 – "two young pigeons, to the priest"
Luk 2:24 – "sacrifice..or two young pigeons"

Pillar

Exo 24:4 – "12 pillars acc. to the 12 tribes of Israel"
Exo 26:32 – "hang it upon 4 pillars..shittim wood"
Exo 26:37 – "five pillars of shittim wood"
Exo 27:10 – "20 pillars thereof & their 20 sockets"
Exo 27:11 – "his 20 pillars and their 20 sockets"
Exo 27:12 – "their pillars 10, and their sockets 10"
Exo 27:14 – "their pillars 3, and their sockets 3"
Exo 27:15 – "their pillars 3, and their sockets 3"
Exo 27:16 – "their pillars 4, and their sockets 4"
Exo 36:36 – "four pillars of shittim wood"
Exo 36:38 – "five pillars of it with their hooks"
Exo 38:19 – "their pillars were four"
Exo 38:10 – "Their pillars were twenty"
Exo 38:11 – "north side..pillars were twenty"
Exo 38:12 – "west side..their pillars ten"

Exo 38:14 – "their pillars 3, and their sockets 3"
Exo 38:15 – "their pillars 3, and their sockets 3"
Exo 38:19 – "pillars were 4..sockets of brass 4"
Jdg 16:29 – "Samson took hold..two middle pillars"
1Ki 7:3 – "beams, that lay on 45 pillars"
1Ki 7:3 – *"fifteen in a row"*
1Ki 7:15 – "two pillars of brass"
1Ki 7:20 – "And the chapiters upon the two pillars"
1Ki 7:20 – "the chapiters upon the two pillars"
1Ki 7:41 – "2 pillars, & the 2 bowls of the chapiters"
1Ki 7:41 – "that were on the top of the two pillars"
2Ki 25:16 – "two pillars, one sea, and the bases"
2Ki 25:17 – "height of the one pillar was 18 cubits"
2Ki 25:17 – "second pillar with wreathen work"
2Ch 3:15 – "he made before the house two pillars"
2Ch 4:12 – "the two pillars and the pommels"
2Ch 4:12 – "chapiters..on the top of the two pillars"
Pro 9:1 – "Wisdom..hath hewn out her 7 pillars"
Jer 52:20 – Neb's temple booty – "two pillars"
Jer 52:21 – "height of one pillar was 18 cubits"
Jer 52:22 – "second pillar..and the pomegranates"
Ezk 40:49 – "pillars by the posts..one on this side"

Pipe

Zec 4:2 – "seven pipes to the seven lamps"
Zec 4:12 – "through the two golden pipes?"

Pity

Deu 7:16 – "thine eye shall have no pity"
2Sa 12:6 – "because he had no pity"
Isa 13:18 – "they shall have no pity"

Place

Gen 1:9 – "waters..gathered..unto one place"
Num 10:14 – "In the first place..standard..Judah"
Num 20:5 – "it is no place of seed, or of figs"
Neh 2:14 – "there was no place for the beast"
Job 16:18 – "let my cry have no place"
Ecc 3:20 – "All go unto one place"
Ecc 6:6 – "do not all go to one place?"
Isa 5:8 – "till there be no place"
Isa 28:8 – "so that there is no place clean"
Jer 7:32 – "bury..till there be no place"
Jer 19:11 – "till there be no place to bury"
Dan 2:35 – "that no place was found for them"
Joh 8:37 – "my word hath no place in you"
Act 2:1 – "all with one accord in one place"
1Co 11:20 – "come together..into one place"
1Co 14:23 – "whole church..into one place"
Heb 8:7 – "no place have been sought"
Heb 12:17 – "found no place of repentance"
Rev 20:11 – "was found no place for them"

Plague

Exo 11:1 – "one plague more upon Pharaoh"
Exo 30:12 – "that there be no plague"
Num 8:19 – "that there be no plague"
1Sa 6:4 – "1 plague was on you all..on your lords"
Rev 15:1 – "angels having the seven last plagues"
Rev 15:6 – "angels..having the seven plagues"
Rev 15:8 – "till the seven plagues..were fulfilled"
Rev 21:9 – "vials full of the 7 last plagues"

Pleasure

Ecc 5:4 – "he hath no pleasure in fools"
Ecc 12:1 – "I have no pleasure in them"
Jer 22:28 – "vessel wherein is no pleasure?"
Jer 48:38 – "vessel wherein is no pleasure"
Eze 18:32 – "I have no pleasure in..death "
Eze 33:11 – "no pleasure..death of the wicked"
Hos 8:8 – "a vessel wherein is no pleasure"
Mal 1:10 – "I have no pleasure in you"
Heb 10:6 – "thou hast had no pleasure"
Heb 10:38 – "soul shall have no pleasure"

Point

Jam 2:10 – "offend in one point..guilty of all

Pomegranate

1Ki 7:20 – "the pomegranates were 200 in rows"
1Ki 7:42 – "400 pomegranates for the 2 networks"
2Ch 3:16 – "100 pomegranates..on the chains"
2Ch 4:13 – "400 pomegranates on the 2 wreaths"
Jer 52:23 – "96 pomegranates on a side"
Jer 52:23 – "the pomegranates..100 round about"

Pommel

2Ch 4:12 – "2 wreaths to cover the two pommels"
2Ch 4:13 – "cover the 2 pommels of the chapiters"

Poor

Deu 15:4 – "there shall be no poor among you"
Isa 14:30 – "the firstborn of the poor shall feed"

Porch

Joh 5:2 – "Bethesda, having five porches"

Porter

1Ch 9:22 – "porters in the gates were 212"
1Ch 9:26 – "4 chief porters, were in their set office"
1Ch 23:5 – "Moreover 4,000 were porters"
1Ch 26:17 – "Eastward were six Levites"
1Ch 26:17 – "northward four a day"
1Ch 26:17 – "southward four a day"
1Ch 26:17 – "toward Asuppim two and two"
1Ch 26:18 – "four at the causeway"
1Ch 26:18 – "two at Parbar"
Neh 7:45 – "porters: the children of Shallum..138"
Neh 11:19 – "porters..that kept the gates..172"

Portion

Gen 48:22 – "I have given to thee 1 portion above"
Num 31:30 – "one portion of fifty"
Num 31:47 – "one portion of fifty..unto the Levites"
Deu 21:17 – "a double portion of all that he hath"
Jos 17:5 – "there fell ten portions to Manasseh"
Jos 17:14 – "Why has thou given me..one portion"
2Ki 2:9 – "double portion of thy spirit be upon me"
Ezr 4:16 – "have no portion on this side the river"
Neh 2:20 – "ye have no portion, nor right"
Ezk 45:7 – "over against one of the portions"
Ezk 47:13 – "Joseph shall have two portions"

Possession

Eze 44:28 – "give them no possession in Israel"

Post

Exo 12:7 – "blood, strike it on the 2 side posts"
Exo 12:22 – "strike the lintel and the 2 side posts"
Exo 12:23 – "the lintel, and on the 2 side posts"
Jdg 16:3 – "Samson..took the doors..the two posts"
Jer 51:31 – "One post shall run to meet another"

Pound

1Ki 10:17 – "3 pound of gold went to one shield"
Ezr 2:69 – "They gave..5000 pound of silver"
Neh 7:71 – "to the treasure..2,200 pound of silver"
Neh 7:72 – "people gave..2000 pound of silver"
Luk 19:13 – "delivered them ten pounds"
Luk 19:16 – "thy pound hath gained ten pounds"
Luk 19:18 – "thy pound hath gained five pounds"
Luk 19:24 – "give it to him that hath ten pounds"
Luk 19:25 – "Lord, he hath ten pounds"
Joh 19:39 – "myrrh..aloes..100 pound weight"

Power

Exo 21:8 – "he shall have no power"
Lev 26:37 – "no power..before your enemies"
Jos 8:20 – "they had no power to flee"
2Ch 14:11 – "them that have no power"
2Ch 22:9 – "Ahaziah..no power to keep..kingdom"
Isa 50:2 – "or have I no power to deliver?"
Dan 3:27 – " the fire had no power"
Dan 8:7 – "no power in the ram to stand"
Joh 19:11 – "no power at all against me"
Rom 13:1 – "there is no power but of God"
Rev 20:6 – "the second death hath no power"

Prayer

Isa 1:15 – "when ye make many prayers"

Preeminence

Ecc 3:19 – "a man hath no preeminence"

Present

1Sa 10:27 – "brought him no presents"
2Ki 17:4 –"brought no present to the king"

President

Dan 6:2 – "And over these three presidents"
Dan 6:2 – "of whom Daniel was the first"

Prey

Amo 3:4 – "a lion..hath no prey?"

Priest

Jos 6:4 – "And 7 priests shall bear..7 trumpets"
Jos 6:6 – "7 priests bear 7 trumpets..rams' horns"
Jos 6:8 – "7 priests bearing the 7 trumpets"
Jos 6:13 – "7 priests bearing 7 trumpets"
2Ki 25:18 – "Zephaniah the second priest"
2Ch 5:12 – "120 priests sounding with trumpets"
2Ch 26:17 – "Azariah..w/ him 80 priests of..LORD"
2Ch 29:34 – "But the priests were too few"
Ezr 3:12 – "many of the priests and Levites"
Ezr 8:24 – "12 of the chief..priests..10 of..brethren"
Neh 7:39 – "The priests..children of Jedaiah..973"
Jer 52:24 – "Zephaniah the second priest"
Hos 4:6 – "thou shalt be no priest to me"
Heb 7:23 – " they truly were many priests"

Prince

Gen 17:20 – "Ishmael..12 princes shall he beget"
Gen 25:16 – "Ishmael..12 princes"
Num 7:3 – "a wagon for two of the princes"
Num 16:2 – "250 princes of the assembly"
Num 17:6 – "every one of..princes gave him a rod"
Num 34:18 – "one prince of every tribe, to divide"
Jos 22:14 – "And with him ten princes"
Jos 22:14 – "princes..each one was an head"
Jdg 7:25 – "2 princes..Midianites, Oreb and Zeeb"
Neh 12:32 – "Hoshaiah, & ½ of the princes..Judah"
Est 1:14 – "seven princes of Media and Persia"
Est 6:9 – "one of the king's most noble princes"
Psa 82:7 – "fall like one of the princes"
Pro 28:2 – "many are the princes thereof"
Ezk 22:6 – "princes of Israel, every one"
Dan 6:1 – "Darius set over..kingdom 120 princes"
Dan 10:13 – "Michael, one of the chief princes"
Dan 11:5 – "one of his princes"
1Co 2:8 – "none of the princes of this world"

Principle

Heb 5:12 – "1st principles of the oracles of God"

Prisoner

Mar 15:6 – "released unto them one prisoner"

Profit

Ecc 2:11 – "was no profit under the sun"
Jer 16:19 – "things wherein there is no profit"
2Ti 2:14 – "about words to no profit"

Proof

Act 1:3 – "alive..by many infallible proofs"

Prophecy

2Pe 1:20 – "no prophecy of the scripture"

Prophet

1Ki 18:4 – "Obadiah took 100 prophets..hid them"
1Ki 18:19 – "the prophets of Baal 450"
1Ki 18:19 – "the prophets of the groves 400"
1Ki 18:22 – "Baal's prophets are 450 men"
1Ki 18:25 – "prophets of Baal..ye are many"
1Ki 18:40 – "prophets..let not one of them escape"
2Ch 18:5 – "king..gathered..of prophets 400 men"

Amo 7:14 – "answered Amos..I was no prophet"
Zec 13:5 – "I am no prophet"
Mat 13:17 – "many prophets and righteous men"
Mat 16:14 – "Jeremias, or one of the prophets"
Mar 6:15 – "or as one of the prophets"
Mar 8:28 – "One of the prophets"
Luk 4:24 – "No prophet is accepted"
Luk 9:8 – "one of the old prophets was risen"
Luk 9:19 – "one of the old prophets is risen"
Luk 10:24 – "many prophets..kings have desired"
Joh 7:52 – "out of Galilee ariseth no prophet"
1Jo 4:1 – "many false prophets are gone out"
Rev 11:10 – "these 2 prophets tormented them"

Proselyte

Mat 23:15 – "sea and land to make one proselyte"
Act 13:43 – "many of the Jews &..proselytes"

Proverb

1Ki 4:32 – Solomon – "spake 3000 proverbs"
Ecc 12:9 – "set in order many proverbs"
Joh 16:29 – "plainly, and speakest no proverb"

Province

Est 1:1 – "Ahasuerus..reigned..over 127 provinces"
Est 8:9 – "India unto Ethiopia, an 127 provinces"
Est 9:30 – "letters..unto all Jews..127 provinces"

Psalm

Act 13:33 – "as it is written in the second psalm"

Publican

Mat 9:10 – "many publicans and sinners"
Mar 2:15 – "many publicans and sinners sat also"

Punishment

1Sa 28:10 – "there shall no punishment happen"

Purpose

Isa 30:7 – "help in vain, and to no purpose"

Purse

Pro 1:14 – "let us all have one purse"

Quaternion

Acts 12:4 – "four quaternions of soliders"

Quarter

Deu 22:12 – "fringes..4 quarters of thy vesture"
1Ch 9:24 – "4 quarters were..porters..east, west"
Jer 49:36 – "four winds from the four quarters"
Rev 20:8 – "nations..in the 4 quarters of..earth"

Queen

Son 6:8 – "There are threescore queens"

Question

Job 9:3 – "he cannot answer him 1 of a 1000"
Mar 11:29 – "I will ask of you one question"
1Co 10:25 – "eat, asking no question"
1Co 10:27 – "no question..conscience sake"

Rain

Deu 11:14 – "I will give..1st rain & the latter rain"
Deu 11:17 – "shut up the heaven..no rain"
2Sa 1:21 – "let there be no dew, neither..rain"
1Ki 8:35 – "When..there is no rain"
1Ki 17:7 – " had been no rain in the land"
2Ch 6:26 – "heaven is shut up..there is no rain"
2Ch 7:13 – "shut up heaven..there be no rain"
Isa 5:6 – "that they rain no rain upon it"
Jer 3:3 – "hath been no latter rain"
Jer 14:4 – "there was no rain in the earth"
Zec 14:17 – "upon them shall be no rain"
Zec 14:18 – "family..that have no rain"

Raisin *(see Bunch & Cluster)*

Rams

1 *Ram*

Exo 29:16 – "Thou shalt also take one ram"
Lev 16:5 – "one ram for a burnt offering"
Num 6:14 – "one ram without blemish"
Num 7:15 – "one ram..for a burnt offering"

Num 7:21 – "one ram..for a burnt offering"
Num 7:27 – "one ram..for a burnt offering"
Num 7:33 – "one ram..for a burnt offering"
Num 7:39 – "one ram..for a burnt offering"
Num 7:45 – "one ram..for a burnt offering"
Num 7:51 – "one ram..for a burnt offering"
Num 7:57 – "one ram..for a burnt offering"
Num 7:63 – "one ram..for a burnt offering"
Num 7:69 – "one ram..for a burnt offering"
Num 7:75 – "one ram..for a burnt offering"
Num 7:81 – "one ram..for a burnt offering"
Num 15:11 – "for one ram, or for a lamb, or a kid"
Num 28:11 – "one ram, 7 lambs of the first year"
Num 28:12 – "flour..oil..for one ram"
Num 28:19 – "two young bullocks, and one ram"
Num 28:27 – "burnt offering...one ram"
Num 28:28 – "meat offering...1 bullock...1 ram"
Num 29:2 – "burnt offering..one ram"
Num 29:9 – "two tenth deals to one ram"
Num 29:36 – "burnt offering..1 bullock, 1 ram"

2 *Rams*

Exo 29:1 – "Take 1 young bullock, and two rams"
Exo 29:3 – "with the bullock and the two rams"
Lev 8:2 – "Aaron and his sons..two rams"
Lev 23:18 – "two rams..for a burnt offering"
Num 29:13 – "burnt offering..two rams"
Num 29:14 – "to each ram of the two rams"
Num 29:17 – "second day ye shall offer..2 rams"
Num 29:20 – "And on the third day..two rams"
Num 29:23 – "And on the fourth day...two rams"
Num 29:26 – "And on the fifth day...two rams"
Num 29:29 – "And on the sixth day...two rams"
Num 29:32 – "And on the seventh day...two rams"

5 *Rams*

Num 7:17 – "five rams..offering of Nashon"
Num 7:23 – "five rams..offering of Nethaneel"
Num 7:29 – "five rams..offering of Eliab"
Num 7:35 – "five rams..offering of Elizur"
Num 7:41 – "five rams..offering of Shelumiel"
Num 7:47 – "five rams..offering of Eliasaph"
Num 7:53 – "five rams..offering of Elishama"
Num 7:59 – "five rams..offering of Gamaliel"
Num 7:65 – "five rams..offering of Abidan"
Num 7:71 – "five rams..offering of Ahiezer"
Num 7:77 – "five rams..offering of Pagiel"
Num 7:83 – "five rams..offering of Ahira"

7 *Rams*

Num 23:1 – "prepare me here 7 oxen..7 rams"
Num 23:29 – "prepare me..7 bullocks and 7 rams"
1Ch 15:26 – "offered 7 bullocks and 7 rams"
2Ch 13:9 – "consecrate himself with..seven rams"
2Ch 29:21 – "brought..7 rams..for a sin offering"
Job 42:8 – "take..now 7 bullocks & 7 rams"
Ezk 45:23 – "offering..7 bullocks and 7 rams"

8+ *Rams*

Gen 32:14 – "twenty rams"
Num 7:87 – "the rams twelve"
Num 7:88 – "the rams sixty"
2Ki 3:4 – "Mesha..100,000 rams, with the wool"
1Ch 29:21 – "sacrificed..1000 rams"
2Ch 29:32 – "congregation brought..100 rams"
2Ch 17:11 – "Arabians brought him..7,700 rams"
Ezr 6:17 – "offered at the dedication..200 rams"
Ezr 8:35 – "burnt offerings..96 rams"
Mic 6:7 – "LORD be pleased with 1000's of rams"

Rank

Num 2:16 – "camp of Reuben..second rank"
Num 2:24 – "camp of Ephraim..third rank"
1Ki 7:4 – "light was against light in three ranks"
1Ki 7:5 – "light was against light in three ranks"

Razor

Num 6:5 – "no razor come upon his head"
Jdg 13:5 – "no razor shall come on his head"
1Sa 1:11 – "no razor come upon his head"

Reckoning

2Ki 22:7 – "there was no reckoning made"
1Ch 23:11 – "they were in one reckoning"

Recompense

Jer 16:18 – "I will recompense..their sin double"

Reed

➤ **Note:** *the measuring reed of Ezekiel 40-48*

Ezk 40:5 – "measuring reed of 6 cubits long"
Ezk 41:8 – "a full reed of six great cubits"

Ezk 40:5 – "breadth of the building, one reed"
Ezk 40:5 – "the building..the height, one reed"
Ezk 40:6 – "gate, which was one reed broad"
Ezk 40:6 – "other threshold..one reed broad"
Ezk 40:7 – "every little chamber..one reed long"
Ezk 40:7 – "every little chamber..one reed broad"
Ezk 40:7 – "gate by the porch..one reed"
Ezk 40:8 – "porch of the gate within was one reed"
Ezk 42:16 – "east side..500 reeds"
Ezk 42:17 – "north side..500 reeds"
Ezk 42:18 – "south side..500 reeds"
Ezk 42:19 – "west side..500 reeds"

Ezk 42:20 – "wall round about, 500 reeds long"
Ezk 42:20 – "wall round about..500 reeds broad"
Ezk 45:1 – "holy portion..length of 25,000 reeds"
Ezk 45:1 – "holy portion..breadth..10,000"
Ezk 45:2 – "for the sanctuary 500 in length"
Ezk 45:2 – "for the sanctuary..500 in breadth"
Ezk 45:3 – "length of 25,000..holy place"
Ezk 45:3 – "breadth of 10,000..holy place"
Ezk 45:5 – "the 25,000 of length..Levites..have"
Ezk 45:5 – "the 10,000 of breadth..Levites..have"
Ezk 45:6 – "appoint..of the city..5,000 broad"
Ezk 45:6 – "appoint..of the city..25,000 long"
Ezk 48:8 – "border..Judah..25,000 reeds..breadth"
Ezk 48:9 – "oblation..25,000 in length"
Ezk 48:9 – "oblation..10,000 in breadth"
Ezk 48:10 – "oblation..north 25,000 in length"
Ezk 48:10 – "oblation..west 10,000 in breadth"
Ezk 48:10 – "oblation..east 10,000 in breadth"
Ezk 48:10 – "oblation..south 25,000 in length"
Ezk 48:13 – "Levites shall have 25,000 in length"
Ezk 48:13 – "Levites..shall have 10,000 in breadth"
Ezk 48:13 – "all the length shall be 25,000"
Ezk 48:13 – "the breadth 10,000"
Ezk 48:15 – "5000, that are left..profane place"
Ezk 48:15 – "over against..25,000..profane place"
Ezk 48:16 – "north side 4,500"
Ezk 48:16 – "south side 4,500"
Ezk 48:16 – "east side 4,500"
Ezk 48:16 – "west side 4,500"
Ezk 48:17 – "suburbs..toward the north 250"
Ezk 48:17 – "suburbs..toward the south 250"
Ezk 48:17 – "suburbs..toward the east 250"
Ezk 48:17 – "suburbs..toward the west 250"
Ezk 48:18 – "holy portion..10,000 eastward"
Ezk 48:18 – "holy portion..10,000 westward"
Ezk 48:20 – "oblation..25,000 by 25,000"
Ezk 48:21 – "over against the 25,000..oblation"
Ezk 48:21 – "25,000 toward the west border"

Remedy

2Ch 36:16 – "wrath..till there was no remedy"

Remembrance

Psa 6:5 – "in death..no remembrance of thee"
Ecc 1:11 – "no remembrance of former things"
Ecc 2:16 – "no remembrance of the wise"

Remission

Heb 9:22 – "shedding of blood is no remission"

Remnant

Ezr 9:14 – "should be no remnant nor escaping"

Jer 11:23 – "shall be no remnant of them"

Repentance

Luk 15:7 – "persons, which need no repentance"

Report

1Sa 2:24 – "it is no good report that I hear"

Reproach

Neh 2:17 – "that we be no more a reproach"

Reproof

Psa 38:14 – "in whose mouth are no reproofs"
Pro 1:25 – "would none of my reproof"

Reputation

Php 2:7 – "made himself of no reputation"

Respect

Rom 2:11 – "no respect of persons with God"
Col 3:25 – "there is no respect of persons"

Respecter

Act 10:34 – "God is no respecter of persons"

Rest

Gen 8:9 – "the dove found no rest"
Job 30:17 – "my sinews take no rest"
Pro 29:9 – "rage or laugh, there is no rest"
Isa 23:12 – "shalt thou have no rest"
Isa 62:7 – "And give him no rest"
Jer 45:3 – "Woe is me..I find no rest"
Lam 1:3 – "Judah..she findeth no rest"
Lam 2:18 – "give thyself no rest"
Lam 5:5 – "we labour, and have no rest"
Mat 12:43 – "seeking rest, and findeth none"
Luk 11:24 – "seeking rest; and finding none"
2Co 2:13 – "I had no rest in my spirit"
2Co 7:5 – "our flesh had no rest"
Rev 14:11 – "they have no rest day nor night"

Restraint

1Sa 14:6 - "there is no restraint to the LORD"

Resurrection

Mat 22:23 – "say that there is no resurrection"
Mar 12:18 – "say there is no resurrection"
Act 23:8 – "say that there is no resurrection"
1Co 15:12 – "is no resurrection of the dead"
1Co 15:13 – "be no resurrection of the dead"
Rev 20:5 – "This is the first resurrection."
Rev 20:6 – "hath part in the first resurrection"

Reward

Pro 24:20 – "no reward to the evil man"
Eze 16:34 – "no reward is given unto thee"
Mat 6:1 – "no reward of your Father"

Rib

Gen 2:21 – "sleep..upon Adam..took 1 of his ribs"
2Sa 2:23 – "smote him under the fifth rib"
2Sa 3:27 – "smote him..under fifth the fifth rib"
2Sa 4:6 – "smote him under the 5th rib"
2Sa 20:10 – "Amasa..smote..in the fifth rib"
Dan 7:5 – "it had three ribs in the mouth of it"

Rich

Mar 12:41 – "many..rich cast in much"

Right

Neh 2:20 – "ye have no portion, nor right"
Heb 13:10 – "whereof they have no right to eat"

Righteous *(as in Righteous Men)*

Gen 18:24 – "50 righteous within the city"
Gen 18:24 – "spare the place for the 50 righteous"
Gen 18:26 – "If I find in Sodom 50 righteous"
Gen 18:28 – "shall lack 5 of the 50 righteous"
Gen 18:28 – "destroy all the city for lack of five?"
Gen 18:28 – "If I find there 45, I will not destroy it"
Gen 18:29 – "Peradventure there..be 40 found"
Gen 18:29 – "I will not destroy it for forty's sake"
Gen 18:30 – "Peradventure..30 be found there"
Gen 18:30 – "I will not do it, if I find 30 there"
Gen 18:31 – "Peradventure..be 20 found there"
Gen 18:31 – "I will not destroy it for twenty's sake"
Gen 18:32 – "Peradventure 10 shall be found there"

Gen 18:32 – "I will not destroy it for ten's sake"

Rings

Exo 25:12 – "thou shalt cast four rings of gold"
Exo 25:12 – "two rings shall be in the one side"
Exo 25:12 – "two rings in the other side of it"
Exo 25:26 – "make for it four rings of gold"
Exo 26:24 – "above the head of it unto one ring"
Exo 27:4 – "upon the net..make four brasen rings"
Exo 28:23 – "make upon the breastplate 2 rings"
Exo 28:23 – "put the two rings on the two ends"
Exo 28:24 – "chains of gold in the two rings"
Exo 28:26 – "make two rings of gold"
Exo 28:27 – "two other rings of gold"
Exo 30:4 – "two golden rings..under the crown"
Exo 36:29 – "coupled together..to one ring"
Exo 37:3 – "cast for it four rings of gold"
Exo 37:3 – "even two rings upon the one side"
Exo 37:3 – "two rings upon the other side of it"
Exo 37:13 – "he cast for it four rings of gold"
Exo 37:27 – "two rings of gold..under the crown"
Exo 39:16 – "they made..two gold rings"
Exo 39:16 – "put the two rings in the two ends"
Exo 39:17 – "2 wreathen chains..in the two rings"
Exo 39:19 – "they made two rings of gold"
Exo 39:20 – "they made two other golden rings"
Ezk 1:18 – "rings..full of eyes round about them 4"

Ripe

Num 18:13 – "whatsoever is first ripe in the land"
Jer 24:2 – "like the figs that are first ripe"

River

Gen 2:13 – "name of the second river is Gihon"
Gen 2:14 – "name of the third river is Hiddekel"
Gen 2:14 – "And the fourth river is Euphrates."
Mic 6:7 – "pleased..with 10,000's of rivers of oil?"

Rod

Num 17:2 – "the house of their fathers 12 rods"
Num 17:3 – "1 rod..for the head..house of..fathers"
Num 17:6 – "their fathers' houses, even 12 rods"
Eze 19:14 – "she hath no strong rod"

Roe

Son 4:5 – "breasts..like two young roes..twins"
Son 7:3 – "breasts..like two young roes..twins"

Roll

Jer 36:28 – "the former words..in the first roll"

Room

Luk 2:7 – "no room for them in the inn"
Luk 12:17 – "no room..to bestow my fruits"

Root

Mat 13:6 – "had no root, they withered away"
Mar 4:6 – "it had no root, it withered away"
Mar 4:17 – "have no root in themselves"
Luk 8:13 – "these have no root"

Row

Exo 28:17 – "four rows of stones"
Exo 28:17 – "first row..sardius, a topaz…"
Exo 28:17 – "carbuncle: this shall be the first row"
Exo 28:18 – "2ⁿᵈ row..emerald..sapphire..diamond"
Exo 28:19 – "third row a ligure..agate..amethyst"
Exo 29:20 – "fourth row a beryl..onyx..jasper"
Exo 39:10 – "they set it in four rows of stones"
Exo 39:10 – "1ˢᵗ row..sardius..topaz..carbuncle"
Exo 39:10 – "this was the first row"
Exo 39:11 – "2ⁿᵈ row..emerald..sapphire..diamond"
Exo 39:12 – "third row..ligure..agate..amethyst"
Exo 39:13 – "fourth row..beryl..onyx..jasper"
Lev 24:6 – "two rows, six on a row..pure tables"
1Ki 6:36 – "built the inner court w/ 3 rows..stone"
1Ki 7:2 – "four rows of cedar pillars"
1Ki 7:4 – "windows in three rows"
1Ki 7:12 – "three rows of hewed stones"
1Ki 7:18 – "made the pillars..2 rows round about"
1Ki 7:18 – "two rows round about..one network"
1Ki 7:24 – "the knops were cast in two rows"
1Ki 7:42 – "2 rows of pomegranates..1 network"
2Ch 4:3 – "two rows of oxen were cast"
2Ch 4:13 – "2 rows..pomegranates..each wreath"
Ezr 6:4 – "3 rows of great stones"

Rule

Pro 25:28 – "no rule over his own spirit"

Ruler

Neh 5:16 – "at my table an 150..Jews and rulers"
Neh 12:40 – "I, and the ½ of the rulers with me"
Pro 6:7 – "having no guide, overseer, or ruler"
Dan 2:10 – "there is no king, lord, nor ruler"
Dan 5:7 – "shall be the third ruler in the kingdom"

Dan 5:16 – "the third ruler in the kingdom"
Dan 5:29 – "he should be the third ruler"
Hab 1:14 – "fishes..that have no ruler"
Mar 5:22 – "one of the rulers of the synagogue"

Sabbath

Lev 23:15 – "seven sabbaths shall be complete"
Lev 23:16 – "morrow after the seventh sabbath"
Lev 25:8 – "seven sabbaths of years"
Lev 25:8 – "space of the seven sabbaths of years"
Isa 66:23 – "from one sabbath to another"
Luk 6:1 – "on the second Sabbath after the first"

Sacrifice

Heb 10:12 – "offered one sacrifice for sins"

Sadducee

Mat 3:7 – "many of the Pharisees & Sadducees"

Saint

Deu 33:2 – "LORD.. Sinai..with 10,000's of saints"
Dan 8:13 – "Then I heard one saint speaking"
Act 26:10 – "many of the saints did I shut up"
Jud 14 – "Lord cometh with 10,000's of his saints"

Sake

Gen 18:29 – "I will not destroy it for forty's sake"
Gen 18:31 – "I will not destroy it for 20's sake"
Gen 18:32 – "I will not destroy it for ten's sake"

Samaritan

Joh 4:39 – "many of the Samaritans..believed"

Sand

Jos 11:4 – "as..sand..on the sea shore in multitude"
2Sa 17:11 – "as the sand..by the sea for multitude"
Jer 33:22 – "neither the sand of the sea measured"
Hos 1:10 – "sand of the sea..cannot be..numbered"
Heb 11:12 – "as..sand..by..seashore innumerable"
Rev 20:8 – "number of whom..as the sand of..sea"

Satisfaction

Num 35:31 – "no satisfaction for..a murderer"
Num 35:32 – "take no satisfaction for him"

Saviour

Isa 43:11 – "beside me there is no saviour"
Isa 45:21 – "a Saviour; there is none beside me"
Hos 13:4 – "for there is no saviour beside me"

Scale

Lev 11:12 – "Whatsoever hath no fins nor scales"
Job 41:16 – "One is so near to another, that no air"
Job 41:17 – "They are joined one to another"

Sceva

Act 19:14 – "sons of one Sceva, a Jew"

Schism

1Co 12:25 – "be no schism in the body"

Scribe

Mar 12:28 – "And one of the scribes came"

Scrip

Mar 6:8 – "no scrip, no bread, no money"

Sea (as in *Laver*)

1Ki 7:44 – "one sea, and 12 oxen under the sea"
2Ki 25:16 – "two pillars, one sea, and the bases"
2Ch 4:15 – "One sea, and twelve oxen under it."
Jer 52:20 – "two pillars, one sea"

Sea (as in *Ocean*)

Act 27:41 – "a place where two seas met"

Seal

Rev 5:1 – "a book written..with 7 seals"
Rev 5:5 – "to loose the seven seals thereof"
Rev 6:1 – "Lamb opened one of the seals"

Rev 6:3 – "when he had opened the second seal"
Rev 6:5 – "when he had opened the third seal"
Rev 6:7 – "when he had opened the fourth seal"
Rev 6:9 – "when he had opened the fifth seal"
Rev 6:12 – "when he had opened the sixth seal"
Rev 8:1 – "when he had opened the 7th seal"

Searching

Isa 40:28 – "no searching of his understanding"

Seat

Rev 4:4 – "round about throne..were 24 seats"

Secret

Eze 28:3 – "no secret that they can hide"
Job 11:6 – "secrets of wisdom..they are double"
Dan 4:9 – "Belteshazzar..no secret troubleth thee"

Seed (as in *Descendants*)

Gen 13:16 – "seed as the dust of the earth"
Gen 13:16 – "number the dust..shall..thy seed be"
Gen 15:3 – "to me thou hast given no seed"
Gen 15:5 – "the stars..So shall thy seed be"
Gen 16:10 – "I will multiply thy seed exceedingly"
Gen 16:10 – "seed..not..numbered for multitude"
Gen 17:2 – "will multiply thy seed exceedingly"
Gen 22:17 – "multiply..seed as..stars..of heaven"
Gen 22:17 – "multiply..seed..as ..sand..sea shore"
Gen 26:4 – "seed to multiply as..stars of heaven"
Gen 32:12 – "seed as the sand of the sea"
Gen 32:12 – "seed..which cannot be numbered"
Job 5:25 – "seed shall be great..as..grass of..earth"
Jer 33:22 – "sand..so will I multiply..seed of David"
Mar 12:20 – "seven brethren.. dying left no seed"
Mar 12:22 – "seven had her, and left no seed"
Gal 3:16 – "And to seeds, as of many"

Sepulchre

2Ch 35:24 – "buried in one of the sepulchres"

Seraphim

Isa 6:2 – "seraphims: each one had six wings"
Isa 6:3 – "and one cried..Holy, holy, holy"
Isa 6:6 – "then flew one of the seraphims"

Servant

Gen 14:14 – "he armed his trained servants..318"
Num 22:22 – "his two servants were with him"
Deu 15:15 – "double hired servant to thee"
1Sa 9:3 – "Take now 1 of the servants with thee"
1Sa 16:18 – "Then answered one of the servants"
1Sa 25:10 – "be many servants now a days"
2Sa 2:15 – "and 12 of the servants of David"
2Sa 9:10 – "Ziba had 15 sons and 20 servants"
2Sa 19:17 – "Ziba..his 15 sons and his 20 servants"
1Ki 2:39 – "2 of the servants of Shimei ran away"
2Ki 1:13 – "let..the life of these 50 thy servants"
2Ki 3:11 – "one of the king of Israel's servants"
2Ki 5:23 – "laid them upon two of his servants"
2Ki 6:12 – "And one of his servants said"
2Ki 7:13 – "And one of his servants answered"
2Ch 8:9 – "did Solomon make no servants"
Ezr 2:65 – "their servants and their maids, 7337"
Neh 4:16 – "½ of my servants wrought in..work"
Neh 4:16 – "other half..held both the spears"
Neh 4:21 – "half of them held the spears"
Neh 7:67 – "manservants..maidservants.. 7,337"
Ezk 46:17 – "gift..inheritance to 1 of his servants"
Mat 21:35 – "took his servants, and beat one"
Luk 15:19 – "make me as one of thy..servants"
Luk 15:26 – "he called one of the servants"
Luk 16:13 – "No servant can serve two masters"
Luk 19:13 – "he called his ten servants"
Luk 19:16 – "Then came the first saying"
Luk 19:18 – "And the second came saying"
Joh 18:26 – "One of the servants of the high priest"
Act 10:7 – "called two of his household servants"
1Ti 6:1 – "as many servants..under the yoke"

Service

Num 8:26 – "shall do no service..Levites"

Seven

Gen 41:20 – "did eat up the first seven fat kine"
Dan 3:19 – "heat the furnace one 7 times more"

Shame

Zep 3:5 – "the unjust knoweth no shame"

Sheep

Exo 22:1 – "If a man steal..restore..four sheep"
Exo 34:19 – "every firstling among thy cattle"
Num 18:17 – "firstling..sheep.. shalt not redeem"
Num 31:32 – "booty...was 675,000 sheep"
Num 31:36 – "went out to war..337,500 sheep"

Num 31:43 – "the congregation..337,500 sheep"
Num 31:37 – "LORD's tribute of..sheep was 675"
Deu 15:19 – "nor shear the firstling of thy sheep"
1Sa 17:28 – "with whom..left those few sheep"
1Sa 25:2 – "man in Maon..he had 3000 sheep"
1Sa 25:18 – "Abigail..took..five sheep"
1Ki 4:23 – "an hundred sheep"
1Ki 8:5 – "sheep..oxen..could not be..numbered"
1Ki 8:63 – "Solomon offered..an 120,000 sheep"
1Ch 5:21 – "of sheep 250,000"
2Ch 7:5 – "Solomon offered..an 120,000 sheep"
2Ch 15:11 – "offered..of the spoil..7000 sheep"
2Ch 29:33 – "consecrated things..3000 sheep"
2Ch 30:24 – "Hezekiah..did give..7000 sheep"
2Ch 30:24 – "princes gave..10,000 sheep"
Neh 5:18 – "prepared for me daily..6 choice sheep"
Job 1:3 – "His substance also was 7000 sheep"
Job 42:12 – "later end of Job..had 14,000 sheep"
Psa 144:13 – "our sheep may bring forth 1000's"
Psa 144:13 – "our sheep may bring forth..10,000's"
Son 4:2 – "sheep..none is barren among them"
Son 6:6 – "sheep..not one barren among them"
Isa 7:21 – "a man shall nourish..two sheep"
Mat 12:11 – "man that shall have one sheep"
Mat 18:12 – "100 sheep, and one..gone astray"
Mat 18:12 – "doth he not leave the ninety and nine"
Mat 18:13 – "the 99 which went not go astray"
Luk 15:4 – "an 100 sheep, if he lose one"
Luk 15:4 – "doth not leave the 99 in the wilderness"

Sheet

Jdg 14:12 – "I will give you 30 sheets"
Jdg 14:13 – "30 sheets..30 change of garments"

Shekel

0-9 *Shekels*

Gen 24:22 – "a golden earring of ½ shekel weight"
Exo 30:13 – "give, every one..half a shekel"
Exo 30:13 – "½ shekel..the offering of the LORD"
Exo 30:15 – "poor..not give less than ½ a shekel"
Exo 38:26 – "a bekah..that is, half a shekel"
Lev 27:6 – "estimation shall be three shekels"
Lev 27:6 – "estimation shall be...five shekels"
Num 3:47 – "five shekels apiece by the poll"
Num 18:16 – "estimation..money of five shekels"

10 *Shekels*

Gen 24:22 – "bracelets..10 shekels weight of gold"
Lev 27:5 – "estimation shall be..ten shekels"
Lev 27:7 – "estimation shall be...ten shekels"
Num 7:14 – "one spoon of ten shekels"
Num 7:20 – "one spoon..gold..10 shekels"
Num 7:26 – "one golden spoon..10 shekels"
Num 7:32 – "one golden spoon..10 shekels"

Num 7:38 – "one golden spoon..10 shekels"
Num 7:44 – "one golden spoon..10 shekels"
Num 7:50 – "one golden spoon..10 shekels"
Num 7:56 – "one golden spoon..10 shekels"
Num 7:62 – "one golden spoon..10 shekels"
Num 7:68 – "one golden spoon..10 shekels"
Num 7:74 – "one golden spoon..10 shekels"
Num 7:80 – "one golden spoon..10 shekels"
Num 7:86 – "spoons..incense..10 shekels apiece"
Jdg 17:10 – "give thee 10 shekels..silver by..year"
2Sa 18:11 – "have given thee 10 shekels of silver"

11-69 *Shekels*

Exo 21:32 – "he shall give..30 shekels of silver"
Lev 27:3 – "estimation shall be fifty shekels"
Lev 27:4 – "estimation shall be thirty shekels"
Lev 27:5 – "estimation shall be..twenty shekels"
Lev 27:7 – "estimation shall be fifteen shekels"
Lev 27:16 – "barley seed..valued at 50 shekels"
Deu 22:29 – "unto the damsel's father 50 shekels"
Jos 7:21 – "wedge of gold of 50 shekels"
2Sa 24:24 – "threshingfloor..oxen for 50 shekels"
2Ki 15:20 – "of each man 50 shekels of silver"
2Ch 3:9 – "weight of the nails..50 shekels of gold"
Neh 5:15 – "taken of them..40 shekels of silver"
Jer 32:9 – "money, even 17 shekels of silver"
Ezk 4:10 – "meat..eat..by weight, 20 shekels a day"
Ezk 45:12 – "20 shekels, 25 shekels, 15 shekels"

70 *Shekels*

Num 7:13 – "silver bowl of 70 shekels"
Num 7:19 – "silver bowl of 70 shekels"
Num 7:25 – "silver bowl of 70 shekels"
Num 7:31 – "silver bowl of 70 shekels"
Num 7:37 – "silver bowl of 70 shekels"
Num 7:43 – "silver bowl of 70 shekels"
Num 7:49 – "silver bowl of 70 shekels"
Num 7:55 – "silver bowl of 70 shekels"
Num 7:61 – "silver bowl of 70 shekels"
Num 7:67 – "silver bowl of 70 shekels"
Num 7:73 – "silver bowl of 70 shekels"
Num 7:79 – "silver bowl of 70 shekels"

100-999 *Shekels*

Gen 23:15 – "land is worth 400 shekels of silver"
Gen 23:16 – "400 shekels of silver, current money"
Exo 30:23 – "spices..cinnamon..250 shekels"
Exo 30:23 – "spices..calamus 250 shekels"
Exo 30:23 – "spices..myrrh 500 shekels"
Exo 30:24 – "spices..cassia 500 shekels"
Num 7:13 – "charger..weight..130 shekels"
Num 7:19 – "charger..weight..130 shekels"
Num 7:25 – "charger..weight..130 shekels"
Num 7:31 – "charger..weight..130 shekels"
Num 7:37 – "charger..weight..130 shekels"
Num 7:43 – "charger..weight..130 shekels"
Num 7:49 – "charger..weight..130 shekels"

Num 7:55 – "charger..weight..130 shekels"
Num 7:61 – "charger..weight..130 shekels"
Num 7:67 – "charger..weight..130 shekels"
Num 7:73 – "charger..weight..130 shekels"
Num 7:79 – "charger..weight..130 shekels"
Num 7:85 – "each charger..weighing 130 shekels"
Num 7:86 – "gold..spoons was 120 shekels"
Deu 22:19 – "amerce him..in 100 shekels of silver"
Jos 7:21 – "200 shekels of silver"
Jdg 17:4 – "200 shekels..made..a graven image"
1Sa 17:7 – "spear's head..600 shekels of iron"
2Sa 14:26 – "hair of his head at 200 shekels"
2Sa 21:16 – "spear weighed 300 shekels of brass"
1Ki 10:16 – "600 shekels of gold went to 1 target"
1Ki 10:29 – "chariot..for 600 shekels of silver"
1Ki 10:29 – *"an horse for an 150"*
1Ch 21:25 – "David gave Ornan..600 shekels..gold"
2Ch 1:17 – "an horse for an 150"
2Ch 1:17 – "a chariot for 600 shekels of silver"
2Ch 9:15 – "600 shekels of beaten gold..1 target"
2Ch 9:16 – "300 shekels of gold went to 1 shield"

1000+ *Shekels*

Exo 38:24 – "gold..29 talents, and 730 shekels"
  ➤   *Thus, 87,730 shekels or 29.24 talents*
Exo 38:25 – "silver..100 talents, & 1,775 shekels"
  ➤   *Thus, 301,775 shekels or 100.59 talents*
Exo 38:28 – "of the 1,775 shekels he made hooks"
Exo 38:29 – "brass..70 talents, and 2,400 shekels"
  ➤   *Thus, 212,400 shekels or 70.8 talents*
Num 3:50 – "firstborn..of Israel..1,365 shekels"
Num 7:85 – "silver vessels weighed 2400 shekels"
Num 31:52 – "gold of the offering..16,750 shekels"
Jdg 8:26 – "weight..golden earrings..1700 shekels"
Jdg 17:2 – "1100 shekels of silver that were taken"
Jdg 17:3 – "restored the 1100 shekels of silver"
1Sa 17:5 – "weight of..coat..5000 shekels of brass"
2Sa 18:12 – "Though I..receive 1000 shekels"

Shepherd

Num 27:17 – "sheep which have no shepherd"
2Ch 18:16 – "sheep that have no shepherd"
Ecc 12:11 – "which are given from one shepherd"
Eze 34:5 – "because there is no shepherd"
Eze 34:8 – "because there was no shepherd"
Ezk 34:23 – "I will set up 1 shepherd over them"
Ezk 37:24 – "they all shall have one shepherd"
Mic 5:5 – "raise against him seven shepherds"
Zec 10:2 – "there was no shepherd"
Zec 11:8 – "Three shepherds..cut off in 1 month"
Mat 9:36 – "as sheep having no shepherd"
Luk 2:15 – "the shepherds said one to another"
Joh 10:16 – "there shall be one shepherd"

Shield

1Ki 10:17 – "he made 300 shields of beaten gold"
1Ki 10:17 – "three pound of gold went to 1 shield"
2Ch 9:16 – "300 shields made he of beaten gold"
2Ch 9:16 – "300 shekels of gold went to 1 shield"

Ship

Dan 11:40 – "king of the north..with many ships"
Luk 5:2 – "two ships standing by the lake"
Luk 5:3 – "he entered into one of the ships"

Shoe

Amo 2:6 – "sold..the poor for a pair of shoes"
Amo 8:6 – "buy..the needy for a pair of shoes"

Shoulder

Exo 28:12 – "upon his two shoulders..memorial"

Shoulderpiece

Exo 28:7 – "shall have two shoulderpieces"

Shouting

Jer 48:33 – "shouting shall be no shouting"

Shrub

Gen 21:15 – "cast the child under 1 of the shrubs"

Sick

Mar 6:13 – "anointed with oil many..sick"

Side

Exo 17:12 – "Aaron and Hur..the 1 on the 1 side"
Exo 25:12 – "2 rings shall be in the one side of it"
Exo 25:32 – "branches..candlestick out of ..1 side"
Exo 26:13 – "a cubit on the one side"
Exo 26:20 – "2nd side of the tabernacle..north side"
Exo 26:23 – "corners of..tabernacle in the 2 sides"
Exo 26:26 – "boards of..1 side of the tabernacle"
Exo 26:27 – "for the two sides westward"
Exo 27:7 – "staves shall be upon the two sides"
Exo 27:9 – "hangings..100 cubits long for one side"

Exo 27:14 – "hangings of one side of the gate"
Exo 28:27 – "put them on the 2 sides of the ephod"
Exo 30:4 – "upon the two sides of it"
Exo 32:15 – "tables..written..on the one side"
Exo 36:28 – "2 boards..the corners..in the 2 sides"
Exo 36:31 – "boards of the one side of..tabernacle"
Exo 37:18 – "three branches..out of the one side"
Exo 37:27 – "two corners of it, upon the two sides"
Exo 38:14 – "hangings of the one side of the gate"
Exo 39:20 – "two sides of the ephod underneath"
Deu 4:32 – "one side of heaven unto the other"
1Sa 14:4 – "a sharp rock on the one side"
1Sa 14:40 – "Be ye on one side..I and Jonathan"
1Sa 17:3 – "Philistines stood..on the one side"
2Sa 2:13 – "one on the one side of the pool"
1Ki 7:7 – "covered w/ cedar from 1 side..to..other"
1Ki 10:20 – "12 lions stood there on 1 side..other"
2Ch 9:19 – "12 lions stood there on the one side"
Ezk 1:8 – "hands of a man..on their 4 sides"
Ezk 1:17 – "they went upon their four sides"
Ezk 10:11 – "they went upon their four sides"
Ezk 41:1 – "posts, six cubits broad..one side"
Ezk 41:2 – "sides..door..5 cubits..one side"
Ezk 41:15 – "galleries thereof on the one side"
Ezk 41:19 – "face of a man..on the one side"
Ezk 41:26 – "windows..palm trees on the one side"
Ezk 42:20 – "He measured it by the four sides"
Ezk 45:7 – "portion..for the prince on..one side"
Ezk 46:19 – "place on the two sides westward"
Ezk 47:7 – "many trees on the 1 side..the other"
Ezk 48:21 – "for the prince, on the one side"
Dan 7:5 – "it raised up itself on one side"

Side Post

Exo 12:7 – "blood, strike it on the 2 side posts"
Exo 12:22 – "strike the lintel and the 2 side posts"
Exo 12:23 – "the lintel, and on the 2 side posts"

Sigh

Lam 1:22 – "for my sighs are many"

Sign

Exo 4:8 – "listen to the voice of the first sign"
Exo 4:9 – "will not believe also these two signs"
Mat 12:39 – "shall no sign be given to it"
Mat 16:4 – "no sign be given unto it"
Mar 8:12 – "There shall no sign be given"
Luk 11:29 – "shall no sign be given it"
Act 2:43 – "many wonders & signs were done"
Act 5:12 – "many signs and wonders wrought"

Silver *(see Pieces, Talents, & Shekels)*

2Sa 21:4 – "have no silver nor gold of Saul"
1Ch 22:16 – "gold..silver..iron, there is no number"
Psa 119:72 – "law..better..than 1000's..gold..silver"
Act 3:6 – "Silver and gold have I none"

Silverling

Isa 7:23 – "were 1000 vines at a 1000 silverings"

Similitude

Deu 4:12 – "heard..voice..but saw no similitude"

Simon

Luk 23:26 – "laid hold upon one Simon..Cyrenian"
Act 9:43 – "many days in Joppa with one Simon"
Act 10:5 – "call for one Simon..surname is Peter"
Act 10:6 – "lodgeth with one Simon a tanner"
Act 10:32 – "the house of one Simon a tanner"

Sin

Num 18:32 – "ye shall bear no sin"
Deu 22:26 – "in..damsel no sin worthy of death"
Deu 23:22 – "it shall be no sin in thee"
Ezk 16:51 – "Samaria commited half thy sins"
Eze 33:16 – "None of his sins..be mentioned"
Luk 7:47 – "Her sins, which are many"
Joh 9:41 – "ye should have no sin"
2Co 5:21 – "who knew no sin"
1Pe 2:22 – "Who did no sin"
1Jn 1:8 – "say that we have no sin"
1Jn 3:5 – "and in him is no sin"

Singer

Ezr 2:65 – "200 singing men and singing women"
Neh 7:44 – "singers: the children of Asaph, 148"
Neh 7:67 – "245 singing men & singing women"

Singing

Isa 16:10 – "there shall be no singing"

Sinner

Ecc 9:18 – "one sinner destroyeth much good"
Mat 9:10 – "many publicans and sinners"
Mar 2:15 – "many publicans and sinners sat also"
Luk 15:7 – "one sinner that repenteth"
Luke 15:10 – "one sinner that repententh"

Sisters

Job 1:4 – "called for their three sisters"

Size

Exo 36:9 – "the curtains were all of one size"
Exo 36:15 – "the eleven curtains were of one size"
1Ki 6:25 – "cherubims were of 1 measure & 1 size"
1Ki 7:37 – "ten bases..one measure, and one size"

Slaughter

1Sa 14:14 – "that first slaughter..about 20 men"

Smith

1Sa 13:19 – "Now there was no smith found"

Socket

Exo 26:19 – "make 40 sockets of silver"
Exo 26:19 – "two sockets..for his two tenons"
Exo 26:19 – "two sockets under another board"
Exo 26:21 – "And their 40 sockets of silver"
Exo 26:21 – "two sockets under one board"
Exo 26:21 – "two sockets under another board"
Exo 26:25 – "eight boards..sixteen sockets"
Exo 26:25 – "two sockets under one board"
Exo 26:25 – "two sockets under another board"
Exo 26:37 – "cast five sockets of brass for them"
Exo 26:32 – "upon the four sockets of silver"
Exo 27:10 – "20 pillars thereof & their 20 sockets"
Exo 27:11 – "his 20 pillars and their 20 sockets"
Exo 27:12 – "their pillars 10, and their sockets 10"
Exo 27:14 – "their pillars 3, and their sockets 3"
Exo 27:15 – "their pillars 3, and their sockets 3"
Exo 27:16 – "their pillars 4, and their sockets 4"
Exo 36:24 – "40 sockets..under the 20 boards"
Exo 36:24 – "two sockets under one board"
Exo 36:24 – "2 sockets..another board..2 tenons"
Exo 36:26 – "their forty sockets of silver"
Exo 36:26 – "two sockets under one board"
Exo 36:26 – "two sockets under another board"
Exo 36:30 – "sockets were 16 sockets of silver"
Exo 36:30 – "under every board two sockets"
Exo 36:36 – "he cast for them 4 sockets of silver"
Exo 36:38 – "their five sockets were of brass"
Exo 38:10 – "their brasen sockets twenty"
Exo 38:11 – "north side..sockets of brass twenty"

Exo 38:12 – "west side..their sockets ten"
Exo 38:14 – "their pillars 3, and their sockets 3"
Exo 38:15 – "their pillars 3, and their sockets 3"
Exo 38:19 – "pillars were 4..sockets of brass 4"
Exo 38:27 – "100 sockets of the 100 talents"

Soldier

1Ch 7:11 – "men of valour..17,200 soldiers"
Joh 19:34 – "one of the soldiers with a spear"
Act 12:6 – "Peter..sleeping between two soldiers"
Act 23:23 – "Make ready 200 soldiers to..Caesarea"

Song

1Ki 4:32 – Solomon – "his songs were 1005"
Psa 137:3 – "Sing us one of the songs of Zion."
Isa 23:16 – "harlot..sing many songs"

Son

Indefinite *Sons*

1Ch 7:4 – "for they had many wives and sons"
1Ch 8:40 – "sons of Ulam..had many sons"
1Ch 23:11 – "Jeush and Beriah had not many sons"
1Ch 23:17 – "sons of Rehabiah were very many"
1Ch 28:5 – "LORD hath given me many sons"
Neh 5:2 – "our sons, and our daughters, are many"
Heb 2:10 – "bringing many sons unto glory"

0 *Sons*

Num 26:33 – "Zelophehad..had no sons"
Num 27:3 – "Our father..had no sons."
Num 27:4 – "our father..hath no son?"
Num 27:8 – "If a man die, and have no son"
Jos 17:3 – "But Zelophehad..had no sons"
2Sa 13:30 – "king's sons..not one of them left"
2Sa 18:18 – "I have no son to keep my name"
2Ki 1:17 – "because he had no son"
1Ch 2:34 – "Now Sheshan had no sons"
1Ch 23:17 – "Eliezer had none other sons"
1Ch 23:22 – "Eleazar died, and had no sons"
1Ch 24:28 – "Eleazar, who had no sons"
Ezr 8:15 – "found there none of the sons of Levi"
Jer 49:1 – "Hath Israel no sons?"

1 *Son*

Gen 10:25 – "sons..name of the one was Peleg"
Gen 36:15 – "Eliphaz the firstborn son of Esau"
Gen 42:13 – "youngest..with our father..one is not"
Gen 44:28 – "and the one went out from me"
Exo 18:3 – "2 sons..name of the 1 was Gershom"
Exo 22:29 – "firstborn of thy sons..give unto me"

Exo 34:20 – "All the firstborn of thy sons..redeem"
Lev 13:2 – "unto one of his sons the priests"
Deu 21:15 – "firstborn son be hers that was hated"
1Ch 6:28 – "sons of Samuel; the firstborn Vashni"
1Ch 8:30 – "And his firstborn son Abdon"
1Ch 23:20 – "sons of Uzziel; Micah the first"
1Ch 23:19 – "sons of Hebron; Jeriah the first"
1Ch 24:21 – "the first was Isshiah"
Lev 7:10 – "sons of Aaron..1 as much as another"
1Ch 23:19 – "sons of Hebron; Jeriah the first"
1Ch 23:20 – "sons of Uzziel; Michah the first"
1Ch 24:21 – "sons of Rehabiah, the first..Isshiah"
1Ch 24:23 – "sons of Hebron; Jeriah the first"
Ezr 10:2 – "Jehiel, one of the sons of Elam"
Neh 10:36 – "firstborn of our sons, and..our cattle"
Neh 13:28 – "one of the sons of Joiada"
Job 1:4 – "feasted in their houses, every one his day"
Mat 1:25 – "she..brought forth her firstborn son"
Mat 20:21 – "the one on thy right hand..other..left"
Mat 21:28 – "man had two sons..came to the first"
Mat 21:31 – "They say unto him, The first"
Mar 12:6 – "having one son, his wellbeloved"
Luk 2:7 – "she brought forth her firstborn son"
Gal 4:22 – "two sons, the one by a bondmaid"

2 *Sons*

Gen 10:25 – "unto Eber were born two sons"
Gen 25:24 – "there were twins in her womb"
Gen 38:27 – "behold, twins were in her womb"
Gen 30:7 – "Bilhah..bare Jacob a second son"
Gen 30:12 – "Zilpah..bare Jacob a second son"
Gen 34:25 – "two of the sons of Jacob..slew..males"
Gen 41:50 – "unto Joseph were born two sons"
Gen 41:52 – "name of the 2nd called he Ephraim"
Gen 42:37 – "Reuben spake..Slay my two sons"
Gen 44:27 – "my wife bare me two sons"
Gen 46:27 – "sons of Joseph..born him..two souls"
Gen 48:1 – "Joseph..with him his two sons"
Gen 48:5 – "thy two sons..shall be mine"
Exo 18:3 – Zipporah – "her two sons"
Exo 18:6 – "thy wife, and her two sons with her"
Lev 16:1 – "after the death of the 2 sons of Aaron"
Rut 1:1 – "he, and his wife, and his two sons"
Rut 1:2 – "his two sons Mahlon and Chilion"
Rut 1:3 – "she was left, and her two sons"
Rut 1:5 – "woman was left of her two sons"
1Sa 1:3 – "two sons of Eli, Hophni and Phinnehas"
1Sa 2:34 – "come upon thy two sons..in one day"
1Sa 4:4 – "2 sons of Eli..were there with the ark"
1Sa 4:11 – "two sons of Eli..were slain."
1Sa 4:17 – "thy two sons also..are dead"
2Sa 14:6 – "thy handmaid had two sons"
2Sa 15:27 – "return into the city..2 sons with you"
2Sa 15:36 – "two sons, Ahimaaz...Jonathan"
2Sa 21:8 – "king took the two sons of Rizpah"
2Ki 4:1 – "take..my two sons to be bondmen"
1Ch 1:19 – "And unto Eber were born two sons"
1Ch 3:15 – "sons of Josiah..the 2nd Jehoiakim"
1Ch 8:39 – "sons of Eshek..Jenush the second"
1Ch 23:19 – "sons of Hebron..Amariah the second"

1Ch 23:20 – "sons of Uzziel..Jesiah the second"
1Ch 24:23 – "sons of Hebron..Amariah the second"
1Ch 26:2 – "sons of Meshelemiah..Jediael the 2nd"
1Ch 26:4 – "sons of Obededom..Jehozabad the 2nd"
1Ch 26:11 – "Hilkiah the second..sons..of Hosah"
Mat 20:21 – "Grant that these my two sons"
Mat 21:28 – "a certain man had two sons"
Mat 21:30 – "he came to the 2nd and said likewise"
Mat 26:37 – "with him Peter..two sons..Zebedee"
Luk 15:11 – "certain man had two sons"
Act 7:29 – "Moses..begat two sons"
Gal 4:22 – "two sons, the one by a bondmaid"

3 *Sons*

Gen 6:10 – "Noah begat three sons"
Gen 9:19 – "These are the 3 sons of Noah"
Gen 29:34 – "I have born him three sons"
Jos 15:14 – "Caleb drove thence..3 sons of Anak"
Jdg 1:20 – "expelled thence the 3 sons of Anak"
1Sa 2:21 – "Hannah..3 sons and two daughters"
1Sa 17:13 – "3 eldest sons of Jesse..followed Saul"
1Sa 17:13 – "names of his 3 sons..went to battle"
1Sa 31:5 – "Saul died, and his three sons"
1Sa 31:8 – "found Saul and his three sons fallen"
2Sa 2:18 – "three sons of Zeruiah"
2Sa 14:27 – "unto Absalom..were born 3 sons"
1Ch 2:3 – "sons of Judah..which three were born"
1Ch 2:16 – "sons of Zeruiah: Abishai..Joab..three"
1Ch 3:15 – "sons of Josiah..the 3rd Zedekiah"
1Ch 3:23 – "And the sons of Neariah..three"
1Ch 7:6 – "The sons of Benjamin..three"
1Ch 8:39 – "sons of Eshek..Eliphelet the third"
1Ch 10:6 – "So Saul died, and his three sons"
1Ch 23:8 – "The sons of Laadan..three"
1Ch 23:9 – "The sons of Shimei...three"
1Ch 23:23 – "The sons of Mushi...three"
1Ch 23:19 – "sons of Hebron..Jahaziel the third"
1Ch 24:23 – "sons of Hebron..Jahaziel the third"
1Ch 26:2 – "sons of Meshelemiah..Zebadiah..3rd"
1Ch 26:4 – "sons of Obededom..Joah the third"
1Ch 26:11 – "Tebaliah the third sons..of Hosah"

4 *Sons*

1Ch 3:15 – "sons of Josiah..the 4th Shallum"
1Ch 7:1 – "sons of Issachar were..four"
1Ch 21:20 – "Ornan..his 4 sons..hid themselves"
1Ch 23:10 – "These four were the sons of Shimei."
1Ch 23:12 – "The sons of Kohath...four"
1Ch 23:19 – "sons of Hebron..Jekameam the 4th"
1Ch 24:23 – "sons of Hebron..Jekameam the 4th"
1Ch 26:2 – "sons of Meshelemiah..Jathniel the 4th"
1Ch 26:4 – "sons of Obededom..Sacar the fourth"
1Ch 26:11 – "Zechariah the fourth..sons..of Hosah"

5 *Sons*

Gen 30:17 – "Leah..bare Jacob the fifth son"
2Sa 21:8 – "king took...the five sons of Michal"

1Ch 2:4 – "All the sons of Judah were five."
1Ch 2:6 – "sons of Zerah..five of them in all"
1Ch 3:20 – "Hashubah..Ohel..five"
1Ch 7:3 – "sons of Izrahiah..five"
1Ch 7:7 – "And the sons of Bela..five"
1Ch 26:3 – "Elam the fifth"
1Ch 26:4 – "sons of Obededom..Nethaneel the 5th"

6 *Sons*

Gen 30:19 – "Leah..bare Jacob the sixth son"
Gen 30:20 – "I have born him six sons"
1Ch 3:22 – "sons of Shemaiah..six"
1Ch 8:38 – "Azel had six sons"
1Ch 9:44 – "Azel had six sons, whose names are"
1Ch 25:3 – "sons of Jeduthun..six"
1Ch 26:3 – "Jehohanan the sixth"
1Ch 26:5 – "Ammiel the sixth"
Neh 3:30 – "Hanun the sixth son of Zalaph"

7 *Sons*

Gen 46:25 – "sons of Bilhah..all the souls were 7"
Rut 4:15 – "which is better to thee than 7 sons"
1Sa 16:10 – "7 of his sons to pass before Samuel"
1Ch 3:24 – "sons of Elioenai..seven"
1Ch 26:3 – "Elioenai the seventh"
1Ch 26:5 – "Issachar the seventh"
Job 1:2 – "born unto him 7 sons and 3 daughters"
Job 42:13 – "He had also 7 sons and 3 daughters."
Act 19:14 – "there were seven sons of one Sceva"

8 *Sons*

1Sa 17:12 – "Jesse..had eight sons"
1Ch 26:5 – "Peulthai the eighth"

10 *Sons*

1Sa 1:8 – "am not I better to thee than ten sons?"
Est 9:10 – "The ten sons of Haman..slew they"
Est 9:12 – "the ten sons of Haman"
Est 9:13 – "let Haman's ten sons be hanged"
Est 9:14 – "they hanged Haman's ten sons"

11 *Sons*

Gen 32:22 – "rose up..and took..his eleven sons"

12 *Sons*

Gen 35:22 – "Now the sons of Jacob were twelve"
1Ch 25:9 – "2nd to Gedaliah..his brethren..sons..12"
1Ch 25:10 – "3rd to Zaccur..sons..brethren..12"
1Ch 25:11 – "4th to Izri..sons..brethren, were 12"
1Ch 25:12 – "5th to Nethaniah..sons..brethren..12"
1Ch 25:13 – "6th to Bukkiah..sons..brethren..12"
1Ch 25:14 – "7th to Jesharelah..sons..brethren..12"
1Ch 25:15 – "8th to Jeshaiah..sons..brethren..12"

1Ch 25:16 – "9th to Mattaniah..sons..brethren..12"
1Ch 25:17 – "10th to Shimei..sons..brethren..12"
1Ch 25:18 – "11th to Azareel..sons..brethren..12"
1Ch 25:19 – "12th to Hashabiah..sons..brethren..12"
1Ch 25:20 – "13th to Shubael..sons..brethren..12"
1Ch 25:21 – "14th to Mattithiah..sons..brethren..12"
1Ch 25:22 – "15th to Jeremoth..sons..brethren..12"
1Ch 25:23 – "16th to Hananiah..sons..brethren..12"
1Ch 25:24 – "17th to Joshbekashah..sons..12"
1Ch 25:25 – "18th to Hanani..sons..brethren..12"
1Ch 25:26 – "19th to Mallothi..sons..brethren..12"
1Ch 25:27 – "20th to Eliathah..sons..brethren..12"
1Ch 25:28 – "21st to Hothir..sons..brethren..12"
1Ch 25:29 – "22nd to Giddalti..sons..brethren..12"
1Ch 25:30 – "23rd to Mahazioth..sons..brethren..12"
1Ch 25:31 – "24th to Romamtiezer..sons..12"

13-50 *Sons*

Gen 46:15 – "sons of Leah..all the souls..were 33"
Gen 46:18 – "sons of Zilpah..even 16 souls"
Gen 46:22 – "sons of Rachel..all the souls were 14"
Jdg 10:4 – "And he had 30 sons..on 30 ass colts"
Jdg 12:9 – "he had 30 sons and 30 daughters"
Jdg 12:14 – "he had 40 sons and 30 nephews"
2Sa 9:10 – "Ziba had 15 sons and 20 servants"
2Sa 19:17 – "Ziba..his 15 sons and his 20 servants"
1Ch 4:27 – "Shimei had 16 sons and six daughters"
1Ch 25:5 – "God gave to Heman 14 sons"
1Ch 26:9 – "Meshelemiah had sons & brethren..18"
1Ch 26:11 – "all the sons & brethren of Hosah..13"
2Ch 11:21 – "begat 28 sons and 60 daughters"
2Ch 13:21 – "begat 22 sons and 16 daughters"
Ezr 8:18 – "sons of Mahli..sons &..brethren, 18"
Ezr 8:19 – "sons of Merari..brethren..sons, 20"

51-99 *Sons*

Gen 46:27 – "all the souls of the house of Jacob..70"
Gen 46:26 – "All the souls..into Egypt..66"
Jdg 8:30 – "Gideon had 70 sons of his body"
Jdg 9:24 – "cruelty..to the 70 sons of Jerubbaal"
2Ki 10:1 – "Ahab had 70 sons in Samaria"
1Ch 15:9 – "sons of Hebron..80"
1Ch 26:8 – "these of the sons of Obededom..62"

100+ *Sons*

1Ch 8:40 – "sons of Ulam..mighty men..an 150"
1Ch 15:5 – "sons of Kohath..an 120"
1Ch 15:6 – "sons of Merari..220"
1Ch 15:7 – "sons of Gershom..130"
1Ch 15:8 – "sons of Elizaphan..200"
1Ch 15:10 – "sons of Uzziel..112"
Neh 11:6 – "sons of Perez..at Jerusalem were 468"
Neh 11:8 – "after him Gabbai, Sallai, 928"

Soothsayer

Mic 5:12 – "shalt have no more soothsayers"

Sorrow

Psa 32:10 – "Many sorrows..to the wicked"
Pro 10:22 – "he addeth no sorrow with it"
1Ti 6:10 – "pierced..with many sorrows"

Soul

Gen 46:15 – "sons of Leah..all the souls..were 33"
Gen 46:18 – "sons of Zilpah..even 16 souls"
Gen 46:22 – "sons of Rachel..all the souls were 14"
Gen 46:25 – "sons of Bilhah..all the souls were 7"
Gen 46:26 – "All the souls..into Egypt..66"
Gen 46:27 – "sons..Joseph..born him..were 2 souls"
Gen 46:27 – "all..souls of the house of Jacob..70"
Exo 1:5 – "of the loins of Jacob were 70 souls"
Lev 17:12 – "No soul of you shall eat blood"
Num 31:28 – "one soul of five hundred"
Act 2:41 – "added unto them about 3000 souls"
Act 4:32 – "were of one heart and of one soul"
Act 7:14 – "Joseph..all his kindred, 75 souls"
Act 27:37 – "we were in all in the ship 276 souls"
1Pe 3:20 – "eight souls were saved by water"
1Pe 3:20 – "few..souls were saved"

Sound

2Ch 5:13 – "to make one sound to be heard"

Soundness

Psa 38:3 – "There is no soundness in my flesh"
Psa 38:7 – "there is no soundness in my flesh"
Isa 1:6 – "there is no soundness in it"

Sparrow

Mat 10:29 – "are not two sparrows sold..farthing?"
Mat 10:29 – "one of them shall not fall"
Mat 10:31 – "more value than many sparrows"
Luk 12:6 – "5 sparrows sold for 2 farthings"
Luk 12:6 – "sparrows..not one..is forgotten"
Luk 12:7 – "more value than many sparrows"

Spearman

Act 23:23 – "to Caesarea..spearmen 200"

Speech

Gen 11:1 – "whole earth was of..one speech"
Psa 19:3 – "There is no speech nor language"

Spirit

2Ch 9:4 – "there was no more spirit in her"
Zec 6:5 – "These are the 4 spirits of the heavens"
Mat 12:45 – "seven other spirits more wicked"
Mar 5:9 – "My name is Legion: for we are many"
Luk 11:26 – "seven other spirits more wicked"
1Co 6:17 – "joined unto the Lord is one spirit"
1Co 12:11 – "worketh that one..selfsame Spirit"
1Co 12:13 – "by one Spirit are we all baptized"
1Co 12:13 – "been made to drink into one Spirit"
Eph 2:18 – "both have access by one Spirit"
Eph 4:4 – "There is..one Spirit"
Phi 1:27 – "stand fast in one spirit"
Rev 1:4 – "the seven Spirits..before his throne"
Rev 3:1 – "he that hath the 7 Spirits of God"
Rev 4:5 – "7 lamps of fire..are the 7 Spirits"
Rev 5:6 – "7 eyes, which are the 7 Spirits"
Rev 16:13 – "three unclean spirits like frogs"

Spoil

Heb 7:4 – "Abraham gave the tenth of the spoils"

Spoon

Num 7:14 – "one spoon of ten shekels"
Num 7:20 – "one spoon..gold..10 shekels"
Num 7:26 – "one golden spoon..10 shekels"
Num 7:32 – "one golden spoon..10 shekels"
Num 7:38 – "one golden spoon..10 shekels"
Num 7:44 – "one golden spoon..10 shekels"
Num 7:50 – "one golden spoon..10 shekels"
Num 7:56 – "one golden spoon..10 shekels"
Num 7:62 – "one golden spoon..10 shekels"
Num 7:68 – "one golden spoon..10 shekels"
Num 7:74 – "one golden spoon..10 shekels"
Num 7:80 – "one golden spoon..10 shekels"
Num 7:84 – "twelve spoons of gold"
Num 7:86 – "golden spoons were twelve"

Spot

Son 4:7 – "there is no spot in thee"

Squares

Ezk 43:16 – "altar..square in the four squares"
              (12x12 cubits)

Ezk 43:17 – "settle..the four squares thereof"
              (14x14 cubits)

Staff/Staves

Zec 11:7 – "I took unto me two staves"
Zec 11:7 – "the one I called Beauty"

Stakes

Isa 33:20 – "not one of the stakes..be removed"

Stall

1Ki 4:26 – "Solomon had 40,000 stalls of horses"
2Ch 9:25 – "Solomon..4000 stalls..horses..chariots"

Stalk

Gen 41:5 – "7 ears of corn came upon on 1 stalk"
Gen 41:22 – "7 ears came up in one stalk"
Hos 8:7 – "it hath no stalk"

Standing

Psa 69:2 – "mire, where there is no standing"

Star

Gen 15:5 – "tell the stars, if..able to number them"
Gen 37:9 – "eleven stars made obeisance to me"
Deu 1:10 – "as the stars of heaven for multitude"
Deu 28:62 – "as the stars of heaven for multitude"
1Ch 27:23 – "Israel like..the stars of the heavens"
Neh 9:23 – "children also..as the stars of heaven"
Psa 147:4 – "He telleth the number of the stars"
Jer 33:22 – "host of heaven cannot be numbered"
Amo 5:8 – "Seek him that maketh the 7 stars"
Nah 3:16 – "merchants above the stars of heaven"
1Co 15:41 – "one star differeth from another"
Heb 11:12 – "so many as the stars of the sky"
Rev 1:16 – "had in his right hand seven stars"
Rev 1:20 – "The mystery of the seven stars"
Rev 1:20 – "7 stars..are angels of the 7 churches"
Rev 2:1 – "holdeth the 7 stars in his right hand"
Rev 3:1 – "saith he that hath..the seven stars"
Rev 12:1 – "upon her head a crown of 12 stars"

State

Mat 12:45 – "last state..worse than the first"
Luk 11:26 – "state of that man..worse than the 1st"

Statute

Dan 6:15 – " no decree nor statute..be changed"

Step

1Ki 10:19 – "The throne had six steps"
1Ki 10:20 – "12 lions stood there on..the 6 steps"
2Ch 9:18 – "there were six steps to the throne"
2Ch 9:19 – "and the other upon the six steps"
Ezk 40:22 – "went up unto it by seven steps"
Ezk 40:26 – "seven steps to go up to it"
Ezk 40:31 – "the going up to it had eight steps"
Ezk 40:34 – "the going up to it had eight steps"
Ezk 40:37 – "the going up to it had eight steps"

Stick

1Ki 17:12 – "I am gathering two sticks"
Ezk 37:16 – "son of man, take thee one stick"
Ezk 37:17 – "join them 1 to another into 1 stick"
Ezk 37:17 – "they shall become one in thy hand"
Ezk 37:19 – "make them one stick"
Ezk 37:19 – "they shall be one in mine hand"

Stir

Act 12:18 – "no small stir among the soldiers"
Act 19:23 – "arose no small stir about that way"

Stone

Exo 28:9 – "thou shalt take two onyx stones"
Exo 28:10 – "Six of their names..one stone"
Exo 28:11 – "shalt thou engrave the two stones"
Exo 28:12 – "put the 2 stones upon the shoulders"
Exo 28:21 – "stones shall be with the names..12"
Exo 39:14 – "stones..12 according to their names"
Jos 4:3 – "out of the midst of Jordan..12 stones"
Jos 4:8 – "12 stones out of the midst of Jordan"
Jos 4:9 – "Joshua..12 stones in the midst of Jordan"
Jos 4:20 – "12 stones..they took out of Jordan"
Jdg 9:5 – "slew his brethren..upon one stone"
Jdg 9:18 – "slain his sons, 70..upon one stone"
1Sa 17:40 – "5 smooth stones out of the brook"
2Sa 17:13 – "until there be not one small stone"
1Ki 6:18 – "there was no stone seen"
1Ki 18:31 – "Elijah took 12 stones"
Zec 3:9 – "upon one stone shall be seven eyes"
Mat 24:2 – "not be left..one stone upon another"
Mar 13:2 – "not be left one stone upon another"
Luk 19:44 – "shall not leave in thee one stone"
Luk 21:6 – "not be left one stone upon another"

Story

Gen 6:16 – "2nd and 3rd stories shalt thou make"
Ezk 41:16 – "galleries round about..their 3 stories"
Ezk 42:3 – "gallery against gallery in three stories"
Ezk 42:6 – "they were in 3 stories..had not pillars"

Straitness

Job 36:16 – "where there is no straitness"

Stranger

Exo 12:43 – "shall no stranger eat thereof"
Lev 22:10 – "no stranger eat of the holy thing"
Num 16:40 – "no stranger.. offer incense"
1Ki 3:18 – "no stranger with us in the house"
2Ch 2:17 – "strangers..in..land of Israel..153,600"
2Ch 2:18 – "70,000 of them..bearers of burdens"
2Ch 2:18 – "80,000 to be hewers in the mountains"
Job 15:19 – "no stranger passed among them"
Eze 44:9 – "No stranger..shall enter..sanctuary"
Joe 3:17 – "shall no strangers pass through"

Straw

Exo 5:16 – "There is no straw given"
Exo 5:18 – "there shall no straw be given you"

Stream

Isa 11:15 – "shall smite it in the seven streams"

Street

Act 12:10 – "passed on through one street"

Strength

1Sa 28:20 – "there was no strength in him"
Job 26:2 – "the arm that hath no strength"
Psa 88:4 – "a man that hath no strength"
Isa 23:10 – "there is no more strength"
Dan 10:8 – "remained no strength in me"
Dan 10:16 – "I have retained no strength"
Dan 10:17 – "remained no strength in me"
Heb 9:17 – "it is of no strength at all"

Strife

Gen 13:8 – " Let there be no strife"

String

Psa 33:2 – "psaltery & an instrument of 10 strings"
Psa 92:3 – "Upon an instrument of ten strings"
Psa 144:9 – "an instrument of ten strings"

Stripe

Deu 25:3 – "40 stripes he may give..& not exceed"
Deu 25:3 – "beat him..with many stripes"
Pro 17:10 – "more than 100 stripes into a fool"
Luk 12:47 – "be beaten with many stripes"
Luk 12:48 – "shall be beaten with few stripes"
Act 16:23 – "had laid many stripes upon them"
2Co 11:24 – "5 times received..40 stripes save 1"

Summer Fruit

2Sa 16:1 – "Ziba..met him, w/..100 of summer fruits"

Supplication

Job 41:3 – "make many supplications unto thee"

Sustenance

Jdg 6:4 – "left no sustenance for Israel"
Act 7:11 – "our fathers found no sustenance"

Swarm

Exo 8:22 – "no swarms of flies shall be there"

Swine

Mat 8:30 – "an herd of many swine feeding"
Mar 5:13 – "swine..they were about 2000"
Luk 8:32 – "herd of many swine feeding"

Sword

1Sa 17:50 – " no sword in the hand of David"
1Sa 21:9 – "sword..for there is no other save that"
1Sa 21:9 – "There is none like that; give it me"
Ezk 21:14 – "let the sword be double the 3rd time"
Luk 22:36 – "hath no sword..buy one"
Luk 22:38 – "Lord..here are two swords"

Synagogue

Luk 13:10 – "teaching in one of the synagogues"

Tabernacle

Exo 26:6 – "it shall be one tabernacle"
Exo 36:13 – "so it became one tabernacle"
1Ch 17:5 – "from one tabernacle to another"
Mat 17:4 – "three tabernacles, one for thee"
Mat 17:4 – "three tabernacles..one for Moses"
Mat 17:4 – "three tabernacles..and one for Elias"
Mar 9:5 – "let us make three tabernacles"
Mar 9:5 – "tabernacles; one for thee"
Mar 9:5 – "tabernacles..one for Moses"
Mar 9:5 – "tabernacles..and one for Elias"
Luk 9:33 – "three tabernacles; one for thee"
Luk 9:33 – "three tabernacles..one for Moses"
Luk 9:33 – "three tabernacles..one for Elias"
Heb 9:2 – "tabernacle made; the first, wherein"
Heb 9:6 – "went always into the first tabernacle"
Heb 9:7 – "But into the second went the..priest"
Heb 9:8 – "while..1st tabernacle was..standing"

Table *(as in Tablet)*

Exo 31:18 – "gave..Moses..2 tables of testimony"
Exo 32:15 – "two tables of the testimony"
Exo 34:1 – "Hew thee 2 tables of stone like the 1st"
Exo 34:1 – "words that were in the first tables"
Exo 34:4 – "he hewed 2 tables..like unto the first"
Exo 34:4 – "took in his hand the 2 tables of stone"
Exo 34:29 – "down..w/ the 2 tables of testimony"
Deu 4:13 – "10 commandments..upon two tables"
Deu 5:22 – "wrote them in two tables of stone"
Deu 9:10 – "2 tables of stone..finger of God"
Deu 9:11 – "two tables of stone..of the covenant"
Deu 9:15 – "two tables..were in my two hands"
Deu 9:17 – "2 tables..cast them out of my 2 hands"
Deu 10:1 – "two tables of stone like unto the first"
Deu 10:2 – "words that were in the first tables"
Deu 10:3 – "two tables of stone like unto the first"
Deu 10:3 – "two tables in mine hand"
1Ki 8:8 – "nothing in..ark save..2 tables of stone"
2Ch 5:10 – "nothing in the ark save the two tables"

Table *(as in Furniture)*

2Ch 4:8 – "made also ten tables..in the temple"
2Ch 4:8 – "5 on the right side, and 5 on the left"
Ezk 40:39 – "in the porch..2 tables on this side"
Ezk 40:39 – "in the porch..2 tables on that side"
Ezk 40:40 – "at the side without..were 2 tables"
Ezk 40:40 – "on the other side..were 2 tables"
Ezk 40:41 – "Four tables were on this side"
Ezk 40:41 – "four tables were on that side"
Ezk 40:41 – "eight tables..slew..sacrifices"

Ezk 40:42 – "four tables were of hewn stone"
Dan 11:27 – "they shall speak lies at one table"

Taches

Exo 26:6 – "shalt make fifty taches of gold"
Exo 26:11 – "thou shalt make fifty taches of brass"
Exo 36:13 – "he made fifty taches of gold"
Exo 36:18 – "he made fifty taches of brass"

Tails

Jdg 15:4 – "firebrand in the midst between 2 tails"
Isa 7:4 – "two tails of these smoking firebrands"

Talebearer

Pro 26:20 – "no talebearer, the strife ceaseth"

Talent

1 *Talent*

Mat 25:15 – "talents..to another one"
Mat 25:18 – "he that had received one"
Mat 25:24 – "which had received the one talent"

2 *Talents*

1Ki 16:24 – "bought..Samaria..for 2 talents..silver"
2Ki 5:23 – "Namaan..Be content, take two talents"
2Ki 5:23 – "bound 2 talents of silver in two bags"
Mat 25:15 – "talents, to another two"
Mat 25:17 – "likewise he that had received two"
Mat 25:17 – "he also gained other two"
Mat 25:22 – "He..that had received two talents"
Mat 25:22 – "deliveredst unto me two talents"
Mat 25:22 – "I have gained two other talents"

5 *Talents*

Mat 25:15 – "unto one he gave five talents"
Mat 25:16 – "he that had received the five talents"
Mat 25:16 – "made them other five talents"
Mat 25:20 – "he that had received five talents"
Mat 25:20 – "brought other five talents"
Mat 25:20 – "deliveredst unto me five talents"
Mat 25:20 – "I have gained..five talents more"

10 *Talents*

2Ki 5:5 – "took with him ten talents of silver"
Mat 25:28 – "unto him which hath 10 talents"

11-99 *Talents*

Exo 38:24 – "gold..29 talents, and 730 shekels"
> *Thus, 87,730 shekels or 29.24 talents*
2Ki 18:14 – "king..appointed..30 talents..gold"
Exo 38:29 – "brass..70 talents, and 2,400 shekels"
> *Thus, 212,400 shekels or 70.8 talents*

100-399 *Talents*

Exo 38:25 – "silver..100 talents, & 1,775 shekels"
> *Thus, 301,775 shekels or 100.59 talents*
Exo 38:27 – "of the 100 talents..cast the sockets"
Exo 38:27 – "100 sockets of the 100 talents"
1Ki 9:14 – "Hiram sent..king 120 talents of gold"
1Ki 10:10 – "gave the king an 120 talents of gold"
2Ki 18:14 – "king..appointed..300 talents..silver"
2Ki 23:33 – "a tribute of 100 talents of silver"
2Ch 9:9 – "gave the king 120 talents of gold"
2Ch 25:6 – "hired.. men..for 100 talents of silver"
2Ch 25:9 – "what shall we do for the 100 talents"
2Ch 27:5 – "Ammon gave..100 talents of silver"
2Ch 36:3 – "condemned..land..100 talents..silver"
Ezr 7:22 – "unto 100 talents of silver"
Ezr 8:26 – "weighed..silver vessels 100 talents"
Ezr 8:26 – "weighed..of gold 100 talents"

400+ *Talents*

1Ki 9:28 – "fetched from thence gold, 420 talents"
1Ki 10:14 – "gold..Solomon in 1 year..666 talents"
2Ki 15:19 – "gave Pul 1000 talents of silver"
1Ch 19:6 – "children of Ammon sent 1000 talents"
1Ch 22:14 – "an 100,000 talents of gold"
1Ch 22:14 – "a 1,000,000 talents of silver"
1Ch 29:4 – "3000 talents of gold..gold of Ophir"
1Ch 29:4 – "7000 talents of refined silver"
1Ch 29:7 – "of gold 5000 talents & 10,000 drams"
1Ch 29:7 – "of silver 10,000 talents"
1Ch 29:7 – "of brass 18,000 talents"
1Ch 29:7 – "100,000 talents of iron"
2Ch 3:8 – "overlaid it with fine gold..600 talents"
2Ch 8:18 – "450 talents of gold..to king Solomon"
2Ch 9:13 – "gold..Solomon in 1 year..666 talents"
Ezr 8:26 – "weighed..650 talents of silver"
Est 3:9 – "I will pay 10,000 talents of silver"
Mat 18:24 – "one..brought..owed..10,000 talents"

Talker

Tit 1:10 – "many unruly..talkers..deceivers"

Target

1Ki 10:16 – "Solomon..200 targets of beaten gold"
1Ki 10:16 – "600 shekels..gold went to one target"
2Ch 9:15 – "Solomon..200 targets of beaten gold"
2Ch 9:15 – "600 shekels..beaten gold..to 1 target"

Tarrying

Psa 40:17 - "make no tarrying, O my God"
Psa 70:5 – "O LORD, make no tarrying"

Tavern

Act 28:15 – "Appii forum, and The three taverns"

Tear

Act 20:19 – "Serving the Lord..with many tears"
2Co 2:4 – "wrote unto you with many tears"

Temple

Rev 21:22 – "And I saw no temple therein"

Temptation

1Co 10:13 – "no temptation taken you"

Tenon

Exo 26:17 – "2 tenons shall there be in one board"
Exo 26:19 – "two sockets..for his two tenons"
Exo 26:19 – "under another board for..2 tenons"
Exo 36:22 – "one board had two tenons"
Exo 36:24 – "2 sockets under 1 board..2 tenons"
Exo 36:24 – "2 sockets..another board..2 tenons"

Tent

Gen 31:33 – "into the two maidservants' tents"
2Ki 7:8 – "went into one tent and did eat..drink"

Ten Thousands

Dan 11:12 – "he shall cast down many 10,000's"

Testament

Heb 9:15 – "transgressions..under..1st testament"
Heb 9:18 – "neither..1st testament was dedicated"

Thanksgiving

2Co 9:12 – "many thanksgivings unto God"

Thief

Mat 27:38 – "two thieves..one on the right"
Mar 15:27 – "two thieves; one on his right"
Luk 12:33 – "where no thief approacheth"

Thing

Indefinite *Things*

Job 16:2 – "I have heard many such things"
Job 23:14 – "many such things are with him"
Ecc 6:11 – "many things that increase vanity"
Isa 42:20 – "Seeing many things"
Mat 13:3 – "many things unto them in parables"
Mat 16:21 – "suffer many things of the elders"
Mat 25:21 – "been faithful over a few things"
Mat 25:21 – "make thee ruler over many things"
Mat 25:23 – "been faithful over a few things"
Mat 25:23 – "make thee ruler over many things"
Mat 27:19 – "I have suffered many things"
Mar 4:2 – "taught them many things by parables"
Mar 5:26 – "suffered many things"
Mar 6:20 – "For Herod..did many things"
Mar 6:34 – "began to teach them many things"
Mar 7:4 – "And many other things there be"
Mar 7:8 – "many other such like things ye do"
Mar 7:13 – "and many such like things do ye"
Mar 8:31 – "Son of man..suffer many things"
Mar 9:12 – "he must suffer many things"
Mar 15:3 – "priests accused him of many things"
Mar 15:4 – "many things they witness against"
Luk 3:18 – "many other things..preached he"
Luk 9:22 – "Son of man must suffer many things"
Luk 10:41 – "troubled about many things"
Luk 11:53 – "provoke him..speak of many things"
Luk 17:25 – "first must he suffer many things"
Luk 22:65 – "many other things..spake they"
Luk 23:8 – "he had heard many things of him"
Joh 8:26 – "I have many things to say..judge"
Joh 16:12 – "yet many things to say unto you"
Joh 20:30 – "many other signs truly did Jesus"
Joh 21:25 – "many other things..Jesus did"
Act 26:9 – "do many things contrary to..Jesus"
2Co 8:22 – "proved diligent in many things"
Gal 3:4 – "suffered so many things in vain"
2Ti 1:18 – "many things he ministered"
Heb 5:11 – "we have many things to say"
Jam 3:2 – "For in many things we offend all."
2Jo 1:12 – "many things to write unto you"
3Jo 1:13 – "I had many things to write"
Rev 2:14 – "I have a few things against thee"
Rev 2:20 – "I have a few things against thee"

0 *Things*

Lev 12:4 – "she shall touch no hallowed thing"
Lev 27:28 – "no devoted thing.. shall be sold"
Deu 23:14 – "no unclean thing in thee"

Jos 23:14 – "that not one thing hath failed"
Jos 23:14 – "and not one thing hath failed"
2Sa 13:12 – "no such thing ought to be done"
Neh 6:8 – "no such things done as thou sayest"
Psa 84:11 – "no good thing will he withhold"
Psa 101:3 – "no wicked thing before mine eyes"
Ecc 1:9 – "no new thing under the sun"
Ecc 8:5 – "shall feel no evil thing"
Ecc 8:15 – "no better thing under the sun"
Isa 15:6 – "there is no green thing"
Isa 52:11 – "touch no unclean thing"
Act 21:25 – "they observe no such thing"
Act 25:26 – "I have no certain thing to write"
Rom 7:18 – "in me..dwelleth no good thing"
2Co 11:15 – "Therefore it is no great thing"
Tit 2:8 – "having no evil thing to say of you"

1 *Thing*

Jos 23:14 – "not 1 thing hath failed of all the good"
Jos 23:14 – "not one thing hath failed thereof"
2Sa 3:13 – "but one thing I require of thee"
Job 9:22 – "This is one thing"
Psa 27:4 – "One thing have I desired of the LORD"
Ecc 3:19 – "even one thing befalleth them"
Ezk 11:5 – "I know the things..every one of them"
Mat 21:24 – "I also will ask you one thing"
Mar 10:21 – "One thing thou lackest"
Luk 6:9 – "I will ask you one thing"
Luk 18:22 – "Yet lackest thou one thing"
Luk 20:3 – "I will also ask you one thing"
Joh 9:25 – "one thing I know..blind, now I see"
Joh 21:25 – "many other things..written every 1"
Act 19:32 – "Some therefore cried one thing"
Act 21:34 – "And some cried one thing"
Phi 3:13 – "this one thing I do, forgetting"
2Pe 3:8 – "be not ignorant of this one thing"

2 *Things*

Job 13:20 – "Only do not two things unto me"
Pro 30:7 – "Two things have I required of thee"
Isa 47:9 – "two things shall come..in one day"
Isa 51:19 – "These two things are come unto thee"
Heb 6:18 – "That by two immutable things"

3 *Things*

2Sa 24:12 – "saith the LORD, I offer thee 3 things"
1Ch 21:10 – "I offer thee 3 things: choose thee 1"
Pro 30:15 – "three things that are never satisfied"
Pro 30:18 – three things..too wonderful for me"
Pro 30:21 – "For 3 things the earth is disquieted"
Pro 30:29 – "There be three things which go well"

4+ **Things**

Psa 104:25 – "things creeping innumerable"
Pro 6:16 – "these six things doth the LORD hate"
Pro 6:16 – "yea, seven are an abomination"

Pro 30:15 – "four things say not, It is enough"
Pro 30:18 – "four which I know not"
Pro 30:21 – "four which it cannot bear"
Pro 30:24 – "four things..little upon the earth"
Pro 30:29 – "four are comely in going"

Thought

Job 42:2 – "no thought..withholden from thee"
Psa 139:18 – "count..more in number than..sand"
Mat 6:25 – "Take no thought for your life"
Mat 6:31 – "Therefore take no thought"
Mat 6:34 – "Take..no thought for the morrow"
Mat 10:19 – "take no thought how..ye..speak"
Mar 13:11 – "take no thought beforehand"
Luk 12:11 – "no thought how..what..answer"
Luk 12:22 – "Take no thought for your life"

Thousands

Num 10:36 – "unto the many thousands of Israel"
Act 21:20 – "many 1000's of Jews..believe"

> *See* **Ten Thousands** *under* **Indefinite Numbers**

Three

2Sa 23:19 – "attained not unto the first three"
2Sa 23:23 – "attained not to the first three"
1Ch 11:21 – "he attained not to the first three"
1Ch 11:25 – "but attained not to the first three"

Throne

Isa 47:1 – "there is no throne, O..Chaldeans"
Mat 19:28 – "ye also shall sit upon 12 thrones"

Thunder

Rev 10:3 – "7 thunders uttered their voices"
Rev 10:4 – "when the 7 thunders had uttered"
Rev 10:4 – "things..the 7 thunders uttered"

Tiding

2Sa 18:20 – "thou shalt bear no tidings"
2Sa 18:22 – "thou hast no tidings ready?"

Time

Indeterminate or 0 *Times*

Neh 9:28 – "many times didst thou deliver"
Psa 106:43 – "Many times did he deliver them"

1 *Time* (see also *Once*)

Gen 43:18 – "money..in our sacks at the 1st time"
Gen 43:20 – "came..the first time to buy food"
Deu 10:10 – "stayed in the mount, acc. to..1st time"
Jos 10:42 – "did Joshua take at one time"
1Ch 11:11 – "his spear against 300..at one time"
Hos 9:10 – "in the fig tree at her first time"

2 *Times* (see also *Twice*)

Gen 22:15 – "angel..called..Abraham..the 2nd time"
Gen 27:36 – "supplanted me these two times"
Gen 41:5 – "dreamed the second time"
Gen 43:10 – "we had returned this 2nd time"
Lev 13:58 – "washed the 2nd time..shall be clean"
Num 10:6 – "blow an alarm the second time"
Jos 5:2 – "circumcise again..Israel the 2nd time"
1Sa 26:8 – "I will not smite him the second time"
2Sa 14:29 – "sent again the 2nd time.. not come"
1Ki 9:2 – "LORD appeared to Solomon..2nd time"
1Ki 18:34 – "Do it the second time"
1Ki 18:34 – "And they did it the second time"
1Ki 19:7 – "angel..came again the second time"
2Ki 10:6 – "wrote a letter the second time"
1Ch 29:22 – "made Solomon..king the 2nd time"
Est 2:19 – "virgins were gathered..the 2nd time"
Isa 11:11 – "the 2nd time to recover the remnant"
Jer 1:13 – "word of the LORD came..the 2nd time"
Jer 13:3 – "word of the LORD came..the 2nd time"
Jer 33:1 – "word of the LORD came..the 2nd time"
Jon 3:1 – "word of the LORD came..the 2nd time"
Nah 1:9 – "affliction shall not rise up the 2nd time"
Mat 26:42 – "away again the 2nd time, and prayed"
Mar 14:72 – "the second time the cock crew"
Joh 3:4 – "enter..2nd time into his mother's womb"
Joh 21:16 – "saith to him again the second time"
Act 7:13 – "at the 2nd time Joseph..made known"
Act 10:15 – "voice spake..again the second time"
2Co 13:2 – "as if I were present, the second time"
Heb 9:28 – "appear the 2nd time without sin"

3 *Times* (see also *Thrice*)

Exo 23:14 – "3 times..keep a feast..in the year"
Exo 23:17 – "3 times in..year..all..males..appear"
Num 22:28 – "smitten me these three times"
Num 22:32 – "Wherefore..smitten..ass..3 times"
Num 22:33 – "ass..turned from me..three times"
Num 24:10 – "blessed them these three times"
Deu 16:16 – "3 times..a year..all thy males appear"
Jdg 16:15 – "thou hast mocked me these 3 times"
1Sa 3:8 – "LORD called Samuel again the 3rd time"

1Sa 19:21 – "Saul sent messengers..third time"
1Sa 20:41 – "David..bowed himself three times"
1Ki 9:25 – "3 times in the year did Solomon offer"
1Ki 17:21 – "stretched..upon the child 3 times"
1Ki 18:34 – "Do it the third time"
1Ki 18:34 – "And they did it the third time"
2Ki 13:18 – "And he smote thrice, and stayed."
2Ki 13:19 – "thou shalt smite Syria but thrice"
2Ki 13:25 – "Three times did Joash beat him"
2Ch 8:13 – "the solemn feasts, 3 times in the year"
Ezk 21:14 – "let the sword be double the 3rd time"
Dan 6:10 – "upon his knees three times a day"
Dan 6:13 – "maketh his petition three times a day"
Mat 26:44 – "went away..prayed the third time"
Mar 14:41 – "he cometh the third time"
Luk 23:22 – "he said unto them the third time"
Joh 21:14 – "third time that Jesus shewed himself"
Joh 21:17 – "saith unto him the third time"
Joh 21:17 – "said unto him the third time"
Act 11:10 – "this was done three times"
2Co 12:14 – "third time I am ready to come"
2Co 13:1 – "This is the third time I am coming"

3½ *Times*

Dan 7:25 – "a time & times & the dividing of time"
Dan 12:7 – "time, times, and an half"
Rev 12:14 – "nourished for a time..times..½ a time"

4 *Times*

2Sa 12:6 – "he shall restore the lamb fourfold"
Neh 6:4 – "sent unto me 4 times after this sort"

5 *Times*

Gen 43:34 – "Benjamin's mess..5 times so much"
2Ki 13:19 – "shouldest have smitten 5 or 6 times"
Neh 6:5 – "Then sent Sanballat..the fifth time"

6 *Times*

2Ki 13:19 – "shouldest have smitten 5 or 6 times"

7 *Times*

Gen 33:3 – "bowed himself to the ground 7 times"
Lev 4:6 – "sprinkle of the blood seven times"
Lev 4:17 – "blood, and sprinkle it seven times"
Lev 8:11 – "sprinkled..upon the altar seven times"
Lev 14:7 – "sprinkle..cleansed..leprosy 7 times"
Lev 14:16 – "oil..seven times before the LORD"
Lev 14:27 – "oil..seven times before the LORD"
Lev 14:51 – "shall sprinkle the house seven times"
Lev 16:14 – "sprinkle of the blood..seven times"
Lev 16:19 – "sprinkle of the blood...seven times"
Lev 26:18 – "seven times more for your sins"
Lev 26:21 – "seven times more plagues"
Lev 26:24 – "seven times for your sins"
Lev 26:28 – "seven times for your sins"

Num 19:4 – "sprinkle of her blood...seven times"
Jos 6:4 – "7ᵗʰ day ye..compass the city 7 times"
Jos 6:15 – "compassed the city..seven times"
Jos 6:15 – "they compassed the city 7 times"
Jos 6:16 – "at the 7ᵗʰ time..priests blew..trumpets"
1Ki 18:43 – "And he said, Go again seven times"
1Ki 18:44 – "it came to pass at the seventh time"
2Ki 4:35 – "the child sneezed seven times"
2Ki 5:10 – "Go and wash in the Jordan 7 times"
2Ki 5:14 – "dipped himself 7 times in Jordan"
Psa 12:6 – "in a furnace of earth, purified 7 times"
Psa 119:164 – "7 times a day do I praise thee"
Pro 24:16 – "a just man falleth seven times..riseth"
Dan 3:19 – "heat the furnace one 7 times more"
Dan 4:16 – "let seven times pass over him"
Dan 4:23 – "till seven times pass over him"
Dan 4:25 – "seven times shall pass over thee"
Dan 4:32 – "seven times shall pass over thee"
Mat 18:21 – "how oft..forgive..till seven times?"
Mat 18:22 – "I say not..Until seven times"
Luk 17:4 – "trespass against thee 7 times"
Luk 17:4 – "seven times in a day turn again"

10+ *Times*

Gen 31:7 – "changed my wages ten times"
Gen 31:41 – hast changed my wages ten times"
Num 14:22 – "tempted me now these ten times"
Deu 1:11 – "make..a 1000 times so many as ye are"
Jos 6:14-15 – 13 times around Jericho (6x1 + 7)
1Ch 21:3 – "The LORD make his people 100 times"
Neh 4:12 – "they said unto us ten times"
Job 19:3 – "ten times have ye reproached me"
Ecc 8:12 – "Though a sinner do evil 100 times"
Dan 1:20 – "10 times better than all the magicians"
Mat 18:22 – "but, Until seventy times seven"
2Co 11:24 – "5 times received..40 stripes save 1"

Tittle

Mat 5:18 – "one jot or one tittle..no wise pass"
Luk 16:17 – "one tittle of the law to fail"

Toes

2Sa 21:20 – "and on every foot six toes"
1Ch 20:6 – "fingers and toes were 24"
1Ch 20:6 – "six on each foot"

Tongue

1Ti 3:8 – "deacons..grave, not doubletongued"
Rev 10:11 – "many..tongues..kings"

Tooth

1Sa 2:13 – "fleshhook of three teeth in his hand"

Transgressions

Pro 28:24 – "It is no transgression"
Jer 5:6 – "their transgressions are many"
Amo 1:3 – "3 transgressions..Damascus, and for 4"
Amo 1:6 – "For 3 transgressions of Gaza, & for 4"
Amo 1:9 – "For 3 transgressions of Tyrus, & for 4"
Amo 1:11 – "3 transgressions of Edom, and for 4"
Amo 1:13 – "3 transgressions of..Ammon, & for 4"
Amo 2:1 – "For 3 transgressions of Moab, & for 4"
Amo 2:4 – "For 3 transgressions of Judah, & for 4"
Amo 2:6 – "For 3 transgressions of Israel, & for 4"
Rom 4:15 – "there is no transgression"

Trees

Exo 15:27 – "Elim..70 palm trees"
Num 33:9 – "Elim..70 palm trees"
Jos 10:26 – "Joshua smote..hanged..on 5 trees"
1Ki 10:12 – "there came no such almug trees"
Isa 10:19 – "trees of his forest shall be few"
Isa 66:17 – "behind one tree in the midst"
Eze 31:14 – "none of..trees..exalt themselves"
Ezk 40:26 – "palm trees, one on this side"
Ezk 47:7 – "very many trees on the one side"
Zec 4:3 – "two olive trees by it"
Zec 4:3 – "one upon the right side of the bowl"
Zec 4:11 – "What are these two olive trees"
Rev 11:4 – "These are the two olive trees"

Tribe

½ *Tribe*

Num 31:33 – "half the tribe of Manesseh"
Num 34:13 – "land..to..the 9 tribes, and ½ tribe"
Num 34:14 – "half the tribe of Manessah"
Num 34:15 – "The 2 tribes and the ½ tribe"
Num 36:9 – "inheritance remove..1 tribe..another"
Deu 3:13 – "the half tribe of Manessah"
Deu 29:8 – "to the half tribe of Manasseh"
Jos 1:12 – "and to half the tribe of Manasseh"
Jos 4:12 – "½..tribe of Manasseh, passed over"
Jos 12:6 – "possession unto..½tribe of Manasseh"
Jos 13:7 – "divide this land..half tribe of Manasseh"
Jos 13:7 – "divide this land..half tribe of Manasseh"
Jos 13:29 – "inheritance unto..½ tribe..Manasseh"
Jos 13:29 – "possession of the ½tribe..Manasseh"
Jos 18:7 – "half the tribe of Manasseh"
Jos 21:6 – "half tribe of Manasseh"
Jos 21:7 – "half tribe of Manasseh"
Jos 21:25 – "half tribe of Manasseh"

Jos 21:27 – "out of the other ½tribe of Manasseh"
Jos 22:1 – "Joshua called..the ½tribe of Manasseh"
Jos 22:7 – "to..½ tribe..Moses had given..Bashan"
Jos 22:7 – "unto the other ½ thereof gave Joshua"
Jos 22:9 – "the half tribe of Manasseh returned"
Jos 22:10 – "½ tribe of Manasseh built..an altar"
Jos 22:11 – "Israel heard..½ tribe.. built an altar"
Jos 22:13 – "the half tribe of of Manasseh"
Jos 22:15 – "the half tribe of of Manasseh"
Jos 22:21 – "the ½ tribe of of Manasseh answered"
1Ch 5:18 – "half the tribe of Manasseh"
1Ch 5:23 – "of the half tribe of Manasseh"
1Ch 5:26 – "the half tribe of Manasseh"
1Ch 6:61 – "were cities given out of the half tribe"
1Ch 6:61 – "namely out of the ½tribe of Manasseh"
1Ch 6:70 – "And out of the half tribe of Manasseh"
1Ch 6:71 – "out of the family of the half tribe"
1Ch 26:32 – "the half tribe of Manasseh"
1Ch 27:20 – "of the ½ tribe..Joel..son of Pedaiah"
1Ch 27:21 – "Of the ½ tribe..in Gilead, Iddo"

1 *Tribe*

Gen 49:16 – "Dan shall judge..as one of the tribes"
Deu 12:14 – "choose in one of thy tribes"
Jdg 21:3 – "to day one tribe lacking in Israel?"
Jdg 21:6 – "one tribe cut off from Israel this day"
1Ki 11:13 – "will give one tribe to thy son"
1Ki 11:32 – "he shall have 1 tribe for..David's sake"
1Ki 11:36 – "unto his son will I give one tribe"

2-11 *Tribes*

Num 34:13 – "land..unto the 9 tribes, and ½ tribe"
Num 34:15 – "2 tribes & the ½ tribe.. side Jordan"
Jos 14:2 – "inheritance..for..9 tribes, and..½ tribe"
Jos 14:3 – "inheritance of 2 tribes and an ½ tribe"
Jos 14:4 – "the children of Joseph were two tribes"
Jos 18:2 – "7 tribes..not yet received..inheritance"
Jos 21:16 – "nine cities out of these two tribes"
1Ki 11:31 – "will give ten tribes to thee"
1Ki 11:35 – "will give it unto thee, even ten tribes"

12 *Tribes*

Gen 49:28 – "these are the 12 tribes of Israel"
Exo 24:4 – "12 pillars acc. To..12 tribes of Israel"
Exo 28:21 – "according to the twelve tribes"
Exo 39:14 – "according to the twelve tribes"
Ezk 47:13 – "inherit the land acc. to..12 tribes"
Mat 19:28 – "ye also..judging..12 tribes of Israel"
Luk 22:30 – "judging the 12 tribes of Israel"
Act 26:7 – "Unto which promise our 12 tribes"
Jam 1:1 – "to the 12 tribes scattered abroad"
Rev 21:12 – "names of the twelves tribes"

Troop

2Sa 2:25 – "became 1 troop..stood..top of an hill"

Trouble

Deu 31:17 – "many evils & troubles..befall them"
Deu 31:21 – "many evils & troubles are befallen"
Job 5:19 – "delivereth thee in 6 troubles: yea, in 7"

Trumpet

Num 10:4 – "blow but with one trumpet"
Num 10:1 – "make thee two trumpets of silver"
Jos 6:4 – "7 priests..bear before..ark 7 trumpets"
Jos 6:6 – "7 priests bear 7 trumpets..rams' horns"
Jos 6:8 – "7 priests..7 trumpets of rams' horns"
Jos 6:13 – "7 priests..7 trumpets of rams' horns"
2Ch 5:12 – *"120 priests sounding with trumpets"*
Rev 8:2 – "to them were given 7 trumpets"
Rev 8:6 – "7 angels which had the 7 trumpets"

Trust

Job 4:18 – "he put no trust in his servants"
Job 15:15 – "he putteth no trust in his saints"

Truth

Hos 4:1 – "there is no truth..in the land"
Joh 8:44 – "because there is no truth in him"

Turtledove

Lev 5:7 – "for his trespass..two turtledoves"
Lev 5:7 – "turtledoves..one for a sin offering
Lev 5:11 – "two turtledoves..bring for his offering"
Lev 12:8 – "two turtles..burnt..sin offering"
Lev 14:22 – "two turtledoves..sin..burnt offering"
Lev 15:14 – "on the eighth day..two turtledoves"
Lev 15:29 – "on the eighth day..two turtles"
Num 6:10 – "on the eighth day..two turtles"
Luk 2:24 – "sacrifice..A pair of turtledoves"

Twelve

Mar 14:10 – "Judas Iscariot, one of the twelve"
Mar 14:20 – "It is one of the twelve"
Mar 14:43 – "Judas, one of the twelve"
Joh 6:70 – "chosen you 12, and one..is a devil"
Joh 6:71 – "Judas Iscariot..one of the twelve"
Joh 20:24 – "Thomas, one of the twelve"

Tyrannus

Act 19:9 – "daily in the school of one Tyrannus"

Undersetter

1Ki 7:34 – "4 undersetters..4 corners of one base"

Understanding

Psa 32:9 – "horse..mule..have no understanding"
Pro 21:30 – "no..understanding..against..LORD"
Isa 27:11 – "it is a people of no understanding"
Isa 29:16 – "He had no understanding?"

Unrighteousness

Lev 19:15 – "do no unrighteousness in judgment"
Lev 19:35 – "do no unrighteousness in judgment"
Psa 92:15 – "no unrighteousness in him"
Joh 7:18 – "no unrighteousness is in him"

Unruly

Tit 1:10 – "many unruly..talkers..deceivers"

Upright

Mic 7:2 – "there is none upright among men"

Usury

Lev 25:36 – "Take thou no usury of him"

Valley

Deu 3:16 – "Gilead..unto Arnon half the valley"

Value

Job 13:4 – "ye are all physicians of no value"

Variableness

Jas 1:17 – "with whom is no variableness"

Veil

Heb 9:3 – "after the second veil, the tabernacle"

Vent

Job 32:19 – "belly is as wine which hath no vent"

Vessel

1Ki 7:47 – "vessels..were exceeding many"
1Ki 10:21 – "vessels of..gold; none were of silver"
2Ki 4:3 – "vessels; borrow not a few"
2Ch 9:20 – "drinking vessels..none were of silver"
Ezr 1:10 – return vessels – "other vessels 1000"
Ezr 1:11 – "all the vessels..gold..silver were 5400"
Ezr 8:27 – "2 vessels of fine copper"
Ezk 4:9 – "put them in one vessel"
Hag 2:16 – "draw out 50 vessels.. were but 20"
Rom 9:21 – "make one vessel unto honour"

Vial

Rev 15:7 – "seven golden vials full..wrath of God"
Rev 17:1 – "angels which had the seven vials"
Rev 21:9 – "angels which had the seven vials"

Village

Neh 6:2 – "let us meet..in some one of the villages"
Act 8:25 – "preached..gospel in many villages"

Vinegar

Num 6:3 – "shall drink no vinegar of wine"

Vine

Isa 7:23 – "were 1000 vines at a 1000 silverings"

Violence

Isa 53:9 – "he had done no violence"
Jer 22:3 – "do no wrong, do no violence"

Virgin

Jdg 21:12 – "four hundred young virgins"
Son 6:8 – "There are..virgins without number"
Mat 25:1 – "heaven likened unto ten virgins"
Mat 25:2 – "five of them were wise"
Mat 25:2 – "five were foolish"

Vision

1Sa 3:1 – "there was no open vision"
Pro 29:18 – "no vision, the people perish"
Lam 2:9 – "prophets..no vision from the LORD"

Voice

Exo 24:3 – "all the people answered with 1 voice"
1Ki 18:26 – "But there was no voice"
Job 3:7 – "let no joyful voice come therein"
Act 19:34 – "all with one voice..cried out"
Act 24:21 – "Except it be for this one voice"
Rev 4:1 – "1st voice which I heard..as..a trumpet"

Vulture

Isa 34:15 – "vultures..every one with her mate"

Wafer

Exo 29:23 – "one wafer out of the basket"
Lev 8:26 – "one wafer" – consecrating Aaron
Num 6:19 – "one unleavened wafer...Nazarite"

Wages

Eze 29:18 – "yet had he no wages, nor his army"

Wagon

Num 7:3 – "six covered wagons"
Num 7:7 – "two wagons and four oxen"
Num 7:8 – "four wagons and eight oxen"

Wall

Lev 25:31 – "villages which have no wall"
1Ki 6:27 – "the wing of the 1 touched the 1 wall"
2Ki 25:4 – "men of war fled..between two walls"
Isa 22:11 – "a ditch between the two walls"
Jer 39:4 – "fled..by the gate betwixt the two walls"
Jer 52:7 – "men of war fled.. between the 2 walls"

Want

Jdg 18:10 – "there is no want of any thing"
Jdg 19:19 – "there is no want of any thing"
Psa 34:9 – "no want to them that fear him"

War

2Ch 14:6 – "he had no war in those years"
2Ch 15:19 – "And there was no more war"
2Ch 17:10 – "no war against Jehoshaphat"

Ward

Act 12:10 – "past the first and second ward"

Watch

Mat 14:25 – "in the fourth watch of the night"
Mar 6:48 – "4th watch of..night..walking upon..sea"
Luk 12:38 – "if he shall come in the second watch"
Luke 12:38 – "or come in the third watch"

Water

Gen 37:24 – "pit..there was no water in it"
Exo 15:22 – "and found no water"
Exo 17:1 – "there was no water for the people"
Num 20:2 – "no water for the congregation"
Num 24:7 – "his seed shall be in many waters"
Num 33:14 – "no water for the people"
Deu 8:15 – "where there was no water"
1Ki 13:22 – "Eat no bread, and drink no water"
2Ki 3:9 – "there was no water for the host"
2Sa 22:17 – "he drew me out of many waters"
Psa 18:16 – "he drew me out of many waters"
Psa 29:3 – "LORD is upon many waters"
Psa 63:1 – "thirsty land, where no water is"
Psa 93:4 – "the noise of many waters"
Son 8:7 – "Many waters cannot quench love"
Isa 1:30 – "a garden that hath no water"
Isa 8:7 – "waters..strong and many"
Isa 17:13 – "like the rushing of many waters"
Isa 41:17 – "seek water, and there is none"
Isa 44:12 – "he drinketh no water, and is faint"
Isa 50:2 – "there is no water..dieth for thirst"
Jer 2:13 – "cisterns, that can hold no water"
Jer 14:3 – "came..and found no water"
Jer 38:6 – "in..dungeon there was no water"
Jer 51:13 – "that dwellest upon many waters"
Ezk 19:10 – "by reason of many waters"
Ezk 43:2 – "like a noise of many waters"
Zec 9:11 – "the pit wherein is no water"
Zec 14:8 – "waters..half..toward the former sea"
Zec 14:8 – "waters..half..toward the hinder sea"
Luk 7:44 – " gavest me no water for my feet"
Rev 1:15 – "voice as,,sound of many waters"
Rev 14:2 – "as the voice of many waters"
Rev 17:1 – "great whore..upon many waters"
Rev 19:6 – "as the voice of many waters"

Waterpot

Joh 2:6 – "set there six waterpots of stone"

Way

Num 22:26 – "where was no way to turn"
Deu 28:7 – "shall come out against thee one way"
Deu 28:7 – "flee before thee seven ways"
Deu 28:25 – "shalt go out one way against them"
Deu 28:25 – "shalt..flee seven ways before them"
1Ki 18:6 – "Ahab went one way by himself"
2Ch 17:3 – "walked in the first ways of..David"
Job 12:24 – "wilderness where there is no way"
Psa 107:40 – "wilderness, where there is no way"
Pro 3:31 – "choose none of his ways"
Jer 25:35 – "shepherds..no way to flee"
Jer 32:39 – "And I will give them..one way"
Ezk 21:16 – "Go thee one way or the other"
Ezk 21:19 – "appoint thee two ways"
Ezk 21:21 – "at the head of the two ways"
Ezk 23:13 – "they took both one way"
Ezk 24:23 – "mourn one toward another"
Mar 11:4 – "place where two ways met"

Weapon

Isa 54:17 – "No weapon..formed..shall prosper"

Weeks

Lev 12:5 – "a maid child..unclean two weeks"
Deu 16:9 – "7 weeks shalt thou number unto thee"
Deu 16:9 – "number the 7 weeks..sickle to..corn"
Dan 9:24 – "70 weeks..determined upon..people"
Dan 9:25 – "commandment..Messiah..7 weeks"
Dan 9:25 – "commandment..Messiah..62 weeks"
Dan 9:26 – "after 62 weeks..Messiah be cut off"
Dan 9:27 – "confirm the covenant..for one week"
Dan 10:2 – "I Daniel was mourning 3 full weeks"
Dan 10:3 – "till three whole weeks were fulfilled"

Well

Exo 15:27 – "Elim, where were 12 wells of water"
2Ch 26:10 – "digged many wells"

Wheel

1Ki 7:30 – "every base had four brazen wheels"
1Ki 7:32 – "under the borders were four wheels"
Ezk 1:15 – "one wheel upon the earth"
Ezk 1:16 – "wheels..they four had one likeness"

Ezk 10:9 – "the four wheels by the cherubim"
Ezk 10:9 – "one wheel by one cherub"
Ezk 10:10 – "they four had one likeness"

Whelp

Ezk 19:3 – "brought up one of her young whelps"

Whore

Deu 23:17 – "no whore of the daughters of Israel"

Whoremonger

Eph 5:5 – "no whoremonger.. in the kingdom"

Wicked

Psa 37:16 – "the riches of many wicked"
Dan 12:10 – "none of the wicked..understand"

Wickedness

Lev 20:14 – "there be no wickedness among you"
Pro 30:20 – "I have done no wickedness"

Widow

Jer 15:8 – "widows..above the sands of the seas"
Luk 4:25 – "many widows were in Israel"
Luk 4:26 – "unto none of them was Elias sent"
Ezk 22:25 – "made her many widows"
Rev 18:7 – "I sit a queen, and am no widow"

Wife

Gen 4:19 – "Lamech took unto him two wives"
Gen 4:19 – "the name of the one was Adah"
Gen 7:13 – "Noah..the three wives of his sons"
Gen 24:41 – "if they give not thee one"
Gen 32:22 – "rose up..and took his two wives"
Deu 21:15 – "2 wives, one beloved..another hated"
Jdg 8:30 – "And Gideon..had many wives"
1Sa 1:2 – "he had two wives..Hannah..Peninnah"
1Sa 27:3 – "David..his 2 wives, Ahinoam..Abigail"
1Sa 30:5 – "David's 2 wives were taken captives"
1Sa 30:18 – "David rescued his two wives"
2Sa 2:2 – "David..and his two wives"
1Ki 11:3 – "he had 700 wives, princesses"
1Ch 4:5 – "Ashur..had 2 wives, Helah and Naarah"
1Ch 7:4 – "for they had many wives and sons"
1Ch 7:15 – "the 2nd was Zelophehad"

2Ch 11:21 – Rehoboam – "took 18 wives"
2Ch 11:23 – "And he desired many wives."
2Ch 13:21 – Abijah – "married 14 wives"
2Ch 24:3 – "Jehoiada took for him two wives"
1Co 7:29 – "have wives..as though..had none"
1Ti 3:2 – "bishop..husband of one wife"
1Ti 3:12 – "deacons..husbands of one wife"
Tit 1:6 – "the husband of one wife"

Wind

Jer 49:36 – "upon Elam..4 winds from..4 quarters"
Ezk 37:9 – "Come from the four winds, O breath"
Dan 7:2 – "four winds of..heaven strove upon..sea"
Dan 8:8 – "toward the four winds of heaven"
Dan 11:4 – "divided toward..4 winds of heaven"
Zech 2:6 – "as the four winds of the heaven"
Mat 24:31 – "gather..elect from the four winds"
Mar 13:27 – "gather..elect from the four winds"
Rev 7:1 – "holding the four winds of the earth"

Wine

Jdg 13:7 – "drink no wine nor strong drink"
Jer 35:6 – "We will drink no wine"
Jer 35:6 – "Ye shall drink no wine"
Jer 35:8 – "to drink no wine all our days"
Jer 35:14 – "wine..unto this day they drink none"
Joh 2:3 – "They have no wine"

Wing

1Ki 6:24 – "5 cubits was the 1 wing of the cherub"
1Ki 6:24 – "from the uttermost part of the 1 wing"
1Ki 8:7 – "cherubims spread forth their 2 wings"
2Ch 3:11 – "one wing of the one cherub"
2Ch 3:12 – "And one wing of the other cherub"
Isa 6:2 – "seraphims: each one had six wings"
Isa 6:2 – "wings; with twain he covered his face"
Isa 6:2 – "wings..with twain he covered his feet"
Isa 6:2 – "wings..with twain he did fly"
Dan 7:6 – "leopard..upon the back of it four wings"
Ezk 1:6 – "every one had four wings"
Ezk 1:9 – "wings were joined one to another"
Ezk 1:11 – "two wings of every one were joined"
Ezk 1:11 – "wings..joined one to another"
Ezk 1:11 – "wings..two covered their bodies"
Ezk 1:23 – "wings straight, the 1 toward the other"
Ezk 1:23 – "every one had two, which covered"
Ezk 1:23 – "and every one had two, which covered"
Ezk 3:13 – "noise of the wings..touched 1 another"
Ezk 10:21 – "and every one four wings"
Rev 4:8 – "four beasts had each..six wings"
Rev 12:14 – "to the woman..2 wings..great eagle"

Wisdom

Job 26:3 – "him that hath no wisdom"
Pro 21:30 – "no wisdom..against the LORD"
Ecc 9:10 – "no..wisdom, in the grave"

Witchcraft

2Ki 9:22 – "Jezebel and her witchcrafts..so many"

With *(as in a **piece of bark**)*

Jdg 16:7 – "If they bind me with 7 green withs"
Jdg 16:8 – "Philistines brought..7 green withs"

Witness

Num 5:13 – "there be no witness against her"
Num 35:30 – "one witness shall not testify"
Deu 17:6 – "mouth of 1 witness..not be put..death"
Deu 17:6 – "At the mouth of two witnesses, or 3"
Deu 19:15 – "1 witness..not rise up against a man"
Deu 19:15 – "at the mouth of three witnesses"
Mat 18:16 – "mouth or two or three witnesses"
Mat 26:60 – "But found none"
Mat 26:60 – "witnesses..yet found they none"
Mat 26:60 – "At the last came two false witnesses."
Mat 26:60 – "though many false witnesses came"
Mar 14:55 – "sought for witness..found none"
2Co 13:1 – "mouth of 2..3 witnesses..established"
1Ti 5:19 – "but before 2 or 3 witnesses"
1Ti 6:12 – "profession before many witnesses"
2Ti 2:2 – "heard of me among many witnesses"
Heb 10:28 – "w/o mercy under 2 or 3 witnesses"
Rev 11:3 – "power unto my two witnesses"

Woe

Rev 9:12 – "One woe is past"
Rev 9:12 – "behold, there come two woes more"
Rev 11:14 – "The second woe is past"
Rev 11:14 – "the third woe cometh quickly"

Woman

Lev 26:26 – "10 women..bake ..bread in one oven"
2Sa 15:16 – "10 women, which were concubines"
2Sa 20:3 – "ten women his concubines"
1Ki 3:17 – "one woman said, O my lord"
1Ki 3:16 – "came..two women, that were harlots"
1Ki 11:1 – "Solomon loved many strange women"
Ezr 2:65 – "200 singing men and singing women"
Job 2:10 – "speakest as one of the foolish women"
Job 42:15 – "no women found so fair"

Isa 4:1 – "7 women shall take hold of one man"
Ezk 16:41 – "in the sight of many women"
Ezk 23:2 – "2 women..daughters of one mother"
Zec 5:9 – "two women..wind was in their wings"
Mat 24:41 – "Two women shall be grinding"
Mat 27:55 – "many women..beholding afar off"
Mar 15:41 – "many other women which came"
Luk 8:3 – "Joanna..Susanna, and many others"
Luk 17:35 – "Two women grinding..one..taken"
Act 17:4 – "of the chief women not a few"

Womanservant

Gen 32:22 – "rose up..took..his 2 womenservants"

Wonder

Job 9:10 – "which doeth..wonders w/out number"
Act 2:43 – "many wonders & signs were done"
Act 5:12 – "many signs and wonders wrought"

Wood

Pro 26:20 – "no wood..the fire goeth out"
Eze 39:10 – "take no wood out of the field"

Wool

Eze 44:17 – "no wool shall come upon them"

Word

1Sa 3:19 – "none of his words fall to the ground"
2Sa 14:12 – "speak 1 word unto my lord the king"
1Ki 8:56 – "hath not failed one word of..promise"
Ecc 5:2 – "therefore let thy words be few"
Ecc 5:7 – "many words..divers vanities"
Jer 36:32 – "added..unto them many like words"
Eze 12:28 – "none of my words be prolonged"
Luk 23:9 – "questioned..him in many words"
Act 2:40 – "And with many other words"
Act 15:32 – "exhorted..with many words"
Act 24:4 – "hear us..a few words.
Act 28:25 – "Paul had spoken one word"
1Co 14:19 – "speak 5 words with..understanding"
1Co 14:19 – "10,000 words in..unknown tongue"
Gal 5:14 – "the law is fulfilled in one word"
Eph 3:3 – "as I wrote afore in few words"
Heb 13:22 – "I have written..you in few words"

Work

Exo 25:36 – "one beaten work of pure gold"

Exo 37:22 – "one beaten work of pure gold"
Lev 16:29 – "do no work at all"
Lev 23:3 – "ye shall do no work therein"
Lev 23:7 –"do no servile work therein"
Lev 23:8 – "do no servile work therein"
Lev 23:21 – "do no servile work therein"
Lev 23:25 – "do no servile work therein"
Lev 23:28 – "do no work in that same day"
Lev 23:35 – "do no servile work therein"
Lev 23:36 – "do no servile work therein"
Num 28:25 – "ye shall do no servile work"
Num 28:26 – "ye shall do no servile work"
Num 29:1 – "ye shall do no servile work"
Num 29:12 – "ye shall do no servile work"
Num 29:35 – "ye shall do no servile work"
Deu 15:19 – "shalt do no work with the firstling"
Deu 16:8 – "thou shalt do no work therein"
Psa 40:5 – "works..cannot be reckoned..in order"
Psa 40:5 – "works.. more than can be numbered"
Psa 40:5 – "Many..are thy wonderful works "
Ecc 9:10 – "no work..in the grave"
Jer 17:24 – "Sabbath..do no work therein"
Eze 15:5 – "it was meet for no work"
Mat 7:22 –"in thy name..many wonderful works"
Mat 13:58 – "he did not many mighty works"
Mar 6:5 – "could there do no mighty work"
Joh 7:21 – "I have done one work..ye all marvel"
Joh 10:32 – "Many good works have I shewed"
Rev 2:5 – "repent, and do the first works"

Wrath

Num 1:53 – "that there be no wrath"
Num 18:5 – "that there be no wrath"

Wreath

2Ch 4:12 – "2 wreaths to cover the 2 pommels"
2Ch 4:13 – "400 pomegranates on the 2 wreaths"

Writing

Deu 10:4 – "wrote..according to the first writing"

Wrong

1Ch 12:17 – "there is no wrong in mine hands"
Jer 22:3 – "do no wrong, do no violence"
Mat 20:13 – "Friend, I do thee no wrong"
Act 25:10 – "to the Jews have I done no wrong"

Year

Indefinite or Less than 1 *Year*

Lev 25:51 – "If there be yet many years"
Lev 25:52 – "few years unto the year of jubilee"
Ezr 5:11 – "house..builded these many years ago"
Neh 9:30 – "many years didst thou forbear them"
Job 16:22 – "When a few years are come"
Pro 4:10 – "years of thy life shall be many"
Ecc 6:3 – "If a man..live many years"
Ecc 11:8 – "But if a man live many years"
Isa 32:10 – "Many days & years..ye be troubled"
Ezk 38:17 – "prophesied..many years"
Zec 7:3 – "as I have done these so many years"
Luk 12:19 – "goods laid up for many years"
Luk 15:29 – "these many years do I serve"
Act 24:10 – "hast been of many years a judge"
Act 24:17 – "Now after many years I came"
Rom 15:23 – "great desire these many years"

1 *Year*

Exo 12:5 – Passover lamb – "male of the 1st year"
Exo 23:29 – "I will not drive them out..in 1 year"
Exo 29:38 – "offer..two lambs of the first year"
Lev 9:3 – "both of the first year" – calf and lamb
Lev 12:6 – "lamb of the first year...burnt offering"
Lev 14:10 – "ewe lamb of the first year"
Lev 23:12 – "he lamb w/out blemish of..1st year"
Lev 23:18 – "7 lambs w/out blemish of..1st year"
Lev 23:19 – "two lambs of the first year"
Num 6:12 – "a lamb of the first year"
Num 6:14 – "one he lamb of the first year"
Num 6:14 – "one ewe lamb of the first year"
Num 7:15 – "one lamb of the first year"
Num 7:17 – "five lambs of the first year"
Num 7:21 – "one lamb of the first year"
Num 7:23 – "five lambs of the first year"
Num 7:27 – "one lamb of the first year"
Num 7:29 – "five lambs of the first year"
Num 7:33 – "one lamb of the first year"
Num 7:35 – "five lambs of the first year"
Num 7:39 – "one lamb of the first year"
Num 7:41 – "five lambs of the first year"
Num 7:45 – "one lamb of the first year"
Num 7:47 – "five lambs of the first year"
Num 7:51 – "one lamb of the first year"
Num 7:53 – "five lambs of the first year"
Num 7:57 – "one lamb of the first year"
Num 7:59 – "five lambs of the first year"
Num 7:63 – "one lamb of the first year"
Num 7:65 – "five lambs of the first year"
Num 7:69 – "one lamb of the first year"
Num 7:71 – "five lambs of the first year"
Num 7:75 – "one lamb of the first year"
Num 7:77 – "five lambs of the first year"
Num 7:81 – "one lamb of the first year"
Num 7:83 – "five lambs of the first year"

Num 7:87 – "the lambs of the first year twelve"
Num 7:88 – the lambs of the first year sixty"
Num 15:27 – "she goat of the 1st year..sin offering"
Num 28:3 – "two lambs of the first year"
Num 28:9 – "two lambs of the first year"
Num 28:11 – "one ram, 7 lambs of the first year"
Num 28:19 – "seven lambs of the first year"
Num 28:27 – "offering..7 lambs of the first year"
Num 29:2 – "7 lambs of ..1st year w/out blemish"
Num 29:8 – "seven lambs of the first year"
Num 29:13 – "fourteen lambs of the first year"
Num 29:17 – "14 lambs of the 1st year w/out spot"
Num 29:20 – "14 lambs..1st year w/out blemish"
Num 29:23 – "14 lambs..1st year w/out blemish"
Num 29:26 – "14 lambs..1st year w/out spot"
Num 29:29 – "14 lambs ..1st year w/out blemish"
Num 29:32 – "14 lambs..1st year w/out blemish"
Num 29:36 – "7 lambs..1st year w/out blemish"
Deu 24:5 – "he shall be free at home one year"
1Sa 13:1 – "Saul reigned one year"
1Ki 10:14 – "weight of gold..to Solomon in 1 year"
2Ki 8:26 – "Ahaziah..reigned 1 year in Jerusalem"
2Ch 9:13 – "gold..Solomon in 1 year..666 talents"
2Ch 22:2 – "Ahaziah..reigned 1 year in Jerusalem"
2Ch 36:22 – "first year of Cyrus king of Persia"
Ezr 1:1 – "in the first year of Cyrus king of Persia"
Ezr 5:13 – "1st year of Cyrus..a decree to build"
Ezr 6:3 – "1st year of Cyrus..a decree concerning"
Jer 25:1 – "1st year of Nebuchadrezzar..king"
Jer 51:46 – "a rumour shall both come one year"
Jer 52:31 – "Evil-merodach..first year of his reign"
Ezk 46:13 – "lamb of the 1st year without blemish"
Dan 1:21 – "unto the first year of king Cyrus"
Dan 4:29 – "At the end of twelve months"
Dan 7:1 – "In the first year of Belshazzar"
Dan 9:1 – "In the first year of Darius"
Dan 9:2 – "In the first year of his reign"
Dan 11:1 – "in the first year of Darius the Mede"

1⅓ *Years*

1Sa 27:7 – "David dwelt..a full year and 4 months"

1½ *Years*

Act 18:11 – "continued there a year and 6 months"

2 *Years*

Gen 11:10 – "begat Arphaxad 2 years after..flood"
Gen 41:1 – "came to pass..end of two full years"
Gen 45:6 – "these two years hath the famine been"
Gen 47:18 – "then came unto him the 2nd year"
1Sa 13:1 – "he had reigned two years over Israel"
2Sa 2:10 – "Ishbosheth..reigned two years"
2Sa 13:23 – "after two full years, Absalom"
2Sa 14:28 – "Absalom..2 full years in Jerusalem"
1Ki 15:25 – "Nadab..began..reign..in the 2nd year"
1Ki 15:25 – "Nadab..reigned over Israel 2 years"
1Ki 16:8 – "Elah..reign over Israel..Tirzah 2 years"

203

1Ki 22:51 – "Ahaziah..reigned 2 years over Israel"
2Ki 1:17 – "Jehoram reigned..in the 2nd year"
2Ki 14:1 – "In the second year of Joash"
2Ki 15:23 – "Pekahiah..reigned two years"
2Ki 15:32 – "2nd year of Pekah..began Jotham"
2Ki 19:29 – "in the 2nd year that which springeth"
2Ki 21:19 – "Amon..reigned 2 years in Jerusalem"
2Ch 21:19 – "end of 2 years..bowels fell out"
2Ch 27:5 – "Ammon..both the 2nd year, & the 3rd"
2Ch 33:21 – "Amon..reigned 2 years in Jerusalem"
Ezr 4:24 – "work..ceased unto..2nd year..of Darius"
Isa 37:30 – "2nd year..which springeth of..same"
Jer 28:3 – "Within two full years..vessels"
Jer 28:11 – "within the space of two full years"
Dan 2:1 – "2nd year of..reign of Nebuchadnezzar"
Amo 1:1 – "two years before the earthquake"
Mat 2:16 – "children..from 2 years old and under"
Act 19:10 – "continued by the space of two years"
Act 24:27 – "after two years Porcius Festus"
Act 28:30 – "Paul dwelt two whole years..house"

3 Years

Gen 15:9 – "Take me an heifer of 3 years old"
Gen 15:9 – "a she goat of 3 years old"
Gen 15:9 – "a ram of 3 years old"
Lev 19:23 – "fruit..3 years..it be uncircumcised"
Lev 25:21 – "bring forth fruit for three years"
Deu 14:28 – "end of 3 years..bring..all the tithe"
Deu 26:12 – "tithes of thine increase the 3rd year"
Jdg 9:22 – "Abimelech..reigned 3 years..Israel"
2Sa 13:38 – "Absalom fled..was there three years"
2Sa 21:1 – "famine in the days of David 3 years"
1Ki 2:39 – "end of 3 years..servants..ran away"
1Ki 10:22 – "once in three years came the navy"
1Ki 15:2 – "Three years reigned he in Jerusalem"
1Ki 15:28 – "in the 3rd year..did Baasha slay him"
1Ki 15:33 – "In the 3rd year of Asa..began Baasha"
1Ki 18:1 – "word of..LORD..to Elijah in..3rd year"
1Ki 22:1 – "3 years without war..Syria & Israel"
1Ki 22:2 – "in..3rd year..Jehoshaphat..came down"
2Ki 17:5 – "king of Assyria..beseiged it 3 years"
2Ki 18:1 – "in the 3rd year of Hoshea..Hezekiah"
2Ki 18:10 – "at the end of 3 years they took it"
2Ki 19:29 – "3rd year sow ye, and reap, and plant"
2Ki 24:1 – "Jehoiakim became his servant 3 years"
1Ch 21:12 – "Either three years' famine"
2Ch 9:21 – "every 3 years..came..ships of Tarshish"
2Ch 11:17 – "made Rehoboam..strong, 3 years"
2Ch 11:17 – "3 years..walked in the way of David"
2Ch 13:2 – "He reigned 3 years in Jerusalem"
2Ch 17:7 – "in the third year of his reign"
2Ch 27:5 – "Ammon..both the 2nd year, & the 3rd"
2Ch 31:16 – "geneology..males, from 3 years old"
Est 1:3 – "third year of his reign..Persia & Media"
Isa 15:5 – "an heifer of three years old"
Isa 16:14 – "3 years..glory of Moab..contemned"
Isa 20:3 – "Isaiah..walked naked..barefoot 3 years"
Isa 37:30 – "in the 3rd year sow ye, and reap"
Jer 48:34 – "as an heifer of three years old"
Dan 1:1 – "third year of the reign of Jehoiakim"

Dan 1:5 – "so nourishing them three years"
Dan 8:1 – "3rd year of the reign of king Belshazzar"
Dan 10:1 – "In the 3rd year of Cyrus king of Persia"
Amo 4:4 – "your tithes after three years"
Luk 13:7 – "three years I come seeking fruit"
Act 20:31 – "three years I ceased not to warn"
Gal 1:18 – "after 3 years I went up to Jerusalem"

3½ Years

Luk 4:25 – "heaven shut up 3 years and 6 months"
Jam 5:17 – "Elias..prayed..rained not..3 yrs & 6 mos"

4 Years

Lev 19:24 – "4th year..fruit thereof shall be holy"
1Ki 6:1 – "in the fourth year of Solomon's reign"
1Ki 6:37 – "In the 4th year was..foundation..laid"
1Ki 22:41 – "Jehoshaphat..began..reign..4th year"
2Ki 18:9 – "4th year of..Hezekiah..Shalmaneser"
Jer 25:1 – "the 4th year of Jehoiakim..son of Josiah"
Jer 36:1 – "the 4th year of Jehoiakim..son of Josiah"
Jer 45:1 – "the 4th year of Jehoiakim..son of Josiah"
Jer 46:1 – "the 4th year of Jehoiakim..son of Josiah"
Jer 51:59 – "Zedekiah..4th year of his reign"

5 Years

Gen 45:6 – "5 years..neither be earing..harvest"
Gen 45:11 – "yet there are 5 years of famine"
Lev 19:25 – "5th year shall ye eat of..fruit thereof"
Lev 27:5 – "from five years old..estimation"
Lev 27:6 – "unto five years old..estimation"
2Sa 4:4 – "lame..five years old..Mephibosheth"
1Ki 14:25 – "5th year..Rehoboam..Shishak..came"
2Ki 8:16 – "5th year..Joram..Jehoram began..reign"
2Ch 12:2 – "5th year of..Rehoboam Shishak..came"

6 Years

Gen 31:41 – "served..six years for thy cattle"
Exo 21:2 – "servant, six years he shall serve"
Exo 23:10 – "six years thou shalt sow thy land"
Lev 25:3 – "Six years thou shalt sow thy field"
Lev 25:3 – "6 years thou shalt prune thy vineyard"
Lev 25:21 – "blessing upon you in the sixth year"
Deu 15:12 – "thy brother..serve thee six years"
Deu 15:18 – "hired servant..serving thee 6 years"
Jdg 12:7 – "Jephthah judged Israel six years"
1Ki 16:23 – "Omri..six years reigned he in Tirzah"
2Ki 11:3 – "was with her hid..six years"
2Ki 18:10 – "even in the 6th year of Hezekiah"
2Ch 22:12 – "hid in the house of God 6 years"
Ezr 6:15 – "6th year..reign of Darius"
Jer 34:14 – "served thee 6 years..let him go free"

7 Years

Gen 29:18 – "I will serve thee 7 years for Rachel"

Gen 29:20 – "Jacob served 7 years for Rachel"
Gen 29:27 – "serve with me yet seven other years"
Gen 29:30 – "served with him yet 7 other years"
Gen 41:26 – "the 7 good kine are 7 years"
Gen 41:26 – "the 7 good ears are 7 years"
Gen 41:27 – "7 thin & ill favoured kine..7 years"
Gen 41:27 – "7 empty ears.. be 7 years..famine"
Gen 41:29 – "there come 7 years of great plenty"
Gen 41:30 – "arise after them 7 years of famine"
Gen 41:34 – "Egypt in the 7 plenteous years"
Gen 41:36 – "food..for store..against the 7 years"
Gen 41:47 – "in the 7 plenteous years"
Gen 41:48 – "gathered up all..food of the 7 years"
Gen 41:53 – "7 years of plenteousness..ended"
Gen 41:54 – "7 years of dearth began to come"
Exo 21:2 – "in the 7th..go out free for nothing"
Exo 23:11 – "the 7th year thou shall let it rest"
Lev 25:4 – "7th year shall be a sabbath of rest"
Lev 25:20 – "What shall we eat the seventh year?"
Num 13:22 – "Hebron..built 7 years before Zoan"
Deu 15:1 – "end of every 7 years...make a release"
Deu 15:9 – "The seventh year, the year of release"
Deu 15:12 – "in the seventh year..let him go free"
Deu 31:10 – "end of every 7 years..year of release"
Jdg 6:1 – "delivered..into..hand of Midian 7 years"
Jdg 6:25 – "even the second bullock of 7 years old"
Jdg 12:9 – Ibzan – "he judged Israel seven years"
2Sa 24:13 – "Shall seven years of famine come"
1Ki 2:11 – "seven years reigned he in Hebron"
1Ki 6:38 – "So he was seven years in building it."
2Ki 8:1 – "famine..upon the land seven years"
2Ki 8:2 – "in the land of the Philistines 7 years"
2Ki 8:3 – "came to pass at the seven years' end"
2Ki 11:4 – "7th year Jehoiada sent and fetched"
2Ki 11:21 – "Seven years old was Jehoash..began"
2Ki 12:1 – "7th year of Jehu Jehoash began"
2Ki 18:9 – "7th year of Hoseha's son of Elah"
1Ch 29:27 – "7 years reigned he in Hebron"
2Ch 23:1 – "in the 7th year Jehoiada strengthened"
2Ch 24:1 – "Joash was 7 years old..began to reign"
Ezr 7:7 – "in the 7th year of Artaxerxes the king"
Ezr 7:8 – "which was in the 7th year of the king"
Neh 10:31 – "we would leave the 7th year..debt"
Jer 34:14 – "end of 7 years let ye go every man"
Jer 52:28 – "carried away captive: in the 7th year"
Ezk 39:9 – "shall burn them with fire seven years"
Luk 2:36 – "Anna..seven years from her virginity"

7½ *Years*

2Sa 2:11 – "David..Hebron..7 years and 6 months"
2Sa 5:5 – "Hebron..reigned..7 years..6 months"
1Ch 3:4 – "Hebron..reigned 7 years and 6 months"

8 *Years*

Lev 25:22 – "ye shall sow the eighth year"
Jdg 3:8 – "served Cushanrishathaim eight years"
Jdg 12:14 – Abdon – "he judged Israel eight years"
2Ki 8:17 – "reigned 8 years in Jerusalem"

2Ki 22:1 – "Josiah was 8 years old..began to reign"
2Ki 24:12 – "king..Babylon took him in..8th year"
2Ch 21:5 – "Jehoram..reigned 8 years..Jerusalem"
2Ch 21:20 – "reigned in Jerusalem 8 years"
2Ch 34:1 – "Josiah was 8 years old..began to reign"
2Ch 34:3 – "8th year..began to seek..God"
2Ch 36:9 – "Jehoiachin..8 years old..began..reign"
Act 9:33 – "Aenas, which had kept his bed 8 years"

9 *Years*

Lev 25:22 – "eat yet of old fruit until the 9th year"
2Ki 17:1 – "Hoshea..reign..nine years"
2Ki 17:6 – "9th year of Hoshea..king..took Samaria"
2Ki 18:10 – "the 9th year of Hoshea's king of Israel"

10 *Years*

Gen 16:3 – "after Abram..dwelt 10 years..Canaan"
Jdg 12:11 – "Elon..judged Israel ten years"
Rut 1:4 – "they dwelled there about ten years"
2Ki 15:17 – "Menahem..reigned 10 years..Samaria"
2Ch 14:1 – "land was quiet ten years"
Jer 32:1 – "10th year of Zedekiah king of Judah"

11 *Years*

1Ki 6:38 – "in..11th year..was the house finished"
2Ki 9:29 – "in..11th year of Joram..began Ahaziah"
2Ki 23:36 – "Jehoiakim..reigned 11 years"
2Ki 24:18 – "Zedekiah..reigned 11 years"
2Ki 25:2 – "city..beseiged..11th year..Zedekiah"
2Ch 36:5 – "Jehoiakim..reigned 11 years"
2Ch 36:11 – "Zedekiah..reigned 11 years"
Jer 52:1 – "Zedekiah..reigned 11 years"
Jer 52:5 – "city was besieged unto the 11th year"

12 *Years*

Gen 14:4 – "12 years they served Chedorlaomer"
1Ki 16:23 – "Omri..reign over Israel, 12 years"
2Ki 3:1 – "Jehoram..reigned twelve years"
2Ki 8:25 – "12th year..Joram.. Ahaziah..begin..reign"
2Ki 17:1 – "In the 12th year of Ahaz..began Hoshea"
2Ki 21:1 – "Manasseh..12 years old..began..reign"
2Ch 33:1 – "Manasseh..12 years old..began..reign"
2Ch 33:21 – "Amon..22 years old..began to reign"
2Ch 34:3 – "12th year..began to purge Judah"
Neh 5:14 – "20th..unto the 32nd..that is, 12 years"
Mat 9:20 – "woman..with..issue of blood 12 years"
Mar 5:25 – "woman..issue of blood 12 years"
Mar 5:42 – "damsel arose..age of 12 years"
Luk 2:42 – "when he was twelve years old"
Luk 8:42 – "daughter, about 12 years of age"
Luk 8:44 – "issue of blood 12 years"

13 *Years*

Gen 14:4 – "in the 13th year they rebelled"
Gen 17:25 – "Ishmael..13 years old..circumcised"

Jer 25:3 – "from..13th year..Josiah..unto..23rd year"
1Ki 7:1 – "Solomon..building his..house 13 years"
Jer 1:2 – "Josiah..in the 13th year of his reign"

14 *Years*

Gen 14:5 – "in the 14th year came Chedorlaomer"
Gen 31:41 – "served..14 years for thy 2 daughters"
2Ki 18:13 – "in the 14th year of..Hezekiah"
Isa 36:1 – "in the 14th year of..Hezekiah"
Ezk 40:1 – "14th year after that..city was smitten"
2Co 12:2 – "I knew a man..above 14 years ago"
Gal 2:1 – "Then 14 years after..again to Jerusalem"

15 *Years*

2Ki 14:17 – "Amaziah..after..Jehoash..15 years"
2Ki 14:23 – "15th year of Amaziah..Jeroboam"
2Ki 20:6 – "I will add unto thy days 15 years"
2Ch 25:25 – "Amaziah..after..Joash..15 years"
Isa 38:5 – "I will add unto thy days 15 years"
Luk 3:1 – "in the 15th year of..Tiberius Caesar"

16 *Years*

2Ki 13:10 – "Jehoash..reigned 16 years"
2Ki 14:21 – "Azariah..16 years old..made him king"
2Ki 15:2 – "16 years old..when he began to reign"
2Ki 15:33 – "reigned 16 years in Jerusalem"
2Ki 16:2 – "Ahaz..reigned 16 years in Jerusalem"
2Ch 26:1 – "Uzziah, who was 16 years old"
2Ch 26:3 – "16 years old..Uzziah..began to reign"
2Ch 27:1 – "Jotham..reigned 16 years..Jerusalem"
2Ch 27:8 – "reigned 16 years in Jerusalem"
2Ch 28:1 – "Ahaz..reigned 16 years in Jerusalem"

17 *Years*

Gen 37:2 – "Joseph being 17 years old"
Gen 47:28 – "Jacob lived in..Egypt 17 years"
1Ki 14:21 – "17 years in Jerusalem"
1Ki 22:51 – "Ahaziah..began to reign..17th year"
2Ki 13:1 – "Jehoahaz..reigned 17 years"
2Ki 16:1 – "In the 17th year of Pekah..Ahaz..began"
2Ch 12:13 – "17 years in Jerusalem"

18 *Years*

Jdg 3:14 – "served Eglon..king of Moab 18 years"
Jdg 10:8 – "vexed...Israel: 18 years"
1Ki 15:1 – "18th year of Jeroboam..reigned Abijam"
2Ki 3:1 – "Jehoram..began to reign..in..18th year"
2Ki 22:3 – "in the 18th year..Josiah..sent Shaphan"
2Ki 23:23 – "18th year of..Josiah..passover..holden"
2Ki 24:8 – "Jehoiachin was 18 years old..to reign"
2Ch 13:1 – "18th year of..Jeroboam began Abijah"
2Ch 34:8 – "18th year..sent Shaphan..to repair"
2Ch 35:19 – "18th year..reign of Josiah..passover"
Jer 32:1 – "was the 18th year of Nebuchadrezzar"
Jer 52:29 – "In the 18th year of Nebuchadrezzar"

Luk 13:11 – "woman..spirit of infirmity 18 years"
Luk 13:16 – "Satan hath bound, lo, these 18 years"

19 *Years*

2Ki 25:8 – "19th year..Nebuchadnezzar"

20 *Years*

Gen 31:38 – "This 20 years have I been with thee"
Gen 31:41 – "I have been 20 years in thy house"
Exo 30:14 – "from twenty years old and above"
Exo 38:26 – "numbered..from 20 years old"
Lev 27:3 – "estimation...from twenty years old"
Lev 27:5 – "unto twenty years old"
Num 1:3 – "twenty years old and upward"
Num 1:18 – "twenty years old and upward"
Num 1:20 – "Reuben..20 years old and upward"
Num 1:22 – "Simeon..20 years old and upward"
Num 1:24 – "Gad..twenty years old and upward"
Num 1:26 – "Judah..twenty years old and upward"
Num 1:28 – "Issachar..20 years old and upward"
Num 1:30 – "Zebulun..20 years old and upward"
Num 1:32 – "Ephraim..20 years old and upward"
Num 1:34 – "Mannaseh..20 years old and upward"
Num 1:36 – "Benjamin..20 years old and upward"
Num 1:38 – "Dan..twenty years old and upward"
Num 1:40 – "Asher..twenty years old and upward"
Num 1:42 – "Naphtali..20 years old and upward"
Num 1:45 – "Israel..20 years old and upward"
Num 14:29 – "20 years old & upward..murmured"
Num 26:2 – "sum..of Israel..20 years old..upward"
Num 26:4 – "sum..from 20 years old and upward"
Num 32:11 – "none..out of Egypt..20 years old"
Jdg 4:3 – "20 years he mightily oppressed"
Jdg 15:20 – Samson – "judged Israel..20 years"
Jdg 16:31 – Samson – "judged Israel..20 years"
1Sa 7:2 – "ark abode in Kirjath-jearim..20 years"
1Ki 9:10 – "at..end of 20 years..Solomon had built"
1Ki 15:9 – "in the 20th year of Jeroboam"
2Ki 15:27 – "Pekah..reigned twenty years"
2Ki 15:30 – "conspiracy..20th year of Jotham"
2Ki 16:2 – "20 years old..began to reign"
1Ch 23:24 – "sons of Levi..20 years and upward"
1Ch 23:27 – "Levites numbered..20 years..above"
1Ch 27:23 – "the number..20 years old..under"
2Ch 8:1 – "end of 20 years..built the house"
2Ch 25:5 – "numbered them..20 years..and above"
2Ch 28:1 – "Ahaz was 20 years old..began to reign"
2Ch 31:17 – "Levites from 20 years old & upward"
Ezr 3:8 – "Levites, from 20 years old and upward"
Neh 1:1 – "in the 20th year, as I was in Shushan"
Neh 2:1 – "in the 20th year of Artaxerxes the king"
Neh 5:14 – "20th year..unto..32nd year..Artaxerxes"

21 *Years*

2Ki 24:18 – "Zedekiah was 21 years old..reign"
2Ch 36:11 – "Zedekiah was 21 years old..reign"
Jer 52:1 – "Zedekiah was 21 years old..reign"

22 *Years*

Jdg 10:3 – "judged Israel 22 years"
1Ki 14:20 – "days..Jeroboam reigned..22 years"
1Ki 16:29 – "Ahab..reigned..in Samaria 22 years"
2Ki 8:26 – "22 years old..Ahaziah..began to reign"
2Ki 21:19 – "Amon..22 years old..began to reign"
2Ch 33:21 – "Amon..22 years old..began to reign"

23 *Years*

Jdg 10:2 – Tola – "he judged Israel 23 years"
2Ki 12:6 – "in the 23rd year of king Jehoash"
2Ki 13:1 – "23rd year of Joash..Jehoahaz..began"
2Ki 23:31 – "Jehoahaz..23 years old..began..reign"
2Ch 36:2 – "Jehoahaz..23 years old..began..reign"
Jer 25:3 – "13th year of Josiah..unto..23rd year"
Jer 52:30 – "In the 23rd year of Nebuchadrezzar"

24 *Years*

1Ki 15:33 – "Baasha..reign over Israel..24 years"

25 *Years*

Num 8:24 – "from 25 years old and upward"
1Ki 22:42 – "Jehoshaphat..reigned 25 years"
2Ki 14:2 – "25 years old..began to reign"
2Ki 15:33 – "25 years old..began to reign"
2Ki 18:2 – "25 years old..began to reign"
2Ki 23:36 – "Jehoiakim..25 years old..began..reign"
2Ch 20:31 – "Jehoshaphat..over Judah..25 years"
2Ch 25:1 – "Amaziah..25 years old..began..reign"
2Ch 27:1 – "Jotham..25 years old..began to reign"
2Ch 27:8 – "was 25 years old..began to reign"
2Ch 29:1 – "Hezekiah began to reign..25 years old"
2Ch 36:5 – "Jehoiakim..25 years old..began..reign"

26-29 *Years*

Gen 11:24 – "Nahor lived 29 years ..begat Terah"
1Ki 16:8 – "In the 26th year of Asa..began Elah"
1Ki 16:10 – "Zimri..smote him..in..27th year of Asa"
1Ki 16:15 – "In..27th year of Asa..did Zimri reign"
2Ki 10:36 – "Jehu reigned over Israel..28 years"
2Ki 14:2 – "reigned 29 years in Jerusalem"
2Ki 15:1 – "27th year of Jeroboam..began Azariah"
2Ki 18:2 – "reigned 29 years in Jerusalem"
2Ch 25:1 – "Amaziah..reigned 29 years.Jersualem"
2Ch 29:1 – "Hezekiah..reigned 29 years"

30 *Years*

Gen 11:14 – "Salah lived 30 years..begat Eber"
Gen 11:18 – "Peleg lived 30 years..begat Reu"
Gen 11:22 – "Serug lived 30 years..begat Nahor"
Gen 41:46 – "Joseph was 30 years old..stood"
Num 4:3 – "From 30 years old..until 50 years old"
Num 4:23 – "From 30 years old..until 50 years old"
Num 4:30 – "From 30 years old..until 50 years old"

Num 4:35 – "From 30 years old..until 50 years old"
Num 4:39 – "From 30 years old..until 50 years old"
Num 4:43 – "From 30 years old..until 50 years old"
Num 4:47 – "From 30 years old..until 50 years old"
2Sa 5:4 – "David was 30 years old..began to reign"
1Ch 23:3 – "Levites..numbered..age of 30 years"
Luk 3:23 – "Jesus..began to be about 30 years"

31-34 *Years*

Gen 11:16 – "Eber lived 34 years..begat Peleg"
Gen 11:20 – "Reu lived 32 years..begat Serug"
2Sa 5:5 – "reigned 33 years over all Israel"
1Ki 2:11 – "33 years reigned he in Jerusalem"
1Ki 16:23 – "In the 31st year of Asa..began Omri"
2Ki 8:17 – "32 years old ..when he began to reign"
2Ki 22:1 – "Josiah..reigned 31 years in Jerusalem"
1Ch 3:4 – "in Jerusalem he reigned 33 years"
1Ch 29:27 – "33 years reigned he in Jerusalem"
2Ch 21:5 – "Jehoram..32 years old..began..reign"
2Ch 21:20 – "32 years old..began to reign"
2Ch 34:1 – "Josiah..reigned in Jerusalem 31 years"
Neh 5:14 – "20th year..unto..32nd year..Artaxerxes"
Neh 13:6 – "in the 32nd year of Artaxerxes..came I"

35-39 *Years*

Gen 11:12 – "Arphaxad..35 years..begat Salah"
Deu 2:14 –"Kadeshbarnea, until Zered..38 years"
1Ki 16:29 – "in the 38th year of Asa..began Ahab"
1Ki 22:42 – "Jehoshaphat..35 years..began..reign"
2Ki 13:10 – "In the 37th year of Joash..Jehoash"
2Ki 15:8 – "38th year of Azariah..Zachariah..reign"
2Ki 15:13 – "Shallum..began..in..39th year..Uzziah"
2Ki 15:17 – "39th year..Azariah..began Menahem"
2Ch 15:19 – "no more war unto..35th year of..Asa"
2Ch 16:1 – "In the 36th year of...Asa"
2Ch 16:12 – "Asa in..39th year.. diseased in his feet"
2Ch 20:31 – "Jehoshaphat.. 35 years old..began"
Joh 5:5 – "certain man..had an infirmity 38 years"

40 *Years*

Gen 25:20 – "Isaac..40 years old..took Rebekkah"
Gen 26:34 – "Esau was 40 years old..took to wife"
Exo 16:35 – "children..Israel..eat manna 40 years"
Num 14:33 – "in the wilderness forty years"
Num 14:34 – "bear your iniquities, even 40 years"
Num 32:13 – "LORD's anger..wilderness 40 years"
Deu 2:7 – "40 years..God hath been with thee"
Deu 8:2 – "God, led thee these forty years"
Deu 8:4 – "raiment waxed not old..these 40 years"
Deu 29:5 – "I have led you 40 years in..wilderness"
Jos 5:6 – "walked forty years in the wilderness"
Jos 14:7 – "40 years old was I..Moses..sent me"
Jdg 3:11 – "the land had rest forty years"
Jdg 5:31 – "And the land had rest forty years."
Jdg 8:28 – "country..quietness 40 years..Gideon"
Jdg 13:1 – "delivered..hand..Philistines 40 years"
1Sa 4:18 – "he had judged Israel 40 years"

2Sa 2:10 – "40 years old..began to reign"
2Sa 5:4 – "David..reigned 40 years"
2Sa 15:7 – "after 40 years, that Absalom said"
1Ki 2:11 – "David reigned over Israel..40 years"
1Ki 11:42 – "Solomon reigned..40 years"
2Ki 12:1 – "Jehoash..40 years reigned.."
1Ch 26:31 – "40th year of the reign of David"
1Ch 29:27 – "reigned over Israel..40 years"
2Ch 9:30 – "Solomon reigned..Jerusalem..40 years"
2Ch 24:1 – "Joash..reigned 40 years in Jerusalem"
Neh 9:21 – "40 years didst thou sustain them"
Psa 95:10 – "40 years long was I grieved w/ this"
Ezk 29:11 – "neither shall..be inhabited 40 years"
Ezk 29:12 – "cities..laid waste..desolate 40 years"
Ezk 29:13 – "At..end of 40 years..gather Egyptians"
Amo 2:10 – "led you 40 years through..wilderness"
Amo 5:25 – "offerings in the wilderness 40 years"
Act 4:22 – "man was above 40 years old"
Act 7:23 – "when he was full 40 years old"
Act 7:30 – "when 40 years were expired"
Act 7:36 – "in the wilderness 40 years"
Act 7:42 – "sacrifices by the space of 40 years"
Act 13:18 – "40 years suffered he their manners"
Act 13:21 – "a king..Saul..by the space of 40 years"
Heb 3:9 – "saw my works forty years
Heb 3:17 – "with whom he was grieved 40 years"

41-49 *Years*

Lev 25:8 – *"seven sabbaths of years"*
Lev 25:8 – *"seven times seven years"*
Lev 25:8 – *"space of the seven sabbaths of years"*
Lev 25:8 – "shall be unto thee 49 years"
Jos 14:10 – "LORD..kept me alive..these 45 years"
1Ki 14:21 – "41 years old..he began to reign"
1Ki 15:10 – "41 years reigned he in Jerusalem"
2Ki 14:23 – "Jeroboam..reigned 41 years"
2Ch 12:13 – "41 years old..he began to reign"
2Ch 16:13 – "Asa..died in the 41st year of his reign"
2Ch 22:2 – "42 years old..Ahaziah..began to reign"
Joh 2:47 – "46 years was this temple in building"

50 *Years*

Lev 25:10 – "ye shall hallow the fiftieth year"
Lev 25:11 – "A jubile shall..50th year be unto you"
Num 4:3 – "From 30 years old..until 50 years old"
Num 4:23 – "From 30 years old..until 50 years old"
Num 4:30 – "From 30 years old..until 50 years old"
Num 4:35 – "From 30 years old..until 50 years old"
Num 4:39 – "From 30 years old..until 50 years old"
Num 4:43 – "From 30 years old..until 50 years old"
Num 4:47 – "From 30 years old..until 50 years old"
Num 8:25 – "from..50 years..cease waiting"
2Ki 15:23 – "50th year of Azariah..Pekahiah..began"
Joh 8:57 – "Thou are not yet 50 years old"

51-69 *Years*

Gen 5:15 – "Mahalaleel lived 65 years and begat"

Gen 5:21 – "Enoch lived 65 years, and begat"
Gen 25:26 – "Isaac..60 years old when she bare"
Lev 27:3 – "estimation...unto sixty years old"
Lev 27:7 – estimation "be from sixty years old"
2Ki 15:2 – "reigned 52 years in Jerusalem"
2Ki 15:27 – "52nd year of Azariah..Pekah..began"
2Ki 21:1 – "Manasseh..reigned 55 years"
1Ch 2:21 – "Hezron..married when..60 years old"
2Ch 26:3 – "Uzziah..reigned 52 years in Jerusalem"
2Ch 33:1 – "Manasseh..reigned 55 years"
Isa 7:8 – "w/in 65 years shall Ephraim be broken"
Dan 5:31 – "Darius..Median..about 62 years old"
1Ti 5:9 – "not a widow..under 60 years old"

70-79 *Years*

Gen 5:12 – "Cainan lived 70 years, and begat"
Gen 11:26 – "Terah lived 70 years..begat Abrahm"
Gen 12:4 – "Abram..75 years old..departed..Haran"
2Ch 36:21 – "she kept Sabbath, to fulfil 70 years"
Psa 90:10 – "days of our years are 70"
Isa 23:15 – "Tyre shall be forgotten 70 years"
Isa 23:15 – "after 70 years..Tyre sing as an harlot"
Isa 23:17 – "after..70 years..LORD will visit Tyre"
Jer 25:11 – "serve the king of Babylon 70 years"
Jer 25:12 – "when 70 years are accomplished'
Jer 29:10 – "after 70 years be accomplished"
Dan 9:2 – "70 years..the desolations of Jerusalem"
Zec 1:12 – "O LORD..indignation these 70 years"
Zec 7:5 – "fasted and mourned..even..70 years"

80-89 *Years*

Gen 16:16 – "Abram..86 years old..Hagar bare"
Exo 7:7 – "Moses..80 years..spake unto Pharaoh"
Exo 7:7 – "Aaron 83 years..spake unto Pharaoh"
Jos 14:10 – "lo, I am this day 85 years old"
Jdg 3:30 – "Moab subdued..land had rest 80 years"
2Sa 19:32 – "Barzillai..very aged..80 years old"
2Sa 19:35 – "I am this day fourscore years old"
Psa 90:10 – "if by reason of strength..be 80 years"
Luk 2:37 – "she was a widow of about 84 years"

90-99 *Years*

Gen 5:9 – "Enos lived 90 years, and begat Cainan"
Gen 17:1 – "Abram..99 years old..LORD appeared"
Gen 17:17 – "shall Sarah..90 years old, bear?"
Gen 17:24 – "Abraham..99 years..circumcised"
1Sa 4:15 – "Now Eli was 98 years old"

100 *Years*

Gen 11:10 – "Shem..100 years..begat Arphaxad"
Gen 17:17 – "child..born unto him..100 years old?"
Gen 21:5 – "Abraham..100 years old..Isaac..born"
Isa 65:20 – "the child shall die an 100 years old"
Isa 65:20 – "sinner..an 100 years old..accursed"
Rom 4:19 – "when he was about an 100 years old"

101-199 *Years*

Gen 5:3 – "Adam lived 130 years..begat"
Gen 5:6 – "Seth lived 105 years and begat"
Gen 5:18 – "Jared lived 162 years and begat"
Gen 5:25 – "Methuselah lived 187 years, & begat"
Gen 5:28 – "Lamech lived 182 years, and begat"
Gen 6:3 – "his days shall be 120 years"
Gen 11:25 – "Nahor..after..begat Terah 119 years"
Gen 23:1 – "Sarah was 127 years old"
Gen 25:7 – "Abraham's life..175 years"
Gen 25:17 – "life of Ishmael..137 years"
Gen 35:28 – "days of Isaac were 180 years"
Gen 47:9 – "years of my pilgrimage are 130 years"
Gen 47:28 – "whole age of Jacob was 147 years"
Gen 50:22 – "Joseph lived an 110 years"
Gen 50:26 – "Joseph died, being an 110 years old"
Exo 6:16 – "years of the life of Levi..137 years"
Exo 6:18 – "years of the life of Kohath..133 years"
Exo 6:20 – "years of the life of Amram..137 years"
Num 33:39 – "Aaron..123 years old when he died"
Deu 31:2 – "I am an 120 years old this day"
Deu 34:7 – "Moses..120 years old when he died"
Jos 24:29 – "Joshua...died being an 110 years old"
Jdg 2:8 – "Joshua...died being an 110 years old"
2Ch 24:15 – "Jehoiada..130 years old..he died"
Job 42:16 – "After this lived Job 140 years"

200-499 *Years*

Gen 5:22 – "Enoch walked with God..300 years"
Gen 5:23 – "all the days of Enoch were 365 years"
Gen 9:28 – "Noah lived after the flood 350 years"
Gen 11:13 – "lived after he begat Salah 403 years"
Gen 11:15 – "Salah..after..begat Eber 403 years"
Gen 11:17 – "Eber..after he begat Peleg 430 years"
Gen 11:19 – "Peleg..after he begat Reu 209 years"
Gen 11:21 – "Reu..after he begat Serug 207 years"
Gen 11:23 – "Serug..after..begat Nahor 200 years"
Gen 11:32 – "days of Terah were 205 years"
Gen 15:13 – "they shall afflict them 400 years"
Exo 12:40 – "sojourning..in Egypt, was 430 years"
Exo 12:41 – "end of the 430 years..selfsame day"
Jdg 11:26 – "Israel dwelt..coasts..Arnon, 300 years"
1Ki 6:1 – "480th year after the children of Israel"
Act 7:6 – "entreat them evil 400 years"
Act 13:20 – "judges about the space of 450 years"
Gal 3:17 – "the law, which was 430 years after"

500-999 *Years*

Gen 5:4 – "days of Adam after..Seth..800 years"
Gen 5:5 – "all the days..Adam..were 930 years"
Gen 5:7 – "Seth..after he begat Enos 807 years"
Gen 5:8 – "all the days of Seth were 912 years"
Gen 5:10 – "Enos lived after he begat..815 years"
Gen 5:11 – "all the days of Enos were 905 years"
Gen 5:13 – "Cainan lived after he begat..840 years"
Gen 5:14 – "all the days of Cainan were 910 years"
Gen 5:16 – "Mahalaleel..after..Jared 830 years"
Gen 5:17 – "days of Mahalaleel were 895 years"
Gen 5:19 – "Jared lived after he begat..800 years"
Gen 5:20 – "all the days of Jared were 962 years"
Gen 5:26 – "Methuselah..after..Lamech 782 years"
Gen 5:27 – "all the days of Methuselah..969 years"
Gen 5:30 – "Lamech lived after..Noah 595 years"
Gen 5:31 – "all the days of Lamech..777 years"
Gen 5:32 – "Noah was 500 years old..begat Shem"
Gen 7:6 – "Noah..600 years old when the flood"
Gen 9:29 – "all the days of Noah were 950 years"
Gen 11:11 – "after he begat Arphaxad 500 years"

1000+ *Years*

Psa 90:4 – "For 1000 years..are but as yesterday"
Psa 102:27 – "thy years shall have no end"
Ecc 6:6 – "though he live 1000 years twice told"
2Pe 3:8 – "one day..as a 1000 years"
2Pe 3:8 – "a 1000 years as one day"
Rev 20:2 – "Satan..bound him 1000 years"
Rev 20:3 – "till the 1000 years should be fulfilled"
Rev 20:4 – "lived..reigned with Christ 1000 years"
Rev 20:5 – "rest of the dead lived not..1000 years"
Rev 20:6 – "shall reign with him 1000 years"
Rev 20:7 – "1000 years are expired..Satan..loosed"

Yoke

1Sa 6:7 – "on which there hath come no yoke"
1Ki 19:19 – "Elisha..plowing with 12 yoke of oxen"
1Ki 19:19 – "and he with the twelfth"
Job 1:3 – "His substance..500 yoke of oxen"
Luk 14:19 – "I have bought five yoke of oxen"

Appendix A
Math Terms and Concepts

The following list is by no means exhaustive, but serves as a foundation for further study of the various numerical and mathematical principles to be found in Scripture. Under each heading one or two representative examples are provided – in most cases, many others exist. Other more complex mathematical concepts involving Bible numbers likewise exist for the mathematicians among us that are beyond the scope of a layman's reference work.

Addition

"Methuselah lived an hundred eighty and seven years, and begat Lamech: And Methuselah lived after he begat Lamech seven hundred eighty and two years, and begat sons and daughters: And all the days of Methuselah were nine hundred sixty and nine years: and he died." Gen 5:25-27

$$187 + 782 = 969$$

Subtraction

"In the fourth year was the foundation of the house of the LORD laid, in the month Zif: And in the eleventh year, in the month Bul, which is the eighth month, was the house finished throughout all the parts thereof, and according to all the fashion of it. So was he seven years in building it." 1Ki 6:37-38

$$11 - 4 = 7$$

Multiplication

"And thou shalt number seven sabbaths of years unto thee, seven times seven years; and the space of the seven sabbaths of years shall be unto thee forty and nine years." Lev 25:8

$$7 \bullet 7 = 49$$

Division

"And divide the prey into two parts; between them that took the war upon them, who went out to battle, and between all the congregation... And the booty, being the rest of the prey which the men of war had caught, was six hundred thousand and seventy thousand and five thousand sheep... Now the half that pertained unto the congregation was three hundred thousand and thirty thousand and seven thousand and five hundred sheep" Num 31:27, 32, 43

$$675,000 / 2 = 337,500$$

Fractions

"And thou, son of man, take thee a sharp knife, take thee a barber's rasor, and cause it to pass upon thine head and upon thy beard: then take thee balances to weigh, and divide the hair. Thou shalt burn with fire a third part in the midst of the city, when the days of the siege are fulfilled: and thou shalt take a third part, and smite about it with a knife: and a third part thou shalt scatter in the wind; and I will draw out a sword after them." Ezk 5:1-2

$$1 / 3 = 3 \bullet \tfrac{1}{3}$$

Percentages

"Or all that about which he hath sworn falsely; he shall even restore it in the principal, and shall add the fifth part more thereto, and give it unto him to whom it appertaineth, in the day of his trespass offering." Lev 6:5

$$\text{Principal} + 20\% = 120\%$$

Pi (π) & Circle Geometry

"And he made a molten sea, ten cubits from the one brim to the other: it was round all about, and his height was five cubits: and a line of thirty cubits did compass it round about." 1Ki 7:23

Many skeptic and atheist websites present IKi 7:23 as a famous Bible "error" that supposedly teaches that $\pi = 3$. Of course they fail to compare scripture with scripture and do not take into account the width of the brim of the laver mentioned in 2 Chronicles:

"Also he made a molten sea of ten cubits from brim to brim, round in compass, and five cubits the height thereof; and a line of thirty cubits did compass it round about... And the thickness of it was an handbreadth, and the brim of it like the work of the brim of a cup, with flowers of lilies; and it received and held three thousand baths." 2Ch 4:2 & 5

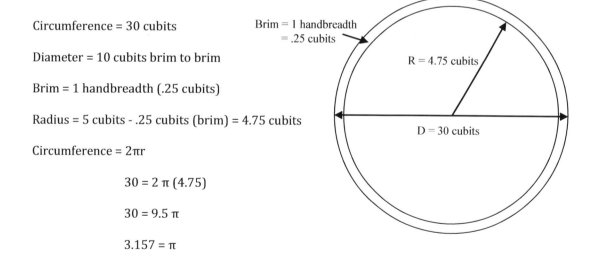

Circumference = 30 cubits

Diameter = 10 cubits brim to brim

Brim = 1 handbreadth (.25 cubits)

Radius = 5 cubits - .25 cubits (brim) = 4.75 cubits

Circumference = $2\pi r$

$$30 = 2 \pi (4.75)$$

$$30 = 9.5 \pi$$

$$3.157 = \pi$$

This is a reasonably close approximation of the true value of pi (3.142) considering the technically unspecific nature of the figures given in these verses.

Two & Three Dimensional Geometry

Area

"Moreover, when ye shall divide by lot the land for inheritance, ye shall offer an oblation unto the LORD, an holy portion of the land: the length shall be the length of five and twenty thousand reeds, and the breadth shall be ten thousand. This shall be holy in all the borders thereof round about." Ezk 45:1

Area = length • width

Holy Oblation = 25,000 reeds • 25,000 reeds = 6.25×10^8 reeds^2

Volume

"And this is the fashion which thou shalt make it of: The length of the ark shall be three hundred cubits, the breadth of it fifty cubits, and the height of it thirty cubits." Gen 6:15

Volume = length • width • height

Noah's Ark = 300 cubits • 50 cubits • 30 cubits = 450,000 cubits^3

Cubes and/or Pyramids

"And he that talked with me had a golden reed to measure the city, and the gates thereof, and the wall thereof. And the city lieth foursquare, and the length is as large as the breadth: and he measured the city with the reed, twelve thousand furlongs. The length and the breadth and the height of it are equal." Rev 21:15-16

If the New Jersualem is a city in the shape of a cube

Volume = any side^3 = (12,000 furlongs)^3 = 1.73 • 10^{12} furlongs^3

If the New Jerusalem is in the shape of a mountain or pyramid (where height, length & width are equal)

Volume = length • width • height / 3 = (12,000 furlongs)^3 / 3 = 5.76 • 10^{11} furlongs^3

The Golden Ratio & Fibonacci Numbers

The golden ratio or golden number (often designated by the Greek letter phi φ) is a ratio important in mathematics and art. This value is found in the human body, throughout nature and is often used by artists and architects in their works as it produces proportions that are pleasing to the eye. The most common expression of the golden ratio is the golden rectangle.

A golden rectangle can be divided into a square (a) and a smaller rectangle (b) where the smaller rectangle (b) is the same shape as the larger rectangle (ab) – in other words the sides of b and ab are proportional.

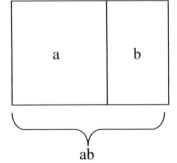

Mathematically   a/b = (a + b)/a

Proportionally   1:1.618

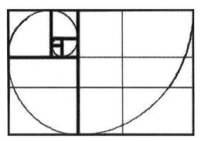

The Fibonacci Numbers are a sequence of numbers (0, 1, 1, 2, 3, 5, 8, 13, 21, etc.) where each number is the sum of the two previous numbers (0+1; 1+1; 1+2; 2+3; 3+5; etc.).   The relationship or proportion of each number in this sequence to the next number is the golden ratio and becomes more exact as the numbers grow larger.

Some examples of golden rectangles in Scripture would include the ark of the covenant (1½ cubits : 2½ cubits = 1.667) and the end of Noah's Ark (30 cubits : 50 cubits = 1.667)

For examples of Fibonacci numbers in Scripture, consult Section One in the **Concordance of Bible Numbers** and look up the Fibonacci Numbers that appear in Scripture: 1, 2, 3, 5, 8, 13, 21, 34, 55, & 144.

Inequalities

"I say unto you, that likewise joy shall be in heaven over one sinner that repenteth, more than over ninety and nine just persons, which need no repentance." Luk 15:7

"A reproof entereth more into a wise man than an hundred stripes into a fool." Pro 17:10

An inequality shows a relation between two values where a is not equal to b.

Sequences

Genesis 1 – seven days of creation (1st day, 2nd day, 3rd day, etc...)

I Chronicles 25 – the 24 courses of Levites that rotated temple worship duties

Ratios, Proportions & Percentages

Numbers 31:25-47 records the conquest of Moab. Many thousands of human captives, sheep, beeves and asses were taken by the armies of Israel. On this occasion, the booty was divided up according to the following formula:

*"And **divide the prey into two parts**; between them that took the war upon them, who went out to battle, and between all the congregation:"* (vs. 27)

*"And **levy a tribute unto the LORD** of the men of war which went out to battle: **one soul of five hundred**, both of the persons, and of the beeves, and of the asses, and of the sheep:"* (vs. 28)

*"And **of the children of Israel's half, thou shalt take one portion of fifty,** of the persons, of the beeves, of the asses, and of the flocks, of all manner of beasts, and give them unto the Levites..."* (vs. 30)

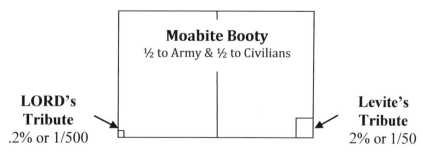

Degrees of a Circle

"And Isaiah said, This sign shalt thou have of the LORD, that the LORD will do the thing that he hath spoken: shall the shadow go forward ten degrees, or go back ten degrees? And Hezekiah answered, It is a light thing for the shadow to go down ten degrees: nay, but let the shadow return backward ten degrees." 2Ki 20:9-10

360° in a circle – Earth rotates 360 degrees (roughly) in 24 hours

24 hours = 1440 minutes

1440 min/360° = 4 min per degree   Therefore, 10° = 40 minutes

Infinity

See the many references to items that were deemed uncountable or infinite in number at the end of Section One under the subheading, **Indefinite Numbers**.

Mathematical Biblical Principles and the Nature of God

1) God is a God of order, in that in every mathematical procedure we must follow a fixed order of operations.
2) God is a God of precision, as evidenced by the exactness of measurements and solutions.
3) God's unchangeableness and dependability are reflected in the certainty of mathematical properties and procedures.
4) God is an infinite God reflected in the infinitude of number sets, space, and functions.
5) Creation shows God's use of mathematical concepts to teach about His nature.
6) Mankind has the God-given ability to discover what God has already ordained and put in place.
7) Mankind has the God-given wisdom and ability to solve complex problems.

Appendix B
Number Differences in the Registers of
Ezra 2 & Nehemiah 7

The books of Ezra and Nehemiah record the return of the captives of the Southern Kingdom of Judah from exile in Babylon. Ezra chapter two and Nehemiah chapter seven specifically record a register of the various families that returned from exile and in most cases they provide a number of the persons from each family making the return to the land Judah.

The obvious problem to students of the word of God is that although the chapters are clearly in parallel to one another, their recorded numbers in roughly half of the instances do not match. The variation in the numbers provided for of any given family can vary by as little as one and by as many as 300. Why is this?

The simplistic answer given by those who do not accept the Bible as their final authority is that there were either scribal errors or transmission errors. Bible believers however begin with the premise that inspiration and preservation are valid Bible doctrines and that *"every word of God is pure"* – even the numbers! Thus differences in numbers in parallel passages of the King James Bible must have a different explanation than being "errors."

Please read the two chapters under discussion and consider the following observations:

1) Nehemiah 7 and Ezra 2 are two different copies of the same register. The specific names and the order in which they are presented show they are recording the same facts – the difference in numbers and name spellings show that they cannot be the exact copies of the same register.

2) In both copies of this register, the total number of *"the whole congregation"* (Ezr 2:64; Neh 7:66) is identical – 42,360.

3) Neither list records an exact number for all of the various constituent families that will allow you to arrive at this total of 42,360 – instead, in both cases, the numbers provided equal about 31,000.

4) The missing 10,000 or so participants in this migration back to Judah included the polluted priests of Neh 7:63-65 that were not numbered with the rest of the Jews pending a decision on their status – being included, but not numbered could result in some possible anomalies. Another factor would be portions of "the whole congregation" that were not individually totalled, and yet included in the final total. The distinction between individual familes that were numbered and those that were not can be seen by comparing Nehemiah 7:8-42 with vs. 43 & 45-62. Some families were treated individually and some collectively.

5) A fine distinction can be seen in some places in the terminology of those being counted – in some places the term "children" is used and other places the term "men."

6) As is so often the case in "apparent" Bible contradictions, time is a major factor. Nehemiah was probably written 100-200 years after Ezra. The simple conclusion is that Nehemiah's register is merely an updated version of that recorded in Ezra. Recounts, people coming and going, people dying enroute, and further information simply meant that the register was updated. Ezra was an early version while Nehemiah provides the later version.

7) The fact that these two records appear in Scripture means that they constitute inspired Scripture, but this does not mean the men who counted and recorded these numbers on the original register or the later, updated register were inspired. Although one could clearly make the case that the first register was in error and faulty before being corrected with the version of Nehemiah, this does not

mean that the Bible itself in error. The Holy Spirit saw fit to engrave for all time as inspired Scripture a flawed human document and an updated version of that same human document – the Holy Spirit did not originally record either of these documents – men did. Think of the parallel ramifications if the Holy Spirit had seen fit to record the front page of tonight's newspaper in the Bible as inspired Scripture. The journalists would not have been inspired - their words would have merely been "perfectly" recorded as is for all eternity.

The Holy Spirit moved Ezra and Nehemiah to copy two registers into our Bible for our learning. The number differences do not mean that God was in any way in error. Rather we can know confidentally that God recorded the two documents exactly as they existed at the time. If anything, their differences are a tremendous proof of inspiration – God faithfully passed on to us what these documents said, differences and all. Most men would have felt obliged to "help God out" and make the figures match. This incidentally is a tremendous flaw often seen in the Septuagint (a corrupt Greek translation of the Hebrew Old Testament) where someone often tried to help out the Holy Spirit by reverse engineering OT quotes to make them match their NT counterparts.

Compare the same manner in which the Holy Spirit moved Moses to record Satan's lie of Genesis 3:1 into inspired Scripture. Satan was not inspired. His lie was not inspired. Satan's lie is still as wrong as the day he uttered it – and yet it is part of inspired Scripture in order to teach and instruct us. One who would charge God with error for recording Satan's lie (an inspired passage of Scripture that is "not true" so to speak) would simply be demonstrating his ignorance of the doctrine of inspiration. Likewise, God is not at fault, in error, or guilty of contradiction for merely recording for our benefit two documents that illustrate the fallibility of men.

Conundrums such as this one appear in Scripture "to separate the men from the boys" – to weed out the Bible believers from the rest of the crowd. A Bible-believer approaches Scripture from a position of faith knowing that an omniscient God who has promised to preserve his word is always right. If something *appears* to be a contradiction, the problem is with me, not with God. My understanding is somehow incomplete and God ALWAYS deserves the benefit of the doubt. The non-Bible believer approaches Scripture from a position of doubt and/or scepticism. A Bible critic will not give God the benefit of the doubt and any *apparent* contradictions are deemed to be valid contradictions until someone can prove otherwise to their satisfaction.

Appendix C
Bible Number Variations Between the King James Bible & Other Bible Translations

Few would disagree with the fact that there exist a a myriad of word differences between the various English Bible translations available on the market. The King James Only position would hold that the AV is the perfect word of God available in English today and cite the twin doctrines of inspiration and preservation as proof. A low view of preservation and/or inspiration results in one holding some other position and citing the oft-repeated mantra that these many word differences "do not affect doctrine." If one sets aside the obvious conclusion such a statement has on the doctrines of inspiration and preservation, the truth is that some word changes do severely affect vital doctrines and others at first glance appear to have little if any effect. Many books have been written on this topic and such a debate is beyond the scope of this volume.

What is often overlooked however are the variations in the numbers recorded in the texts of the various English Bible versions. Just as words are different in different translations and versions, so too are the actual numbers recorded as inspired Scripture. One can endlessly debate how important any given difference in wording may be between two versions; however, numbers are unyielding and uncompromising in such a discussion. When version A says "2" and version B says "5", the chance that both could be right are virtually non-existent.

Most of us remember from our school days that a teacher may have given us some latitude when it came to our answers in English, science or social studies, but not in math. Arithmetic presents the stark reality that an answer is either right or wrong – rarely is there room for leniency in interpretation in arithmetic.

The net effect of this phenomenon is that when dealing with various Bible versions, numbers can and will often provide conclusive and immediate proof that a suspect version "is in error." People are often cagey about "judging" a translation as defective and they will often use ambiguous language rather than plainly stating that a version has known problems. Numbers however can provide a harsh wakeup call that a particular version has incontrivable errors and hence cannot be deemed trustworthy. Such a conclusion is not open to whim, interpretation and bias because the numbers do not easily lie – they are either right or wrong!

Below are several examples where the various versions disagree on a number and thereby some of them conclusively prove themselves to be in error. Ironically, the issue is rarely translation – eg. does this Hebrew word mean 10 or 100? Instead, the root problem is either the use of a text with known corruptions or someone is guilty of trying to "help God out" because they did not understand the meaning of the text they were attempting to translate.

How Many Kohathites – 8,600 or 8,300?

Numbers 3:28 in a King James Bible records the number of males over a month old in the family of Kohath as being 8,600. Several translations such as the ERV "adjust" this number to 8,300. Other versions such as the NIV complete the same task through their marginal notes – an asterix next to this number takes the reader to a misleading marginal note that says, *"Hebrew; some Septuagint manuscripts 8,300."* The Hebrew Masorretic Text however clearly says 8,600.

הקדש משמרת שמרי מאות ושש **אלפים שמנת ומעלה** חדש-מבן זכר-כל במספר

What is going on here?

Levi had three sons: Gershon, Kohath and Merari. When the temple was constructed in the wilderness, the family of Aaron became the priests, but the "Levites" that erected, deconstructed and carried the tabernacle came from these three families. Each family had a different set of tasks. Each family had all of their males above a month old counted as follows:

Num 3:22	Gershonites	7,500
Num 3:28	Kohathites	8,600
Num 3:34	Merarites	6,200
		22,300

Herein lies the problem. Although these three numbers add up to 22,300, verse 39 says that the total of these three families is the round figure of 22,000. After being so exact, God adds up the total and misplaces 300 men? This is where some of the new versions, the Septuagint and others step in to "help God out" by fudging one of the numbers to make the totals match.

About the time someone makes the feeble attempt to cover for the Holy Spirit by saying that maybe He rounded the figure off to the nearest thousand, a second issue arises toward the end of the chapter. God is going to swap the firstborn of Israel for the tribe of Levi. Instead of every firstborn Jewish male becoming a priest, only one tribe will become the priests of God. For this swap to work in God's greater plan, the numbers must match – any extra people would have to be "redeemed" (v. 46). The chapter records that the non-Levite firstborn over a month old totaled 22,273 – this is certainly an exact figure with no rounding!

This total of the non-Levite firstborn however raises a terrible conundrum:

God said there were 22,000 Levites – there are 22,273 non-Levite firstborn – thus there are an extra 273 firstborn with no Levite to take their place; therefore these 273 firstborn must be redeemed. An elaborate procedure is enacted in Num 3:46-51 to accomplish this whereby five shekels of "redemption money" is collected for each of these 273 "extras" and given to Aaron and his sons.

But hold on! None of this should be necessary because ***there really are 22,300 Levites*** if the figures for Gershon, Kohath and Merari are correct in vs. 22, 28 & 34. Instead of redeeming 273 firstborn Jews, we should have had zero people to redeem and instead 27 Levites to spare (22,300 – 22,273 = 27). Figured this way, there is no redemption money necessary and this whole redemption exercise is unnecessary!

Issue #1 – Why do these three figures not add up correctly to 22,300, but to 22,000 as God claims?
Issue #2 – Why have this redemption money ceremony when the problem it is attempting to solve is only the result of incorrect addition?
Issue #3 – Could the King James Bible be in error here? Should the total for one of these three families be adjusted downward by 300 to make the math work?

This is an apparent contradiction of Scripture that sorely tests the faith of the Bible-believer where he is being asked to trust God's math – figures that at first glance do not appear to add up! As mentioned, several Bible versions have taken this matter into their own hands and "provided cover" for God by tweaking one figure downward by 300 to make it all work out. In doing so however, they have missed a blessing and introduced an error into their versions that clearly nullifies them as being valid "bibles."

The key to whole problem is that this chapter is not describing **three** groups of priests, but **four**!

Num 3:22	**Gershonites**	7,500		7,500
Num 3:28	**Kohathites**	8,600	Less **Aaron & his Sons** (-300)	8,300
Num 3:34	**Merarites**	6,200		6,200
		22,300		22,000

Aaron and his sons may have been physical descendants of Levi through Kohath, but they were a distinct and separate group from the Levites in general. The Gershonites, Kohathites and Merarites were known collectively as "the Levites" and did everything but the offerings and tabernacle/temple worship ceremonies – this was the domain of Aaron and his sons alone who were collectively known as "the priests." Note how many times in the Bible Aaron and his sons have their distinctiveness maintained in the simple phrase "priests and Levites" in such verses as 1Ch 23:2 & John 1:19). In Numbers 4 the Levites are divided into these four groups and slept on the four different sides of the tabernacle. In I Chronicles 27:17 the "Levites" and "Aaronites" are mentioned in the same verse as two different groups.

At this point in history, there were 300 members of Aaron and his "sons." They were descended from Kohath and therefore numbered among the 8,600, but when the matter of priestly duties was raised, they were not numbered with the 22,000 Levites.

One cannot tamper with God's words (even the numbers!) and win. The Lord knew exactly what he was doing when he performed his addition in Numbers 4 and always deserves the benefit of the doubt!

Trouble With Saul's Reign in I Samuel 13:1

The King James Bible begins to record King Saul's departure from sanity when it gives the time frame of his problems in I Samuel 13:1 – *"Saul reigned **one** year; and when he had reigned **two** years over Israel..."* Consider the "wisdom" of an alternative version:

ASV   Saul was **40** years old when he began to reign; and when he had reigned **2** years over Israel,

CJB   Sha'ul was --- years old when he began his reign, and he had ruled Israel for **2** years.

CEV   Saul was a **young** man when he became king, and he ruled Israel **2** years.

DRA   Saul was a child of **1** year when he began to reign, and he reigned **2** years over Israel.

MSG   Saul was a **young** man when he began as king. He was king over Israel **many** years.

NIV   Saul was **30** years old when he became king, And he reigned over Israel **42** years.

NLV   Saul was **40** years old when he began to rule. He ruled over Israel **32** years.

WYC   Saul was a son of **1** year...when he began to reign; and he reigned upon Israel **22** years.

Anyone see a problem here? The King James Bible is so simple! King Saul reigned a year and all was fine. When he had reigned two years, he began his slide into insanity. Trusting God's preserved word will never led you astray!

The convoluted and contradictory efforts of modern translations to deal with Bible number "problems" by alteration, omission or covering them up with ambiguity illustrates just how important it is that we get the issue of Bible numbers correct. Atheist, Skeptic and Muslim websites abound with examples such these as "proof" that Christianity is a fraudulent belief system full of contradictions. We can certainly help ourselves in this war for the souls of men by using a Bible that is consistent with its numbers.

Appendix D
Apparent Contradictions & Bible Numbers

There are only two mentalities with which one can approach the written word of God:

1)   This book is the inspired, preserved word of God – it is infallible and ***cannot*** be improved upon.
2)   This book is something less than the inspired preserved word of God and ***can*** be improved upon.

Understanding these two mindsets is crucial to understanding the subject of apparent contradictions in the Bible. If the Bible cannot be improved upon, than anything in Scripture that appears to be a contradiction is just that – only the *appearance* of a contradiction that does indeed have a resolution if one will seek God's face and search the Scriptures. If one has the opposite mindset, the basis has already been laid to admit that there are errors in the Bible and that we can help God out by "tweaking" his words for Him.

The first mindset approaches a "problem text" by faith with the admission that if two things appear to not match, the problem is with me and not with the Lord. God is always given the benefit of the doubt until I gain some wisdom on the apparent contradiction.

The second mindset does not have any room to give God the benefit of the doubt. Scripture is read with a sceptical or critical eye and the problem is assumed to be a "mistake" or "error" until conclusive proof is provided otherwise – see any atheist or "Bible contradiction" website to illustrate the point! Unfortunately, many very sincere Christians have been primed with this mindset after years of sitting in churches where the Bible is questioned, corrected, and improved upon with references to Greek, Hebrew, multiple Bible versions and man's opinions.

A significant number of these apparent contradictions deal with Bible numbers. In the vast majority of cases, **context** provides the simple resolution. Failing to read a passage in its context is the source of most Bible problems and unfortunately is not something that only the cults are guilty of. Always read the verses before and after the passage with the "problem" number in it; carefully compare cross references and in an amazing number of cases your "problem" will be solved.

The other most common cause of these apparent contradictions is **time**. Because we read the Bible in the present, we often fail to appreciate that "the past" may cover quite a bit of ground and that details often change over time. For example, if you obtained two quotes from me where I first claim that my weight is 170lbs and then that my weight is 220lbs, it would be simple to conclude that I may be lying or playing loose with the facts. The other possibility is that there is a twenty year time span between my two quotes. The numbers contradict, but they are in fact both true – just in two different time contexts. This dilemma of time lies at the core of many Bible problems that involve numbers.

The following examples are by no means exhaustive, but they serve as a sampling of Bible problem texts that involve numbers. Some of them rank among the most perplexing apparent contradictions to be found in Scripture. In each case it is imperative that the student of God's word approach the Bible from a position of belief, seeking the assistance of God's Holy Spirit of whom we have been promised that He will lead and guide us into all truth!

How Many Israelites Died At Baal-Peor?

*"And those that died in the plague were **twenty and four thousand**."* Num 25:9

*"Neither let us commit fornication, as some of them committed, and fell in one day **three and twenty thousand**."* 1Co 10:8

Both verses describe the same event in the same context – Moses says that 24,000 died in Numbers while Paul tells the Corinthians it was 23,000.   However, Moses gives no time reference and implies that 24,000 was the total number of Moabites killed – Paul reports that 23,000 died *"in one day."*

Too Many Deaths in Bethshemesh?

*"And he smote the men of Bethshemesh, because they had looked into the ark of the LORD, even he smote of the people **fifty thousand and threescore and ten men**: and the people lamented, because the LORD had smitten many of the people with a great slaughter."* 1Sa 6:19

This is a relatively famous supposed contradiction. The idea here is that Bethshemesh was a small town and it would have been impossible for 50,070 men to have lived there and for all of them to have looked into the ark.   Because of the supposed awkwardness of the number, many claim this was a scribal error and the real number was probably 70, 570 or 5,070 – anything but believe what it says!   Several versions such as the NIV, MSG, & ESV say it must have been only 70 men. The CSB comes up with the private interpretation of "70 men out of 50,000."

A careful reading of the verse reveals that the Lord did indeed smite the men of Bethshemesh – but this is further qualified with *"even he smote of the people."* The group slain by the Lord was wider than just the men of Bethshemesh.   A tourist attraction like the ark of the covenant would have drawn tremendous numbers of tourists to a never before seen sight.   The passage is not difficult to understand as is – only difficult to believe!

How Many Horsemen?

*"David smote also Hadadezer, the son of Rehob, king of Zobah, as he went to recover his border at the river Euphrates. And David took from him a thousand chariots, and **seven hundred horsemen**, and twenty thousand footmen: and David houghed all the chariot horses, but reserved of them for an hundred chariots."* 2Sa 8:3-4

*"And David smote Hadarezer king of Zobah unto Hamath, as he went to stablish his dominion by the river Euphrates. And David took from him a thousand chariots, and **seven thousand horsemen**, and twenty thousand footmen: David also houghed all the chariot horses, but reserved of them an hundred chariots."* 1Chr 18:3-4

One passage says that David captured 700 horsemen and the other says 7,000 horsemen. The contexts seem similar, but the numbers do not match. If these numbers were 575 and 6,945 no one would be worried and simply assume that the context was dealing with several different battles in the same war campaign. Because however the larger number is off by a factor of ten, the assumption is made that this must be a scribal error – somebody added a zero!

A careful reading of the two passages shows a subtle difference in wording.   David's interaction with Hadadezer was more than just one battle. Apparently 6,300 were captured as a group while the remaining 700 were captured at a different time.   As we stated at the beginning of this appendix, when one approaches the Bible with the mentality it has errors, it is easy to assume every apparent discrepancy must be an error – when one trusts God and his word, credible answers to these problem texts are not difficult to find.   However these scenarios played out, both records given must be accurate.

Absalom's Forty Years

*And on this manner did Absalom to all Israel that came to the king for judgment: so Absalom stole the hearts of the men of Israel. And it came to pass **after forty years**, that Absalom said unto the king, I pray thee, let me go and pay my vow, which I have vowed unto the LORD, in Hebron." 2Sa 15:6-7*

The problem in this verse concerns the forty years being referred to. Absalom was not even forty years old at this point, and yet the verse clearly says that he set his power grab into motion *"after forty years."* Although they do not know what God is referring to, many new versions simply change "forty" to "four" to make the passage sound more plausible.

Whether forty or four, the reference cannot be referring to Absalom's age – what then does it refer to? The assumption made by those who advocate the number "four" assume it refers to Absalom's plotting for power behind the scenes before going public – although there is no statement of this in the passage.

The key to understanding the number forty is verse six. Absalom stole the hearts of the men of Israel. Before this happened, the hearts of the men of Israel belonged to David. Since Israel first saw him defeat Goliath, gain the victory over the Philistines and sang his praises in the streets while watching Saul devolve into insanity, the hearts of the men of Israel had followed David. How long had it been since the nation fell in love with David after the events of Goliath and the Philistines? Forty years! After forty years of loving and following David, now the mood of the nation was falling into step behind Absalom.

How Long Was the Famine in the Days of David?

*"So Gad came to David, and told him, and said unto him, Shall **seven years of famine** come unto thee in thy land? or wilt thou flee three months before thine enemies, while they pursue thee? or that there be three days' pestilence in thy land? now advise, and see what answer I shall return to him that sent me." 2Sa 24:13*

*"Either **three years' famine**; or three months to be destroyed before thy foes, while that the sword of thine enemies overtaketh thee; or else three days the sword of the LORD, even the pestilence, in the land, and the angel of the LORD destroying throughout all the coasts of Israel. Now therefore advise thyself what word I shall bring again to him that sent me." 1Chr 21:12*

Was David offered seven years of famine or three years of famine for his sin of numbering Israel? The NIV, GNB, RSV and many other new versions simply make the verses match by changing the reference in 2Sa 24:13 to "three years."

In 2Sa 21:1 David had already had three years of famine because of Saul's sin of killing the Gibeonites. 2Sa 24:13 says, *"Shall seven years of famine come unto thee..."* At the time this was spoken, Israel had already gone through three years of famine, was in the fourth year, and David was being offered three more years of famine (1Ch 21:12) for a total of seven years. Note how 2Sa 24:1 says, *"**And again** the anger of the LORD was kindled against Israel..."* Both accounts are correct, but spoken in different contexts.

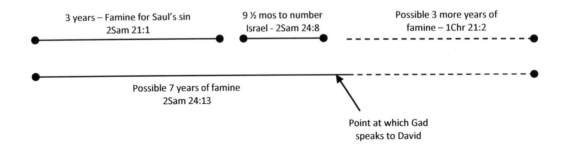

222

How Many Horse Stalls?

*"And Solomon had **forty thousand stalls** of horses for his chariots, and twelve thousand horsemen."* 1Ki 4:26

*"And Solomon had **four thousand stalls** for horses and chariots, and twelve thousand horsemen; whom he bestowed in the chariot cities, and with the king at Jerusalem."* 2Ch 9:25

Was it 4,000 or 40,000 stalls for the chariot horses? Note very carefully the difference between *"40,000 stalls OF horses FOR his chariots"* versus *"4,000 stalls FOR horses AND chariots."* Comparing these two verses simply teaches us that each chariot had ten horses. One passage give the overall number of stalls (counting one stall per horse) while the other passage groups these by tens as assigned to each chariot.

How old was Ahaziah When He Began to Reign?

*"**Two and twenty years old** was Ahaziah when he began to reign; and he reigned one year in Jerusalem. And his mother's name was Athaliah, the daughter of Omri king of Israel."* 2Ki 8:26

*"**Forty and two years old** was Ahaziah when he began to reign, and he reigned one year in Jerusalem. His mother's name also was Athaliah the daughter of Omri."* 2Chr 22:2

This is the "holy grail" of Bible problem texts and is probably the most difficult problem text in all of Scripture dealing with numbers. Two problems are presented when comparing these verses:

1)   Two different ages are given for Ahaziah's ascension to the throne
2)   2Chr 22:2 presents an additional problem stating that Ahaziah's father died at the age of 40 making Ahaziah two years older than his father - compare 2Ki 8:16-17

Many solutions are proposed, but the four major ones are:

1)   ***One of the verses contains a mistake in translation.*** The NIV and many other versions make this assumption and change 2Ch 22:2 to read "twenty-two" although no Hebrew text states this.
2)   ***There was a 20 year gap between Ahaziah's coronation and the beginning of his*** reign – i.e. Ahaziah was anointed king at 22, but did not take the throne until he was 42.
3)   ***The 42 years is not Ahaziah's age, but the beginning of a wicked family dynasty;*** thus the 42 years do not start with Ahaziah's birth, but with the beginning of the reign of King Omri or Ahab of the Northern Kingdom of Israel.
4)   ***There are two Ahaziahs*** – both were sons of Athaliah and both reigned for one year.

We reject the first option because of our belief in God's ability to inspire and preserve his holy word. The same "problem" exists in the Hebrew text which means that any version like the NIV that changes one of these numbers is guilty of INTENTIONALLY mistranslating the Hebrew texts!

Many of the problem texts found in Scripture occur during the time of the divided kingdom. This was a very complex time in Israel's history. The house of Ahab and house of Jehoshaphat had "joined affinity" marking the only real time between Rehoboam and the Babylonian captivity that anyone attempted to rejoin the two halves of the divided nation of Israel. The records of the kings detail a number of intermarriages between the two kingdoms, overlapping reigns, men with identical or similar names, and several men with multiple names.

The background to the reign of Ahaziah begins with the reign of Ahab who starts to rule Israel in the 38th year of Asa, king of Judah. Asa's son, Jehoshaphat, begins to reign in Ahab's 4th year – he is 35 and reigns for 25 years Ahab is so wicked that the prophet tells him his posterity will be cut off (1Kin 21:21); but he humbles himself so that God postpones this judgment until the days of his sons (1Kin 21:29).

Despite the wickedness of Ahab and the northern kingdom of Israel, Jehoshaphat of Judah "joins affinity" with Ahab (2Chr 18:1) by allowing his son Jehoram to marry Ahab's daughter (2Chr 21:5-6).

Ahab has a son named Ahaziah and Ahab makes his son co-regent in the 17th year of Jehoshaphat of Judah (1Kin 22:51).   This Ahaziah only reigns two years, eventually falling through a lattice and dying of his injuries. (not the Ahaziah mentioned in either of our problem text passages!) While Ahaziah is still alive, but almost dead and incapable of fulfilling his royal duties, Ahab (his father) names Jehoram (his brother) as the new co-regent. For a short time Israel has three kings reigning which takes place in the 2nd year of Ahaziah and in the 18th year of Jehoshaphat – 2Kin 3:1.

This Jehoram of Israel will rule 12 years. Note that there are two Jehorams – one each in both Israel and Judah, reigning at the same time. Jehoram of Judah had been anointed just a year or two prior to Jehoram of Israel becoming king. Jehoram of Judah co-reigns with his father (Jehoshaphat) for five years before being crowned as sole king. Until Ahaziah dies, Ahab is still reigning with Jehoram of Israel who has been installed as his co-regent.

After the death of Ahaziah, Ahab convinces Jehoshaphat of Judah to go to battle with him. Ahab dies in battle leaving Jehoram as the sole king of Israel (*1Kin 22:26*). Then Jehoshaphat dies, leaving his Jehoram as the sole king of Judah (2Chr 21:2-4). Remember that Jehoram of Judah is the son-in-law of Ahab.

Jehoram of Judah consolidates his kingdom by killing many of the other princes. This implies that some of them may have had a claim to throne of Judah.   This may have been possible because of intermarriage problems.   Nonetheless, God is displeased with this wicked son-in-law of Ahab and Jehoram dies when his bowels fall out (2Chr 21:15). God subsequently stirred up enemies that killed all of Jehoram's sons but one (2Chr 21:16-17).

Jehoram of Judah dies at 40 years of age with one remaining son named Ahaziah who is 22 years old - see 2Chr 21:20 and then 2Kin 8:17 & 26.   This brings us to our problem text, specifically 2Chr 22:1 which says that Ahaziah is forty-two years old.   These background details effectively rule out the second and third options listed previously for this problem text: there is no evidence of a 20 year gap between Ahaziah of Judah's coronation and reign; neither does 42 years fit for an evil dynasty.   Omri began his reign 38 years before this Ahaziah and Ahab roughly 32 years before Ahaziah.   The only option remaining is that there were two kings named Ahaziah in Judah!

Could this be possible? Regardless of whether the answer to this question is yes or no, remember not to confuse the following information with the previous Ahaziah of Israel, the son of Ahab (and brother of Athaliah!), who had already died by this time.

Both problem texts say that Ahaziah reigned one year.   However **TWO** different times are given for the beginning of the reign of Ahaziah in the SAME book:

*"In the **twelfth** year of Joram the son of Ahab king of Israel did Ahaziah the son of Jehoram king of Judah begin to reign."* 2Ki 8:25

*"And in the **eleventh** year of Joram the son of Ahab began Ahaziah to reign over Judah."* 2Ki 9:29

Note that both references to this problem text cite Ahaziah as reigning one year – something hard to do when your reign begins in the eleventh year of Joram as well as in the twelfth year of Jehoram.   Also note the difference in identification: one verse includes that Ahaziah was *"the son of Jehoram king of Judah"* while the other passage does not – a minor, but potentially significant difference.

The verses certainly appear to be pointing at two men named Ahaziah. Further collaboration is found in 2Kin 10:13 where Ahaziah has brethren which contradicts 2Chr 21:17 & 22:1 that clearly state there was only one son of Jehoshaphat remaining. One Ahaziah had brethren, the other did not.

Another point of difference that indicates two different men is how the mother of Ahaziah is described in our problem text verses. Of the 42 year old Ahaziah, it is said, *"his mother's name **ALSO** was Athaliah the daughter of Omri."* This can only mean that two kings of Judah had Athaliah for their mother.

Regardless of how many Ahaziahs there may be, we know that the 42 year old Ahaziah of 2Chr 22:2 could not be Jehoram's son – the previous verses (21:16-22:1) clearly describe a king named Jehoram who died at 40 years old and thus could not be immediately succeeded by a 42 year old son.

The scenario that best fits and does not contradict the verses given to us is that there were two Ahaziahs that each reigned for a year over Judah. One is the youngest biological son of Jehoram and Athaliah, is also known as Jehoahaz, and is described in 2Chr 21:16-21. The other is a stepson or previous son of Athaliah that was much older, an import brought with Athaliah from the northern kingdom, and the man described in 2Chr 22:2 and the subsequent verses.

Jehoram of Judah was stricken with bowel disease in the last two years of his eight year reign. Jehoram made the 22 year old Ahaziah (also known as Jehoahaz) co-regent in the 11th year of the king of Israel – this son lasted one year and died. The 42 year old Ahaziah is then made co-regent in the 12th year of the king of Israel. Jehoram then died; this second Ahaziah then reigned one year and died as well. Thus 2Chr 22 is alternating between two men named Ahaziah who reigned in a very messy, semi-triumvirate with Jerhoam during an incredibly volatile two years of Judah's history that ended in a coup with an angry, Northern Kingdom import usurping power over the nation of Judah.

Note the strange wording of 2Chr. 22:10 where *"her son"* (the 42 year old Israelite Ahaziah) is dead, so Athaliah takes vengeance on the Judah royal line. Note also the strange wording in 2Chr. 22:11 – Jeshoshabeath is the daughter of "the king" and yet turns out to be the "daughter of king Jehoram." She was the sister of the 22 year old Ahaziah. Her brother's son (i.e. her nephew) becomes the next king when Queen Athaliah is finally killed.

This explanation is not simple and it requires serious study and attention to detail. No one has ever come up with a conclusive, ironclad explanation for this problem text – however there is a very plausible and likely scenario that fits all of the relevant verses without having to resort to accusations of mistakes and mistranslations. God could have cleared up matter such as this, but did not. Problem texts try the faith of the reader and force him to study, as well as choosing between trusting God and his own intellect. The student of God's word would be wise to always believe the Holy Spirit over the words and explanations of men who seek to correct God's word.

The Song of Songs

Song of Songs is the title the Holy Spirit assigns to the Song of Solomon in its very first verse. Few can deny the poetic beauty and majesty of the Song of Solomon – but what did the Holy Spirit intend for us to understand in this challenging, but intriguing book?

Song of Songs is a verse-by-verse commentary for Bible believers. Where many expositions consider the Song of Solomon from only a devotional perspective, Dr. Williams has attempted to uncover the doctrinal teachings of the book as well as examining its historical setting and practical applications. Where many have succumbed to the temptation to spiritualize this poetic masterpiece, the author has endeavored to follow a literal approach in Bible interpretation, allowing the Scriptures to speak for themselves.

Song of Songs will not only help you to understand this portion of Scripture better, but it will help you to grasp just how much our Saviour loves us and desires us to walk ever closer with Him.

Available in the Following Formats!

 Softcover Book

 Online Digital Download

 Kindle E-Book at Amazon.com

For ordering contact:

Verity & Charity Publications
PO Box 422
Portage, WI 53901

www.veritycharity.com

226

Line Upon Line

Dr JG Williams

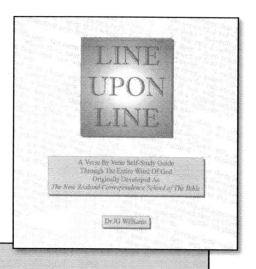

The self-study system that will take you verse-by-verse through the ENTIRE English Bible!

Originally developed by missionary Jeff Williams as
The New Zealand Correspondence School of the Bible

For Self-Study
Study every verse of the Bible at your own pace, developing a thorough understanding of the entire Word of God.

For Homeschoolers
A self-maintaining, four-year high school Bible curriculum.
Quizzes, tests and answer key included.

As a Sunday School Guide or Discipleship Course
Bible verse explanations for people with little or no Bible knowledge.
Increasingly challenging material.

As a Bible Commentary
Commentary and cross-references given for virtually every verse of Scripture.
The "hard" passages and issues have NOT been ignored!

- King James Bible based study program
- 107 lessons cover the entire Bible, book by book, in an ascending order of doctrinal difficulty
- Includes all relevant quizzes, tests and answer keys
- Fundamental, conservative, dispensational
- Emphasis on the literal method of Bible interpretation
- Suitable for adult small group study or self-study of God's word
- Available in four different formats: book in handy ringbinder system; digital files on CD; entire course in online digital download; or online download *one book at a time!*

Available at

Verity & Charity Publications
PO Box 422, Portage, WI 53901

www.veritycharity.com

Book Format in Ringbinder Study System

**Instant Online
Download**

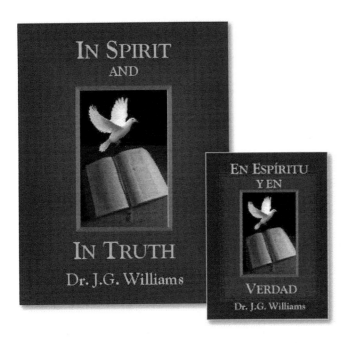

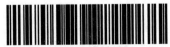

Made in the USA
Lexington, KY
03 March 2016